CAPTURED AT ARNHEM

CAPTURED AT ARNHEM

Men's Experiences in Their Own Words

Peter Green

Pen & Sword
MILITARY
AN IMPRINT OF PEN & SWORD BOOKS LTD.
YORKSHIRE – PHILADELPHIA

First published in Great Britain in 2022 by
PEN AND SWORD MILITARY
An imprint of
Pen & Sword Books Limited
Yorkshire – Philadelphia

ISBN 978 1 39908 837 4

A CIP catalogue record for this book is available from the British Library.

Typeset in Times New Roman 10/12 by
SJmagic DESIGN SERVICES, India.
Printed and bound in the UK by CPI Group (UK) Ltd.

Pen & Sword Books Limited incorporates the imprints of Atlas, Archaeology,
Aviation, Discovery, Family History, Fiction, History, Maritime, Military, Military
Classics, Politics, Select, Transport, True Crime, Air World, Frontline Publishing,
Leo Cooper, Remember When, Seaforth Publishing, The Praetorian Press,
Wharncliffe Local History, Wharncliffe Transport, Wharncliffe True Crime and
White Owl.

For a complete list of Pen & Sword titles please contact
PEN & SWORD BOOKS LIMITED
47 Church Street, Barnsley, South Yorkshire S70 2AS, United Kingdom
E-mail: enquiries@pen-and-sword.co.uk
Website: www.pen-and-sword.co.uk

Or
PEN AND SWORD BOOKS
1950 Lawrence Rd, Havertown, PA 19083, USA
E-mail: Uspen-and-sword@casematepublishers.com
Website: www.penandswordbooks.com

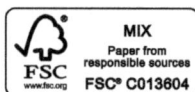

Contents

Capture at Arnhem is dedicated to my Mother, Marjorie Green, and all the other loved ones who waited in the Autumn of 1944, for news of their men, initially reported as missing, often also known to have been wounded.

Foreword

"In the annals of the British Army... there can be few episodes more glorious than the epic of Arnhem." Field Marshal Montgomery's tribute to the men of the 1st Airborne Division, who in September 1944 battled heroically but unsuccessfully for the bridge over the Lower Rhine at Arnhem, has stood the test of time. Few battles are still commemorated with the same defiant pride as Operation Market Garden, and few are able to inspire men today, especially the Parachute Regiment, quite as much as that single word "Arnhem."

There were, of course, more men at Arnhem than "just" the Paras. Besides the support arms and services – gunners, sappers, signals, supply, medical etc – there were the glider-borne infantry of 1st Air-landing brigade, and the men of the Glider Pilot Regiment who after landing (usually crash-landing) their flimsy aircraft fought as infantry, some 1260 of them. As an officer in the successor regiment to the Border Regiment, whose first battalion was one of the three air-landing infantry units at Arnhem, I was proud to wear the glider badge on the sleeve of my service dress. The distinction was awarded to the Borders not for Arnhem but earlier, for Sicily, the first major airborne operation of the war. However, we all basked in the glowing "operational heritage" won by the regiment at Arnhem. Indeed, as I write these words, the last Border veteran of the battle, Sergeant Wilf Oldham, has just been lain to rest, aged 101, and with military honours furnished by his successor (twice amalgamated) regiment. Such is the thread of regimental comradeship over the years, and of course the enduring power of the epic Arnhem story.

But Corporal Oldham was one who got away. The battalion having been ordered, with the rest of the division, to breakout from near-encirclement and get back across the river as best they could, Oldham managed to find an Dutch rowing boat and get himself and several others to safety. Fewer than a third from 1 Border managed to, however. And the division as a whole fared no better. Some units, like the remnants of 2 Para at the bridge itself, were captured almost to a man, having been surrounded and out of ammunition. Of the 12,000 men of the 1st Airborne Division, Glider Pilot Regiment and Polish Parachute Brigade who landed by parachute or glider, fewer than 4,000 came out at the end of that extraordinary nine-day battle – a battle expected to last just two days before ground forces reached the Rhine to relieve them.

The story of Arnhem doesn't therefore end that night, 25 September, when the last bedraggled red beret reached the allied bank of the Lower Rhine. Or, indeed, when the hurly burly of operational analysis – and recriminations – was done. The story continues with the record of those captured, which until now has not been comprehensively collated or appraised. Peter Green, whose own father, Lieutenant Alan Green of 1 Border, wounded and captured at Arnhem, is part of that record, now takes up that hitherto sketch story. His work in assembling the MI9 debriefs held in the National Archives and then interpreting the bigger picture they collectively present, will be invaluable to researchers, as well as to those with family or regimental connections. Judging from the National Archives trove, MI9 – Military Intelligence Branch 9, the organization set up at the outbreak of the war to help escape and evasion – managed to debrief nearly a third of those captured, which in the circumstances was an astonishing feat. Green reckons that in all probability the questionnaires completed by released PoWs and now held at Kew are the entire MI9 archive; and I think he's probably right, for MI9 were always about attention to detail, and completeness. But whatever the case, 2,357 questionnaires gives a pretty good general picture of what was going on – certainly more than opinion pollsters go on today.

Above all, though, this is a record of men of valour and fortitude who, except for a very dwindling few, are now dead. Montgomery said of the men of the 1st Airborne Division, "In years to come it will be a great thing for a man to be able to say, 'I fought at Arnhem'." In that, he was right, and this book is a significant contribution to keeping alive and understanding the full import of their "great thing", fighting at Arnhem.

Allan Mallinson

Acknowledgements

This study would have not been possible to produce in any sensible timescale without the generous help of John Howes with access to his collection of questionnaires and for his time on my behalf at the National Archives. Paul Pariso has made available his encyclopedic knowledge of people and places at Arnhem, without complaint no matter how trivial the question may have appeared to him.

Niall Cherry has pointed me in positive directions when research avenues dried up. Stefan Geck has shared his knowledge of Dulag Luft. Rolf Keller has provided access to his research into *arbeitskommandos* and Philip Reinders his knowledge of the Glider Pilot Regiment.

The families of former prisoners have been invaluable in providing details of men's lives as prisoners of war. In particular:

Ray Barnard
Roderick Barron
Grenville Bint
Paul Brindley
Jean James
Alastair Taylor
Barbara Lorne
Phil Welham

Finally, friends in Germany, Harald Schlanstedt and Hajo Neubert, for their advice on pre-1945 German place names.

As ever, any errors are my responsibility.

Introduction

MI9 and MI-X, the British and American units responsible for liaison with prisoner of war camps and training in the event of capture and evasion techniques, were tasked to produce questionnaires that every returning former prisoner would be required to complete.

It was expected that the questionnaires would show: the successes and failures of pre-captivity training; highlight men whose excellent behaviour in captivity should be rewarded or whose experience could be valuable in the future; or whose behaviour required punishment; or identify war crimes committed by their captors.

MI9 and MI-X had no illusions about the response returning former POWs would give to a paperwork exercise. This was how the announcement that they were to create the questionnaires was described in Foot and Langley's history of MI9:

> Nelson and Langley looked at one another, the same picture for me in each of their minds: row upon row of released prisoners, many of them prisoners since May 1940 and some embittered by the fiasco that followed the 'standfast order' in Italy sitting like schoolboys at an examination to answer questions which the majority would feel was a waste of time and utterly pointless now the war was over. 'I don't think,' said Nelson' that they will take kindly to such treatment. They will regard it as one more maddening obstacle delaying their return home. I think we will have a lot of trouble on our hands.'[1]

In many cases they were right, only a third of men completed questionnaires. Others returned to the UK without seeing one.

Nevertheless, the 2,357 that have survived from men captured as a result of Operation Market Garden in 1944 give an extra dimension to the tragic story of the destruction of an elite unit in a bid to end the war by Christmas 1944.

All the men's answers and comments are direct quotations, however obvious spelling errors in place names have been corrected.

---

1 Foot and Langley, *MI9: Escape and Evasion 1939–1945*, Bodley Head, 1979, p. 289.

Chapter 1

Questionnaires and Other Sources

Introduction

Operation Market Garden failed to provide the highway into Germany that would end the war in the autumn of 1944. Instead, more than 6,000 men from the 1st Airborne Division, the Glider Pilot Regiment and the Polish Independent Parachute Brigade became prisoners of war, along with men from 4th Battalion, Dorset Regiment, who had crossed the Rhine in a failed attempt to secure the bridgehead.

At the end of the Second World War in Europe, men captured at Arnhem, like all returning Allied POWs, were asked to complete questionnaires about their experience of captivity. There are 2,358 of these questionnaires, roughly a third of the potential total, in the National Archives at Kew. The questionnaires record the men's experience of life in Germany during the last few months of the war, often in their own words. They do not cover all men captured at Arnhem. There is, for example, only one Polish questionnaire. This account uses the questionnaires that were completed or survived to give an overview of what failure at Arnhem meant for one of the Allies' elite formations close to the war's end.

> Private Roland Swinburn, 2nd Battalion, South Staffordshire Regiment, 'We were under fed. Rations being 900 grams of bread a day and 25 grams of marge a day and a bowl of soup a day.'

As well as the Silesian coal mines where Private Swinburn laboured, the men worked in artificial oil plants in the Sudetenland, mines in the Harz Mountains, salt mines and factories, and repaired sewers or the heavily bombed German railways. The men describe transport by packed and insanitary boxcars across Germany and the fear of massacre at the war's end. Many would experience appalling winter marches westwards from Poland through the snow away from the advancing Russians. For all it meant little food and often poor medical attention.

They record the life led by concentration camp prisoners working alongside them:

> Private Russell Daye, 7th Battalion, King's Own Scottish Borderers, '[Concentration camp workers] Worked 12 hrs a day and they were that weakened by their work, that when they were working, they held each other up.'

The men captured at Arnhem were the largest single number of men captured at one go, around a fortnight, by the Germans since the fall of France; more than Dieppe, more than Crete. What is apparent is that despite the chaos into which Germany was descending in the last autumn of the war, the Germans coped, but that this was often achieved by taking little account of the needs of their prisoners:

> Private John Godden, 1st Battalion, Parachute Regiment, 'During that period we were locked in cattle trucks with almost no ventilation, we were allowed no exercise during journey.'

German procedures were based on regulations that covered the whole of the Wehrmacht, not just the army or the air force, but prisoners were still handled in different ways; some facilities were little used, others were over-used; and interrogation was carried on long after any information gained would have been out of date. Most surprising are the blunt comments from the German interrogators to their captives about Germany's military and political prospects:

> Captain Frederick Gibbs, 156th Battalion, Parachute Regiment, 'Political Interrogation by Foreign Office Official in civilian clothes. Required information as to what we would do with Germany after the war ...'.

General Questionnaires for British/American Ex-Prisoners of War

The Liberation Questionnaires were created by Military Intelligence 9. MI9 had the responsibility for training men in evasion and escape techniques, and in communication with men in prison camps. The questionnaires were intended to provide information on their captivity; to identify war crimes, collaborators or other prisoners whose actions required further investigation; and to gauge the effectiveness of MI9's work to provide escape and evasion training, and support for prisoners.

The questionnaires formed part of the programme to repatriate former prisoners, Operation Endor. The intention was that the returning men, Recovered Allied Military Personal or RAMPs, would complete questionnaires at repatriation centres established in mainland Europe before being returned to the UK. Some men were repatriated before Endor got underway or returned to Britain by unofficial routes, so they never saw a questionnaire. Others, no doubt impatient with army bureaucracy, ignored them. MI9 estimated that only a third of all the potential questionnaires from British and Commonwealth POWs captured in Europe were completed. Of the 6,000 plus men who were captured at Arnhem, there are 2,357 questionnaires in the National Archives at Kew. There may be more. Searches are done manually and are immensely time-consuming, however, the number is comparable with MI9's estimate of a third being returned.

QUESTIONNAIRES AND OTHER SOURCES

On the ground, the exercise was supervised by MI9 teams operating as Intelligence School 9 (Western European Area) – IS9 (WEA). IS9 had supervised the evasion and escape school in Highgate, London. IS 9 (WEA) was disbanded in August 1945. Allied bombing destroyed the main German POW records and many camp commandants destroyed their own files as camps were evacuated, so the questionnaires, together with the War Office's list of POWs and the reports by the Swiss of their camp visits as the protecting power, are the primary sources available that provide a general view of the life of the prisoners. They sit alongside a rich collection of detailed autobiographies and biographies that provide very specific information about an individual's experience.

Each questionnaire took up two and a half foolscap pages. Oddly, during the austerity of wartime, one and a half sides of paper were blank. Although the teams took 100lb of paperwork with them to Europe, some ran out of questionnaires and had to resort to using duplicated copies of typed forms. There are four of these duplicated forms in the Arnhem series.

The questions on the printed questionnaire are:

Part I
Question 1
Service Number
Rank
Surname
Christian Names
Decorations

Question 2
Ship (RN, USN or Merchant Navy)
Unit (Army)
Squadron (RAF or AAF)

Question 3
Division (Army), Command (RAF or AAF)

Question 4
Date of birth

Question 5
Date of enlistment

Question 6
Civilian trade or profession (or examinations passed while P/W)

Question 7
Private address

Question 8
Place and date of original capture

Question 10
Main camps or hospitals in which imprisoned
Camp number
Location
From
Till

Question 11
Were you in a working camp?
Location
From
Till
Nature of work

Question 12
Did you suffer any serious illnesses as a P/W?
Nature of illness
Cause
Duration
Did you receive adequate medical treatment?

Part II
Question 1 Interrogation after capture

Service number
Rank
Surname
Christian names

Question 2
Lectures before capture
Were you lectured in your unit on how to behave in the event of
capture? (State where, when and by whom).

Were you lectured on escape and evasion? (State where, when
and by whom).

Question 3
Were you specially interrogated by the enemy? (State where, when
and methods used by enemy).

Question 4
Escapes attempted
Did you make any attempted or partly successful escapes? (Give details
of each attempt separately, stating where, when, method employed,
names of your companions, where and when recaptured and by
whom.) Were you physically fit? What happened to your companions?

Question 5
Sabotage
Did you do any sabotage or destruction of enemy factory plant, war material, communications, etc, when employed on working parties or during escape? (Give details, places and dates).

Question 6
Collaboration with enemy
Do you know of any British or American personnel who collaborated with the enemy or in any way helped the enemy against other Allied Prisoners of War? (Give details, names of person(s) concerned, camp(s), dates and nature of collaboration or help given to the enemy).

Question 7
War Crimes
If you have any information or evidence of bad treatment by the enemy to yourself or to others, or knowledge of any enemy violation of Geneva Convention you should ask for a copy of 'Form Q' on which to make your statement.

[Note: Form Q is a separate form inviting information on 'War Crimes' and describes the kinds of offences coming under this title.]

Question 8
Have you any other matter of any kind you wish to bring to notice?

Security Undertaking
I fully realize that all information relating to the matters covered by the questions in Part II are of a highly secret and official nature.

I have had explained to me and fully understand that under Defence Regulations or USAR 380-5 I am forbidden to publish or communicate any information concerning these matters.

Date
Signature

What's Missing

The 2,358 Arnhem questionnaires discovered in the National Archives are filed in batches alphabetically by surname and then by service number. Individual questionnaires are not catalogued: they have to be found by laborious manual searches. This work has been undertaken by members of the Arnhem Fellowship, who have used their background knowledge to assist with work in the archives. The number of questionnaires by unit are:

Glider Pilot Regiment – 179
1st Airborne Division – 2,130
4th Battalion, Dorset Regiment – 48
1st Independent Polish Parachute Brigade Group – 1

It is possible therefore that other questionnaires remain to be discovered, however, the percentage of Arnhem ones is close to the National Archives' estimate that they hold only 33 per cent of the possible number of questionnaires. So where are the remainder?

In 1944 MI9 understood that the returning men would not appreciate being made to fill out forms when they wanted to be home. Getting men to complete the forms was, therefore, not going to be easy. In a bureaucratic contradiction, the MI9 teams tasked with overseeing the completion of the forms were also instructed that, 'No interrogations by IS 9 (WEA) officers shall be allowed to hold up the return to the UK of any British or American prisoner of war.'

Private Victor Gregg, 10th Battalion, Parachute Regiment, recorded his frustration at army bureaucracy. His questionnaire is dated 15 May 1945 and refers to being 'abroad for one week' after liberation, although his biography has 'six or seven weeks'. In his account of his wartime experiences[2] he described his experience of returning to the UK, 'I was sent to a camp to be sorted out. I got asked the usual crap: Who was I? Where have I come from? How had I managed to get there?' Gregg was an extreme case. Unashamedly anti-establishment, after liberation he spent time with the Russian army. On his return to Britain, he joined the Communist Party.

Foot and Langley believed that many questionnaires were used by former prisoners to vent their grievances of all kinds in long rambling accounts of capture, camp life and unsuccessful escapes. These, Foot and Langley believed, had 'been mercifully pulped'. The Arnhem series include two officers who were accused of betraying their men over escape equipment, and of several prisoners profiteering:

> Private Stanley Trevelyn Harvey, 11th Battalion, Parachute Regiment,
> 'British POWs sold us Red Cross food for rings and watches, this
> was reported at my last camp Limberg 12A.'

There are questionnaires missing from many high-profile Arnhem POWs, who were unlikely to avoid paperwork or vent their anger at the system. These include men who were liberated without passing through the repatriation centres at Antwerp, Brussels or Reims. Lieutenant Colonel John Frost, 2nd Battalion, Parachute Regiment, and Lieutenant James Cleminson, 3rd Battalion, Parachute Regiment, were liberated from the hospital at Obermaßfeld, near Kassel, on 5 April and flown to RAF Lyneham by the Americans. There are no questionnaires either for any men held at Oflag IX A/H, which was liberated on 4 April. But questionnaires do exist from its sister camp, Oflag IX A/Z, which was liberated on 13 April. Oflag IX A/H

---

2   Gregg and Stroud, *Rifleman: a front-line life from Alamein and Dresden to the fall of the Berlin Wall*, Bloomsbury, 2011.

was flown out by the Americans on 8 April. They returned via a US transit camp in France to RAF Westcott in Oxfordshire. Men from Oflag IX A/Z, however, were flown to Belgium by the Americans on 16 April, but then passed through the British repatriation centre at Brussels before the RAF returned them to the UK.

Oflag 79 at Braunschweig was repatriated over several days from 16 April. Some men were flown directly to the UK, others returned via the Brussels repatriation centre. Lieutenant Edmund Scrivener, 1st Battalion, Border Regiment, returned via Brussels, as did Major Victor Dover, 2nd Battalion, Parachute Regiment; both their questionnaires exist.

Lieutenant Colonel Tommy Haddon, 1st Battalion, Border Regiment, who had been Senior British Officer at Dulag XII B, was moved to Oflag XII B in March 1945 after the Dulag had been bombed. The Oflag was evacuated by the Germans but liberated by the Americans 50km to the east at Giessen. The men were flown straight back to England. There is no questionnaire for Haddon.

It was not just officers who were liberated in this way. Sapper Tom Hicks, 1st Parachute Squadron, Royal Engineers, was flown directly back to Britain by the Americans. He landed at RAF Hurn near Bournemouth on 22 April without passing through a repatriation centre. He has no questionnaire. Nor has Private Colin Hall, 10th Battalion, Parachute Regiment, who returned to Great Missenden from Munster.

However, at least one man who did pass through a repatriation centre is missing a questionnaire. Captain Bernard Briggs, 1st Parachute Brigade, kept a record of his time in captivity. This shows that after liberation, while being marched from Moosburg, he passed through Reims. There is no questionnaire for Captain Briggs.

It is not easy to prove a negative but it can be reasonably assumed that the 2,357 Arnhem questionnaires used in this account are close to the total number of questionnaires that exist for men from 1st Airborne Division, Glider Pilot Regiment, and 4th Battalion, Dorset Regiment, captured around Arnhem and Oosterbeek during Operation Market Garden, and that the majority of missing ones are from men who arrived back in the UK without passing through the repatriation system on mainland Europe.

The questionnaires provided an opportunity for men to describe their British training in case of captivity, interrogation, their medical support and work undertaken as a POW. The Arnhem men went to camps that already held men captured in Norway and France in spring 1940; from North Africa, Greece and Crete in 1941 and 1942; and the disasters at Dieppe in 1942 and the Dodecanese in 1943. However, the experience of a newly arrived prisoner at Stalag IV B in Silesia was in essence the same as one of the veteran prisoners or as they called themselves 'Kriegies' – the nickname came from the German word for prisoners of war, 'Kriegsgefangene'. It is also clear that there was no attempt to separate the Arnhem men from each other and, where the questionnaires list fellow POWs, they are often from 1st Airborne Division:

> Private Victor Cawrey, 21st Independent Parachute Company, 'Started marching and ducked column in company of Pte Humphreys 2nd Para Batt, Pte Finglass 21st Ind Para ...'

The questionnaires show the intelligence concerns of the German security services and Foreign Office. Many Germans had no illusions about the future either. The documents include comments by German interrogators on German defeat.

To the airborne men, it was clear that the war could not go on for much longer. On arriving at their permanent camps, many were told by fellow prisoners that escaping was not worth the risk with victory so close:

> Corporal William Watson, 1st Airborne Reconnaissance Squadron, 'We were advised by a Flying Officer of the RAF not to escape owing to the progress of the allied troops. He said that the senior British officer had disbanded the Escape committee to avoid taking unnecessary risks.'

Questionnaires and Work

German industry and agriculture were dependent on forced and slave labour, including POWs. The Geneva Convention expected NCOs and Other Ranks to work:

> Geneva Convention Article 27 – General Belligerents may employ as workmen prisoners of war who are physically fit, other than officers and persons of equivalent status, according to their rank and their ability. Nevertheless, if officers or persons of equivalent status ask for suitable work, this shall be found for them as far as possible. Non-commissioned officers who are prisoners of war may be compelled to undertake only supervisory work, unless they expressly request remunerative occupation. During the whole period of captivity, belligerents are required to admit prisoners of war who are victims of accidents at work to the benefit of provisions applicable to workmen of the same category under the legislation of the detaining Power. As regards prisoners of war to whom these legal provisions could not be applied by reason of the legislation of that Power, the latter undertakes to recommend to its legislative body all proper measures for the equitable compensation of the victims.
>
> Article 28 – Organization of work.
> The detaining Power shall assume entire responsibility for the maintenance, care, treatment and the payment of the wages of prisoners of war working for private individuals.
>
> Article 29 – No prisoner of war may be employed on work for which he is physically unsuited.
>
> Article 30 – The duration of the daily work of prisoners of war, including the time of the journey to and from work, shall not

be excessive and shall in no case exceed that permitted for civil workers of the locality employed on the same work. Each prisoner shall be allowed a rest of twenty-four consecutive hours each week, preferably on Sunday.

Article 31 – Prohibited work
Work done by prisoners of war shall have no direct connection with the operations of the war. In particular, it is forbidden to employ prisoners in the manufacture or transport of arms or munitions of any kind, or on the transport of material destined for combatant units.

In the event of violation of the provisions of the preceding paragraph, prisoners are at liberty, after performing or commencing to perform the order, to have their complaints presented through the intermediary of the prisoners' representatives' whose functions are described in Articles 43 an 44, or, in the absence of a prisoners' representative, through the intermediary of the representatives of the protecting Power.

Article 32
It is forbidden to employ prisoners of war on unhealthy or dangerous work. Conditions of work shall not be rendered more arduous by disciplinary measures.

The questionnaires include only one where a man was required to carry out direct war work. Sergeant Hayes was held at Stalag IX C/Z at Mühlhausen:

Sergeant William Hayes, 156th Battalion, Parachute Regiment, 'Breaking Geneva Convention by making men dig anti-tank ditches and building road blocks.'

That men's employment should not support the war effort was a requirement that was difficult to meet during a period of total war and Arnhem POWs would find themselves employed in repairing bomb damage as well as mines, factories, railways and agriculture.

Questionnaires and Transport to Camps

Men were mostly transferred to camps by train. The questionnaires have no question on how men were moved, but the final question, 'Any other matter, etc' provided an opportunity for some to describe the applying conditions under which men were moved by train:

Lance Corporal Blockwell, 7th Battalion, King's Own Scottish Borderers, 'During movements from camps were locked in boxcars for as long as 10–14 days ...'

The camp a man went to from the Dulag was not necessarily his only camp. The Germans moved men west away from the Russians and men might also move camps as the German need for labour changed. This was particularly the case in Silesia, where men were transferred between the many Stalags in District IV.

Questionnaires and Winter Marches

Prison camps, including those holding men captured at Arnhem, were marched away from the Russians in Arctic conditions lacking proper clothing and food. In POW autobiographies marches from the East form a major part of the narrative. In the questionnaires, they are less significant. One reason for this was that there was no specific question about evacuations on the original forms. Four questionnaires have an extra question: 'MARCHES. Have you taken part in any marches in or into GERMANY? If so please write names of any personnel who you saw fall out, giving if possible, place, name and date.' These questions were added using a stencil duplicator. The evacuation marches from the East in early 1945 were known at a high level in Britain before the end of the war, but in Foot and Langley's history of MI9 they receive only a short mention in their summary of the final days of their work. All the questionnaires with the extra question are dated in May, suggesting that this question was added late in the repatriation process.

No man answered the march question. Men's remarks on the marches come in the final catch-all general question:

> Staff Sergeant Bennett Sayles, Glider Pilot Regiment, 'Very bad treatment received from guards of Stalag Luft. 7 whilst on March from Bankau to Luckenwalde ...'

Quality of the Data

Questionnaires were not moderated and not checked on completion: there were just too many men, too much paper and too little time. Men were anxious to get home.

The questionnaires are a mixed-bag of information. Questions were open to different interpretations. For example, the questionnaire asked if a man had been specially interrogated and many answered 'No' to this. Staff Sergeant Peter Aitken, Glider Pilot Regiment, answered 'No' to special interrogation, while recording almost two months at the Luftwaffe's interrogation centre, Dulag Luft. However, Lance Corporal Albert Aldcroft, Royal Engineers, described his time at Dulag Luft as special, 'Yes, at Luftwaffe interrogation centre threatened with solitary followed by attempts to gain confidence and showing reports by other POWs.'

Question 10 specifically asked for the 'Main camps or hospitals in which imprisoned', but then failed to define 'Main'. Some men listed all the camps that they passed through, including battlefield collection points. Others ignored all the transit camps and gave only their fixed camps. Private Arthur Applin, 2nd Battalion, Parachute Regiment, gave his only camp as Stalag IV B from 10 October 1944 until 22 April 1945, though he does list the working party that he was allocated to in Leipzig, from January.

Question 2 asked, 'What was a man's unit?' Thirty-three men gave their unit as 'Parachute Regiment' without a battalion number. Other replies give only a brigade. Men from the Royal Engineers or Royal Signals or other specialist units, often give only their Corps designation. As a result, they cannot be allocated to a brigade, or their capture related to a specific time or part of the battlefield.

Place Name Problems

It was expecting too much for men to spell German place names correctly. Dulag Luft West at Oberursel caused particular problems. Corporal Roland McFarlane, 'HQ Airborne Troops' described being interrogated at 'Uberest'. Staff Sergeant Richard Grant, Glider Pilot Regiment, spelt it Oberwerzel, while Private Clifford Harvey, 181st Airlanding Field Ambulance RAMC, gives 'Oberfue-lle'. It was not just enlisted men who found German names challenging. Officers too had problems with the Dulag Luft. Major Rev. Albert Harlow, Royal Army Chaplains' Department, described being at 'Ober Ouzel'. The Dulag Luft transit camp at Wetzlar was no easier. Private John Elliott, 4th Parachute Brigade HQ, spells it as 'Werson'.

Place names in the Sudetenland pose an additional problem in the twenty-first century. What were German names in 1945 now have completely different Czech ones. Seestadtl was the German name for Ervínice, which to add a further layer of complication has been destroyed by open-cast mining. Tschausch, south-east of Chemnitz, was a large open-cast mine site that features in eighteen questionnaires. Private Gilbert Braithwaite, 2nd Battalion, South Staffordshire Regiment, spelt it 'Chouse'. Private John Acton, 1st Battalion, Border Regiment, gave 'Choiuse' and Private Norman Connold, 3rd Battalion, Parachute Regiment, has 'Tchowts'. In the Czech Republic it is known as Souš.

The Problem of Dates

The dates in the questionnaires are sometimes unreliable. Twenty-one men gave a date for capture before Market Garden started:

Private Thomas Forsyth, 7th Battalion, King's Own Scottish Borderers, 19 March 1944

CAPTURED AT ARNHEM

Sergeant Albert Palmer, Glider Pilot Regiment, 20 March 1944

Sergeant Henry Clark, 1st Airlanding Light Regiment Royal Artillery, 18 July 1944

Lance Corporal Thomas Travers, 2nd Battalion, The Parachute Regiment, 21 July 1944

Lance Corporal Stanley Barron, 250th Airborne Light Company, Royal Army Service Corps, 23 July 1944

Private William Hughes, 2nd Battalion, South Staffordshire Regiment, 15 August 1944

Lance Corporal George McLean, 1st Battalion, The Parachute Regiment, 19 August 1944

Private George Bellas, 7th Battalion, King's Own Scottish Borderers, 20 August 1944

Private Joseph Heath, 10th Battalion, The Parachute Regiment, 21 August 1944

Lance Corporal James Ransom, 250th Airborne Light Company, Royal Army Service Corps, 21 August 1944

Corporal Roy Davey, 2nd Battalion, South Staffordshire Regiment, 22 August 1944

Gunner Robert Dixon, 1st Airlanding Light Regiment Royal Artillery 26 August 1944

Private John Fox, 2nd Battalion, South Staffordshire Regiment, 26 August 1944

Private Kenneth Reading, 21st Independent Company, The Parachute Regiment, 26 August 1944

Private Matthew Skelly, Royal Army Medical Corps, 27 August 1944

Private Alfred Murphy, 2nd Battalion, The Parachute Regiment, 28 August 1944

Private William McKee, The Parachute Regiment, 9 September 1944

Private James Horsfield, 2nd Battalion, The Parachute Regiment, 10 September 1944

QUESTIONNAIRES AND OTHER SOURCES

Gunner Albert Such, 1st Airlanding Light Regiment, Royal Artillery, 15 September 1944

Private Ernest Blades, 1st Battalion, The Border Regiment 16 September 1944

Private John Caldwell, 2nd Battalion, South Staffordshire Regiment, 16 September 1944

The questionnaire asked for the dates they were at camps. In the immediate stages of captivity, and with it taking several days to travel from Arnhem to their camp, it is understandable that arrival dates are not precise enough to identify specific transports. But the eight who gave dates for their arrival at Stalag XI B or Stalag XII A before Market Garden are puzzling:

Private Charles Marriott, 1st Battalion, The Border Regiment, 29 July 1940

Lance Corporal Stanley Barron, 250th Airborne Light Company, Royal Army Service Corps, 23 July 1944

Private Robert O'Brian, 1st Battalion, The Parachute Regiment, 28 August 1944

Private George Bellas, 7th Battalion, King's Own Scottish Borderers, 1 September 1944

Private William Callaghan, 1st Battalion, The Border Regiment, 6 September 1944

Private Alfred Murphy, 2nd Battalion, The Parachute Regiment, 6 September 1944

Lance Corporal George McLean, 1st Battalion, The Parachute Regiment, 9 September

Private Ernest Mackay, 2nd Battalion, The Parachute Regiment, 10 September 1944

Three gave dates for arriving at Stalag XII A that were after the end of the war:

Private Robert Kitchener, 2nd Battalion, Parachute Regiment, 25 September 1945

Private James Hope, 2nd Battalion, South Staffordshire Regiment, 25 September 1945

Lance Corporal Eric Potts, 181st Airlanding Field Ambulance, RAMC, 1 November 1945

One man listed his escape and recapture in August 1945. This, like other bizarre dates, must result from men's impatience at army bureaucracy and the questionnaires not being scrutinized:

> Private Harry Palmer, 3rd Battalion, Parachute Regiment, 'Yes on 23.8.45 till the 29.8.45 recaptured at Wurzen 29.8.45.'

The unreliability of the dates on the questionnaires prevents groups of men transported together being identified either when being moved from the battlefield or later as they were sent to fixed camps. Liberation dates, which were of immense significance to the men and very recent, are likely to be more reliable, though as already noted, one questionnaire was dated 1928 by the signatory.

The questionnaires did not record men's German POW numbers. These show where and when men were registered. They were of no interest to MI9, today they are useful aids to research. The ones that have been added here are taken from various miscellaneous German files and men's biographies, but most of all the War Office record, *Prisoners of War British Army 1939–1945*, republished by HMSO in 1990 and now available online, which is a snapshot of British records at the end of March 1945.

Men with sequential POW numbers give different dates for transfer to permanent camps. Private Harry Thompson, 4th Battalion, Dorset Regiment, has the German number 17537 and Lance Corporal Albert Hogger, 4th Battalion, Dorset Regiment, is 17538. Private Thompson records leaving Limburg on 27 October 1944 and arriving at Stalag IV B at Muhlberg on 2 November 1944. Lance Corporal Hogger left Limburg on 24 October 1944 and arrived at Stalag IV B on 29 October 1944. Without more data it is not possible to distinguish between men giving the wrong dates and multiple transports close together. But the questionnaires suggest multiple transports.

> Private Albert Quinn, 1st Battalion, Border Regiment 75350 – arrived Stalag IVB 21 November
>
> Private William Scott, 2nd Battalion, South Staffordshire Regiment 75351 – arrived Stalag IVB 1 November
>
> Private James Davis, 7th Battalion, King's Own Scottish Borderers 75352 – arrived November, no day given
>
> Lance Corporal Stanley Lines, 2nd Battalion, South Staffordshire Regiment 75356 – arrived Stalag IVB 4 November

The transport of prisoners should be seen against the background of a German railway system that was struggling to cope with delivering essential raw materials to the armaments industry and supplies to the armed forces. The group above were all members of the Airlanding Brigade, but members of the Parachute Regiment are recorded with numbers close to this group.

Table 1: Prisoners' Details

Names, rank and service number as given on Liberation Questionnaires. The units include those of men on attachment to units on the Divisional roll. German POW numbers from other sources. The locations are all the camps or hospitals men passed through as given on their questionnaires. Obvious errors have been corrected, for example 'Stalag XII B' amended to 'Oflag XII B'.

Family name	Forename	Rank	Unit as given on Questionnaire	Army number	POW number	Wounded on capture?	Camps
Ackerman	Donald Henry Edwin	Gunner	1st Airborne Div, Light Regiment, Royal Artillery	14334539	88742		Stalag XII A, Stalag IV D
Acton	John	Private	1st Battalion, Border Regiment	3605400		Yes	Stalag XII A, Stalag IV C
Adams	Arthur Richard	Lance Corporal	7th Battalion, King's Own Scottish Borderers Regiment	14211553	18661	Yes	Stalag VII A
Adams	Donald	Staff Sergeant	Glider Pilot Regiment	136331			Stalag XII A, Stalag IV B
Addis	John	Private	1st Battalion, Border Regiment	4697979	92114	Yes	Stalag XII A, Stalag IV C
Agar	Godfrey Stewart	Staff Sergeant	Glider Pilot Regiment	2151406	118668	Yes	Apeldoorn Hospital, Stalag XI B, Stalag VIII C, Stalag IV B
Aggleton	Michael John	Private	2nd Battalion, South Staffordshire Regiment	4929070	91754		Stalag XII A, Stalag IV B
Airey	John	Private	11th Battalion, Parachute Regiment	3596766	91574		Stalag XII A, Stalag IV C
Aitcheson	Frederick George	Private	2nd Battalion, Parachute Regiment	2931605	140150	Yes	Arnhem Municipal Hospital, St Elizabeth's Hospital, Apeldoorn Hospital, Stalag VII A

Family name	Forename	Rank	Unit as given on Questionnaire	Army number	POW number	Wounded on capture?	Camps
Aitken	George Cecil	Private	1st Battalion, Parachute Regiment	4208372			Stalag XII A, Stalag XI B
Aitken	John	Private	7th Battalion, King's Own Scottish Borderers Regiment	14415429			Stalag XII A, Stalag IV B
Aitken	Peter	Staff Sergeant	Glider Pilot Regiment	28799361			Dulag Luft – Wetzlar, Stalag Luft 7, Stalag III A
Alcock	Norman	Driver	250th Airborne Light Company, Royal Army Service Corps	136798	88757		Stalag XII A, Stalag IV C
Aldcroft	Albert	Lance Corporal	Royal Engineers	2020229			Dulag Luft, Stalag XII A, Stalag IV B, Stalag IV B
Allchurch	Charles Cedric	Driver	1st Airlanding Anti-Tank Battery, Royal Artillery	14565660	92011		Stalag XII A, Stalag IV B
Allchurch	William Henry	Private	133rd Parachute Field Ambulance	7360747			Dulag Luft, Stalag IX C
Allen	Arthur	Signalman	1st Parachute Brigade, Royal Signals	2594068	89409		Stalag XII A, Stalag IV B
Allen	Ernest William	Lance Corporal	10th Battalion, Parachute Regiment	117618			Stalag IV B, Stalag IV C
Allen	Geoffrey Richard Ernest	Sergeant	Glider Pilot Regiment	2579984			Stalag XII A, Stalag IV B
Allen	John Charles	Private	Parachute Regiment	5349777	117477	Yes	Apeldoorn Hospital, Stalag XI B, Stalag III A, Stalag XI A
Allen	Robert Arthur	Corporal	3rd Battalion, Parachute Regiment	2080592	89462		Stalag XII A, Stalag II A
Allen	Ronald Harry	Gunner	Royal Artillery	14325639	229759		Stalag XII A, Stalag IV B, Stalag IV A

16

Surname	First name	Rank	Regiment/Unit	Service number	POW number	Camps
Allen	Wilfred	Private	2nd Battalion, South Staffordshire Regiment	1815415		Stalag XII A, Stalag IV B
Alletson	Edward Charles Walter	Private	21st Independent Parachute Company	5832371	118900	Stalag XI B
Allingham	Edward	Private	2nd Battalion, South Staffordshire Regiment	1815416	91758	Stalag XII A, Stalag IV B
Allison	Thomas	Private	7th Battalion, King's Own Scottish Borderers Regiment	14414347		Stalag IV D
Allwood	Henry	Gunner	Royal Artillery	15267128	15245	Stalag XIII D, Stalag IV D
Allwright	Charles Norman	Sergeant	7th Battalion, King's Own Scottish Borderers Regiment	4751022		Stalag XII A, Stalag II A
Amos	Henry	Private	2nd Battalion, South Staffordshire Regiment	5125455	75909	Stalag XII A, Stalag IV B
Anderson	Arthur	Private	2nd Battalion, Parachute Regiment	5783569		Stalag XII A, Stalag IV B
Anderson	Alexander	Sergeant	Royal Army Service Corps	292574	118863	Stalag XI B, Stalag VIII C, Stalag IX B
Anderson	Alexander Kennedy	Sergeant	1st Battalion, Parachute Regiment	5679174		Stalag XII A, Stalag II A
Anderson	Ivor Douglas	Private	7th Battalion, King's Own Scottish Borderers Regiment	3189214		Stalag XII A, Stalag IV B
Anderson	William	Private	7th Battalion, King's Own Scottish Borderers Regiment	3190405		Stalag XI B
Anderson	William Henry	Private	Royal Army Service Corps	14244352		Stalag XII A, Stalag IV B, Stalag IV B
Andrews	John	Gunner	1st Airlanding Light Regiment, Royal Artillery	14326582	92218	Stalag XII A, Stalag IV B

Family name	Forename	Rank	Unit as given on Questionnaire	Army number	POW number	Wounded on capture?	Camps
Angell	Donald Francis	Private	1st Battalion, Border Regiment	14237266	91882		Stalag XII A, Stalag IV B
Ansell	Lawrence Frank	Sergeant	2nd Battalion, Parachute Regiment	2042803	89854		Stalag XII A, Stalag II A
Anson	Joseph William	Private	10th Battalion, Parachute Regiment	14332028	92125		Stalag XII A, Stalag IV B
Anson	John Edward	Lance Corporal	1st Parachute Brigade, Royal Signals	2576520			Stalag XII A, Stalag IV B
Appleby	John	Private	1st Battalion, Border Regiment	14579657	75433		Stalag XII A, Stalag IV B, Stalag IV A
Applin	Arthur George	Private	2nd Battalion, Parachute Regiment	14421867	88787		Stalag IV B
Archer	Cyril	Gunner	1st Airlanding Light Regiment, Royal Artillery	14507454	75998		Stalag XII A, Stalag IV B, Stalag IV F
Arnold	Jack Thomas	Gunner	1st Airlanding Light Regiment, Royal Artillery	985649	118061		Stalag XI B
Ash	Arthur Charles	Driver	Royal Electrical and Mechanical Engineers	14412395			Stalag IV B
Ash	Alfred George	Lance Corporal	3rd Battalion, Parachute Regiment	14200328	90030		Stalag XII A, Stalag IV B, Stalag IV F
Ashcroft	Stanley	Private	156th Battalion, Parachute Regiment	321781	90117		Stalag XII A, Stalag IV B
Ashfield	Cyril Douglas	Private	2nd Battalion, Parachute Regiment	5837161			Stalag IV B, Stalag IV C
Ashington	George	Private	2nd Battalion, South Staffordshire Regiment	5109173	117515	Yes	Stalag XI B
Ashley	Neville Leonard	Sergeant	2nd Battalion, Parachute Regiment	4124109			Stalag XII A, Stalag XVIII C

Surname	First Name(s)	Rank	Unit	Service No.	POW No.	Questionnaire	Camps
Ashton	Frederick	Gunner	2nd Airlanding Anti-Tank Battery, Royal Artillery	3530609	92233		Stalag XII A, Stalag IV B
Ashton	Frederick John	Private	1st Battalion, Border Regiment	3771829	117682	Yes	Stalag XI B
Ashton	Gerard	Private	1st Battalion, Border Regiment	3603315			Stalag XII A, Stalag IV B, Stalag IV D
Ashworth	Harvey	Sapper	1st Parachute Squadron, Royal Engineers	1881677			Stalag XII A, Stalag IV B, Stalag IV C
Askew	Thomas Richard	Private	1st Parachute Brigade	14229144	89259		Stalag IV B
Aston	George Frederick	Private	11th Battalion, Parachute Regiment	4927881			Stalag XII A, Stalag IV B, Stalag IV C
Atherton	George Frederick	Private	1st Battalion, Border Regiment	14583624	91476		Stalag IV F
Atkinson	Frederick	Corporal	Parachute Regiment	3447850	118756		Stalag XI B, Stalag XI B
Austen	James	Private	Parachute Regiment	6399160			Stalag XII A, Stalag IV B, Stalag IV A
Austin	Albert Henry	Corporal	Light Warning Set No. 6080, RAF	919538			Stalag XI B, Dulag Luft, Stalag Luft 7, Stalag III A
Austin	Norris	Corporal	1st Battalion, Border Regiment	4455267			Stalag XII A, Stalag IV B, Stalag IV A
Auty	Sam	Sergeant	Glider Pilot Regiment	4617488			Dulag Luft – Oberusel, Stalag Luft 7, Stalag III A
Avann	Thomas Alfred Spencer	Private	3rd Battalion, Parachute Regiment	7617647	89724	Yes	Stalag XII A, Stalag XI B
Avis	Jack Robb	Sergeant	2nd Battalion, Parachute Regiment	5672958			Stalag XII A, Stalag II A
Ayres	David Ivor	Lance Corporal	250th Airborne Light Company, Royal Army Service Corps	123373		Yes	Hema, nr Enschede, Stalag XI B, Oflag 79
Baal	Lloyd Wilson	Private	10th Battalion, Parachute Regiment	93872	89594		Stalag IV C
Back	Harold Ernest	Lance Corporal	2nd Battalion, Parachute Regiment	6473851			Stalag XII A, Stalag II A, Stalag III A

Family name	Forename	Rank	Unit as given on Questionnaire	Army number	POW number	Wounded on capture?	Camps
Bacon	Arthur Henry	Private	2nd Battalion, Parachute Regiment	6142669			Stalag XI B
Bacon	Sydney Thomas	Corporal	156th Battalion, Parachute Regiment	6012161			Ermelo Hospital, Stalag IV B
Badger	Peter George	Private	2nd Battalion, Parachute Regiment	469960	117561	Yes	Stalag XI B, Stalag II A
Baggott	Ronald	Private	2nd Battalion, South Staffordshire Regiment	14654405	91176		Stalag IV B
Bailey	Albert Herbert Charles	Driver	253rd Airborne Light Company, Royal Army Service Corps	170899			Stalag XII A, Stalag IV B
Bailey	Walter Clement	Trooper	1st Airborne Reconnaissance Squadron	10603469			Stalag XII A, Stalag IV B, Dulag IV A
Baldwin	John	Lieutenant	Glider Pilot Regiment	269414			Dulag Luft, Stalag Luft 1
Baldwin	Ronald George	Private	11th Battalion, Parachute Regiment	4980004	92118		Stalag XII A, Stalag IV C
Ball	Donald	Private	Parachute Regiment	3973863	118487	Yes	Stalag XI B
Ball	Eric	Lance Corporal	10th Battalion, Parachute Regiment	865470	118290	Yes	Apeldoorn Hospital, Stalag XI B
Ball	George	Signalman	1st Airlanding Light Regiment, Royal Signals	2122492	118122		Apeldoorn Hospital, Stalag XI B
Ball	Richard Patrick	Gunner	1st Airlanding Light Regiment, Royal Artillery	1084454	117397		Stalag XI B
Ballingall	Peter	Private	16th Parachute Field Ambulance, Royal Army Medical Corps	97004292	118595		Stalag XI B
Barclay	Robert	Lance Corporal	1st Battalion, Parachute Regiment	3131984	140156	Yes	Stalag IV A
Barham	Leonard Charles	Sergeant	1st Battalion, Parachute Regiment	6026001			Stalag IV B
Barling	Anthony Seymour	Captain	133rd Parachute Field Ambulance, Royal Army Medical Corps	306036	40		Dulag Luft, Wetzlar, Oflag IX A/Z

Surname	First name	Rank	Regiment	Number	Number	Q	Camps
Barlow	Leslie George	Private	3rd Battalion, Parachute Regiment	7908100	91599	Yes	Stalag XII A, Stalag IV B
Barnard	Harry	Private	3rd Battalion, Parachute Regiment	5511669			Stalag IV B, Stalag IV F
Barnbrook	James Stanley	Sergeant	2nd Battalion, Parachute Regiment	6016887			Stalag IV B
Barnes	George	Private	2nd Battalion, Parachute Regiment	6145484	88941		Stalag XII A, Stalag IV B
Barningham	Sydney	Private	7th Battalion, King's Own Scottish Borderers Regiment	14414368			Stalag IV B
Barr	John Dobbin	Private	7th Battalion, King's Own Scottish Borderers Regiment	14211045	75959		Stalag XII A, Stalag IV B
Barraclough	Charles	Private	2nd Battalion, Parachute Regiment	883950			Stalag XII A, Stalag IV B
Barrett	Dennis George	Sergeant	1st Battalion, Parachute Regiment	5338896			Stalag XII A, Stalag II A
Barrett	Robert Ernest	Gunner	1st Airlanding Light Regiment, Royal Artillery	869862	92115		Stalag XII A, Stalag IV B
Barritt	Harry Charlie	Lance Corporal	10th Battalion, Parachute Regiment	6412557			Stalag IV B, Stalag IV C
Barron	Stanley	Lance Corporal	250th Airborne Light Company, Royal Army Service Corps	175762			Stalag XII A, Stalag IV B
Barry	Philip Hanbury	Lieutenant	2nd Battalion, Parachute Regiment	240444	2182	Yes	Reserve Lazarett Obermaßfeld, Reserve Lazarett Meiningen, Oflag IX A/Z
Barstow	Robert	Sergeant	3rd Battalion, Parachute Regiment	3392250			Stalag XII A, Interrogation centre Dietz, Stalag II A
Bashford	Stanley Thomas Howard	Sergeant	11th Battalion, Parachute Regiment	4857599	89784		Stalag XII A, Stalag II A

Family name	Forename	Rank	Unit as given on Questionnaire	Army number	POW number	Wounded on capture?	Camps
Bass	Bertram	Gunner	1st Airlanding Anti-Tank Battery, Royal Artillery	998089		Yes	Stalag XII A, Stalag IV B
Bastow	James Arthur	Signalman	1st Parachute Brigade, Royal Signals	6216630	117880	Yes	Stalag XI B, Stalag III A, Stalag XI A, Stalag IV D
Bates	John Bernard	Staff Sergeant	Glider Pilot Regiment	912044			Dulag Luft – Oberusel, Stalag Luft 7, Stalag III A
Bateson	Robert James	Private	1st Battalion, Border Regiment	3776362	975499		Stalag XII A, Stalag IV B, Stalag IV C
Batten	John Samuel	Sergeant	Parachute Regiment	5435891	117981	Yes	Stalag XI B, Stalag VIII C
Battley	John Harold	Private	16th Parachute Field Ambulance, Royal Army Medical Corps	7387449	89574		Stalag XII A, Stalag IV B
Baudrey	Henry William	Private	156th Battalion, Parachute Regiment	841838	75328		Stalag XII A, Stalag IV B
Baxendale	Michael Kenneth	Private	156th Battalion, Parachute Regiment	6849050	117855	Yes	Lingen Hospital, Stalag XI B, Oflag 79
Baxter	Robert Valentine	Private	Parachute Regiment	2760375			Stalag IV B, Stalag IV C
Bayford	George William	Regimental Sergeant Major	Glider Pilot Regiment	6843827			Dulag Luft – Oberusel, Stalag Luft 7, Stalag III A
Bayley	Len Edward	Private	10th Battalion, Parachute Regiment	14646018		Yes	Stalag XII A, Stalag XI B
Baylis	George Sidney	Staff Sergeant	Glider Pilot Regiment	6206242			Dulag Luft – Wetzlar, Stalag Luft 7, Stalag III A
Baylis	Richard William Charles	Private	2nd Battalion, South Staffordshire Regiment	978278	140084	Yes	Hospital Holland, Stalag VII A

Surname	First name(s)	Rank	Unit	Number	Number		Camps
Beach	James William Alfred	Private	3rd Battalion, Parachute Regiment	14203487			Stalag XII A, Stalag IV F, Stalag IV B
Beasley	Walter Leslies	Private	156th Battalion, Parachute Regiment	6981219	75509		Stalag XII A, Stalag IV B, Stalag IV F
Beattie	James	Private	7th Battalion, King's Own Scottish Borderers Regiment	3197491	88795		Stalag XII A, Stalag IV B
Beckett	Owen Charles	Lance Corporal	10th Battalion, Parachute Regiment	7346270			6 Panzer Grenadier HQ, Stalag XII A, Stalag IV B
Beckett	Sydney Reginald Barker	Private	4th Battalion, Dorset Regiment	1506674	21874		Stalag XII A, Stalag IV B
Bedder	Walter Thomas	Private	7th Battalion, King's Own Scottish Borderers Regiment	1539436	90497		Stalag XII A, Stalag IV B, Stalag IV C
Beddoe	William Glyndwr	Lieutenant	7th Battalion, King's Own Scottish Borderers Regiment	285618	524		Stalag XII A, Oflag XII B, Oflag VII B, Stalag VII A
Bedford	Douglas Leslie	Private	1st Battalion, Parachute Regiment	14658474			Stalag XII A, Stalag IV B
Bedford	Francis Henry	Private	2nd Battalion, Parachute Regiment	7013778			Stalag XII A Stalag IV B
Bedford	Stanley William	Private	2nd Battalion, South Staffordshire Regiment	4925203			Stalag XII A, Stalag IV B
Beeston	John Richard	Private	2nd Battalion, Parachute Regiment	11050096			Stalag XII A, Stalag IV B
Beet	Charles	Lance Corporal	2nd Battalion, South Staffordshire Regiment	5125139	99999	Yes	Stalag XII A, Stalag IV F
Beet	Walter Reginald	Private	10th Battalion, Parachute Regiment	6400246	754454	Yes	Stalag XII A, Stalag IV B, Stalag IV C
Beezum	Gordon	Sergeant	Glider Pilot Regiment	7904031			Stalag XII A, Stalag IV B
Bell	Albert Percy	Private	16th Parachute Field Ambulance, Royal Army Medical Corps	69089	89949		Stalag XII A, Stalag IV B

Family name	Forename	Rank	Unit as given on Questionnaire	Army number	POW number	Wounded on capture?	Camps
Bell	John Mitchell Kenyon	Lieutenant	156th Battalion, Parachute Regiment	217392		Yes	Stalag XII A, Dulag XII B, Oflag VII B, Stalag VII A
Bell	Keith Foster	Lieutenant	11th Battalion, Parachute Regiment	172259	2179	Yes	Reserve Lazarett Obermaßfeld, Oflag IX A/Z
Bell	Robert	Aircraftman	Light Warning Set Unit No. 6080, RAF	1373392			Stalag XII A, Stalag IV B
Bell	Robert	Private	7th Battalion, King's Own Scottish Borderers Regiment	3191588		Yes	Stalag XIII B
Bellamy	John Desmond	Sergeant/W	16th Parachute Field Ambulance	7381695	89795		St Elizabeth's Hospital, Dulag Luft – Frankfurt, Stalag XII A, Stalag II A
Bellas	George Geoffrey	Private	7th Battalion, King's Own Scottish Borderers Regiment	3325532			Stalag XII A, Stalag IV B
Bellew	Cyril	Craftsman	Royal Electrical and Mechanical Engineers	4081359	75843		Stalag XII A, Stalag IV B
Benham	Arthur James	Private	2nd Battalion, Parachute Regiment	58357880		Yes	Stalag XI B
Bennett	Arthur	Private	2nd Battalion, South Staffordshire Regiment	4928716		Yes	Stalag XII A, Stalag IV C, Stalag IV G
Bennett	Edward Harry	Private	156th Battalion, Parachute Regiment	14416157	90647		Stalag XII A, Stalag IV B
Bennett	Harold George	Private	133rd Parachute Field Ambulance, Royal Army Medical Corps	7378123			Stalag IV B
Bennett	Thomas	Private	3rd Battalion, Parachute Regiment	4129244	89557		Stalag XII A, Stalag IV B

Surname	First name	Rank	Regiment	Number	Number	Q	Camps
Bennett	William James (?)	Private	Parachute Regiment	3459818		Yes	Stalag XII A, Stalag IV B, Stalag IV A
Bent	William	Private	1st Battalion, Border Regiment	3596732	75926		Stalag XII A, Stalag IV F
Berg	Alfred Ernest	Lance Corporal	250th Airborne Light Company, Royal Army Service Corps	6219285	91140		Stalag XII A, Stalag IV B, Stalag IV F
Berg	Edward Horace	Private	2nd Battalion, South Staffordshire Regiment	6400036			Stalag IV B
Bernstein	Cyril	Lance Corporal	11th Battalion, Parachute Regiment	954033	92135	Yes	Stalag XII A, Stalag IV B
Berry	Cecil John	Lance Corporal	2nd Battalion, South Staffordshire Regiment	4921888			Stalag XII A, Stalag IV B, Stalag IV C
Berry	George Albert	Lance Bombardier	1st Airlanding Anti-Tank Battery, Royal Artillery	3524816	92014		Stalag XII A, Stalag IV B
Berry	Joseph Edward	Private	11th Battalion, Parachute Regiment	1428100	294932		Apeldoorn Hospital, Stalag XII A, Stalag IV B
Berry	O'Neill Ferguson	Lance Corporal	7th Battalion, King's Own Scottish Borderers Regiment	3188546			Dulag XII A, Stalag XI B
Best	Lawrence	Driver	250th Airborne Light Company, Royal Army Service Corps	10694171	76000		Stalag XII A, Stalag IV B
Bett	John Myles	Sergeant, Lance	7th Battalion, King's Own Scottish Borderers Regiment	3196624	140133	Yes	St Liduina Hospital Apeldoorn, St Joseph's Hospital Enschede, Stalag VII A, Stalag 383, Stalag VII A
Betts	George	Sergeant	Glider Pilot Regiment	14233066			Stalag XII A, Stalag IV B
Betts	Henry	Private	156th Battalion, Parachute Regiment	4345218			Stalag XII A, Stalag IV B
Beveridge	Thomas McLeod	Lance Corporal	9th Field Company (Airborne), Royal Engineers	2113967	75856		Stalag XII A, Stalag IV D

Family name	Forename	Rank	Unit as given on Questionnaire	Army number	POW number	Wounded on capture?	Camps
Beveridge	William	Private	1st Battalion, Parachute Regiment	2885410	140117		Apeldoorn Hospital, Stalag VII A, Augsburgh, Ettringen
Bevington	Bernard Leslie	Private	2nd Battalion, South Staffordshire Regiment	14397682			Dulag Luft, Stalag VIII C
Bicker	George Stanley	Corporal	Royal Signals	2324374			Stalag XII A, Stalag VIII C
Biddulph	James	Private	2nd Battalion, South Staffordshire Regiment	5051428			Stalag XII A, Stalag VIII C
Bilsland	John	Private	3rd Battalion, Parachute Regiment	3196036			Stalag IV B
Binge	Dudley Albert George	Sergeant	2nd Battalion, Parachute Regiment	1612710			Stalag XII A, Stalag XVIII C
Binns	Arthur	Staff Sergeant	Glider Pilot Regiment	3390495			Stalag XII A, Stalag IV B
Birchenough	Richard Alfred Godsal	Captain	11th Battalion, Parachute Regiment	112810	18650	Yes	Lazarett Ruttenmunster, Stalag V B, Oflag VII B
Bird	Charles Randle	Lance Corporal	5th Battalion, Dorset Regiment	4923658	93369		Stalag XII A, Stalag XI B
Bird	Frederick Rudd	Gunner	1st Airlanding Light Regiment, Royal Artillery	14290006	118217	Yes	Stalag XI B
Bird	Roy Alexander	Corporal	16th Parachute Field Ambulance, Royal Army Medical Corps	85750	89654		Stalag XII A, Stalag II A
Birtwistle	Sam	Gunner	1st Airlanding Light Regiment, Royal Artillery	14254706	75966		Stalag XII A, Stalag IV B, Stalag IV D
Bishop	Frank	Private	2nd Battalion, South Staffordshire Regiment	5681913	117804	Yes	Stalag XI B, Stalag III A, Stalag XI A, Stalag IV D
Bishop	Walter William	Lance Corporal	156th Battalion, Parachute Regiment	6086564			Stalag XII A, Stalag IV B, Stalag IV A?

Surname	First name	Rank	Unit				Camps
Black	Bernard	Staff Sergeant	Glider Pilot Regiment	884545	7596		Sammelstelle Woerden, Dulag Luft – Oberusel, Dulag Luft – Wetzlar, Stalag Luft 1
Black	John	Private	156th Battalion, Parachute Regiment	2939792			Stalag XII A, Stalag IV B, Stalag IV A
Black	James Charles	Sapper	1st Parachute Squadron, Royal Engineers	1986005			Stalag XII A, Stalag IV B
Blackie	James	Corporal	7th Battalion, King's Own Scottish Borderers Regiment	3185739			Stalag XII A, Stalag IV B
Blackmore	John David	Private	10th Battalion, Parachute Regiment	4447335			Stalag XII A, Stalag IV B, Stalag IV F
Blackmore	Sydney George	Private	1st Battalion, Parachute Regiment	6853726	117793	Yes	Stalag XI B, Stalag III A, Stalag XI A
Blacow	Ronald	Sergeant	156th Battalion, Parachute Regiment	3710567			Stalag XII A, Stalag II A
Blades	Ernest	Private	1st Battalion, Border Regiment	3602778	91628		Stalag IV B
Bland	Percy	Private	156th Battalion, Parachute Regiment	4208563			Stalag XII A, Stalag XI B
Blanks	Joseph	Private	156th Battalion, Parachute Regiment	6146068	75506		Stalag IV C
Blinko	George Henry	Private	21st Independent Parachute Company	5391704		Yes	Stalag XI B, Stalag III A, Stalag XI A
Blockwell	Albert Leslie	Lance Corporal	7th Battalion, King's Own Scottish Borderers Regiment	7622135	26090		Stalag XII A, Stalag IV B, Stalag IV F
Blouet	Donald	Private	133rd Parachute Field Ambulance, Royal Army Medical Corps	7349318	90112		Stalag IV B
Bloys	William	Private	2nd Battalion, Parachute Regiment	6029487			Stalag XII A, Stalag IV B

Family name	Forename	Rank	Unit as given on Questionnaire	Army number	POW number	Wounded on capture?	Camps
Blundell	Kenneth	Staff Sergeant	Glider Pilot Regiment	4460360			Stalag XII A, Stalag IV B
Boddington	Wilfred	Private	156th Battalion, Parachute Regiment	103738			Stalag XII A, Stalag IV B
Boe	John Allan	Private	3rd Battalion, Parachute Regiment	5442182	117309	Yes	Stalag XI B, Oflag 79
Bollington	Robert	Gunner	1st Airlanding Light Regiment, Royal Artillery	14326060	118631	Yes	Arnhem Hospital, Apeldoorn Hospital, Stalag XI B
Bolton	Joseph	Private	2nd Battalion, Parachute Regiment	1086471	117914		Stalag XI B, Stalag III A, Stalag II A
Bonser	Frank	Private	11th Battalion, Parachute Regiment	4800484	117591		Stalag XI B
Boorman	Percy	Lance Corporal	4th Parachute Brigade	6286352	117660		Stalag XI B, Stalag III A, Stalag XI A, Stalag IV D
Booth	Eric Charles	Driver	1st Parachute Squadron, Royal Engineers	1951655			Stalag XII A, Stalag IV B, Stalag IV D
Booth	Harry	Private	3rd Battalion, Parachute Regiment	892682			Stalag XII A, Stalag IV B
Bourne	Derrick Arthur	Private	2nd Battalion, South Staffordshire Regiment	4925767			Stalag XII A, Stalag IV B
Bourne	Ernest Frederick	Lance Corporal	2nd Battalion, South Staffordshire Regiment	4918790	91638		Stalag XII A, Stalag IV B, Stalag IV C
Boushear	James	Private	156th Battalion, Parachute Regiment	14255636			Stalag XII A, Stalag IV B, Stalag IV F
Boustead	Albert Edward	Lieutenant	2nd Battalion, South Staffordshire Regiment	434	91844	Yes	Enschede Hospital, Stalag XII A, Oflag XII B, Oflag VII B, Stalag VII A
Bowden	Samuel Kenneth	Sergeant	Glider Pilot Regiment	71237			Stalag Luft 3, Stalag III A

Surname	First names	Rank	Regiment	Number	Number	Questionnaire	Camps
Bower	Stanley	Sapper	4th Parachute Squadron, Royal Engineers	1951358	90698	Yes	Stalag XII A, Stalag IV B
Bowers	Raymond Francis	Captain Reverend	10th Battalion, Parachute Regiment	291627	140115	Yes	Stalag VII A
Bowes	James Michael	Private	156th Battalion, Parachute Regiment	3653641	75343		Stalag XII A, Stalag IV B, Stalag IV D, Stalag IV F
Bowie	Alexander John	Private	3rd Battalion, Parachute Regiment	3318961			Stalag XII A, Stalag IV B
Bowles	Charles Edward	Private	2nd Battalion, Oxfordshire and Buckinghamshire Light Infantry Regiment	5383183	118070	Yes	Stalag XI B, Oflag 79
Bowles	Dennis Arthur	Gunner	1st Airlanding Light Regiment, Royal Artillery	14257583		Yes	Stalag XII A, Stalag IV B, Stalag IV F
Boyd	Douglas	Private	7th Battalion, King's Own Scottish Borderers Regiment	3197623			Stalag XII A, Stalag IV B, Stalag IV F
Boydell	Edward	Private	2nd Battalion, Parachute Regiment	2757701			Stalag IV B
Boyle	Peter Bernard	Staff Sergeant	Glider Pilot Regiment	4983193			Stalag XII A, Stalag IV B
Boyle	Ronald James	Private	2nd Battalion, Parachute Regiment	3598564	117376	Yes	Stalag XI B, Stalag III A, Stalag XI A
Boynes	Albert Percival Michael	Private	10th Battalion, Parachute Regiment	5619030	26082		Stalag XII A, Stalag IV B
Brackenboro	John Leonard	Private	Parachute Regiment	4123948			Stalag IV D
Bradbeer	Albert Leslie	Sergeant	Glider Pilot Regiment	14230534	76284		Stalag XII A, Stalag IV B
Bradbury	John Alfred	Sergeant	Glider Pilot Regiment	14547304			Dulag Luft – Frankfurt, Stalag Luft 7, Stalag II A
Bradbury	William Henry George	Sapper	1st Parachute Squadron, Royal Engineers	14203066			Stalag XII A, Stalag IV B
Bradley	Edward	Sergeant	2nd Battalion, South Staffordshire Regiment	4913836	89848		Stalag XII A, Stalag II A

Family name	Forename	Rank	Unit as given on Questionnaire	Army number	POW number	Wounded on capture?	Camps
Bradley	Leslie	Sergeant	1st Battalion, Parachute Regiment	3654679	140113	Yes	Stalag VII A
Bradley	Thomas Phazie	Lance Corporal	9th Field Company (Airborne), Royal Engineers	2012016			Stalag XII A, Stalag IV B
Braithwaite	Gilbert Edmund	Private	2nd Battalion, South Staffordshire Regiment	6016356			Stalag XII A, Stalag IV B, Stalag IV C
Braithwaite	Robert Raymond	Private	The Parachute Regiment	2084621			Stalag XII A, Stalag IV B, Stalag IV C
Bramwell	Paul Eric	Gunner	1st Airlanding Light Regiment, Royal Artillery	935154	92068		Stalag XII A, Stalag IV B
Breen	Thomas Francis	Lance Corporal	1st Airborne Provost Company	1917769			Dulag Luft – Frankfurt, Stalag IX C
Bremner	Francis Reginald John	Private	156th Battalion, Parachute Regiment	5348811			Stalag XII A, Stalag IV B, Stalag IV D
Brett	Frank Arthur	Gunner	1st Airlanding Anti-Tank Battery, Royal Artillery	1103757	75561		Stalag XII A, Stalag IV B, Stalag IV D
Brett	Thomas	Lance Corporal	1st Battalion, Border Regiment	3596764	91625		Stalag XII A, Stalag IV (?)
Brewin	Thomas Frderick	Private	2nd Battalion, South Staffordshire Regiment	14662825	91503		Stalag XII A, Stalag IV C
Bricker	Denis Herbert	Driver	250th Airborne Light Company, Royal Army Service Corps	175632	118617	Yes	Apeldoorn Hospital, Stalag XI B, Oflag 79
Bridge	Joseph Edward	Private	2nd Battalion, South Staffordshire Regiment	4923097	89444		Stalag XII A, Dulag Luft – Oberusel, Stalag IV B
Bridgewater	Ernest Edward	Corporal	11th Battalion, Parachute Regiment	7262084		Yes	Stalag IV B, Stalag II A
Briggs	Kenneth William	Lance Corporal	1st Battalion, Border Regiment	4346036	75674		Stalag XII A, Stalag IV B

Bright	Stanley	Private	2nd Battalion, South Staffordshire Regiment	5734258			Stalag IV B
Bristow	Frank James	Private	156th Battalion, Parachute Regiment	6291433			Stalag XII A, Stalag IV B
Britland	Sydney	Leading Aircraftman	Light Warning Set Unit No. 6080, RAF	1750457	1055		Dulag Luft, Stalag Luft 7, Stalag III A
Britnev	Vladimir Alexandroitcn	Lieutenant	1st Battalion, Parachute Regiment	162044	534		Oflag 79
Britton	Daniel James	Private	1st Battalion, Parachute Regiment	5672278	140088	Yes	Stalag VII A, Reserve Lazarette Freising
Broadfoot	Robert	Private	156th Battalion, Parachute Regiment	3189292			Stalag XII A, Stalag IV B
Broadhurst	William	Private	11th Battalion, Parachute Regiment	889617	9166		Stalag XII A, Stalag IV C
Broadley	David Smith	Staff Sergeant	Glider Pilot Regiment	1468299			Stalag XII A, Dulag Luft, Stalag Luft 7, Stalag III A
Brock	Edwin Ward	Regimental Sergeant Major	16th Parachute Field Ambulance, Royal Army Medical Corps	7522897			Stalag XII A, Stalag II A
Brodie	James	Gunner	1st Airlanding Light Regiment, Royal Artillery	14957653			Stalag XII A, Stalag IV B, Stalag IV C
Brodrick	Thomas Robert	Corporal	Army Catering Corps	7369184	140055		Stalag VII A
Bromfield	Arthur	Sergeant	2nd Battalion, Parachute Regiment	6014527	88939		Stalag XII A, Stalag XVIII C
Bromilow	Willis Vincent	Private	1st Battalion, Border Regiment	14653229	117623	Yes	Stalag XI B, Stalag III A, Stalag XI A
Brook	William Henry	Driver	63rd Company, Royal Army Service Corps	163198	75501	Yes	Stalag XI B, Stalag IV B, Stalag IV F
Brooker	Ronald James	Trooper	1st Airborne Reconnaissance Squadron	6354463	91435		Arnhem Hospital, Stalag XII A, Stalag IV B, Stalag IV F

Family name	Forename	Rank	Unit as given on Questionnaire	Army number	POW number	Wounded on capture?	Camps
Brookes	Dennis Lionel	Corporal	11th Battalion, Parachute Regiment	4123596			Stalag XII A, Stalag II A
Brookfield	John	Staff Sergeant	Glider Pilot Regiment	85942	76289		Stalag XII A, Stalag IV B
Brooks	Arthur	Private	2nd Battalion, South Staffordshire Regiment	5125767	92898		Stalag XII A, Stalag VIII C, Stalag IX B
Brooks	Clarence	Sergeant	Glider Pilot Regiment	7590893			Dulag Luft, Stalag Luft 7, Stalag III A
Brooks	David Arthur	Sergeant	2nd Battalion, Parachute Regiment	6349289			Stalag II A
Brooks	Edward Charles	Corporal	156th Battalion, Parachute Regiment	5437863			Stalag II A
Brooks	Jack	Private	1st Battalion, Border Regiment	14650833	117535	Yes	Stalag XI B, Stalag III A, Stalag XI A, Stalag IV D
Brooks	Jack Douglas	Driver	250th Airborne Light Company, Royal Army Service Corps	242720	91417		Stalag XII A, Stalag IV B, Stalag IV A
Brooks	Stanley Donald	Private	2nd Battalion, Parachute Regiment	6104511	117266		Arnhem Municipal Hospital, Lingen Hospital, Stalag XI B
Broome	Alfred James	Private	10th Battalion, Parachute Regiment	6022185			Stalag XII A, Stalag IV B
Brophy	Thomas	Private	156th Battalion, Parachute Regiment	65890			Stalag XII A, Stalag IV B
Brotherton	Arthur	Private	156th Battalion, Parachute Regiment	5054413			Stalag IV B
Brotherton	Donald	Private	3rd Battalion, Parachute Regiment	6018336	117523		Stalag XI B, Stalag III A, Stalag XI A

Surname	First name(s)	Rank	Unit	Service no.		Questionnaire	Camps
Brotherton	Walter	Craftsman	Royal Electrical and Mechanical Engineers	4273439	91760		Stalag XII A, Stalag IV B, Stalag IV A
Brown	Arthur	Private	2nd Battalion, Parachute Regiment	7357412			Stalag XII A, Stalag IV B
Brown	Andrew Peddie Dunlop	Private	3rd Battalion, Parachute Regiment	3191772	65303		Stalag XII A, Stalag IV B, Stalag IV C
Brown	Cyril	Private	2nd Battalion, Parachute Regiment	920584			Stalag IX B
Brown	Charles Francis Leighton	Private	4th Battalion, Dorset Regiment	5956239			Stalag IV B, Stalag IV C
Brown	Duncan	Corporal	3rd Battalion, Parachute Regiment	2931228	89926		Stalag XII A, Stalag II A
Brown	Edward Hubart	Gunner	1st Airlanding Light Regiment, Royal Artillery	1096863	118214	Yes	Stalag XI B
Brown	George Andrew	Corporal	3rd Battalion, Parachute Regiment	3129190	75318		Stalag XII A, Stalag IV B
Brown	George Reginald	Sergeant, Lance	2nd Battalion, South Staffordshire Regiment	4917565	89468		Stalag XII A, Stalag II A
Brown	Harry	Private	156th Battalion, Parachute Regiment	91516			Stalag XII A, Stalag IV F
Brown	Henry	Gunner	1st Airlanding Light Regiment, Royal Artillery	937082	75977		Stalag XII A, Stalag IV B
Brown	Harold Stanley	Driver	253rd Airborne Light Company, Royal Army Service Corps	2897665			Stalag XII A, Stalag IV B
Brown	James	Private	4th Parachute Brigade	2987572	90626		Stalag XII A, Stalag IV B
Brown	John	Sapper	Royal Engineers	1895443	118186	Yes	Stalag XI B
Brown	Joseph Potter	Lance Corporal	1st Battalion, Border Regiment	4542186	77754		Stalag XII A, Stalag IV B, Stalag IV F
Brown	John Redshaw	Private	11th Battalion, Parachute Regiment	4452924	91729	Yes	Stalag XII A, Stalag IV B

Family name	Forename	Rank	Unit as given on Questionnaire	Army number	POW number	Wounded on capture?	Camps
Brown	Leonard	Private	7th Battalion, King's Own Scottish Borderers Regiment	14211781	89851		Stalag XII A, Stalag XI B
Brown	Norman	Private	2nd Battalion, South Staffordshire Regiment	4918535			Stalag XII A, Stalag IV B
Brown	Norman	Private	7th Battalion, King's Own Scottish Borderers Regiment	3190181			Stalag XII A, Stalag IV B
Brown	Peter	Private	3rd Battalion, Parachute Regiment	3058097			Stalag XII A, Stalag IV B
Brown	Robert Miller	Private	16th Parachute Field Ambulance, Royal Army Medical Corps	14633706	90560		Stalag XII A, Stalag IV B
Brown	Thomas Watson	Private	Para	3858124	91582		Stalag XII A, Stalag IV B, Stalag IV C
Brown	William Harold	Private	10th Battalion, Parachute Regiment	4535118	75502		Stalag IV B, Stalag IV D
Browne	Daniel James	Private	1st Battalion, Border Regiment	14550679	14186		Stalag XII A, Stalag IV B, Stalag IV F
Browne	Edward William	Staff Sergeant	Glider Pilot Regiment	5730039			Stalag XII A, Dulag Luft – Oberusel, Stalag Luft 7, Stalag III A
Browne	Patrick	Private	7th Battalion, King's Own Scottish Borderers Regiment	1711838			Stalag XII A, Stalag IV B
Brownsell	Anthony	Corporal	156th Battalion, Parachute Regiment	5670619			Stalag XII A, Stalag II A
Bruce	Arnold	Private	2nd Battalion, South Staffordshire Regiment	4919516	92113		Stalag XII A, Stalag IV B
Bruce	Jack	Sergeant	Glider Pilot Regiment	6211584			Stalag XII A, Stalag IV B

Brunt	Derek	Private	1st Battalion, Parachute Regiment	4748060	92120		Stalag XII A, Stalag IV B, Stalag IV A
Bryan	Stephen Arthur	Lance Corporal	2nd Battalion, South Staffordshire Regiment	4919029	117965		Stalag XI B
Bryans	William Howard	Private	2nd Battalion, Parachute Regiment	3325884	75427		Stalag XII A, Stalag IV B, Stalag IV C
Bryant	Reginald Ernest	Private	156th Battalion, Parachute Regiment	14428514		Yes	Stalag XII A, Stalag IV B, Stalag IV F
Bryce	Charles	Staff Sergeant	Glider Pilot Regiment	3254730			Stalag Luft 7, Stalag III A
Bryson	Lionel Henry	Regimental Sergeant Major	Royal Army Medical Corps	7259229			Reserve Lazarett Obermaßfield, Reserve Lazarett Hildburghausen, Reserve Lazarette Freising
Buchanan	Peter Rhodes	Sergeant	2nd Battalion, Parachute Regiment	2931641			Stalag XII A, Stalag II A
Buck	Charles Reginald Harold	Craftsman	Advanced Workshop Detachment, Royal Electrical and Mechanical Engineers	7387240	89268		Stalag XII A, Stalag IV B, Stalag IV D
Buck	Lawrence Fredrick	Corporal	1st Parachute Squadron, Royal Engineers	1883034			Stalag XII A, Stalag XVIII C
Buckley	Charles	Private	1st Battalion, Border Regiment	3597954	91982		Stalag XII A, Stalag IV B, Stalag IV A
Budd	Frederick John	Lance Corporal	181st Airlanding Field Ambulance, Royal Army Medical Corps	7364587			Koning Willem III Kazerne Apeldoorn, Apeldoorn Hospital
Budibent	Clement Bryan	Private	156th Battalion, Parachute Regiment	7674669	18655	Yes	Utrecht Hospital, Reserve Lazarett Burgsteinfurt, Reserve Lazarett Rottemunster, Stalag V B, Stalag V A

Family name	Forename	Rank	Unit as given on Questionnaire	Army number	POW number	Wounded on capture?	Camps
Buglass	James	Private	3rd Battalion, Parachute Regiment	4975389			Stalag IV C, Stalag IV C
Bull	Henry James	Private	156th Battalion, Parachute Regiment	6092624			Stalag XII A, Stalag IV B
Bull	Thomas James	Private	2nd Battalion, South Staffordshire Regiment	14200023	89515		Stalag XII A, Stalag IV B, Stalag IV D
Bullas	Jack	Private	156th Battalion, Parachute Regiment	3387227			Stalag XII A, Stalag IV B
Bunkall	Cecil Norman	Sergeant	Glider Pilot Regiment	911333			Stalag IV B
Burdon	Jack Forster	Private	1st Battalion, Border Regiment	3191498	75438		Stalag XII A, Stalag IV B, Stalag IV C
Burgess	Leonard	Private	3rd Battalion, Parachute Regiment	14693144	91690		Stalag IV B
Burgoyne	William Ralph	Sergeant	Glider Pilot Regiment	4749099			Stalag XII A, Stalag IV B
Burns	Peter	Private	3rd Battalion, Parachute Regiment	14569564	117458		Stalag XI B, Stalag III A, Stalag XI A, Stalag IV D
Burns	Robert Speed	Private	4th Parachute Brigade HQ	3452456	117659	Yes	Stalag XI B, Stalag III A, Stalag XI A
Burrell	Reginald George	Gunner	1st Airlanding Anti-Tank Battery, Royal Artillery	1109220			Stalag IV G
Burridge	Bernard William	Sergeant	1st Battalion, Parachute Regiment	2620969	89213		Stalag XII A, Stalag XVIII C
Burridge	Thomas William	Private	7th Battalion, King's Own Scottish Borderers Regiment	1076009	89213		Stalag XII A, Stalag IV B, Stalag IV F
Burton	Albert	Sapper	4th Parachute Squadron, Royal Engineers	1882104	140144	Yes	Apeldoorn 'Civvis' (Civilian) Hospital, Stalag VII A

Surname	First name	Rank	Unit	Service number		Questionnaire	Camps
Burton	George	Corporal	3rd Battalion, Parachute Regiment	4921199			Dulag Luft, Stalag IV B
Burton	Thomas	Private	7th Battalion, King's Own Scottish Borderers Regiment	3450209	90249		Stalag XII A, Stalag XI B
Butler	Dennis John	Private	1st Battalion, Parachute Regiment	14409701			Stalag XII A, Stalag IV B, Stalag IV F
Butter	Arthur Anthony	Private	Parachute Regiment	7960360	294117		Stalag IV B, Stalag IV C
Butterly	John James	Lance Corporal	1st Parachute Brigade, Royal Signals	796225	880906		Stalag XII A, Stalag IV B
Buttriss	George	Gunner	Forward Observation Unit, Royal Artillery	946892	90711		Stalag XII A, Stalag IV B
Buxey	William Thomas	Sergeant	Glider Pilot Regiment	1876657			Utrecht Hospital, Dulag Luft – Oberusel, Stalag Luft 7, Stalag III A
Byrne	John	Private	1st Battalion, Parachute Regiment	4206915			Stalag XII A, Stalag IV C
Byrne	Michael	Private	1st Battalion, Border Regiment	3782510	118304		Stalag XI B
Byrne	Philip Stafford	Private	1st Battalion, Parachute Regiment	4206124	89957		Stalag IV B, Stalag IV F
Caddick	Ernest	Lance Corporal	156th Battalion, Parachute Regiment	3770832			Stalag IV B, Stalag IV B, Stalag IV E
Cain	John	Private	1st Battalion, Parachute Regiment	3189138	75363		Stalag XII A, Stalag IV B, Stalag IV C
Cairns	William	Corporal	7th Battalion, King's Own Scottish Borderers Regiment	3190460			Stalag II A
Calder	Ronald	Staff Sergeant	Glider Pilot Regiment	3859441			Dulag Luft – Oberusel, Stalag Luft 7, Stalag III A
Caldwell	John Gibson McCoy	Private	2nd Battalion, South Staffordshire Regiment	274850		Yes	Stalag IV B
Callaghan	William	Private	1st Battalion, Border Regiment	3708684	75699		Stalag XII A, Stalag IV B
Cameron	Andrew	Sapper	9th Field Company (Airborne), Royal Engineers	2073139			Stalag XII A, Stalag IV B

Family name	Forename	Rank	Unit as given on Questionnaire	Army number	POW number	Wounded on capture?	Camps
Cameron	Alan James	Trooper	4th Parachute Brigade HQ	3536624	117367		Stalag XI B, Stalag III A, Stalag XI A
Cameron	Hugh McKenzie	Gunner	1st Airlanding Light Regiment, Royal Artillery	890053	75919		Stalag XII A, Stalag IV B, Stalag IV E
Camp	Thomas Everard	Private	1st Battalion, Border Regiment	2619360	118320	Yes	Stalag XI B
Campbell	Henry	Sergeant	2nd Battalion, Parachute Regiment	3055067			Stalag XII A, Stalag XVIII C
Campbell	John Joseph	Private	7th Battalion, King's Own Scottish Borderers Regiment	4539373	90498		Stalag XII A, Stalag IV B, Stalag IV C
Campbell	Robert Stewart	Lance Bombardier	1st Airlanding Light Regiment, Royal Artillery	1578886			Dulag Luft, Stalag XII A, Stalag IV B
Campbell	Sidney Alex Albers	Gunner	1st Airlanding Light Regiment, Royal Artillery	6099334			Stalag IV B, Stalag IV C
Campbell	Alec	Staff Sergeant	Glider Pilot Regiment	2694009			Dulag Luft – Frankfurt, Stalag VII A, Stalag III A
Cannon	Leonard Alexander	Private	1st Battalion, Parachute Regiment	3964252			Stalag XII A, Stalag XI B, Stalag 357
Cansfield	Peter Evens	Signalman	1st Parachute Brigade, Royal Signals	4927573	91328		Stalag XII A, Stalag IV B, Stalag IV F
Canty	Roy	Private	3rd Battalion, Parachute Regiment	6015492			Stalag XII A, Stalag IV D
Capewell	Edward	Private	2nd Battalion, South Staffordshire Regiment	14642798	92703		Stalag XII A, Stalag IV A, Stalag IV A
Cardwell	Edward Alfred	Sapper	4th Parachute Squadron, Royal Engineers	1952670	117909		Stalag XI B, Stalag III A, Stalag XI A, Stalag IV D
Carlier	Leonard Thomas	Private	2nd Battalion, Parachute Regiment	5835317	89827		Stalag XII A, Stalag XI B

Surname	First name	Rank	Unit	Number	Number	Yes	Camps
Carmichael	John	Private	1st Battalion, Parachute Regiment	2879115	91559	Yes	Stalag XII A, Stalag IV B, Stalag IV A
Carpenter	Richard	Private	11th Battalion, Parachute Regiment	5954520			Stalag XII A, Stalag IV D
Carr	Jack	Sergeant	2nd Battalion, Parachute Regiment	2182264			Stalag XII A, Stalag 317, Stalag XVIII C
Carr	Joseph Stuart	Private	2nd Battalion, Parachute Regiment	6147869			Stalag XII A, Stalag II A, Stalag III A
Carr	Stephen Francis	Sapper	1st Parachute Squadron, Royal Engineers	2135069	117444	Yes	Stalag XI B, Stalag III A, Stalag XI A
Carr	William	Signalman	4th Parachute Brigade, Royal Signals	4279044	91677		Stalag XII A, Stalag IV B, Stalag IV A
Carroll	Albert	Lance Corporal	2nd Battalion, South Staffordshire Regiment	14668753	89367		Stalag IV B, Stalag IV C
Carroll	William James	Private	11th Battalion, Parachute Regiment	2932551	117761		Stalag XI B
Carruthers	William George	Private	7th Battalion, King's Own Scottish Borderers Regiment	3194917	91509		Stalag XII A, Stalag IV B, Stalag IV A
Carter	Frederick George Henry	Private	16th Parachute Field Ambulance, Royal Army Medical Corps	14264103	90150		Stalag IV B
Carter	George Richard	Private	7th Battalion, King's Own Scottish Borderers Regiment	3326436			Stalag XII A, Stalag IV B, Stalag IV C
Carter	James Henry	Driver	1st Airlanding Anti-Tank Battery, Royal Artillery	1142052			Stalag XII A, Stalag IV C
Carter	Stephen William	Private	181st Airlanding Field Ambulance, Royal Army Medical Corps	7392998			Stalag XII A, Stalag IV B
Cartledge	Albert	Private	2nd Battalion, Parachute Regiment	14550580			Stalag IV D
Cartmell	James	Private	156th Battalion, Parachute Regiment	3447716	118308		Stalag XI B

Family name	Forename	Rank	Unit as given on Questionnaire	Army number	POW number	Wounded on capture?	Camps
Cartwright	Hugh Harry Langdon	Lieutenant	2nd Battalion, South Staffordshire Regiment	269402	2171	Yes	Apeldoorn, Stalag XI B, Oflag IX A/Z
Case	Alfred Ernest	Private	156th Battalion, Parachute Regiment	5380977	91759		Stalag XII A, Stalag VIII C
Cassells	William	Gunner	1st Airlanding Light Regiment, Royal Artillery	14283055	92092		Stalag XII A, Stalag IV B, Stalag IV C
Cattell	Frederick	Private	2nd Battalion, South Staffordshire Regiment	1557871	91751		Stalag IV B, Stalag IV F
Cave	William Herbert	Driver	250th Airborne Light Company, Royal Army Service Corps	176447	118898	Yes	Apeldoorn Hospital, Stalag XI B, Oflag 79
Cawley	John	Driver	253rd Airborne Light Company, Royal Army Service Corps	10680840	90968		Stalag XII A, Stalag IV B, Stalag IV D
Cawood	Donald Samuel	Private	1st Battalion, Border Regiment	14202522	91629		Stalag XII A, Stalag IV B
Cawrey	Victor Frank	Private	21st Independent Parachute Company	4975875	118305		Stalag XI B, Stalag III A, Stalag XI A
Chamberlain	Stanley Arthur	Private	3rd Battalion, Parachute Regiment	557436	89733		Stalag XII A, Stalag XI B, Stalag 357
Chambers	Talbot Alexander	Sergeant	89th Parachute Field Security Section	118933	93637		Stalag XII A, Stalag VIII C, Stalag III A
Chandler	Brian Gerald	Private	2nd Battalion, South Staffordshire Regiment	7607105			Stalag XII A, Stalag IV B, Stalag IV A
Chandler	William Francis	Trooper	1st Airborne Reconnaissance Squadron	6091692	118711	Yes	Stalag XI B, Oflag 79
Channon	William	Company Quartermaster Sergeant Major	4th Parachute Brigade HQ	5567123	88745		Stalag XII A, Stalag XVIII C

Surname	Forename	Rank	Unit	Number		Questionnaire	Camps
Chant	James Stephen	Private	2nd Battalion, South Staffordshire Regiment	5498826	89337		Stalag XII A, Stalag IV B
Chaplin	Donald Arthur	Sergeant	11th Battalion, Parachute Regiment	3970424			Stalag II A
Chapman	Albert Henry	Gunner	1st Airlanding Light Regiment, Royal Artillery	1470053			Stalag XII A, Stalag VIII C
Chapman	Harold	Trooper	GHQ Liaison Regiment (Phantom)	14521821			Stalag XII A, Stalag IV B, Stalag IV F
Chapman	Harry Arthur Frederick	Staff Sergeant	Glider Pilot Regiment	4267802			Stalag XII A, Stalag IV B
Chapman	Ronald Anthony Francis	Private	3rd Battalion, Parachute Regiment	4914786			Stalag IV B
Chapman	Walter Frederick	Private	7th Battalion, King's Own Scottish Borderers Regiment	4751017			Stalag XII A, Stalag IV B
Charles	Ernest	Private	1st Battalion, Parachute Regiment	5679630		Yes	Stalag XII A, Stalag IV B, Stalag IV D
Chesterton	Eric	Sergeant, Lance	Royal Signals	2330939			Stalag XII A, Stalag VIII C
Chilcott	Frederick Henry	Bombardier	1st Airlanding Anti-Tank Battery, Royal Artillery	780594			Stalag XII A, Stalag XVIII C
Chilton	Edward	Private	1st Battalion, Border Regiment	3191430	75497		Stalag XII A, Stalag IV B, Stalag IV C
Chilton	Herbert James	Staff Sergeant	1st Airlanding Brigade	2012822	118889	Yes	Stalag XI B, Stalag VIII C, Stalag III D
Chilvers	George Williams	Lance Corporal	7th Battalion, King's Own Scottish Borderers Regiment	6922969			Stalag IV B, Stalag IV C
Chivers	Laurence Herbert James	Sergeant	156th Battalion, Parachute Regiment	5673491			Stalag XII A, Stalag IV B
Chivers	William Ernest	Private	2nd Battalion, South Staffordshire Regiment	4917934			Dulag Luft, Stalag XII A, Stalag XI B

Family name	Forename	Rank	Unit as given on Questionnaire	Army number	POW number	Wounded on capture?	Camps
Christie	George	Private	7th Battalion, King's Own Scottish Borderers Regiment	3190220	90556		Stalag XII A, Stalag IV D
Christopher	James	Private	156th Battalion, Parachute Regiment	14425251	75700		Stalag IV B, Stalag IV D
Clamp	George Edward	Corporal	2nd Battalion, Parachute Regiment	4859690		Yes	Stalag XII A, Stalag II A
Clancey	Philip Stafford	Private	10th Battalion, Parachute Regiment	6091449		Yes	Arnhem Hospital, Apeldoorn Hospital, Stalag VII A
Clapham MC	Edward Eric	Lieutenant	1st Airlanding Anti-Tank Battery, Royal Artillery	258481	2175	Yes	Reserve Lazarett Obermaßfeld, Meiningen Con Depot, Oflag IX A/Z
Clark	Andrew Basil	Company Quartermaster Sergeant Major	11th Battalion, Parachute Regiment	6397607			Stalag XII A, Stalag II A
Clark	Clifford Samuel	Leading Aircraftman	Light Warning Set Unit No. 6341, RAF	1675207			Stalag XII A, Stalag IV B
Clark	Henry Pullman	Sergeant	1st Airlanding Light Regiment, Royal Artillery	997188	88740		Stalag XII A, Stalag XVIII C
Clark	James	Private	7th Battalion, King's Own Scottish Borderers Regiment	3245281	90528		Stalag XII A, Stalag VIII C
Clark	John William	Private	3rd Battalion, Parachute Regiment	14219515	89172		Stalag XII A, Stalag IV B, Stalag IV D
Clarke	Alfred Charles James	Private	3rd Battalion, Parachute Regiment	122644			Stalag XII A, Stalag XI B
Clarke	Christopher	Private	3rd Battalion, Parachute Regiment	2049999	91517		Stalag XII A, Stalag IV B

Surname	First name	Rank	Unit	Service no.	POW no.	Q	Camps
Clarke	Donald	Sergeant	11th Battalion, Parachute Regiment	4450139	88788	Yes	Stalag XII A, Stalag XVIII C
Clarke	Edward	Private	10th Battalion, Parachute Regiment	3191917	118830	Yes	Stalag XI B, Oflag 79
Clarke	George	Driver	250th Airborne Light Company, Royal Army Service Corps	290806			Stalag XII A, Stalag IV B
Clarke	Peter	Staff Sergeant	Glider Pilot Regiment	7356321	118129		Konig Willem III Kazerne Apeldoorn, Stalag XI B, Stalag VIII C, Stalag 357
Clarke	Reginald Eric	Sergeant	Glider Pilot Regiment	7949735			Stalag XII A, Stalag IV B
Clarkson	Gordon	Private	2nd Battalion, Parachute Regiment	14682836			Stalag XII A, Stalag IV B, Stalag IV C
Clegg	Thomas	Private	Royal Army Medical Corps	73918145			Stalag IV B
Clements	Robert Stanley	Private	156th Battalion, Parachute Regiment	6293276	117709	Yes	Stalag XI B, Stalag III A, Stalag IX A
Clements	Sydney Peter	Private	11th Battalion, Parachute Regiment	14411807	117346		Stalag XI B, Stalag III A, Stalag XI A
Clifton	William	Corporal	9th Field Company (Airborne), Royal Engineers	2077843	91313	Yes	Stalag XII A, Stalag II A
Clowes	Albert	Private	1st Battalion, Border Regiment	3780000	26085		Stalag XII A, Stalag IV B, Stalag IV G
Coates	John Robert	Sergeant	2nd Battalion, Parachute Regiment	3771565			Stalag XII A, Stalag XVIII C
Cobbold	George Arthur	Staff Sergeant	Glider Pilot Regiment	2575349			Dulag Luft – Oberusel, Stalag Luft 7, Stalag III A
Cockroft	Frederick	Driver	1st Airborne Division, Royal Signals	14503023			Stalag XII A, Stalag IV C
Cocks	Cecil	Private	1st Battalion, Border Regiment	14642494	91707		Stalag XII A, Stalag IV C
Coggins	Percy	Private	1st Battalion, Parachute Regiment	5047437	89331		Stalag IV B

43

Family name	Forename	Rank	Unit as given on Questionnaire	Army number	POW number	Wounded on capture?	Camps
Coid	William	Private	7th Battalion, King's Own Scottish Borderers Regiment	3190234	75372		Stalag XII A, Stalag IV B
Coidan	Denis Gabriel Andrew	Sapper	4th Parachute Squadron, Royal Engineers	1986027	117355	Yes	Stalag XI B
Colaluca	Angelo	Private	3rd Battalion, Parachute Regiment	4809747	117819	Yes	Stalag XI B
Cole	John Henry	Private	156th Battalion, Parachute Regiment	6896445			Stalag XII A, Stalag IV B, Stalag IV D
Cole	Stanley Reginald	Lance Bombardier	Royal Artillery	14262654	93708	Yes	Stalag XII A, Stalag VIII C
Coleman	Richard	Private	10th Battalion, Parachute Regiment	3658412	90520		Stalag XII A, Stalag IV B?
Colkin	Billy	Private	7th Battalion, King's Own Scottish Borderers Regiment	11000947	91778		Stalag XII A, Stalag IV B, Stalag IV C
Collier	Dennis	Private	156th Battalion, Parachute Regiment	5734402			Stalag XII A, Stalag IV B, Stalag IV C
Collins	Herbert	Lance Corporal	7th Battalion, King's Own Scottish Borderers Regiment	3325401	99999		Stalag XII A, Stalag IV B, Stalag IV A
Collins	Sydney George	Private	2nd Battalion, South Staffordshire Regiment	4699064	89288		Stalag IV B, Stalag IV C
Colls	Douglas	Sergeant, Lance	1st Airlanding Anti-Tank Battery, Royal Artillery	1514892			Stalag XII A, Stalag II A
Colmer	Donald Bernard	Private	3rd Battalion, Parachute Regiment	2067681			Dulag Luft, Stalag IV B
Coltart	David	Private	7th Battalion, King's Own Scottish Borderers Regiment	3191054			Stalag IV C

Combey	Simpson Alfred	Lance Corporal	4th Parachute Squadron, Royal Engineers	125981	117794	Yes	Stalag XI B
Common	Albert	Private	1st Battalion, Border Regiment	3191433	91457		Stalag XII A, Stalag IV B, Stalag IV C
Condon	George Walter	Private	11th Battalion, Parachute Regiment	7263856			Stalag XII A, Stalag IV B
Connelly	Edward	Private	7th Battalion, King's Own Scottish Borderers Regiment	3325781			Stalag XII A, Stalag IV B, Stalag IV C
Connely	James Joseph	Gunner	1st Airlanding Anti-Tank Battery, Royal Artillery	3055590	91734	Yes	Stalag XII A, Stalag IV B
Connold	Norman Thomas	Private	3rd Battalion, Parachute Regiment	14427804			Stalag IV B
Connolly	John	Private	4th Battalion, Dorset Regiment	14710015	17562		Stalag XII A, Stalag IV B, Stalag IV D
Connor	Frank	Private	7th Battalion, King's Own Scottish Borderers Regiment	144336225	25479		Stalag IV B
Conway	James Joseph	Staff Sergeant	Glider Pilot Regiment	7043131	117320		Stalag XI B
Coogan	Allan McKenzie Smith	Gunner	1st Airlanding Light Regiment, Royal Artillery	1084529			Stalag XII A, Stalag IV B, Stalag IV F
Cook	George	Private	3rd Battalion, Parachute Regiment	6214569	89173		Stalag XII A, Stalag IV B
Cook	James	Sapper	9th Field Company (Airborne), Royal Engineers	2069925	91491		Stalag IV C
Cook	Noel	Sapper	4th Parachute Squadron, Royal Engineers	1903563	26021		Stalag XII A, Stalag IV B, Stalag IV F
Cook	William Mark	Lance Corporal	11th Battalion, Parachute Regiment	903583	92143		Stalag XII A, Stalag IV B, Stalag IV C
Cooke	Archie William George	Lance Corporal	1st Parachute Squadron, Royal Engineers	1881045			Stalag IV B, Stalag IV D

Family name	Forename	Rank	Unit as given on Questionnaire	Army number	POW number	Wounded on capture?	Camps
Cooke	Charles Edward	Private	2nd Battalion, South Staffordshire Regiment	4917571			Stalag XII A
Cooke	Clifford Kenneth	Private	11th Battalion, Parachute Regiment	10666764	89804		Stalag XII A, Stalag XI B
Cooke	Eric Finney	Private	2nd Battalion, Parachute Regiment	4197475	117278	Yes	Arnhem, Reserve Lazarett Gronau, Stalag XI B, Oflag 79
Cooke	Peter Sidney Victor	Corporal	3rd Battalion, Parachute Regiment	2080407	294120		Stalag IV B
Coombe	Herbert Dorrien	Sergeant	3rd Battalion, Parachute Regiment	5435865	140301	Yes	Stalag VII A Freising Hospital
Cooper	Benjamin John Richard	Sergeant, Lance	2nd Battalion, South Staffordshire Regiment	4077803			Stalag XII A, Stalag II A
Cooper	Cyril	Driver	Airborne Light Company, Royal Army Service Corps	114167	140093	Yes	Lochem Hospital, Stalag VII A
Cooper	Dennis Patrick	Private	1st Battalion, Border Regiment	1437623	75685		Stalag XII A, Stalag IV B
Cooper	Gordon Michael	Private	4th Battalion, Dorset Regiment	14556629			Stalag IV B
Cooper	Herbert George	Private	2nd Battalion, South Staffordshire Regiment	5057632	91673		Stalag XII A, Stalag IV B
Cooper	James	Trooper	1st Airborne Reconnaissance Squadron	14671335	117414	Yes	Stalag XI B
Cooper	John Robert	Corporal	11th Battalion, Parachute Regiment	863102	140123	Yes	Stalag VII A, Stalag 383
Cooper	Robert Dudley	Private	10th Battalion, Parachute Regiment	1461847			Stalag XII A, Stalag IV B, Stalag IV A
Cooper	Ronald Victor	Lance Corporal	1st Parachute Brigade, Royal Signals	5348617			Stalag IV F

Surname	First name	Rank	Unit	Number		Questionnaire	Camps
Cooper	Stanley	Private	181st Airlanding Field Ambulance, Royal Army Medical Corps	7368352			Apeldoorn Hospital, Stalag XII A, Stalag IV B
Cooper	Thomas John	Private	10th Battalion, Parachute Regiment	897853	75654	Yes	Stalag XII A, Stalag IV B
Copley	Stanley George	Signalman	1st Parachute Brigade, Royal Signals	2587283	117839	Yes	Stalag XI B
Coppack	Philip Maurice	Staff Sergeant	Glider Pilot Regiment	937504			Dulag Luft – Oberursel, Stalag Luft 7, Stalag III A
Corfield	Ronald	Sergeant	Glider Pilot Regiment	14344873			Stalag Luft 7, Stalag III A
Cormack	George Burnet	Private	181st Airlanding Field Ambulance, Royal Army Medical Corps	7347023	140059		Stalag VII A
Cornish	Denis	Sergeant	Glider Pilot Regiment	903724		Yes	Dulag Luft – Frankfurt, Stalag Luft 7, Stalag III A
Corns	Charles Eric	Lance Corporal	2nd Battalion, South Staffordshire Regiment	4918495	91746		Stalag XII A, Stalag IV B
Cortmann	Alexander	Private	3rd Battalion, Parachute Regiment	2890203	92100		Stalag XII A, Stalag IV B, Stalag IV F
Corton	Bernard	Private	1st Battalion, Border Regiment	14591265	91520		Stalag XII A, Stalag IV B
Cottam	John Philip	Private	4th Battalion, Dorset Regiment	14664309	25027		Stalag IV F
Cotten	George Henry Charles	Sapper	1st Parachute Squadron, Royal Engineers	14892438			Stalag XII A, Stalag IV B
Cottrell	William John	Bombardier	1st Airlanding Anti-Tank Battery, Royal Artillery	1514708			Stalag XII A, Stalag XVIII C
Couch	Stanley Hugh	Private	2nd Battalion, South Staffordshire Regiment	5440744			Stalag XII A, Stalag IV B
Coupe	Harold	Sapper	1st Parachute Squadron, Royal Engineers	1922268	89229		Stalag XII A, Stalag IV B

Family name	Forename	Rank	Unit as given on Questionnaire	Army number	POW number	Wounded on capture?	Camps
Courcha	William Alexander	Private	10th Battalion, Parachute Regiment	14665231	75407		Stalag XII A, Stalag IV B
Course	Charles Joseph	Private	10th Battalion, Parachute Regiment	4986412			Stalag XII A, Stalag IV B
Courtie	Thomas	Company Sergeant Major	10th Battalion, Parachute Regiment	3768595	140153	Yes	Apeldoorn Hospital, Stalag VII A Reserve Lazarett Freising, Stalag 383
Courtney	Richard William	Gunner	2nd Airlanding Anti-Tank Battery, Royal Artillery	14268331	90921		Stalag XII A, Stalag IV B
Courtney	Thomas Richard Brian	Major	133rd Parachute Field Ambulance, Royal Army Medical Corps	112406	91202		Stalag XII A, Interrogation centre Dietz, Oflag 79, Reserve Lazarett Leipzig-Wahren, Reserve Lazarett Halle
Cousins	Eric Robert	Sergeant	7th Battalion, King's Own Scottish Borderers Regiment	4751138	89427		Stalag XII A, Stalag II A
Cowie	David	Sergeant	2nd Battalion, Parachute Regiment	7886460			Stalag XII A, Stalag XVIII C
Cox	Basil	Private	10th Battalion, Parachute Regiment	5671559	91757		Stalag XII A, Stalag IV B
Cox	Denis Herbert	Sergeant, Acting	2nd Battalion, South Staffordshire Regiment	5051692	89424	Yes	Stalag XII A, Stalag II A
Cox	Ronald Charles Percival	Private	2nd Battalion, Parachute Regiment	5832882			Stalag XII A, Stalag IV B
Cox	Wilfred Douglas	Private	156th Battalion, Parachute Regiment	49191598	89935		Stalag XII A, Stalag XI B

Coxon	Frank	Private	1st Battalion, Parachute Regiment	825718			Stalag IV B
Craig	Daniel	Private	7th Battalion, King's Own Scottish Borderers Regiment	14211595	90557		Stalag XII A, Stalag IV B
Craig	Daniel	Lance Bombardier	Forward Observation Unit, Royal Artillery	855981	75340		Stalag XII A, Stalag IV B
Craig	James	Sergeant	2nd Battalion, Parachute Regiment	3246833	89139		Stalag XII A, Stalag XVIII C
Craig	John Alexander	Private	1st Battalion, Parachute Regiment	7046503	92185		Stalag XII A, Stalag IV C
Craig	Thomas John Lawson	Private	7th Battalion, King's Own Scottish Borderers Regiment	3194287	117380	Yes	Stalag XI B, Stalag III A, Stalag XI A, Stalag IV D
Craig	William	Private	3rd Battalion, Parachute Regiment	14246464		Yes	St Joseph's Hospital Enschede, Reserve Lazarett Teupitz, Dulag Luft Hospital, Reserve Lazarett Obermaßfield, Reserve Lazarett Meiningen, Stalag IX C
Craik	James	Private	7th Battalion, King's Own Scottish Borderers Regiment	3190194			Stalag XII A, Stalag IV B, Stalag IV D
Cram	James Wilson	Sergeant	7th Battalion, King's Own Scottish Borderers Regiment	3193062	89988		Stalag XII A, Stalag II A
Crandles	Austin	Private	2nd Battalion, South Staffordshire Regiment	14340452	89261		Stalag XII A, Stalag IV B, Stalag IV C
Crane	Douglas Broadway	Private	1st Battalion, Parachute Regiment	14577150	75160		Stalag XII A, Stalag IV B
Crane	Ernest	Private	156th Battalion, Parachute Regiment	14420927	18658	Yes	Utrecht Hospital, Reserve Lazarett Burgsteinfurt, Reserve Lazarett Rottenmunster, Stalag VII A

Family name	Forename	Rank	Unit as given on Questionnaire	Army number	POW number	Wounded on capture?	Camps
Crane	William	Private	2nd Battalion, Parachute Regiment	4398812	117851	Yes	Stalag XI B, Stalag III A, Stalag XI A
Crawford	Bert Victor	Private	2nd Battalion, Parachute Regiment	5731255		Yes	Stalag XII A, Stalag IV B
Crawley	Leslie Stanley	Private	2nd Battalion, Parachute Regiment	1677621	75439		Stalag XII A, Stalag IV B, Stalag IV A
Creasy	Reginald George	Corporal	3rd Battalion, Parachute Regiment	5623140	90102		Stalag XII A, Stalag II A
Cressey	Charles	Lance Corporal	1st Airborne Provost Company	2053082	14909		Stalag XII A, Stalag IV B
Critchley	Arthur	Private	3rd Battalion, Parachute Regiment	7888645			Stalag XII A, Stalag IV B, Stalag IV A
Crittenden	Robert Claude	Lieutenant	1st Battalion, Border Regiment	264942	2176	Yes	Oflag IX A/Z
Crockett	Dennis George	Private	7th Battalion, King's Own Scottish Borderers Regiment	11001185	916141		Stalag XII A, Stalag IV B, Stalag IV C
Crockford		Sergeant	Glider Pilot Regiment	2063433			Stalag XII A, Stalag IV B
Cronshaw	Albert	Private	1st Battalion, Border Regiment	6471864			Stalag XII A, Stalag IV B, Stalag IV F
Crook	John Williams	Lance Bombardier	1st Airlanding Light Regiment, Royal Artillery	14256319			Stalag XII A, Stalag IV B, Stalag IV F
Cross	Bernard	Private	1st Battalion, Border Regiment	1146496	18654	Yes	Stalag VII A
Crossland	Stanley	Lance Corporal	1st Battalion, Border Regiment	4691419	117619	Yes	Apeldoorn Hospital, Stalag XI B
Crowe	Ronald Harry	Sergeant	1st Parachute Brigade, Royal Signals	2323334	18679	Yes	Utrecht Hospital, Reserve Lazarett Münster, Reserve Lazarett Rottenmunster, Stalag VII A, Stalag 383

Surname	First name	Rank	Unit	Number	Number	Yes	Sources
Crudginton		Private	1st Battalion, Parachute Regiment	5439376		Yes	Apeldoorn Hospital, Stalag IV C
Cuckle	Lionel	Private	11th Battalion, Parachute Regiment	4896515	75995		Stalag XII A, Stalag IV B
Cull	George William	Private	1st Parachute Brigade	14410678			Stalag XII A, Stalag IV B, Stalag XIII B
Cull	Peter Patrick	Private	1st Battalion, Border Regiment	3608321	14935	Yes	Stalag XII A, Stalag IV B, Stalag IV C
Culliton	Patrick	Private	3rd Battalion, Parachute Regiment	13098369			Stalag XII A
Cully	Christopher	Private	7th Battalion, King's Own Scottish Borderers Regiment	3196678	75541		Stalag XII A, Stalag IV B, Stalag IV C
Culpan	Eric Hopkinson	Sergeant	Glider Pilot Regiment	2081536			Dulag Luft – Oberusel, Stalag Luft 7, Stalag III A
Cund	Edwin	Sergeant	2nd Battalion, South Staffordshire Regiment	4914618			Stalag XII A, Stalag II A
Cunliffe	Roger	Private	1st Battalion, Border Regiment	14402790			St Elizabeth's Hospital, Stalag XII A, Stalag IV B, Stalag IV F
Cunningham	Alexander	Corporal	10th Battalion, Parachute Regiment	4481938	90824		Stalag XII A, Stalag II A
Cunningham	Thomas	Lance Corporal	156th Battalion, Parachute Regiment	345429	90500		Stalag XII A, Stalag IV F
Curtin	William Victor	Lance Corporal	11th Battalion, Parachute Regiment	62945308	95390		Stalag XII A, Stalag IV B
Curtis	Arthur	Private	11th Battalion, Parachute Regiment	6399339			Stalag XII A, Stalag IV B
Curtis	George	Private	1st Battalion, Border Regiment	3597790	118189	Yes	Apeldoorn Hospital, Stalag XI B
Curtis	Leonard Arthur Cecil	Private	3rd Battalion, Parachute Regiment	2047378	117875		Arnhem Municipal Hospital, Stalag XI B, Stalag III A, Stalag XI A

Family name	Forename	Rank	Unit as given on Questionnaire	Army number	POW number	Wounded on capture?	Camps
Cuthbertson	Malcolm	Private	4th Battalion, Dorset Regiment	3770561	91903		Stalag XII A, Stalag IV B, Stalag IV A
Cuthell	Stanley	Private	181st Airlanding Field Ambulance, Royal Army Medical Corps	7388028		Yes	Apeldoorn Hospital, Stalag XII A, Stalag IV B
Cuttill	George Frederick	Corporal	10th Battalion, Parachute Regiment	6025196			Stalag XII A, Stalag II A
Dagwell	David Nicol	Private	156th Battalion, Parachute Regiment	5349578			Stalag XII A, Stalag IV B
Dale	John Arthur	Lance Corporal	2nd Battalion, South Staffordshire Regiment	4914922	89487		Stalag XII A, Stalag IV B, Stalag IV C
Dale	Ronald Richard	Staff Sergeant	Glider Pilot Regiment	5112070	900		Dulag Luft – Oberusel, Stalag Luft 7, Stalag III A
Daley	Joseph	Private	1st Battalion, Border Regiment	3599017	24651		Stalag XII A, Stalag IV B, Stalag IV G
Dalton	Christopher	Private	1st Battalion, Parachute Regiment	4348459			Stalag XII A, Stalag IV B
Dance	Kenneth George	Private	2nd Battalion, South Staffordshire Regiment	4927983	25553		Stalag XII A, Stalag IV B
Dane	Ernest Victor	Sapper	9th Field Company (Airborne), Royal Engineers	2135629	117886		Stalag XI B, Stalag III A, Stalag XI A
Daniels	Stanley	Private	2nd Battalion, South Staffordshire Regiment	14682944	89138		Stalag XII A, Stalag IV C
Darkins	Arthur Robert	Private	156th Battalion, Parachute Regiment	6474749			Stalag XII A, Stalag IV B
Davey	Edward Thomas	Private	181st Airlanding Field Ambulance	7358134	90173		Stalag XII A, Stalag IV B

Surname	Forename	Rank	Regiment	Number	Number	Q	Camps
Davey	Roy	Corporal	2nd Battalion, South Staffordshire Regiment	5348839	89921		Stalag XII A, Stalag II A
Davidson	Charles	Private	10th Battalion, Parachute Regiment	4536073	75493		Stalag XII A, Stalag IV B
Davidson	Robert Mason	Private	156th Battalion, Parachute Regiment	61519	117713	Yes	Stalag XI B
Davies	Desmond Godfrey	Private	2nd Battalion, Parachute Regiment Royal Army Medical Corps	14389667	89420		Stalag IV B
Davies	Eric	Private	1st Battalion, Parachute Regiment	4195158	117835	Yes	Stalag XI B, Stalag III A, Stalag VI A
Davies	Henry	Private	4th Battalion, Dorset Regiment	14723652			Stalag IV B
Davies	Robert William	Private	1st Battalion, Border Regiment	1454411	75695		Stalag IV F
Davies	Sydney	Private	2nd Battalion, Parachute Regiment	14309397			Stalag XII A, Stalag VIII C, Stalag II C, Stalag X C Marlag-Milag
Davies	William Peter	Private	3rd Battalion, Parachute Regiment	41796618			Stalag XII A, Stalag XI B
Davis	Alexander	Private	1st Battalion, Parachute Regiment	818745			Stalag XII A, Stalag IV B, Stalag IV A
Davis	George Ernest	Staff Sergeant	Glider Pilot Regiment	2045543			Dulag Luft, Stalag Luft 7, Stalag III A
Davis	John Harold	Private	3rd Battalion, Parachute Regiment	5625908			Stalag XII A, Dulag Luft – Wetzlar, Stalag IV B, Stalag IV F
Davis	James Robert	Private	7th Battalion, King's Own Scottish Borderers Regiment	11251840	75352	Yes	Stalag XII A, Stalag IV B, Stalag IV F
Davis	Samuel Wilfred	Private	181st Airlanding Field Ambulance, Royal Army Medical Corps	7362406	93720		Dulag Luft, Stalag XII A, Stalag VIII C, Stalag XIII C

Family name	Forename	Rank	Unit as given on Questionnaire	Army number	POW number	Wounded on capture?	Camps
Dawson	Herbert	Private	2nd Battalion, South Staffordshire Regiment	1714784	89717		Stalag XII A, Stalag XI B, Stalag 357
Dawson	John Harold	Private	2nd Battalion, Parachute Regiment	11407811	75336		Stalag XII A, Stalag IV B
Dawson	Leonard William	Sergeant/W	156th Battalion, Parachute Regiment	800747			Stalag XII A, Stalag II A
Dawson	Robert Ridley	Corporal	Royal Army Medical Corps	7266914			Stalag IV B
Dawson	William Felix	Private	2nd Battalion, South Staffordshire Regiment	5053162	91698		Stalag XII A, Stalag IV B, Stalag IV C
Day	Frank Graham	Driver	261st Field Park Company, Royal Engineers	2013286			Stalag XII A, Stalag IV B, Stalag IV F?
Daye	Russell Robert	Private	7th Battalion, King's Own Scottish Borderers Regiment	14620635	118419	Yes	Stalag XI B
Deacon	James	Corporal	7th Battalion, King's Own Scottish Borderers Regiment	3190690			Stalag XII A, Stalag II A
Deakin	Albert	Private	2nd Battalion, South Staffordshire Regiment	2621911	91483		Stalag XII A, Stalag IV B, Stalag IV F
Dean	William Arthur	Private	156th Battalion, Parachute Regiment	4974106			Stalag XII A, Stalag IV B
Deasy	William Roy	Staff Sergeant	Glider Pilot Regiment	985314	118164		Stalag XI B, Stalag VIII C, Stalag IV B
Debnam	Thomas James	Private	3rd Battalion, Parachute Regiment	5435791	117979	Yes	Stalag XI B, Oflag 79
Deeley	George Alfred	Sergeant	Glider Pilot Regiment	5127622			Dulag Luft – Oberusel, Stalag Luft 7, Stalag III A
Delea	Eric Michael Desmond	Private	156th Battalion, Parachute Regiment	3778794			Stalag XII A, Dulag Luft – Wetzlar, Stalag IV B, Stalag IV G

Dell	Edward	Corporal	2nd Battalion, Parachute Regiment	6203748			Stalag XII A, Stalag II A, Stalag III A
Denholm	James	Private	11th Battalion, Parachute Regiment	3314746	119639		Apeldoorn Hospital, Stalag XI B
Dennis	Bernard George	Gunner	1st Airlanding Light Regiment, Royal Artillery	1076427	77371		Stalag IV B
Dennis	Frank	Sergeant	Glider Pilot Regiment	5887705			Dulag Luft, Stalag Luft 7, Stalag III A
Dennis	Ronald Francis	Private	4th Battalion, Dorset Regiment	14710022	26048		Stalag XII A, Stalag IV B, Stalag IV F
Dennison	Wilfred	Private	7th Battalion, King's Own Scottish Borderers Regiment	4539145	90639		Stalag XII A, Stalag IV B
Denny	Thomas Bernard Philip	Private	2nd Battalion, South Staffordshire Regiment	14554721			Stalag XII A, Stalag IV B, Stalag IV C
Derbyshire	Stanley	Private	3rd Battalion, Parachute Regiment	14375898	52885		Queen Wilhelmina Barracks, Konig Willem III Kazerne Apeldoorn, Stalag IX C
Devey	John Raymond	Staff Sergeant	Glider Pilot Regiment	3601654	903		Dulag Luft – Oberusel, Stalag Luft 7, Stalag III A
Devine	John	Signalman	1st Parachute Brigade, Royal Signals	2574778	88905		Stalag XII A, Stalag IV B
Devlin	James	Private	7th Battalion, King's Own Scottish Borderers Regiment	14410841			Stalag IV D
Di Paola	Joseph	Private	7th Battalion, King's Own Scottish Borderers Regiment	3323806			Stalag XII A, Stalag IV B, Stalag IV F
Dicken	Henry	Private	10th Battalion, Parachute Regiment	14410900	90516	Yes	Stalag XII A, Stalag IV B, Reserve Lazarett II Dresden, Hospitals (see notes), Stalag XIII C

Family name	Forename	Rank	Unit as given on Questionnaire	Army number	POW number	Wounded on capture?	Camps
Dickens	John Raymond	Captain	2nd Battalion, South Staffordshire Regiment	180222	2201		Apeldoorn Hospital, Stalag XI B, Oflag IX A/Z, Reserve Lazarett Obermaßfeld, Oflag IX A/Z
Dickin	James Leon	Private	2nd Battalion, South Staffordshire Regiment	4927982			Stalag XII A, Stalag IV B
Dickinson	John Burley	Captain	1st Airlanding Light Regiment, Royal Artillery	138257	2199		Stalag XI B, Oflag IX A/Z
Dickson	Richard	Private	3rd Battalion, Parachute Regiment	4546716	92122		Stalag IV B
Didsbury	Noran	Sergeant	Glider Pilot Regiment	14576025			Stalag XII A, Stalag IV B
Dinwiddie	Gordon Maidland	Major	7th Battalion, King's Own Scottish Borderers Regiment	90195	2195	Yes	Apeldoorn Hospital, Oflag IX A/Z
Dixon	Eric Joseph	Private	2nd Battalion, South Staffordshire Regiment	4201186	75872	Yes	Stalag XII A, Stalag IV B
Dixon	Frank Edwin	Lance Corporal	16th Parachute Field Ambulance, Royal Army Medical Corps	7381047			Stalag XII A, Stalag IV B
Dixon	George	Corporal	1st Airborne Reconnaissance Squadron	14272599			Stalag II A
Dixon	John	Private	7th Battalion, King's Own Scottish Borderers Regiment	14203067	90692		Stalag XII A, Stalag IV B
Dixon	Joseph Albert	Private	3rd Battalion, Parachute Regiment	3915723			Stalag IV B, Stalag IV C
Dixon	John Francis	Private	1st Battalion, Border Regiment	3602801			Stalag XII A, Stalag IV B

Surname	Forename	Rank	Unit	Number	Number 2	Questionnaire	Camps
Dixon	Robert Richard	Gunner	1st Airlanding Light Regiment, Royal Artillery	14600654			Stalag XII A, Stalag VIII C, Stalag IV B
Dixon	Thomas	Private	133rd Parachute Field Ambulance, Royal Army Medical Corps	7361998	89925		Stalag XII A, Stalag XI B, Stalag V A, Marching
Dodd	William Ronald	Private	3rd Battalion, Parachute Regiment	6404195			Stalag XII A, Stalag IV B, Stalag IV D
Doig	Charles	Lieutenant	7th Battalion, King's Own Scottish Borderers Regiment	268306			Stalag XII A, Dulag XII B Hadamar, Oflag 79
Doig	John	Private	156th Battalion, Parachute Regiment	14407490			Stalag XII A, Stalag IV B
Dolaghan	Thomas Noel William Dowie	Private	4th Parachute Brigade	6977906	89826		Stalag XII A, Stalag XI B
Donald	Colin	Private	Parachute Regiment	1467192	117417		Stalag XI B, Stalag III A, Stalag XI A
Donaldson	Edward	Private	7th Battalion, King's Own Scottish Borderers Regiment	14656612	89231		Stalag IV B
Donnelly	Moses	Private	1st Battalion, Parachute Regiment	4538622	91461		Stalag XII A, Stalag IV B
Donnelly	Thomas Baker	Private	1st Battalion, Parachute Regiment	2981809			Stalag XII A, Stalag IV B, Stalag IV F
Donovan		Private	2nd Battalion, Parachute Regiment	5953014	89358		Stalag XII A, Stalag IV B, Stalag IV C
Donowho	William	Private	7th Battalion, King's Own Scottish Borderers Regiment	3190801			Stalag XI B
Doughty	Leslie	Sergeant	1st Airlanding Anti-Tank Battery, Royal Artillery	842123	90131		Stalag XII A, Stalag II A
Douglas	Joseph	Lance Corporal	1st Parachute Squadron, Royal Engineers	1886957			Apeldoorn Hospital, Stalag XI B
Douglas	William	Private	156th Battalion, Parachute Regiment	3189703	91481	Yes	Stalag XII A, Stalag IV B, Stalag IV A, Stalag IV E

Family name	Forename	Rank	Unit as given on Questionnaire	Army number	POW number	Wounded on capture?	Camps
Douthwaite	Fred	Private	1st Battalion, Parachute Regiment	14587525	117657	Yes	Stalag XI B
Dove	William Kenneth	Private	156th Battalion, Parachute Regiment	6981695			Stalag XII A, Stalag IV B, Stalag IV D, Stalag IV F
Dover	Victor	Major	2nd Battalion, Parachute Regiment	113514	521		Dulag XII B Hadamar, Oflag 79
Down	Percy	Corporal	1st Battalion, Parachute Regiment	5671339	118257	Yes	Arnhem Hospital, Konig Willem III Kazerne Apeldoorn, Stalag XI B, Stalag VIII C, Brunswick
Downton	William Henry	Private	2nd Battalion, South Staffordshire Regiment	14316550	92022		Stalag XII A, Stalag IV A
Drayton	Frank	Private	2nd Battalion, Parachute Regiment	408160	89525		Stalag XII A, Stalag II A
Dredge	Norman Victor	Private	2nd Battalion, South Staffordshire Regiment	14700066	92215		Stalag XII A, Stalag IV B
Drew	Douglas John Archer	Private	3rd Battalion, Parachute Regiment	6468336			Stalag XII A, Stalag IV B
Drewitt	Arthur William	Private	11th Battalion, Parachute Regiment	518429	117485	Yes	Stalag XI B, Stalag III A, Stalag XI A, Stalag IV D
Driscoll	Edward Dennis	Corporal	7th Battalion, King's Own Scottish Borderers Regiment	2751006	90567		Stalag XII A, Stalag II A
Drury	Robert	Private	10th Battalion, Parachute Regiment	5726456			Stalag XII A, Stalag IV B, Stalag IV D
Dryden	John James	Private	11th Battalion, Parachute Regiment	4451109			Stalag XII A, Stalag IV B

Surname	First name(s)	Rank	Unit				Camps
Duck	John	Signalman	4 Para Brigade, Royal Signals	2573508	90737		Stalag XII A, Stalag IV B, Stalag IV A
Duddy	George Victor	Private	181st Airlanding Field Ambulance, Royal Army Medical Corps	7402718	89573		Stalag XII A, Stalag IV B
Dudley	Frank Thomas	Craftsman	Royal Electrical and Mechanical Engineers	5574814	91497		Stalag XII A, Stalag IV B, Stalag IV A
Duffell	Edward George	Private	2nd Battalion, Parachute Regiment	5835781	89688		Stalag XII A, Stalag XI B
Duffy	John	Sergeant	1st Parachute Brigade	7662893	90033		Stalag XII A, Stalag III A
Dukes	Benjamin William	Private	181st Airlanding Field Ambulance, Royal Army Medical Corps	7380299			Stalag XII A, Stalag IV B
Dunbar	William Shearer	Sergeant	Glider Pilot Regiment	2572042			Apeldoorn, Dulag Luft – Oberusel, Stalag Luft 3
Dunford	Reginald Charles	Private	10th Battalion, Parachute Regiment	555639	77099	Yes	Stalag XII A, Stalag IV B, Stalag IV A, Stalag IV C
Dunlop	John Paterson	Lance Bombardier	1st Airlanding Light Regiment, Royal Artillery	1084223	117403	Yes	Stalag XI B, Stalag III A, Stalag XI A, Stalag IV D
Dunn	Kenneth Harold	Private	2nd Battalion, Parachute Regiment	1828301			Stalag XII A, Stalag IV B
Durant	George Edwin	Gunner	1st Airlanding Light Regiment, Royal Artillery	14284494	91884		Stalag XII A, Dulag Luft – Oberusel, Stalag XII A, Stalag IV B, Stalag IV C
Durkin	James	Private	1st Battalion, Border Regiment	4614317	26024	Yes	Stalag XII A, Stalag IV B
Durnin	Charles	Private	1st Battalion, Border Regiment	4347257	91969		Stalag XII A, Stalag IV B, Stalag IV A

Family name	Forename	Rank	Unit as given on Questionnaire	Army number	POW number	Wounded on capture?	Camps
Dyall	William	Sergeant	Glider Pilot Regiment	853162			Stalag XII A, Stalag IV B, Stalag IV D
Dyer	Albert Jack	Private	2nd Battalion, Parachute Regiment	206567			Stalag XII A, Stalag IV B, Stalag IV C
Dyer	Thomas	Private	2nd Battalion, Parachute Regiment	4543023	89946		Stalag XII A, Stalag IV B, Stalag IV F
Eagleton	John	Private	1st Battalion, Border Regiment	14671556	91521		Stalag XII A, Stalag IV B, Stalag IV F
Easton	William	Private	3rd Battalion, Parachute Regiment	5781435			Stalag XII A, Stalag IV B, Stalag IV C
Eatwell	Horace Arthur	Regimental Sergeant Major	1st Battalion, Parachute Regiment	2613152	89402		Dulag Luft, Stalag XII A, Stalag VIII C
Eccles	Cyril	Private	156th Battalion, Parachute Regiment	7617196			Stalag IV B
Edwards	Charles Percy	Lance Corporal	7th Battalion, King's Own Scottish Borderers Regiment	4921302	90763		Arnhem, Stalag XII A, Stalag IV B
Edwards	James	Lance Corporal	2nd Battalion, South Staffordshire Regiment	4927985	76661		Stalag XII A, Stalag IV C
Edwards	John Iver	Gunner	1st Airlanding Light Regiment, Royal Artillery	14679928	118175	Yes	Apeldoorn Hospital, Stalag XI B
Edwards	John William Edward	Private	2nd Battalion, Parachute Regiment	5511508	117955		Stalag XI B, Stalag III A, Stalag XI A
Edwards	Thomas	Corporal	2nd Battalion, Parachute Regiment	4699004			Stalag XII A, Stalag IV B
Edwards	William	Private	[Unit not given]	2100175			Stalag IV C
Elder	Paul	Lance Corporal	4 Parachute Brigade, Royal Signals	2981146	118597	Yes	Stalag XI B

Surname	First name(s)	Rank	Regiment / Unit	Service no.	POW no.	Questionnaire	Camps
Eley	John	Private	1st Airlanding Light Regiment, Royal Artillery	14316068	75818		Stalag XII A, Stalag VIII C
Ellard	Joseph James	Sapper	4th Parachute Squadron, Royal Engineers	4448884	140111	Yes	Konig Willem III Kazerne Apeldoorn, Stalag VII A
Elletson	John Edward	Lance Corporal	1st Parachute Brigade, Royal Signals	2591334	91296		Stalag XII A, Stalag IV B
Elliott	Albert James	Private	3rd Battalion, Parachute Regiment	6207794			Stalag XII A, Stalag IV B
Elliott	Arthur Lewis Shaw	Bandsman	1st Battalion, Border Regiment	3759659	118321	Yes	Stalag XI B
Elliott	Charles Bridgeman	Private	156th Battalion, Parachute Regiment	4279607			Stalag XII A, Stalag IV B
Elliott	Frederick Robert George	Corporal	10th Battalion, Parachute Regiment	5773317			Stalag XII A, Stalag II A
Elliott	John	Private	4th Parachute Brigade HQ	839439	90625	Yes	Dulag Luft – Wetzlar, Stalag XII A, Stalag IV B
Elliott	Robert	Private	1st Battalion, Border Regiment	3608489		Yes	Stalag XII A, Stalag IV B, Stalag IV D
Elliott	Sidney Charlie Edwin	Private	2nd Battalion, Parachute Regiment	6153666	140131		Stalag VII A
Ellis	Desmond	Private	2nd Battalion, South Staffordshire Regiment	6409401			Stalag XII A, Stalag IV B, Stalag IV F
Ellis	John Aloysius	Staff Sergeant	Glider Pilot Regiment	1901936			Dulag Luft – Oberusel, Stalag Luft 7, Stalag III A
Ellis	Leslie Henry	WO II	1st Parachute Squadron, Royal Engineers	1869692			Stalag XII A, Stalag XVIII C
Ellis	William George	Gunner	2nd Airlanding Anti-Tank Battery, Royal Artillery	1094054			Stalag XII A, Stalag IV B
Ellison	Anthony	Private	1st Battalion, Border Regiment	4277251	91930		Stalag XII A, Stalag IV B, Stalag IV A

Family name	Forename	Rank	Unit as given on Questionnaire	Army number	POW number	Wounded on capture?	Camps
Ellwood	Michael	Private	2nd Battalion, Parachute Regiment	14272883		Yes	Stalag XII A, Stalag IV C
Elsey	George Douglas Jack	Craftsman	Royal Electrical and Mechanical Engineers	1574063	21901		Stalag XII A, Stalag IV B
Emmerton	Thomas Horace	Lance Corporal	2nd Battalion, Parachute Regiment	5831766			Stalag IV D
Entwistle	John	Private	1st Battalion, Border Regiment	14674222	91780		Stalag IV C
Erangey	Patrick Joseph	Gunner	2nd Airlanding Anti-Tank Battery, Royal Artillery	1147917			Stalag IV B
Evans	Ernest Philip	Signalman	4th Parachute Brigade, Royal Signals	14580106	117881	Yes	Stalag XI B, Stalag III A, Stalag XI A
Evans	Frank	Private	1st Battalion, Border Regiment	3864100	91881		Stalag XII A, Dulag Luft – Wetzlar, Stalag IV C
Evans	Kenneth Charles	Lieutenant	4th Parachute Squadron, Royal Engineers	267949	2178		Apeldoorn Hospital, Oflag IX A/Z
Evans	Robert George	Private	1st Battalion, Parachute Regiment	6108197		Yes	Dulag Luft – Wetzlar, Stalag XII A, Stalag IV B
Evans	Thomas	Private	3rd Battalion, Parachute Regiment	4031655		Yes	Stalag XII A, Stalag XI B
Evans	Trevor Parry	Sergeant, Lance	2nd Battalion, Parachute Regiment	3966276	89810		Stalag XII A, Stalag II A
Evans	William Henry	Corporal	1st Battalion, Border Regiment	3602813	140142	Yes	Apeldoorn Hospital, Stalag VII A, Stalag 383
Evans	Walter John	Private	156th Battalion, Parachute Regiment	5679918			Stalag XII A, Stalag IV B

Surname	First name(s)	Rank	Unit	Number			Camps
Evans	William James	Private	181st Airlanding Field Ambulance, Royal Army Medical Corps	7361934			Stalag XII A, Stalag IV B, Stalag IV D
Evans	Wilfred Richard	Driver	1st Airlanding Light Regiment, Royal Artillery	14320758	75312		Stalag XII A, Stalag IV B
Everest	Sydney John	Private	3rd Battalion, Parachute Regiment	6214961	90470	Yes	Stalag XII A, Stalag XI B, Stalag 357
Eves	Edward	Private	1st Parachute Brigade	3977266	75448		Stalag XII A, Stalag IV B, Stalag IV A
Ewing	Archibald	Private	2nd Battalion, Parachute Regiment	2937469			Stalag XII A, Stalag IV B
Exley	Brian Harding	Gunner	1st Airlanding Light Regiment, Royal Artillery	14296963	75830		Stalag XII A, Stalag IV B
Fail	Adam	Gunner	1st Airlanding Anti-Tank Battery, Royal Artillery	1491362	75543	Yes	Stalag XII A, Stalag IV B
Fairbrass	Jack	Private	2nd Battalion, South Staffordshire Regiment	989345	17526		Stalag XII A, Stalag IV B, Stalag IV F
Fairmington	Matthew	Lance Corporal	10th Battalion, Parachute Regiment	10602075			Dulag XII A, Stalag IV B
Fairweather	Clifford	Corporal	250th Airborne Light Company, Royal Army Service Corps	229170	118846		Apeldoorn Hospital, Stalag XI B, Stalag VIII C
Faithorn	Peter	Private	21st Independent Parachute Company	5772762			Stalag XII A, Stalag IV B
Farley	Peter	Private	1st Battalion, Border Regiment	3190506			Stalag XII A, Stalag IV B
Farmer	Samuel	Private	10th Battalion, Parachute Regiment	6854355	92168		Stalag XII A, Stalag IV B
Farr	Victor	Private	[Unit not given]	14650326			
Farrell	Alexander	Private	7th Battalion, King's Own Scottish Borderers Regiment	2884841	91898	Yes	Stalag XII A, Stalag IV B

Family name	Forename	Rank	Unit as given on Questionnaire	Army number	POW number	Wounded on capture?	Camps
Farrington	Bernard Haig	Private	2nd Battalion, South Staffordshire Regiment	4918377	118721	Yes	Stalag XI B
Farrow	Kenneth Ronald	Private	21st Independent Parachute Company	4928276	117550	Yes	Stalag XI B, Stalag III A, Stalag XI A
Faulkner	Maurice Arthur	Private	2nd Battalion, South Staffordshire Regiment	4917591	91647		Stalag XII A, Stalag IV B, Stalag IV A
Fellows	James	Private	1st Battalion, Border Regiment	14584168			Stalag XII A, Stalag IV B, Stalag XIII B
Fenton	John	Lance Corporal	2nd Battalion, South Staffordshire Regiment	491469	89849		Stalag XII A, Stalag XI B
Fenwick	George Rae	Corporal	250th Airborne Light Company, Royal Army Service Corps	108381	91188		Stalag XII A, Stalag II A
Fergus	Gerard John	Trooper	1st Airborne Reconnaissance Squadron	14282358	52935		Queen Wilhelmina Barracks, Reserve Lazarett Obermaßfeld, Stalag IX C/Z Mühlhausen
Ferguson	David Drummond	Private	7th Battalion, King's Own Scottish Borderers Regiment	14210564	25480		Stalag XII A, Stalag IV B
Ferguson	John	Sergeant, Lance	7th Battalion, King's Own Scottish Borderers Regiment	3190459			Stalag XII A, Stalag II A
Ferguson	Samuel	Sergeant	156th Battalion, Parachute Regiment	2754337			Stalag XII A, Stalag II A
Ferrari	Henry Felix	Signalman	Royal Signals	6352602			Stalag XII A, Stalag IV A
Few	Ted	Private	156th Battalion, Parachute Regiment	5257174			Stalag XII A, Stalag IV B, Stalag IV F

Surname	First name(s)	Rank	Unit	Number	Number	Questionnaire	Camps
Fickling	Kenneth Bruce	Private	1st Battalion, Parachute Regiment	14568820			Stalag XII A, Stalag IV B, Stalag IV F
Field	Albert Henry	Private	2nd Battalion, South Staffordshire Regiment	11006127	140211	Yes	Stalag VII A
Finglass	Gordon	Private	21st Independent Parachute Company	6346424	117784	Yes	Stalag XI B, Stalag III A, Stalag XI A
Finlinson	Edwin	Private	10th Battalion, Parachute Regiment	1593916	294918	Yes	Reserve Lazarett Siegburg, Stalag IV B
Fisher	Donald Edwin	Private	10th Battalion, Parachute Regiment	5890901	91687		Stalag XII A, Stalag IV B
Fisher	Patrick	Private	2nd Battalion, Parachute Regiment	5630343	294160		Stalag XII A, Stalag IV B, Stalag IV C
Fisher	Sidney Eugene	Private	2nd Battalion, Parachute Regiment	5771570			Stalag XII A, Stalag IV B
Fishwick	William	Private	2nd Battalion, Parachute Regiment	3774446	91425		Stalag XII A, Stalag IV B
Fitchett	Reginald Frank	Lance Corporal	3rd Battalion, Parachute Regiment	5337096	117876	Yes	Stalag XI B, Stalag III A
Fitzgerald	Michael	Driver	1st Airlanding Anti-Tank battery	6854732		Yes	Dulag Luft, Stalag XII A, Stalag VIII C, Stalag II C, Marlag-Milag North
Fitzgibbons	Maurice	Corporal	156th Battalion, Parachute Regiment	4617001			Stalag XII A, Stalag II A
Fitzpatrick	John Francis	Private	2nd Battalion, Parachute Regiment	4198450		Yes	Stalag XII A, Stalag IV B
Flanaghan	Andrew	Private	11th Battalion, Parachute Regiment	1609685	91482		Stalag XII A, Stalag IV B, Stalag IV C
Fleming	James	Private	2nd Battalion, Parachute Regiment	2985559			Dulag Luft, Stalag IV B

Family name	Forename	Rank	Unit as given on Questionnaire	Army number	POW number	Wounded on capture?	Camps
Fleming	Joseph	Private	7th Battalion, King's Own Scottish Borderers Regiment	14211103	75937		Stalag XII A, Stalag IV B
Fleming	William James	Sergeant	2nd Battalion, Parachute Regiment	2989834			Stalag XVIII C
Fletcher	Dugald	Private	156th Battalion, Parachute Regiment	2766219			Stalag XII A, Stalag IV B
Fletcher	Ernest Leslie	Bombardier	2nd Airlanding Anti-Tank Regiment, Royal Artillery	1525244	89756		Stalag XII A, Stalag II A
Flint	Thomas Joseph	Private	2nd Battalion, South Staffordshire Regiment	14682857	92093		Stalag XII A, Stalag IV B, Stalag IV C
Flynn	Christopher Alexander	Private	1st Battalion, Border Regiment	3602818	53397		Stalag IX C
Flynn	James	Private	1st Battalion, Border Regiment	3595760	140070		Stalag VII A
Fogarty	Christopher Winthrop	Lieutenant	1st Airlanding Light Regiment, Royal Artillery	237353	93296	Yes	Dulag Luft, Oflag XII B, Oflag VII B, Stalag VII A
Ford	Harry Gardner	Private	2nd Battalion, Parachute Regiment	14650990	91571	Yes	Stalag XII A, Stalag IV B
Ford	Jesse	Lance Corporal	Provost Company, 1st Airborne Division	7691865			Stalag XII A, Stalag IV B
Ford	William	Lance Corporal	7th Battalion, King's Own Scottish Borderers Regiment	3188138	90720		Stalag XII A, Stalag IV B
Forman	John Henry	Private	2nd Battalion, South Staffordshire Regiment	4920555	91701		Stalag XII A, Stalag IV B, Stalag IV C
Forman	Michael Bertram	Major	7th Battalion, King's Own Scottish Borderers Regiment	91061	90861	Yes	Stalag XII A, Interrogation Centre Diez, Oflag XII B, Oflag 79

Surname	First name(s)	Rank	Unit	Service No.	POW No.	Questionnaire	Camps
Forsyth	Thomas Thomson	Private	7th Battalion, King's Own Scottish Borderers Regiment	14210830	90168	Yes	
Fort	Eric Joseph	Corporal	2nd Battalion, South Staffordshire Regiment	4923320	89551		Stalag XII A, Stalag II A
Forwood	Charles	Corporal	7th Battalion, King's Own Scottish Borderers Regiment	3136134	88797		Stalag XII A, Stalag XVIII C
Foster	Andrew	Private	156th Battalion, Parachute Regiment	3190000		Yes	Stalag XI B
Foster	David William	Leading Aircraftman	Light Warning Set Unit No. 6080, RAF	1652764			Stalag XI B, Dulag Luft – Oberursel, Dulag Luft – Wetzlar, Stalag Luft 7, Stalag III A
Foster	Eric	Staff Sergeant	Glider Pilot Regiment	6401145			Stalag XII A, Stalag IV B
Foster	Edward James	Private	2nd Battalion, Parachute Regiment	6028848			Stalag XII A, Stalag IV B
Foster	Harry	Private	1st Battalion, Border Regiment	14584171	75688		Stalag XII A, Stalag IV B, Stalag IV F
Foster	James Henry	Private	7th Battalion, King's Own Scottish Borderers Regiment	144339540	91774		Stalag XII A, Stalag IV B, Stalag IV F, Stalag IV B
Foster	Kenneth	Private	156th Battalion, Parachute Regiment	320416	140138	Yes	Apeldoorn Hospital?, Stalag VII A
Foster	Williams	Gunner	1st Airlanding Light Regiment, Royal Artillery	14337091	975967		Stalag XII A, Stalag IV B, Stalag IV F
Foulke	Harold Bernard	Private	181st Airlanding Field Ambulance, Royal Army Medical Corps	7382422	140061		Stalag VII A
Fowler	Colin	Private	1st Battalion, Border Regiment	4546551	91931		Stalag XII A, Stalag IV B
Fowler	James Edward	Lance Corporal	3rd Battalion, Parachute Regiment	4076697	117176		Stalag XI B, Stalag 357
Fowler	Sydney John	Lance Corporal	3rd Battalion, Parachute Regiment	870732	89224	Yes	Stalag XII A, Stalag IV B, Stalag IV D

Family name	Forename	Rank	Unit as given on Questionnaire	Army number	POW number	Wounded on capture?	Camps
Fox	George	Private	Royal Engineers	14435314			Stalag XII A, Stalag IV B
Fox	John	Private	2nd Battalion, South Staffordshire Regiment	14437468	76799		Stalag XII A, Stalag IV B
Fox	Wilfred George	Private	2nd Battalion, South Staffordshire Regiment	4697023	92167		Stalag XII A, Stalag IV B
Foxon	James Arthur	Signalman	Royal Signals	2378460	91899		Stalag XII A, Stalag IV B
Franzel	Frank Charles	Private	11th Battalion, Parachute Regiment	3661561			Stalag XII A, Stalag IV B, Stalag IV A
Frary	Dennis	Private	133rd Parachute Field Ambulance, Royal Army Medical Corps	14351195			Stalag XII A, Stalag XI B
Fraser	Homer Newell	Staff Sergeant	Glider Pilot Regiment	2135945	140099	Yes	Apeldoorn Hospital, Stalag VII A, Stalag 383
Freemantle	Albert Brendon	Private	156th Battalion, Parachute Regiment	888204			Stalag XII A, Stalag IV B
Frewin	Eric Sidney	Private	1st Battalion, Border Regiment	1150793	25560		Stalag XII A, Stalag IV B
Funnell	Harry Ronald	Private	10th Battalion, Parachute Regiment	6411360			Stalag XII A, Stalag IV B
Furber	Tom	Private	2nd Battalion, South Staffordshire Regiment	14682861			Stalag XII A, Stalag IV B, Stalag IV C
Furniss	Thomas	Driver	250th Airborne Light Company, Royal Army Service Corps	10694184	117594	Yes	Stalag XI B
Gaitero	Allan	Corporal	3rd Battalion, Parachute Regiment	6466565	89523		Stalag XII A, Stalag II A
Garbutt	William Martyn	Sergeant	Glider Pilot Regiment	816515	76327	Yes	Stalag XII A, Stalag IV B
Gardner	Cyril	Private	7th Battalion, King's Own Scottish Borderers Regiment	14204693	90577		Stalag XII A, Stalag IV B, Stalag IV D

Surname	First name(s)	Rank	Unit	Service no.	POW no.	Questionnaire	Camps
Gardner	Eric Sidney	Private	Royal Army Medical Corps	7382362	9171		Stalag IV B
Garnham	Ronald Arthur Douglas	Sergeant	Glider Pilot Regiment	3966566			Stalag XII A, Stalag IV B
Garnsworthy	Leslie George	Sergeant	1st Airlanding Anti-Tank Battery, Royal Artillery	5671600			Stalag XII A, Stalag II A
Garrard	Stephen Walter	Sergeant	Glider Pilot Regiment	10677268			Stalag Luft 7, Stalag III A
Garvey	Thomas	Private	1st Battalion, Border Regiment	3596852	91984		Stalag XII A, Stalag IV B
Gascoyne	John William	Private	10th Battalion, Parachute Regiment	5734588	294913		Stalag IV G
Gaunt	James	Sergeant, Lance	2nd Battalion, South Staffordshire Regiment	4913313	90025		Stalag XII A, Dulag Luft, Stalag II A
Gavin	Patrick Charles	Regimental Quartermaster Sergeant	133rd Parachute Field Ambulance, Royal Army Medical Corps	7263776			Stalag XII A, Stalag IV B
Gaz	Jozef	Private	1st Polish Parachute Brigade	3143169			Stalag XII A, Stalag IV B
Geoghan	Thomas	Private	2nd Battalion, South Staffordshire Regiment	1561803	91634		Stalag XII A, Stalag IV B, Stalag IV C
Gethin	James Thomas	Private	1st Battalion, Parachute Regiment	4757644			Stalag IV B
Gibb	Archibald Allan	Private	2nd Battalion, South Staffordshire Regiment	2880575	89435		Stalag XII A, Stalag IV B, Stalag IV C
Gibb	William	Private	181st Airlanding Field Ambulance, Royal Army Medical Corps	7396628	90571		Stalag XII A, Stalag IV B
Gibbins	Leonard Albert	Corporal	3rd Battalion, Parachute Regiment	2181072			Stalag IV B
Gibbons	Ernest James Scott	Sergeant	9th Field Company (Airborne), Royal Engineers	1867057	117182	Yes	Stalag XI B, Stalag 357
Gibbs	Frederick Michael	Captain	156th Battalion, Parachute Regiment	114084	91015		Stalag XII A, Oflag XII B, Oflag 79
Gibbs	Ronald Williams	Gunner	1st Airlanding Light Regiment, Royal Artillery	932645	118095	Yes	Stalag XI B

Family name	Forename	Rank	Unit as given on Questionnaire	Army number	POW number	Wounded on capture?	Camps
Gibney	James	Sergeant Major	Royal Signals	2582457	91575		Stalag XII A, Stalag IV B, Stalag IV C
Gibson	John	Signalman	4th Parachute Brigade, Royal Signals	2933959	117437	Yes	Reserve Lazarett Gronau, Stalag XI B, Stalag III A, Stalag XI A
Gibson	Robert	Private	156th Battalion, Parachute Regiment	14509289	90773	Yes	Stalag XII A, Stalag IV B
Gick	Bernard Joseph	Lieutenant	1st Battalion, Parachute Regiment	186283	91009		Oflag 79
Gilbert	William Ernest	Private	3rd Battalion, Parachute Regiment, Royal Army Medical Corps	7372770	93701		Dulag XII A, Stalag VIII C, Stalag 344, Stalag XIII C
Gilchrist	David Alexander	Major/T	11th Battalion, Parachute Regiment	95588	545		Oflag XII B, Oflag VII B
Gilchrist	James Gibson	Private	156th Battalion, Parachute Regiment	14415465	975697		Stalag XII A, Stalag IV B, Stalag IV F
Gilchrist	William	Lance Corporal	7th Battalion, King's Own Scottish Borderers Regiment	14110114	140136	Yes	Almalo, Stalag VII A
Giles	Dennis	Private	16th Parachute Field Ambulance, Royal Army Medical Corps	14548345	118432		Stalag XI B
Giles	Jess	Private	2nd Battalion, South Staffordshire Regiment	1686196			Stalag XII A, Stalag IV B, Stalag IV F
Gill	Stanley Albert	Private	2nd Battalion, South Staffordshire Regiment	4209968			Stalag XII A, Stalag IV B
Gillard	Owen William	Private	156th Battalion, Parachute Regiment	295319			Stalag XII A, Stalag IV B
Gillespie	George Whyte	Private	10th Battalion, Parachute Regiment	1478056	90535		Stalag XII A, Stalag IV A

Surname	First name	Rank	Unit	Number	Number		Camps
Gillespie	Stanley	Lieutenant	3rd Battalion, Parachute Regiment	273249	556		Oflag XII B, Oflag 79
Gillies	Peter	Private	7th Battalion, King's Own Scottish Borderers Regiment	3196959	89449		Stalag IV C
Gillies	William	Private	1st Battalion, Border Regiment	1799012	92007		Stalag XII A, Stalag IV B
Gillow	Charles	Staff Sergeant	Glider Pilot Regiment	894370			Stalag XII A, Dulag Luft, Stalag Luft 7, Stalag III A
Girgan	James	Private	7th Battalion, King's Own Scottish Borderers Regiment	3191075	294539		Stalag XII A, Stalag IV B, Stalag IV D
Girvin	Robert	Staff Sergeant	Glider Pilot Regiment	7022767			Stalag XII A, Dulag Luft – Oberusel, Stalag Luft 7, Stalag III A
Gleave	William	Private	2nd Battalion, Parachute Regiment	3855379	118637	Yes	Stalag XI B, Stalag II D, Stalag II E
Gledhill	Tom	Private	1st Battalion, Parachute Regiment	14333598	117528		Stalag XI B
Glenn	John	Private	1st Battalion, Border Regiment	14401972	118102	Yes	Stalag XI B
Glenn	James Joseph	Driver	250th Airborne Light Company, Royal Army Service Corps	6984399	91784		Stalag XII A, Stalag IV B
Glennon	Thomas	Private	7th Battalion, King's Own Scottish Borderers Regiment	3191300			Stalag XII A, Stalag IV B
Glover	George H	Private	10th Battalion, Parachute Regiment	3913168	89593		Stalag XII A, Stalag IV B
Glover	James	Staff Sergeant	Glider Pilot Regiment	6970561			Stalag XII A, Stalag IV B
Godbold	John William	Private	1st Battalion, Parachute Regiment	6215765	92131	Yes	Stalag XII A, Stalag IV B, Stalag IV C
Goddard	Lawrence George	Lance Corporal	250th Airborne Light Company, Royal Army Service Corps	200409	89943		Stalag XII A, Stalag XI B
Godden	John Herbert	Private	1st Battalion, Parachute Regiment	912836			Stalag XII A, Stalag IV B

Family name	Forename	Rank	Unit as given on Questionnaire	Army number	POW number	Wounded on capture?	Camps
Godden	Sidney James	Private	1st Battalion, Parachute Regiment	6352588			Stalag XI B
Gofton	Andrew Kay	Private	16th Parachute Field Ambulance, Royal Army Medical Corps	7390953	93686		Arnhem Hospital, Stalag XII A, Dulag Luft, Stalag VIII C, Stalag 344
Goldstein	Sidney	Private	7th Battalion, King's Own Scottish Borderers Regiment	1527851			Stalag XII A, Stalag IV B
Goode	Eric Henry	Sapper	1st Parachute Squadron, Royal Engineers	2073137	118286	Yes	Apeldoorn Hospital, Stalag XI B
Goodger	Osmond Geoffrey	Private	2nd Battalion, South Staffordshire Regiment	14295823	91674		Stalag XII A, Stalag IV B, Stalag IV A
Goodrich	Horace William	Corporal	1st Parachute Brigade	81635			Stalag XII A, Stalag II A
Goodwin	Roger	Private	3rd Battalion, Parachute Regiment	14434753	90028		Stalag XII A, Stalag IV B, Stalag IV A
Gordon	William Dalziel	Staff Sergeant	Glider Pilot Regiment	934643	118350	Yes	Stalag XI B, Stalag 357
Gordon	William James	Staff Sergeant	GHQ Liaison Regiment (Phantom)	5391601			Stalag XII A, Stalag IV B
Gore	Denis Edmund	Private	4th Battalion, Dorset Regiment	14723664	14948		Stalag XII A, Stalag IV B
Gorman	Alfred	Private	1st Battalion, Border Regiment	3186358	117406	Yes	Stalag XI B, Stalag III A
Gough	Charles Frederick Howard	Major	1st Airborne Reconnaissance Squadron	31420	595		Dulag Luft – Oberusel, Oflag XII B, Oflag VII B
Gough	Samuel	Private	Forward Observation Unit, Royal Artillery	981355	89226		Stalag XII A, Stalag IV B, Stalag IV D
Gould	Jack	Private	156th Battalion, Parachute Regiment	14204155			Stalag XII A, Stalag IV B, Stalag IV A

Surname	First name(s)	Rank	Unit	Number	Questionnaire	Camps
Goulding	Denis	Sergeant	1st Battalion, Border Regiment	3599543	Yes	Reserve Lazarett V B Villingen, Stalag VII A, Stalag 383
Gower	Geoffrey Ernest	Private	1st Battalion, Parachute Regiment	14418468	91373		Stalag XII A, Stalag IV B, Stalag IV G
Grainger	Frederick	Private	7th Battalion, King's Own Scottish Borderers Regiment	14416704	90637		Stalag XII A, Stalag IV B
Grant	Anthony	Private	1st Battalion, Parachute Regiment	2939381			Stalag XII A, Stalag IV B
Grant	Alexander	Private	7th Battalion, King's Own Scottish Borderers Regiment	14210847	91393		Stalag XII A, Stalag IV B
Grant	Gerard	Private	1st Battalion, Border Regiment	3607117	91473		Stalag XII A, Stalag IV B
Grant	Patrick	Private	156th Battalion, Parachute Regiment	2820322			Stalag XII A, Stalag IV B, Stalag IV D
Grant	Robert Henry	Private	156th Battalion, Parachute Regiment	14418394			Stalag XII A, Stalag IV B, Stalag IV F
Grant	Richard Sydney	Staff Sergeant	Glider Pilot Regiment	6474934			Dulag Luft – Oberusel, Stalag Luft 7, Stalag III A
Gray	Frederick	Private	156th Battalion, Parachute Regiment	6980488			Stalag XII A, Stalag IV B, Stalag IV A
Gray	James	Private	1st Battalion, Parachute Regiment	14417442			Stalag XII A, Stalag IV B
Gray	Joseph Patrick	Private	11th Battalion, Parachute Regiment	697843	91588		Stalag XII A, Stalag IV C
Gray	John Robert	Private	2nd Battalion, Parachute Regiment	5835364			Stalag XII A, Stalag IV B, Stalag IV D
Gray	Percy Norman	Private	1st Battalion, Border Regiment	3603654	92033	Yes	Stalag XII A, Stalag IV B, Stalag IV F
Gray	Robert	Driver	2nd Airlanding Anti-Tank Battery, Royal Artillery	1441987			Stalag XII A, Stalag IV B, Stalag IV F

Family name	Forename	Rank	Unit as given on Questionnaire	Army number	POW number	Wounded on capture?	Camps
Green	Alan Thomas	Lieutenant	1st Battalion, Border Regiment	247201	2177	Yes	Koning Willem III Kazerne Apeldoorn, Stalag XI B, Oflag IX A/Z
Green	George	Private	2nd Battalion, South Staffordshire Regiment	7523335	90559		Stalag XII A, Stalag IV B, Stalag IV B
Green	George Stanley	Lance Corporal	1st Battalion, Parachute Regiment	2929195			Stalag XII A, Stalag IV B, Stalag IV D
Green	John	Driver	250th Airborne Light Company, Royal Army Service Corps	10698160	117845	Yes	Stalag XI B
Green	James Webster	Private	4th Parachute Brigade HQ	14403355	118728	Yes	Stalag XI B, Oflag 79
Green	Paul James	Private	11th Battalion, Parachute Regiment	2930629	91996		Stalag XII A, Stalag IV B
Green	Stanley Clifford	Aircraftman	Light Warning Set Unit No. 6080, RAF	1877382			Stalag XII A, Stalag IV B
Green	Walter	Corporal	181st Airlanding Field Ambulance, Royal Army Medical Corps	7399587	77329		Apeldoorn Hospital, Stalag XII A, Stalag VIII C, Stalag 344, Stalag IV C
Green	William Henry	Gunner	1st Airlanding Light Regiment, Royal Artillery	14326093	75829		Stalag XII A, Stalag IV B
Greenall	John	Private	1st Battalion, Border Regiment	3606248	75398		Stalag XII A, Stalag IV B, Stalag IV F
Greenbaum	Frank Ashley	Sergeant	Glider Pilot Regiment	14417002			Dulag Luft – Oberusel, Stalag Luft 7, Stalag III A
Greenhill	Douglas Crump	Private	16th Parachute Field Ambulance, Royal Army Medical Corps	7368666	284148		Stalag IV B

Greensill	Joseph	Signalman	1st Parachute Brigade, Royal Signals	5572988	90035	Stalag XII A, Stalag IV B, Stalag IV F
Greenslade	George Charles	Staff Sergeant	Glider Pilot Regiment	6086559	75462	Dulag Luft – Oberusel, Stalag XII A, Stalag Luft 7, Stalag III A
Gregg	Victor	Private	10th Battalion, Parachute Regiment	6913933	92043	Stalag XII A, Stalag IV B, Stalag IV A
Gregory	Nicholas	Driver	1st Airlanding Anti-Tank Battery, Royal Artillery	1526957	91295	Stalag XII A, Stalag IV B
Grewcock	Walter Kenneth	Corporal	1st Parachute Brigade, Royal Signals	2591584	89179	Stalag XII A, Stalag XVIII C
Grieveson	John	Signalman	Royal Signals	862338		Stalag XII A, Stalag IV B, Stalag IV C
Griffin	Joseph	Private	10th Battalion, Parachute Regiment	5619645	90078	Stalag XII A, Stalag XI B
Griffith	Thomas David	Corporal	1st Battalion, Parachute Regiment	1695912		Stalag IV B
Griffith	William Gordon	Sergeant	Glider Pilot Regiment	4192348		Dulag Luft, Stalag XII A, Stalag Luft 7, Stalag III A
Griffiths	Alan	Private	4th Battalion, Dorset Regiment	14723668	26032	Stalag IV F
Griffiths	George William	Sergeant	1st Battalion, Parachute Regiment	4194806		Stalag XII A, Stalag II A
Griffiths	John Douglas	Sergeant	Glider Pilot Regiment	2570423		Stalag XII A, Stalag IV B
Griffiths	William Henry	Private	7th Battalion, King's Own Scottish Borderers Regiment	14648339	90580	Stalag XII A, Stalag IV B
Grindrod	John	Private	1st Battalion, Border Regiment	1739180		Stalag IV F
Gristwood	William John	Driver	1st Airlanding Anti-Tank Battery, Royal Artillery	1524980		Stalag XII A, Stalag IV B
Grounsell	William Charles Francis	Private	156th Battalion, Parachute Regiment	5672628		Stalag XII A, Stalag IV B

Family name	Forename	Rank	Unit as given on Questionnaire	Army number	POW number	Wounded on capture?	Camps
Grove	Philip Nigel	Captain/T	1st Battalion, Parachute Regiment	85684	597		Apeldorn, Dulag Luft – Oberusel, Stalag XII A, Dulag XII B Hadamar, Oflag 79
Grundy	Benjamin	Private	2nd Battalion, Parachute Regiment	4748425			Stalag XII A, Stalag IV B, Stalag IV D
Guidi	David	Private	7th Battalion, King's Own Scottish Borderers Regiment	14435105			Stalag XII A, Stalag IV B
Guyatt	Eric George	Lance Bombardier	1st Airlanding Light Regiment, Royal Artillery	935260	92081		Stalag XII A, Stalag IV B, Stalag IV C
Guyon	George Edmund	Lieutenant	1st Battalion, Parachute Regiment	184696	2183	Yes	Stalag XI B, Oflag IX A/Z
Gwilliam	William Henry	Private	4th Battalion, Dorset Regiment	14207817			Stalag XII A, Stalag IV B
Hackett	Andrew Dennistoun	Lance Corporal	Provost Company, 1st Airborne Division	3320391	117430	Yes	Apeldoorn Hospital, Stalag XI B
Hackett	Henry	Gunner	Forward Observation Unit, Royal Artillery	876593			Stalag XII A, Stalag IV B
Hadfield	Frank Charles	Gunner	1st Airlanding Light Regiment, Royal Artillery	14399107	117708	Yes	Stalag XI B, Stalag III A, Stalag XI A, Stalag IV D
Hadfield	George Frederick	Sergeant	Glider Pilot Regiment	3531592	140112	Yes	Stalag VII A, Stalag 383
Hailes	George Greener	Private	11th Battalion, Parachute Regiment	4470510	117933	Yes	Stalag XI B, Stalag III A
Hale	George John	Private	1st Battalion, Parachute Regiment	5989841	92054		Stalag XII A, Stalag IV B
Hale	Roland John	Private	2nd Battalion, Parachute Regiment	5512642			Stalag XII A, Stalag IV B, Stalag IV D
Hales	Albert Charles	Lance Corporal	4th Battalion, Dorset Regiment	6014349	91914		Stalag XII A, Stalag IV B

Surname	Forename	Rank	Unit	Number	POW No.	Questionnaire	Camps
Hales	Clifford	Signalman	1st Parachute Brigade, Royal Signals	3782726	91929		Dulag Luft, Stalag XII A, Stalag IV B
Haley	John Michael William	Private	156th Battalion, Parachute Regiment	14391649			Stalag XII A, Stalag IV B
Halford	Fred Victor	Gunner	2nd Airlanding Anti-Tank Battery, Royal Artillery	4917794			Stalag XII A, Stalag IV B, Stalag IV F
Hall	Bertie Kenneth	Private	2nd Battalion, South Staffordshire Regiment	4032739	89187		Stalag XII A, Stalag IV C
Hall	David	Private	2nd Battalion, South Staffordshire Regiment	5124942	90257		Stalag XI B
Hall	Edward	Driver	250th Airborne Light Company, Royal Army Service Corps	213094	117844	Yes	Reserve Lazarett Lingen, Stalag XI B
Hall	Harry George	Private	2nd Battalion, South Staffordshire Regiment	4928572	93202		Stalag XII A, Stalag VIII C
Hall	Joseph Kenneth	Private	2nd Battalion, Parachute Regiment	975632			Stalag IV B, Stalag IV C, Komotau Hospital
Hall	Joseph Stanley	Private	16th Parachute Field Ambulance, Royal Army Medical Corps	7366937			Stalag XII A, Stalag IV B
Hall	Kevin Kenneth	Private	156th Battalion, Parachute Regiment	4344015			Stalag XII A, Stalag IV B, Stalag IV A
Haller	Bernard John Frederick	Staff Sergeant	Glider Pilot Regiment	14291815			Apeldoorn Hospital
Hallett	Hugh Anthony	Private	2nd Battalion, Parachute Regiment	6465318	89693		Stalag XII A, Stalag XI B
Halley-Frame	Thomas Sidney	Lance Corporal	3rd Battalion, Parachute Regiment	6013288	91532		Stalag XII A, Stalag IV B
Halliday	Leslie Albert	Private	3rd Battalion, Parachute Regiment	5952211	118495	Yes	Stalag XI B, Oflag 79
Halliwell	Stanley	Sergeant, Lance	1st Parachute Squadron, Royal Engineers	2000549	89623		Stalag XII A, Stalag II A

77

Family name	Forename	Rank	Unit as given on Questionnaire	Army number	POW number	Wounded on capture?	Camps
Halmshaw	Raymond	Gunner	1st Airlanding Light Regiment, Royal Artillery	1155912	75562		Stalag XII A, Stalag IV B
Halstead	Richard Angus	Lieutenant	1st Battalion, Parachute Regiment	203705	2198	Yes	Apeldoorn Hospital, Stalag XI B, Offlag IX A/Z
Hamer	Mal Dwyn	Lance Corporal	1st Parachute Brigade	6921343	75451		Stalag XII A, Stalag IV B, Stalag IV C
Hamilton	John	Gunner	1st Airlanding Light Regiment, Royal Artillery	14709137	75912		Stalag XII A, Stalag IV B
Hamilton	Reginald Thomas	Private	7th Battalion, King's Own Scottish Borderers Regiment	14437879			Stalag XII A, Stalag IV B
Hamlett	Ernest	Private	1st Battalion, Border Regiment	4462122	118075	Yes	Apeldoorn Hospital, Stalag XI B
Hampton	Leslie Robert	Gunner	1st Airlanding Light Regiment, Royal Artillery	14249030	75969		Stalag XII A, Stalag IV B, Stalag IV F
Hancock	Kenneth	Private	2nd Battalion, South Staffordshire Regiment	14642711			Stalag XII A
Handforth	John Collin	Private	7th Battalion, King's Own Scottish Borderers Regiment	3325396	90714		Stalag XII A, Stalag IV B
Hann	Alfred John	Signalman	Royal Signals	2384029	91967		Stalag XII A, Stalag IV B
Hann	Stanley	Staff Sergeant	Glider Pilot Regiment	44692164	76307	Yes	Stalag XII A, Stalag IV B
Hannah	Andrew	Private	1st Battalion, Border Regiment	3192167	140096	Yes	Stalag VIII C
Hannah	James Alexander	Private	1st Battalion, Border Regiment	3192337	117450	Yes	Stalag XI B, Stalag III A, Stalag XI A
Harbour	Frederick Spencer	Sergeant	10th Battalion, Parachute Regiment	6402134			Amersfoot, Stalag XII A, Stalag XVIII C

QUESTIONNAIRES AND OTHER SOURCES

Surname	First name	Rank	Regiment	Number	Number 2		Camps
Hardie	John	Driver	112th Field Regiment Royal Artillery	873582			Stalag IX C
Harding	Henry	Private	10th Battalion, Parachute Regiment	14623902	88779		Stalag XII A, Stalag IV B, Stalag IV C
Harding	Kenneth Arthur Gordon	Private	2nd Battalion, Parachute Regiment	6148830			Stalag XII A, Stalag IV B
Hardwick	John Geoffrey	Sergeant	Glider Pilot Regiment	3054186			Stalag XII A, Stalag IV B
Hardy	Harry	Private	156th Battalion, Parachute Regiment	4343700	117894		Stalag XI B
Hare	Ronald	Gunner	1st Airlanding Anti-Tank Battery, Royal Artillery	4698349	92013		Stalag XII A, Stalag IV B
Hares	Myrddin Edward	Trooper	1st Airborne Reconnaissance Squadron	6852442	75683		Stalag XII A, Stalag IV B, Stalag IV F
Hargrave	Francis Richard	Private	2nd Battalion, South Staffordshire Regiment	7013354	89576		Stalag XII A, Stalag IV B
Hargreaves	Alan Wilson	Sergeant	Glider Pilot Regiment	1922641			Stalag XII A, Stalag IV B
Harley	William Douglas	Lance Corporal	2nd Battalion, South Staffordshire Regiment	14202780	118289	Yes	Stalag XI B
Harlow	Albert Wiliam(?) Harrison	Major Reverend	Royal Army Chaplains' Department	131946	640		Hospitals in Holland, Dulag Luft – Wetzlar, Oflag XII B, Oflag VII B
Harper	Charles	Private	7th Battalion, King's Own Scottish Borderers Regiment	3190813	75984		Stalag XII A, Stalag IV B
Harper	Gordon Thomas	Private	2nd Battalion, South Staffordshire Regiment	14692209	17566		Stalag XII A, Stalag IV B
Harper	John Everard	Lance Corporal	2nd Battalion, Parachute Regiment	497226	88485		Stalag XII A, Stalag IV B
Harris	Douglas George	Private	3rd Battalion, Parachute Regiment	3967311			Stalag XII A, Stalag IV B, Reserve Lazarett Komotau, Reserve Lazarett Bilin

Family name	Forename	Rank	Unit as given on Questionnaire	Army number	POW number	Wounded on capture?	Camps
Harris	George William	Staff Sergeant	Army Physical Training Corps	3767430	89164		Stalag XII A, Stalag XVIII C
Harris	John Edward	Private	2nd Battalion, South Staffordshire Regiment	1786237	89999		Stalag XII A, Stalag IV B, Stalag IV F
Harris	James Phillip	Private	1st Battalion, Parachute Regiment	854121	117846	Yes	Stalag XI B, Stalag III A, Stalag XI A, Stalag IV D
Harris	Kenneth Wesley	Private	10th Battalion, Parachute Regiment	14425014	80092		Harskamp, Stalag XII A, Stalag IV B
Harris	Norman	Lance Corporal	1st Parachute Brigade	83502			Stalag XII A, Stalag IV B
Harris	Percy Victor	Private	4th Battalion, Dorset Regiment	5735127			Stalag IV B, Stalag IV F
Harris	Ronald Maxwell	Sergeant	Parachute Regiment	911930	89342		Stalag XII A, Stalag XVIII C
Harrison	Alan Aubrey	Private	3rd Battalion, Parachute Regiment	4624721	89838		Stalag XII A, Stalag XI B, Stalag 357
Harrison	Eric George	Private	1st Battalion, Border Regiment	14579662	175991		Stalag XII A, Stalag IV B
Harrison	Ivan	Lance Corporal	1st Battalion, Border Regiment	3603444	91800		Stalag XII A, Stalag IV C
Harrison	James William	Private	4th Parachute Brigade	4697029			Stalag XII A, Stalag IV F
Harrison	Robert	Private	7th Battalion, King's Own Scottish Borderers Regiment	14210604	90725		Stalag XII A, Stalag IV D
Harrison	Thomas	Private	3rd Battalion, Parachute Regiment	4273328	91739		Stalag XII A, Stalag IV C
Harrop	James Edward	Private	4th Battalion, Dorset Regiment	1723369	25988		Stalag XII A, Stalag IV F

Surname	First name	Rank	Unit	Number	Number	Questionnaire	Camps
Hart	George Briggs	Private	7th Battalion, King's Own Scottish Borderers Regiment	1115868	75425		Stalag XII A, Stalag IV B
Hartley	Alfred Harold	Private	156th Battalion, Parachute Regiment	14413724	14069		Stalag XII A, Stalag IV B, Stalag IV A, Stalag IV B
Hartley	Benjamin	Driver	1st Airlanding Anti-Tank Battery, Royal Artillery	3712207			Stalag XII A, Stalag IV B
Hartley	Kenneth Wrightson	Lance Corporal	9th Field Company (Airborne), Royal Engineers	2017149	75812		Stalag XII A, Stalag IV B, Stalag IV F
Hartley	William	Driver	1st Airlanding Anti-Tank Battery, Royal Artillery	1514908	919294		Stalag XII A, Stalag IV B
Hartman	John Victor	Corporal	2nd Battalion, Parachute Regiment	14231235			Stalag XII A, Stalag IV B
Harvey	Arthur Edwin	Private	2nd Battalion, South Staffordshire Regiment	4918973	91640		Stalag XII A, Stalag IV B, Stalag IV C
Harvey	Clifford	Private	181st Airlanding Field Ambulance, Royal Army Medical Corps	7263046	93691		Stalag XII A, , Stalag VIII C, Stalag VIII B, Stalag XIII C
Harvey	Robert	Private	2nd Battalion, South Staffordshire Regiment	5192902	117318	Yes	Stalag XI B
Harvey	Richard	Sapper	9th Field Company (Airborne), Royal Engineers	2152263			Stalag XII A, Stalag IV B
Harvey	Stanley Trevelyan	Private	11th Battalion, Parachute Regiment	865935	91530		Stalag XII A, Stalag IV B
Harwood	Alfred George	Private	2nd Battalion, South Staffordshire Regiment	5391715		Yes	Stalag XII A, Stalag 357
Haslam	Reginald Alfred	Bombardier	1st Airlanding Anti-Tank Battery, Royal Artillery	1115969			Stalag XII A, , Stalag IV B
Hastings	Benjamin	Driver	253rd Airborne Light Company, Royal Army Service Corps	993266	140078	Yes	Hospital Holland – unspecified, Stalag VII A

Family name	Forename	Rank	Unit as given on Questionnaire	Army number	POW number	Wounded on capture?	Camps
Hastings	Thomas Ernest	Corporal	Royal Army Medical Corps Parachute	7381574	118445		Stalag XI B, Stalag VIII C, Stalag 344, Stalag XIII C, Stalag VII A
Hatcher	Arthur	Corporal	16th Parachute Field Ambulance, Royal Army Medical Corps	7264821			Stalag XII A, Stalag II A
Hately	John Frederick	Private	156th Battalion, Parachute Regiment	6896966	221694	Yes	Stalag XII A, Stalag IV B, Stalag IV D, Stalag IV F
Haunch	George William Edgar	Lance Corporal	7th Battalion, King's Own Scottish Borderers Regiment	3325597	90713		Stalag XII A, Stalag IV B, Stalag IV F
Hawkins	Benjamin Edward	Private	2nd Battalion, South Staffordshire Regiment	4922840	91639	Yes	Stalag XII A, Stalag IV B, Stalag IV A
Hawley	Ernest William	Lance Bombardier	1st Airlanding Anti-Tank Battery, Royal Artillery	1545256	92036	Yes	Arnhem Hospital, Stalag XII A, Stalag IV B
Hayes	Frederick George	Sergeant	156th Battalion, Parachute Regiment	5249918		Yes	Stalag XII A, Stalag II A
Hayes	George	Driver	250th Airborne Light Company, Royal Army Service Corps	183151	75950		Stalag XII A, Stalag IV B, Stalag IV G
Hayes	Joseph	Private	11th Battalion, Parachute Regiment	2984852	92028	Yes	Stalag XII A, Stalag IV B
Hayes	William Jack	Sergeant	156th Battalion, Parachute Regiment	5108162	52932	Yes	Reserve Lazarett Obermaßfeld, Reserve Lazarett Meiningen, Stalag IX C Mühlhausen
Hayman	Ronald Walter	Private	3rd Battalion, Parachute Regiment	602704	117823	Yes	Stalag XI B, Stalag III A, Stalag XI A, Stalag IV D

Haynes	John Henry	Private	11th Battalion, Parachute Regiment	7888568	75980		Stalag XII A, Stalag IV B, Stalag IV F
Haysom	James	Signalman	1st Parachute Brigade, Royal Signals	2573777		Yes	Stalag XII A, Stalag IV B
Hayward	Charles Henry	Private	7th Battalion, King's Own Scottish Borderers Regiment	14649274			Stalag XII A, Stalag IV B
Hayward	John Spencer Victor	Private	250th Airborne Light Company, Royal Army Service Corps	107853	140066	Yes	Apeldoorn Hospital, Stalag VII A, Stalag 383
Hayward	William Charles	Gunner	2nd Airlanding Anti-Tank Battery, Royal Artillery	781029	117653	Yes	Stalag XI B, Stalag III A
Headland	William George	Private	3rd Battalion, Parachute Regiment	1435227		Yes	Stalag IV B, Stalag IV C
Healey	Edwin	Staff Sergeant	Glider Pilot Regiment	3775315			Dulag Luft – Oberusel, Stalag Luft 7, Stalag III A
Heaney	Kevin Joseph	Private	Royal Army Ordnance Corps	14335886			Stalag IV D
Heath	Joseph Henry	Private	10th Battalion, Parachute Regiment	945801			Stalag XII A, Stalag IV A
Heaton	Joseph	Private	2nd Battalion, Parachute Regiment	7899398			Stalag XII A, Stalag XI B
Hedgecock	Leonard	Staff Sergeant	Glider Pilot Regiment	2584748		Yes	Stalag XII A, Stalag IV B
Hedley	John	Private	11th Battalion, Parachute Regiment	4279331	75974		Stalag XII A, Stalag IV B
Hellier	Wally James	Private	2nd Battalion, Parachute Regiment	6148710			Stalag XII A, Stalag IV B
Henderson	Duncan	Private	156th Battalion, Parachute Regiment	853860			Stalag XII A, Stalag IV B
Hendry	John	Gunner	1st Airlanding Light Regiment, Royal Artillery	877914	118044	Yes	Stalag XI B
Hendy	Arthur Sydney	Lance Corporal	1st Parachute Squadron, Royal Engineers	1874248			Stalag XII A, Stalag IV B, Stalag IV C

Family name	Forename	Rank	Unit as given on Questionnaire	Army number	POW number	Wounded on capture?	Camps
Henley	Reginald French	Private	10th Battalion, Parachute Regiment	5568074	89389		Stalag XII A, Stalag IV B, Stalag IV D
Hepworth	Jack	Private	156th Battalion, Parachute Regiment	7263996	90926		Stalag XII A, Stalag IV B
Herbert	Allan George	Private	2nd Battalion, South Staffordshire Regiment	4915809	118538		Stalag XI B
Herbert	Henry Charles	Private	11th Battalion, Parachute Regiment	14405294		Yes	Stalag XII A, Stalag IV B, Stalag IV A
Hewerdine	Walter	Driver	1st Airlanding Anti-Tank Battery, Royal Artillery	1527073			Stalag XII A, Stalag IV B, Stalag IV G
Hewish	Robert Harvey	Lance Corporal	4th Parachute Brigade, Royal Signals	6469323			Stalag XII A, Stalag IV B, Stalag IV D
Heyes	Stanley	Signalman	1st Parachute Brigade, Royal Signals	4132010	118696	Yes	Stalag XI B
Hickman	Thomas Victor	Lance Corporal	1st Airlanding Anti-Tank Battery, Royal Artillery	893124	75855	Yes	Stalag XII A, Stalag IV B
Hicks	Albert Edward	Driver	63 Company, Royal Army Service Corps	14318934	91432		Stalag XII A, Stalag IV B, Stalag IV G
Higginbotham	James	Staff Sergeant	Glider Pilot Regiment	905927			Dulag Luft – Oberusel, Stalag Luft 7, Stalag III A
Higginbottom	Ernest	Lance Corporal	2nd Battalion, Parachute Regiment	1798347			Stalag XII A, Stalag IV B, Stalag IV C
Higgins	Geoffrey	Sergeant	Glider Pilot Regiment	7911243			Stalag XII A, Stalag IV B
Higginson	Walter	Private	11th Battalion, Parachute Regiment	3452978	117687		Stalag XI B, Stalag III A, Stalag XI A, Stalag IV D

Surname	First name	Rank	Unit	Number	Number		Camps
Hill	Cecil	Corporal	2nd Battalion, Parachute Regiment	6401664			Stalag IV B, Stalag IV C
Hill	David McNair	Private	7th Battalion, King's Own Scottish Borderers Regiment	14210611	75837		Stalag XII A, Stalag IV B, Stalag IV G
Hill	Francis Edwin	Private	3rd Battalion, Parachute Regiment	5389890	75327		Stalag XII A, Stalag IV B, Stalag IV C
Hill	Henry Samuel	Driver	253rd Airborne Light Company, Royal Army Service Corps	5949386			Stalag XII A, Stalag IV B
Hill	Leslie Thomas	Private	2nd Battalion, Parachute Regiment	5391983	117847		Stalag XI B, Stalag III A, Stalag XI A, Stalag IV D/Z
Hill	Norris Williams	Private	1st Parachute Brigade	11007637			Stalag XII A, Stalag IV B
Hill	William	Lance Corporal	16th Parachute Field Ambulance, Royal Army Medical Corps	7264147			Stalag IV B
Hill	William	Lance Corporal	1st Airlanding Brigade	14283573	91724		Stalag XII A, Stalag IV B
Hill	William	Private	Royal Army Medical Corps	7376940	75664		Stalag XII A, Stalag IV B, Reserve Lazarett H57 Hohenstein
Hillman	Albert Edward	Private	2nd Battalion, Parachute Regiment	14207392	117308	Yes	Stalag XI B, Oflag 79
Hills	James Alfred	Private	7th Battalion, King's Own Scottish Borderers Regiment	2883680			Stalag XII A, Stalag IV B, Stalag IV A
Hilton	Harry	Lance Corporal	4th Battalion, Dorset Regiment	5962248	26050		Stalag XII A, Stalag IV B
Hilton	Wallace George	Private	7th Battalion, King's Own Scottish Borderers Regiment	1542155	90499		Stalag XII A, Stalag IV B
Hindmarsh	Henry	Private	2nd Battalion, Parachute Regiment	4461927			Stalag XII A, Stalag IV B
Hinsley	William Alfred	Private	4th Battalion, Dorset Regiment	1584800	14223		Stalag IV B, Stalag IV C
Hippisley	William James	Company Quartermaster Sergeant Major	156th Battalion, Parachute Regiment	5671303			Stalag XII A, Stalag II A

Family name	Forename	Rank	Unit as given on Questionnaire	Army number	POW number	Wounded on capture?	Camps
Hoare	Leonard Leslie	Private	2nd Battalion, Parachute Regiment	6351050	90672	Yes	Stalag XII A, Stalag IV B, Stalag IV F
Hobson	Frank	Private	7th Battalion, King's Own Scottish Borderers Regiment	14415862	75921		Stalag XII A, Stalag IV B, Stalag IV D
Hockley	Ernest Harold	Sergeant	Glider Pilot Regiment	2323238			Stalag XII A, Stalag IV B
Hoddinott	Brinkley	Private	11th Battalion, Parachute Regiment	14284895	117763	Yes	Stalag XI B, Stalag XI A
Hodge	Donald Hugh	Private	1st Battalion, Border Regiment	3866321	15231	Yes	Stalag XII A, Stalag IV B, Stalag VIII C, Stalag VIII D
Hodges	Joseph	Private	Royal Army Ordnance Corps	10573941			Stalag XII A, Stalag IV B
Hodgkins	Basil Royston	Lieutenant	4th Battalion, Dorset Regiment	315216	583		Oflag XII B, Oflag 79
Hodgson	Frank Douglas	Corporal	1st Airborne Provost Company	4537324	15450		Stalag XII A, Stalag VIII C, Stalag IV B
Hodgson	Geoffrey	Private	156th Battalion, Parachute Regiment	14291625		Yes	Apeldoorn Hospital, Reserve Lazarett 6/689/1 Ermelo, Amersfoort Transit Camp, Stalag XII A, Stalag IV B, Stalag IV F
Hogan	Michael Patrick William	Private	10th Battalion, Parachute Regiment	14429149	75748		Stalag XII A, Stalag IV B, Stalag IV F
Hogger	Albert Cornelius	Lance Corporal	4th Battalion, Dorset Regiment	5888643	17538		Stalag XII A, Stalag IV B
Hogwood	Ralph Herbert	Sergeant	7th Battalion, King's Own Scottish Borderers Regiment	5052938	88746		Stalag XII A, Stalag XVIII C

Holcombe	John	Private	3rd Battalion, Parachute Regiment	2089989	91616		Stalag XII A, Stalag IV B, Stalag IV A, Stalag IV C
Holden	James	Private	Parachute Regiment	3458392	92147		Stalag XII A, Stalag IV B, Stalag IV D
Holding	Thomas Wilfred	Private	1st Battalion, Border Regiment	3782686			Stalag XII A, Dulag Luft – Wetzlar, Stalag IV B, Stalag IV C
Holdsworth	Kenneth	Lance Corporal	181st Airlanding Field Ambulance, Royal Army Medical Corps	7399450			Apeldoorn Hospital, Stalag XII A, Stalag IV B
Hole	Edward Stanley	Private	3rd Battalion, Parachute Regiment	5672174			Dulag Luft, Stalag IV B
Holgate	Norman	Private	4th Battalion, Dorset Regiment	1767939			Stalag XII A, Stalag IV F
Holland	Donald Kitson	Sergeant	2nd Battalion, South Staffordshire Regiment	4921819			Stalag XII A, Stalag II A
Holland	James	Driver	Royal Artillery	14321655	75880		Stalag XII A, Stalag IV B
Hollands	Frank Richard	Private	156th Battalion, Parachute Regiment	6104597			Stalag XII A, Stalag IV B, Stalag IV F
Hollinshead	Douglas	Private	11th Battalion, Parachute Regiment	844968	118171		Stalag XI B
Hollis	William	Private	1st Battalion, Parachute Regiment	14367454	118051	Yes	Stalag XI B
Holmes	Robert	Private	1st Battalion, Parachute Regiment	5891275	92008		Stalag XII A, Stalag IV B, Stalag IV C
Holmes	William John	Private	11th Battalion, Parachute Regiment	2821375	140126		Transit?, Stalag VII A
Holt	Arthur	Private	7th Battalion, King's Own Scottish Borderers Regiment	3716068	90489		Stalag XII A, Stalag IV B, Stalag IV A
Holt	Ronald Charles Neville	Private	2nd Battalion, Parachute Regiment	2766005	93727		Stalag VIII C, Stalag XI B
Hooker	Gerald Sidney Herbert	Sergeant	Glider Pilot Regiment	2600495	117490		Stalag XI B, Stalag VIII C

Family name	Forename	Rank	Unit as given on Questionnaire	Army number	POW number	Wounded on capture?	Camps
Hooper	James Michael	Staff Sergeant	Glider Pilot Regiment	2584037			Dulag Luft, Stalag Luft 7, Stalag III A
Hooper	Tom	Private	1st Battalion, Border Regiment	3599167	92110		Stalag XII A, Stalag IV B, Stalag IV A
Hooson	Gwilyn	Private	7th Battalion, King's Own Scottish Borderers Regiment	14374202	89535		Stalag XII A, Stalag IV B
Hope	James	Private	2nd Battalion, South Staffordshire Regiment	14340464	91504		Stalag XII A, Stalag IV B, Stalag IV C
Hope	John William	Driver	250th Airborne Light Company, Royal Army Service Corps	241767	90820		Stalag XII A, Stalag IV B, Stalag IV D
Hope	Thomas Rogers	Lance Corporal	1st Airborne Provost Company	6206756			Stalag XII A
Hope-Jones	Ronald Christopher	Lieutenant	1st Battalion, Border Regiment	187403	602		Stalag XII A, Dulag of Oflag XII B, Oflag 79
Hopkins	Kenneth Arthur	Private	181st Airlanding Field Ambulance, Royal Army Medical Corps	14672266			Enschede, Stalag XII A, Stalag IV B, Stalag IV D
Hornbuckle		Private	4th Battalion, Dorset Regiment	4922862	26054		Stalag XII A, Stalag IV B, Stalag IV F
Horne	George Minta	Signalman	1st Parachute Brigade, Royal Signals	2598143	91952		Stalag XII A, Stalag IV B
Horne	Robert William Peter	Private	156th Battalion, Parachute Regiment	6087103	90562		Stalag XII A, Stalag VIII C
Horsburgh	Robert	Corporal	7th Battalion, King's Own Scottish Borderers Regiment	3192345	91334		Stalag II A
Horsfield	James	Private	10th Battalion, Parachute Regiment	14632609	17		Stalag XIII C, Stalag IV B, Stalag IV G

Surname	Forename	Rank	Unit	Number	Number	Questionnaire	Camps
Horsley	James	Private	11th Battalion, Parachute Regiment	6010893		Yes	Apeldoorn Hospital, Stalag XI B
Horton	Charles Henry	Private	16th Parachute Field Ambulance, Royal Army Medical Corps	7357394	93681		Dulag Luft – Oberusel, Stalag XII A, Stalag VIII C
Horton	John	Sergeant	Glider Pilot Regiment	14413159	21		Stalag XII A, Dulag Luft – Oberusel, Stalag Luft 7, Stalag III A
Hosker	Thomas Herbert	Private	7th Battalion, King's Own Scottish Borderers Regiment	14573434			Stalag IV B, Stalag IV A
Hotine	Robert Edward	Driver	4th Parachute Brigade, Royal Signals	2600066	90802		Stalag XII A, Stalag IV B
Houghton	Norman Edwin	Private	11th Battalion, Parachute Regiment	996560			Stalag XII A, Stalag IV B
Hounslow	Edward Charles	Private	3rd Battalion, Parachute Regiment	5502730	89562		Stalag IV B
Hounslow	Harold	Private	2nd Battalion, Oxfordshire and Buckinghamshire Light Infantry Regiment	5385947			Stalag IV C
Howard	Ernest	Corporal	156th Battalion, Parachute Regiment	5884952	90688		Stalag XII A, Stalag II A
Howard	Harold	Lance Corporal	4th Parachute Squadron, Royal Engineers	1904106	117582	Yes	Stalag XI B, Stalag III A, Stalag XI A, Stalag IV B
Howard	John James	Lance Corporal	1st Battalion, Parachute Regiment	3598966	89855		Stalag XI B, Stalag 357
Howard	Leslie Frederick	Private	1st Battalion, Parachute Regiment	15327223			Stalag XII A, Stalag IV B
Howard	Stanley Victor	Private	2nd Battalion, Parachute Regiment	6029634			Stalag XII A, Stalag IV B
Howard	Thomas Henry	Private	10th Battalion, Parachute Regiment	14417045			Stalag XII A, Stalag IV B
Howe	Henry	Private	181st Airlanding Field Ambulance, Royal Army Medical Corps	14679982			Stalag XII A, Stalag IV B

Family name	Forename	Rank	Unit as given on Questionnaire	Army number	POW number	Wounded on capture?	Camps
Howell	Derek Martin	Gunner	1st Airlanding Anti-Tank Battery, Royal Artillery	5835348	118694	Yes	Stalag XI B
Howells	John	Lance Corporal	1st Airborne Provost Company	4078592	118226	Yes	Stalag XI B
Howes	Raymond Cuthbert	Lance Corporal	2nd Battalion, South Staffordshire Regiment	4919552	118205	Yes	Stalag XI B
Howson	Victor	Private	11th Battalion, Parachute Regiment	14499916	75690		Stalag XII A, Stalag IV B, Stalag IV D, Stalag IV F
Hoyer Millar MC	Francis Kinglake	Captain	2nd Battalion, Parachute Regiment	85213	90872		Stalag XII A, Dulag XII B Hadamar, Oflag 79
Hoyland	Frank Charles	Private	4th Parachute Brigade HQ	14292326			Stalag XII A, Stalag IV B
Hoyle	Kenneth H	Private	7th Battalion, King's Own Scottish Borderers Regiment	14424034			Stalag XII A, Stalag VIII C, Stalag IV B
Hoyne	William	Sergeant	1st Battalion, Border Regiment	3596668	140120	Yes	Stalag VII A, Stalag 383
Hudson	Arthur George	Private	2nd Battalion, Parachute Regiment	1507796	75409		Stalag XII A, Stalag IV B
Hudson	Francis	Lance Corporal	2nd Battalion, South Staffordshire Regiment	5046543	91637	Yes	Stalag XII A, Stalag IV B, Stalag IV C
Hudson	Frederick Philip	Sergeant	Glider Pilot Regiment	14218054			Dulag Luft – Oberusel, Stalag Luft 1
Hudson	George Ernest	Sapper	9th Field Company, Royal Engineers	2124141	75840		Stalag XII A, Stalag IV B
Huggett	William Arthur	Lance Corporal	1st Parachute Brigade, Royal Signals	5572488	89408		Stalag IV D
Hughes	Anthony Cecil	Private	3rd Battalion, Parachute Regiment	5125630	77095	Yes	Stalag XII A, Stalag IV B, Stalag IV G

Surname	Forename	Rank	Unit	Number	Number	Q	Camps
Hughes	Edward	Lance Corporal	1st Battalion, Border Regiment	3596264	75689		Stalag XII A, Stalag IV B, Stalag IV F
Hughes	Ernest	Corporal	11th Battalion, Parachute Regiment	3718667	140294		Reserve Lazarett Freising Stalag VII A
Hughes	Ernest Edward	Sapper	1st Parachute Squadron, Royal Engineers	14644896	140116	Yes	Stalag VII A
Hughes	Gwyn	Gunner	2nd Airlanding Anti-Tank Battery, Royal Artillery	14519116			Stalag XII A, Stalag IV B
Hughes	Michael Frederick	Private	2nd Battalion, South Staffordshire Regiment	5891442			Stalag IV C Brux
Hughes	Peter	Private	7th Battalion, King's Own Scottish Borderers Regiment	14212001			Stalag XII A, Stalag IV B, Stalag IV A
Hughes	Richard Francis	Private	Parachute Regiment	4127229	75676		Stalag XII A, Stalag IV B
Hughes	Thomas	Private	11th Battalion, Parachute Regiment	4127126	117585	Yes	Osterbeek Hospital, Apeldoorn, Stalag XI B
Hughes	Thomas	Private	2nd Battalion, Parachute Regiment	3969834	91184		Stalag XII A, Stalag IV B, Stalag XIII B
Hughes	William Horace	Private	2nd Battalion, South Staffordshire Regiment	14316562	92212		Stalag XII A, Stalag IV B
Hull	Charles Cecil	Private	181st Airlanding Field Ambulance, Royal Army Medical Corps	7387687			Apeldoorn Hospital, Stalag XII A, Stalag IV B
Hume	William	Private	7th Battalion, King's Own Scottish Borderers Regiment	3190812	90486		Stalag XII A, Stalag IV B, Stalag IV C
Humpherson	Stanley Richmond	Private	7th Battalion, King's Own Scottish Borderers Regiment	3197733	90684		Stalag XII A, Stalag IV B
Humphreys	William	Private	2nd Battalion, Parachute Regiment	5835367	117578	Yes	Stalag XI B, Stalag III A, Stalag XI A

Family name	Forename	Rank	Unit as given on Questionnaire	Army number	POW number	Wounded on capture?	Camps
Hunt	Harry James	Private	2nd Battalion, Parachute Regiment	6848386			Stalag XII A, Stalag IV B, Stalag IV C
Hunt	William	Private	1st Battalion, Border Regiment	4626714	91979	Yes	Stalag XII A, Stalag IV B
Hunter	Edward Donaldson	Private	7th Battalion, King's Own Scottish Borderers Regiment	14204706	117703	Yes	Stalag XI B
Hunter	Robert	Private	156th Battalion, Parachute Regiment	3128295	89547		Stalag XII A, Stalag IV B
Hunton	Alfred Frederick	Gunner	2nd Airlanding Anti-Tank Battery, Royal Artillery	1094022	90896		Stalag XII A, Stalag IV B
Hurst	Norman Frank	Private	1st Battalion, Parachute Regiment	4123041	91749		Stalag IV B
Husband	Desmond John	Private	156th Battalion, Parachute Regiment	14519026			Stalag XII A, Stalag IV B, Stalag IV D
Hutchinson	George Albert	Driver	250 Company, Royal Army Service Corps	10671025			Stalag XII A, Stalag IV B
Hutchinson	Ronald	Private	2nd Battalion, Parachute Regiment	4455745	89908		Stalag XII A, Stalag XI B
Hutton	James Brownlie	Private	156th Battalion, Parachute Regiment	14350633	90762		Stalag XII A, Stalag IV A
Hutton	James Gordon	Private	Royal Army Medical Corps	7365933	90826		Stalag XII A, Stalag IV B
Hutton	Matthew	Private	2nd Battalion, Parachute Regiment	4467557	75411		Stalag XII A, Stalag IV B, Stalag IV G
Hutton	William Alfred	Private	2nd Battalion, South Staffordshire Regiment	4923158	25554		Stalag IV B
Hyams	Meyer John	Private	10th Battalion, Parachute Regiment	6410376	117971		Stalag XI B, Stalag III A

Surname	First name(s)	Rank	Unit	Number	Number	Questionnaire	Camps
Hyde	Thomas	Private	7th Battalion, King's Own Scottish Borderers Regiment	975812	90578		Stalag XII A, Stalag IV B
Hyland	Thomas	Sapper	Royal Engineers	2004091			Stalag XII A, Stalag IV B
Hymes	Douglas	Private	1st Battalion, Parachute Regiment	7402136			Stalag XII A, Stalag IV B
Hyslop	Eric	Sergeant	7th Battalion, King's Own Scottish Borderers Regiment	3190541	75874	Yes	Stalag XII A, Stalag VIII C, Stalag IV B
Infield	Gerald Maurice	Lieutenant	3rd Battalion, Parachute Regiment	174451	522		Oflag XII B, Oflag 79
Ingham	Herbert	Private	156th Battalion, Parachute Regiment	14382007	117977	Yes	Stalag XI B, Stalag III A, Stalag XI B
Ingham	Hubert Leslie	Private	1st Battalion, Border Regiment	3718775	975357	Yes	Zutphen Hospital, Stalag XII A, Stalag IV B, Stalag IV C
Ingham	Ralph Taylor	Private	11th Battalion, Parachute Regiment	147330064			Stalag XII A, Stalag XI B
Ingle	John Ernest	Driver	Royal Army Service Corps	14506862			Stalag XII A, Stalag IV B, Stalag IV C
Ingram	Stanley	Lance Bombardier	1st Airlanding Light Regiment, Royal Artillery	14306817	75871		Stalag XII A, Stalag IV B, Stalag IV D
Install	Alfred Charles	Sergeant	Glider Pilot Regiment	5734412			Stalag XII A, Stalag IV B
Ireland	Albert	Private	181st Airlanding Field Ambulance, Royal Army Medical Corps	7372142	140054		Stalag VII A
Isherwood	Reginald	Sergeant	1st Battalion, Parachute Regiment	893585			Stalag XII A, Stalag VIII C
Ives	Andrews Robert	Private	11th Battalion, Parachute Regiment	5576559	117581	Yes	Stalag XII A, Stalag III A, Stalag XI A, Stalag IV B
Ivey	Alan Wilfred	Staff Sergeant	Glider Pilot Regiment	1480721		Yes	Stalag XII A, Stalag IV B
Izzard	Cyril James	Private	2nd Battalion, Parachute Regiment	6029653	91397		Stalag XII A, Stalag IV B

Family name	Forename	Rank	Unit as given on Questionnaire	Army number	POW number	Wounded on capture?	Camps
Jackson	Albert	Private	156th Battalion, Parachute Regiment	4278961			Stalag XII A, Dulag Luft – Wetzlar, Stalag IV B
Jackson	Arthur	Private	Royal Army Service Corps	10694198			Stalag XII A, Stalag IV B, Stalag IV G
Jackson	Arthur Henry	Private	133rd Parachute Field Ambulance, Royal Army Medical Corps	7357319	90690		Stalag IV B
Jackson	Arnold Phillip	Private	181st Airlanding Field Ambulance, Royal Army Medical Corps	14275901			Koning Willem III Kazerne Apeldoorn, Reserve Lazarett IV/686, Meer en Bosch Klinik Heemstede
Jackson	Charles James	Sergeant	Glider Pilot Regiment	2583498	76300		Stalag XII A, Stalag IV B
Jackson	Empsall	Private	HQ 1st Parachute Brigade	2042543			Stalag XII A, Stalag IV B, Stalag IV A, Stalag IV A
Jackson	Fred Duncan	Private	10th Battalion, Parachute Regiment	81614	117524		Stalag XI B
Jackson	John Henry	Corporal	7th Battalion, King's Own Scottish Borderers Regiment	4750981			Stalag XII A, Stalag II A
Jackson	Peter Joseph	Private	181st Airlanding Field Ambulance, Royal Army Medical Corps	7260275			Apeldorn, Stalag XII A, Stalag IV B
Jackson	Sydney	Lance Corporal	2nd Battalion, South Staffordshire Regiment	4124815			Stalag XII A, Stalag IV B, Stalag IV D

Surname	Forename	Rank	Regiment				Camps
Jackson	William Marshall	Private	7th Battalion, King's Own Scottish Borderers Regiment	3194093	117852	Yes	Stalag XI B, Stalag III A, Stalag XI A, Stalag IV D
James	Alec Arnold	Sergeant	Glider Pilot Regiment	5891664	140210	Yes	Apeldoorn Hospital, Reserve Lazarett Freising
James	Arthur Bert	Private	21st Independent Parachute Company	7022654	75364		Stalag XII A, Stalag IV B
James	David William Mervyn	Staff Sergeant	Glider Pilot Regiment	944489			Dulag Luft – Oberusel, Stalag Luft 7, Stalag III A
James	Edward Henry	Private	21st Independent Parachute Company	1602953	75365		Stalag XII A, Stalag IV B
James	George	Private	2nd Battalion, Parachute Regiment	6153238	89279		Stalag IV C
James	Joseph James	Lance Corporal	2nd Battalion, South Staffordshire Regiment	4929053	75839		Stalag IV B
James	Robert John	Private	2nd Battalion, South Staffordshire Regiment	6095111			Stalag XII A, Stalag XI B, Stalag 357
James	Stanley Ernest George	Private	11th Battalion, Parachute Regiment	14051444	52921	Yes	1288 Meiningen
Jamieson	Peter Dunlop	Sergeant	156th Battalion, Parachute Regiment	2884343			Stalag XII A, Stalag II A
Janovsky	Roland	Private	2nd Battalion, Parachute Regiment	6848274			Stalag XII A, Stalag IV D
Jarvis	Ronald Eric	Sergeant	11th Battalion, Parachute Regiment	6292520	92145		Stalag XII A, Stalag VIII C, Stalag IV G, Stalag IV F
Jeavons	Sidney Thomas	Private	2nd Battalion, South Staffordshire Regiment	4923382			Stalag XII A, Stalag IV B, Stalag IV C
Jebbitt	David Owen	Private	181st Airlanding Field Ambulance, Royal Army Medical Corps	7265533			Apeldoorn Hospital, Stalag XII A, Stalag IV B
Jeffery	Norman Dennis	Private	4th Battalion, Dorset Regiment	14592676	17581		Stalag XII A, Stalag IV B, Stalag IV F

Family name	Forename	Rank	Unit as given on Questionnaire	Army number	POW number	Wounded on capture?	Camps
Jeffries	John Patrick	Signalman	Royal Signals	2379610	117314		Stalag XI B, Stalag III A, Stalag XI A
Jenkins	Griffith	Private	1st Battalion, Parachute Regiment	929213	91462	Yes	Stalag XII A, Stalag IV B
Jenkins	Kenneth George	Gunner	1st Airlanding Anti-Tank Battery, Royal Artillery	14384421	75957		Stalag XII A, Stalag IV B
Jenkins	Ronald William	Lance Corporal	156th Battalion, Parachute Regiment	7437345			Stalag XII A, Stalag IV B
Jenkinson	Horace	Private	2nd Battalion, Oxfordshire and Buckinghamshire Light Infantry Regiment	5891203	920009		Stalag XII A, Stalag IV B, Stalag IV A
Jenkinson	Wilfred	Driver	223 Company, Royal Army Service Corps	3860067			Stalag IV B
Jervis	Harold	Private	2nd Battalion, South Staffordshire Regiment	5067977			Stalag XII A, Stalag IV B, Stalag IV C
Jessup	Geoffrey Frederick George	Private	156th Battalion, Parachute Regiment	6460489	118209		Stalag XI B
Jeuchner	Albert George	Private	2nd Battalion, Parachute Regiment	6352988	91162		Stalag XII A, Stalag IV B, Stalag IV G
John	John Edward	Private	Royal Army Medical Corps	7357904	88911		Stalag XII A, Stalag IV B
Johnson	Arthur	Private	2nd Battalion, South Staffordshire Regiment	1568699	92045		Stalag IV D
Johnson	Douglas Frederick William	Private	2nd Battalion, South Staffordshire Regiment	867876			Stalag XII A, Stalag IV B, Stalag IV C
Johnson	Horace	Private	2nd Battalion, South Staffordshire Regiment	4923187	9190		Stalag XII A, Stalag IV B

Johnson	Peter	Private	1st Battalion, Parachute Regiment	5388969	89242		Stalag XII A, Stalag IV B
Johnston	Harold	Private	4th Battalion, Dorset Regiment	3709037	17569		Stalag XII A, Stalag IV B
Johnstone	Robert	Private	Parachute Regiment	4279221	117304		Stalag XI B
Johnstone	William Tait	Signalman	1st Parachute Brigade, Royal Signals	2378622			Stalag XII A, Stalag IV B
Jolly	Arthur Charles Edward	Private	156th Battalion, Parachute Regiment	320647			Stalag IV B
Jolly	Frank Ronald	Signalman	1st Airlanding Light Regiment, Royal Artillery	14280533	92067	Yes	Stalag XII A, Stalag IV B, Stalag IV C
Jonas	John James	Corporal	2nd Battalion, Parachute Regiment	1876407	93725		Stalag XII A, Stalag VIII C
Jones	Arthur	Corporal	1st Battalion, Parachute Regiment	3957377			Stalag IV B
Jones	Anthony	Private	2nd Battalion, Parachute Regiment	1595342	117692	Yes	Stalag XI B, Stalag III A, Stalag XI A, Stalag IV D
Jones	Alfred Redgewell	Corporal	2nd Battalion, South Staffordshire Regiment	4922888	89509		Stalag XII A, Stalag II A
Jones	Cyril	Gunner	2nd Airlanding Anti-Tank Battery, Royal Artillery	14319790	91777		Stalag XII A, Stalag IV B, Stalag IV D
Jones	Conway Thomas	Sapper	1st Parachute Squadron, Royal Engineers	1909450		Yes	Enschede Hospital, Tirpitz, Dulag Luft – Oberusel, Omark, Reserve Lazarett Meiningen, Stalag IX C/Z
Jones	Donald	Sergeant	Glider Pilot Regiment	14395807			Stalag XII A, Stalag IV B
Jones	Dewi Llewellyn	Sergeant	1st Airlanding Brigade, Royal Signals	2362597	91555		Stalag XII A, Stalag VIII C
Jones	Edgar	Driver	1st Airlanding Anti-Tank Battery, Royal Artillery	11053201	118272	Yes	Stalag XI B

Family name	Forename	Rank	Unit as given on Questionnaire	Army number	POW number	Wounded on capture?	Camps
Jones	Ernest George	Lance Corporal	21st Independent Parachute Company	7360854	117260		Stalag XI B
Jones	George	Sapper	1st Parachute Squadron, Royal Engineers	2193549	91490		Stalag XII A, Stalag IV B
Jones	Hugh	Private	10th Battalion, Parachute Regiment	4199324	140154		Arnhem Hospital, Apeldoorn Hospital, Reserve Lazarett Freising, Stalag VII A
Jones	Howard Franklyn	Lance Corporal	16th Parachute Field Ambulance, Royal Army Medical Corps	7518016	89789		Dulag Luft, Stalag XII A, Stalag II A
Jones	Harry Thomas	Private	1st Battalion, Parachute Regiment	5192697			Apeldoorn Hospital, Stalag IV C
Jones	John	Private	1st Battalion, Parachute Regiment	14418927			Stalag XII A, Stalag IV B
Jones	John Alfred	Gunner	2nd Airlanding Anti-Tank Battery, Royal Artillery	14281117	91703		Stalag XII A, Stalag IV C
Jones	John Campbell	Signalman	4th Parachute Brigade, Royal Signals	324396	77367		Dulag Luft, Stalag XII A, Stalag IV B, Stalag IV F
Jones	John Richard	Private	156th Battalion, Parachute Regiment	14316790	75691		Stalag IV B, Stalag IV F
Jones	Peter	Private	2nd Battalion, Parachute Regiment	3388690	52922		Reserve Lazarett Obermaßfield, Reserve Lazarett 1 May 1945
Jones	Robert	Sapper	Royal Engineers	5733483	88932		Stalag XII A, Stalag IV B
Jones	Robert Hobdell	Sergeant	2nd Battalion, Parachute Regiment	4975220	88902		Stalag XII A, Stalag XVIII C
Jones	Robert John	Corporal	2nd Battalion, South Staffordshire Regiment	5886650			Stalag XII A, Stalag II A, Stalag XII A

Surname	First names	Rank	Regiment	Number	Number	Camps
Jones	Stephen Samuel	Private	156th Battalion, Parachute Regiment	5575919	21903	Stalag XII A, Stalag IV B
Jones	Thomas Edward	Driver	250th Airborne Light Company, Royal Army Service Corps	277972	91094	Stalag XII A, Stalag IV B, Stalag IV A
Jones	Thomas Leslie	Private	3rd Battalion, Parachute Regiment	3911512		Stalag IV B
Jones	William Arthur	Driver	Royal Army Service Corps	14435505	91795	Stalag XII A, Stalag IV G
Jones	Wilfred Richard George	Private	181st Airlanding Field Ambulance, Royal Army Medical Corps	7364540	90558	Stalag XII A, Stalag IV B
Jordan	William Edwin	Private	4th Battalion, Dorset Regiment	14227233	17594	Stalag IV B
Jorden	Leonard	Private	2nd Battalion, South Staffordshire Regiment	1655164	91558	Stalag XII A, Stalag IV B
Jorimann	Reginald Percy	Private	2nd Battalion, South Staffordshire Regiment	5504266		Stalag XII A, Stalag IV B
Josephs	Daniel	Private	156th Battalion, Parachute Regiment	6849171		Stalag XII A, Dulag Luft – Frankfurt, Stalag IV B
Jukes	George William	Signalman	1st Parachute Brigade, Royal Signals	2069539		Stalag XII A, Stalag IV B
Kane	John Patrick	Private	2nd Battalion, Parachute Regiment	4690202		Stalag XII A, Stalag IV B, Stalag IV A
Kane	Lawrence Patrick	Lieutenant	7th Battalion, King's Own Scottish Borderers Regiment	482	569	Dulag XII B Hadamar, Oflag 79
Kay	George Edward	Private	3rd Battalion, Parachute Regiment	4974938	88758	Stalag XII A, Stalag XVIII C
Kay	John	Private	Parachute Regiment	915487	89731	Stalag XII A, Stalag XI B, Stalag 357
Kaye	Stanley Lawrence	Captain	16th Parachute Field Ambulance, Royal Army Medical Corps	246299	618	Oflag 79, Stalag XVII B

Family name	Forename	Rank	Unit as given on Questionnaire	Army number	POW number	Wounded on capture?	Camps
Kean	Alexander Brown	Lance Corporal	1st Parachute Brigade, Royal Signals	2699469			Stalag XII A, Stalag IV B, Stalag IV F
Kearns	James Thomas	Private	1st Battalion, Parachute Regiment	4808363	89495		Stalag XII A, Stalag IV B, Stalag IV D
Keddie	John	Private	10th Battalion, Parachute Regiment	2758803			Stalag XII A, Stalag IV B, Stalag IV C
Keeler	Norman Arthur	Sergeant, Lance	4th Parachute Squadron, Royal Engineers	2031950	21705	Yes	Stalag XII A, Stalag VIII C, Linden School Hanover
Keenan	James Mullan	Private	156th Battalion, Parachute Regiment	3189614	118364		Stalag XI B
Keens	Norman	Private	2nd Battalion, Parachute Regiment	14310355			Stalag IV B, Stalag IV C
Kellett	Edgar	Trooper	1st Airborne Reconnaissance Squadron	14253215	75684		Stalag XII A, Stalag IV B
Kelly	Charles	Gunner	1st Airlanding Anti-Tank Battery, Royal Artillery	14504062	75468		Stalag XII A, Stalag IV B, Stalag IV C
Kelly	Dennis	Private	2nd Battalion, Parachute Regiment	4616630			Stalag XII A, Stalag IV B
Kelly	James	Lance Corporal	10th Battalion, Parachute Regiment	2930968	90505		Stalag XII A, Stalag IV B, Stalag IV C
Kelly	Patrick Joseph	Sergeant	1st Battalion, Parachute Regiment	7012461			
Kemley	Peter William	Private	2nd Battalion, Parachute Regiment	14584652	118154	Yes	Stalag XI B, Stalag III A, Stalag XI A, Stalag IV D/Z
Kennedy	George	Lance Corporal	7th Battalion, King's Own Scottish Borderers Regiment	2930509			Stalag XII A, Stalag IV B, Stalag IV C

Surname	First name(s)	Rank	Unit	Number	Number	Q	Camps
Kennedy	Simon James	Private	11th Battalion, Parachute Regiment	5885331	92158		Stalag XII A, Stalag VIII A, Stalag IX B
Kennedy	Wilfred	Private	156th Battalion, Parachute Regiment	2877369	90579		Stalag XII A, Stalag IV B
Kenworthy	Joseph	Private	1st Battalion, Border Regiment	4467370	118066	Yes	Apeldoorn Hospital, Stalag XI B
Kerr	Charles Cole	Private	7th Battalion, King's Own Scottish Borderers Regiment	3188450			Stalag XII A, Stalag IV B
Kerr	Harry Alexander	Trooper	1st Airborne Reconnaissance Squadron	7020098	118345	Yes	Apeldoorn Hospital, Stalag XI B
Kerr	James Edward	Sergeant, Lance	1st Battalion, Border Regiment	3602996	118836	Yes	Stalag XI B, Stalag 357
Kerswell	William John	Sergeant	Royal Army Medical Corps	7523088	77338		Stalag XII A, Stalag VIII C, Stalag 344, Stalag XIII C, Stalag XIII D
Keys	Harry	Private	2nd Battalion, South Staffordshire Regiment	4208715			Stalag XII A, Stalag XI B
Kidd	James	Private	7th Battalion, King's Own Scottish Borderers Regiment	3194226	89317		Stalag XII A, Stalag IV B
Kidds	Charles Frederick	Private	2nd Battalion, Parachute Regiment	7021470	294155		Stalag IV B, Stalag IV C
Kidley	Jack	Private	2nd Battalion, South Staffordshire Regiment	14441082			Stalag XII A, Stalag IV B
Kilbryde	George Howard	Sergeant	Glider Pilot Regiment	4922900			Dulag Luft – Oberursel, Stalag Luft 7, Stalag III A
Kill	William	Sergeant, Lance	1st Airlanding Anti-Tank Battery, Royal Artillery	1107611	89415		Stalag XII A, Dulag Luft, Stalag II A
Killick	John Edward	Captain	89th Parachute Field Security Section	137467	628		Zutphen Transit Camp, Stalag XII A, Oflag XII B, Oflag 79

Family name	Forename	Rank	Unit as given on Questionnaire	Army number	POW number	Wounded on capture?	Camps
Kilner	Melville Gordon	Corporal	1st Battalion, Parachute Regiment	3910374			Stalag XII A, Stalag XVIII C
King	Charles	Private	156th Battalion, Parachute Regiment	5338048	75537		Stalag XII A, Stalag IV B, Stalag IV D
King	Charles Davis	Lance Corporal	1st Airborne Reconnaissance Squadron	5347510	118626	Yes	Stalag XI B, Oflag 79
King	David John	Private	1st Battalion, Parachute Regiment	6148512	92159		Stalag IV B
King	Frank Douglas	Captain	11th Battalion, Parachute Regiment	138204	585		Stalag XII A, Oflag XII B, Oflag 79
King	George Richard	Private	Parachute Regiment	5510137		Yes	Lochem Hospital, Interrogation Camp Germany, Dulag Luft – Wetzlar, Stalag XII A, Stalag IV B, Stalag IV F
King	Joseph Bertie	Corporal	16th Parachute Field Ambulance, Royal Army Medical Corps	7347201	118427	Yes	Stalag XI B, Stalag VIII C
King	Leonard William	Signalman	4th Parachute Brigade, Royal Signals	2588983			Utrecht Hospital, Apeldoorn Hospital, Stalag XII A, Stalag IV B
Kirk	Duncan	Private	7th Battalion, King's Own Scottish Borderers Regiment	14211437	91487		Stalag XII A, Stalag IV B
Kirk	George Milton	Sapper	1st Parachute Squadron, Royal Engineers	1948638			Stalag XII A, Stalag IV B
Kirk	Stanley Harry	Lance Corporal	16th Parachute Field Ambulance, Royal Army Medical Corps	7349841			Stalag XII A, Stalag IV B
Kirlew	Alfred Harry	Private	156th Battalion, Parachute Regiment	405893			Stalag XII A, Stalag IV B, Stalag IV F

Surname	First name(s)	Rank	Unit / Regiment	Number	Number	Q	Camps
Kirlow	Alfred	Private	2nd Battalion, Parachute Regiment	14437450			Stalag XII A, Stalag IV B, Stalag IV A
Kitchener	Robert Anthony	Private	2nd Battalion, Parachute Regiment	6145647		Yes	Stalag XII A, Stalag IV B
Kite	George Anthony	Sergeant, Lance	2nd Battalion, South Staffordshire Regiment	5498368			Stalag II A
Klamph	Samuel	Private	156th Battalion, Parachute Regiment	5953101			Stalag XII A, Stalag IV B
Knapp	Frederick Frank	Private	11th Battalion, Parachute Regiment	14670639			Stalag XII A, Stalag IV B
Knight	James	Private	2nd Battalion, Parachute Regiment	5735190	117865	Yes	Stalag XI B, Stalag III A, Stalag XI A, Stalag IV D
Knight	James Downie	Private	7th Battalion, King's Own Scottish Borderers Regiment	14211438	75939		Stalag IV B
Knight	Joseph William	Sapper	9th Field Company (Airborne), Royal Engineers	2058280	91610	Yes	Stalag XII A, Stalag IV B, Stalag IV G
Knight	Lawrence Alfred	Sergeant, Lance	2nd Battalion, Parachute Regiment	7016898			Stalag XII A, Stalag XVIII C
Knight	Leonard Davies	Signalman	1st Parachute Brigade, Royal Signals	14200119	89308		Stalag XII A, Stalag IV B
Knox	William Hutchinson	Sergeant	Glider Pilot Regiment	11000594	1070		Dulag Luft – Frankfurt, Stalag Luft 7, Stalag III A
Lacey	Sidney Herbert	Sergeant, Lance	2nd Battalion, South Staffordshire Regiment	4917620	89474		Stalag XII A, Stalag II A
Laidlaw	Robert James	Private	7th Battalion, King's Own Scottish Borderers Regiment	3194137	140238	Yes	Apeldoorn Hospital, Reserve Lazarett Freising, Stalag VII A
Laing	Herbert Alexander	Private	21st Independent Parachute Company	879322	118030		Osterbeek Hospital, Arnhem Hospital, Apeldoorn Hospital, Stalag XI B

Family name	Forename	Rank	Unit as given on Questionnaire	Army number	POW number	Wounded on capture?	Camps
Laing	Robert	Private	1st Battalion, Parachute Regiment	888389			Stalag IV B
Laing	Robert Hutt	Lance Bombardier	2nd Airlanding Anti-Tank Battery, Royal Artillery	14554942	91695		Stalag XII A, Stalag IV B, Stalag IV A
Lakin	Bernard Lamplugh	Private	Royal Army Medical Corps	7522252	88910		Stalag XII A, Stalag IV B
Lamb	Lionel Edward	Private	10th Battalion, Parachute Regiment	1806297	117689		Stalag XI B, Stalag III A, Stalag XI A, Stalag IV D
Lancaster	Alexander Albert	Corporal	9th Field Company (Airborne), Royal Engineers	1899732			Stalag XII A, Stalag II A
Lancaster	Clarke Albert	Corporal	Parachute Regiment	4389325	117978		Stalag XI B, Stalag VIII C
Lancaster	Joseph	Private	11th Battalion, Parachute Regiment	935934			Stalag XII A, Stalag IV B, Stalag IV D
Lane	Henry Sidney	Private	181st Airlanding Field Ambulance, Royal Army Medical Corps	7384160			Stalag XII A, Stalag IV B, Stalag IV D
Lane	Philip George Oliver	Corporal	1st Parachute Squadron, Royal Engineers	2009968			Stalag XII A, Stalag XVIII C
Lang	Robert	Private	1st Battalion, Border Regiment	3606642	117504	Yes	Stalag XI B
Langford	Alfred Joseph	Private	2nd Battalion, South Staffordshire Regiment	4919269			Stalag XII A, Stalag IV B
Langford	John Adair	Captain	Forward Observation Unit, Royal Artillery	158269	90871		Interrogation centre Dietz, Oflag 79
Langford	Samuel	Private	2nd Battalion, Parachute Regiment	5952886	91076		Stalag XII A, Stalag IV D?
Lasenby	James Joseph	Lieutenant	1st Battalion, Parachute Regiment	297337	91000	Yes	Stalag XII A, Oflag XII B, Dulag Luft, Oflag 79

Surname	First Name(s)	Rank	Unit	Number	Number 2	Questionnaire	Camps
Lashmar	Reginald Douglas	Private	156th Battalion, Parachute Regiment	6446980			Stalag XII A, Stalag IV B
Latto	James	Lance Corporal	1st Battalion, Parachute Regiment	6353770	118810	Yes	Stalag XI B
Laughland	Thomas Anderson	Sergeant	2nd Battalion, Parachute Regiment	2989237			Stalag XII A, Stalag II A
Launder	Philip Ernest Stephen	Private	2nd Battalion, South Staffordshire Regiment	14673092	77081		Stalag IV B
Law	Sidney Albert	Private	2nd Battalion, South Staffordshire Regiment	1790572			Stalag IV B
Lawrence	Henry Philip	Private	2nd Battalion, South Staffordshire Regiment	4922180			Stalag IV F
Lawson	Albert	Private	2nd Battalion, South Staffordshire Regiment	1789246	91169		Stalag XII A, Stalag IV B
Lawson	George Steele	Signalman	Royal Signals	2382692			Stalag XII A, Stalag IV B, Stalag IV A
Lawson	Wilfred McLellen	Private	156th Battalion, Parachute Regiment	7948335	118001		Stalag XI B
Lawton	John William	Lance Corporal	1st Airborne Provost Company	7691899			Stalag XII A, Stalag IV B
Layland	Frederick	Gunner	2nd Airlanding Anti-Tank Battery, Royal Artillery	1092475	92062		Dulag Luft, Stalag IV D
Layton	Ernest	Private	Parachute Regiment	14224910			Stalag XII A, Stalag IV B
Ledger	James	Staff Sergeant	Glider Pilot Regiment	5111304	140080	Yes	Stalag VII A, Stalag 383
Lee	Idwal	Driver	1st Airlanding Anti-Tank Battery, Royal Artillery	5188617	75540		Stalag IV B
Lee	John Henry Dixon	Captain	1st Airlanding Light Regiment, Royal Artillery	94122	587		Stalag XII A, Oflag XII B, Oflag 79
Leece	Albert Edward	Gunner	Royal Artillery	14667137	91887		Stalag XII A, Stalag IV B, Stalag IV C

Family name	Forename	Rank	Unit as given on Questionnaire	Army number	POW number	Wounded on capture?	Camps
Leech	James	Private	156th Battalion, Parachute Regiment	4343831			Stalag XII A, Stalag IV B
Leeder	Roberto Cedric	Sergeant	Glider Pilot Regiment	6293746		Yes	Stalag XII A, Stalag IV B
Lees	Fred	Sergeant	Glider Pilot Regiment	109626			Stalag XII A, Stalag IV B
Lees	Herbert	Corporal	10th Battalion, Parachute Regiment	7014234			Stalag XII A, Stalag II A
Lees	Norman Alfred	Lance Corporal	156th Battalion, Parachute Regiment	14377390	90542		Stalag XII A, Stalag IV B, Stalag IV D, Stalag IV F
Lees	Robert Brownlee	Corporal	156th Battalion, Parachute Regiment	3190642			Stalag XII A, Stalag IV B
Leggett	Clarence Leslie	Corporal	11th Battalion, Parachute Regiment	4691420	75986		Stalag XII A, Stalag IV B, Stalag IV G
Leith	James Park	Lance Corporal	7th Battalion, King's Own Scottish Borderers Regiment	14211442	118744		Stalag XI B
Lemon	Arthur	Private	7th Battalion, King's Own Scottish Borderers Regiment	14633797	88770		Stalag XI B, Stalag IV B, Stalag IV C
Lemmie	George Dougan	Private	3rd Battalion, Parachute Regiment	3187549			Stalag IV B
Leslie	John	Lance Corporal	10th Battalion, Parachute Regiment	2930008	75795		Stalag XII A, Stalag IV B
Leslie	James	Private	10th Battalion, Parachute Regiment	14432451	92072		Stalag XII A, Stalag IV B, Stalag IV C
Leslie	Thomas Mackie	Sergeant	2nd Battalion, Parachute Regiment	7343202			Stalag XIII C
Letchford	Arthur Nugent	Private	2nd Battalion, Parachute Regiment	6854730			Stalag XII A, Stalag IV B, Stalag IV F

Surname	First name	Rank	Unit	Number	Number	Q	Camps
Lever	Benjamin	Lance Corporal	1st Battalion, Border Regiment	3776422	26083		Stalag IV B, Stalag IV G
Levien	Robert Hugh	Lieutenant	2nd Battalion, Parachute Regiment	73127	554		10 Panzer HQ, Dulag XII B Hadamar, Oflag 79
Lewington	John William	Private	10th Battalion, Parachute Regiment	14641541			Stalag XII A, Stalag IV B, Stalag IV G
Lewington	William Bert	Lance Corporal	4th Battalion, Dorset Regiment	5953107	17534		Stalag XII A, Stalag IV B, Stalag IV A
Lewis	Harry	Private	[No unit given]	2939511			Stalag XII A, Stalag XI B
Lewis	Harry Leslie	Private	4th Battalion, Dorset Regiment	14702331	20533		Stalag IV B
Lewis	John	Corporal	1st Battalion, Parachute Regiment	4032087	92129		Stalag XII A, Stalag IV B, Stalag IV A
Lewis	Stanley Edward	Lance Corporal	Parachute Regiment	2929796	118522	Yes	Stalag XI B
Lewis	Vivian	Corporal	1st Battalion, Parachute Regiment	890079			Stalag XII A, Stalag II A
Lewis	William	Private	1st Battalion, Border Regiment	14431937	92111		Stalag XII A, Stalag IV B, Stalag IV C
Linden	Jack Alfred	Corporal	89th Parachute Field Security Section	918417			Stalag XII A, Stalag XVIII C
Linden	Thomas	Private	7th Battalion, King's Own Scottish Borderers Regiment	3197468	90495		Stalag XII A, Stalag IV B, Stalag IV A
Lindley	Francis William	Major	10th Battalion, Parachute Regiment	226192	2194	Yes	Oflag IX A/Z, Reserve Lazarett Obermaßfeld, Reserve Lazarett Meiningen, Oflag IX A/Z
Lindsay	Allan Barr	Staff Sergeant	Glider Pilot Regiment	918329	76335		Stalag XII A, Stalag IV B
Lines	Stanley	Lance Corporal	2nd Battalion, South Staffordshire Regiment	5440800	75356		Stalag XII A, Stalag IV B
Lintern	Ronald Jack	Corporal	156th Battalion, Parachute Regiment	3959419		Yes	Stalag XII A, Stalag II A

107

Family name	Forename	Rank	Unit as given on Questionnaire	Army number	POW number	Wounded on capture?	Camps
Lister	Benjamin	Corporal	250th Airborne Light Company, Royal Army Service Corps	178990	17547		Stalag XII A, Stalag VIII C
Little	David Richardson	Private	3rd Battalion, Parachute Regiment	3190427			Stalag IV B
Little	Wilfred	Private	1st Battalion, Border Regiment	4621936	91710		Stalag XII A, Stalag IV B
Littlewood	Harold	Lance Corporal	156th Battalion, Parachute Regiment	4127282			Stalag XII A, Stalag IV B
Livesey	Stanley	Lance Corporal	7th Battalion, King's Own Scottish Borderers Regiment	14427536			Stalag IV D
Livesey	Trevor John	Captain	1st Parachute Squadron, Royal Engineers	222702	611		Stalag XII A, Oflag XII B, Oflag 79
Lloyd	Arthur	Lance Corporal	156th Battalion, Parachute Regiment	5888980			Enschede, Reserve Lazarett Teupitz, Reserve Lazarett Obermaßfeld, Reserve Lazarett Meiningen, Stalag IX C/Z
Lloyd	Clifford Walter	Private	4th Battalion, Dorset Regiment	5726668	20035		Stalag IV B, Stalag IV F
Lloyd	Philip Isaac	Signalman	Royal Signals	558280	90805		Stalag XII A, Stalag IV B
Lloyd	Samuel	Gunner	1st Airlanding Anti-Tank Battery, Royal Artillery	14268055			Stalag IV C
Lochery	John Aiken	Private	7th Battalion, King's Own Scottish Borderers Regiment	14327588	91779		Stalag VI C, Stalag IV B
Lock	Bert Edward	Private	11th Battalion, Parachute Regiment	2081300	117961	Yes	Stalag XI B, Stalag III A, Stalag XI B
Lockwood	Joseph William	Gunner	1st Airlanding Light Royal Artillery	14329838			Stalag XII A, Stalag IV B, Stalag IV D, Stalag IV F

Logan	Thomas Davison	Private	2nd Battalion, Parachute Regiment	1433668	118681	Yes	Queen Wilhelmina Barracks, Apeldoorn Hospital, Stalag XI B, Oflag 79
Long	Albert Edward	Private	4th Battalion, Dorset Regiment	5950672			Stalag VIII B
Long	Reginald Arthur	Staff Sergeant	Glider Pilot Regiment	10538193			Stalag Luft 7, Stalag III A
Long	Thomas Edwin	Private	2nd Battalion, Parachute Regiment	14918167	117576	Yes	Stalag XI B, Stalag III A, Stalag XI A, Repatriation Camp Annaberg
Longson	James	Private	1st Battalion, Border Regiment	3782025	75994		Stalag XII A, Stalag IV B, Stalag IV C
Losty	Patrick Alfred	Sergeant	Glider Pilot Regiment	1436976			Stalag XII A, Stalag IV B
Lothian	James Charles Ogilvie	Lance Corporal	7th Battalion, King's Own Scottish Borderers Regiment	14212249	75383		Stalag XII A, Stalag IV B
Lott	George Henry	Company Sergeant Major	10th Battalion, Parachute Regiment	6395878			Stalag XII A, Stalag XVIII C
Lovatt	George	Private	7th Battalion, King's Own Scottish Borderers Regiment	14201968	90691		Stalag XII A, Stalag IV B, Stalag IV A
Lovett	James	Staff Sergeant	Glider Pilot Regiment	128577			Dulag Luft, Stalag Luft 7, Stalag III A
Lowe	Alfred	Private	2nd Battalion, South Staffordshire Regiment	14700220		Yes	Dulag XII A, Stalag VIII A
Lowe	David Borwell	Staff Sergeant	Glider Pilot Regiment	2084363	76332		Stalag XII A, Stalag IV B
Lowe	Eric Leslie	Gunner	1st Airlanding Light Regiment, Royal Artillery	14552349	91444		Stalag XII A, Stalag IV B
Lowrie	James	Lance Corporal	1st Parachute Brigade, Royal Signals	2351489			Stalag XII A, Stalag IV B
Lumb	Donald	Corporal	3rd Battalion, Parachute Regiment	3780397			Stalag XII A, Stalag II A

Family name	Forename	Rank	Unit as given on Questionnaire	Army number	POW number	Wounded on capture?	Camps
Lumb	Vernon	Sergeant	3rd Battalion, Parachute Regiment	137755			Stalag XII A, Stalag XVIII C
Lumsden	Albert Edward	Private	2nd Battalion, Parachute Regiment	941821			Stalag XII A, Stalag IV B
Lund	James	Private	2nd Battalion, Parachute Regiment	843710			Stalag XII A, Stalag IV B
Lund	Robert	Staff Sergeant	Glider Pilot Regiment	2005243			Dulag Luft – Oberursel, Stalag Luft 7, Stalag VI A
Lune	Albert	Private	181st Airlanding Field Ambulance, Royal Army Medical Corps	14672958	140058		Stalag IV B
Lupton	Thomas	Private	7th Battalion, King's Own Scottish Borderers Regiment	3195317	90508		Stalag XII A, Stalag IV B
Lynch	Peter Patrick	Sergeant	7th Battalion, King's Own Scottish Borderers Regiment	3192399	89987		Stalag II A
Lyndon	Edwin Charles	Sapper	9th Field Company (Airborne), Royal Engineers	2115530			Stalag XII A, Stalag IV B, Stalag IV F
Lynes	Frank Herbert	Lance Corporal	7th Battalion, King's Own Scottish Borderers Regiment	2563317			Stalag XII A, Stalag IV B
Lyon	Archibald Davidson	Sergeant	Glider Pilot Regiment	14216954	15246	Yes	Enschede Hospital, Reserve Lazarett Nürnberg, Stalag XIII C, Dulag Luft – Oberursel, Stalag Luft 7, Stalag III A
Lyons	Charles Howard Cecil	Sergeant	Glider Pilot Regiment	427924	118524		Ede Stalag XI B, Stalag VIII C, Stalag IV B, Stalag IX A

Surname	First name(s)	Rank	Unit	Number	Number	Camp(s)
Lyons	Leslie William Herbert	Sergeant	Parachute Regiment	5573769		Stalag XII A, Stalag IV B
Lyons	Robert	Private	7th Battalion, King's Own Scottish Borderers Regiment	4698363	90786	Stalag XII A
Macdonald	John Forbes	Sergeant	Glider Pilot Regiment	2881342		Dulag Luft – Oberusel, Stalag Luft 7, Stalag III A
Macdonnell	Charles James	Lieutenant	2nd Battalion, South Staffordshire Regiment	294983	2173	Apeldoorn Hospital, Stalag XI B, Oflag IX A/Z
Mackay	Ernest Henry	Private	2nd Battalion, Parachute Regiment	6922282	91676	Apeldoorn Hospital, Apeldoorn, Dulag Luft, Stalag XII A, Stalag IV B?
Mackenzie	John Alexander	Private	3rd Battalion, Parachute Regiment	2820366	89961	Stalag XII A, Stalag IV B
Madden	Harald	Private	Parachute Regiment	14658029		Stalag IV C
Magee	Alfred	Private	156th Battalion, Parachute Regiment	1439453		Stalag IV F
Maguire	Joseph	Private	1st Battalion, Border Regiment	14583475	24938	Stalag XII A, Stalag IV B
Maidens	William Edward	Private	16th Parachute Field Ambulance, Royal Army Medical Corps	7403380		Stalag XII A, Stalag IV B
Mallett	William John	Captain	Forward Observation Unit, Royal Artillery	249340	568	Stalag XII A, Oflag XII B, Oflag 79
Malley	James	Private	7th Battalion, King's Own Scottish Borderers Regiment	14211489		Stalag XII A, Stalag IV B
Mallison	Geoffrey Norman	Staff Sergeant	Glider Pilot Regiment	4348337		Apeldoorn Hospital
Maloney	Robert	Signalman	1st Parachute Brigade, Royal Signals	2328785		Stalag XII A, Stalag XI B
Manders	Jesse Ewart	Leading Aircraftman	Light Warning Set Unit No. 6080, RAF	1206626	1255	Apeldoorn Hospital, Stalag XIII D, Stalag XIII C

Family name	Forename	Rank	Unit as given on Questionnaire	Army number	POW number	Wounded on capture?	Camps
Manley	George	Private	7th Battalion, King's Own Scottish Borderers Regiment	10602371	91781		Stalag IV B, Stalag IV F
Manley	John	Private	3rd Battalion, Parachute Regiment	5833839			Stalag IV B
Mann	Sydney George	Corporal	1st Battalion, Border Regiment	4276920	18675	Yes	Stalag V B, Stalag VII A, Stalag 383
Manning	Alfred Ernest	Gunner	2nd Airlanding Anti-Tank Battery, Royal Artillery	1155826			Stalag XII A, Stalag IV B
Manuel	Henry Thomas	Private	11th Battalion, Parachute Regiment	320899	140073		Apeldoorn Hospital, Stalag VII A
Mapplebeck	Thomas	Private	3rd Battalion, Parachute Regiment	2067264	118599		Stalag XI B
Mardell	George Henry	Sergeant	2nd Battalion, South Staffordshire Regiment	6201240	89425		Stalag XII A, Stalag II A
Markham	Leonard	Private	Parachute Regiment	5962142	89799		Stalag XII A, Stalag XI B, Stalag 357
Marks	Geoffrey George	Private	1st Battalion, Parachute Regiment	6853688			Stalag XII A, Stalag IV C
Marr	William	Sapper	1st Parachute Squadron, Royal Engineers	2110349	89232		Stalag XII A, Stalag IV B
Marriott	Charles Edward	Private	1st Battalion, Border Regiment	4277974	117642	Yes	Stalag XI B
Marriott	Charles Edward	Private	11th Battalion, Parachute Regiment	4399906			Stalag XII A, Stalag IV B, Stalag IV F, Reserve Lazarett Wermsdorf
Marriott	James Harold	Private	156th Battalion, Parachute Regiment	4987520			Stalag XII A, Stalag IV F

Surname	Forename	Rank	Unit	Number	Number	Questionnaire	Camps
Marsden	James	Gunner	2nd Airlanding Anti-Tank Battery, Royal Artillery	1152480		Yes	Stalag XII A, Stalag IV B, Stalag IV F
Marshall	James	Private	7th Battalion, King's Own Scottish Borderers Regiment	14608077	90576		Stalag XII A, Stalag IV B
Marshall	Reginald	Private	7th Battalion, King's Own Scottish Borderers Regiment	3326129	91782		Stalag IV C
Martin	Frederick George	Company Sergeant Major	1st Battalion, Parachute Regiment	6285361	89411		Stalag XII A, Stalag II A
Martin	Joseph	Private	1st Battalion, Parachute Regiment	2615745	118725	Yes	Oflag 79
Martin	Reginald Alfred	Lance Corporal	253rd Airborne Light Company, Royal Army Service Corps	171029		Yes	Arnhem Hospital, St Joseph's Hospital Enschede, Stalag XI B, Stalag IV F
Martin	Reginald	Driver	Advanced Workshop Detachment Royal Electrical and Mechanical Engineers	115945	91173		Stalag XII A, Stalag IV B
Maskell	William	Private	7th Battalion, King's Own Scottish Borderers Regiment	14403967	118174		Stalag XI B
Mason	Arthur	Private	7th Battalion, King's Own Scottish Borderers Regiment	1525984	88754		Stalag XII A, Stalag IV D
Mason	Edward	Private	1st Battalion, Border Regiment	3660775	91524		Stalag XII A, Stalag IV B, Stalag IV A
Mason	Herbert Advad	Staff Sergeant	181st Airlanding Field Ambulance, Royal Army Medical Corps	7249904	77340		Apeldoorn Hospital, Stalag XII A, Stalag VIII C, Stalag 344, Stalag XVII B
Mason	Harry Pearson	Corporal	1st Battalion, Parachute Regiment	3601962			Stalag II A
Mason	Peter Brown	Lieutenant	7th Battalion, King's Own Scottish Borderers Regiment	176	15258	Yes	Apeldoorn Hospital, Stalag XIII D, Oflag 64, Stalag III A

Family name	Forename	Rank	Unit as given on Questionnaire	Army number	POW number	Wounded on capture?	Camps
Mason	William Frederick	Private	2nd Battalion, Parachute Regiment	11002192	75309		Stalag XII A, Stalag IV B, Stalag IV C
Maston	Edward Peel	Private	156th Battalion, Parachute Regiment	14414353			Stalag XII A, Stalag IV C
Mather	Denis	Private	3rd Battalion, Parachute Regiment	14221140	91745		Stalag XII A, Stalag IV B, Stalag IV C
Matthew	Douglas	Private	Parachute Regiment	2884596	294131		Stalag IV G
Matthews	Frederick George	Private	1st Battalion, Border Regiment	3392036	117499		Stalag XI B
Matthews	Ronald George	Private	7th Battalion, King's Own Scottish Borderers Regiment	4750960			Stalag XII A, Stalag IV A
Matthews	William Lawrence	Corporal	1st Battalion, Parachute Regiment	2618797			Stalag II A
Maughan	Albert Sidney	Sergeant	Glider Pilot Regiment	4270235			Stalag Luft 7, Stalag III A
Mawditt	Norman Denis	Lance Corporal	181st Airlanding Field Ambulance, Royal Army Medical Corps	7519050			Koning Willem III Kazerne Apeldoorn, Reserve Lazarett Appeldoorn
Mawhinney	Herbert	Sergeant	156th Battalion, Parachute Regiment	5109805			Stalag XII A, Stalag II A
Maxwell	John	Private	3rd Battalion, Parachute Regiment	2928375	75316		Stalag XII A, Stalag IV B
Maxwell	Thomas Williams	Private	2nd Battalion, South Staffordshire Regiment	987046	118027		Apeldoorn Hospital, Stalag XI B
May	Dennis Roy	Private	2nd Battalion, Parachute Regiment	14331381		Yes	Enschede, Stalag XII A, Stalag IV B
May	Kenneth	Sergeant, Lance	156th Battalion, Parachute Regiment	1430419	90746	Yes	Stalag XII A, Stalag II A

Surname	First names	Rank	Regiment				Camps
May	William Albert Henry	Staff Sergeant	Glider Pilot Regiment	854844			Stalag XII A, Stalag IV B
McAlindon	Joseph	Private	10th Battalion, Parachute Regiment	7346837	89950		Stalag XII A, Stalag IV B
McAndrew	John Edward	Driver	250th Airborne Light Company, Royal Army Service Corps	70518	117962		Stalag XI B
McCall	Jack Miller	Corporal	7th Battalion, King's Own Scottish Borderers Regiment	14211456			Stalag XII A, Stalag XVIII C
McCallum	John	Private	133rd Parachute Field Ambulance, Royal Army Medical Corps	7348139	90691		Stalag XII A, Stalag IV B
McCalmont	Edwin John Terance	Corporal	11th Battalion, Parachute Regiment	1136790			Stalag IV B, Stalag III B, Stalag III A
McCandlish	Andrew Holen	Sergeant	Glider Pilot Regiment	3320419	88476		Stalag XII A, Stalag XVIII C
McCarner	William Hector	Sergeant	1st Airlanding Anti-Tank Battery, Royal Artillery	3711379	91316		Stalag XII A, Stalag II A
McCarron	Joseph Gerald	Private	1st Battalion, Parachute Regiment	6985449			Stalag XII A, Stalag IV B
McClure	Robert Hammond	Corporal	7th Battalion, King's Own Scottish Borderers Regiment	14211457	118754	Yes	Stalag XI B, Stalag 357
McClure	William	Private	2nd Battalion, Parachute Regiment	7022065			Stalag XII A, Stalag IV B
McCluskie	John	Sergeant	1st Battalion, Border Regiment	3596965	117454		Apeldoorn Hospital, Stalag XI B, Stalag VIII C, Stalag IX B
McCooke	John Brewster	Captain	2nd Battalion, South Staffordshire Regiment	140490	91006		Enschede, Dulag Luft – Oberusel, Stalag XII A, Oflag XII B, Oflag 79
McCool	John Gerald	Gunner	2nd Airlanding Anti-Tank Battery, Royal Artillery	5392324	117398	Yes	Stalag XI B

Family name	Forename	Rank	Unit as given on Questionnaire	Army number	POW number	Wounded on capture?	Camps
McCormack	James Laurence	Private	2nd Battalion, Parachute Regiment	6983201			Stalag XII A, Stalag IV B
McCourt	James Frederick	Captain	7th Battalion, King's Own Scottish Borderers Regiment	465	465		Stalag XII A, Dulag Luft – Oberusel, Oflag XII B, Oflag VII B, Stalag VII A
McCreedy	Richard James	Lance Bombardier	1st Airlanding Anti-Tank Battery, Royal Artillery	3711048			Stalag XII A, Stalag IV B, Stalag IV F
McDonald	Allan Gosland	Private	7th Battalion, King's Own Scottish Borderers Regiment	3326607			Stalag XII A, Stalag IV B
McDonald	John	Sapper	1st Parachute Squadron, Royal Engineers	2931360		Yes	Stalag XII A, Stalag IV B
McDonald	James Pennie	Private	Parachute Regiment	879673	75692		Stalag XII A, Stalag IV B
McDonald	Robert Hector	Private	1st Battalion, Border Regiment	3772203	914753		Stalag IV C
McDonald	Thomas	Private	7th Battalion, King's Own Scottish Borderers Regiment	3189884			Stalag XII A, Stalag IV B
McDonnell	Patrick	Private	2nd Battalion, Parachute Regiment	7047377			Stalag IV D
McDowell	James	Private	7th Battalion, King's Own Scottish Borderers Regiment	3193938	91896		Stalag XII A, Stalag IV B, Stalag IV A
McEvoy	Anthony	Private	21st Independent Parachute Company	14002666	75314		Stalag XII A, Stalag IV B
McFarlane	Roland	Corporal	Royal Army Medical Corps	7377807	77327		Stalag XII A, Stalag VIII C, Stalag 344, Stalag XIII C
McGaugie	Robert	Private	7th Battalion, King's Own Scottish Borderers Regiment	33233736	90068		Stalag XII A, Stalag IV B, Stalag IV F

Surname	First Name	Rank	Unit				Camps
McGaw	John Sibbald	Lance Corporal	1st Airborne Provost Company	7691875			Stalag XII A, Stalag II A
McGivern	George Simon Patrick	Lance Corporal	1st Parachute Squadron, Royal Engineers	2000959	117217	Yes	Reserve Lazarett Gronau, Stalag XI B
McGowan	Walter	Private	181st Airlanding Field Ambulance, Royal Army Medical Corps	7407324	90158		Zutphen POW Transit Camp, Stalag XII A, Stalag IV B
McGrath	Terence Ronald Forbes	Sergeant	4th Parachute Squadron, Royal Engineers	1875005	21753		Stalag VIII C
McGurk	John	Private	7th Battalion, King's Own Scottish Borderers Regiment	3194113	99999		Stalag XII A, Stalag IV B
McHale	John	Private	2nd Battalion, Parachute Regiment	14563648	75428		Stalag XII A, Stalag IV B
McHardy	Charles	Private	7th Battalion, King's Own Scottish Borderers Regiment	14214324	90579		Stalag XII A, Stalag IV B
McHugh	James	Private	1st Battalion, Border Regiment	3599165	91948	Yes	Stalag XII A, Stalag IV B, Stalag IV D
McInally	John Andrew	Private	7th Battalion, King's Own Scottish Borderers Regiment	3190240	118035	Yes	Apeldoorn Hospital, Stalag XI B
McIntosh	Donald Dinnie	Private	1st Battalion, Parachute Regiment	2880411			Stalag XII A, Stalag IV B
McIntosh	William Downie	Private	3rd Battalion, Parachute Regiment	5191914			Stalag IV B, Stalag IV C
McIntyre	Hugh	Corporal	7th Battalion, King's Own Scottish Borderers Regiment	3187559			Stalag XII A, Stalag II A
McIvor	Hugh	Sergeant	2nd Airlanding Anti-Tank Battery, Royal Artillery	3179804			Stalag XII A, Stalag II A
McKail	William	Private	7th Battalion, King's Own Scottish Borderers Regiment	14415428	91789		Stalag XII A, Stalag IV B, Stalag IV F
McKay	James Maxwell	Staff Sergeant	Glider Pilot Regiment	2823181			Stalag XII A, Dulag Luft, Stalag Luft 7, Stalag III A

Family name	Forename	Rank	Unit as given on Questionnaire	Army number	POW number	Wounded on capture?	Camps
McKee	William	Private	Parachute Regiment	1445760			Stalag IV B
McKendrick	John Lindsay	Private	7th Battalion, King's Own Scottish Borderers Regiment	14211200	18657	Yes	Stalag V B
McKenna	William Tarrant	Sapper	4th Parachute Squadron, Royal Engineers	3055480	140103		Stalag VII A
McKnight	John	Private	133rd Parachute Field Ambulance, Royal Army Medical Corps	7360808			Stalag XII A, Dulag Luft, Stalag IV B
McKnight	John	Lance Corporal	7th Battalion, King's Own Scottish Borderers Regiment	3715834	26062		Stalag XII A, Stalag IV B
McLachlan	Frederick	Gunner	Royal Artillery	14587240	19535		Stalag XII A, Stalag IV B
McLaren	Ernest	Lance Corporal	7th Battalion, King's Own Scottish Borderers Regiment	14211475			Stalag XII A, Stalag IV B
McLay	James	Corporal	7th Battalion, King's Own Scottish Borderers Regiment	14211476	90563		Stalag XII A, Stalag II A
McLean	Charles Harris	Corporal	Royal Army Medical Corps	7517370	118377	Yes	Stalag XI B, Stalag VIII C, Stalag XI B
McLean	Duncan	Captain	2nd Battalion, Parachute Regiment	94824	616		Stalag XII A, Oflag XII B, Oflag 79
McLean	George Falconer	Lance Corporal	1st Battalion, Parachute Regiment	2937656	118411		Stalag XI B
McLeavy	Donald	Sergeant	Glider Pilot Regiment	0	117758		Stalag XI B, Stalag VIII C, Reserve Lazarett Falkenberg Stalag VIII C, Stalag IV B
McLellan	John	Private	7th Battalion, King's Own Scottish Borderers Regiment	3190228	15460		Stalag XII A, Stalag VIII C, Stalag IV C

Surname	Forename	Rank	Regiment	Service No.			Camps
McLoughlin	David	Private	2nd Battalion, Parachute Regiment	7047407			Stalag XII A, Stalag XI B
McLoughlin	Patrick Bernard	Private	10th Battalion, Parachute Regiment	6412159	75600	Yes	Stalag XII A, Stalag IV B
McLure	James	Private	156th Battalion, Parachute Regiment	2454564			Stalag XII A, Stalag VIII C
McNeilage	Robert	Private	7th Battalion, King's Own Scottish Borderers Regiment	14327083	90490		Stalag XII A, Stalag IV B, Stalag IV A
McNeill	George Cuthill	Corporal	1st Battalion, Parachute Regiment	3130965			Stalag XII A, Stalag II A
McQuilian	Alexander	Private	11th Battalion, Parachute Regiment	7901172	91663		Stalag XII A, Stalag IV C
McTavish	Alexander	Gunner	1st Airlanding Light Regiment, Royal Artillery	1156883	75563		Stalag XII A, Stalag IV B
McVicar	Archibald Lamont	Private	10th Battalion, Parachute Regiment	2933355			Stalag XII A, Stalag IV B, Stalag IV C
McWilliam	Thomas Andrew	Corporal	156th Battalion, Parachute Regiment	3771531			Stalag XII A, Stalag II A
McWilliams	Robert	Private	Royal Army Medical Corps	7378039	118405	Yes	Stalag XI B
Mead	Kenneth Andrew	Sergeant	Glider Pilot Regiment	1878306		Yes	Stalag XII A, Stalag IV B
Meakin	Reginald	Lieutenant	Glider Pilot Regiment	314146			Stalag XII A, Stalag Luft 1
Meakings	Frank Howard	Lance Corporal	16th Parachute Field Ambulance	861740	90088		Stalag XII A, Stalag XI B
Meen	Bernard George Henry	Lance Corporal	3rd Battalion, Parachute Regiment	6025548			Stalag XII A, Stalag IV B, Stalag IV C
Meiklejohn	John	Private	7th Battalion, King's Own Scottish Borderers Regiment	3185236	80652		Stalag XII A, Stalag IV B
Meiklejon	Robert Smith	Private	11th Battalion, Parachute Regiment	2990761	75434	Yes	Stalag IV B

119

Family name	Forename	Rank	Unit as given on Questionnaire	Army number	POW number	Wounded on capture?	Camps
Mellor	William Frederick	Private	Royal Army Medical Corps attached 2nd Battalion, Parachute Regiment	14381095	294176		Stalag IV B
Mellors	Wilfred	Lance Corporal	2nd Battalion, South Staffordshire Regiment	5052769	89599		Stalag XII A, Stalag IV B
Melrose	William George	Staff Sergeant	Glider Pilot Regiment	1464667			Dulag Luft – Wetzlar, Stalag Luft 7, Stalag III A
Melvin	Ronald Cameron	Corporal	2nd Battalion, South Staffordshire Regiment	4923341	90415		Stalag XII A, Stalag II A
Menzies	Alastair Charles Vass	Captain Reverend	Royal Army Chaplains' Department	205975	90860		Stalag XII A, Oflag XII B, Oflag 79
Menzies	Harry	Corporal	2nd Battalion, Parachute Regiment	3247104			Stalag XII A, Stalag VIII C
Mercer	Kenneth Walter	Private	4th Battalion, Dorset Regiment	14656451	14227		Stalag XII A, Stalag IV B
Meredith	Clifford Desmond	Private	2nd Battalion, South Staffordshire Regiment	5260457			Stalag XII A, Stalag IV B
Merignac	Louis	Private	7th Battalion, King's Own Scottish Borderers Regiment	3184987			Stalag XII A, Stalag IV B
Merrick	Albert John	Driver	1st Parachute Brigade, Royal Signals	7896485	91619		Stalag XII A, Stalag IV B
Metcalfe	Edwin	Private	1st Battalion, Border Regiment	3602861	118844	Yes	Dortmund Hospital, Stalag XI B
Middleton	Alan James	Driver	250th Airborne Light Company, Royal Army Service Corps	10680515			Stalag XII A, Stalag IV B, Stalag IV A
Middleton	Horace	Private	156th Battalion, Parachute Regiment	5048758	117507		Stalag XI B, Stalag III A, Stalag XI A

Surname	First name	Rank	Unit	Number	Number	Q	Camps
Midgley	Jack	Private	2nd Battalion, Parachute Regiment	1597944		Yes	Stalag XII A, Stalag IV B
Miles	Ashley Bertram	Private	1st Parachute Brigade HQ	888755	75517	Yes	Stalag XII A, Stalag IV B
Miles	Ronald Frederick	Trooper	1st Airborne Reconnaissance Squadron	6853948	118494		Apeldoorn Hospital, Stalag XI B
Millard	Jack	Private	3rd Battalion, Parachute Regiment	3388645	294177		Dulag Luft, Stalag IV B
Miller	Brian	Staff Sergeant	16th Parachute Field Ambulance, Royal Army Medical Corps	7349554	89671		Stalag XII A, Stalag II A
Miller	Christopher Alfred	Staff Sergeant	Glider Pilot Regiment	937499	117770	Yes	Stalag XI B, Stalag VIII C
Miller	George	Lance Corporal	1st Battalion, Border Regiment	2980246	918718		Stalag XII A, Dulag Luft – Oberusel, Stalag XII A, Stalag IV B
Miller	Philip Anthony Alfred	Sapper	1st Parachute Squadron, Royal Engineers	1947386			Stalag XII A, Stalag IV B
Miller	Percy Frank	Private	1st Battalion, Parachute Regiment	14503578	75406		Stalag XII A, Stalag IV B
Miller	Thomas Visgen	Captain	4th Parachute Brigade Royal Artillery	89054	608	Yes	Reserve Lazarett Siegburg, Stalag XII A, Oflag XII B, Oflag 79
Miller	Walter	Private	2nd Battalion, Parachute Regiment	4926652	75339		Stalag IV B, Stalag IV B
Milligan	William John	Private	7th Battalion, King's Own Scottish Borderers Regiment	3197078	117381	Yes	Arnhem Hospital, Stalag XI B, Stalag III A, Stalag XI A
Millington	Arthur	Private	1st Battalion, Border Regiment	3856104	91880		Stalag XII A, Stalag IV B, Stalag IV C
Mills	James	Driver	16th Parachute Field Ambulance, Royal Army Medical Corps	3973384	118439	Yes	Stalag XI B

Family name	Forename	Rank	Unit as given on Questionnaire	Army number	POW number	Wounded on capture?	Camps
Mills	Kenneth Henry George	Staff Sergeant	Glider Pilot Regiment	551404		Yes	Stalag XII A, Stalag IV B
Milne	Alexander Noble	Gunner	1st Airlanding Light Regiment, Royal Artillery	919655	75976		Stalag XII A, Stalag IV B, Stalag IV D, Stalag IV B
Milne	George	Private	7th Battalion, King's Own Scottish Borderers Regiment	2878859	117412		Stalag XI B, Stalag III A, Stalag XI A
Milner	Charles	Private	7th Battalion, King's Own Scottish Borderers Regiment	14327609			Stalag XII A, Stalag IV B
Milner	Denis Herbert	Private	16th Parachute Field Ambulance, Royal Army Medical Corps	7397106	90554	Yes	Stalag XII A, Stalag IV B
Milner	Eric	Driver	1st Airlanding Anti-Tank Battery, Royal Artillery	1144982	75098		Stalag XII A, Stalag IV B
Milner	Ernest Leonard	Private	156th Battalion, Parachute Regiment	5334959	140129		Stalag VII A
Minto	James Henry	Private	7th Battalion, King's Own Scottish Borderers Regiment	14204716	91485		Stalag XII A, Stalag IV B, Stalag IV C
Mirylees	Geoffrey Keith	Private	1st Battalion, Parachute Regiment	6898405	75819		Stalag IV B
Mitchell	Alan	Sergeant	Glider Pilot Regiment	10538003	858		Dulag Luft – Oberusel, Stalag Luft 7, Stalag III A
Mitchell	Charles Maurice	Private	7th Battalion, King's Own Scottish Borderers Regiment	14636263	25194		Stalag XII A, Stalag XIII B
Mitchell	Edward	Sergeant	Glider Pilot Regiment	10555051	76321		Stalag XII A, Stalag IV B
Mitchell	Geoffrey Ernest	Private	2nd Battalion, Parachute Regiment	5782772	89423		Stalag IV B

Surname	First name(s)	Rank	Unit				Camps
Mitchell	Harry	Private	21st Independent Parachute Company	6986281	117626		Stalag XI B, Stalag III A, Stalag XI A
Mitchell	James	Private	7th Battalion, King's Own Scottish Borderers Regiment	3186927			Stalag XII A, Stalag IV B, Stalag IV C
Mitchell	William	Driver	250th Airborne Light Company, Royal Army Service Corps	80574	91351		Stalag XII A, Stalag IV B, Stalag IV F
Mitchelmore	Albert Henry	Private	3rd Battalion, Parachute Regiment	6460413	75317		Stalag XII A, Stalag IV B, Stalag IV F
Mobsby	William	Private	3rd Battalion, Parachute Regiment	6410136	92032		Stalag IV B
Mock	George	Gunner	1st Airlanding Anti-Tank Battery, Royal Artillery	14708487	92012		Stalag IV B
Moffat	Alexander	Lance Corporal	1st Parachute Squadron, Royal Engineers	2067621	117420	Yes	Reserve Lazarett Lingen, Stalag XI B
Moffat	Walter	Private	Parachute Regiment	14255679	75417		Stalag XII A, Stalag IV B
Monsell	John Humphrey Arnold	Lieutenant	2nd Battalion, Parachute Regiment	112889	562		Dulag XII B Hadamar, Oflag 79
Montgomery	Samuel	Private	2nd Battalion, South Staffordshire Regiment	7013157	90005		Stalag XII A, Stalag IV B, Stalag IV F, French Reveir Plauen
Montgomery	Terence	Private	1st Battalion, Parachute Regiment	7013242	92037		Stalag XII A, Stalag IV B
Moody	Albert Donald Urquhart	Signalman	Royal Signals	6349280	140217		Reserve Lazarette Freising, Stalag VII A
Moon	Raymond Jack	Private	250th Airborne Light Company, Royal Army Service Corps	14566626	91459		Stalag XII A, Stalag IV B, Stalag IV F
Moore	Alfred George Golden	Sergeant	1st Battalion, Parachute Regiment	6461833	140083	Yes	Enschede Hospital, Oflag VII C
Moore	Albert James	Lance Corporal	3rd Battalion, Parachute Regiment	5832722			Dulag Luft, Stalag IV B

Family name	Forename	Rank	Unit as given on Questionnaire	Army number	POW number	Wounded on capture?	Camps
Moore	Arthur Reginald	Private	Parachute Regiment	14218858	75324		Stalag XII A, Stalag IV B, Stalag IV C
Moore	Eric Charles Arthur	Sergeant	2nd Airlanding Anti-Tank Battery, Royal Artillery	868114	91788		Stalag XII A, Stalag VIII C
Moore	William	Private	7th Battalion, King's Own Scottish Borderers Regiment	14201431	90694		Stalag XII A, Stalag IV A
Morait	Peter John	Private	156th Battalion, Parachute Regiment	59816			Stalag XII A, Stalag IV B
Moran	Joseph	Signalman	1st Parachute Brigade, Royal Signals	2320146	91620		Stalag XII A, Stalag IV B, Stalag IV C
Mordle	Alfred Augustus	Corporal	7th Battalion, King's Own Scottish Borderers Regiment	14204397	118624		Stalag XI B, Stalag VIII C
Morgan	Edward	Gunner	1st Airlanding Light Regiment, Royal Artillery	1116829	92937	Yes	Stalag XII A, Stalag IV B, Stalag IV F
Morgan	Michael Joseph	Gunner	1st Airlanding Anti-Tank Battery, Royal Artillery	868311	91479		Stalag XII A, Stalag IV B
Morgan	Stephen	Private	2nd Battalion, Parachute Regiment	14436780			Stalag XII A, Stalag IV B
Morris	David	WO II	11th Battalion, Parachute Regiment	5946742			St Elizabeth's Hospital, Apeldoorn Hospital, Stalag XII A, Interrogation Centre Dietz, Stalag VIII C, Stalag IX B
Morris	Edmund Barker	Lance Corporal	1st Airborne Reconnaissance Squadron	14279106		Yes	Apeldoorn Hospital, Stalag XI B
Morris	Gordon Hollister	Private	11th Battalion, Parachute Regiment	14339316	118673	Yes	Stalag XI B

Surname	First name	Rank	Regiment	Number	Number		Camps
Morris	John Alyn	Private	3rd Battalion, Parachute Regiment	4198194	92170		Stalag XII A, Stalag IV B, Stalag IV C
Morrison	George	Private	10th Battalion, Parachute Regiment	2981937	92038	Yes	Stalag XII A, Stalag IV B
Morrison	John Alexander	Captain	Glider Pilot Regiment	88880	5979	Yes	Dulag Luft, Stalag Luft 1
Morrison	Roderick Dickson	Driver	1st Airlanding Light Regiment, Royal Artillery	882484			Stalag XII A, Stalag IV B, Stalag IV F
Morton	Albert Alfred	Private	2nd Battalion, Parachute Regiment	6853588	117956		Stalag XI B, Stalag III A, Stalag XI A
Moscou	David Beaconsfield	Lance Corporal	7th Battalion, King's Own Scottish Borderers Regiment	14610927			Stalag XII A, Stalag II A
Moses	Ernest	Sergeant	10th Battalion, Parachute Regiment	4124796	117856		Stalag XI B, Stalag VIII C
Mossie	Robert	Private	2nd Battalion, South Staffordshire Regiment	3191185	92058		Stalag IV A
Mountford	William Frederick	Lance Corporal	2nd Battalion, South Staffordshire Regiment	5439497	91644		Stalag XII A, Stalag IV B
Mowat	Billy Bruce	Leading Aircraftman	Light Warning Set Unit No. 6341, RAF	-168468			Apeldoorn, Stalag XI B, Dulag Luft – Oberusel, Dulag Luft – Wetzlar, Stalag Luft 7, Stalag III A
Mowat	John Robert	Staff Sergeant	Glider Pilot Regiment	2818874			Stalag XII A, Stalag IV B
Muirhead	Archibald	Sergeant	7th Battalion, King's Own Scottish Borderers Regiment	3187718	89533		Stalag XII A, Stalag II A
Mulcahy	Thomas	Private	1st Battalion, Parachute Regiment	3393711			Stalag XIII B
Mullender	James William	Private	11th Battalion, Parachute Regiment	4399431	52908		Apeldoorn Hospital, Reserve Lazarett Obermaßfeld, Reserve Lazarett Meiningen, Stalag IX C/Z

Family name	Forename	Rank	Unit as given on Questionnaire	Army number	POW number	Wounded on capture?	Camps
Mullineux	William	Private	3rd Battalion, Parachute Regiment	3866182			Dulag Luft – Wetzlar, Stalag XII A, Stalag IV B, Stalag IV C
Mullins	Thomas Harald	Private	Parachute Regiment	1691988			Stalag XII A, Stalag IV B, Stalag IV G, Stalag IV F
Mumford	Ernest Frank	Private	16th Parachute Field Ambulance, Royal Army Medical Corps	7266759	118628		Stalag XI B
Munro	Alexander	Private	11th Battalion, Parachute Regiment	7370319	117167		Stalag XI B
Munro	James L	Private	10th Battalion, Parachute Regiment	3318030			Stalag XII A, Stalag IV B, Stalag IV F
Murphy	Andrew	Private	7th Battalion, King's Own Scottish Borderers Regiment	14327614	93376		Stalag XII A, Stalag IV B, Stalag IV A
Murphy	Alfred Victor	Private	2nd Battalion, Parachute Regiment	14218919	25964		Stalag XII A, Stalag IV F
Murray	Alistair George	Private	2nd Battalion, Parachute Regiment	2926439			Stalag IV B
Murray	James	Private	Parachute Regiment?	14530543			Stalag XII A, Stalag IV B
Murray MC	Douglas Campbell	Major/T	1st Parachute Squadron, Royal Engineers	106883	607	Yes	Stalag XII A, Oflag XII B, Oflag 79
Mustard	Alfred	Private	156th Battalion, Parachute Regiment	3770819			Stalag XII A, Stalag IV B
Musto	Ronald Herbert	Private	11th Battalion, Parachute Regiment	924313			Stalag XII A, Stalag IV B
Mynett	Leonard	Private	11th Battalion, Parachute Regiment	6985800	91412		Stalag XII A, Stalag IV B

Surname	First name(s)	Rank	Unit	Number	Number	Q	Camps
Nadin	George Edmund	Private	1st Battalion, Border Regiment	3866328			Stalag XII A, Stalag IV D
Naish	Bernard Cyril	Private	4th Battalion, Dorset Regiment	14376654	17588		Stalag XII A, Stalag IV B, Stalag IV F
Nash	William	Private	250th Airborne Light Company, Royal Army Service Corps	2597427			Stalag XII A, Stalag IV B, Stalag IV A
Naylor	Alfred	Private	10th Battalion, Parachute Regiment	6349458	89595		Stalag XII A, Stalag VIII C, Stalag IV G
Needham	George Henry	Sapper	1st Parachute Squadron, Royal Engineers	2133390			Stalag XII A, Stalag IV B
Neil	George Currie	Corporal	1st Battalion, Parachute Regiment	7394382			Stalag XII A, Stalag II A
Neild	Harry	Private	156th Battalion, Parachute Regiment	4539879			Stalag XII A, Stalag IV B, Stalag IV A
Nelson	Albert	Gunner	Royal Artillery (Field) Airborne	14264847	75838	Yes	Stalag XII A, Stalag IV B
Neve	George Thomas	Private	181st Airlanding Field Ambulance, Royal Army Medical Corps	7370817			Stalag XII A, Stalag IV B
Nevins	Daniel	Private	10th Battalion, Parachute Regiment	4275543		Yes	Stalag XI B, Stalag III A, Stalag XI A
Newell	Cecil	Private	2nd Battalion, Parachute Regiment	1559998			Stalag XII A, Stalag IV C
Newell	Douglas George Valentine	Lance Corporal	11th Battalion, Parachute Regiment	165223	89349		Stalag IV B
Newham	Leslie	Driver	1st Airlanding Light Regiment, Royal Artillery	14609703			Stalag XII A, Stalag IV B
Newhouse	Frank	Private	10th Battalion, Parachute Regiment	14557569	14188		Stalag XII A, Stalag IV A
Newman	Arthur Royston 'Roy'	Private	16th Parachute Field Ambulance, Royal Army Medical Corps	198333	22044		Stalag IV B

Family name	Forename	Rank	Unit as given on Questionnaire	Army number	POW number	Wounded on capture?	Camps
Newman	James	Private	181st Airlanding Field Ambulance, Royal Army Medical Corps	7397436		Yes	Stalag XII A, Stalag IV B
Newman	Robert Eugène	Private	Royal Army Medical Corps	7533134			Stalag XII A, Stalag IV B, Stalag IV G
Newman	Walter Roy	Lance Corporal	10th Battalion, Parachute Regiment	6407101	118206		Queen Wilhelmina Barracks, Apeldoorn Hospital, Stalag XI B
Newport	Edward Selwyn	Lieutenant	1st Battalion, Border Regiment	96393	630	Yes	Dulag XII B Hadamar, Oflag 79
Newton	Arthur	Staff Sergeant	Glider Pilot Regiment	913044			Stalag XII A, Stalag Luft 7, Stalag III A
Newton	George Robert	Private	Royal Army Medical Corps	7262642	140300	Yes	Hospital Holland, Reserve Lazarett Freising, Stalag VII A
Newton	Herbert Leonard	Trooper	1st Airborne Reconnaissance Squadron	6028646	118477	Yes	Stalag XI B
Newton	Kenneth Ernest	Private	181st Airlanding Field Ambulance, Royal Army Medical Corps	14672306			Stalag XII A, Stalag IV B, Stalag IV F
Newton	Peter	Private	156th Battalion, Parachute Regiment	3194733			Stalag XII A, Stalag IV B
Newton	William Ewart	Private	2nd Battalion, South Staffordshire Regiment	1714799	89400		Stalag XII A, Stalag IV B
Nichollas	Lewis	Private	2nd Battalion, Parachute Regiment	4390380	117336		Stalag XI B, Stalag III A, Stalag XI A
Nichols	Henry William	Private	2nd Battalion, Parachute Regiment	2083033			Stalag XII A, Stalag IV B

Surname	Forename	Rank	Unit	Number	Number	Camps
Nicholson	John	Private	Parachute Regiment	10601868	75341	Stalag XII A, Stalag IV B
Nicholson	William John Ainsley	Driver	63 Company, Royal Army Service Corps	10662795		Stalag XII A, Stalag IV B, Stalag IV F
Nicklin	George Lewis	Sergeant	Glider Pilot Regiment	7955175	117174	Stalag XI B, Stalag VIII C
Nicklin	William Harry	Lance Corporal	Royal Army Service Corps	290769	90584	Stalag XII A, Stalag IV B
Niel	Marshall	Private	3rd Battalion, Parachute Regiment	4461059	118193	Stalag XI B
Nightingale	Cyril	Private	3rd Battalion, Parachute Regiment	4694319	91511	Stalag XII A, Stalag IV B
Nimmo	Tristram	Private	1st Battalion, Parachute Regiment	2938274		Stalag XII A, Stalag IV B, Stalag IV D
Nixon	Charles	Private	1st Battalion, Border Regiment	3600613	91944	Stalag XII A, Stalag IV B
Noble	Barry Denis	Private	156th Battalion, Parachute Regiment	14641561		Stalag XII A, Stalag IV B
Noble	Charles Bruce	Captain	133rd Parachute Field Ambulance, Royal Army Medical Corps	279738		Gestapo Prison Utrecht, Gestapo Prison Doetinchem, Stalag XI B
Noble	Jeffrey Fraser	Lieutenant	156th Battalion, Parachute Regiment	276375	91017	Stalag XII A, Oflag XII B, Oflag 79
Nolan	Harold	Lance Corporal	1st Battalion, Border Regiment	767839	118802	Stalag XI B
Nolan	William Gregory	Lance Corporal	2nd Battalion, South Staffordshire Regiment	4919088		Stalag XII A, Stalag IV B, Stalag IV C
Norris	Donald Eric	Staff Sergeant	Glider Pilot Regiment	1470905	118693	Stalag XI B, Stalag 357
North	Albert Joseph William	Sergeant	Glider Pilot Regiment	14269986	118614	Stalag XI B, Stalag VIII C, Stalag IV B
Noton	Montagu John	Private	156th Battalion, Parachute Regiment	899551		Stalag XII A, Stalag IV B, Stalag IV F
Nullis	John Robert	Lance Corporal	2nd Battalion, South Staffordshire Regiment	5729659		Stalag XII A, Stalag XI B

129

Family name	Forename	Rank	Unit as given on Questionnaire	Army number	POW number	Wounded on capture?	Camps
Nurse	George	Private	156th Battalion, Parachute Regiment	3977282			Stalag XII A, Stalag IV B
Nyman	Hugo Oscar	Private	4th Battalion, Dorset Regiment	14512195	14176		Stalag XII A, Stalag IV B, Stalag IV G
O'Brian	Robert Gerard	Private	1st Battalion, Parachute Regiment	2049245			Stalag XII A, Stalag IV B
O'Brien	Cyril	Private	1st Parachute Brigade	14411394			Stalag IV B
O'Brien	Michael	Driver	16th Parachute Field Ambulance, Royal Army Medical Corps	1466843	90151	Yes	Stalag XII A, Stalag IV B
O'Brien	William Arthur	Private	11th Battalion, Parachute Regiment	5989720	72149		Stalag XII A, Stalag IV B, Stalag IV D
O'Dell	Charles John	Private	11th Battalion, Parachute Regiment	866848	118054		Stalag XI B
O'Donnell	Edward	Private	Parachute	3065854			Stalag XII A, Stalag IV B, Stalag IV C
O'Hanlon	Henry	Private	1st Battalion, Border Regiment	3783776			Stalag XII A, Stalag IV B
O'Leary	Peter	Sergeant	1st Battalion, Parachute Regiment	4206855	140128		St Liduina Hospital Apeldoorn, Stalag VII A, Stalag 383
O'Malley	Hamilton Joseph Keyes	Captain	Glider Pilot Regiment	44556		Yes	Lochem Hospital, Dulag Luft – Oberusel, Dulag Luft – Wetzlar, Stalag Luft 1
O'Neill	Peter	Private	1st Battalion, Border Regiment	3772654			Stalag IV B
O'Neill	William	Private	7th Battalion, King's Own Scottish Borderers Regiment	3195748	14202		Stalag XII A, Stalag IV B, Stalag IV A
O'Quinn	Bernard Patrick	Lance Corporal	1st Airborne Provost Company	7687579			Stalag XII A, Stalag IV B

Surname	First name	Rank	Regiment	Number	Number		Camps
Oakes	William Arthur	Sergeant	Glider Pilot Regiment	14573970			Dulag Luft – Oberusel, Stalag Luft 7, Stalag III A
Oakley	Albert William Frank	Private	10th Battalion, Parachute Regiment	14204428	92042		Stalag XII A, Stalag IV B, Stalag IV A
Oakley	Harry	Corporal	2nd Battalion, South Staffordshire Regiment	5124863			Stalag XII A, Stalag II A
Oates	Jack	Private	Parachute Regiment	2089524			Stalag XII A, Stalag IV B, Stalag IV C
Ogden	Ernest Alvin	Trooper	1st Airborne Reconnaissance Squadron	3599015	117719		Stalag XI B, Stalag III A, Stalag XI A
Oldbury	James Thomas	Sapper	1st Parachute Squadron, Royal Engineers	1871921			Stalag IV B
Oldfield	William Thomas	Gunner	Royal Artillery	1457697	91538		Stalag XII A, Stalag IV B, Stalag IV C
Oliver	Edward James	Corporal	1st Parachute Squadron, Royal Engineers	2093811			Stalag XII A, Stalag XVIII C
Oliver	James	Private	2nd Battalion, Parachute Regiment	3189025	140079	Yes	Stalag VII A
Oliver	Leslie	Private	1st Battalion, Border Regiment	3537403	91793		Stalag XII A, Stalag IV B, Stalag IV C
Oram	Arthur William	Sergeant	Glider Pilot Regiment	14416890			Dulag Luft – Frankfurt, Stalag Luft 7, Stalag III A
Orchard	Edward John	Private	7th Battalion, King's Own Scottish Borderers Regiment	14209984	117553		Stalag XI B
Orrell	Herbert	Private	2nd Battalion, Parachute Regiment	14643075	91319		Stalag XII A, Stalag IV B
Osborn	Frank	Private	2nd Battalion, South Staffordshire Regiment	14316895	75927		Stalag XII A, Stalag IV F, Stalag IV F
Osborne	Raymond Frederick	Staff Sergeant	Glider Pilot Regiment	922174			Dulag Luft – Oberusel, Stalag Luft 7, Stalag III A

131

Family name	Forename	Rank	Unit as given on Questionnaire	Army number	POW number	Wounded on capture?	Camps
Owen	Albert	Private	10th Battalion, Parachute Regiment	14367248			Stalag XII A, Stalag IV B
Owen	Frederick Richard	Private	2nd Battalion, South Staffordshire Regiment	993170	89600		Stalag XII A, Stalag IV B
Owen	Geoffrey Grenvelle Jonfi	Lance Corporal	181st Airlanding Field Ambulance, Royal Army Medical Corps	7399699		Yes	Koning Willem III Kazerne Apeldoorn, Reserve Lazarett IV/686
Owen	Russell	Signalman	1st Parachute Brigade, Royal Signals	7013739	117877		Stalag XI B, Stalag III A, Stalag XI A, Stalag IV D
Owens	Cecil	Private	7th Battalion, King's Own Scottish Borderers Regiment	14201305	90045		Stalag XII A, Stalag IV B
Oxford	Cecil James	Sergeant	Glider Pilot Regiment	4859963			Dulag Luft, Stalag Luft 7, Stalag III A
Paddon	Walter Charles Frank	Lance Corporal	2nd Battalion, Parachute Regiment	6153239			Stalag XII A, Stalag VIII C, Stalag IV B
Padfield	Harold	Sergeant, Lance	1st Parachute Squadron, Royal Engineers	1873564			Stalag XII A, Stalag XVIII C
Paffett	James Henry	Sergeant	9th Field Company (Airborne), Royal Engineers	1870477	117208		Stalag XI B, Stalag 357
Paine	Frank Thomas	Sapper	Royal Engineers	2090115	140152	Yes	Reserve Lazarett Freising, Stalag VII A
Painter	Frederick Thomas	Private	2nd Battalion, Parachute Regiment	7893694			Stalag XII A, Stalag IV B, Stalag IV A
Painting	Harold	Lance Corporal	2nd Battalion, South Staffordshire Regiment	5111673	91422		Stalag XII A, Stalag IV B, Stalag IV G
Palframan	Arthur Kenneth	Gunner	1st Airlanding Light Regiment, Royal Artillery	14312127	91541		Stalag XII A, Stalag IV B

Surname	First name	Rank	Unit	Number	Number		Camps
Palmer	Albert Edgar	Sergeant	Glider Pilot Regiment	4803786			Dulag Luft – Oberusel, Stalag Luft 7, Stalag III A
Palmer	Charles Thomas Albert	Lance Corporal	7th Battalion, King's Own Scottish Borderers Regiment	4750869	91083		Stalag IV B, Stalag IV A
Palmer	David Edward	Lance Corporal	11th Battalion, Parachute Regiment	6343456	89812		Stalag XII A, Stalag II A
Palmer	Harry	Private	3rd Battalion, Parachute Regiment	5382027			?
Palmer	Raymond	Private	4th Battalion, Dorset Regiment	4399530	75898		Stalag XII A, Stalag IV B
Panter	Stanley Charles	Captain	2nd Battalion, Parachute Regiment	165617	91002	Yes	Stalag XII A, Oflag XII B, Oflag 79
Parfitt	Cecil	Gunner	2nd Airlanding Anti-Tank Battery, Royal Artillery	5392331	91790		?
Pargeter	Albert Raymond	Private	2nd Battalion, South Staffordshire Regiment	4917639	91734		Stalag IV B
Park	William	Gunner	Forward Observation Unit, Royal Artillery	1152141			Stalag XII A, Stalag IV B, Stalag IV A
Parker	Donald Sydney	Sergeant	Glider Pilot Regiment	5886465			Stalag XII A, Dulag Luft – Oberusel, Stalag Luft 7, Stalag III A
Parker	Frederick John	Lance Corporal	4th Parachute Brigade, Royal Electrical and Mechanical Engineers	7623305	117862	Yes	Stalag XI B
Parker	George	Private	1st Battalion, Border Regiment	14560262			Stalag IV C
Parker	Thomas	Private	156th Battalion, Parachute Regiment	14632653	90745		Stalag XII A, Stalag IV B
Parker MM	Harry Frank	Corporal	3rd Battalion, Parachute Regiment	4620407			Stalag XII A, Stalag II A
Parkes	William Henry	Sergeant	2nd Battalion, South Staffordshire Regiment	4917868			Stalag II A

Family name	Forename	Rank	Unit as given on Questionnaire	Army number	POW number	Wounded on capture?	Camps
Parkin	Godfrey	Sapper	9th Field Unit, Royal Engineers	2135831	117638	Yes	Reserve Lazarett Linden, Stalag VI C, Stalag XI B, Stalag III A, Stalag II A
Parkin	Harold Cosford	Private	2nd Battalion, Parachute Regiment	910905		Yes	Stalag IV B, Stalag IV F
Parkin	William	Corporal	7th Battalion, King's Own Scottish Borderers Regiment	47509191	90784		Stalag XII A, Stalag VIII C, Stalag III A
Parrack	Peter Adolphus	Private	156th Battalion, Parachute Regiment	5113809			Stalag XII A, Stalag IV B
Parrish	George Frederick	Private	3rd Battalion, Parachute Regiment	14661418	117895	Yes	Stalag XI B, Stalag VIII C
Parry	George	Private	2nd Battalion, South Staffordshire Regiment	4919190			Stalag XII A, Stalag IV B, Stalag IV C
Parry	William Reginald	Private	16th Parachute Field Ambulance, Royal Army Medical Corps	97005169			St Elizabeth's Hospital, Enschede, Dulag Luft – Oberusel, Stalag XII A, Stalag XI B
Parsons	Maurice Charles	Sergeant	1st Battalion, Parachute Regiment	6018096	89455		Stalag II A
Partridge	Felix Frederick	Sapper	Royal Engineers	1915238			Stalag XII A, Stalag IV B
Paterson	George	Private	11th Battalion, Parachute Regiment	2820870	117263	Yes	Stalag XI B
Paterson	Robert	Sergeant	156th Battalion, Parachute Regiment	3244907	89820		Stalag XII A, Stalag II A
Paterson	Robert	Sapper	4th Parachute Squadron, Royal Engineers	14644253	118403	Yes	Apeldoorn, Stalag XI B
Paterson	William	Signalman	1st Parachute Brigade, Royal Signals	2348020	91340		Stalag XII A, Stalag IV B, Stalag IV F

Surname	First names	Rank	Unit	Number	Number	Escaped	Camps
Patterson	Donald	Lance Corporal	7th Battalion, King's Own Scottish Borderers Regiment	3193858	91477		Stalag XII A, Stalag IV C
Patterson	Kenneth	Driver	Royal Artillery	14321751	91372		Stalag XII A, Stalag IV
Pattle	Reginald Stanley	Driver	133rd Parachute Field Ambulance, Royal Army Medical Corps	5124019	90849		Stalag XII A, Stalag IV B, Stalag IV D ZW
Pauling	Leonard James	Gunner	1st Airlanding Light Regiment, Royal Artillery	14376919			Stalag XII A, Stalag IV B, Stalag IV A
Paull	George Arthur	Lieutenant	2nd Airlanding Anti-Tank Battery, Royal Artillery	268829	90870		Stalag XII A, Oflag 79
Pavey	Charles	Gunner	2nd Airlanding Anti-Tank Battery, Royal Artillery	6400146	91702		Stalag XII A, Stalag IV C
Payne	Albert Stanley	Private	2nd Battalion, Parachute Regiment	5835225			Stalag XII A, Stalag IV B, Stalag IV C
Peacock	Claude Victor	Lance Corporal	11th Battalion, Parachute Regiment	6142921	117771	Yes	Stalag XI B, Stalag III A, Stalag II A, Stalag IV D
Peacock	Frederick William	Private	1st Battalion, Border Regiment	4808802	25559		Stalag XII A, Stalag IV B, Stalag IV ?
Peacock	Frank William	Sapper	4th Parachute Squadron, Royal Engineers	2070914	117908	Yes	Stalag XI B, Stalag III A, Stalag XI A, Stalag IV D
Pearce	Leslie James	Lance Corporal	3rd Battalion, Parachute Regiment	4917641	117826		Stalag XI B
Pearce	Reginald	Private	156th Battalion, Parachute Regiment	5826606	117615		Stalag XI B, Stalag III A, Stalag XI A
Pearce	William Charles	Private	11th Battalion, Parachute Regiment	4750999	117233		Stalag XI B
Pearson	Ambrose	Private	1st Battalion, Parachute Regiment	4695232	90779		Stalag XII A, Stalag IV B, Stalag IV A
Pearson	Herbert James	Private	4th Battalion, Dorset Regiment	14723722	17597		Stalag XII A, Stalag IV B

Family name	Forename	Rank	Unit as given on Questionnaire	Army number	POW number	Wounded on capture?	Camps
Pearson	Michael David	Private	Parachute Regiment	4699298	75445		Stalag XII A, Stalag IV B
Pearson	George William	Private	1st Battalion, Border Regiment	3602871	75470		Stalag IV B
Peck	Jack	Lance Corporal	1st Parachute Brigade, Royal Signals	4803722	91314		Stalag XII A, Stalag IV B
Peers	James	Corporal	Provost Company, 1st Airborne Division	1735900	89866		Stalag XII A, Stalag II A
Peet	Charles William	Private	3rd Battalion, Parachute Regiment	14242974	117281		Stalag XI B, Oflag 79
Penfold	Kenneth	Private	2nd Battalion, Parachute Regiment	4865420			Stalag XII A, Stalag IV B, Stalag IV F
Penman	James	Private	Army Catering Corps attached 1st Airborne Div	29990978			Stalag XII A, Stalag IV B
Penney	Ronald Edward	Private	11th Battalion, Parachute Regiment	860215	14218		Stalag XII A, Stalag IV B, Stalag IV A
Pennington	Alfred	Private	1st Battalion, Border Regiment	3390631	118309		Stalag XI B
Pentney	Trevor George Harcourt	Lance Corporal	Provost Company, 1st Airborne Division	14688685			Stalag XII A, Stalag IV B, Stalag IV A
Pepper	Maurice Raymond	Sergeant	Glider Pilot Regiment	7595239			Dulag Luft – Oberusel, Stalag Luft 7, Stalag III A
Percy	Victor Douglas	Staff Sergeant	Glider Pilot Regiment	5951478	118488	Yes	Stalag XI B, Stalag VIII C
Perkins	Arthur Wallace	Gunner	1st Airlanding Light Regiment, Royal Artillery	14245682			Stalag XII A, Stalag IV B
Perkins	George	Private	7th Battalion, King's Own Scottish Borderers Regiment	14422898	117785		Stalag XI B
Perks	Victor	Private	133rd Parachute Field Ambulance, Royal Army Medical Corps	14630044	90042		Dulag Luft, Stalag IV B

Surname	First name	Rank	Unit	Service number	POW number	Camps
Perrin-Brown	Christopher	Major	1st Battalion, Parachute Regiment	121945	572	Oflag XII B, Oflag 79
Perry	Charles Edward	Private	3rd Battalion, Parachute Regiment	14207893	75531	Stalag XII A, Stalag IV B
Perry	George Herbert	Corporal	3rd Battalion, Parachute Regiment	4622196		Dulag Luft, Stalag IV B
Perry	Norman	Private	2nd Battalion, South Staffordshire Regiment	4916676		Stalag XII A, Stalag IV D
Perry	Stanley	Lance Corporal	2nd Battalion, Parachute Regiment	6353005	89792	Stalag XII A, Stalag XI B
Perse	Peter John	Captain	11th Battalion, Parachute Regiment	148840	2200	Apeldoorn Hospital, Reserve Lazarett Burgsteinfurt, Reserve Lazarett Lingen, Stalag XI B, Oflag 79
Peters	Thomas Charles	Private	2nd Battalion, Parachute Regiment	14343574	117799	Stalag XII A, Stalag III A, Stalag XI A
Petrie	Lewis	Sergeant	7th Battalion, King's Own Scottish Borderers Regiment	3185683		Stalag XII A, Stalag XVIII C
Pettitt	Thomas Joseph	Private	2nd Battalion, Parachute Regiment	14397946		Stalag XII A, Stalag IV B, Stalag IV G
Phillips	Alfred Henry	Private	156th Battalion, Parachute Regiment	14578642	118212	Stalag XI B
Phillips	Bernard	Corporal	1st Airborne Provost Company	7373821	89395	Stalag XII A, Stalag IV B
Phillips	Edward Leigh	Captain Reverend	3rd Battalion, Parachute Regiment	163854	558	Dulag XII B Hadamar, Oflag 79
Phillips	Patrick Mannix	Private	2nd Battalion, Parachute Regiment	6462931	117509	Stalag XI B, Stalag III A, Stalag XI A, Stalag IV D
Phillips	Ronald John	Private	2nd Battalion, Parachute Regiment	5510064	117829	Reserve Lazarett Gronau, Stalag XI B, Hildesheim Hospital

137

Family name	Forename	Rank	Unit as given on Questionnaire	Army number	POW number	Wounded on capture?	Camps
Phillips	Thomas John	Private	181st Airlanding Field Ambulance, Royal Army Medical Corps	7374379			Apeldoorn Hospital, Stalag XII A, Stalag IV B
Phipps	Dennis Edward	Private	Parachute Regiment	14539342			Stalag XII A, Stalag IV B, Stalag IV B
Pick	Robert Baxter Paterson	Private	1st Battalion, Parachute Regiment	7367569	91495		Dulag Luft – Oberusel, Stalag XII A, Stalag IV B
Pierce	Gordon Basil	Corporal	7th Battalion, King's Own Scottish Borderers Regiment	4750968	89154		Stalag XII A, Stalag XVIII C
Pilbeam	Henry Frank James	Craftsman	Royal Electrical and Mechanical Engineers	7590939	91494		Stalag XII A, Stalag IV B, Stalag IV A
Pilbeam	Reginald	Private	133rd Parachute Field Ambulance, Royal Army Medical Corps	7361895	118451		Stalag XI B
Pinguet	Robert Sidney Paul	Sergeant	89th Parachute Field Security Section	10350914			Apeldoorn Hospital, Stalag VII A, Stalag 383
Pitcher	Richard Eric	Private	10th Battalion, Parachute Regiment	7369253			Stalag IV B
Pitman	Kenneth Frederick	Driver	1st Airlanding Anti-Tank Battery, Royal Artillery	1462957			Stalag IV B
Pitt	Fred	Private	3rd Battalion, Parachute Regiment	3455442	140134		Stalag VII A
Pitt	Harry	Private	7th Battalion, King's Own Scottish Borderers Regiment	3197317			Stalag XII A, Stalag IV B, Stalag IV D
Plenderleith	John	Private	3rd Battalion, Parachute Regiment	3449604			Stalag XII A, Stalag IV B, Stalag IV D

Surname	First name(s)	Rank	Unit	No.	No.	Q	Camps
Plunton	Charles Frederick	Sapper	1st Parachute Squadron, Royal Engineers	1912650	118771	Yes	Stalag XI B
Pocklington	George Edward	Lance Corporal	3rd Battalion, Parachute Regiment	4754286			Stalag XII A, Stalag XI B
Ponting	Joseph Bernard	Private	3rd Battalion, Parachute Regiment	5193231	91656		Stalag XII A, Stalag IV B
Poole	Granville	Gunner	2nd Airlanding Anti-Tank Battery, Royal Artillery	14583325	91888		Stalag XII A, Stalag IV C
Pooley	Kenneth Walter	Private	Royal Army Ordnance Corps	14235531	117502		Stalag XI B
Pope	Robert Edward	Private	2nd Battalion, Parachute Regiment	5385849	75412		Stalag XII A, Stalag IV B, Stalag IV F
Poplett	William Alfred	Private	3rd Battalion, Parachute Regiment	5113895	91512		Stalag XII A, Stalag IV B, Stalag IV C
Postans	Charles	Sapper	9th Field Company (Airborne), Royal Engineers	1867233	117153	Yes	Stalag XI B
Pott	Robert Lailett John	Major	156th Battalion, Parachute Regiment	95241	2193		Reserve Lazarett Gronau, Oflag 79
Potter	Joseph William Dominic	Signalman	1st Airborne Division, Royal Signals	2590125	118138	Yes	Apeldoorn Hospital, Stalag XI B
Potts	Dennis	Private	1st Parachute Brigade HQ	6354479	75519		Stalag XII A, Stalag IV B, Stalag IV F
Potts	Edmund	Private	11th Battalion, Parachute Regiment	10582732	117943	Yes	Stalag XI B
Potts	Eric	Lance Corporal	181st Airlanding Field Ambulance, Royal Army Medical Corps	7399495			Stalag XII A, Stalag IV B
Potts	John Reginald	Private	1st Parachute Brigade HQ	5962036	89583		Stalag XII A, Stalag IV B
Poulton	William Lawrence	Private	2nd Battalion, South Staffordshire Regiment	4929079	91738		Stalag XII A, Stalag IV B, Stalag IV F

Family name	Forename	Rank	Unit as given on Questionnaire	Army number	POW number	Wounded on capture?	Camps
Powell	Charles	Lance Corporal	2nd Battalion, Parachute Regiment	4035583	117800	Yes	Reserve Lazarett Lingen, Stalag XI B, Stalag III A, Stalag XI A
Powell	Francis	Sergeant	Glider Pilot Regiment	190364			Stalag XII A, Dulag Luft – Oberusel, Stalag Luft 7, Stalag III A
Poynton	Joseph	Private	1st Airlanding Anti-Tank Battery, Royal Artillery	3386146	92076		Stalag XII A, Stalag IV B
Prentice	Eric	Sergeant	1st Airlanding Light Royal Artillery	838595	118523		Apeldoorn Hospital, Stalag XI B, Stalag VIII C, Stalag IV B
Presley	Leslie	Private	1st Battalion, Parachute Regiment	5672364	92261		Stalag XII A, Stalag IV B
Pressly	Ian Leith	Private	10th Battalion, Parachute Regiment	14420876	93261		Dulag Luft – Wetzlar, Stalag XII A, Stalag IV B
Preston	Lawrence	Private	1st Battalion, Border Regiment	3600079	75484		Stalag XII A, Stalag IV B, Stalag IV A
Preston	Tom	Corporal	7th Battalion, King's Own Scottish Borderers Regiment	3715814	88747		Stalag XII A, Stalag XVIII C
Price	Douglas	Private	3rd Battalion, Parachute Regiment	14286857	75429		Stalag XII A, Stalag IV B, Stalag IV C
Price	Raymond	Trooper	1st Airborne Reconnaissance Squadron	4919635	118715	Yes	Stalag XI B
Price	Raymond William	Private	3rd Battalion, Parachute Regiment	5252678	91598	Yes	Stalag XII A, Stalag IV C
Price	Sidney Robert	Sergeant	Glider Pilot Regiment	2388139			Stalag Luft 7, Stalag III A
Prigmore	Frederick	Private	10th Battalion, Parachute Regiment	5512177			Stalag IV D

Surname	Forename	Rank	Unit	Number	Number	Q	Camps
Prince	Charles Henry	Private	181st Airlanding Field Ambulance, Royal Army Medical Corps	14672756			Stalag XII A, Stalag IV B, Stalag IV D
Prior	Mark James	Sergeant/W	3rd Battalion, Parachute Regiment	6094195			Stalag XII A, Stalag II A
Pritchard	Thomas	Private	1st Battalion, Parachute Regiment	4802222	92155		Stalag XII A, Stalag IV B
Prosho	Thomas George	Private	1st Parachute Brigade	6148592		Yes	Stalag XII A, Stalag IV B, Stalag IV F
Prosser	John Edward	Private	4th Parachute Brigade	6202091	117339		Stalag XI B, Stalag III A
Proudfoot	William	Staff Sergeant	Glider Pilot Regiment	922985	76320		Stalag XII A, Stalag IV B
Proudlock	James	Private	156th Battalion, Parachute Regiment	101687			Stalag XII A, Stalag IV B
Proven	Robert	Private	7th Battalion, King's Own Scottish Borderers Regiment	3192121	140107		Stalag VII A
Pruden	Ernest Edward	Quartermaster Sergeant	16th Parachute Field Ambulance, Royal Army Medical Corps	7348767			Stalag XII A, Stalag II A
Pryce	John Ivor	Lieutenant	3rd Battalion, Parachute Regiment	177861	550		Dulag XII B Hadamar, Oflag 79
Pugh	George Everton	Quartermaster Sergeant	Army Physical Training Corps	3710537	140127	Yes	Apeldoorn, Stalag XI B, Stalag VII A
Pullen	Arthur Harvey	Private	2nd Battalion, Parachute Regiment	5445475		Yes	Arnhem Hospital, Reserve Lazarett Obermaßfield, Stalag IX C
Pullinger	Albert	Private	2nd Battalion, Parachute Regiment	5836763			Stalag XII A, Stalag IV B
Pummell	Joseph Walter	Lance Corporal	1st Airborne Provost Company	6025654		Yes	Ziekenhuis van de Vereeniging, Apeldoorn, Reserve Lazarett Ibbenburg? nr Munster, Stalag XI B

Family name	Forename	Rank	Unit as given on Questionnaire	Army number	POW number	Wounded on capture?	Camps
Purdie	John	Corporal	7th Battalion, King's Own Scottish Borderers Regiment	3193054			Stalag XII A, Stalag II A
Purdy	Harry	Private	3rd Battalion, Parachute Regiment	6203365	89831		Stalag XII A, Stalag XI B, Stalag 357
Purnell	Desmond James George	Gunner	1st Airlanding Anti-Tank Battery, Royal Artillery	4194052	117351	Yes	Apeldoorn Hospital, Stalag XI B, Stalag III A, Stalag XI A, Stalag IV B
Purnell	William Tom	Private	7th Battalion, King's Own Scottish Borderers Regiment	3190949	90350		Stalag XII A, Stalag XI B
Purvis	James Anderson	Private	2nd Battalion, South Staffordshire Regiment	557747			Stalag IV B
Pusser	David Stanley James	Sergeant	Royal Army Medical Corps	7370765			Stalag XII A, Stalag II A
Pye	George	Staff Sergeant	181st Airlanding Field Ambulance, Royal Army Medical Corps	7261693			Stalag XII A, Stalag VIII C
Quigley	Edmund	Sergeant	Light Warning Set Unit No. 6341, RAF	1149134	943		Stalag Luft 7, Stalag III A
Quinn	Albert Edward	Private	1st Battalion, Border Regiment	4546937	75350	Yes	Stalag XII A, Stalag IV B
Quinn	Hugh	Lance Corporal	4th Parachute Squadron, Royal Engineers	1875356	117372		Stalag XI B
Rafferty	Henry	Lance Corporal	1st Battalion, Border Regiment	3597639	118090	Yes	Apeldoorn Hospital, Stalag XI B
Rafferty	William	Private	1st Battalion, Border Regiment	14642750		Yes	Stalag XII A, Stalag IV B, Stalag IV F
Rainbow	Edmund Hubert	Private	181st Airlanding Field Ambulance, Royal Army Medical Corps	7401241			Stalag XII A, Stalag IV B, Stalag IV D

Surname	First name(s)	Rank	Regiment	Number			Camps
Rainford	Arthur	Gunner	1st Airlanding Light Regiment, Royal Artillery	14302795		Yes	Stalag XII A, Stalag IV B
Ralph	Edward Ernest Sidney	Staff Sergeant	Glider Pilot Regiment	1434775	117299	Yes	Stalag XI B, Stalag VIII C, Stalag IV B
Ramsbottom	Harold Bocek?	Private	2nd Battalion, South Staffordshire Regiment	4207102	75682		Stalag XII A, Stalag IV B
Ramsbottom	Walter James	Staff Sergeant	Glider Pilot Regiment	920299			Dulag Luft, Stalag Luft 7, Stalag III A
Ramsey	Sydney	Private	2nd Battalion, Parachute Regiment	3249012			Stalag IV B
Randle	Oliver	Sapper	4th Parachute Squadron, Royal Engineers	2009716	117588	Yes	Stalag XI B, Stalag III A, Stalag XI A, Stalag IV D
Rands	Leslie Briton	Driver	Royal Army Service Corps	14425027			Stalag XII A, Stalag IV B, Stalag IV D
Rankin	William John Begg	Private	7th Battalion, King's Own Scottish Borderers Regiment	3190180	117583	Yes	Stalag XI B, Stalag III A, Stalag XI A, Stalag IV D
Ransom	James Leslie	Lance Corporal	250th Airborne Light Company, Royal Army Service Corps	10694205	91189		Stalag XII A, Stalag IV B
Ratchford	William	Private	11th Battalion, Parachute Regiment	14400554			Stalag XII A, , Stalag IV B, Stalag IV F
Rathband	Herbert Henry	Sergeant/W	Glider Pilot Regiment	1544344	103967		Dulag Luft, Stalag Luft 7, Stalag III A
Raven	William James	Private	3rd Battalion, Parachute Regiment	5679281	117827		Stalag XI B, Stalag III A, Stalag XI A, Stalag IV D
Rawding	Harold	Private	2nd Battalion, South Staffordshire Regiment	4910663	17593		Stalag XII A, Stalag IV B
Rea	Henry William	Signalman	1st Airborne Division, Royal Signals	10547340	91900		Stalag XII A, Stalag IV B, Stalag IV C

Family name	Forename	Rank	Unit as given on Questionnaire	Army number	POW number	Wounded on capture?	Camps
Read	Lewis Allen	Sergeant	10th Battalion, Parachute Regiment	6402998		Yes	Dulag Luft – Oberusel, Stalag VIII C, Stalag XI B
Read	Victor Henry William	Signalman	1st Parachute Brigade, Royal Signals	2586247	89797	Yes	Dulag Luft – Frankfurt, Stalag XII A, Stalag XI B
Reading	Charles	Private	Parachute Regiment	262549			Stalag XII A, Stalag IV B, Stalag IV F
Reading	Kenneth	Private	21st Independent Parachute Company	14313329	91380		Stalag IV C
Reast	Stanley Albert Barradell	Lance Corporal	1st Airborne Provost Company	986562	14904		Stalag XII A, Stalag IV B
Reay	Harrison James	Private	11th Battalion, Parachute Regiment	3716400	75990		Stalag XII A, Stalag IV B, Stalag IV G
Reay	John James	Private	16th Parachute Field Ambulance, Royal Army Medical Corps	4451377	88937		Stalag XII A, Stalag IV B
Redman	Ernest	Private	3rd Battalion, Parachute Regiment	3862185	117983	Yes	Stalag XI B, Stalag III A, Stalag XI A
Reed	Ronald	Private	1st Battalion, Border Regiment	4469834	118362	Yes	Stalag XI B
Reed	Samuel	Private	4th Parachute Brigade HQ	64180	118177		Stalag XI B
Reeves	Richard George	Private	3rd Battalion, Parachute Regiment	3968883	92171		Stalag XII A, Stalag IV C
Reeves	Reginald Henry	Sapper	9th Field Company (Airborne), Royal Engineers	1883104	75854		Stalag XII A, Stalag IV B, Stalag IV F
Reid	George	Sapper	4th Parachute Squadron, Royal Engineers	2067721			Stalag XII A, Stalag IV B, Stalag IV C
Reid	James Bruce	Private	7th Battalion, King's Own Scottish Borderers Regiment	14416765			Stalag XII A, Stalag IV B, Stalag IV G

Surname	First name(s)	Rank	Unit	Number		Camps
Reid	William	Private	156th Battalion, Parachute Regiment	3131283		Stalag XII A, Stalag IV B, Stalag IV A
Reilly	John	Craftsman	Royal Electrical and Mechanical Engineers	889575		Stalag XII A, Stalag VIII C, Stalag VIII A, Stalag IV C
Rendle	William	Private	181st Airlanding Field Ambulance, Royal Army Medical Corps	7399502		Stalag XII A, Stalag IV B
Rennie	David Brown	Private	10th Battalion, Parachute Regiment	14423029		Stalag XII A, Stalag IV D
Renton	John	Private	1st Battalion, Border Regiment	3192256	75503	Stalag XII A, Stalag IV B, Stalag IV C
Reynolds	Cyril Wilfred	Private	1st Battalion, Border Regiment	14645531		Stalag XII A, Stalag IV B
Reynolds	Jack	Lieutenant	2nd Battalion, South Staffordshire Regiment	190738	538	Oflag XII B, Oflag 79
Rhydderch	Verdun	Private	250th Airborne Light Company, Royal Army Service Corps	190586		Stalag XII A, Stalag IV B
Rice	Ronald Edward	Corporal	2nd Battalion, South Staffordshire Regiment	5627473	89382	Stalag XII A, Stalag II A
Richards	John Thomas	Sergeant	1st Battalion, Parachute Regiment	4195046		Stalag XII A, Stalag VIII C
Richardson	Ernest James	Private	Parachute Regiment	4979999		Stalag IV B
Richey	James	Captain	1st Battalion, Parachute Regiment	151648	547	Oflag XII B, Oflag 79
Riding	Cedric Kenneth	Private	1st Battalion, Border Regiment	3606398	118052	Yes	Stalag XI B
Rigby-Jones MC	Guy	Major/T	181st Airlanding Field Ambulance, Royal Army Medical Corps	216228		Konig Wilhelm III Kazerne Apeldoorn, Kriegslazarett 4/686, Heemstede
Riley	Bernard	Private	1st Battalion, Border Regiment	4546122	118191	Stalag XI B

Family name	Forename	Rank	Unit as given on Questionnaire	Army number	POW number	Wounded on capture?	Camps
Riley	Hugh	Private	1st Battalion, Border Regiment	3866213	75496		Stalag XII A, Stalag IV B
Ring	Ronald	Private	156th Battalion, Parachute Regiment	4345252		Yes	Stalag IV B
Roan	Cyril Charles	Lance Corporal	2nd Battalion, Parachute Regiment	5891392			St Elizabeth's Hospital, Apeldoorn Hospital, Dulag-Luft, Stalag XII A, Stalag IV B, Stalag IV F
Robbie	William George	Private	10th Battalion, Parachute Regiment	2879256			Stalag XII A, Stalag IV B, Stalag IV F
Robbins	James	Lance Corporal	181st Airlanding Field Ambulance, Royal Army Medical Corps	7366512	76659		Stalag XII A, Stalag IV B
Roberts	Andrew	Lieutenant	2nd Battalion, Parachute Regiment	251878			Dulag XII B Hadamar, Oflag 79
Roberts	Christopher William	Private	156th Battalion, Parachute Regiment	5253355			Stalag XII A, Stalag XII B
Roberts	David Norman	Private	1st Battalion, Parachute Regiment	1678453			Stalag XII A, Stalag IV B
Roberts	Geoffrey William	Private	7th Battalion, King's Own Scottish Borderers Regiment	14434693	92103		Stalag XII A, Stalag IV C
Roberts	Harry Royston	Lieutenant	1st Airborne Divisional Workshop Royal Electrical and Mechanical Engineers	281104	2188		Apeldoorn Hospital, Stalag XI B, Oflag IX A/Z
Roberts	John	Lance Corporal	2nd Battalion, South Staffordshire Regiment	4913467			Zutphen Transit Camp, Stalag IV B
Roberts	Leslie	Driver	Royal Signals	14532593	90430		Stalag XII A, Stalag XI B
Roberts	Robert William	Lance Bombardier	Forward Observation Unit, Royal Artillery	924830	92050		Stalag XII A, , Stalag IV B, Stalag IV A

Surname	First name(s)	Rank	Unit	Number	POW No.	Q	Camps
Roberts	Wilfred Clifford	Corporal	3rd Battalion, Parachute Regiment	7343865	118551		Stalag XI B, Stalag VIII C, Stalag VIII B, Stalag VII A
Robertson	Arthur	Gunner	2nd Airlanding Anti-Tank Battery, Royal Artillery	5392231			Stalag IV B
Robertson	Matthew	Corporal	7th Battalion, King's Own Scottish Borderers Regiment	3192156			Stalag XII A, Stalag II A
Robertson	Robert Dickson	Corporal	7th Battalion, King's Own Scottish Borderers Regiment	3195880	118369	Yes	St Joseph's Hospital Apeldoorn, Stalag XI B, Stalag VIII C
Robertson	Stanley	Private	1st Parachute Brigade HQ	3603869	75447		Stalag XII A, Stalag IV B
Robertson	Thomas Hood	Lance Corporal	156th Battalion, Parachute Regiment	91664			Stalag XII A, Stalag IV B
Robinson	Cyril Bernard	Sergeant Major	1st Parachute Brigade	4698977			Stalag XII A, Stalag IV B, Stalag IV F
Robinson	Cyril Frederick	Sergeant	Glider Pilot Regiment	5830482		Yes	Bismarck School Hanover, Stalag XI B
Robinson	Michael William Patrick	Sapper	9th Field Company (Airborne), Royal Engineers	1944654	76252		Enschede Hospital, Dulag Luft – Wetzlar, Stalag IV C
Robson	Joseph	Lance Corporal	11th Battalion, Parachute Regiment	14644631	92139		Stalag XII A, Stalag IV B, Stalag IV A
Robson	Ronald	Driver	253rd Airborne Light Company, Royal Army Service Corps	174394			Stalag XII A, Stalag IV B
Rock	Ernest	Private	2nd Battalion, Parachute Regiment	3607396			Stalag XII A, Stalag XI B
Roddick	Roy Alistair	Corporal	10th Battalion, Parachute Regiment	6403044			Stalag XII A, Stalag II A
Rodgers	Harry	Lance Corporal	1st Parachute Brigade HQ	886051	89080		Stalag XII A, Stalag XI B
Roger	James Charles	Private	10th Battalion, Parachute Regiment	4619865	117190		Stalag XI B

Family name	Forename	Rank	Unit as given on Questionnaire	Army number	POW number	Wounded on capture?	Camps
Rogers	Arthur	Private	2nd Battalion, South Staffordshire Regiment	1811751	91421		Stalag XII A, Stalag IV B
Roissetter	Fredrick	Private	2nd Battalion, Parachute Regiment	875919	117234		Reserve Lazarett Gronau, Stalag XI B
Rollins	Robert	Private	156th Battalion, Parachute Regiment	4748127			Stalag XII A, Stalag IV B, Stalag IV C
Rook	Walter Ernest	Private	2nd Battalion, Parachute Regiment	5956703			Stalag XII A, Stalag IV B, Stalag IV D
Rose	John William	Private	181st Airlanding Field Ambulance, Royal Army Medical Corps	7404654	90026		Stalag XII A, Stalag IV B
Rose	Stanley Edward	Private	11th Battalion, Parachute Regiment	6854552	117584	Yes	Stalag XI B, Stalag III A, Stalag XI A, Stalag IV D
Ross	John	Private	156th Battalion, Parachute Regiment	2823352	75658		Stalag IV B, Stalag IV F
Ross	Ronald	Sergeant	7th Battalion, King's Own Scottish Borderers Regiment	3184652	88798		Stalag XII A, Stalag XVIII C
Roughton	John Kenneth	Corporal	10th Battalion, Parachute Regiment	7886696			Stalag XII A, Stalag IV B
Rouse	Edwin	Corporal	7th Battalion, King's Own Scottish Borderers Regiment	3191861	91783		Stalag XII A, Stalag VIII C, Stalag XI B
Rouse	Ronald	Sergeant	11th Battalion, Parachute Regiment	4981946			Stalag XII A, Stalag XVIII C
Routledge	James	Sergeant	3rd Battalion, Parachute Regiment	4275722			Stalag XII A, Stalag II A
Rowan	Gerald	Private	181st Airlanding Field Ambulance, Royal Army Medical Corps	144401865			Queen Ethelburgers Barracks, Stalag IV F

Rowbottom	Frank	Lance Corporal	2nd Battalion, South Staffordshire Regiment	5050824	52836		Stalag IX C
Rowley	Ernest	Private	10th Battalion, Parachute Regiment	5347202			Stalag XII A, Stalag IV B
Rowthorn	Aubrey Owen	Corporal	3rd Battalion, Parachute Regiment	5890319			Stalag XII A, Stalag II A, Stalag II A
Royall	Arthur Robert	Lieutenant	1st Battalion, Border Regiment	269802	632		Dulag of Oflag XII B, Oflag 79
Royle	James Harold Ernest	Private	2nd Battalion, Parachute Regiment	3454348	140132	Yes	Apeldoorn Hospital, Stalag VII A
Rubin	Leonard Sidney	Private	181st Airlanding Field Ambulance, Royal Army Medical Corps	7403928			Stalag XII A, Stalag IV B
Rumney	Albert Edward	Gunner	1st Airlanding Light Regiment, Royal Artillery	1103814	118160	Yes	Apeldoorn Hospital, Stalag XI B
Rumsey	Reginald	Private	10th Battalion, Parachute Regiment	6407115	117600	Yes	Stalag XI B, Stalag III A, Stalag IV D/Z, Stalag XI A
Rushforth	George	Lance Corporal	250th Airborne Light Company, Royal Army Service Corps	99987			Stalag XII A, Stalag IV B
Russell	Arthur Eli	Private	10th Battalion, Parachute Regiment	2048220	75423		Stalag XII A, Stalag IV B
Russell	Andrew McCallum	Private	7th Battalion, King's Own Scottish Borderers Regiment	14607803	15459		Stalag XII A, Stalag IV B
Russell	Ralph Frederick	Private	2nd Battalion, Parachute Regiment	5731487	89294		Stalag XII A, Stalag IV D
Russon	John Edward	Private	2nd Battalion, Parachute Regiment	4928328	140076		Stalag VII A
Rutter	Jeffrey Raymond	Private	10th Battalion, Parachute Regiment	5836591			Stalag XII A, Stalag IV B, Stalag IV D, Stalag IV D

Family name	Forename	Rank	Unit as given on Questionnaire	Army number	POW number	Wounded on capture?	Camps
Ryan	Edward	Private	10th Battalion, Parachute Regiment	3961505			Stalag XII A, Stalag IV B
Ryan	Edward Joseph	Private	10th Battalion, Parachute Regiment	6914029	118579	Yes	Stalag XI B
Ryan	Ronald William	Sergeant	Glider Pilot Regiment	2589852			Stalag XII A, Stalag IV B
Saabye	Jack	Sapper	Royal Engineers	1864157	118238	Yes	Apeldoorn Hospital, Stalag XI B
Sadler	Charles	Sergeant	156th Battalion, Parachute Regiment	4387908			Stalag XII A, Stalag II A
Salt	Bernard Frederick	Private	2nd Battalion, Parachute Regiment	14660885	117150	Yes	Reserve Lazarett Emmerich, Reserve Lazarett Hanover, Stalag XI B, Oflag 79
Saltman	Jack	Private	7th Battalion, King's Own Scottish Borderers Regiment	14213424	89885		Stalag XII A, Stalag XI B, Stalag 357
Salton	James	Private	10th Battalion, Parachute Regiment	3056379	75694		Stalag XII A, Stalag IV B
Sander	Gustave	Private	11th Battalion, Parachute Regiment	13807937	91694		Stalag XII A, Stalag IV B
Sanders	Samuel John Frederick	Staff Sergeant	181st Airlanding Field Ambulance, Royal Army Medical Corps	7348718	77583	Yes	Dulag Luft – Oberusel, Stalag XII A, Oflag VII C, Stalag 344, Stalag XIII C, Stalag XIII D, Stalag VII A
Sanderson	Ellison	Sergeant	Glider Pilot Regiment	937039			Dulag Luft, Stalag Luft 7, Stalag III A
Sankey	Walter	Private	2nd Battalion, South Staffordshire Regiment	14480882	91180		Stalag XII A, Stalag IV B, Stalag IV D

Surname	First name	Rank	Regiment	Number			Camps
Sargant	Raymond	Sergeant	Glider Pilot Regiment	4617321			Dulag Luft – Oberusel, Dulag Luft – Wetzlar, Stalag Luft 7, Stalag II A
Sargent	Reginald Arthur	Driver	181st Airlanding Field Ambulance, Royal Army Medical Corps	199690			Dulag Luft, Stalag XII A, Stalag IV B
Saunders	Charles Stanley	Private	3rd Battalion, Parachute Regiment	5381500	1249	Yes	Reserve Lazarett Obermaßfeld, Reserve Lazarett Meiningen, Stalag IX C/Z
Saunders	John Richard	Private	2nd Battalion, South Staffordshire Regiment	14397706	92173		Stalag XII A, Stalag IV C
Saunders	Leslie Percy	Sergeant	Glider Pilot Regiment	4804127			Stalag XII A, Stalag IV B
Saunders	William	Private	2nd Battalion, Parachute Regiment	7018194			Stalag XII A, Stalag XI B
Savage	Henry Owen	Corporal	1st Battalion, Parachute Regiment	2057101			Stalag XII A, Stalag II A
Sawyer	John	Private	2nd Battalion, South Staffordshire Regiment	5047154	89803		Stalag XII A, Stalag XI B
Sawyer	James George	Lance Corporal	250th Airborne Light Company, Royal Army Service Corps	289543	91153		Stalag XII A, Stalag IV B, Stalag IV A
Sawyers	Edward	Private	3rd Battalion, Parachute Regiment	4456749			Dulag Luft, Stalag IV B, Stalag IV G
Sayles	Bennett	Staff Sergeant	Glider Pilot Regiment	850767			Stalag Luft 7, Stalag III A
Scholfield	John	Private	181st Airlanding Field Ambulance, Royal Army Medical Corps	7407356			Enschede, Stalag XII A, Stalag IV B
Scott	Andrew	Sergeant	7th Battalion, King's Own Scottish Borderers Regiment	3191998			Stalag XII A, Stalag II A
Scott	Arnold	Private	156th Battalion, Parachute Regiment	4746709			Stalag XII A, Reserve Lazarett Stalag II A, Stalag II A

151

Family name	Forename	Rank	Unit as given on Questionnaire	Army number	POW number	Wounded on capture?	Camps
Scott	Joseph James	Private	1st Battalion, Border Regiment	3603978	118152	Yes	Apeldoorn Hospital, Stalag XI B
Scott	Joseph Rowland	Gunner	1st Airlanding Light Regiment, Royal Artillery	14322051			Stalag XII A, Stalag IV B, Stalag IV F
Scott	William Mawhinnie	Private	2nd Battalion, South Staffordshire Regiment	997574	75351		Stalag XII A, Stalag IV B, Stalag IV F
Scrivener	Edmund Filford	Lieutenant	1st Battalion, Border Regiment	292013	601	Yes	Stalag XII A, Dulag of Oflag XII B, Oflag 79
Scutt	Henry John	Private	10th Battalion, Parachute Regiment	6395492			Stalag XII A, Stalag IV B, Stalag IV D
Seabridge	Thomas Cyril	Private	2nd Battalion, South Staffordshire Regiment	5050452	117514	Yes	Stalag XI B
Seale	Joseph Alexander	Private	1st Battalion, Border Regiment	14645417	118574	Yes	Stalag XI B
Seaman	Frederick George	Sergeant	Glider Pilot Regiment	876231			Dulag Luft – Oberusel, Stalag Luft 7, Stalag III A
Searle	Ivan John	Private	2nd Battalion, Parachute Regiment	562071	75305		Stalag XII A, Stalag IV B, Stalag IV C
Sefton	Stanley	Private	11th Battalion, Parachute Regiment	4042163	90948		Amersfoort Transit Camp, Stalag XII A, Stalag IV B, Stalag IV D
Seymour	George Harry	Private	11th Battalion, Parachute Regiment	6464228	118672	Yes	Stalag XI B, Stalag III A, Stalag XI A, Stalag IV D
Seymour	Tom Henry	Lance Corporal	1st Battalion, Border Regiment	14574818	75687		Stalag IV B
Sharkey	James	Private	2nd Battalion, Parachute Regiment	14540464	294149		Stalag IV B

152

Surname	First name(s)	Rank	Regiment/Unit	Service No.	POW No.	Questionnaire	Camps
Sharlott	Ronald Cyril Walter	Private	21st Independent Parachute Company	14663891	117627	Yes	Stalag XI B, Stalag III A, Stalag XI A, Stalag IV D/Z
Shaw	Albert	Private	7th Battalion, King's Own Scottish Borderers Regiment	10602461		Yes	Reserve Lazarett Meiningen, Stalag IX C
Shaw	Neil Buchanan	Corporal	7th Battalion, King's Own Scottish Borderers Regiment	14435379	89618		Stalag XII A, Stalag II A
Shaw	Robert	Private	2nd Battalion, Parachute Regiment	13041806			Stalag XII A, Stalag II A
Shearer	George	Lance Corporal	7th Battalion, King's Own Scottish Borderers Regiment	4268582	91488		Stalag XII A, Stalag IV B
Shears	Charles Eli	Private	10th Battalion, Parachute Regiment	5623548			Stalag XII A, Stalag IV B
Shedden	William	Lance Corporal	7th Battalion, King's Own Scottish Borderers Regiment	3191038	90550		Stalag XII A, Stalag IV B
Sheilds	John Williams	Private	16th Parachute Field Ambulance, Royal Army Medical Corps	14272469	91321		Stalag XII A, Stalag IV B
Shelbourne	James Ernest	Private	1st Battalion, Parachute Regiment	6914183			Stalag XII A, Stalag IV B, Stalag IV D
Sheldon	Walter	Private	1st Battalion, Border Regiment	14201232	91951		Stalag XII A, Stalag IV B, Stalag IV A
Shell	Lionel	Sergeant	Glider Pilot Regiment	319389			Stalag XII A, Stalag IV B
Shelton	Albert Stanley	Lance Corporal	1st Parachute Brigade	6107546		Yes	Arnhem, Dulag Luft, Stalag XII A, Stalag IV B
Shephard	Wallis James	Private	1st Battalion, Border Regiment	3604890	91785		Stalag XII A, Stalag IV B, Stalag IV C
Shepherd	Frank	Staff Sergeant	Glider Pilot Regiment	932328			Stalag XII A, Stalag IV B
Shepherd	Joseph	Private	11th Battalion, Parachute Regiment	14647522	75987		Stalag XII A, Stalag IV B

Family name	Forename	Rank	Unit as given on Questionnaire	Army number	POW number	Wounded on capture?	Camps
Shepherd	Robert	Driver	250th Airborne Light Company, Royal Army Service Corps	240955	89511		Stalag XII A, Stalag IV B, Stalag IV D
Shepley	Arthur	Sergeant, Lance	156th Battalion, Parachute Regiment	4344978	52919	Yes	Arnhem Hospital, Apeldoorn Hospital, Reserve Lazarett Obermaßfeld, Reserve Lazarett Meiningen, Stalag IX C/Z
Sherret	Richard	Private	7th Battalion, King's Own Scottish Borderers Regiment	3196547	91333		Stalag XII A, Stalag IV B
Sherwood	Reginald Douglas	Gunner	1st Airlanding Light Regiment, Royal Artillery	904283	117636	Yes	Stalag XI B, Stalag III A, Stalag XI A, Stalag IV D
Short	Edward Richard	Private	11th Battalion, Parachute Regiment	5954640	117579	Yes	Stalag XI B, Stalag III A, Stalag XI A, Stalag IV B
Silvester	Vernon John Bellis	Lieutenant	156th Battalion, Parachute Regiment	204917	91013		Stalag XII A, Oflag XII B, Oflag 79
Simonds	William Robert	Private	156th Battalion, Parachute Regiment	5884494	75416		Stalag XII A, Stalag IV B, Stalag IV C
Simons	Denis Harold	Staff Sergeant	Glider Pilot Regiment	119641			Dulag Luft – Oberusel, Stalag Luft 7, Stalag III A
Simpson	Albert	Staff Sergeant	Glider Pilot Regiment	856791			Apeldoorn Hospital, Dulag Luft, Stalag Luft 7, Stalag III A
Simpson	David Anderson	Captain	Glider Pilot Regiment	193137	8494		Dulag Luft – Wetzlar, Dulag Luft – Oberusel, Stalag Luft 3, Stalag III A
Simpson	David Richard	Trooper	1st Airborne Reconnaissance Squadron	4807155	91436		Stalag XII A, Stalag IV B, Stalag IV F

154

Surname	First name	Rank	Regiment	Number	Number		Camps
Skelly	Matthew	Private	Royal Army Medical Corps	59586	118404		Stalag XI B, Stalag V A
Skidmore	Leonard	Private	2nd Battalion, South Staffordshire Regiment	14286891	92165		Stalag XII A, Stalag IV A
Slatter	Reginald	Private	2nd Battalion, South Staffordshire Regiment	5509858	91700		Stalag XII A, Stalag IV B, Stalag IV F
Sloan	Alexander	Private	7th Battalion, King's Own Scottish Borderers Regiment	3189499	92645	Yes	Stalag XII A, Stalag IV B, Stalag IV G
Small	Eric Lyng	Private	10th Battalion, Parachute Regiment	5682652	88909		Stalag XII A, Stalag XVIII C
Small	William Desmond	Private	1st Battalion, Parachute Regiment	2616873			Stalag IV B, Stalag IV D
Smallwood	Leonard	Bombardier	1st Airlanding Anti-Tank Battery, Royal Artillery	2077387	91537		Stalag XII A, Stalag VIII C
Smart	Daniel Penman	Lance Corporal	4th Battalion, Dorset Regiment	4923884			Stalag XII A, Stalag IV B
Smith	Arthur John Alan	Staff Sergeant	Glider Pilot Regiment	14206556			Stalag XII A, Stalag IV B
Smith	Claude Albert	Sergeant	Glider Pilot Regiment	6400991			Stalag XII A, Stalag IV B
Smith	Frederick Lawrence Spencer	Private	Royal Army Medical Corps	7349477			Stalag XII A, Stalag IV B
Smith	Gerald	Private	2nd Battalion, Parachute Regiment	895906	90561		Stalag XII A, Stalag IV B
Smith	Hugh	Private	3rd Battalion, Parachute Regiment	972248	117441	Yes	Reserve Lazarett Lingen, Stalag XI B, Stalag III A, Stalag XI A, Stalag IV D
Smith	James	Private	2nd Battalion, Parachute Regiment	14206353			Stalag XII A, Stalag IV B
Smith	John Lawrence	Private	156th Battalion, Parachute Regiment	3781730	75511		Stalag XII A, Stalag IV B

Family name	Forename	Rank	Unit as given on Questionnaire	Army number	POW number	Wounded on capture?	Camps
Smith	John Thomas	Private	156th Battalion, Parachute Regiment	14665924	90483		Stalag XII A, Stalag IV B, Stalag IV F
Smith	Leslie	Private	10th Battalion, Parachute Regiment	6103769	117868	Yes	Stalag XI B, Oflag 79
Smith	Norman	Private	2nd Battalion, Parachute Regiment	7367390	89422		Stalag XII A, Stalag IV B
Smith	Norman Peter	Private	7th Battalion, King's Own Scottish Borderers Regiment	3191832	90175		Stalag XII A, Stalag IV B, Stalag IV D, Reserve Lazarett Leipzig, Stalag IV D
Smith	Richard Arthur	Private	11th Battalion, Parachute Regiment	14406654	118292	Yes	Stalag XI B
Smith	Reginald Albert	Driver	250th Airborne Light Company, Royal Army Service Corps	6405247	90822		Stalag IV B
Smith	Ronald Arthur	Private	4th Parachute Brigade	5891105			Stalag XII A, Stalag IV B, Stalag IV A
Smith	Stanley	Private	11th Battalion, Parachute Regiment	6286753	140256	Yes	Hospital, Stalag VII A
Smith	Stephen Knowles	Sergeant	1st Parachute Squadron, Royal Engineers	869950			Stalag XII A, Stalag II A
Smith	Thomas	Private	3rd Battalion, Parachute Regiment	3244188	75318		Stalag XII A, Stalag IV B
Smith	William	Private	4th Battalion, Dorset Regiment	3245456	17563		Stalag XII A, Stalag IV B
Smith	William Henry	Private	2nd Battalion, South Staffordshire Regiment	14700136			Stalag XII A, Stalag IV B
Smithson	Douglas	Sergeant	Glider Pilot Regiment	1886189			Stalag XII A, Stalag Luft 7, Stalag III A

Surname	First Name	Rank	Unit	Number	Number	Q	Camps/Sources
Smyth	John Michael	Private	10th Battalion, Parachute Regiment	3961524	75686		Stalag XII A, Stalag IV B, Stalag IV D, Stalag IV F
Snape	William	Private	11th Battalion, Parachute Regiment	4200916	140074	Yes	Queen Wilhelmina Barracks, Stalag VII A
Snell	William	Private	3rd Battalion, Parachute Regiment	14395715			Stalag IV B, Stalag IV C
Snelson	John Alfred	Private	4th Battalion, Dorset Regiment	3654902	19485		Stalag IV B
Snoding	Victor Henry	Private	16th Parachute Field Ambulance, Royal Army Medical Corps	14679808			Stalag XII A, Stalag IV B
Southwell	Frank	Trooper	1st Airborne Reconnaissance Squadron	10601898	88786		Stalag XII A, Stalag IV B
Speedie	William	Gunner	1st Airlanding Light Regiment, Royal Artillery	14297015	77092		Stalag IV B
Spencer	John Robert	Private	156th Battalion, Parachute Regiment	3448672			Stalag XII A, Stalag IV B, Stalag IV D, Stalag IV B
Spicer	Joseph Henry	Private	3rd Battalion, Parachute Regiment	3773429			Stalag XII A, Stalag IV B, Stalag IV D
Sproson	Ernest Travis	Private	156th Battalion, Parachute Regiment	5109576			Stalag IV F
Staddon	Roy Glinn	Lieutenant	1st Airlanding Light Regiment, Royal Artillery	258888	2203	Yes	Reserve Lazarett Meiningen, Oflag IX A/Z
Staff	Harry Victor William	Private	1st Battalion, Parachute Regiment	6015570			Stalag XII A, Dulag Luft – Oberusel, Stalag XII A, Stalag IV B
Stanislaus	George	Private	3rd Battalion, Parachute Regiment	5672402			Stalag XII A, Stalag IV B
Stanley	Dennis	Private	7th Battalion, King's Own Scottish Borderers Regiment	5255876			Stalag XII A, Stalag IV B
Stark	Ronnie Leslie	Major	1st Battalion, Parachute Regiment	167154	531		Dulag Luft – Oberusel, Interrogation centre Dietz, Oflag VII B

Family name	Forename	Rank	Unit as given on Questionnaire	Army number	POW number	Wounded on capture?	Camps
Start	Arthur Edward	Driver	Royal Army Service Corps	106686628	25680		Stalag XII A, Stalag IV B, Stalag IV F
Stead	John Edward	Staff Sergeant	Glider Pilot Regiment	794717			Dulag Luft, Stalag Luft 7, Stalag III A
Steel	Henry	Private	7th Battalion, King's Own Scottish Borderers Regiment	3190845	75879	Yes	Stalag XII A, Stalag IV B, Stalag XIII B
Steel	James	Lieutenant	Royal Engineers	256839	11453		Dulag of Oflag XII B, Oflag XII B, Oflag VII B
Steer	George William	Captain	7th Battalion, King's Own Scottish Borderers Regiment	121441	580		Stalag XII A, , Oflag XII B, Oflag VII B, Stalag VII A
Steirn	Aubrey Edward	Private	4th Battalion, Dorset Regiment	5734516	117345	Yes	Stalag XI B, Oflag 79
Stephens	Douglas	Driver	Royal Army Service Corps	10689300	91454		Stalag XII A, Stalag IV B
Stephens	John Howard	Lieutenant	Glider Pilot Regiment	166162	5868	Yes	Dulag Luft – Oberusel, Dulag Luft – Wetzlar, Stalag Luft 1
Stephenson	Charles Richard	Lance Corporal	4th Parachute Brigade HQ	3711558			Dulag Luft, Stalag IV B, Stalag IV F
Stephenson	Fredrick John	Private	2nd Battalion, Parachute Regiment	4461913		Yes	Stalag XII A, Stalag IV B
Stephenson	James Airen	Sergeant	Glider Pilot Regiment	4616329			Dulag Luft – Oberusel, Stalag Luft 7, Stalag III A
Stevens	Charles Edward	Signalman	1st Parachute Brigade, Royal Signals	2587250	91335		Stalag XII A, Stalag IV B, Stalag IV F
Stevens	Daniel Donne	Sapper	4th Parachute Squadron, Royal Engineers	1877687	90690		Stalag XII A, Stalag IV B, Stalag IV A

Surname	Forename	Rank	Unit	Number	Number	Q	Camps
Stevens	Reginald Charles	Sergeant	3rd Battalion, Parachute Regiment	3908419			Stalag IV B
Stevens	Reginald John	Private	1st Airlanding Brigade	5441106	91453		Stalag XII A, Stalag IV B, Stalag IV F
Stevens	Thomas Birdsall	Sergeant	Glider Pilot Regiment	3713627			Stalag Luft 7, Stalag III A
Stevens	Walter Wiliam	Private	2nd Battalion, Parachute Regiment	6203483	91187		Stalag XII A, Stalag IV B, Stalag IV F
Stewart	Edward	Private	4th Parachute Brigade HQ	2882576	90551		Stalag XII A, Stalag IV B
Stewart	Lachlan McIntyre	Private	2nd Airlanding Anti-Tank Battery, Royal Artillery	1440083	91696		Stalag XII A, Stalag IV B, Stalag IV A
Stidson	Bert James George	Lance Corporal	3rd Battalion, Parachute Regiment	859567	91531		Stalag XII A, Stalag IV B
Still	Blake Edwin Charles	Private	10th Battalion, Parachute Regiment	2323483			Stalag XII A, Stalag IV C, Stalag IV B, Stalag IV A
Stillwell	John James	Private	10th Battalion, Parachute Regiment	6412179			Stalag IV B
Stimpson	John William	Private	1st Battalion, Border Regiment	4756947	91797		Stalag XII A, Stalag IV B, Stalag IV C
Stockbridge	Stanley Gordon	Lance Corporal	1st Battalion, Parachute Regiment	5050289	90411		Stalag XII A, Stalag XI B
Stokes	Jack	Private	2nd Battalion, Parachute Regiment	5726302	140087	Yes	Stalag VII A
Stokes	Reginald	Private	2nd Battalion, South Staffordshire Regiment	5051452	89713		Stalag XII A, Stalag XI B, Stalag 357
Stone	Charles	Private	3rd Battalion, Parachute Regiment	5125422	118806	Yes	Stalag XI B, Oflag 79
Stone	Frank John	Corporal	250th Airborne Light Company, Royal Army Service Corps	176054	117625	Yes	Stalag XI B, Stalag VIII C, Stalag XI B
Stones	Horace Ryan	Sergeant	Glider Pilot Regiment	4337089			Dulag Luft – Oberusel, Stalag Luft 7, Stalag III A

159

Family name	Forename	Rank	Unit as given on Questionnaire	Army number	POW number	Wounded on capture?	Camps
Storey	Sidney Joseph	Private	2nd Battalion, South Staffordshire Regiment	4922800	89283		Stalag XII A, Stalag IV B
Stott	William Patrick	Lieutenant	1st Battalion, Border Regiment	228611	619		Dulag XII B Hadamar, Oflag 79
Streeter	Fred Henry	Private	1st Battalion, Border Regiment	14319170	91725		Stalag XII A, Stalag IV B
Stripp	Ronald Sidney	Private	1st Battalion, Border Regiment	6412612	75518		Arnhem Hospital, Stalag XII A, Stalag IV B, Stalag IV F
Strong	Gordon Thomas Piney	Sergeant	1st Battalion, Parachute Regiment	7901320	89413		Stalag XII A, Stalag II A
Stubbs	Herbert Henry	Lance Corporal	Provost Company, 1st Airborne Division	4803335	90844		Stalag XII A, Stalag IV B
Such	Albert George	Gunner	1st Airlanding Light Regiment, Royal Artillery	14318215	52917	Yes	Stalag IX C/Z
Suffolk	Douglas Evan Gabe	Driver	250th Airborne Light Company, Royal Army Service Corps	243335			Stalag IV D
Sullivan	David	Private	133rd Parachute Field Ambulance, Royal Army Medical Corps	14584840	90705		Stalag IV B
Sullivan	Edward	Private	11th Battalion, Parachute Regiment	4124947	91723		Stalag XII A, Stalag IV B
Sullivan	Henry	Private	2nd Battalion, Parachute Regiment	5445367			Stalag XII A, Stalag IV B, Stalag IV A
Sullivan	John Anthony	Sergeant	Glider Pilot Regiment	6915850	118814	Yes	Stalag XI B, Stalag 357
Sullivan	Joseph Vincent	Private	133rd Parachute Field Ambulance, Royal Army Medical Corps	7265333	90387		Dulag Luft, Stalag XII A, Stalag IV B

Sully	Reginald Gordon	Lance Corporal	3rd Battalion, Parachute Regiment	7958094			Stalag XII A, Stalag IV B, Stalag IV F
Sumner	James	Private	1st Battalion, Parachute Regiment	4206313	75167		Stalag XII A, Stalag IV B, Stalag IV G
Sunderland	Abram	Private	4th Battalion, Dorset Regiment	3658220	26067		Stalag XII A, Stalag IV B
Sutherberry	Stanley	Trooper	1st Airborne Reconnaissance Squadron	37775079	118190		Stalag XI B
Sutton	Peter Francis	Private	1st Battalion, Parachute Regiment	1509534	52880		Stalag IX C/Z
Swan	John	Private	10th Battalion, Parachute Regiment	2986583	140114	Yes	Enschede Hospital, Stalag VII A
Sweeney	Frederick Thomas	Lance Corporal	2nd Battalion, Parachute Regiment	4128770	89687		Stalag XI B
Sweeney	James	Private	2nd Battalion, Parachute Regiment	14314297	119302	Yes	Stalag XI B
Sweeney	Joseph	Private	3rd Battalion, Parachute Regiment	7015510		Yes	Stalag XII A, Stalag IV B
Swinburn	Roland Alfred	Private	2nd Battalion, South Staffordshire Regiment	4914462	89281		Stalag IV B
Swiney	George Henry	Private	181st Airlanding Field Ambulance, Royal Army Medical Corps	2366607			Stalag XII A, Stalag IV B
Swire	Leonard Robert	Private	1st Battalion, Border Regiment	14677968	75557		Stalag IV B
Sykes	Jack	Corporal	10th Battalion, Parachute Regiment	4613278	88923		Stalag XII A, Stalag XVIII C
Symes	Donald Douglas	Private	4th Parachute Brigade HQ	3969910			Utrecht Hospital, Stalag XII A, Stalag IV B, Stalag IV F
Tait	Thomas Henry	Private	2nd Battalion, Parachute Regiment	1700964			Stalag IV B

Family name	Forename	Rank	Unit as given on Questionnaire	Army number	POW number	Wounded on capture?	Camps
Tall	Anthony Harold	Private	Parachute Regiment	5509604	91419	Yes	Stalag XII A, Stalag IV B, Stalag IV C
Tallant	George William	Private	133rd Parachute Field Ambulance, Royal Army Medical Corps	14580854			Stalag XII A, Stalag XI B, Stalag V A
Tams	Leonard James	Private	2nd Battalion, South Staffordshire Regiment	4918801			Stalag XII A, Stalag IV B, Stalag IV D
Tandy	Bernard Raymond	Private	4th Battalion, Dorset Regiment	4922073	117679	Yes	Stalag XI B
Tarbitten	John Walter	Staff Sergeant	Glider Pilot Regiment	7363554			Stalag XII A, Stalag IV B
Tasker	David Ritchie	Company Sergeant Major	2nd Battalion, Parachute Regiment	2882737			Stalag XII A, Stalag XVIII C
Tate	Alfred	Private	2nd Battalion, Parachute Regiment	4747547	117923	Yes	Stalag XI B
Tate	George Cooper	Private	1st Battalion, Border Regiment	3602897	24253		Stalag XII A, Stalag IV B, Stalag IV D
Taylor	Amos	Private	Parachute Regiment	4127008	91561	Yes	Stalag XI B, Stalag IV B
Taylor	Clifford James	Lance Corporal	2nd Battalion, South Staffordshire Regiment	4919628	89432		Stalag XII A, Stalag IV B, Stalag IV C
Taylor	Eric	Gunner	1st Airlanding Light Regiment, Royal Artillery	974904	118496	Yes	Stalag XI B
Taylor	Frederick	Gunner	1st Airlanding Anti-Tank Battery, Royal Artillery	1684407	92087		Stalag IV B
Taylor	Gordon Erich	Corporal	1st Parachute Squadron, Royal Engineers	5184742		Yes	Dulag Luft – Wetzlar, Stalag IV B
Taylor	Harry	Private	1st Battalion, Border Regiment	1560536	117656	Yes	Stalag XI B, Stalag III A

Surname	Forename	Rank	Unit	Number	Number	Q	Camps
Taylor	John Alfred	Driver	Royal Army Service Corps	14403352	25803		Stalag XII A, Stalag IV B, Stalag IV F
Taylor	James William	Lieutenant	7th Battalion, King's Own Scottish Borderers Regiment	489	2197		Apeldoorn Hospital, Stalag XI B, Oflag IX A/Z
Taylor	Kenneth Joseph	Private	21st Independent Parachute Company	6148344	93412		Stalag XII A, Stalag IV B, Revier-Wurzen
Taylor	Kenneth	Gunner	2nd Airlanding Anti-Tank Battery, Royal Artillery	14545649			Stalag IV B, Stalag IV C
Taylor	Perry	Private	11th Battalion, Parachute Regiment	6095347	91577		Stalag IV B
Taylor	William Mons	Private	156th Battalion, Parachute Regiment	14625060	90423		Stalag XII A, Stalag XI B, Stalag 357
Tebbutt	Richard Henry	Gunner	1st Airlanding Light Regiment, Royal Artillery	14329479	75820		Stalag XII A, Stalag IV F
Tedds	Frederick Arthur	Private	3rd Battalion, Parachute Regiment	5116659	91534		Stalag XII A, Stalag IV B, Stalag IV C
Teece	Percy James	Lance Corporal	1st Airborne Provost Company	7398111	118232	Yes	Stalag XI B
Telfer	James	Private	10th Battalion, Parachute Regiment	10583514			Stalag XII A, Stalag IV B, Stalag IV A
Temple	Stanley James	Sapper	1st Parachute Squadron, Royal Engineers	1876271	117889	Yes	Reserve Lazarett Lingen, Stalag XI B, Stalag III A, Stalag XI A, Stalag IV D/Z
Tennet	Arthur	Lance Corporal	2nd Battalion, Parachute Regiment	4271165			Stalag XII A, Stalag IV B
Terry	Fred Dolphin	Sergeant	1st Battalion, Border Regiment	3602936		Yes	Utrecht Hospital, Reserve Lazarett Bocholt, Marlag-Milag North, Stalag XI B, Stalag 357
Tew	Leonard Ira	Lance Corporal	2nd Battalion, South Staffordshire Regiment	1603718	89146		Stalag XII A, Stalag IV B, Stalag IV C

Family name	Forename	Rank	Unit as given on Questionnaire	Army number	POW number	Wounded on capture?	Camps
Thackeray	Charles Louis	Staff Sergeant	Glider Pilot Regiment	87484			Stalag XII A, Stalag IV B
Thatcher	Laurence Albion	Private	2nd Battalion, Parachute Regiment	14270226			Stalag IV B
Thelwell	Arthur	Lance Corporal	Provost Company, 1st Airborne Division	3976695			Stalag XII A, Stalag IV B, Stalag IV C
Thickens	Trevor	Gunner	1st Airlanding Brigade, Royal Signals	14319564			Stalag IV B, Stalag IV F
Thomas	Frederick George	Private	Parachute Regiment	6089619			Dulag Luft, Stalag IV B, Stalag IV C
Thomas	Frederick H G	Private	10th Battalion, Parachute Regiment	4749339	75495		Stalag XII A, Stalag IV B
Thomas	Geoffrey Ramsden	Leading Aircraftman	Light Warning Set Unit No. 6080, RAF	1009701	92596		Stalag XII A, Stalag IV B
Thomas	Jack	Private	1st Battalion, Parachute Regiment	2616730	117732	Yes	Reserve Lazarett Lingen, Stalag XI B
Thomas	John Arthur	Lance Corporal	1st Airborne Reconnaissance Squadron	7664756		Yes	Rhede hospital, Stalag XII A, Stalag IV B
Thomas	Thomas David	Lance Corporal	Royal Army Medical Corps	7402758			Stalag XII A, Stalag VIII C
Thomas	William	Lance Corporal	16th Parachute Field Ambulance, Royal Army Medical Corps	90752	89991		Stalag XII A, Stalag IV B
Thompson	Albert	Sergeant	3rd Battalion, Parachute Regiment	4802925	89546		Stalag XII A, Stalag II A
Thompson	Harold	Corporal	10th Battalion, Parachute Regiment	4372953	90421		Stalag XII A, Stalag II A
Thompson	Horace	Private	3rd Battalion, Parachute Regiment	1513648			Stalag XII A, Stalag IV B

Surname	First name	Rank	Unit	Service no.	POW no.	Questionnaire	Camps
Thompson	Harry	Private	4th Battalion, Dorset Regiment	5953745	17537		Stalag XII A, Stalag IV B
Thompson	Harry	Sapper	9th Field Company (Airborne), Royal Engineers	4858665		Yes	Enschede Hospital, Dulag Luft, Stalag XII A, Stalag VIII C
Thompson	John	Corporal	156th Battalion, Parachute Regiment	5725314	117361		Stalag XI B, Stalag VIII C, Stalag IV B, Stalag IX A
Thompson	William Robert	Driver	250th Airborne Light Company, Royal Army Service Corps	75968	91124		Stalag XII A, Stalag IV B
Thomson	John	Staff Sergeant	Glider Pilot Regiment	3194205			Stalag Luft 7, Stalag III A
Thomson	John	Private	Royal Army Medical Corps	3052830	118773	Yes	Stalag XI B
Thornley	Robert	Private	1st Battalion, Border Regiment	3598842	75560		Stalag XII A, Stalag IV B
Thornton	Cyril Williams	Private	1st Battalion, Parachute Regiment	6408334	75789		Stalag XII A, Stalag IV B
Thornton	Frederick George	Driver	1st Parachute Brigade, Royal Signals	2572006	92249		Stalag XII A, Stalag IV B
Thorpe	Russell Ambrose	Private	2nd Battalion, South Staffordshire Regiment	4914617		Yes	Stalag XII A, Stalag IV B
Thrussell	Joseph	Private	7th Battalion, King's Own Scottish Borderers Regiment	3191825			Stalag XII A, Stalag IV B, Stalag IV C
Tidball	Ronald	Private	Royal Army Medical Corps attached 1st Battalion, Parachute Regiment	14590201	294182		Stalag IV B
Tidswell	Peter James	Private	2nd Battalion, South Staffordshire Regiment	4928642	91743		Stalag XII A, Stalag IV B, Stalag IV F
Tidy	Harold	Private	3rd Battalion, Parachute Regiment	3858993			Stalag IV B
Tillotson	John Willie	Private	133rd Parachute Field Ambulance, Royal Army Medical Corps	168025	89206		Stalag XII A, Stalag IV B, Stalag IV D/Z
Timothy	John	Major	1st Battalion, Parachute Regiment	164812	530		Dulag Luft – Oberursel, Oflag XII B, Oflag VII B

Family name	Forename	Rank	Unit as given on Questionnaire	Army number	POW number	Wounded on capture?	Camps
Tims	Eric	Sergeant	3rd Battalion, Parachute Regiment	3526756			Dulag Luft, Stalag IV B
Tindale	William	Private	7th Battalion, King's Own Scottish Borderers Regiment	3194092	89484		Stalag XII A, Stalag IV B
Tingey	Aubrey Henry	Private	2nd Battalion, South Staffordshire Regiment	14695003	75848		Stalag XII A, Stalag IV B, Stalag IV G
Tipler	Jack	Sapper	9th Field Company (Airborne), Royal Engineers	1875910			Stalag IV B, Stalag IV F
Tobin	John O'Hara	Captain	Royal Army Medical Corps	263459	90863		Dulag Luft – Oberusel, Stalag XII A, Oflag 79, Stalag III C, Stalag IV A, Stalag IV D
Tobin	Montague	Staff Sergeant	Glider Pilot Regiment	7596863	76330		Stalag XII A, Stalag IV B
Tolcher	Cecil	Private	3rd Battalion, Parachute Regiment	5109776	117899	Yes	Stalag XI B
Tomblin	Bryan Alan	Sergeant	Glider Pilot Regiment	14259326	1005		Dulag Luft – Oberusel, Stalag Luft 7, Stalag III A
Tomlinson	John William	Sergeant	2nd Battalion, Parachute Regiment	3457129		Yes	Stalag XII A, Stalag XVIII C
Tonks	Jack	Sergeant	Glider Pilot Regiment	1533350			Stalag XII A, Stalag IV B
Topp	Edward	Private	Royal Army Medical Corps attached 11th Battalion, Parachute Regiment	7366381			Stalag XII A, Stalag IV B
Towler	Walter	Private	3rd Battalion, Parachute Regiment	1452410	90034		Stalag XII A, Stalag XI B
Towns	Spencer Albert	Corporal	2nd Battalion, Parachute Regiment	4035901	89439	Yes	Stalag XII A, Stalag II A

Surname	First name	Rank	Unit	Number	Number	Questionnaire	Camps
Townsend	Arthur Sidney	Private	2nd Battalion, South Staffordshire Regiment	4928172			Stalag XII A, Stalag IV B
Townsend	Reginald George	Driver	1st Airlanding Anti-Tank Battery, Royal Artillery	14260506	91712		Stalag XII A, Stalag IV B, Stalag IV C
Townsley	Arthur	Private	156th Battalion, Parachute Regiment	14632673	90526		Stalag XII A, Stalag IV B
Tracey	Daniel Edward	Private	4th Battalion, Dorset Regiment	3663292	19473		Stalag XII A, Stalag IV B, Stalag IV F
Tracy	John	Private	7th Battalion, King's Own Scottish Borderers Regiment	14205520	90686		Stalag XII A, Stalag IV B
Travers	Thomas	Lance Corporal	2nd Battalion, Parachute Regiment	14290146	91395		Stalag IV B
Travis	Geoffrey Edwards	Private	1st Battalion, Border Regiment	3783718	92124		Stalag XII A, Stalag IV B, Stalag IV C
Travis-Davison	Kenneth	Sergeant	Glider Pilot Regiment	1779501			Stalag XII A, Stalag IV B
Trayfoot	Albert John	Private	2nd Battalion, South Staffordshire Regiment	6098705			Stalag XII A, Stalag IV B, Stalag IV C
Treherne	Leslie Edward Sidley	Lieutenant	10th Battalion, Parachute Regiment	224515	91219		Stalag XII A, Dulag XII B Hadamar, Oflag 79
Trevis	John Thomas	Private	4th Battalion, Dorset Regiment	5050843	17552		Stalag XII A, Stalag IV B, Stalag IV F
Trim	Henry George	Lance Corporal	261st Field Park Company Royal Engineers	2077679	90624		Stalag XII A, Stalag IV B, Stalag IV F
Trotter	Andrew Carmochan?	Corporal	7th Battalion, King's Own Scottish Borderers Regiment	19414344	88788		Stalag XII A, Stalag XVIII C
Troughear	John Joseph	Private	1st Battalion, Border Regiment	14206269	75419		Stalag XII A, Stalag IV B
Troy	Sidney Richard	Gunner	2nd Airlanding Anti-Tank Battery, Royal Artillery	1524961	117721	Yes	Stalag XI B, Stalag III A, Stalag XI A

167

Family name	Forename	Rank	Unit as given on Questionnaire	Army number	POW number	Wounded on capture?	Camps
Trueman	Arthur	Sergeant	Glider Pilot Regiment	101997	52909	Yes	Reserve Lazarett Obermaßfeld, Reserve Lazarett Meiningen, Stalag IX C/Z
Truscott	James Sidney	Private	2nd Battalion, Parachute Regiment	5732326			Stalag IV B, Stalag IV C
Tucker	Percy Henry	Corporal	1st Battalion, Parachute Regiment	5436835	118466	Yes	Stalag XI B, Stalag VIII C, Stalag IV B
Tucker	Sidney Francis	Lance Corporal	2nd Battalion, South Staffordshire Regiment	5672376			Stalag XII A, Stalag IV B, Stalag IV D
Tuckwood	Robert George	Private	1st Battalion, Parachute Regiment	2082225			Stalag XII A, Stalag IV B, Stalag IV A
Tunningley	Adino	Sapper	9th Field Company (Airborne), Royal Engineers	2126746	91350		Stalag XII A, Stalag IV F
Turnbull	Albert	Signalman	1st Airlanding Anti-Tank Battery, Royal Artillery	14321818			Stalag XII A, Stalag IV B, Stalag IV C
Turner	Arthur	Sergeant	1st Battalion, Parachute Regiment	2612567			Stalag II A
Turner	Henry Charles	Private	10th Battalion, Parachute Regiment	14429950	75473		Stalag XII A, Stalag IV B, Stalag IV C
Turner	John Henry	Private	10th Battalion, Parachute Regiment	4126773	90517		Stalag XII A, Stalag IV B
Turner	Ronald	Sapper	9th Field Company (Airborne), Royal Engineers	2006480			Stalag XII A, Stalag IV B, Stalag IV F
Turner	Stanley Reginald	Craftsman	Royal Electrical and Mechanical Engineers	5124014	75833		Stalag XII A, Stalag IV B, Stalag IV F
Turner	William	Driver	250th Airborne Light Company, Royal Army Service Corps	11057252	91122		Stalag XII A, Stalag IV B

Turnnidge	Benjamin Basil	Private	1st Battalion, Parachute Regiment	6012580			Stalag XII A, Stalag IV B, Stalag IV A
Turrell	Leslie	Private	11th Battalion, Parachute Regiment	3770461	117767	Yes	Stalag XI B
Twort	James Alfred	Lance Corporal	3rd Battalion, Parachute Regiment	2037852			Stalag XII A, Stalag II A
Tyson	Geoffrey	Gunner	1st Airlanding Light Regiment, Royal Artillery	4390649			Stalag XII A, Stalag IV B
Underwood	Frederick Ernest	Signalman	1st Airlanding Brigade, Royal Signals	10579286	118893		Heymer Hospital, Stalag XI B, Oflag 79
Ungi	Albert	Private	16th Parachute Field Ambulance, Royal Army Medical Corps	14560365	90154		Dulag Luft, Stalag XII A, Stalag IV B, Stalag IV C
Unsworth	Joseph	Lance Corporal	1st Airborne Provost Company	19411962			Stalag XII A, Stalag IV B
Urquhart	David	Sergeant, Lance	1st Parachute Squadron, Royal Engineers	2136258	89621		Stalag XII A, Stalag II A
Urquhart	James Alex	Staff Sergeant	Glider Pilot Regiment	5185152			Dulag Luft – Oberusel, Stalag Luft 7, Stalag III A
Vale	Edwin John	Private	2nd Battalion, Parachute Regiment	13026704			Stalag XII A, Stalag IV B
Vardy	Harold	Private	2nd Battalion, Parachute Regiment	4747822	89909		Stalag XII A, Stalag XI B
Varney	Charles Norman	Bombardier	Royal Artillery	14311471	117328		Stalag XI B, Stalag VIII C, Stalag XI B
Vaugan	Thomas	Signalman	4th Parachute Brigade, Royal Signals	4034124	90845		Stalag XII A, Stalag VIII C, Stalag VIII A, Stalag IV C
Vaughan	Peter	Trooper	1st Airborne Reconnaissance Squadron	13116352	75803	Yes	Stalag XII A, Dulag Luft – Oberusel, Dulag Luft – Wetzlar, Stalag III D, Reserve Lazarett 119 Neuköln

Family name	Forename	Rank	Unit as given on Questionnaire	Army number	POW number	Wounded on capture?	Camps
Vaughan	Thomas Charles	Private	2nd Battalion, South Staffordshire Regiment	4928042	93418		Stalag XII A, , Stalag VIII C, Stalag XI B
Veal	Robert William	Private	4th Battalion, Dorset Regiment	14441359			Stalag IV B, Stalag IV F
Vernon	Stanley	Lance Corporal	2nd Battalion, Parachute Regiment	1427411			Stalag IV B
Verrall	Cyril Albert Douglas	Private	1st Battalion, Border Regiment	7023138	75483		Stalag XII A, Stalag IV B
Vick	Arthur James	Sergeant, Lance	7th Battalion, King's Own Scottish Borderers Regiment	4750885	89592		Stalag XII A, Stalag II A
Vincent	Stanley Maurice	Private	2nd Battalion, Parachute Regiment	549942			Stalag IV B
Vine	James	Private	1st Battalion, Border Regiment	3771185			Stalag IV B, Stalag IV D
Vooght	Leslie John	Lance Corporal	2nd Battalion, Parachute Regiment	6402898			Stalag XII A, Stalag IV B
Vowles	Frederick Harry	Private	10th Battalion, Parachute Regiment	53337249	75677		Stalag XII A, Stalag IV B
Wade	Richard Samuel	Staff Sergeant	Glider Pilot Regiment	6969360	117350	Yes	Stalag XI B, Stalag VIII C, Stalag IV B
Wadling	Ronald Francis	Private	2nd Battalion, South Staffordshire Regiment	5631222	118222	Yes	Stalag XI B, Stalag III A, Stalag XI A
Wagstaff	Jack	Private	2nd Battalion, South Staffordshire Regiment	4955931	89186		Stalag XII A, Stalag IV B
Wainright	Lawrence	Lance Corporal	2nd Battalion, Parachute Regiment	5783535			Stalag IV D
Wake	Lewis James	Lance Corporal	4th Battalion, Dorset Regiment	5725542	99899		Stalag XII A, Stalag IV B

Surname	First name	Rank	Unit	Number	Number 2	Q	Camps
Walker-Cook	Alfred	Staff Sergeant	Army Physical Training Corps	4689266		Yes	Stalag XII A, Stalag II A
Wallace	Samuel	Private	1st Battalion, Border Regiment	14671726	24363		Stalag XII A, Stalag IV B, Stalag IV D
Wallis	Stanley Percival	Private	1st Battalion, Parachute Regiment	14565828			Dulag Luft, Stalag XII A, Stalag IV B, Stalag IV F
Wallis	William	Sergeant	3rd Battalion, Parachute Regiment	5048129			Stalag XII A, Stalag XVIII C
Walpole	Robert Holland	Lieutenant	1st Parachute Squadron, Royal Engineers	299883	570		Dulag XII B Hadamar, Oflag 79
Walsh	Richard	Private	2nd Battalion, Parachute Regiment	6409551			Lochem Hospital, Dulag Luft, Stalag XII A, Stalag IV B
Walsh	William Marston	Driver	1st Parachute Brigade	3975544			Stalag XII A, Stalag IV B, Stalag IV F
Walters	Ernest Frederick	Lieutenant	2nd Battalion, South Staffordshire Regiment	247035	625		Stalag XII A, Dulag XII B Hadamar, Oflag 79
Walton	Frank Thomas	Private	1st Battalion, Parachute Regiment	6015864			Dulag Luft – Wetzlar, Stalag XII A, Stalag VIII C, Stalag VIII A, Stalag IV C
Ward	Cyril Thomas James	Driver	253rd Airborne Light Company, Royal Army Service Corps	191887	91660		Stalag XII A, Stalag IV B
Ward	Douglas Edward Newman	Staff Sergeant	Glider Pilot Regiment	1878308		Yes	Stalag XII A, Stalag IV B
Ward	Frederick Ernest	Private	4th Battalion, Dorset Regiment	5959729	17577		Stalag XII A, Stalag IV B
Ward	Jack	Corporal	10th Battalion, Parachute Regiment	4122698			Stalag IV B
Ward	Kenneth Alan	Private	2nd Battalion, Parachute Regiment	14401199	90990		Stalag XII A, Stalag IV B, Stalag IV C

Family name	Forename	Rank	Unit as given on Questionnaire	Army number	POW number	Wounded on capture?	Camps
Ward	Raymond John	Staff Sergeant	Glider Pilot Regiment	961033	117493		Stalag XI B, Stalag VIII C, Stalag IV B
Ward	William Edward	Private	10th Battalion, Parachute Regiment	6026817			Stalag XII A, Stalag IV B
Wardle	George Henry	Private	181st Airlanding Field Ambulance, Royal Army Medical Corps	7399634	77376		Stalag XII A, Stalag IV B
Wardle	Harry	Private	2nd Battalion, South Staffordshire Regiment	14386178	92096		Stalag XII A, Stalag IV A
Wareham	James Anthony	Signalman	1st Parachute Brigade, Royal Signals	14650390	90046	Yes	Stalag XII A, Stalag IV B, Stalag IV F
Warren	Ernest Edward	Corporal	1st Parachute Brigade	2736584			Stalag XII A, Stalag XVIII C
Warren	Horace	Driver	1st Airlanding Light Regiment, Royal Artillery	797724	118215		Apeldoorn Hospital, Stalag XI B
Warren	Hector George	Corporal	2nd Battalion, Parachute Regiment	5836132	117205		Stalag XI B
Warren	James William Sidney	Private	156th Battalion, Parachute Regiment	5826438			Stalag XII A, Stalag IV B
Warrender	Alfred George	Private	2nd Airlanding Anti-Tank Battery, Royal Artillery	1469862		Yes	Reserve Lazarett Lochem, Stalag IV B, Reserve Lazarett H57 Hohenstein, Stalag IV F
Warrener	Reginald	Private	1st Battalion, Border Regiment	4279142			Stalag XII A, Stalag IV B
Warwick	Herbert	Private	156th Battalion, Parachute Regiment	3448671			Stalag XII A, Stalag IV B, Stalag IV D

Surname	Forename	Rank	Regiment	Number	Number	Camps
Washer	Kenneth Edwin	Trooper	1st Airborne Reconnaissance Squadron	14370214	75816	Stalag XII A, Stalag IV B, Stalag XIII B
Wassell	Douglas	Driver	800th Company Air Despatch Royal Army Service Corps	407727	117432	Stalag XI B
Waters	John	Gunner	1st Airlanding Light Regiment, Royal Artillery	14311629	75333	Stalag XII A, Stalag IV B
Watkins	Herbert	Staff Sergeant	Glider Pilot Regiment	3660659		Stalag Luft 7, Stalag III A
Watkinson	Charles Rollett	Staff Sergeant	Glider Pilot Regiment	809931		Dulag Luft – Oberusel, Stalag Luft 7, Stalag III A
Watson	Charles Garth	Sergeant	Glider Pilot Regiment	1591231		Stalag Luft 7, Stalag III A
Watson	Frank Campbell	Sergeant	Glider Pilot Regiment	2082989	15256	Stalag XIII D, Stalag Luft 7, Stalag III A
Watson	Horace Richard	Private	Army Catering Corps	1712902	91708	Stalag XII A, Stalag IV C
Watson	John	Private	7th Battalion, King's Own Scottish Borderers Regiment	14327664		Stalag XII A, Stalag IV B
Watson	John Leslie	Private	2nd Battalion, South Staffordshire Regiment	14573619	90414	Stalag XII A, Stalag 357
Watson	Raymond	Private	3rd Battalion, Parachute Regiment	11425065		Stalag XII A, Stalag XI B
Watson	Thomas	Private	1st Battalion, Border Regiment	3533468	75696	Stalag XII A, Stalag IV B, Stalag IV F
Watson	William Alexander	Corporal	1st Airborne Reconnaissance Squadron	10603591	89835	Stalag XII A, Stalag II A
Watt	William	Private	1st Battalion, Parachute Regiment	923891	118445	Stalag XI B
Watton	Norman Ralph	Private	2nd Battalion, South Staffordshire Regiment	14265948	91508	Stalag XII A, Stalag IV C
Watts	James Percival	Private	2nd Battalion, Parachute Regiment	2061552		Stalag XII A, Stalag IV B, Stalag IV C

Family name	Forename	Rank	Unit as given on Questionnaire	Army number	POW number	Wounded on capture?	Camps
Wayte	Frederick John	Lance Corporal	3rd Battalion, Parachute Regiment	5890044			Dulag Luft, Stalag IV B
Weallans	Arthur Edward	Sergeant	11th Battalion, Parachute Regiment	2660102			Stalag II A, Stalag II E
Weatherburn	Eric	Private	4th Battalion, Dorset Regiment	3780290	14985		Stalag IV B
Weaver	Raymond Ernest	Driver	93rd Company, Royal Army Service Corps	14368841			Stalag XII A, Stalag IV B
Webb	Alan Kenneth	Private	1st Battalion, Border Regiment	14424829	91622		Stalag XII A, Stalag IV B, Stalag IV A
Webb	Arthur Stanley	Private	181st Airlanding Field Ambulance, Royal Army Medical Corps	7387237	77358		Stalag XII A, Stalag IV B
Webb	Charles	Private	11th Battalion, Parachute Regiment	11001276	117762	Yes	Stalag XI B, Stalag III A, Stalag XI A
Webb	Maurice William	Private	2nd Battalion, Parachute Regiment	5392996			Stalag XII A, Stalag IV B, Stalag IV F
Webb	Norman Harold	Lance Corporal	2nd Battalion, Parachute Regiment	5391635			Stalag XII A, Stalag VII C
Webber	Daniel Robert Wynham	Major	11th Battalion, Parachute Regiment	63580	552		Dulag XII B Hadamar, Oflag 79
Wedgbury	Albert Edward	Private	2nd Battalion, South Staffordshire Regiment	4039812	75936		Stalag XII A, Stalag IV B
Weiland	Douglas	Lance Corporal	156th Battalion, Parachute Regiment	6896313			Stalag XII A, Stalag IV B, Stalag IV D, Stalag IV F
Welch	William Gordon	Captain	1st Battalion, Border Regiment	132473	2186		Apeldoorn Hospital, Oflag IX A/Z

Surname	First name	Rank	Unit	Number	POW no.	Questionnaire	Camps
Welham	Hubert Edward	Lance Corporal	1st Airborne Reconnaissance Squadron	6854308			Lochem Hospital, Stalag XII A, Stalag IV B, Stalag IV G
Wellington	William	Private	7th Battalion, King's Own Scottish Borderers Regiment	4622033	91769		Stalag IV C
Wells	Joseph	Private	4th Battalion, Dorset Regiment	14631903	14221		Stalag IV B
Welsh	James	Driver	800th Company Air Despatch, Royal Army Service Corps	11251580	91794	Yes	Stalag XII A, Stalag IV B, Stalag IV C
Wesson	Harry	Private	2nd Battalion, South Staffordshire Regiment	14660102	91753		Stalag XII A, Stalag IV B, Stalag IV F
West	George	Corporal	11th Battalion, Parachute Regiment	4460064			Stalag XII A, Stalag II A
West	Percy	Private	156th Battalion, Parachute Regiment	558672			Stalag XII A, Stalag IV B, Stalag IV F
West	William Samuel	Private	1st Battalion, Parachute Regiment	10582814	118148	Yes	Stalag XI B
Wetherall	John Aubrey Bruce	Sergeant	Glider Pilot Regiment	14414511	1087		Dulag Luft, Stalag Luft 7, Reserve Lazarett 344, Stalag 383
Wetherall		Private	2nd Battalion, South Staffordshire Regiment	14334858	90347		Stalag XII A, Stalag XI B
Whadcoat	Ernest Frederick	Private	10th Battalion, Parachute Regiment	6351604			Stalag XII A, Stalag IV D
Whaites	Albert George	Signalman	Royal Signals	14264165	91554		Stalag XII A, Stalag IV C
Whalley	Walter	Lance Corporal	Advanced Workshop Detachment, Royal Electrical and Mechanical Engineers	5950306	75041		Stalag XII A, Stalag IV F
Wharam	Denis	Driver	250th Airborne Light Company, Royal Army Service Corps	268832	75385		Stalag XII A, Stalag IV B

Family name	Forename	Rank	Unit as given on Questionnaire	Army number	POW number	Wounded on capture?	Camps
Whatmore	Reginald	Private	2nd Battalion, Parachute Regiment	5110657			Stalag XII A, Stalag IV B, Stalag IV C
Wheeler	Henry	Private	3rd Battalion, Parachute Regiment	6089379	91565		Stalag XII A, Stalag IV B, Stalag IV D
Wheeler	Leonard Ernest	Sergeant	2nd Battalion, South Staffordshire Regiment	7014846	117552	Yes	Stalag XI B, Stalag VIII C, Stalag III E
Wheeler	William	Lance Corporal	1st Battalion, Border Regiment	4693666	91950		Stalag XII A, Stalag IV B
Whelan	John James	Private	156th Battalion, Parachute Regiment	14436631			Stalag XII A, Stalag IV B
Wheldon	Roland Alfred	Staff Sergeant	Glider Pilot Regiment	3715219			Dulag Luft – Oberusel, Stalag Luft 7, Stalag III A
Whippy	John Walter	Sergeant	Glider Pilot Regiment	2044661			Dulag Luft – Oberusel, Stalag Luft 7, Stalag III A
White	Bernard	Private	1st Battalion, Border Regiment	4547299	117501	Yes	Stalag XI B
White	George	Regimental Sergeant Major	10th Battalion, Parachute Regiment	4387779		Yes	Stalag XII A, Stalag XVIII C
White	Kenneth Grayston	Lieutenant	1st Airlanding Light Regiment, Royal Artillery	258890	2200		St Elizabeth's Hospital, Apeldoorn Hospital, Stalag XI B, Oflag IX A/Z
White	Kenneth James	Sergeant	Glider Pilot Regiment	1891554	140212	Yes	Reserve Lazarett Freising, Stalag VII A
White	Leslie Philip	Lance Corporal	Royal Army Service Corps	276402	90997		Stalag XII A, Stalag IV B, Stalag IV C
White	Wilfred	Private	1st Battalion, Border Regiment	4467262	92004		Stalag XII A, Stalag IV D
Whitlock	Sydney Edward	Private	11th Battalion, Parachute Regiment	231982	91309		Stalag XII A, Stalag IV B, Stalag IV A

Surname	First name(s)	Rank	Unit	Service No.	No.	Q	Camps
Whittaker	James	Lance Corporal	4th Battalion, Dorset Regiment	4271899	17582		Stalag XII A, Stalag IV B
Whittaker	Solomon	Private	2nd Battalion, South Staffordshire Regiment	4914442	92098		Stalag IV B
Whittaker	Stanley James	Private	4th Parachute Brigade	14618322			Stalag XII A, Stalag IV B, Stalag IV C
Whittaker	Thomas	Private	10th Battalion, Parachute Regiment	3655345			Stalag IV B
Whittam	Albert	Gunner	1st Airlanding Light Regiment, Royal Artillery	1791277	118695		Stalag XI B
Whyatt	Norman	Lance Corporal	1st Battalion, Parachute Regiment	5504900	92150		Stalag XII A, Stalag IV B
Widdowson	George	Major	10th Battalion, Parachute Regiment	49397	91001		Dulag XII B Hadamar, Dulag Luft, Oflag VII B, Stalag VII A
Widdowson	Herbert	Lance Corporal	2nd Battalion, South Staffordshire Regiment	5050919			Stalag XII A, Stalag IV B
Wiedericks	Benjamin James	Private	156th Battalion, Parachute Regiment	2766217			Stalag XII A, Stalag IV A
Wild	John Richard Wilcock	Sergeant	Glider Pilot Regiment	14428935	76319		Stalag XII A, Stalag IV B
Wilde	Cyril	Private	3rd Battalion, Parachute Regiment	14207950	75585		Stalag XII A, Stalag IV B
Wilde	Jack	Private	2nd Battalion, South Staffordshire Regiment	14682977	89140		Stalag XII A, Stalag XI B
Wilder	Leslie Maurice	Lance Corporal	1st Parachute Brigade, Royal Signals	2583200			Stalag XII A, Stalag IV G
Wilding	Albert Geoffrey	Signalman	Royal Signals	5125376	91668		Stalag XII A, Stalag IV C
Wildman	John Alfred	Private	1st Battalion, Parachute Regiment	14227447	140242	Yes	Arnhem Hospital Friesing (sic?), Stalag VII A

Family name	Forename	Rank	Unit as given on Questionnaire	Army number	POW number	Wounded on capture?	Camps
Wilkinson	Richard	Sergeant, Lance	3rd Battalion, Parachute Regiment	408654		Yes	Stalag II A
Willcock	Douglas Brian	Lieutenant	156th Battalion, Parachute Regiment	176224	76777		Oflag XII B, Oflag VII B
Willcocks	Arthur Hambly	Captain	2nd Battalion, South Staffordshire Regiment	187080	544		Oflag XII B, Oflag 79
Willett	Lewis Alfred	Driver	250th Airborne Light Company, Royal Army Service Corps	64737			Stalag XII A, Stalag IV B
Williams	Arthur	Private	2nd Battalion, South Staffordshire Regiment	14389591	92044		Stalag XII A, Stalag IV B, Stalag IV C
Williams	Arthur Morley	Sergeant	Glider Pilot Regiment	4208939			Stalag XII A, Stalag IV B
Williams	Dennis Harold	Private	7th Battalion, King's Own Scottish Borderers Regiment	14313606	140068		St Elizabeth's Hospital, Alemelo, Stalag VII A
Williams	David Meredith	Private	10th Battalion, Parachute Regiment	14219148	52884		Apeldoorn Hospital, Reserve Lazarett Obermaßfeld, Stalag IX C/Z
Williams	Jeffrey Arthur James	Trooper	1st Airborne Reconnaissance Squadron	14208949	117735	Yes	Stalag XI B, Stalag III A, Stalag XI A, Stalag IV B
Williams	Kenneth	Private	2nd Battalion, South Staffordshire Regiment	5829632	89601		Stalag XII A, Stalag IV B, Stalag IV C
Williams	Mervyn Lionel	Private	156th Battalion, Parachute Regiment	14664091			Stalag XII A, Stalag IV B, Stalag IV F
Williamson	John	Private	1st Battalion, Parachute Regiment	14251983	140072		Arnhem Hospital, Stalag VII A, Augsburgh, Ettringen

Surname	Forename	Rank	Unit	Number	Number 2	Questionnaire	Camps
Williamson	Robert Hugh	Private	1st Battalion, Border Regiment	3596704	75948		Stalag XII A, Stalag IV (B?)
Willis	Jack	Private	3rd Battalion, Parachute Regiment	843584			Stalag XII A, Stalag IV C
Willoughby	Bryan	Private	1st Battalion, Parachute Regiment	5679967	140110	Yes	Hospital Holland - Unspecified, Stalag VII A hospital
Willoughby	Leslie	Private	3rd Battalion, Parachute Regiment	4466448			Stalag IV B, Reserve Lazarett Bilin
Willoughby	Norman	Private	1st Parachute Brigade HQ	4699350	75162		Stalag XII A, Stalag IV B
Wilmot	Harold Francis Thomas	Staff Sergeant	Glider Pilot Regiment	7016404			Stalag XII A, Stalag IV B
Wilson	Alexander Outridge	Private	10th Battalion, Parachute Regiment	5873605			Stalag XII A, Stalag IV B, Stalag IV C
Wilson	Baldwin	Captain	1st Battalion, Border Regiment	182276	2192		Oflag IX A/Z
Wilson	Clement John	Sapper	9th Ind Company Royal Engineers	1896106	81179	Yes	Arnhem Hospital, Stalag XII A, Stalag IV F
Wilson	Ernest	Private	2nd Battalion, South Staffordshire Regiment	4919216			Stalag XII A, Stalag IV B, Stalag IV D
Wilson	John	Private	21st Independent Parachute Company	14551208	91672		Stalag XII A, Stalag IV B, Stalag IV C
Wilson	James Archibald	Sergeant	Glider Pilot Regiment	3247627			Stalag XII A, Stalag IV B
Wilson	Joseph Leonard	Sergeant	Glider Pilot Regiment	1675969			Dulag Luft, Stalag Luft 7, Stalag III A
Wilson	James McWhirter	Private	7th Battalion, King's Own Scottish Borderers Regiment	3131140			Stalag XII A, Stalag IV B
Wilson	Kenneth	Corporal	16th Parachute Field Ambulance, Royal Army Medical Corps	7263793		Yes	Stalag XII A, Stalag II A
Wilson	Rayment John	Sergeant	Glider Pilot Regiment	7366948			Dulag Luft – Oberusel, Stalag Luft 7, Stalag III A

Family name	Forename	Rank	Unit as given on Questionnaire	Army number	POW number	Wounded on capture?	Camps
Wilson	Thomas Alan	Private	1st Battalion, Parachute Regiment	7366147	89418		Stalag XII A, Stalag IV B
Wilson	Thomas Frederick	Corporal	1st Parachute Brigade, Royal Signals	2583477			Stalag XII A, Stalag II A
Wilson	William Herbert	Sapper	9th Field Company (Airborne), Royal Engineers	6461773	118897		Apeldoorn Hospital, Stalag XI B, Oflag 79
Wiltshire	Reginald William	Lance Corporal	4th Parachute Brigade HQ	7349096			Stalag XII A, Stalag IV B
Windsor	Ronald	Gunner	Forward Observation Unit, Royal Artillery	14261766			Stalag XII A, Dulag Luft, Stalag VIII C, Stalag IV C
Wink	John	Private	7th Battalion, King's Own Scottish Borderers Regiment	14554656			Stalag XII A, Stalag IV B, Stalag IV D
Winslow	Jack Robert	Lance Corporal	156th Battalion, Parachute Regiment	6896410			Stalag XII A, Stalag XVIII C
Winter	Victor Norman	Private	181st Airlanding Field Ambulance, Royal Army Medical Corps	7370800	140060		Stalag VII A
Winterbottom	Leslie	Private	3rd Battalion, Parachute Regiment	14218354			Stalag IV B
Wise	Ernest Leslie	Private	3rd Battalion, Parachute Regiment	870497			Stalag XII A, Stalag IV B, Stalag IV C
Wise	Thomas James	Private	2nd Battalion, South Staffordshire Regiment	4928047	91742		Stalag XII A, Stalag IV B, Stalag IV C
Witham	Cornelius Robert	Private	11th Battalion, Parachute Regiment	14411380	118537		Stalag XI B
Withey	Leslie George	Lance Corporal	250th Airborne Light Company, Royal Army Service Corps	277631	14201		Stalag XII A, Stalag IV B, Stalag IV A
Withnall	Patrick Brereton	Staff Sergeant	Glider Pilot Regiment	2332442			Stalag XII A, Dulag Luft, Salag Luft 7, Stalag III A

Surname	First name	Rank	Regiment	Number	Number		Camps
Withmall	William Charles	Lieutenant	2nd Battalion, South Staffordshire Regiment	5050853	548		Dulag of Oflag XII B, Oflag 79
Witty	Thomas Alfred	Private	7th Battalion, King's Own Scottish Borderers Regiment	4540232	75958		Stalag XII A, Stalag IV B, Stalag IV F
Wood	Albert Edward	Private	156th Battalion, Parachute Regiment	5672565			Stalag IV B
Wood	Alfred Robert	Private	3rd Battalion, Parachute Regiment	1498245			Stalag XII A, Stalag IV B
Wood	David	Private	2nd Battalion, South Staffordshire Regiment	4928653	118699	Yes	Stalag XI B
Wood	Ernest	Private	1st Battalion, Border Regiment	3603488	93263		Stalag XII A, Stalag IV B, Stalag IV C
Wood	Ernest John	Private	1st Battalion, Border Regiment	14671738	26084		Stalag XII A, Stalag IV B, Stalag IV G
Wood	Harold George	Corporal	2nd Battalion, Parachute Regiment	6350557			Stalag VIII C, Stalag IV B
Wood	Joseph	Private	1st Battalion, Parachute Regiment	1440598	117745	Yes	Stalag XI B, Stalag III A, Stalag XI A
Wood	Jack	Private	2nd Battalion, South Staffordshire Regiment	4914111			Stalag XII A, Stalag IX B
Woodard	Ronald Alan George	Private	156th Battalion, Parachute Regiment	5826728			Stalag XII A, Stalag IV B, Stalag IV C
Woodhouse	Francis	Lance Bombardier	1st Airlanding Light Regiment, Royal Artillery	14249662	52921		Apeldoorn Hospital, Reserve Lazarett Obermaßfeld, Stalag IX C
Woodland	Alfred Arthur	Private	4th Battalion, Dorset Regiment	6150553	26069		Stalag XII A, Stalag IV B, Stalag IV A
Woodmansey	Frederick	Sergeant	10th Battalion, Parachute Regiment	4537265		Yes	Stalag II D
Woods	Kenneth	Driver	253rd Airborne Light Company, Royal Army Service Corps	10683067			Stalag XII A, Stalag IV B
Woods	Leslie Harold	Corporal	2nd Battalion, Parachute Regiment	5949111			Stalag IV B

181

Family name	Forename	Rank	Unit as given on Questionnaire	Army number	POW number	Wounded on capture?	Camps
Woodward	Robert Lisle	Private	156th Battalion, Parachute Regiment	3711157			Stalag XII A, Stalag IV B, Stalag IV F
Woolford	Stanley Benjiman	Driver	Royal Artillery	11050415			Stalag XII A, Stalag IV B
Woolrich	Herbert	Driver	4th Parachute Brigade, Royal Signals	10698347	90741		Stalag XII A, Stalag IV B, Stalag IV A
Worrall	James Ambrose	Private	2nd Battalion, Parachute Regiment	5835036	91659		Dulag Luft, Stalag XII A, Stalag IV B, Stalag IV G
Worsfold	Gerald Percy	Private	7th Battalion, King's Own Scottish Borderers Regiment	14440258	91478		Stalag XII A, Stalag VIII C, Stalag VIII A, Stalag IV C
Wren	Jack Francis	Private	2nd Battalion, Parachute Regiment	6853864	75337		Stalag XII A, Stalag IV B
Wright	David	Captain	1st Parachute Brigade HQ	218952	571		Dulag XII B Hadamar, Oflag 79
Wright	Gerald Arthur	Private	3rd Battalion, Parachute Regiment	6346044	91484		Stalag XII A, Stalag IV B, Stalag IV C
Wright	James Holt	Sapper	1st Parachute Squadron, Royal Engineers	2182781	91493		Dulag Luft – Wetzlar, Stalag XII A, Stalag IV B
Wright	Leslie Edward	Private	Royal Army Ordnance Corps	14655624	118678	Yes	Apeldoorn Hospital, Stalag XI B, Stalag II D
Wright	Leonard William	Lieutenant	3rd Battalion, Parachute Regiment	276874	90944	Yes	Dulag Luft – Oberusel, Stalag XII A, Dulag XII B Hadamar, Oflag 79
Wright	Stanley Winston	SergeantMajor	2nd Battalion, South Staffordshire Regiment	4913782		Yes	Stalag XII A, Stalag VIII C, Stalag XI ?
Wrighton	Raymond Bernard	Private	1st Battalion, Border Regiment	14595060			Stalag XII A, Stalag IV B, Stalag IV F

Surname	First name(s)	Rank	Unit	Number	Number	Questionnaire	Camps
Wyard	Raymond Russell	Private	156th Battalion, Parachute Regiment	7344919			Stalag XII A, Stalag IV B
Wyke	Peter	Private	10th Battalion, Parachute Regiment	14219746	75336		Stalag XII A, Stalag IV B, Stalag IV F
Yarman	Andrew	Private	1st Battalion, Border Regiment	3597286	75659		Stalag XII A, Stalag IV B
Yates	Dewar Galloway	Private	7th Battalion, King's Own Scottish Borderers Regiment	14211034	118414	Yes	Stalag XI B
Young	Graham Ferguson	Leading Aircraftman	Light Warning Set Unit No. 6341, RAF	971682		Yes	Hospital nr Arnhem, Utrecht Hospital, Reserve Lazarett Burgsteinfurt, Reserve Lazarett Rottenmunster, Dulag Luft – Oberusel, Dulag Luft – Wetzlar
Young	John	Private	7th Battalion, King's Own Scottish Borderers Regiment	3192130	75941		Stalag XII A, Stalag IV B, Stalag IV F
Young	John James	Private	1st Battalion, Border Regiment	4547346	91971	Yes	Stalag XII A, Stalag IV B, Stalag IV A
Young	James Walker	Lance Corporal	Royal Army Service Corps	220847	14097	Yes	Arnhem Hospital, Apeldoorn Hospital, Stalag VII A, Stalag 383, Stalag VII A
Young	William Gibb	Private	7th Battalion, King's Own Scottish Borderers Regiment	3190173	117451	Yes	Stalag XI B, Stalag III A, Stalag XI A
Younger	John Charles	Private	2nd Battalion, South Staffordshire Regiment	4913643	89465		Stalag XII A, Stalag IV C
Youngman	Ronald	Lance Corporal	2nd Battalion, Parachute Regiment	6354216	75338		Stalag XII A, Stalag IV B

Chapter 2

Becoming a POW

Preparation

Training in how to respond to being taken prisoner had been part of the British Army's procedures from the start of the war. The fundamental was that men should give their captors only their name, rank and army number. This was enshrined in the Geneva Convention that Britain and Germany had signed.

The training covered responding to interrogation, and, as the war progressed, evasion. The trainers could be unit officers, the intelligence officer or platoon commander, an MI9 officer or a successful escaper as part of a programme organized by MI9. Capture training is recorded by two-thirds of the questionnaires, while evader training is recorded by just over half, 1,239.

The capture training included a film *Name, rank and number*, that showed new POWs being interrogated by the Germans and giving away information through answering apparently innocuous questions. Since the training included a film, cinemas were a favourite location for training sessions. In Grantham this was the slightly confusingly called State Cinema. It was not government-owned; State was its name. The film was supported by lectures:

> Private Gilbert Braithwaite, 2nd Battalion, South Staffordshire Regiment, 'Film and lecture by Coy Commander, England 1944.'

Capture and evasion training could be used to fill in a blank space in the regimental timetable. And not necessarily in the UK:

> Corporal Edward Brooks, 156th Battalion, Parachute Regiment, 'On the boat from Italy [by] an escaped officer.'

Surprisingly, one man credits the Germans. Presumably Private Farrell meant the camp leader of the POWs, the Man of Confidence:

> Private Alexander Farrell, 7th Battalion, King's Own Scottish Borderers, 'Dresden camp commandant.'

British policy was to encourage escape and men were taught that the best time to do so was as soon after being captured as possible. Escape aids, maps and money were issued, though some were not impressed:

> Staff Sergeant John Stead, Glider Pilot Regiment, 'Attempted escape immediately after capture was rendered difficult due the enemy knowing all our escape aids and the fact that the RAF issued us with French escape packet and money when it was known we were to land in Holland.'

Or this comment on the other escape aids:

> Private William Parry, 16th Parachute Field Ambulance, 'I consider that material given to us before the operation for escape purposes was not very satisfactory. I have tried the hacksaw blade on barbed wire & it was US [unserviceable].'

Once captured it was difficult to retain the escape materials issued before the operation:

> Herbert Laing, 21st Independent Parachute Company, 'At Apeldoorn hospital still being in possession of escape material we were ordered by the R.A.M.C. RSM of the block to hand in all escape kit. He said the Germans were about to search and if anyone was found with such kit reprisals would be taken on the seriously wounded.'

The failed attempt to reinforce the Oosterbeek perimeter at the end of the operation led to men from 4th Battalion, Dorset Regiment, being captured. Their questionnaires allow a comparison to be made between the training given to airborne troops, who were likely to be landed behind enemy lines and therefore were at greater risk of capture than ordinary infantry.

Of the forty-eight Dorset questionnaires, only two men record evasion training, but twenty-two (45 per cent record capture training). The comparable figures for 1st Battalion, Border Regiment (Airlanding), were recorded sixteen evasion training (10 per cent) and ninety-eight (64 per cent) for capture training, and for 1st Battalion, Parachute Regiment, twenty-five evasion (19 per cent) and ninety-four (73 per cent) capture. Although the Dorset's questionnaires are a very small sample, it suggests that airborne troops received more training in evasion and how to handle being captured.

Information from Prisoners

The Geneva Convention required that new prisoners be recorded and the information passed by the International Red Cross to the home authorities. This meant prisoners were interrogated, but the Germans had other priorities. Answers to questions about the enemies' units, their weapons and their objectives were always useful, but by late 1944 the Germans had a need for another type of information: the economic situation in Britain and the political attitudes of the Allies. Any snippets that might inform, or better still support, the policy of splitting the Allies and forging a new anti-Soviet alliance with Germany, which, many senior members of the Nazi Party now believed, was the only way to salvage something from the war.

CAPTURED AT ARNHEM

The American journalist Edward Beattie[3] was captured a month before Market Garden and, because he had been a correspondent in Germany in 1940, was considered a significant prisoner. He was interviewed by a senior member of the Party, who told Beattie that:

> German military policy during this critical period aims frankly at playing for time and a split between Russia and the Western powers. Such a split, the Nazis hope, would open the way for the compromise peace which is their only hope.

Managing their Prisoners

Airborne troops might be captured behind the front line and there was the possibility that these men might not be soldiers but saboteurs or spies. As such, they would have been the responsibility of the Gestapo and did not fall within the terms of the Geneva Convention. The threat of handing men over to the Gestapo was one used when would-be escapers were captured.

Captain Charles Noble, 133rd Parachute Field Ambulance, discovered that it was no mere threat. He was an evader who had escaped from the Apeldoorn hospital and was with the Dutch underground when recaptured. He was eventually transferred to the POW system at Fallingbostel:

> Captain Charles Noble, 133rd Parachute Field Ambulance, 'Arnhem, (Velp, 1st Parachute Div, Counter Intelligence). Gestapo Prison in Utrecht and Doetinchem (Holland). Methods: Prolonged questioning. Threatening.'

The Geneva Convention required that captives be managed by the equivalent troops of the capturing power. Since all German airborne troops formed part of the Luftwaffe, it was the air force that had experience of airborne warfare and, therefore, they had the expertise and responsibility for interrogating new airborne prisoners. However, as members of the British Army, they were the German Army's responsibility. The High Command of the German Armed Forces ruled on the position of Allied airborne prisoners:[4]

> Paratroopers, airborne and anti-aircraft troops in the British and American armed forces are part of the army, not the air force. Prisoners of war from these branches of service are not to be counted as Air Force prisoners of war as specified in 'Regulations about the prisoners of war' from 05.30.1943 No. 2000 43g. They are therefore not to be held in Air Force camps, but in those of the OKW. Their use as a workforce follows

---

3   Beattie, Edward W., *Diary of a Kriegie*, Thomas Crowell Company, 1946.
4   BA-MA RW 6/270,15/1/44 OKW Az. 2 f 24.11 a Kreigsgefangen Org. (1) Nr. 5607/43. Britsche und amerikanischen Fallschirmjäger, Luftlandtruppen und Flaksoldaten, in Vourkoutiotis, V., *The Prisoners of War and German High Command*, Palgrave, 2003.

the current guidelines on POWs in accordance with their nationality. Paratroopers are only to be employed under special supervision.

Since in the German armed forces, these types of prisoners would be part of the air force, their interrogation for intelligence gathering purposes is the responsibility of the Air Force.

Newly captured British and American paratroopers, airborne troops and members of anti-aircraft units should be sent to the air force reception camp, Dulag Luft West at Oberursel, for questioning in small groups (up to a total of 20 prisoners). For groups of over 20 prisoners, Oberursel West should be consulted on whether the prisoners of war are to be transferred to Oberursel or whether an interrogation unit should be sent to the capture area.

After questioning, the POW will be transferred to OKW POW camps.

Arnhem POWs were routinely employed by the Germans and there is no evidence that they were under special supervision. At least one Luftwaffe interrogator failed to follow orders:

> Private John Hatley, 156th Battalion, Parachute Regiment, 'Luftwaffe officer at Stalag XII A. I was informed that it was only a routine statement that was being taken in order to ascertain whether I belonged to an A/B Div so that he could be sent to a Stalag Luft.'

One man recorded remaining close to the battlefield and being used to help the Germans remove Dutch equipment and property:

> Staff Sergeant Walter Ramsbottom, Glider Pilot Regiment, 'In direct contravention of the Geneva Convention I was put in charge of a working party of 75 men of the 1st British Airborne Division in the front line i.e. Arnheim, from 26.9.44 – 9.10.44 approx. for the purpose of stripping Dutch factories and railway yards e.g. one dynamo factory and one extremely large boot and shoe factory.'

The OKW camps were maintained by the army (Heer), with guards provided by the Ersatzheer (Reserve Army) from the Wehrkreis (military district) where they were located. Specialist camp staff were provided by other parts of the German military. Until the middle of the war OKW camps were identified by the number of the Wehrkreis on which they were located. But camps created later had Arabic numerals.

Captured aircrew were held in Luftwaffe camps, Stalag Lufts, maintained by the High Command of the Air Force – Oberkommando der Luftwaffe. They had Luftwaffe guards. These camps were identified by numbers that had no relation to their location in a Wehrkreis. Officers and men were held in the same camps. Aircrew were among the most prized of German captives. They were not allowed to work and were held in camps in Poland and eastern Germany to make escape to the UK as difficult as possible.

First Camps

The German name for battlefield collection points was *sammelstelle*, but only one man includes it on his questionnaire. Staff Sergeant Bernard Black, Glider Pilot Regiment, was an evader who recorded being held at a *sammelstelle* at 'Woerden, Holland' on 20 December 1944. Woerden is 50 miles west of Arnhem. Black was transferred from Woerden to the Luftwaffe interrogation centre Dulag Luft and then to Stalag Luft 1.

Apart from hospitals, the places that occur most frequently in the few accounts of the early days of men's captivity are Zutphen and Ede. Zutphen was 30km northeast of Arnhem in the area where 9th SS Panzer had been concentrated. It became a railhead for moving men to reception camps. The only description of any kind of Zutphen was by Captain John Killick.

> Captain John Killick, 89 Parachute Security Section, 'the only interrogation was three days after capture in a PW cage at Zutphen'.

Other references to this early stage of captivity are to the subject and methods of interrogation, or to the headquarters of German units without a specifically named location. The other *sammelstelle* that is referred to was at Ede. Most records of Ede are from evaders, but a small number come from men captured during the battle. In his separate diary Staff Sergeant George Greenslade, Glider Pilot Regiment, described his early captivity in detail:

> 22nd Taken to the Barracks at Ede where we had further searching etc. No food from the Germans, fed by the Dutch Red Cross. Straw paillasses, no blankets, bloody cold.

> 23rd Still in the Barracks. More prisoners arrive.

> 24th Marched to Harscamp, a disused Riding School. Still fed by Dutch Red Cross on a little bread with jam spread and a bowl of mashed potatoes. Very cold, slept on straw, no blankets.

Table 2: First Locations

The first places where men were held before transfer to permanent camps. The number of men is the number of individuals who refer to the site either in the list of camps or in answers to other questions on the questionnaire. If not otherwise specified, locations are reception camps.

Location as on Liberation Questionnaire	Number of men	Notes
10 Panzer HQ	1	10 SS Panzer Division 'Frundsberg', originally its HQs was at Beekbergen, between Apeldoorn and Arnhem.
6 Panzer Grenadier *(sic)* HQ	1	No. 6 Panzer Grenadier recorded, possibly Fallschirmjäger Regiment 6; puzzling because they were operating south of Arnhem during the battle.

Location as on Liberation Questionnaire	Number of men	Notes
Amersfoot	3	Includes 'Amersfoot Transit Camp'.
Apeldoorn Hospital	124	Hospitals that initially took prisoners of war, but also German casualties by the end of the war. By then it was staffed by men from 181 Airlanding Field Ambulance, 16 and 133 Para Field Ambulances. Includes alternate names and sites in the Apeldoorn area as 'Apeldoorn Hospital', 'Apeldoorn 'Civvis' [civilian] Hospital', 'Apeldorn', 'Konig Wilhelm III Kazerne Apeldoorn' (and spelling variants), 'Kriegslazarett 4/686', 'Reserve Lazarett Appeldoorn', 'Reserve Lazarett IV/686', 'St Joseph's Hospital Apeldoorn', 'St Liduina Hospital Apeldoorn', 'Ziekenhuis van de Vereeniging Apeldoorn', 'Queen Wilhelmina Barracks' and 'Queen Ethelburger's Barracks'.
Arnhem Hospital	33	Includes 'Arnhem Hospital', 'Arnhem Hospital Frieing' *sic*, 'Arnhem Municipal Hospital' and 'St Elizabeth's Hospital'.
Bismarck School Hanover	1	Used as a Reserve Lazarett.
Dortmund Hospital	1	
Dulag Luft	200	Includes Dulag Luft – Frankfurt, Dulag Luft – Oberusel, Dulag Luft – Wetzlar and Dulag Luft Hospital. All three sites were north-west of Frankfurt.
Dulag XII B Hadamar	26	Includes men using the name Dulag of Oflag XII B. It was north-west of Frankfurt.
Ede	1	Possibly Harskamp, a former Dutch Army Barracks.
Enschede	31	Hospital, includes Hema, nr Enschede, Enschede Hospital, Hema, nr Enschede, Heymer *(sic)* Hospital and St Joseph's Hospital Enschede.
Gestapo Prison Doetinchem	1	An evader, escaped from captivity in September, recaptured 2 January 1945.
Gestapo Prison Utrecht	1	See above.
Harskamp	2	A former Dutch Army Barracks.
Hospital unspecified	1	
Interrogation centre Dietz	7	The army centre at Dulag Oberbefehlshaber West – Supreme Commander West's Interrogation Centre at Diez Castle, north-west of Frankfurt. Includes 'Military Barracks Diez', 'Interrogation Camp Germany' and plain 'Diez'.

Location as on Liberation Questionnaire	Number of men	Notes
Marlag-Milag North	1	The permanent Kriegsmarine Camps for Royal Navy and Merchant Navy prisoners.
Oosterbeek Hospital	2	
Reserve Lazarett Bocholt	2	Includes Rhede Hospital, attached to Stalag IV F.
Reserve Lazarett Burgsteinfurt	4	South-east of Enschede.
Reserve Lazarett Emmerich	4	German Army hospital close to the Netherlands border.
Reserve Lazarett Freising	16	Includes Stalag VII A Freising Hospital, Stalag VII A Hospital, Stalag VII A Reserve. Lazarett Freising and Reserve Lazarett Freising.
Reserve Lazarett Gronau	6	German Army Hospital close to Münster.
Reserve Lazarett Hanover	1	
Reserve Lazarett Linden	1	
Reserve Lazarett Lingen	3	
Reserve Lazarett Lochem	6	
Reserve Lazarett Meiningen	13	Major POW Hospital in Hesse specialising in eye surgery, managed by Stalag IX C.
Reserve Lazarett Münster	2	Includes 'Reserve Lazarett Ibbenburg? nr Munster'.
Reserve Lazarett Nürnberg	1	
Reserve Lazarett Obermaßfeld	16	Major orthopaedic POW Hospital in Hesse, with, by the War's end, 181 Field Ambulance medical staff. Managed by Stalag IX C.
Reserve Lazarett Rottenmunster	5	Attached to Stalag V B.
Reserve Lazarett Siegburg	2	
Reserve Lazarett Teupitz	2	In Brandenburg, includes 'Tirpitz Hospital'.
Reserve Lazarett Villingen	1	Attached to Stalag V B.
Sammelstelle Woerden	1	*Sammelstelle* was the German term for battlefield collection points for POWs.
Stalag XI B	424	The main Dulag for walking wounded who arrived by hospital train from Apeldoorn
Stalag XII A	1,513	Includes Dulag XII A and Stalag XII A. The camp was at Limburg an der Lahan, north-west of Frankfurt. It was the major reception centre for all POWs captured in north-western Europe.
Utrecht Hospital	8	
Zutphen POW Camp	4	Includes Zutphen Hospital. Zutphen was a major railhead for moving men to Stalag XII A at Limburg.

Battlefield sites

Interrogation and holding sites as
recorded in Questionnaires

[H] Hospital

◉ Interrogation site

The Netherlands

Amsterdam

Almalo [H]

[H]
Heemstede   [H] Ermelo   Enschede [H]
Amersfoort ◉ Appledoorn [H]   [H] Lochem
Utrecht [H]
Harskamp ◉   Zutphen [H]   ◉ Doetinchem
Rotterdam Oosterbeek[H]   ◉ Velp
Arnhem

Nijmegen

Germany

Eindhoven

Belgium

Hamburg

X

Stalag XI B ●

Hanover

VI   XI

Köln   Kassel

Dulag XII B   Dulag Luft Wetzlar   ● Oflag IX A/H
Hadamar   Dulag XII A ◉   ● Oflag IX A/Z
Limburg an der Lahn ◉   IX
Obervefehlshaber West
Diez Castle   [H] Dulag Luft Hohemark
Dulag Luft Oberursal ◉

XII   Frankfurt

Metz   **Dulag sites**   Nürnberg

Camps registering men off the
battlefield

[H] Hospital

◉ Dulag

● Camp acting as a Dulag

○ Wehrkreis headquarters

X Wehrkreis number

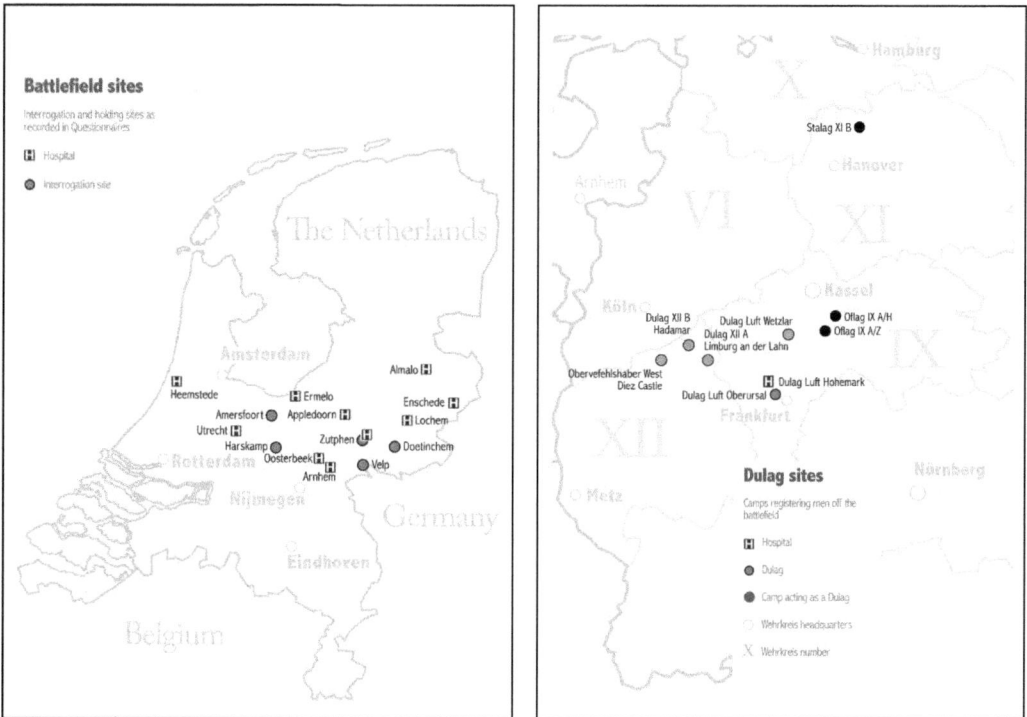

Above left: Map 1: Battlefield locations recorded in questionnaires.

Above right: Map 2: Dulags

POW Camps – Reception Centres

Prisoners were received into the POW system formally at *Durchgangslager* (Dulags) – reception camps that were away from the battlefield. In the autumn of 1944 there were two in the West. One, for NCOs and Other Ranks, was a compound within the permanent POW, Stalag XII A, camp at Limburg an der Lahn, 160 miles from Arnhem. A second for officers was at Hadamar close to Oflag XII B, 5 miles to the west of Limburg. Fifteen officers record time at Stalag XII A, followed almost immediately by transfer to Oflag XII B. It is possible that the stipulation on the questionnaire to record 'Main camps' means that many more officers travelled this route.

One trainload of walking wounded was sent to Limburg before the British medical staff were able to secure better treatment for such cases from the Germans. This led to the Germans creating two temporary Dulags for Arnhem men. Stalag XI B Fallingbostel was the destination for the hospital trains and the camp where wounded NCOs and Other Ranks were registered. Wounded officers were transferred to Oflag IX A/H or its subsidiary camp Oflag IX A/Z, both near Kassel.

Unlike Limburg, NCOs and Other Ranks who were registered at the temporary Dulag at Fallingbostel might be retained at the camp, and all the officers who went to Oflag IX A/H or IX A/Z stayed there until liberation, unless they required treatment at a hospital, which is what Lieutenant Colonel John Frost, 2nd Battalion, Parachute Regiment, and Lieutenant James Cleminson, 3rd Battalion, Parachute Regiment, experienced, transferring to Obermaßfeld, when their wounds required specialist treatment after spending time at Spangenberg and Rotenburg.

Seriously wounded men were held in Reserve Lazaretts – military hospitals – often managed by Stalags, before they were fit enough for transfer to permanent camps. In some cases these men only reached their regular camp early in 1945.

The army's specialist interrogation centre of the High Commander in the West, Dulag Oberbefehlshaber West close to Limburg at Dietz, was little used. Only six men record passing through the centre, unlike the Luftwaffe's centre, Dulag Luft, which was heavily used.

Transport to Dulags and then later to permanent camps took a long time. By the autumn of 1944 the German railway system was beginning to find it difficult to cope:

> Staff Sergeant John Devey, Glider Pilot Regiment, 'Train journey of 4 days after capture without food or water.'

> Private Harry Lewis, [unit not given], 'On train from Zutphen – Limburg camp 4 days 5 nights.'

Devey's journey was from the battlefield to Oberursel: Lewis's journey was to Limburg. Both journeys of around 200 miles.

Dulag XII A, Limburg

The Limburg Dulag had been created during 1944. It was on the same site as Stalag XII A, at Limburg an der Lahn, between Frankfurt and Köln. Limburg was a Dulag for the whole Western Front and not just for men captured at Arnhem. Over 60 per cent (1,507) of questionnaires record time at Limburg. Limburg registered able-bodied NCOs and Other Ranks: officers passed through the camp before transfer to the officers' Dulag XII B at Hadamar, 5km to the west. Typically a man would spend two months at Limburg.

The first arrival date on a questionnaire is an example of how misleading they can be for dates. Six men give dates before the start of Market Garden, one in July. Men appear to have arrived at Limburg in increasing numbers after 20 September 1944. The last date for leaving the camp is Christmas Day.

Stalag XII A at Limburg was a very large camp holding men of many nationalities. To cope with the sudden influx of new prisoners, the Germans erected marquees with straw to sleep on. The men had to cope with inadequate food, poor washing and sanitary conditions:

Private Thomas Avann, 3rd Battalion, Parachute Regiment, noted, 'Bad sanitary conditions at Limburg.'

Private Leonard Cannon, 1st Battalion, Parachute Regiment, 'Living conditions bad. Very little food water shortage. No lights. Sanitation poor. Only one blanket issued.'

Dulag XII B, Hadamar

The Dulag was in a wooden building in the yard of a former school on the hill below Oflag XII B. The Oflag itself was housed in a former monastery and held senior British officers. In May 1944 there was a major general, ten brigadiers and twenty-three lieutenant colonels among the 314 prisoners. The Dulag had been created in July 1944 mainly to hold officers captured in Normandy.

In November 1944, when visited by the Swiss in the role of a Protecting Power, the camp held fifty-six officers and ten orderlies. The appointment of Lieutenant Colonel Tommy Haddon, 1st Battalion, Border Regiment, as permanent Senior British Officer followed the Swiss visit. The Swiss had noted that:

> The majority of the present strength are airborne Officers captured in the Arnhem region, now awaiting transport to a proper Oflag. Unfortunately up to the present time there has been no permanent senior British officer, those having acted as such during their stay here sooner or later left for other camps in Germany. Thus it has been impossible to organise the camp in a manner as to correspond with the British point of view, each senior British officer having had to start anew.

The questionnaires record eighty-nine men spending time at the Dulag. The camp is variously described as Oflag XII B, Stalag XII B or Dulag XII B.

Lieutenant Colonel Haddon stayed at Hadamar until March 1945, when the site was bombed. By this time the camp was no longer very active. Haddon, 'I was left with a British doctor and the eleven Frenchman ... other British officers passed through, but the stream was drying up.' Following the bombing, Haddon moved into the main Oflag.

Dulag Luft West, Oberursel, Wetzlar and Hohemark

The Luftwaffe had been the first of the German armed forces to organize the systematic gathering of intelligence from prisoners, by establishing two permanent transit camps, Durchgangslagers der Luftwaffe – Dulag Luft: one on the Eastern Front; the other in the West.

Dulag Luft West was located at three sites: the main interrogation centre at Oberursel in the north-western suburbs of Frankfurt, with a hospital close by at Hohemark; and a transit camp at Wetzlar 50km to the north. By late 1944 interrogations were also taking place at Wetzlar. The centre had an airborne warfare specialist on its staff: Major Georg Helm, Iron Cross First Class, who had fought in Crete. He was supported by Feldwebel Fade. The burden of interrogating, or at least managing the interrogation, of all the men who passed through the Dulag fell on these two men. The questionnaires record 110 men passing through. On the basis that the questionnaires represent a third of all men captured, Helm and Fade interrogated over 300 men.

Men usually describe Dulag Luft as a Luftwaffe centre, some even as an 'RAF Centre'. Several questionnaires fail to include Dulag Luft as a camp that men had passed through but mention it in answer to the interrogation question.

The Germans could distinguish most airborne troops from other Allied forces from their uniform and insignia. German photographs of POWs show some with regimental insignia. Glider pilot's wings were very like RAF aircrew's wings. Two-thirds of glider pilot questionnaires show them being sent to Luftwaffe camps, one-third to army Stalags. The other easily confused group were the RAF Light Warning Units. A picture taken after the battle at Nijmegen shows Squadron Leader Howard Coxon, the Commanding Office of Light Warning Set Unit No. 6080, RAF wearing battle dress with no obvious sign that he was RAF rather than army. Of the ten questionnaires from men in 6080 Unit Light Warning, five show men sent to army camps and five to Luftwaffe ones.

The centre was well-known in Britain and it featured in briefings for Allied aircrew. Dulag Luft's use of heated airless rooms to persuade prisoners to talk led to a war crimes trial in 1946. Four questionnaires include some references to heat treatment. The war crime trials did not include any evidence from men taken prisoner at Arnhem. Instead, the trial focused on events in 1943.

Stalag XI B, Fallingbostel

The first transfers of wounded men were to Limburg. They were moved in boxcars and in conditions that took no account of their wounds. Objections by Colonel Warrack, the senior British Medical Officer, led to later groups going by ambulance train to Stalag XI B at Fallingbostel. The Germans now improvised and Fallingbostel became a Dulag for the walking wounded, but only NCOs and Other Ranks: officers arriving at Fallingbostel were transferred after a few days to Oflag IX A/H or A/Z, which acted as officers' Dulags. Stalag XI B was a large camp with several nationalities and in that sense was similar to Limburg.

A total of 226 questionnaires record Stalag XI B as a POW's first camp. Representatives of the Swiss Foreign Office, as protecting power, inspected the hospital on 9 November 1944. They reported 'that the hospital equipment was good on the whole, it was not anticipated that there would be a constant arrival of severely wounded from the front, which is now the case'.

If men recorded time at Fallingbostel it was usually described as Stalag XI B. Sergeant Cyril Robinson, Glider Pilot Regiment, who spent a month at Fallingbostel, is the only man to describe it as a Dulag.

Perhaps because Fallingbostel was not a dedicated Dulag, some men were retained at the camp and in some cases men were transferred from Limburg to Fallingbostel.

Dulag Oberbefehlshaber West, Dietz

Dulag OB West had been established in autumn 1943. Initially this was alongside a transit camp at Châlons-sur-Marne in France, but by autumn 1944, as the Allies advanced, it had moved east, to the castle at Diez close to Limburg. The first formal notice of OB West at Dietz to reach Britain was in a telegram from the British Embassy in Berne to London on 27 December 1944:

> During recent short visit to Oflag 12B now organised as transit camp, Swiss representative learned existence of interrogation camp at Dietz on Lahn in addition to Oberursel.

> Man of confidence at Oflag 12B informed Swiss representative that interrogation at Dietz is severer than that Oberursel as far as the length of time is concerned. Accommodation is good and there has been no ill-treatment.

Edward Beattie, an American war correspondent for United Press, was captured west of Belfort on 12 September 1944. He arrived at Stalag XII A Limburg in early October. After three days he was transferred to Diez. He spent seven days there:

> Dietz Castle is the typical storybook Rhineland burg which juts up in a confusion of angled Greystone walls, battlements and steep moves from the cluster of old houses at its base. Even today, the massive keep looks capable of protecting the town from marauding robber bands, but the picture books stuff went out of date generations ago, and the keep for many years has been used as a prison.

In questionnaires, OB West is described as Diez or Diez castle, never by its German title. Major Michael Forman, 7th Battalion, King's Own Scottish Borderers Regiment, comes closest, describing it as 'Interrogation Camp Diez'. Only six questionnaires have references to the camp. The six consisted of four officers, one NCO and one private. Two who spent time at Diez, Major George Widdowson, 10th Battalion, Parachute Regiment, and Major Charles Gough, 1st Airborne Reconnaissance Squadron, also spent time at Dulag Luft.

Oflag IX A/H and IX A/Z

Officers who were able to walk were transferred in a few days from Fallingbostel to Oflag IX A/H at Spangenberg and many then travelled on to its subsidiary camp, Oflag IX A/Z at Rotenburg, where they were registered. Wehrkreis IX included two major POW hospitals at Obermaßfeld and Meiningen. Presumably the proximity of the hospitals was the reason for handling walking wounded officers at Oflag IX A, rather than sending them to Oflag 79 and the able-bodied officers from Hadamar to Spangenberg. Airborne medics provided most of the medical staff at Obermaßfeld. They formed a *kommando* managed by Stalag IX C at Bad Sulza, 80 miles to the east.

Men whose wounds did not heal as expected were transferred from Spangenberg and Rotenburg to one of the two hospitals. These included Lieutenant Colonel John Frost, 2nd Battalion, Parachute Regiment, who spent time at Obermaßfeld after first being sent to Oflag IX A/H. Lieutenant James Cleminson, 3rd Battalion, Parachute Regiment, remained at Obermaßfeld until he was liberated in March 1945. The absence of any questionnaires from men held at Oflag IX A/H or Obermaßfeld, including those of Frost and Cleminson, makes it impossible to gauge the total number of those who went to Oflag IX A/H or the hospital.

Twenty-one questionnaires record time at Oflag IX A/Z, while there are thirty-five references to spending time at Meiningen and or Obermaßfeld. Officers were transferred after treatment to Oflag IX A/H or A/Z, NCOs and Other Ranks were sent to Bad Sulza's subsidiary camp at Mühlhausen, Stalag IX C/Z. This was 40 miles east of Oflag IX A/H.

Registration

The questionnaires have very little information on the registration process. References to being registered are limited to comments about their interrogation:

> Company Sergeant Major Frederick Martin, 1st Battalion, Parachute Regiment, 'Yes I was interrogated by officers of the Luftwaffe. I stated my No., Rank & Name. I was temporarily refused registration because I refused to give further information.'

> Private Stanley Crouch, 2nd Battalion, South Staffordshire Regiment, 'Interrogated under the guise of registering with the Red Cross at 12A Limburg.'

> Private Albert Lawson, 2nd Battalion, South Staffordshire Regiment, 'Limberg – 28 September 1944 – A German Officer tried to persuade us that we were being registered for Luft camps.'

The questionnaires did not ask for POW numbers and they are not referred to in any of the men's answers. Where known, POW numbers are included in the War Office list of POWs and occasionally from men's autobiographies and rare camp files that have survived. The most useful of the latter is the miscellaneous collection of papers from Stalag XI B that appear to have come from the British Man of Confidence's papers and provided movement lists to and from *kommandos* managed by Stalag XI B.[5]

---

5 National Archives, Kew, WO 361/1797/1 and 2.

Chapter 3

Interrogation

We Know Everything

Interrogation began in the Netherlands and continued in some cases until men were at their permanent prison camps. The basic technique was always the same, 'We know already so there is no need to keep silent.'

> Private John Rose, 181st Airlanding Field Ambulance, 'Yes at Arnhem. Enemy already knew where we left from, the name of plane & glider and also names of units.'

> Sergeant John Bellamy, 16th Parachute Field Ambulance, 'Was taken to The Dulag Luft for interrogation given to air-crews, and questioned 26/9/1944. The method was one of "We know it already".'

> Private Colin Fowler, 1st Battalion, Border Regiment, '[Stalag] IV B Dec 44. I was asked questions in a normal sort of way. If I couldn't supply the answers they could. They were two German army and one flying officer.'

The German air force and army both had interrogation centres separate from the POW transit camps, where more thorough military interrogation could take place. Given the leading role of the Luftwaffe in the interrogations, it is not surprising that 202 men record passing through Dulag Luft, but only six through the Army Centre, Dulag Oberbefehlshaber West.

Interrogation was usually just questioning. There are three records of violence. Two are from Dulag Luft. Men sent to Dulag Luft or the army's OB West would be kept in solitary confinement:

> Driver John Taylor, RASC, 'Heelsum. Holland. 8.9.44 kicked in stomach by officer for not divulging name of O.C Division.'

> Private William Mullineux, 3rd Battalion, Parachute Regiment, 'Wetzlar [part of Dulag Luft]. Sept 44. Kept without food in effort to extract information. Also struck in face.'

> Private John Elliott, 4th Parachute Brigade HQ, 'Werson (sic) [part of Dulag Luft] 29-9-44 Solitary confinement no food clothing hit with sticks and fist.'

By late 1944 the state security services – *Reichssicherheitshauptamt* (RSHA) and The German Foreign Office – were also taking an increasing interest in political and economic information that could be gleaned from newly arrived POWs. The Geneva Convention required that new prisoners be recorded and the information passed by the International Red Cross for forwarding to the POWs' home authorities. All this meant prisoners were interrogated to one degree or another .

Interrogators

The questionnaires show Luftwaffe interrogators were present on the battlefield alongside the Division's SS opponents.

> Bombardier Frederick Chilcott, 1st Airlanding Anti-Tank Battery, 'At Arnhem by Luftwaffe Officers who promised admission to Luft camps if given information, which they didn't get.'

After men had been transferred to Germany the competitive nature of Nazi bureaucracy meant that Luftwaffe and army interrogators were joined by Gestapo, Foreign Office officials and nameless civilians, who appear in the questionnaire answers. One man recorded a surprising interrogator: an officer from the German Navy, the Kriegsmarine, presumably helping the other armed services, but with the way the Nazi party encouraged competition, it was also possible that the Navy wanted to make sure it had a presence.

> Lance Corporal Albert Hales, 4th Battalion, Dorset Regiment, 'Interrogated at Stalag XII A during Oct '44 by German Naval Officer ...'

Some of the questionnaires containing references to threats of Gestapo interrogation, relate to this:

> Private Charles Hull, 181st Airlanding Field Ambulance, 'Informed that we would be treated as agents on refusing to answer any except three stipulated questions (i.e. Name Rank No.).'

Men found it difficult to distinguish which organisation the 'civilian' interrogators belonged. Sergeant Chambers was interrogated at Limburg in October 1944:

> Sergeant Talbot Chambers, 89 Parachute Security Section, 'By a civilian occasionally wearing Luftwaffe Major's uniform and who said he was from German Foreign Office or Red Cross Rep ...'

Newly captured men were assembled in temporary sites close to the battlefield, from where they were transferred to reception camps for registration, before being moved to their permanent camp. Unfortunately, few questionnaires describe the early stages of captivity. The request for information on 'Main Camps' meant that most men did not record their immediate capture or in some cases the reception camps where they were held close to the battlefield.

INTERROGATION

The Geneva Convention required that prisoners need only provide their name, rank or number, and training emphasized this.

Geneva Convention Article 5

Every prisoner of war is required to declare, if he is interrogated on the subject, his true names and rank, or his regimental number. If he infringes this rule, he exposes himself to a restriction of the privileges accorded to prisoners of his category. No pressure shall be exercised on prisoners to obtain information regarding the situation in their armed forces or their country. Prisoners who refuse to reply may not be threatened, insulted, or exposed to unpleasantness or disadvantages of any kind whatsoever. If, by reason of his physical or mental condition, a prisoner is incapable of stating his identity, he shall be handed over to the Medical Service.

The most common German interrogation technique to gain more information was to impress the man with their existing knowledge and ask for its confirmation. This was coupled with incentives and threats. The incentives were of being sent to a 'better camp,' that is a Luftwaffe one, where men would not be asked to work, or getting information back more quickly to the man's family. The verbal threats used were of being shot or a being sent to a poor army camp, or even concentration camp. Ironically, men sent to Luftwaffe camps were subjected to the worst of the winter marches, since the camps were in Poland:

Sergeant William Griffith, Glider Pilot Regiment, 'Near Frankfurt on Maine, by Luftwaffe, Oct 1944 solitary confinement, bread & water, threatened with firing squad for withholding information.'

Sapper Philip Miller, 1st Parachute Squadron Royal Engineers, 'Yes, threats of concentration camps used, and shooting. Interrogated at (12A) Limburg.'

Many answers to the interrogation question emphasize that men refused to answer, but one adds a little background to this situation:

Private Jack Wood, 2nd Battalion, South Staffordshire Regiment, 'Just a few questions on where we flew from and when. They were browned off of insults by the time it was my turn.'

And there was duplication in the questioning:

Sergeant William John Kerswell, Royal Army Medical Corps, 'Enschede 18th October 1944. Questioned Luft Interrogation camp 27th October. Questioned after 24 hours solitary confinement, XII A on 1st November 44 Questioned.'

Little use was made of the OB West Interrogation Centre at Diez, but when it was used it duplicated interrogation elsewhere. Major Ronnie Stark, 1st Battalion,

Parachute Regiment, and Major David Gilchrist, 11th Battalion, Parachute Regiment, both recorded interrogation at Dulag Luft before being moved to Diez.

Apart from glider pilots being sent to Dulag Luft, the only other group singled out for interrogation were men from the Light Warning Units of the RAF, with their potential technical knowledge. The question that needs answering here is how did the interrogators know Quigley was a radar specialist?

> Sergeant Edmund Quigley, 6341st Unit Light Warning RAF, 'Oberursel Nr Frankfurt – towards end of Sept 44. I was held there a week pending the arrival of a Radar Officer from Berlin.'

Aircrew or Soldiers?

Why others were selected for Dulag Luft or why the two officers and four Other Ranks were singled out to go to OB West at Diez is not clear. The Germans could distinguish between men to be treated as army or as air force by the unit badges on men's battle dress. The glider pilots' double wings badge was very similar to that of RAF pilots:

> Staff Sergeant Herbert Mason, 181st Airlanding Field Ambulance, 'They knew all about us. ie they knew our unit by our shoulder flash and colour.'

Photographs of POWs show that some men did wear their regimental and divisional badges. Of the 179 glider pilots with questionnaires, eighty-six went to army camps and ninety-one to Luftwaffe-managed ones.

The time that the Luftwaffe devoted to interrogation of Arnhem men was greater than the German Army. The air war was a technological one and information on new equipment was an important part of that war. The Luftwaffe had taken a similar view regarding men captured in Sicily in 1943. Many of these were also sent to Dulag Luft, for example Corporal Palmer, captured at Catania on 14 July 1943:

> Corporal Edward Palmer, 2nd Battalion, Parachute Regiment, 'Dulag Luft Frankfurt. Firstly bogus Red Cross official who presents a supposed Red Cross form containing questions of military nature. Secondly softening up process of solitary confinement for eight days with minimum rations culminating in interrogation.'

The army appears to have concentrated their efforts on a small number of individuals, why it is not clear, and as result, few men passed through OB West at Diez. Market Garden was an intelligence windfall on their own doorstep for the Luftwaffe and they took every advantage of it. While Allied airborne tactics and equipment remained fundamental intelligence targets, by the autumn of 1944 the Luftwaffe procedures also allowed the Germans to explore political and economic intelligence.

Battlefield Interrogation

The questionnaire's request was for information if a man was 'specially interrogated by the enemy'. This should have eliminated answers about routine questioning on capture, although what was routine and what was special were not defined. Even so, some men do refer to early interrogations:

> Lance Corporal Edmund Morris, 1st Airborne Reconnaissance Squadron, 'I was interrogated by an enemy officer immediately I was captured, but as I was in a bad condition he left me, quite dissatisfied.'

> Private Walter McGowan, 181st Airlanding Field Ambulance, interrogated, 'By filling in form at Zuphund (sic).'

And most descriptions of these early interrogations describe them taking place at a German headquarters:

> Private Michael Aggleton, 2nd Battalion, South Staffordshire Regiment, 'At Div HQ Arnhem Sept 22nd. Normal questions asked ie have you been in action before, where? etc. No force used.'

> Lieutenant Robert Levien, 2nd Battalion, Parachute Regiment, 'Was separated from ORs at 10th Panzer Div HQ near Arnhem for interrogation & also was interrogated by an SS Oberst. Otherwise normal routine.'

> Corporal Dennis Brookes, 11th Battalion, Parachute Regiment, 'September 44 just north of Arnhem in a Luftwaffe HQ.'

> Captain Charles Noble, 133rd Parachute Field Ambulance, 'Arnhem, (Velp, 1st Parachute Div, Counter Intelligence).'

At the western edge of the pocket Ede was the other transit camp mentioned in interrogations. This was a former Dutch Army barracks, 'Harscamp'. Although it was a convenient site to hold men captured on the western edge of the Arnhem/Oosterbeek pocket, not all men captured in Oosterbeek were held here. There are five records of interrogations at Ede, of which these are examples:

> Sergeant Charles Lyons, Glider Pilot Regiment, 'Ede (Holland) ordinary interrogating by Luftwaffe officer who asked questions about units and casualties during Airborne landing.'

> Private Kenneth Harris, 10th Battalion, Parachute Regiment, 'Harscamp. Holland Sept 24 1944. By word of mouth.'

> CQSM William Channon, 4th Parachute Brigade, 'Ede near Arnhem, Holland. Taken to German GHQ and accused of shooting a German Red Cross nurse. Supposed to have been recognised by an officer, also offered drinks in an Offs Mess and told I should go to a concentration camp.'

The men record interrogations at Arnhem that range from 'blustering and threatening' to 'kindness' and 'very easy interrogation'. However, the kindness could be tinged with threats:

> Lance Bombardier Richard McCreedy, 1st Airlanding Anti-Tank Battery, 'Arnheim. Sept. given wine and food etc and told that if questions were answered correctly could proceed to hospital and have wounds dressed.'

> Private John Lochery, 7th Battalion, King's Own Scottish Borderers Regiment, 'Amensfoot Holland. Sept 20th 45. Promised better conditions and if no results this way they said they would use force.'

> Staff Sergeant Stanley Hann, Glider Pilot Regiment, 'Zutphen, near Arnheim (sic). Method given food, drink and cigarettes. Later a slight bullying attitude by SS officer who tried to make me speak over radio transmitter.'

The only questionnaires with an descriptions of violence or other third degree methods are these:

> Driver John Taylor, RASC, 'Heelsum. Holland. 8.9.44(sic) kicked in stomach by officer for not divulging name of O. C Division.'

> Private Thomas Askew, 1st Parachute Brigade, 'Yes by 21 Pz [21st Panzer Grenadier Regiment was part of 10 SS Panzer Division] around [illegible] used bright lights and 2 days starvation – tried to ascertain objectives.'

The incentive of being sent to a Luftwaffe camp, where men would not have to work, is a common feature:

> Bombardier William Cottrell, 1st Airlanding Anti-tank Battery, 'Zutphen. Method – Questions & promises of being sent to a Luft Stalag which was considered better camps than normal.'

> Private Thomas Bennett, 3rd Battalion, Parachute Regiment, 'Kindness. At Arnhem allowed to retain razor blades promised better Luftwaffe billets if I could prove I was a parachutist.'

Several German units are recorded at this early stage of captivity: '21 Panzer', '9th Panzer (SS) Div HQ' and '6th Panzer Grenadier HQ'. The 6th Panzer Grenadier Regiment was part of 7 Panzer Division and not involved in Market Garden. Several men record being interrogated by SS officers. The main opposition to the British were SS troops from the two SS Panzer Division that were re-forming in the Arnhem area after Normandy:

> Captain Trevor Livesey, 1st Parachute Squadron Royal Engineers, 'Questioned by S.S. officer the day after capture at Zutphen.'

> Sergeant James Craig, 2nd Battalion, Parachute Regiment, recorded being interrogated by 'an American German at SS Div HQ in Arnhem.'

The British medical teams who continued to work, having been captured, aroused German interest. The questionnaire of one Royal Army Medical Corps man also includes a reference to the Gestapo close to the battlefield:

> Lance Corporal Owen Becket, 10th Battalion, Parachute Regiment, 'Arnhem 19.9.44 – 23.9.44. By Gestapo officer whilst working as a medical orderly at 6th Panzer Grenadier HQ. Direct Questions.'

> Lance Corporal Stanley Kirk, 16th Parachute Field Ambulance, 'At Zutphen Holland on 26/9/44 by German SS officers. I was told names of senior officers of my division who had surrendered with their men in an attempt to draw me into argument.'

Luftwaffe interrogators were also present at the battlefield, but the smaller number of references to them in the questionnaires suggests there were fewer of them and that their activity focused on Dulag Luft and Limburg.

Hospital Interrogations

Men in hospitals were also questioned. Lieutenant Evans mentions a 'group interrogation', which cannot have been very exhaustive:

> Lieutenant Kenneth White, 1st Airlanding Light Regiment, 'Not specially but I was informed in hospital at Apeldoorn that my next of kin could not be informed about me unless I gave fuller particulars (unit) than I was prepared to give.'

> Driver Cyril Cooper, Airborne Light Company, RASC, 'Yes in hospital at Lockom nr Arnhem. Was given coffee and cigs at hospital and ask strength of 6th Airborne Div also transport planes but I did not tell.'

> Lieutenant Kenneth Evans, 4th Parachute Squadron, Royal Engineers, '[questioned] only in group at Emergency Hospital at Apeldoorn in Holland.'

Battlefield to Dulag

Men could be marched from the place of capture to battlefield collection points but reaching a Dulag required rail transport. Troop transport in Europe at the time used what to British eyes were goods wagons; boxcars. They were marked as being able to carry forty *hommes* and eight *chevaux*. At the start of the war, the BEF used them to move men across France. So although in Britain troops were used to travelling in passenger coaches, using boxcars was not completely new. What was new and extremely unpleasant was that the Germans locked men in, with little or no food and very few, if any toilet stops:

> Private Thomas Dolaghan, 4th Parachute Brigade, 'spent 4 days in a rlwy freight van with 49 other companions without food or water or a blanket. The van door was locked the whole 4 days.'

> Lieutenant Lawrence Kane, 7th Battalion, King's Own Scottish Borderers, 'After capture I was moved from Zutphen to Limberg in a boxcar which was locked throughout the trip or four nights and three days. We were allowed no sanitary facilities, Given approximately 1/4 loaf of bread and about one pint of water during that time.'

The distance from Arnhem to Stalag XII A at Limburg was around 150 miles in a straight line. The journey, delayed by troop and supply trains for a prioritized German Army and by Allied Air attacks, took four days. Limburg to Stalag IV B in Silesia is almost twice the distance. Sergeant Jack Avis took five days to reach Stalag II A at Neubrandenburg from Limburg, a journey of over 350 miles:

> Private Norman Smith, 7th Battalion, King's Own Scottish Borderers Regiment, 'Journies (sic) to different Stalags made under very bad conditions. In cattle wagons (about 40 men in each) and with practically no food. When we reached Limburg we were too weak to do anything.'

The hospital trains from Apeldoorn also drew a complaint:

> Captain John Dickens, 2nd Battalion, South Staffordshire Regiment, 'But when travelling by ambulance train 5–9 Oct 1944 there was inadequate provision of dressings etc for wounded, and my condition deteriorated considerably as a result.'

There is one reference to men being moved by passenger train to a Dulag. On Christmas Day six men were taken from Teupitz hospital, south-east of Berlin, to Dulag Luft.

Interrogation at Limburg and Dulag Luft

There were two main types of interrogation: simple questions or a bogus Red Cross form for men to complete. Coercion, solitary confinement and threats occurred rarely and then mainly at Dulag Luft. Men sent to Dulag Luft were routinely held in solitary confinement, with little food and threats, before being questioned:

> Captain James McCourt, 7th Battalion, King's Own Scottish Borderers Regiment, 'solitary confinement, terrible conditions, poor food ...'

> Sergeant Raymond Sargant, Glider Pilot Regiment, 'Solitary Confinement, 'Hot treatment' & then by suggestive treatment (Not employed).'

Sergeant Ralph Hogwood, 7th Battalion, King's Own Scottish Borderers Regiment, described his interrogation at Limburg as 'Gestapo method by questioning'. It is unclear if he is implying anything more than stern questioning. Military matters still predominated in Luftwaffe interrogations. Questions were combined with telling the prisoner that the answers to their questions were already known and it was only confirmation that was required.

Men were impressed by the standard of the English of some of their interrogators:

> Sergeant Henry Clark, 1st Airlanding Light Regiment, 'Conversation attitude adopted by a civilian dressed officer speaking perfect English rather like trying to be introduced into a debate Limburg Camp (Stalag 12 A) Germany.'

> Private Arthur Webb, 181st Airlanding Field Ambulance, 'Stalag XII A Limburg. October 1944. Individual interviews with person dressed in civilian clothes who spoke good English.'

Two men commented unfavourably on German interrogation techniques:

> Major Charles Gough, 1st Airborne Reconnaissance Squadron, 'Yes by Luftwaffe at Ober Oerzel near Frankfurt. 3 days, with solitary confinement. By Wehrmacht at Diez. 6 days solitary two interrogations one at 2 am and one at 7.30 am two days later. Threats about hot rooms & other things. References to cruelty to German POWs by British at Maison Blanche near Algiers & vague references to Tower of London. All rather theatrical.'

> Captain John Killick, 89 Parachute Security Section, 'The interrogation was lackadaisical, and made no attempt to break us down: he had a large printed pro-forma, on which he tried to fill in as many points as possible.'

A very few men record solitary confinement at Limburg. And one of 'rough handling':

> Private Clifford Cooke, 11th Battalion, Parachute Regiment, '24/9/44 Limburg. Information sought under threats of Gestapo reprisals. Men given solitary confinement on refusal to talk.'

> Corporal Thomas Edwards, 2nd Battalion, Parachute Regiment, 'Stalag XII A Oct 1944. Solitary confinement. No food for 68 hours. And rough handling by German guards.'

Staff at the Dulag Luft were tried on war crime charges for using closed and overheated rooms to torture aircrew. None of the charges related to airborne POWs. Four men describe being subjected to heat treatment:

> Sergeant James Barnbrook, 2nd Battalion, Parachute Regiment, 'Put in a "sweat" cell at Dulag for not answering questions.'

None of the men identified this treatment as a war crime.

The Bogus Red Cross Form

The 'Usual "Red Cross" form' is a common element in men's comments about interrogations. The Germans claimed that it had been provided by the Red Cross. The British pamphlet 'Responsibilities of Prisoners of War' included a warning about this form:

> 9. Bogus Forms may be produced in the hope that the prisoner will answer the questions which they ask. They may appear to be genuine Red Cross forms or official documents. Put your pen through every question except Name, Rank and Number – otherwise the Enemy may fill in the answers above your signature in order to bluff other prisoners. (Note. –Failure to fill in a Red Cross form does not delay notification to relatives, who are informed through official channels.)

Presumably, the standard Luftwaffe 'arrival report form' was used by interrogators on the battlefield:

> Private Walter McGowan, 181st Airlanding Field Ambulance, interrogated, 'By filling in form at Zuphund (sic).'

Their interrogators claimed that its completion was essential if news of the man's capture was to reach home. The form asked for far more than the name, rank and number authorized under the Geneva Convention.

Flight Sergeant Albert Barnes, RAF, described the original that he was given at Dulag Luft at the end of September 1944 as having the heading 'Red Cross Form – Geneva' and 'Printed in Switzerland' at the bottom. Use of the form was not confined to the Dulag Luft:

Captain John Kilick, 89 Parachute Security Section, at Zutphen, 'he had a large printed pro-forma, on which he tried to fill in as many points as possible.'

Sergeant David Cowie, 2nd Battalion, Parachute Regiment, was handed the form at Limburg. 'They said they were Red Cross representatives and asked us to fill forms giving names of unit, planes we dropped from and what we did in our company.'

Despite warnings, it appears that some men did complete the form. Driver Raymond Weaver, 93rd Company RASC, completed a form at Limburg. 'Each man filled in a form. British Sergeant assured us everything was in order.'

Military Questions

As well as keeping their Allied order of battle up to date, the Luftwaffe had to overcome the loss of their radar sites in France and with them their ability to track incoming aircraft. If the Allies were using airfields in northern France instead of the UK for their airborne troops, their ability to intervene further east into Germany itself became a possibility:

Private George Milne, 7th Battalion, King's Own Scottish Borderers Regiment, 'What a certain type of glider carried … by explaining that they knew what it carried was their method.'

Private Henry Scutt, 10th Battalion, Parachute Regiment, 'Limberg few days after capture. I was shown maps, types of aircraft, told where my billets were in England. They tried to give me the impression that they knew all about us before we started on the operation.'

Private John Jones, 1st Battalion, Parachute Regiment, 'He asked what airfields flew from and also tried to get strength of Bn.'

One of the reasons for the Luftwaffe's early interest in formal interrogations was the increasingly technological nature of air warfare. Men from the two RAF Light Warning Units that accompanied the division had specific technical knowledge of interest that was definitely of interest to the Luftwaffe. Some were sent to Dulag Luft from hospitals three months after their capture. Yet only one man describes being singled out for detailed interrogation. None of the other questionnaires from eight other men from the two units who passed through the Dulag specifically record technical questions.

Leading Aircraftman Graham Young from 6341st Unit Light Warning reached the centre in March 1945 after time in five hospitals, when the war was almost over. Three others from the Light Warning Units, who had been wounded, arrived in December from Stalag XI B:

Leading Aircraftman David Foster, Light Warning Set Unit No. 6080, RAF, 'At Oberursel from Dec 5/44 to Dec 19/44 questioned 6 times by 4 different German officers.'

Economic and Political Questions

It is at the Dulags that political and economic questions appear alongside the purely military. The Germans were keen to learn of the effect that the new V1 flying bombs and V2 rockets were having on London:

> Gunner Alexander Noble, 1st Airlanding Light Regiment, was interrogated at Stalag XII A, 'A German in civilian clothes asked questions on damage to London by flying bombs, also about civilian rationing system, and the prices of articles.'

> Corporal Charles Forwood, 7th Battalion, King's Own Scottish Borderers Regiment, 'Limburg An English speaking civilian using English sporting events as a base to extract information of V2 Damage and civilian morale in London.'

> Private Thomas Hughes, 2nd Battalion, Parachute Regiment, was questioned at Limburg 'interrogated by civilian: he asked what unit I was in and then asked about London and the buzz bomb and then about what Russia would do to Germany after the war was over.'

Allied plans for Germany after the war suggest a surprising honesty on the part of the questioners:

> Captain Frederick Gibbs, 156th Battalion, Parachute Regiment, 'Political Interrogation by "Foreign Office Official" in civilian clothes. Required information as to what we would do with Germany after the war, and our attitude to Russians ...'

At least one man with Irish connections appear to have been selected for political discussions during interrogations. Sergeant Conway was an Irish citizen:

> Staff Sergeant James Conway, Glider Pilot Regiment, was interrogated after transfer from Stalag XI B to a fixed camp, Stalag IV B, 'Asked damage done by V1. Why I fight for England.'

And one man was questioned about his potential support for the fight against Communism:

> Corporal Dennis Brookes, 11th Battalion, Parachute Regiment, 'Limburg by the Luftwaffe NCOs. Trying to elicit sympathy for German calls in battle against communism.'

The Common Wealth Party, a Labour Party splinter group with overtly socialist objectives founded by J. B. Priestley among others, attracted an interrogator's interest:

> Driver George Hayes, 250th Airborne Light Company, RASC, 'German Interrogation Officer at St. XII A was unusually interested in the British political party known as The Common Wealth Party. He questioned (a) my opinion of it (b) did it receive much popularity c) did it get much publicity.'

Interrogation At Stalag XI B, Fallingbostel

Few of the prisoners sent to Stalag XI B at Fallingbostel record being interrogated at the camp. The officers were moved in a couple of days to a fixed camp, Oflag IX A/H or A/Z, while NCOs and Other Ranks were transferred from Fallingbostel's hospital over the rest of the autumn and early winter to their permanent camps. Interrogations continued at these camps:

> Private Michael Baxendale, 156th Battalion, Parachute Regiment, 'Yes at Fallingbostel. Methods rather quick owing to wounds.'

> Private Victor Cawrey, 21st Independent Para Company, '11B Fallingbostel promises of clothing extra food cigarettes.'

Interrogation at Oflag IX A/H and A/Z

Wounded officers who had spent only a couple of days at Fallingbostel were interrogated at Oflag IX A/Z at Rotenburg. Presumably, men sent to its parent camp, Oflag IX A/H, were also interrogated, but the absence of any liberation questionnaires from this group prevent this being confirmed:

> Major Gordon Dinwiddie, 7th Battalion, King's Own Scottish Borderers Regiment, 'Normal only on arrival at Oflag asked for, type of commission, profession, status of commission and nationality of parents as well as routine questions.'

> Lieutenant Alan Green, 1st Battalion, Border Regiment, 'Only routine interrogation as to name, rank, unit, father's and mother's names ...'

Interrogation At Dulag XII B

There are few records of interrogation at Dulag XII B. Many who passed through the camp responded to the interrogation question with a 'No' or a line through the question, presumably because they did not feel their interrogation was 'special':

Captain James Richey, 1st Battalion, Parachute Regiment, 'at Hadamar – again very easy – the interrogators took 'No' for an answer. (This 2nd interrogation was by the LUFTWAFFE).'

Interrogation at Dulag Oberbefehlshaber West

OB West matched the other Dulags for conditions that men were held in. And as at the other specialist centre, Dulag Luft, men were kept in solitary confinement before being interrogated. There are fewer threats recorded than at Dulag Luft and no mention of that centre's use of heat treatment:

> Major Michael Forman, 7th Battalion, King's Own Scottish Borderers Regiment, 'Yes at Diez near Limburg. I was in solitary confinement for 8 days. German rations were short, and Red Cross cigarettes and food were withdrawn.'

> Private Gustave Sander, 11th Battalion, Parachute Regiment, 'Interrogated at Military Barracks Diez by military and civil authorities after having been singled out at XII A as a paratrooper, solitary confinement for 24 hours.'

Only six questionnaires refer to OB West, which conforms to the German policy of giving the Luftwaffe the lead for interrogations. Major Charles Gough, 1st Airborne Reconnaissance Squadron, and Major George Widdowson, 10th Battalion, Parachute Regiment, passed through both Dulag Luft West and Diez. Was it their senior rank that made them of special interest? Certainly Lieutenant Colonel Haddon, 1st Battalion, Border Regiment, who lacks a questionnaire, in his personal papers describes being sent to Diez.

The only man to record spending time in the Kriegsmarine camp described a version of the Red Cross trick used at Dulag Luft and Stalag XII A, before he was transferred to Stalag XI B at Fallingbostel:

> Sergeant Fred Terry, 1st Battalion, Border Regiment, '[Interrogation] Yes Malag (sic) Bremen Nov 8 Dec 1944. Information required for notifying next of kin. Civilian masquerading as a Canadian Red Cross Representatives. Solitary confinement (6 days).'

Kommando 806, Stalag III D

Kommando 806 was part of a German project to recruit British prisoners to an anti-Soviet crusade. The camp was spread over several sites in and around Berlin. Trooper Vaughan is one of four men who record time at the camp. The British Frei Korps were also based at the complex. Only Vaughan refers to the camp's special purpose:

Trooper Peter Vaughan, 1st Airborne Recce Squadron, 'I have fairly extensive and detailed information relating to the endeavour and methods of a special department of the German Foreign office and military to gain the collaboration of Allied POWs. For information on that subject I also beg to refer to other officers and ORs of the American and British Forces who – against their wish – were kept in the Berlin Interrogation Commando.'

Interrogation at Prison Camps

The Germans continued to interrogate men after they had arrived at their permanent camps. The value of the military questioning a month after the operation had finished is puzzling:

Private John Aitken, 7th Battalion, King's Own Scottish Borderers Regiment, 'I was interrogated by the Luftwaffe at Muhlberg on 20 Oct 1944. He asked where I had left England and what Div I was in. All I gave him was Number, Rank, Name.'

Private Robert Veal, 4th Battalion, Dorset Regiment, 'Yes at Mühlburg by a German Officer on 10/10/44 who asked a variety of questions both military and personal.'

The answers to questioning on political and social issues at permanent camps would have produced more relevant answers, though not necessarily ones that the Germans hoped for:

Private Ted Few, 156th Battalion, Parachute Regiment, 'At IV B Mulburg. Taken into a room and spoken to nicely by English-speaking German and advised to accept trade job instead of ordinary labouring which I finally did so.'

Staff Sergeant Alfred Walker-Cook, Army Physical Training Corps, 'Yes. Neubrandenburg 22.9.44. German interpreter. Spoke to myself and 3 ORs of places in England. (socially).'

Corporal Charles Harris McLean, Royal Army Medical Corps, 'Sagan Dec 44. Informal talk with civilians.'

Not all men were specially interrogated. Rather than answering 'no', many put a line through the question. It is unfortunate that Lance Corporal Thelwell did not give an explanation of his answer. Perhaps the answer lies in his training as part of the Division's police force:

Lance Corporal Arthur Thelwell, Provost Company, 1st Airborne Division, 'No, avoided it.'

Table 3: Interrogation

The answers given to Question 3, 'Were you specially interrogated by the enemy? (State where, when and methods used by enemy).' Most answers on the form are preceded by 'Yes'. This has been removed to avoid duplication.

Name	Forename	Rank	Unit	Army number	POW number	Answer given on Questionnaire
Ackerman	Donald Henry Edwin	Gunner	1st Airborne Div Light Regiment, Royal Artillery	14334539	88742	At Limburg (XII A) in September 1944. By asking what work I had done. If I should like a good job, and as to what was happening in London about this time.
Addis	John	Private	1st Battalion, Border Regiment	4697979	92114	At XII A in Sept 44. We were not forced in any way to answer the questions.
Aggleton	Michael John	Private	2nd Battalion, South Staffordshire Regiment	4929070	91754	At Div HQ Arnhem Sept 22nd. Normal questions asked ie have you been in action before, where? etc. No force used.
Aitken	John	Private	7th Battalion, King's Own Scottish Borderers Regiment	14415429		I was interrogated by the Luftwaffe at Muhlberg on 20 Oct 1944. He asked where I had left England and what Div I was in. All I gave him was Number, Rank, Name.
Aldcroft	Albert	Lance Corporal	Royal Engineers	2020229		At Luftwaffe interrogation centre threatened with solitary followed by attempts to gain confidence and showing reports by other POWS.
Allchurch	William Henry	Private	133rd Battalion, Parachute Regiment Field Ambulance	7360747		Dulag Luft. Method used. 1. Said already knew everything about my unit. Special. Ref – about DZ time of take off time of drop.
Allen	Robert Arthur	Corporal	3rd Battalion, Parachute Regiment	2080592	89462	Arnhem 20.9.44 questioned by SS. Limberg 28.9.44 questioned by Luftwaffe Officer.
Allen	Arthur	Signalman	1st Parachute Brigade, Royal Signals	2594068	89409	At Limburg asked name only – told the rest by them [ie the Germans].

Surname	First Name	Rank	Unit	Number		Interrogation
Anderson	Ivor Douglas	Private	7th Battalion, King's Own Scottish Borderers Regiment	3189214		Limburg XII A on 23/8/1944 (sic).
Angell	Donald Francis	Private	1st Battalion, Border Regiment	14237266	91882	Normal.
Ashley	Neville Leonard	Sergeant	2nd Battalion, Parachute Regiment	4124109		Limburg Sept 1944, Methods – bribery cajolery and threats.
Askew	Thomas Richard	Private	1st Parachute Brigade	14229144	89259	By 21 Pz in [illegible], used bright lights and 2 days starvation – tried to ascertain objectives. Forced to march 23 km in bare feet – Could have been at 21 Pz HQ. Period 17-20 Sept.
Austen	James	Private	Parachute Regiment	6399160		Frankfort on Main 23 9 44 solitary confinement
Austin	Albert Henry	Corporal	Light Warning Set Unit No. 6080, RAF	919538		Oberursal 5-12-44 – 22-12-44 solitary confinement.
Auty	Sam	Sergeant	Glider Pilot Regiment	4617488		Oberursal. Direct questioning Solitary confinement.
Baldwin	John	Lieutenant	Glider Pilot Regiment	269414		Direct.
Barnbrook	James Stanley	Sergeant	2nd Battalion, Parachute Regiment	6016887		On capture at Arnhem bullying methods also at Dulag Luft III Bullying and frightening methods used.
Barraclough	Charles	Private	2nd Battalion, Parachute Regiment	883950		Interrogated at Linberg in September 1944, first by soft soaping, and then threatening us verbally.
Barritt	Harry Charlie	Lance Corporal	10th Battalion, Parachute Regiment	6412557		At Interrogation Centre Dulag Luft near Frankfort.
Barron	Stanley	Lance Corporal	250th Airborne Light Company, RASC	175762		Arnhem Holland and name and rank taken.
Barstow	Robert	Sergeant	3rd Battalion, Parachute Regiment	3392250		Limburg Interrogation by confinement.
Bashford	Stanley Thomas Howard	Sergeant	11th Battalion, Parachute Regiment	4857599	89784	Interrogated at Limburg by Luftwaffe Intelligence Officer.

Name	Forename	Rank	Unit	Army number	POW number	Answer given on Questionnaire
Bates	John Bernard	Staff Sergeant	Glider Pilot Regiment	912044		Oberuselle Oct 22/44.
Baxter	Robert Valentine	Private	Parachute Regiment	2760375		Writing.
Bayley	Len Edward	Private	10th Battalion, Parachute Regiment	14646018		Ordinary.
Beddoe	William Glyndwr	Lieutenant	7th Battalion, King's Own Scottish Borderers Regiment	285618	524	Airforce interrogation centre Wetzler (Nr Frankfurt) 26-28 Sept 44. Instead of direct questioning they kept giving me all sorts of information concerning my unit and occasionally asking for confirmation.
Beet	Walter Reginald	Private	10th Battalion, Parachute Regiment	6400246	75454	Stalag IV B. November 1944. Methods employed. Nil.
Bell	John Mitchell Kenyon	Lieutenant	156th Battalion, Parachute Regiment	217392		Obeursell (S of Frankfurt) End of September 1944 – continual solitary confinement and short rations for 10 days.
Bellamy	John Desmond	Sergeant/W	16th Parachute Field Ambulance	7381695	89795	Was taken to the Dulag Luft for interrogation given to air-crews, and questioned 26/9/1944. The method was one of 'We know it already'.
Bennett	Thomas	Private	3rd Battalion, Parachute Regiment	4129244	89557	Kindness. At Arnhem allowed to retain razor blades promised better Luftwaffe billets if I could prove I was a parachutist.
Berry	George Albert	Lance Bombardier	1st Airlanding Anti-Tank Battery	3524816	92014	Limburg Germany. September 1944 by answering questions put to me.
Berry	O'Neill Ferguson	Lance Corporal	7th Battalion, King's Own Scottish Borderers Regiment	3188546		Yes. Limberg. Sept. Normal.
Berry	Joseph Edward	Private	11th Battalion, Parachute Regiment	1428100	294932	On recapture. Wehrmacht at Ede. Gestapo at Apeldoorn. Luftwaffe at Enschede. Threats of shooting, questioning and flattery.

Betts	George	Sergeant	Glider Pilot Regiment	14233066		Normal at Arnhem.
Beveridge	Thomas McLeod	Lance Corporal	9th Field Company, Royal Engineers Airborne	2113967	75856	Interrogated by Luftwaffe Officers Oct 44.
Bevington	Bernard Leslie	Private	2nd Battalion, South Staffordshire Regiment	14397682		Zutzen Blustering + threatening. Frankfort solitary.
Bicker	George Stanley	Corporal	Royal Signals	2324374		Frankfurt 21 Oct 44. 7 days solitary, was captured in civilian clothes attempting to re-cross the Rhine.
Bishop	Walter William	Lance Corporal	156th Battalion, Parachute Regiment	6086564		I was interrogated at Lindberg in Germany, by members of the German Air Forces. On the day 26/9/1944.
Black	James Charles	Sapper	1st Parachute Squadron, Royal Engineers	1986005		Interrogation 'Arnhem and Limburg. Immediately after capture and on arrival at Limburg. Offered better treatment for information required.'
Blackmore	John David	Private	10th Battalion, Parachute Regiment	4447335		SS Troops Div HQ.
Blouet	Donald	Private	133rd Parachute Field Ambulance	7349318	90112	General interrogation. Method was to tell you that information was of no importance, others had given it.
Bloys	William	Private	2nd Battalion, Parachute Regiment	6029487		Yes. Wine and food.
Booth	Eric Charles	Driver	1st Parachute Squadron, Royal Engineers	1951655		By Luftwaffe + Army Officers Threats of concentration camps if truth was not told.
Bourne	Ernest Frederick	Lance Corporal	2nd Battalion, South Staffordshire Regiment	4918790	91638	No special interrogation by the Enemy. Usual questions asked. No information given.
Bowie	Alexander John	Private	3rd Battalion, Parachute Regiment	3318961		Oberursel Sept. Promised of being sent to Luft Stalag.

Name	Forename	Rank	Unit	Army number	POW number	Answer given on Questionnaire
Bradbury	William Henry George	Sapper	1st Parachute Squadron, Royal Engineers	14203066		Stalag XII B German Airforce Officer.
Bradbury	John Alfred	Sergeant	Glider Pilot Regiment	14547304		At RAF (sic) interrogation centre nr Frankfurt Sept 44. Solitary for three days – threatened with starvation – threats are not carried out.
Bradley	Edward	Sergeant	2nd Battalion, South Staffordshire Regiment	4913836	89848	Interrogation crossed out 'At Dulag XII A (Limberge) by Luftwaffe officer'.
Braithwaite	Gilbert Edmund	Private	2nd Battalion, South Staffordshire Regiment	6016356		Promise of not going to an RAF Stalag. (sic).
Breen	Thomas Francis	Lance Corporal	1st Airborne Provost Company	1917769		Ordinary interrogation Dulag Luft Frankfurt (M).
Bridge	Joseph Edward	Private	2nd Battalion, South Staffordshire Regiment	4923097	89444	Oberstusel – Oct 1944 – solitary confinement. Shortage of food and then offers of Red Cross parcels, cigarettes, etc for information. Threats of violence (unfulfilled).
Bridgewater	Ernest Edward	Corporal	11th Battalion, Parachute Regiment	7262084		Werslau 25.9.44 threatened to hand me over to the Gestapo if I did not answer their questions and placed in solitary confinement no food.
Bristow	Frank James	Private	156th Battalion, Parachute Regiment	6291433		At his Div HQ, Partly on day of capture and more so on 4 days after. He made statements about our formation and armament which were correct in the main part, then he asked for confirmation from us.
Britland	Sydney	Leading Aircraftman	Light Warning Set Unit No. 6080, RAF	1750457	1055	Dulag Luft Oct 1944 Solitary confinement.

Surname	First name(s)	Rank	Unit	Service No.	No.	Notes
Broadfoot	Robert	Private	156th Battalion, Parachute Regiment	3189292		Oberursel 5th 10 44 Threatening method.
Brock	Edwin Ward	Regimental Sergeant Major	16th Parachute Field Ambulance	7522897		Dulag Luft Frankfurt on Maine 20.9.44 Question by Luft Officer, treated politely & asked about unit. He said he had interviewed my CO already. I referred them to my CO and was dismissed.
Brodie	James	Gunner	1st Airlanding Light Regiment, Royal Artillery	14957653		Arnhem and Limberg Questioning in normal manner.
Bromfield	Arthur	Sergeant	2nd Battalion, Parachute Regiment	6014527	88939	Limburg 29/9/44. Luftwaffle (sic) threatened two keep us at transit camp in cells. 2 by civilian questioned on factories and transport in London 30/9/44.
Brook	William Henry	Driver	63 Company RASC	163198	75501	Ede Holland by German intelligence officer. No rough methods used, but was threatened to be shot by German soldier previously.
Brooker	Ronald James	Trooper	1st Airborne Reconnaissance Squadron	6354463	91435	Arnhem. Enemy talked of various subjects. Each time working round to military topics. Tried to get us intoxicated with raw spirits.
Brookes	Dennis Lionel	Corporal	11th Battalion, Parachute Regiment	4123596		On September 44 just north of Arnhem in a Luftwaffe HQ and at Limburg by the Luftwaffe NCOs. Trying to elicit sympathy for German calls in battle against communism.
Brooks	Arthur	Private	2nd Battalion, South Staffordshire Regiment	5125767	92898	Interrogation 'Frankfurt on Main solitary confinement' Sabotage 'Broke up [illegible] – bed boards and fused lights'.
Brooks	Clarence	Sergeant	Glider Pilot Regiment	7590893		
Brown	Harold Stanley	Driver	253rd Airborne Light Company, RASC	2897665		Limburg and Mühlberg just questioned.
Brown	Harry	Private	156th Battalion, Parachute Regiment	91516		Interrogated by Luftwaffe at XII A, 'I was interrogated at my first camp Stalag XII A by the Luftwaffe. They were very polite.'

Name	Forename	Rank	Unit	Army number	POW number	Answer given on Questionnaire
Brown	Norman	Private	2nd Battalion, South Staffordshire Regiment	4918535		Nothing special although some were placed in solitary confinement for three days on bread and water others enjoyed luxury in a Luftwaffe camp.
Brown	Norman	Private	7th Battalion, King's Own Scottish Borderers Regiment	3190181		Interrogated by Luftwaffe Officers at Limberg 26/9/44. They spoke very good English but employed no 3rd degree methods.
Browne	Edward William	Staff Sergeant	Glider Pilot Regiment	5730039		Aircrew Interrogation Centre Oberursal solitary confinement and light diet.
Brownsell	Anthony	Corporal	156th Battalion, Parachute Regiment	5670619		Limberg 28-9-44 by Luftwaffe personnel.
Brunt	Derek	Private	1st Battalion, Parachute Regiment	4748060	92120	Interrogation 'Yes told we were being registered.'
Bryan	Stephen Arthur	Lance Corporal	2nd Battalion, South Staffordshire Regiment	4919029	117965	Ordinary.
Bryson	Lionel Henry	Regimental Sergeant Major	Royal Army Medical Corps	7259229		Interrogated at Dulag Luft Frankfurt about a fortnight after capture only questioned on [illegible] & have photo taken and fingerprints taken, treatment wall there was not in my opinion correct. Kept standing up all night in small-cell with five other protected personnel.
Buck	Charles Reginald Harold	Craftsman	Advanced Workshop Detachment, REME	7387240	89268	Just trick questions no ill treatment or solitary confinement.
Buck	Lawrence Fredrick	Corporal	1st Parachute Squadron, Royal Engineers	1883034		Limburg. By Luftwaffe staff refusing to answer statements, brought threats of being sent to bad camp or shot.
Budd	Frederick John	Lance Corporal	181st Airlanding Field Ambulance	7364587		Interrogation kit searched no special methods employed.

Surname	First name	Rank	Regiment	Number	Number	Notes
Buglass	James	Private	3rd Battalion, Parachute Regiment	4975389		'Persuasive' at Luftwaffe HQ.
Burton	George	Corporal	3rd Battalion, Parachute Regiment	4921199		Normal.
Butler	Dennis John	Private	1st Battalion, Parachute Regiment	14409701		Limburg Oct Promised to take us to special Luft camp.
Butter	Arthur Anthony	Private	Parachute Regiment	7960360	294117	
Caddick	Ernest	Lance Corporal	156th Battalion, Parachute Regiment	3770832		Limburg.
Cairns	William	Corporal	7th Battalion, King's Own Scottish Borderers Regiment	3190460		Normal at Arnhem.
Calder	Ronald	Staff Sergeant	Glider Pilot Regiment	3859441		Interrogation at Dulag Luft Oberursel.
Cameron	Alan James	Trooper	4th Parachute Brigade HQ	3536624	117367	Apeldoorn Holland.
Campbell	Sidney Alex Albers	Gunner	1st Airlanding Light Regiment	6099334		Arnhem Holland Just a few questions.
Campbell	Robert Stewart	Lance Bombardier	1st Airlanding Light Regiment	1578886		Interrogated at camp outside Frankfurt on Maine. In Oct methods single confinement.
Campbell	Henry	Sergeant	2nd Battalion, Parachute Regiment	3055067		Diez nr Limburg 26th Sept 1944, solitary confinement for four days in a cell, then interrogated at 01.00 hrs on the morning(date unknown).
Campbell	Alec	Staff Sergeant	Glider Pilot Regiment	2694009		Solitary confinement for 7 days then cigs and a 'friendly' chat.
Cannon	Leonard Alexander	Private	1st Battalion, Parachute Regiment	3964252		Stalag XII A by Luftwaffe Officers. Given a cig. Told to sit down and make ourselves comfortable.
Carlier	Leonard Thomas	Private	2nd Battalion, Parachute Regiment	5835317	89827	By Luftwaffe Officers at XII A. Casual talking.

Name	Forename	Rank	Unit	Army number	POW number	Answer given on Questionnaire
Carmichael	John	Private	1st Battalion, Parachute Regiment	2879115	91559	Vechlau. Confronted me with a list of CO, 2 i/c, etc was offered cigarettes and drink when I refused to give anything but name rank number was placed in solitary with no food.
Carr	Jack	Sergeant	2nd Battalion, Parachute Regiment	2182264		Frankfurt on Main. 20-9-44. Placed 3 days in solitary confinement for not divulging information meal of soup per day. I refused all information asked.
Carroll	Albert	Lance Corporal	2nd Battalion, South Staffordshire Regiment	14668753	89367	Arnhen (Holland) methods good.
Carter	Stephen William	Private	181st Airlanding Field Ambulance	7392998		'Enchede'. Officer asked for division, names of officers, travelled by Horsa or parachute (rations 48 hr packs).
Cawley	John	Driver	253rd Airborne Light Company, RASC	10680840	90968	Enemy officer speaking perfect English. Method employed by him, he pretended to know everything in hope that I should part with information.
Cawrey	Victor Frank	Private	21st Independent Parachute Company	4975875	118305	11 B Fallingbostel promises of clothing extra food cigarettes.
Chamberlain	Stanley Arthur	Private	3rd Battalion, Parachute Regiment	557436	89733	Limburg. Ger. Sept 1944 Method normal.
Chambers	Talbot Alexander	Sergeant	89 Parachute Security Section	118933	93637	Stalag XII A Early Oct '44. By a civilian occasionally wearing Luftwaffe Major's uniform and who said he was from German Foreign Office or Red Cross Rep. Friendly methods. Questions varied from opinions on the war to what you thought of Russia. Mostly political. Tried to find out civilian background.

Surname	First Name	Rank	Unit	Number		Notes
Channon	William	Company Quartermaster Sergeant Major	4th Parachute Brigade HQ	5567123	88745	At Ede near Arnhem, Holland. Taken to German GHQ and accused of shooting a German Red Cross nurse. Supposed to have been recognised by an officer, also offered drinks in an Offrs Mess and told I should go to a concentration camp.
Chapman	Albert Henry	Gunner	1st Airlanding Light Regiment	1470053		At Limberg Oct 44 by questions.
Chapman	Harold	Trooper	GHQ Liaison Regiment (Phantom)	14521821		Interrogated in Holland and Germany just asked questions.
Charles	Ernest	Private	1st Battalion, Parachute Regiment	5679630		Limburg 29-9-44 Trade interrogation, no [number] questions regarding trade chiefly food problems, Flying Bomb damage, politics.
Chesterton	Eric	Sergeant, Lance	Royal Signals	2330939		Limburg - 15 Oct 44-20 Oct 44 5 days' solitary confinement.
Chilcott	Frederick Henry	Bombardier	1st Airlanding Anti-Tank Battery	780594		At Arnhem by Luftwaffe Officers who promised admission to Luft camps if given information, which they didn't get.
Chivers	Laurence Herbert James	Sergeant	156th Battalion, Parachute Regiment	5673491		9 days solitary (Luftwaffe camp) October 44. Not allowed to wash or shave. No books poor food. Name of camp Dulag Luft.
Chivers	William Ernest	Private	2nd Battalion, South Staffordshire Regiment	4917934		Frankfurt-an-Main, Lindburgh, Fallingbostel immediately after arrival. Cigarette & chocolates at first but if no info forthcoming 24hr solitary confinement with no food. This sequence continued for 3-4 days.
Clark	Andrew Basil	Company Quartermaster Sergeant Major	11th Battalion, Parachute Regiment	6397607		Limburg Military questions.
Clark	James	Private	7th Battalion, King's Own Scottish Borderers Regiment	3245281	90528	Limburg 28.9.44. They told me who I was, my unit, and Division and how I landed in Holland.

Name	Forename	Rank	Unit	Army number	POW number	Answer given on Questionnaire
Clark	Henry Pullman	Sergeant	1st Airlanding Light Regiment	997188	88740	Conversation attitude adopted by a civilian dressed officer speaking perfect English rather like trying to be introduced into a debate Limburg Camp Stalag 12 A Germany.
Clarke	Alfred Charles James	Private	3rd Battalion, Parachute Regiment	122644		Limburg Stalag XII A in Sept 44 Interrogation by an officer of the Luftwaffe.
Cobbold	George Arthur	Staff Sergeant	Glider Pilot Regiment	2575349		3 days solitary they claimed to know all the answers.
Coleman	Richard	Private	10th Battalion, Parachute Regiment	3658412	90520	Yes as to strength and equipment.
Colls	Douglas	Sergeant, Lance	1st Airlanding Anti-Tank Battery	1514892		Routine.
Connelly	Edward	Private	7th Battalion, King's Own Scottish Borderers Regiment	3325781		At Limburg tried to trap using clever questions.
Connely	James Joseph	Gunner	1st Airlanding Anti-Tank Battery	3055590	91734	Just interview.
Conway	James Joseph	Staff Sergeant	Glider Pilot Regiment	7043131	117320	At Stalag XII A. Asked about damage done by V1. Why I fight for England.
Cook	James	Sapper	9th Field Company, Royal Engineers Airborne	2069925	91491	Oberursel. October 1944. Luftwaffe HQ by bribes ie cigarettes, easy treatment, also by cheap and empty threats.
Cooke	Clifford Kenneth	Private	11th Battalion, Parachute Regiment	10666764	89804	24/9/44 Limburg. Information sought under threats of Gestapo reprisals. Men given solitary confinement on refusal to talk.
Cooper	Cyril	Driver	Airborne Light Company, RASC	114167	140093	In hospital at Lochom nr Arnhem Given cigs and coffee and asked strength of 6th Airborne Div also transport planes but I did not tell.

Surname	First names	Rank	Unit	Number		Notes
Cooper	Stanley	Private	181st Airlanding Field Ambulance	7368352		Interrogation separately re conditions at home, employment conditions in my trade at the moment.
Cooper	Thomas John	Private	10th Battalion, Parachute Regiment	897853	75654	At Stalag XII A by German Officer general questions about unit strength and types of aircraft used on operation. I refused to answer questions and was not pressed.
Coppack	Philip Maurice	Staff Sergeant	Glider Pilot Regiment	937504		Luftwaffe Interrogation Centre Oberursal Oct 1st (approx) threats promises of being imprisoned with personal friends.
Cornish	Denis	Sergeant	Glider Pilot Regiment	903724		I was specially interrogated by German Luftwaffe Officer at an interrogation centre near Frankfort. Date approx 29/9/44. I was placed in solitary confinement for 6 days prior to interrogation.
Cottrell	William John	Bombardier	1st Airlanding Anti-Tank Battery	1514708		At Zutphen. Method - Questions & promises of being sent to a Luft Stalag which was considered better camps than normal.
Couch	Stanley Hugh	Private	2nd Battalion, South Staffordshire Regiment	5440744		Interrogated under the guise of registering with The Red Cross at 12A Limburg.
Coupe	Harold	Sapper	1st Parachute Squadron, Royal Engineers	1922268	89229	12A German Air Force Officer.
Courtney	Richard William	Gunner	2nd Airlanding Anti-Tank Battery	14268331	90921	Limberg Sept 1944 Luftwaffe told us they would give us good food and put us in a good camp.
Courtney	Thomas Richard Brian	Major	133rd Parachute Field Ambulance	112406	91202	At Castle Dietz. Solitary confinement followed by conversations of 2-3 hours during which I was fed with British Red Cross food.
Cowie	David	Sergeant	2nd Battalion, Parachute Regiment	7886460	?	They said they were Red Cross representatives and asked us to fill forms giving names of unit, planes we dropped from and what we did in our company.

Name	Forename	Rank	Unit	Army number	POW number	Answer given on Questionnaire
Cox	Denis Herbert	Sergeant, Acting	2nd Battalion, South Staffordshire Regiment	5051692	89424	Yes by Luftwaffe Officers. Tried promise of a good camp if information given as to airborne methods.
Craig	William	Private	3rd Battalion, Parachute Regiment	14246464		Ordinary.
Craig	James	Sergeant	2nd Battalion, Parachute Regiment	3246833	89139	By an American German at SS Div HQ in Arnhem. By Luftwaffe Officers at Limberg XII A – also asked questions and filled in precis whether you answered or not.
Creasy	Reginald George	Corporal	3rd Battalion, Parachute Regiment	5623140	90102	Yes. I was offered preferential treatment by Luftwaffe interrogation officer. When I wouldn't talk was threatened but afterwards dismissed.
Cressey	Charles	Lance Corporal	1st Airborne Provost Company	2053082	14909	Limburg by German Airforce Officers.
Cuckle	Lionel	Private	11th Battalion, Parachute Regiment	4896515	75995	Muhlberg – fairly direct questions.
Cull	George William	Private	1st Parachute Brigade	14410678		Not specifically, same as everyone. Limberg about 24th Sept. Passed cigarettes & speaking nice. But mostly by saying names of our kites & weapons or trying to catch us.
Culliton	Patrick	Private	3rd Battalion, Parachute Regiment	13098369		At XII A Limburg on 26/9/1944. They stated that they knew all about our operation. They told us all about ourselves and they were right.
Culpan	Eric Hopkinson	Sergeant	Glider Pilot Regiment	2081536		Oberhursal. Solitary confinement and questions. Also a form for Red Cross use (according to Germans) to be filled in. Only next of kin given although the form requested details of squadron, etc.

Surname	Forename	Rank	Unit	Service No	POW No	Notes
Cund	Edwin	Sergeant	2nd Battalion, South Staffordshire Regiment	4914618		Limburg Stalag XII A.
Cunningham	Alexander	Corporal	10th Battalion, Parachute Regiment	4481938	90824	German IO Officers knew everything.
Dagwell	David Nicol	Private	156th Battalion, Parachute Regiment	5349578		Limburg Sept 1944. A German civilian.
Dalton	Christopher	Private	1st Battalion, Parachute Regiment	4348459		Interrogated at Dulag Luft nr Frankfurt (Main) excuse used information would help the Red Cross to get word of your capture to relatives.
Daniels	Stanley	Private	2nd Battalion, South Staffordshire Regiment	14682944	89138	Limburg September.
Davey	Roy	Corporal	2nd Battalion, South Staffordshire Regiment	5348839	89921	At Limburg. Method by giving me good food and trying to get me to drink wine.
Davies	Desmond Godfrey	Private	2nd Battalion, Parachute Regiment. Royal Army Medical Corps	14389667	89420	Not specially interrogated.
Davies	William Peter	Private	3rd Battalion, Parachute Regiment	41796618		German air force officer. NO food two days tried to entice asking all about home then threatening.
Davis	John Harold	Private	3rd Battalion, Parachute Regiment	5625908		Locked in cell for four days barely any food or water near Wetzlar Oct 1944.
Davis	Samuel Wilfred	Private	181st Airlanding Field Ambulance	7362406	93720	In an RAF interrogation camp 11 Kilo from Limburg. Food very poor solitary confinement for 7 days.
Davis	George Ernest	Staff Sergeant	Glider Pilot Regiment	2045543		At RAF interrogation centre near Frankfurt Sept. 44. Solitary for four days. Threatened for longer period if not talk. Threat not carried out.
Dawson	Robert Ridley	Corporal	Royal Army Medical Corps	7266914		Wetzlar.

Name	Forename	Rank	Unit	Army number	POW number	Answer given on Questionnaire
Dawson	Herbert	Private	2nd Battalion, South Staffordshire Regiment	1714784	89717	By Luftwaffe Officers who gave us a fag and tried to make us comfortable Stalag 12 A.
Dawson	John Harold	Private	2nd Battalion, Parachute Regiment	11407811	75336	Muhlberg.
Daye	Russell Robert	Private	7th Battalion, King's Own Scottish Borderers Regiment	14620635	118419	Ordinary.
Deeley	George Alfred	Sergeant	Glider Pilot Regiment	5127622		Oberursel. A/C Interrogation Centre. Solitary confinement. Question and answer.
Delea	Eric Michael Desmond	Private	156th Battalion, Parachute Regiment	3778794		Wetzlar 30/9/44–5/10/44 in solitary confinement.
Dell	Edward	Corporal	2nd Battalion, Parachute Regiment	6203748		Arnhem Sept 21 1944.
Dennis	Frank	Sergeant	Glider Pilot Regiment	5887705		Oberusel, 3rd to 7th Oct. 1944. Threatened to be put into the hands of the Gestapo and solitary confinement.
Devey	John Raymond	Staff Sergeant	Glider Pilot Regiment	3601654	903	Oberursel 25 Sept 1944. Interviewed by friendly German Pilot. Usual 'Red Cross Form' supplied asking for Squadron aircraft flown and tug aircraft used. Sweat Box 3 days.
Dickson	Richard	Private	3rd Battalion, Parachute Regiment	4546716	92122	Holland locked in cellar for 7 days with no lights small hole in door.
Dinwiddie	Gordon Maidland	Major	7th Battalion, King's Own Scottish Borderers Regiment	90195	2195	Normal only on arrival at Oflag. asked for, type of commission, profession, status of commission and nationality of parents as well as routine questions.
Dixon	John	Private	7th Battalion, King's Own Scottish Borderers Regiment	14203067	90692	Limburg 23 Sept 44 Name of place captured and Division.

Surname	First names	Rank	Unit	Number		Remarks
Dixon	Thomas	Private	133rd Parachute Field Ambulance	7361998	89925	ADA. Holland Sept 22/44. Threatened with solitary confinement.
Dodd	William Ronald	Private	3rd Battalion, Parachute Regiment	6404195		Limburg 12A Promised better treatment if would tell them names of units on operation (Arnhem).
Doig	John	Private	156th Battalion, Parachute Regiment	14407490		Limburg Sept 1944. Told that I would be sent to an Army Camp not RAF if I did not tell them the aerodrome I left from in England.
Dolaghan	Thomas Noel William Dowie	Private	4th Parachute Brigade	6977906	89826	At Stalag XII A Limbourg (sic) Germany by Luftwaffe officers who said that the interrogation was normal routine for registration as a POW. 30/9/1944.
Donnelly	Moses	Private	1st Battalion, Parachute Regiment	4538622	91461	In Holland 1 day after capture NCO took him for a walk gave him a cigarette and asked questions about his private life, then told me what unit I was in and the home location.
Donowho	William	Private	7th Battalion, King's Own Scottish Borderers Regiment	3190801		[Just answererd] Yes.
Dover	Victor	Major	2nd Battalion, Parachute Regiment	113514	521	At Arnhem immediately after capture. I was taken away by staff car and 'talked at' for some hours.
Dredge	Norman Victor	Private	2nd Battalion, South Staffordshire Regiment	14700066	92215	Interrogation 'Yes just formal routine'.
Drew	Douglas John Archer	Private	3rd Battalion, Parachute Regiment	6468336		At Stalag XII Limburg (Lahn) method was mainly to try and draw you out by pretending to know all about our unit and saying is not such and such correct.
Drury	Robert	Private	10th Battalion, Parachute Regiment	5726456		Threats of concentration camps were used and shooting at (Limberg Stalag XII A) if the truth was not told.
Dunbar	William Shearer	Sergeant	Glider Pilot Regiment	2572042		At Oberursal. 3 days solitary confinement then questioned re squadron markings? On refusing information returned to solitary for 1 day before being sent to permanent camp.

Name	Forename	Rank	Unit	Army number	POW number	Answer given on Questionnaire
Durant	George Edwin	Gunner	1st Airlanding Light Regiment	14284494	91884	Oberursal 15 October 1944 solitary confinement 6 days.
Easton	William	Private	3rd Battalion, Parachute Regiment	5781435		Limburg Stalag XII A Sept 28. Type of aircraft weapons and taking off places.
Eatwell	Horace Arthur	Regimental Sergeant Major	1st Battalion, Parachute Regiment	2613152	89402	Oberursal Nr Frankurt-Main Luftwaffe Interrogation Camp for aircrews, solitary confinement, etc.
Edwards	Thomas	Corporal	2nd Battalion, Parachute Regiment	4699004		At Stalag XII A Oct 1944. Solitary confinement. No food for 68 hours. And rough handling by German guards.
Elliott	John	Private	4th Parachute Brigade HQ	839439	90625	Werson (sic) 29-9-44 Solitary confinement no food clothing hit with sticks and fist.
Ellis	John Aloysius	Staff Sergeant	Glider Pilot Regiment	1901936		Oberursal Sept 1944 solitary confinement for 2 days.
Evans	Kenneth Charles	Lieutenant	4th Parachute Squadron, Royal Engineers	267949	2178	No only in group at Emergency Hospital at Apeldoorn in Holland.
Evans	Robert George	Private	1st Battalion, Parachute Regiment	6108197		2 weeks at Dulag Luft - attempt to gain confidence over this period by 'friendly discussions' with unknown civilians – questions normally general not applied to particular organisation.
Evans	Thomas	Private	3rd Battalion, Parachute Regiment	4031655		At Luftwaffe camp Frankfurt on Main solitary confinements no treatment for wounds.
Evans	Walter John	Private	156th Battalion, Parachute Regiment	5679918		Limburg 24/9/1944.
Evans	Frank	Private	1st Battalion, Border Regiment	3864100	91881	German Air Force Camp (Oct 44) received 24 hrs solitary confinement.

Everest	Sydney John	Private	3rd Battalion, Parachute Regiment	6214961	90470	Normal.
Fairweather	Clifford	Corporal	250th Airborne Light Company, RASC	229170	118846	Interrogated at Sagan on 29 December 1944 Method very casual.
Faulkner	Maurice Arthur	Private	2nd Battalion, South Staffordshire Regiment	4917591	91647	Ordinary Limburg Oct 1944.
Ferguson	David Drummond	Private	7th Battalion, King's Own Scottish Borderers Regiment	14210564	25480	Refused to answer only gave rank name no.
Ferguson	Samuel	Sergeant	156th Battalion, Parachute Regiment	2754337		By German Luftwaffe officers at Stalag XII A Transit Camp. Interrogated individually.
Few	Ted	Private	156th Battalion, Parachute Regiment	5257174		At IV B Mulburg. Taken into a room and spoken to nicely by English-speaking German and advised to accept trade job instead of ordinary labouring which I finally did so.
Fitzgerald	Michael	Driver	1st Airlanding Anti-Tank battery	6854732		Nine days in a cell at Frankfurt with American pilots Luft Camp.
Fleming	James	Private	2nd Battalion, Parachute Regiment	2985559		Dulag Luft 24th Sept.
Fletcher	Ernest Leslie	Bombardier	2nd Airlanding Anti-Tank Battery	1525244	89756	Questioned by Luftwaffe at Stalag XII A.
Fletcher	Dugald	Private	156th Battalion, Parachute Regiment	2766219		Limburg. By German Officer who asked my No, Rank and Names, where and when captured and entered these particulars on paper form.
Ford	William	Lance Corporal	7th Battalion, King's Own Scottish Borderers Regiment	3188138	90720	By Luftwaffe officers at Limberg questions were about Bn, Division, what type of planes we flew in.
Forman	Michael Bertram	Major	7th Battalion, King's Own Scottish Borderers Regiment	91061	90861	At Diez near Limburg. I was in solitary confinement for 8 days. German rations were short, and Red Cross cigarettes and food were withdrawn.

Name	Forename	Rank	Unit	Army number	POW number	Answer given on Questionnaire
Forsyth	Thomas Thomson	Private	7th Battalion, King's Own Scottish Borderers Regiment	14210830	90168	Interrogated concerning where I worked, what type of work. Tried to persuade one to talk by reprisals. Casual Interrogation at Frankfurt.'
Forwood	Charles	Corporal	7th Battalion, King's Own Scottish Borderers Regiment	3136134	88797	Limburg An English speaking civilian using English sporting events as a base to extract information of V2 Damage and civilian morale in London.
Foster	James Henry	Private	7th Battalion, King's Own Scottish Borderers Regiment	144339540	91774	Interrogation 'Yes at Limburg during Oct by civilian. Questions and bribery'.
Foster	David William	Leading Aircraftman	Light Warning Set Unit No. 6080, RAF	1652764		Oberursel from Dec 5/44 to Dec 19/44. Questioned six times by four different German officers.
Fowler	Colin	Private	1st Battalion, Border Regiment	4546551	91931	IV B Dec 44. I was asked questions in a normal sort of way. If I couldn't supply the answers they could. They were two German army and one flying officer.
Foxon	James Arthur	Signalman	Royal Signals	2378460	91899	Interrogated at Limburg. Stock questions asked – type of aircraft used, etc.
Frary	Dennis	Private	133rd Parachute Field Ambulance	14351195		Holland.
Furber	Tom	Private	2nd Battalion, South Staffordshire Regiment	14682861		Limburg.
Gaitero	Allan	Corporal	3rd Battalion, Parachute Regiment	6466565	89523	Interrogated at Linburg 25.9.44 We were told that if we answered all questions we would go to a Luftwaffe camp If we did not we would go to an Army camp.
Garbutt	William Martyn	Sergeant	Glider Pilot Regiment	816515	76327	Yes Oosterbreck [sic] Holland immediately after capture. Starvation.

230

Surname	First name(s)	Rank	Unit	Service No.	Camp No.	Notes
Gardner	Cyril	Private	7th Battalion, King's Own Scottish Borderers Regiment	14204693	90577	At Limburg usual questions regarding identification.
Gaunt	James	Sergeant, Lance	2nd Battalion, South Staffordshire Regiment	4913313	90025	Dulagluft. Oberursal. Threatened with Gestapo and solitary confinement.
Gavin	Patrick Charles	Regimental Quartermaster Sergeant	133rd Parachute Field Ambulance	7263776		Luftwaffe Centre, nr Frankfurt-on-Maine. Solitary confinement.
Gibb	Archibald Allan	Private	2nd Battalion, South Staffordshire Regiment	2880575	89435	XII B 20/9/44 No.
Gibb	William	Private	181st Airlanding Field Ambulance	7396628	90571	31/9/1944 By 2 questions.
Gibbs	Frederick Michael	Captain	156th Battalion, Parachute Regiment	114084	91015	Political Interrogation by Foreign Office Official in civilian clothes. Required information as to what we would do with Germany after their war, and our attitude to Russians, Sept 1944.
Gibney	James	Sergeant Major	Royal Signals	2582457	91575	Interrogated at Limburg (XII A) Oct/44.
Gilbert	William Ernest	Private	3rd Battalion, Parachute Regiment	7372770	93701	Place not known Methods used mainly solitary confinement.
Gilchrist	David Alexander	Major/T	11th Battalion, Parachute Regiment	95588	545	Oberursal & Dietz. In October Chiefly displaying their own knowledge and trying to get confirmation of this knowledge being Correct.
Gilchrist	James Gibson	Private	156th Battalion, Parachute Regiment	14415465	975697	Normal At Mulberg on Nov 21.11.44.
Gillespie	George Whyte	Private	10th Battalion, Parachute Regiment	1478056	90535	Limburgh 25 Sept Questions.
Gillow	Charles	Staff Sergeant	Glider Pilot Regiment	894370		At Dulag Luft – I was in solitary confinement for 1 day only & did not undergo any rigorous interrogation whatever.

Name	Forename	Rank	Unit	Army number	POW number	Answer given on Questionnaire
Girvin	Robert	Staff Sergeant	Glider Pilot Regiment	7022767		OBERURSAL 26.9.44 to 30.9.44 Solitary confinement with little food and then interrogated on the 30th.
Gledhill	Tom	Private	1st Battalion, Parachute Regiment	14333598	117528	Stalag XI B.
Glenn	James Joseph	Driver	250th Airborne Light Company, RASC	6984399	91784	Frankfurt 27/9/1944. Confinement for two days (and living on bread and water).
Godden	John Herbert	Private	1st Battalion, Parachute Regiment	912836		Yes. Stalag XII A Limburg by Luftwaffe on 4-10-44 Flattery & Persuasion.
Gofton	Andrew Kay	Private	16th Parachute Field Ambulance	7390953	93686	Interrogated at Luftwaffe POW Camp near Frankfurt Germany. Formal questioning [This added in a second hand].
Gough	Charles Frederick Howard	Major	1st Airborne Reconnaissance Squadron	31420	595	By Luftwaffe at Ober Oerzel near Frankfurt. 3 days, with solitary confinement. By Wehrmacht at Diez. 6 days solitary two interrogations one at 2 am and one at 7.30 am two days later. Threats about hot rooms & other things. References to cruelty to German POWs by British at Maison Blanche near Algiers & vague references to Tower of London. All rather theatrical.
Gough	Samuel	Private	Forward Obs Unit, Royal Artillery	981355	89226	Slight interrogation they had already found out everything they wanted to know.
Grant	Alexander	Private	7th Battalion, King's Own Scottish Borderers Regiment	14210847	91393	Stalag IV B Mulberg Nov. 1944 Normal interrogation.
Grant	Richard Sydney	Staff Sergeant	Glider Pilot Regiment	6474934		Aircrew interrogation centre, Oberwerzel Nr Frankfurt 29 Sept. 1944. Methods employed questioning with threats.

Gray	Frederick	Private	156th Battalion, Parachute Regiment	6980488		Limberg Sept. Question.
Green	George Stanley	Lance Corporal	1st Battalion, Parachute Regiment	2929195		At Limburg. Bullying & promise of good treatment if we came across.
Green	George	Private	2nd Battalion, South Staffordshire Regiment	7523335	90559	Frankfort – Questions only on War matters, also food rationing in England, also political matters.
Greenbaum	Frank Ashley	Sergeant	Glider Pilot Regiment	14417002		Obersursal Use of threats & solitary confinement 2 days.
Greenslade	George Charles	Staff Sergeant	Glider Pilot Regiment	6086559	75462	At Obersursal October 1944 Solitary confinement their n questions.
Grieveson	John	Signalman	Royal Signals	862338		Sept 30th Luftwaffe. questions Limberg.
Griffith	William Gordon	Sergeant	Glider Pilot Regiment	4192348		Near Frankfurt on Maine, by Luftwaffe, Oct 1944 solitary confinement, bread & water, threatened with firing squad for withholding information.
Grove	Philip Nigel	Captain/T	1st Battalion, Parachute Regiment	85684	597	Air Force interrogation centre, Oberursel September 1944. Given a form to fill in and asked several questions by a Luftwaffe Sgt & their n by a German civilian.
Guyatt	Eric George	Lance Bombardier	1st Airlanding Light Regiment	935260	92081	Limburg Oct 1944 Solitary confinement bread and water.
Hackett	Henry	Gunner	Forward Obs Unit Royal Artillery	876593		Limburg September Stating it was already known their information required. Being kind & offering cigarettes.
Hales	Clifford	Signalman	1st Parachute Brigade, Royal Signals	3782726	91929	Although not personally interrogated at Frankfurt. I did 9 day solitary confinement.
Haley	John Michael William	Private	156th Battalion, Parachute Regiment	14391649		Stammlager XII B. Limberg. Normal methods of questioning.

Name	Forename	Rank	Unit	Army number	POW number	Answer given on Questionnaire
Hallett	Hugh Anthony	Private	2nd Battalion, Parachute Regiment	6465318	89693	No Limburg XII A Ask normal questions.
Hamer	Mal Dwyn	Lance Corporal	1st Parachute Brigade	6921343	75451	No. At Arnhem. No special way.
Hamilton	Reginald Thomas	Private	7th Battalion, King's Own Scottish Borderers Regiment	14437879		Limburg Friendliness.
Hampton	Leslie Robert	Gunner	1st Airlanding Light Regiment	14249030	75969	No. Short interrogation by Luftwaffe Officers. When refusing information I was not pressed.
Hann	Stanley	Staff Sergeant	Glider Pilot Regiment	44692164	76307	Zutphen, near Arnhen. Method given food, drink and cigarettes. Later a slight bullying attitude by SS officer who tried to make me speak over radio transmitter.
Harbour	Frederick Spencer	Sergeant	10th Battalion, Parachute Regiment	6402134		Amersfoot. Holland. Sept 20th 1944. Interrogated singly, by a Colonel, after a handshake, given a cigarette and promises of being sent to a good camp, if right answers given.
Hardwick	John Geoffrey	Sergeant	Glider Pilot Regiment	3054186		Immediately on capture. Holland Normal.
Hargrave	Francis Richard	Private	2nd Battalion, South Staffordshire Regiment	7013354	89576	Lindberg Threatened to be handed over to Gestapo.
Harlow	Albert William Harrison	Major Reverend	Royal Army Chaplains' Department	131946	640	Solitary confinements. Dulag Luft Wezlar & Ober-Ouzel.
Harper	Gordon Thomas	Private	2nd Battalion, South Staffordshire Regiment	14692209	17566	In every different place I was moved to. Usual questions.

Surname	First name	Rank	Unit	Service No.	POW No.	Notes
Harper	John Everard	Lance Corporal	2nd Battalion, Parachute Regiment	497226	88485	A Director of Iron and Steel Works tried to discover what was being made at my previous employment [He was a fitter – general iron work] but, discovering that I had been in their army such a long time gave me up.
Harris	Norman	Lance Corporal	1st Parachute Brigade	83502		A short interrogation on arrival at Limburg.
Harris	Kenneth Wesley	Private	10th Battalion, Parachute Regiment	14425014	80092	Harscamp. Holland Sept 24 1944. By word of mouth.
Harris	Percy Victor	Private	4th Battalion, Dorset Regiment	5735127		At Muhlberg by asking all sorts of tricky questions and slight threats.
Harris	Douglas George	Private	3rd Battalion, Parachute Regiment	3967311		Linburg. Asking questions ?-9-44.
Harris	George William	Staff Sergeant	Army Physical Training Corps	3767430	89164	No ordinary interrogation.
Harrison	Eric George	Private	1st Battalion, Border Regiment	14579662	175991	Arnhem, 1 day after capture.
Harrison	Robert	Private	7th Battalion, King's Own Scottish Borderers Regiment	14210604	90725	Questions asked Stalag XII A Limburg 5.10.44.
Hartley	Benjamin	Driver	1st Airlanding Anti-Tank Battery	3712207		Interrogated by well spoken English using only cigs and promises of good treatment, Limburg Sept 1944.
Hartley	Alfred Harold	Private	156th Battalion, Parachute Regiment	14413724	14069	Germans revealed as much as I knew + more.
Harvey	Clifford	Private	181st Airlanding Field Ambulance	7263046	93691	Luftwaffe Interrogation Centre Oberfue-lle by offer of special treatment, bullying and threats of punishment such as solitary confinement.
Harwood	Alfred George	Private	2nd Battalion, South Staffordshire Regiment	5391715		Linburg Trick questions.

Name	Forename	Rank	Unit	Army number	POW number	Answer given on Questionnaire
Haslam	Reginald Alfred	Bombardier	1st Airlanding Anti-Tank Battery	1115969		At Interrogation Centre near Frankfort on Main. Method employed sweat box cells.
Hately	John Frederick	Private	156th Battalion, Parachute Regiment	6896966	221694	By Luftwaffe officer at Stalag XII A. I was informed that it was only a routine statement that was being taken in order to ascertain whether I belonged to an A/B Div so that he could be sent to a Stalag Luft.
Hawkins	Benjamin Edward	Private	2nd Battalion, South Staffordshire Regiment	4922840	91639	Not severely 12A Stalag.
Hayes	Joseph	Private	11th Battalion, Parachute Regiment	2984852	92028	Limburg By questions.
Hayward	John Spencer Victor	Private	250th Airborne Light Company, RASC	107853	140066	Appledorne Holland, Oct 1944 Questions on strength of Airborne etc. I refused to answer.
Headland	William George	Private	3rd Battalion, Parachute Regiment	1435227		At Arnhem German building – method by giving me information that he already had.
Healey	Edwin	Staff Sergeant	Glider Pilot Regiment	3775315		Auber Ruzel – Sept 30th- Oct 13th 1944 solitary confinement.
Hendy	Arthur Sydney	Lance Corporal	1st Parachute Squadron, Royal Engineers	1874248		Limberg. Routine questioning.
Henley	Reginald French	Private	10th Battalion, Parachute Regiment	5568074	89389	Limburg (4) four days at Stalag. Promised good treatment. Kind of planes used. Arms used.
Hewish	Robert Harvey	Lance Corporal	4th Parachute Brigade, Royal Signals	6469323		Sense of humour played on very effectively in many cases at Limburg – Stamlager XII A Sept 44.
Higginbotham	James	Staff Sergeant	Glider Pilot Regiment	905927		Oberusel – by threats of Gestapo punishment Sept 1944.

Surname	First name	Rank	Regiment	Number	No.	Notes
Hill	Cecil	Corporal	2nd Battalion, Parachute Regiment	6401664		Luftwaffe HQ in their field. Sept 23-25? Maps of flight with times, units engaged in operation & statements supposedly from other prisoners.
Hill	William	Lance Corporal	16th Parachute Field Ambulance	7264147		At Frankforte. In a room with others. Microphoned threatening with death, politics book of your home concentration camps.
Hindmarsh	Henry	Private	2nd Battalion, Parachute Regiment	4461927		Arnhen. 21/9/44. Verbal.
Hogwood	Ralph Herbert	Sergeant	7th Battalion, King's Own Scottish Borderers Regiment	5052938	88746	1. At Deatrich, 2. Limbourg 3. Gestapo method by questioning. Generally on their conditions of living and conditions in England, and their threat of Bolshevikism against Europe.
Holding	Thomas Wilfred	Private	1st Battalion, Border Regiment	3782686		Wetzlar (Germany) 5.10.44 solitary confinement.
Hole	Edward Stanley	Private	3rd Battalion, Parachute Regiment	5672174		Frankfurt on Main 24/9/1944 confined for one day for not explaining gammon bomb.
Holland	James	Driver	Royal Artillery	14321655	75880	At Limbourg.
Holland	Donald Kitson	Sergeant	2nd Battalion, South Staffordshire Regiment	4921819		Dulag Luft Oberursal, Limburg XII A, Neubranden their enemy tried to force out information.
Holt	Arthur	Private	7th Battalion, King's Own Scottish Borderers Regiment	3716068	90489	Lindberg By Luftwaffe Officers.
Holt	Ronald Charles Neville	Private	2nd Battalion, Parachute Regiment	2766005	93727	Dulag Luft [crossed out and interrogation centre entered, same hand], nr Hanover Oct 1944 Confined to cells and after a space of a few days interrogated. Threatened Strafe Lager
Hooper	James Michael	Staff Sergeant	Glider Pilot Regiment	2584037		Dulag Luft nr Frankfurt solitary confinement.

Name	Forename	Rank	Unit	Army number	POW number	Answer given on Questionnaire
Hooson	Gwilyn	Private	7th Battalion, King's Own Scottish Borderers Regiment	14374202	89535	Limberg September 44.
Hope	Thomas Rogers	Lance Corporal	1st Airborne Provost Company	6206756		Limburg German air force officer after capture.
Hopkins	Kenneth Arthur	Private	181st Airlanding Field Ambulance	14672266		Enshede, Holland, October 1944 Questions.
Horsfield	James	Private	10th Battalion, Parachute Regiment	14632609	17	(Frankfurt) (Nov 1944) (No food).
Horsley	James	Private	11th Battalion, Parachute Regiment	6010893		Ordinary interrogation.
Horton	Charles Henry	Private	16th Parachute Field Ambulance	7357394	93681	Solitary confinement. Obercurfel. Luftwaffe Interrogation Centre Shown photographs. Interrogation on dropping. Usual RAF Int.
Horton	John	Sergeant	Glider Pilot Regiment	14413159	21	4 days solitary confinement at Oberootsal interrogation by Luftwaffe.
Hosker	Thomas Herbert	Private	7th Battalion, King's Own Scottish Borderers Regiment	14573434		At Arnhem. As usual.
Houghton	Norman Edwin	Private	11th Battalion, Parachute Regiment	996560		Was interrogated at Air Corps camp. Location unknown in Sept 1944.
Hounslow	Edward Charles	Private	3rd Battalion, Parachute Regiment	5502730	89562	Not specially interrogated. They told me all about my unit. When we dropped and their planes we used.
Howard	John James	Lance Corporal	1st Battalion, Parachute Regiment	3598966	89855	Main interrogation centre near Frankfurt. Dulag Luft questioned separately. Cross examination method with cigarettes and kindness.

Surname	First Name	Rank	Unit	Number	Number	Notes
Howard	Thomas Henry	Private	10th Battalion, Parachute Regiment	14417045		Limburg.
Hoyer Millar MC	Francis Kinglake	Captain	2nd Battalion, Parachute Regiment	85213	90872	Only immediate interrogation carried out = Questions & Method of interrogation were unoriginal & insufficiently carried out.
Hoyland	Frank Charles	Private	4th Parachute Brigade HQ	14292326		Yes No Lemburg.
Hudson	Francis	Lance Corporal	2nd Battalion, South Staffordshire Regiment	5046543	91637	Not specially interrogation asked usual questions. No information given XII A Linberg Germany.
Hudson	Frederick Philip	Sergeant	Glider Pilot Regiment	14218054		Middleharnis Overflakke O/Lt Afrika Korps threat of shooting and hanging 16/12/1944. Brielle Oberst German Army Threat of hanging 18/12/1944. Oberursal Solitary Confinement 4/1/1945 [Hudson was an evader and only captured in December].
Hughes	Anthony Cecil	Private	3rd Battalion, Parachute Regiment	5125630	77095	Luftwaffe Camp near Frankfurt solitary confinement.
Hughes	Peter	Private	7th Battalion, King's Own Scottish Borderers Regiment	14212001		Lindburgh 25 Sept 44 Questioned by a German officer.
Hughes	Thomas	Private	2nd Battalion, Parachute Regiment	3969834	91184	Interrogated by civilian: he asked what unit I was in and then asked about London and the buzz bomb and then about what Russia would do to Germany after their war was over.
Hughes	William Horace	Private	2nd Battalion, South Staffordshire Regiment	14316562	92212	Arnhem September threatened for Internment camp.
Hull	Charles Cecil	Private	181st Airlanding Field Ambulance	7387687		Direct questioning Limburg. Questions dealt mainly with conditions at home and particulars of Airborne Div. Informed that we would be treated as agents on refusing to answer any except three stipulated questions (i.e. Name Rank No).

Name	Forename	Rank	Unit	Army number	POW number	Answer given on Questionnaire
Hume	William	Private	7th Battalion, King's Own Scottish Borderers Regiment	3190812	90486	At Limburg with their normal procedure and no force at all.
Humphreys	William	Private	2nd Battalion, Parachute Regiment	5835367	117578	Fallingbostel.
Hunt	Harry James	Private	2nd Battalion, Parachute Regiment	6848386		Not specially just asked questions.
Hutchinson	Ronald	Private	2nd Battalion, Parachute Regiment	4455745	89908	At XII A Limburg. Questioned on type of transport arms.
Hyslop	Eric	Sergeant	7th Battalion, King's Own Scottish Borderers Regiment	3190541	75874	At Limberg, Oct 44, Friendship with Russia, Food in England (Political questions). Questions were not answered by me.
Ingham	Ralph Taylor	Private	11th Battalion, Parachute Regiment	147330064		Limburg-Lahn by Luftwaffe. No methods.
Ingram	Stanley	Lance Bombardier	1st Airlanding Light Regiment	14306817	75871	Interrogated at Lindberg only asked Division, Bty, Tp. I gave no reply and was let go.
Isherwood	Reginald	Sergeant	1st Battalion, Parachute Regiment	893585		At Wetzlar from 23/9/44. Given extraordinary good treatment, and questioning on England political and economical situation, relations with Russia and plans for post war Germany.
Izzard	Cyril James	Private	2nd Battalion, Parachute Regiment	6029653	91397	Limbergh 24.9.44. Threatened with separation from other prisoners, and not being sent to a proper camp.
Jackson	Arthur	Private	Royal Army Service Corps	10694198		Limbergh Sept. If we gave good information of our Div. what aircraft were used and strengths of different Batts we would be sent to a Luft camp and better treated. WE DID NOT.

Surname	First name(s)	Rank	Unit/Regiment	Number	Number	Interrogation details
Jackson	Empsall	Private	1st Parachute Brigade	2042543		Interrogated at their Luft Camp at Frankfurt. Method keeping you in solitary confinement, very little food, and nothing to pass your days with.
Jackson	Peter Jackson	Private	181st Airlanding Field Ambulance	7265275		Limburg during October. Methods employed consisted of questions concerning English rationing system also what firm I worked for at home.
James	George	Private	2nd Battalion, Parachute Regiment	6153238	89279	Arnhiem Holland usual questions.
James	Arthur Bert	Private	21st Independent Parachute Company	7022654	75364	By SS interrogation officer. At Arnhem. Methods were gentle at first. Afterwards threats were used which proved to be bluff.
James	David William Mervyn	Staff Sergeant	Glider Pilot Regiment	944489		At Luftwaffe Interrogation Centre Oberursel (Nr Frankfurt-on-Main) Solitary confinement for three days. Threatened with Gestapo.
Jamieson	Peter Dunlop	Sergeant	156th Battalion, Parachute Regiment	2884343		Limburg Camp, Germany, Sept 1944. By Luftwaffe Personnel. Questionnaire.
Jenkins	Ronald William	Lance Corporal	156th Battalion, Parachute Regiment	7437345		Limburg.
Jeuchner	Albert George	Private	2nd Battalion, Parachute Regiment	6352988	91162	By Luftwaffe Officer on rationing bomb damage from V-1 in England.
Johnson	Peter	Private	1st Battalion, Parachute Regiment	5388969	89242	At Limburg 26.9.44.
Johnson	Douglas Frederick William	Private	2nd Battalion, South Staffordshire Regiment	867876		Methods used when under interrogation were by threats of Gestapo interrogation, buy confinement with bread and water. Name of place, Holland, Date 21-9-44.

Name	Forename	Rank	Unit	Army number	POW number	Answer given on Questionnaire
Johnstone	William Tait	Signalman	1st Parachute Brigade, Royal Signals	2378622		Oct 44 Limburgh asked about Div and also where other airborne units were. Did not answer their questions.
Jones	Alfred Redgewell	Corporal	2nd Battalion, South Staffordshire Regiment	4922888	89509	Lindberg – military.
Jones	John	Private	1st Battalion, Parachute Regiment	14418927		At Cologne, after capture. He asked what airfields flew from and also tried to get strength of Bn.
Jones	John Campbell	Signalman	4th Parachute Brigade, Royal Signals	324396	77367	Luft camp near Frankfurt (Ruhr) Solitary confinement followed by interrogation disarming manner used plus flattery.
Jones	Dewi Llewellyn	Sergeant	1st Airlanding Brigade, Royal Signals	2362597	91555	Not especially interrogated.
Jones	Conway Thomas	Sapper	1st Parachute Squadron, Royal Engineers	1909450		Ober Roosel Dulag Luft nr Frankfurt on Main. Confinement for one day still weak from wound. Just plain method + questions.
Jones	Robert	Sapper	Royal Engineers	5733483	88932	Interrogation 'Yes Arnhem'.
Jones	Cyril	Gunner	2nd Airlanding Anti-Tank Battery	14319790	91777	I was put in cells for two days in October can not remember [illegible] dates not known.
Jones	Robert Hobdell	Sergeant	2nd Battalion, Parachute Regiment	4975220	88902	Limburg. 29/9/1944. By questioning and threats to stop food and take reprisals etc if Q's not answered.
Jones	Howard Franklyn	Lance Corporal	16th Parachute Field Ambulance	7518016	89789	At Dulag Luft Frankfurt 26/27-9-44 by Luftwaffe personnel who endeavoured to discover information on their Arnhem operation – formation, training, transport, etc of Airborne Divisions.

Surname	First names	Rank	Regiment	Service No.	No.	Details
Jones	Robert John	Corporal	2nd Battalion, South Staffordshire Regiment	5886650		Frankfurt Germany Luft Camp.
Josephs	Daniel	Private	156th Battalion, Parachute Regiment	6849171		Dulag Luft Frankfurt/Maine Nove :1944 (sic) By threats of more confinement and less rations.
Kane	John Patrick	Private	2nd Battalion, Parachute Regiment	4690202		At Arnhem shortly after capture, methods employed were good in such as to gain confidence so you would talk.
Kay	John	Private	Parachute Regiment	915487	89731	St12A Yes by Luftwaffe Officers Given fag told to sit down and make ourselves comfortable.
Kay	George Edward	Private	3rd Battalion, Parachute Regiment	4974938	88758	Yes.
Kaye	Stanley Lawrence	Captain	16th Parachute Field Ambulance	246299	618	Practically none.
Kearns	James Thomas	Private	1st Battalion, Parachute Regiment	4808363	89495	We were interrogated but it was not strict.
Kelly	Patrick Joseph	Sergeant	1st Battalion, Parachute Regiment	7012461	?	Normal.
Kennedy	Wilfred	Private	156th Battalion, Parachute Regiment	2877369	90579	Muhlberg. By civilian on my trade. General questions about shipyards.
Kerswell	William John	Sergeant	Royal Army Medical Corps	7523088	77338	Enschede 18th October 1944. Questioned. Luft Interrogation camp 27th October. Questioned after 24 hours solitary confinement, XII A on 1st November 44 Questioned.
Kidds	Charles Frederick	Private	2nd Battalion, Parachute Regiment	7021470	294155	Ordinary questions.
Kilbryde	George Howard	Sergeant	Glider Pilot Regiment	4922900		At Dulag Luft interrogation centre (Oberursel), 23.9.44 (approx) for one hr by civilian. Propaganda ie 'Soviet menace' etc and spoke about a glider scheme alleged to have taken place in England, He knew quite a lot of details, very friendly.

Name	Forename	Rank	Unit	Army number	POW number	Answer given on Questionnaire
Kill	William	Sergeant, Lance	1st Airlanding Anti-Tank Battery	1107611	89415	Oberursel 1st October 1944. Questions about unit offices and general description of battery. On refusal to answer threatened with shooting but return to camp after further refusal.
Killick	John Edward	Captain	89 Parachute Security Section	137467	628	The only interrogation was three days after capture in a PW cage at Zutphen, their interrogation was lackadaisical, and made no attempt to break us down: he had a large printed pro-forma, on which he tried to fill in as many points as possible.
King	Leonard William	Signalman	4th Parachute Brigade, Royal Signals	2588983		At Limburg, Germany I was committed to 7 days solitary confinement commencing 7.12.44 + ending 14.12.44.
King	George Richard	Private	Parachute Regiment	5510137		Interrogated at Luft camp. Solitary Conf. Civilian Interrogation. Kindness.
Kirk	Stanley Harry	Lance Corporal	16th Parachute Field Ambulance	7349841		At Zutphen Holland on 26/9/44 by German SS officers. I was told claims of senior officers of my Division who had surrendered with their men in an attempt to draw me into an argument sent on working parties.
Kirk	Duncan	Private	7th Battalion, King's Own Scottish Borderers Regiment	14211437	91487	At Frankfurt one week after capture we were kept in solitary confinement for five days during which time we were interrogated by German officers. … [illegible]
Kitchener	Robert Anthony	Private	2nd Battalion, Parachute Regiment	6145647		Normal Arnhem (SS) Limburg.
Klamph	Samuel	Private	156th Battalion, Parachute Regiment	5953101		At Limberg 26-9-44. Ref to questionnaire papers done by previous POW and their admittance two military warfare.
Knight	Lawrence Alfred	Sergeant, Lance	2nd Battalion, Parachute Regiment	7016898		Limburg (Transit Camp) About 30 Sept 1944. Threatened to be shot if we did not tell the truth.

Surname	First Name	Rank	Unit	Service No.	POW No.	Notes
Knight	Leonard Davies	Signalman	1st Parachute Brigade, Royal Signals	14200119	89308	Normal Limburg Normal questioning.
Knight	Joseph William	Sapper	9th Field Company, Royal Engineers Airborne	2058280	91610	Near Frankfurt, no food for 24 hours. German Officer played with a revolver during interrogation.
Knox	William Hutchinson	Sergeant	Glider Pilot Regiment	11000594	1070	Oberhausen (Frankfurt) 22 Oct 44. Solitary confinement. Threatening interrogation.
Laing	Robert Hutt	Lance Bombardier	2nd Airlanding Anti-Tank Battery	14554942	91695	Arnhem 26 Sept 1944 No methods.
Lakin	Bernard Lamplugh	Private	Royal Army Medical Corps	7522252	88910	Limburg.
Lane	Philip George Oliver	Corporal	1st Parachute Squadron, Royal Engineers	2009968		Limburg by air force personnel.
Langford	John Adair	Captain	Forward Obs Unit, Royal Artillery	158269	90871	At Diez September 27 – Oct 3rd 1944. 5 Days Solitary confinement followed by interrogation by questioning only.
Lasenby	James Joseph	Lieutenant	1st Battalion, Parachute Regiment	297337	91000	At Oberursel (near Frankfurt on Maine) in Oct 44. In close solitary confinement on poor rations for 48 hrs. Both by Wehrmacht and civil interrogators.
Lawson	Albert	Private	2nd Battalion, South Staffordshire Regiment	1789246	91169	Limberg – 28 – September 1944 – A German Officer tried to persuade us that we were being registered for Luft camps.
Layland	Frederick	Gunner	2nd Airlanding Anti-Tank Battery	1092475	92062	At Bad Homburg put in rooms, their n brought as cigarettes, chocolate and food.
Lee	John Henry Dixon	Captain	1st Airlanding Light Regiment	94122	587	No – after a straightforward questionnaire at XII B by their Luftwaffe officer at which we were not pressed to answer any questions a few officers were selected for special interrogation.

Name	Forename	Rank	Unit	Army number	POW number	Answer given on Questionnaire
Lee	Idwal	Driver	1st Airlanding Anti-Tank Battery	5188617	75540	By question.
Leggett	Clarence Leslie	Corporal	11th Battalion, Parachute Regiment	4691420	75986	Frankfurt 19th Oct 44 Solitary confinement Bread + water.
Levien	Robert Hugh	Lieutenant	2nd Battalion, Parachute Regiment	73127	554	Was separated from ORs at 10th Panzer Div HQ near Arnhem for interrogation & also was interrogated by an SS Oberst. Otherwise normal routine.
Lewis	John	Corporal	1st Battalion, Parachute Regiment	4032087	92129	Arnhem Just asked.
Lewis	Vivian	Corporal	1st Battalion, Parachute Regiment	890079		Oflag in Germany. Date unknown. Wanted to know length of time I was on a lorry from my location in England to airdrome.
Linden	Jack Alfred	Corporal	89 Parachute Security Section	918417		No, Individual interrogation by Sergeants of Luftwaffe.
Linden	Thomas	Private	7th Battalion, King's Own Scottish Borderers Regiment	3197468	90495	Limburgh questioning.
Livesey	Trevor John	Captain	1st Parachute Squadron, Royal Engineers	222702	611	Questioned by S.S. officer their day after capture at Zutphen. No third degree methods used. Officer seemed in possession of confidential information as to personalities in units of my division.
Lothian	James Charles Ogilvie	Lance Corporal	7th Battalion, King's Own Scottish Borderers Regiment	14212249	75383	Muhlberg Nov 44 Questioning.
Lott	George Henry	Company SergeantMajor	10th Battalion, Parachute Regiment	6395878		By Luftwaffe personnel, warned that I would be sent to an inferior camp for not answering questions.
Lovett	James	Staff Sergeant	Glider Pilot Regiment	128577		Frankfurt 24.9.44. Solitary confinement.

Surname	First name	Rank	Regiment	Number	POW No.	Remarks
Lowe	Alfred	Private	2nd Battalion, South Staffordshire Regiment	14700220		Interrogation at Limburg in Oct 44 by two civilian men who came to their camp they could talk English and one had been in London.
Lowe	David Borwell	Staff Sergeant	Glider Pilot Regiment	2084363	76332	Merely asked for Name, Rank, No, Rgt.
Lowrie	James	Lance Corporal	1st Parachute Brigade, Royal Signals	2351489		Interrogated at Limburg. German officer wished to know unit, where we flew from, type of playing used. When information refused threatened to retain us in Limburg.
Lumb	Vernon	Sergeant	3rd Battalion, Parachute Regiment	137755		By Luftwaffe Intelligence, at Stalag XII A, Limburg Sept 1944.
Lumsden	Albert Edward	Private	2nd Battalion, Parachute Regiment	941821		By Luftwaffe Officers.
Lupton	Thomas	Private	7th Battalion, King's Own Scottish Borderers Regiment	3195317	90508	Stalag XII A All questions asked, but not pressed for answer (There was no need to reply as they knew answers).
Lyndon	Edwin Charles	Sapper	9th Field Company, Royal Engineers Airborne	2115530		Nothing special.
Lyon	Archibald Davidson	Sergeant	Glider Pilot Regiment	14216954	15246	At Oberursel in December 1944. Spent two days solitary confinement.
Lyons	Charles Howard Cecil	Sergeant	Glider Pilot Regiment	427924	118524	Ede (Holland) ordinary interrogating by Luftwaffe officer who asked questions about units and casualties during Airborne landing.
Macdonald	John Forbes	Sergeant	Glider Pilot Regiment	2881342		Oberursel. Direct only method. No rough treatment although it was promised if we failed to talk. Very little food and very filthy conditions.
Mackay	Ernest Henry	Private	2nd Battalion, Parachute Regiment	6922282	91676	To a camp for airforce personnel. Method confinement (Outside Frankfurt).
Magee	Alfred	Private	156th Battalion, Parachute Regiment	1439453		Limburg 28/9/44 Nothing particular.

Name	Forename	Rank	Unit	Army number	POW number	Answer given on Questionnaire
Malley	James	Private	7th Battalion, King's Own Scottish Borderers Regiment	14211489		Limburg 25/8/44.
Maloney	Robert	Signalman	1st Parachute Brigade, Royal Signals	2328785		Limburg – on arrival. Verbal questions by interrogator.
Manley	John	Private	3rd Battalion, Parachute Regiment	5833839		Place not known. Ordinary questioning no rough stuff.
Mardell	George Henry	Sergeant	2nd Battalion, South Staffordshire Regiment	6201240	89425	Limberg. Tried to force information from me.
Marks	Geoffrey George	Private	1st Battalion, Parachute Regiment	6853688		Yes.
Marr	William	Sapper	1st Parachute Squadron, Royal Engineers	2110349	89232	Limberg, 26-9-44, Normal, Luftwaffe interrogation.
Marshall	James	Private	7th Battalion, King's Own Scottish Borderers Regiment	14608077	90576	I was interrogated by their Luftwaffe at Muhlberg 20th Oct 1944. He asked me when I left England and what division I was in.
Martin	Reginald Alfred	Lance Corporal	253rd Airborne Light Company, RASC	171029		Solitary confinement Nov.
Martin	Frederick George	Company Sergeant Major	1st Battalion, Parachute Regiment	6285361	89411	I was interrogated by officers of their Luftwaffe. I stated my No. Rank + Name. I was temporarily refused registration because I refused to give further information.
Mason	Harry Pearson	Corporal	1st Battalion, Parachute Regiment	3601962		Limburg (No. + Rank).

Surname	First name	Rank	Regiment	Number	Number	Details
Mason	Arthur	Private	7th Battalion, King's Own Scottish Borderers Regiment	1525984	88754	Limburg 20.9.44 Verbal.
Mason	Herbert Advad	Staff Sergeant	181st Airlanding Field Ambulance	7249904	77340	At Limburg, but they knew all about us. ie they knew our unit by our shoulder flash and colour.
Maston	Edward Peel	Private	156th Battalion, Parachute Regiment	14414353		Mass interrogation.
Matthews	Ronald George	Private	7th Battalion, King's Own Scottish Borderers Regiment	4750960		Limbourg and Arnhem. Tried to pump us letting us think he knew all about us and in several cases he was right.
May	Kenneth	Sergeant, Lance	156th Battalion, Parachute Regiment	1430419	90746	XII A Limberg questionnaire by Luftwaffe personnel 29.9.44.
May	Dennis Roy	Private	2nd Battalion, Parachute Regiment	14331381		Enschede Solitary confinement for 3 or 4 days.
McCall	Jack Miller	Corporal	7th Battalion, King's Own Scottish Borderers Regiment	14211456		At Dulag 12 A Limburg. Enemy stated that I would be sent to airforce camp if questions were answered truthfully and in details.
McCalmont	Edwin John Terance	Corporal	11th Battalion, Parachute Regiment	1136790		In an interrogation camp near Frankfurt. Confined in a very small sound proofed cell on bread and water.
McCandlish	Andrew Holen	Sergeant	Glider Pilot Regiment	3320419	88476	By Luftwaffe personnel. Method used was threats of being sent to a punishment camp.
McClure	William	Private	2nd Battalion, Parachute Regiment	7022065		Mostly by direct questioning.
McCooke	John Brewster	Captain	2nd Battalion, South Staffordshire Regiment	140490	91006	At Oberursel Interrogation Camp. Not very directly questioned. Only a few questions about my unit, transport and those were not pressed, when I declined to answer.
McCormack	James Laurence	Private	2nd Battalion, Parachute Regiment	6983201		Limberg Germany October Questioned.
McCourt	James Frederick	Captain	7th Battalion, King's Own Scottish Borderers Regiment	465	465	Solitary confinement, terrible conditions, poor food and verbal interrogation at OBERURSEL, Germany.

Name	Forename	Rank	Unit	Army number	POW number	Answer given on Questionnaire
McCreedy	Richard James	Lance Bombardier	1st Airlanding Anti-Tank Battery	3711048		Arnhem. Sept. given wine and food etc and told that if questions were answered correctly called proceed to hospital and have wounds dressed. Limburg. Sept. Air Force and documentation.
McDonald	Thomas	Private	7th Battalion, King's Own Scottish Borderers Regiment	3189884		By questions.
McFarlane	Roland	Corporal	Royal Army Medical Corps	7377807	77327	Uberest. Luft Interrogation HQ. Normal questioning.
McGowan	Walter	Private	181st Airlanding Field Ambulance	7407324	90158	By filling in form at Zuphund.
McGurk	John	Private	7th Battalion, King's Own Scottish Borderers Regiment	3194113	99999	Muhlberg Nov 44 Questionnaire.
McHardy	Charles	Private	7th Battalion, King's Own Scottish Borderers Regiment	14214324	90579	No. I was interrogated at Muhlburg.
McHugh	James	Private	1st Battalion, Border Regiment	3599165	91948	I was interrogated at Limberg. I was given a little extra food. 'The food situation in England.'
McIntosh	William Downie	Private	3rd Battalion, Parachute Regiment	5191914		Interrogated by German flying personnel.
McIntyre	Hugh	Corporal	7th Battalion, King's Own Scottish Borderers Regiment	3187559		Normal No. Rk Name.
McKay	James Maxwell	Staff Sergeant	Glider Pilot Regiment	2823181		Normal interrogation at Dulag Luft 25.9.44.
McKnight	John	Private	133rd Parachute Field Ambulance	7360808		Frankfurt-on-Main October 1944 Solitary confinement.

Surname	First name	Rank	Regiment	Service No.	POW No.	Interrogation
McLaren	Ernest	Lance Corporal	7th Battalion, King's Own Scottish Borderers Regiment	14211475		Limberg (Stalag XII A) September 28th. Questions regarding Aircraft used, units, landing zones, how many units used.
McLay	James	Corporal	7th Battalion, King's Own Scottish Borderers Regiment	14211476	90563	Linberg. Sept 1944. They questioned me on what division I was in their regiment where we took off from they told me if I told them I would get to better camp with better conditions and food.
McLean	Charles Harris	Corporal	Royal Army Medical Corps	7517370	118377	Sagan Dec 44. Informal talk with civilians.
McLean	Duncan	Captain	2nd Battalion, Parachute Regiment	94824	616	No. Very brief interrogation & after giving Name, rank & number & having stated I could answer no further questions, their interrogation ended.
McLoughlin	Patrick Bernard	Private	10th Battalion, Parachute Regiment	6412159	75600	Economical situation in England.
McLure	James	Private	156th Battalion, Parachute Regiment	2454564		Linburg. Threats were made but not carried out.
McQuilian	Alexander	Private	11th Battalion, Parachute Regiment	7901172	91663	In XII A.
McWilliam	Thomas Andrew	Corporal	156th Battalion, Parachute Regiment	3771531		Questioned by Luftwaffe Officers.
Meen	Bernard George Henry	Lance Corporal	3rd Battalion, Parachute Regiment	6025548		Limburg (Stalag XII A). Sept 28(?). 1944 Questions as to information as regards unit, type of weapons, of aircraft and aerodrome we left. Luftwaffe officers did interrogation.
Meiklejohn	John	Private	7th Battalion, King's Own Scottish Borderers Regiment	3185236	80652	By commanding officer Stalag IV B 29.9.44. Questions.
Melrose	William George	Staff Sergeant	Glider Pilot Regiment	1464667		VETSLAU Interrogation centre shortly after capture. I spent 7 days in solitary confinements.

Name	Forename	Rank	Unit	Army number	POW number	Answer given on Questionnaire
Menzies	Harry	Corporal	2nd Battalion, Parachute Regiment	3247104		8C.
Mercer	Kenneth Walter	Private	4th Battalion, Dorset Regiment	14656451	14227	Questions asked about flashes on uniform.
Merrick	Albert John	Driver	1st Parachute Brigade, Royal Signals	7896485	91619	Solitary confinement for three days.
Miller	George	Lance Corporal	1st Battalion, Border Regiment	2980246	918718	Overursile nr Frankfurt (Amien (sic) Solitary confinement.
Miller	Philip Anthony Alfred	Sapper	1st Parachute Squadron, Royal Engineers	1947386		Threats of concentration camps used, and shooting. Interrogated at (12A) Limburg.
Miller	Brian	Staff Sergeant	16th Parachute Field Ambulance	7349554	89671	By questionnaire – solitary confinement in cell. Questioned by Luft. Officers.
Miller	Christopher Alfred	Staff Sergeant	Glider Pilot Regiment	937499	117770	Not specially.
Millington	Arthur	Private	1st Battalion, Border Regiment	3856104	91880	Lindberg. Germany. Questions.
Milne	Alexander Noble	Gunner	1st Airlanding Light Regiment	919655	75976	A German in civilian clothes asked questions on damage to London by flying bombs, also about civilian rationing system, and their prices of articles.
Milne	George	Private	7th Battalion, King's Own Scottish Borderers Regiment	2878859	117412	What a certain type of glider carried. In Munster Only by explaining that they knew what it carried was their method.
Milner	Charles	Private	7th Battalion, King's Own Scottish Borderers Regiment	14327609		Limberg 28 Sept. First they gave us cigarettes and their n told us they would give us good food if we told them their truth.

Surname	First name	Rank	Unit	Number	POW No.	Interrogation
Mitchell	Charles Maurice	Private	7th Battalion, King's Own Scottish Borderers Regiment	14636263	25194	Interrogation 'Yes Larg[ER?] Holland. 18th-9-1944. By asking questions concerning military matters and hinting at what might happen if I did not answer. Also given some form to fill in.'
Mitchell	James	Private	7th Battalion, King's Own Scottish Borderers Regiment	3186927		Near Apledorne 20 Sept 1944 By being friendly and 5 day solitary confinement.
Mitchell	William	Driver	250th Airborne Light Company, RASC	80574	91351	Yes.
Mitchell	Alan	Sergeant	Glider Pilot Regiment	10538003	858	Oberursel (Dulag Luft) Sept 27th 44. Solitary confinement – threatening interrogation.
Mitchell	Edward	Sergeant	Glider Pilot Regiment	10555051	76321	Just after capture was threatened with schmeiser asking where machine gun nests were. Next day interrogated and given cigarettes and bread when German officer try to find out about loads of gliders.
Moffat	Walter	Private	Parachute Regiment	14255679	75417	Limburg Questions.
Morait	Peter John	Private	156th Battalion, Parachute Regiment	59816		Interrogation by their enemy in Stalag XII A. Spoke as if they knew all about us and our division.
Moran	Joseph	Signalman	1st Parachute Brigade, Royal Signals	2320146	91620	Int. SS HQ Arnhem. Normal methods used first. Secondly – given tea, their n attempted Int. by means of casual conversation.
Morris	David	WO II	11th Battalion, Parachute Regiment	5946742		I was put into 'Solitary Confinement' at Dietz nr Limburg for a period of 10 days.
Morris	Edmund Barker	Lance Corporal	1st Airborne Reconnaissance Squadron	14279106		I was interrogated by an enemy officer immediately I was captured, but as I was in a bad condition he left me, quite dissatisfied.
Morrison	John Alexander	Captain	Glider Pilot Regiment	88880	5979	Five interrogations gliders 24/9/1944.
Mowat	Billy Bruce	Leading Aircraftman	Light Warning Set Unit No. 6341, RAF	168468		At Oberursel from Dec 5/44 to Dec 19/44 questioned 6 times by 4 different German officers.

Name	Forename	Rank	Unit	Army number	POW number	Answer given on Questionnaire
Mullineux	William	Private	3rd Battalion, Parachute Regiment	3866182		Wetzlar. Sept 44. Kept without food in effort to extract information. Also struck in face.
Munro	James L	Private	10th Battalion, Parachute Regiment	3318030	?	Yes.
Murphy	Andrew	Private	7th Battalion, King's Own Scottish Borderers Regiment	14327614	93376	Limburg 9 Oct 44.
Murray	Alistair George	Private	2nd Battalion, Parachute Regiment	2926439		When captured and going through the usual interrogation it was very evident that their German Command was very well informed about our Division and the operation, even to the fact we were a week late.
Murray MC	Douglas Campbell	Major/T	1st Parachute Squadron, Royal Engineers	106883	607	At Zutphen straight forward questions.
Mustard	Alfred	Private	156th Battalion, Parachute Regiment	3770819		At Limburg on 3rd Oct. Just asked normal questions.
Naylor	Alfred	Private	10th Battalion, Parachute Regiment	6349458	89595	Not specially. Just gave them the name, rank, number stuff.
Needham	George Henry	Sapper	1st Parachute Squadron, Royal Engineers	2133390		Yes.
Newell	Cecil	Private	2nd Battalion, Parachute Regiment	1559998		An HQ outside Arnhem and later at Limberg, because of not giving information was told I would be set to work immediately, if information given would go to a Dulag Luft where there was no work.
Newham	Leslie	Driver	1st Airlanding Light Regiment	14609703		At a camp just outside of Frankfurt. date unknown. Solitary confinement.

Newman	Walter Roy	Lance Corporal	10th Battalion, Parachute Regiment	6407101	118206	By SS officer but when I declined to give any other information than that authorised they desisted. No force used.
Newman	James	Private	181st Airlanding Field Ambulance	7397436		Limburge – no special methods.
Newman	Robert Eugène	Private	Royal Army Medical Corps	7533134		Limberg. Just plain questions.
Newport	Edward Selwyn	Lieutenant	1st Battalion, Border Regiment	96393	630	Yes, by officer of SS Germania division. Gave me a form and treated me well at first, their n after failure to get anything from me threatened and tried to browbeat me. Nil result so he gave it up as a bad job.
Newton	Arthur	Staff Sergeant	Glider Pilot Regiment	913044		Normal interrogation.
Newton	Peter	Private	156th Battalion, Parachute Regiment	3194733		Yes Limburg.
Nicholson	William John Ainsley	Driver	63 Company RASC	10662795		Yes.
Nicklin	George Lewis	Sergeant	Glider Pilot Regiment	7955175	117174	Fallingbostel and Sagan after arrival. No particular system employed. Mainly an attempt make NCOs volunteer for work.
Noble	Charles Bruce	Captain	133rd Battalion, Parachute Regiment Field Ambulance	279738		Arnhem (Velp). 1st Parachute Div Counter Intelligence Gestapo Prison in Utrecht and Doetrincheim (Holland). Methods prolonged questioning. Threatening.
Nullis	John Robert	Lance Corporal	2nd Battalion, South Staffordshire Regiment	5729659		Limburg Stalag XII A September 1944 German Airforce Officer.
O'Brian	Robert Gerard	Private	1st Battalion, Parachute Regiment	2049245		In Limburg, their usual interrogation.

Name	Forename	Rank	Unit	Army number	POW number	Answer given on Questionnaire
O'Brien	Cyril	Private	1st Parachute Brigade	14411394		Outside Arnhem, by SS Officer.
O'Donnell	Edward	Private	Parachute	3065854		Two days after capture straightforward.
O'Malley	Hamilton Joseph Keyes	Captain	Glider Pilot Regiment	44556		1. Hospital – Ordinary conversation. 2. Overeusal – Ordinary conversation. 3. Weislaw – Ordinary conversation. General tone Bolshevik menace and attempts to speak detrimentally about USA.
O'Neill	William	Private	7th Battalion, King's Own Scottish Borderers Regiment	3195748	14202	Lemberg Sep 29th 44. Asked for rank & army number. Date of capture & place. No other questions asked.
O'Quinn	Bernard Patrick	Lance Corporal	1st Airborne Provost Company	7687579		By German Air Force Officers at 12A Limburg Camp Oct 1944.
Oakes	William Arthur	Sergeant	Glider Pilot Regiment	14573970		Oberusel, 1-10-44 Filling in forms.
Oakley	Harry	Corporal	2nd Battalion, South Staffordshire Regiment	5124863		At Limberg. Their methods were that we would be shot if we did not give information.
Oates	Jack	Private	Parachute Regiment	2089524		Place not known. Offered cigarettes. Tried to bribe. Told him nothing. They seemed to know everything. They told us a lot.
Ogden	Ernest Alvin	Trooper	1st Airborne Recommaissance Squadron	3599015	117719	Was found with maps and magnetic buttons, these were taken off me. I was asked if anyone else had their se things. Frontline area after capture, normal method of Interrogation.

Surname	First Name	Rank	Unit	Number	Number	Notes
Oliver	Edward James	Corporal	1st Parachute Squadron, Royal Engineers	2093811		We were lectured and interrogated by G.A.F. Officers who told us that we would go to a nice Stalag if we answered their questions.
Oliver	Leslie	Private	1st Battalion, Border Regiment	3537403	91793	Mulhberg Stalag IV A a civilian who was very friendly very interested in the food and transport situation in England.
Oram	Arthur William	Sergeant	Glider Pilot Regiment	14416890		Dulag Luft Frankfurt. Solitary confinement 7 days. Periodical snap questioning and promises of the early release from solitary for information.
Oxford	Cecil James	Sergeant	Glider Pilot Regiment	4859963		Dulag Luft near Frankfurt on Main. Usual threat of solitary confinement etc.
Padfield	Harold	Sergeant, Lance	1st Parachute Squadron, Royal Engineers	1873564		Interrogation by Luftwaffe Officer. By answering the questions you were promised to be sent to a Luftwaffe camp with our friends.
Palmer	Charles Thomas Albert	Lance Corporal	7th Battalion, King's Own Scottish Borderers Regiment	4750869	91083	Arnhem, Sept 1944 Just ordinary questions.
Palmer	Albert Edgar	Sergeant	Glider Pilot Regiment	4803786		Oberhursel. Solitary Confinement + Questions.
Panter	Stanley Charles	Captain	2nd Battalion, Parachute Regiment	165617	91002	Arnhem 23-9-44 9th Panzer (SS) Div HQ Normal methods.
Parker	Donald Sydney	Sergeant	Glider Pilot Regiment	5886465		Oberusel 2/11/44 solitary confinement.
Parry	William Reginald	Private	16th Parachute Field Ambulance	97005169		At the Luftwaffe interrogation camp at Oberüssel. Date 24.9.44. I was questioned by an NCO – fluent English – he had pro formas ready and read out list of questions & frequently attempted to try to trap me by giving me correct or nearly correct and [illegible] questions. [Illegible] like all second Battalion [illegible] were employed.

257

Name	Forename	Rank	Unit	Army number	POW number	Answer given on Questionnaire
Partridge	Felix Frederick	Sapper	Royal Engineers	1915238		Interrogated for information on airborne strength and where stationed.
Paterson	William	Signalman	1st Parachute Brigade, Royal Signals	2348020	91340	Stalag XII A.
Paterson	Robert	Sergeant	156th Battalion, Parachute Regiment	3244907	89820	Interrogation was carried out at Lindberg on arrival. Methods used. By saying they knew everything. The mentioning of various names in the Bn. The promise of better treatment.
Paterson	Kenneth	Driver	Royal Artillery	14321751	91372	Normal.
Pepper	Maurice Raymond	Sergeant	Glider Pilot Regiment	7595239		Oberursal Sept 24th solitary confinement 2 days.
Perks	Victor	Private	133rd Parachute Field Ambulance	14630044	90042	At Frankfurt September 1944. By trying to make you believe they already knew everything and that it didn't matter.
Perry	George Herbert	Corporal	3rd Battalion, Parachute Regiment	4622196		No. [Only answer, but he spent time at Dulag Luft]
Phillips	Bernard	Corporal	1st Airborne Provost Company	7373821	89395	No special interrogation.
Pick	Robert Baxter Paterson	Private	1st Battalion, Parachute Regiment	7367569	91495	Oberursel Nr Frankfurt Sept '44. Solitary confinement & soft soap.
Pierce	Gordon Basil	Corporal	7th Battalion, King's Own Scottish Borderers Regiment	4750968	89154	Limburgh 27 Sept 44 Questions.
Pitt	Harry	Private	7th Battalion, King's Own Scottish Borderers Regiment	3197317		Questions asked Stalag XII A-Limburg 5/10/44.

Surname	First Name	Rank	Regiment	Number	Number	Notes
Pocklington	George Edward	Lance Corporal	3rd Battalion, Parachute Regiment	4754286		Limburg.
Pope	Robert Edward	Private	2nd Battalion, Parachute Regiment	5385849	75412	By asking personal questions then suddenly switching over to military.
Potts	Eric	Lance Corporal	181st Airlanding Field Ambulance	7399495		Interrogated by civilian at Limburg. Interested in our political views and opinions.
Potts	John Reginald	Private	1st Parachute Brigade	5962036	89583	Interrogated by Luftwaffe officers at Limburg on the 26th of September 1944. Questioned as to unit, type of aircraft used on operation and from which area drawn took off. Was not compelled to answer any questions.
Powell	Francis	Sergeant	Glider Pilot Regiment	190364		At Oberesual (?) solitary confinement for three days.
Pressly	Ian Leith	Private	10th Battalion, Parachute Regiment	14420876	93261	At Frankfurt/Main, threats, and solitary confinement.
Preston	Tom	Corporal	7th Battalion, King's Own Scottish Borderers Regiment	3715814	88747	Once at German HQ in Droitrech in Holland, once at Stalag XII A. Bog standard word of mouth, no force used.
Price	Sidney Robert	Sergeant	Glider Pilot Regiment	2388139		Normal interrogation only.
Prigmore	Frederick	Private	10th Battalion, Parachute Regiment	5512177		Easy methods.
Prince	Charles Henry	Private	181st Airlanding Field Ambulance	14672756		Muhlberg on Elbe 30-8-45 questions asked.
Prior	Mark James	Sergeant/W	3rd Battalion, Parachute Regiment	6094195		Lindburg Stalag 12 A Questions Luft Intg Officers.
Proven	Robert	Private	7th Battalion, King's Own Scottish Borderers Regiment	3192121	140107	At Arnhem.
Pullinger	Albert	Private	2nd Battalion, Parachute Regiment	5836763		Yes No No.

Name	Forename	Rank	Unit	Army number	POW number	Answer given on Questionnaire
Purdy	Harry	Private	3rd Battalion, Parachute Regiment	6203365	89831	At Stalag 12A by Luftwaffe personally.
Purnell	William Tom	Private	7th Battalion, King's Own Scottish Borderers Regiment	3190949	90350	Stalag XII A Limburg. Sept 1944. Threatening attitude.
Quigley	Edmund	Sergeant	Light Warning Set Unit No. 6341, RAF	1149134	943	Oberursel Nr Frankfurt – towards end of Sept 44. I was held there a week pending the arrival of a Radar Officer from Berlin. Also interrogated by resident radio engineer there.
Rafferty	William	Private	1st Battalion, Border Regiment	14642750		Normal procedure.
Rainbow	Edmund Hubert	Private	181st Airlanding Field Ambulance	7401241		Frankfort.
Ramsey	Sydney	Private	2nd Battalion, Parachute Regiment	3249012		Ordinary normal interrogation on capture.
Ratchford	William	Private	11th Battalion, Parachute Regiment	14400554		At Frankfurt. I was placed in solitary cell for five days.
Rathband	Herbert Henry	Sergeant/W	Glider Pilot Regiment	1544344	103967	Swet (sic) box Dulag Luft.
Read	Victor Henry William	Signalman	1st Parachute Brigade, Royal Signals	2586247	89797	Dulag Luft Oberhausel nr Frankfurt on Main 22-9-44 to 27-9-44 by solitary confinement.
Read	Lewis Allen	Sergeant	10th Battalion, Parachute Regiment	6402998		Yes at Oberhausel near Frankfurt on Main interrogation camp by being placed in solitary confinement for 8 days on very little rations. Large staff employed, each department grilling PW in turn.
Reay	Harrison James	Private	11th Battalion, Parachute Regiment	3716400	75990	Usual interrogation enemy did not need any special means they seem to know all the answers!

Reay	John James	Private	16th Parachute Field Ambulance	4451377	88937	Limburg & Arnhen. Not specially interrogated only questioned.
Reid	James Bruce	Private	7th Battalion, King's Own Scottish Borderers Regiment	14416765		Usual.
Reid	William	Private	156th Battalion, Parachute Regiment	3131283		At Limberg Sept 29th 30th 44. Two Germany MOI person on internal affairs & food situation in England also morale of Eng civilians and VI damage.
Reid	George	Sapper	4th Parachute Squadron, Royal Engineers	2067721		Frankfurt. Asked how many men were wounded on the drop, etc.
Reilly	John	Craftsman	REME	889575		Frankfurt Solitary confinement and starvation Sept 1944.
Rendle	William	Private	181st Airlanding Field Ambulance	7399502		At Limberg Oct 44. By questions.
Richards	John Thomas	Sergeant	1st Battalion, Parachute Regiment	4195046		As paratroops we were taken to Stalag Luft Wetzlar from 23.9.44 to 26.9.44. We were questioned on England's economical and political situation. Relations with Russia and plans for post-War Germany.
Richardson	Ernest James	Private	Parachute Regiment	4979999		Not nice by putting me in a darkroom and left for two days with no food or water.
Richey	James	Captain	1st Battalion, Parachute Regiment	151648	547	
Roan	Cyril Charles	Lance Corporal	2nd Battalion, Parachute Regiment	5891392		Ob inf [Obermaßfeld Infirmary].
Robbins	James	Lance Corporal	181st Airlanding Field Ambulance	7366512	76659	12 hours solitary confinement.
Roberts	Robert William	Lance Bombardier	Forward Obs Unit, Royal Artillery	924830	92050	At Oberusal 8/10/44. General questioning and attempt to obtain information by bribery in so that they offered prisoners cigarettes and solitary confinement for unsatisfactory replies by prisoners.

Name	Forename	Rank	Unit	Army number	POW number	Answer given on Questionnaire
Roberts	John	Lance Corporal	2nd Battalion, South Staffordshire Regiment	4913467		I was interrogated at Zutphen in September [1] stating that they knew my unit's number, Division, so that they may eventually get the correct issue.
Robinson	Michael William Patrick	Sapper	9th Field Company, Royal Engineers Airborne	1944654	76252	Weztlar, 12.10.44 questioning.
Robson	Joseph	Lance Corporal	11th Battalion, Parachute Regiment	14644631	92139	Only usual interrogation. At 12 A Limburg. Method soft soap.
Rollins	Robert	Private	156th Battalion, Parachute Regiment	4748127		We were interrogated at Limberg they wanted to know where we lived back in England as they had been told (Good).
Rose	John William	Private	181st Airlanding Field Ambulance	7404654	90026	At Arnhem. Enemy already knew where we left from, the name of plane & glider and also names of units.
Roughton	John Kenneth	Corporal	10th Battalion, Parachute Regiment	7886696		Limburg 1.10.44 Coaxing and threats.
Rouse	Ronald	Sergeant	11th Battalion, Parachute Regiment	4981946		Satisfactory.
Rowthorn	Aubrey Owen	Corporal	3rd Battalion, Parachute Regiment	5890319		Interrogated at LIMBERG about 25-9-44. We were told that if we answered all questions satisfactorily we would go to a Luftwaffe camp, if we didn't answer to an Army camp.
Royall	Arthur Robert	Lieutenant	1st Battalion, Border Regiment	269802	632	Interrogated by Luftwaffe representative in common with all airborne POWs.
Rumsey	Reginald	Private	10th Battalion, Parachute Regiment	6407115	117600	Fallingbostel Germany Oct 10th/10/44. Interrogation routine methods used.
Sadler	Charles	Sergeant	156th Battalion, Parachute Regiment	4387908		Limberg, 28-9-44. Luftwaffe, officer, ques.

Surname	Forename	Rank	Regiment	Service Number	No.	Notes
Sander	Gustave	Private	11th Battalion, Parachute Regiment	13807937	91694	Interrogated at Military Barracks Diez by military and civil authorities after having been singled out at XII A as a paratrooper, solitary confinement for 24 hours.
Sanders	Samuel John Frederick	Staff Sergeant	181st Airlanding Field Ambulance	7348718	77583	At an interrogation centre at Oberursal (Germany) – solitary confinement.
Sanderson	Ellison	Sergeant	Glider Pilot Regiment	937039		Oberusel Sept 25th-29th 44. Threats of handing over to Gestapo.
Sargant	Raymond	Sergeant	Glider Pilot Regiment	4617321		Breskins Oberusal. Solitary Confinement, 'Hot treatment' & then by suggestive treatment (Not employed).
Sargent	Reginald Arthur	Driver	181st Airlanding Field Ambulance	199690		At Frankfurt Interrogation camp Sept 21 1944, German Officer.
Saunders	John Richard	Private	2nd Battalion, South Staffordshire Regiment	14397706	92173	I was interrogated at Linbergh by the enemy but I told them nothing. He was not too rough.
Saunders	Leslie Percy	Sergeant	Glider Pilot Regiment	4804127		20 kilometers from Arnhem 25 Sept 44 ordinary questions by SS Commanders and Luftwaffe Officers (No violence).
Scholfield	John	Private	181st Airlanding Field Ambulance	7407356		Not specially but interrogated with my unit in (Enchede) Holland beginning October he appeared to know everything before he starts on you (and tells you so first).
Scott	Arnold	Private	156th Battalion, Parachute Regiment	4746709		Limburg Germany in solitary confinement without food 48 hrs.
Scott	Andrew	Sergeant	7th Battalion, King's Own Scottish Borderers Regiment	3191998		Limburg. Oct 1944. Asked questions on Unit Div where landed.
Scutt	Henry John	Private	10th Battalion, Parachute Regiment	6395492		Limberg few days after capture. I was shown maps, types of aircraft, told where my billets were in England they tried to give me the impression that they knew all about us before we started on the operation.

Name	Forename	Rank	Unit	Army number	POW number	Answer given on Questionnaire
Seaman	Frederick George	Sergeant	Glider Pilot Regiment	876231		Oberusel: Sept 1944: Close confinement.
Searle	Ivan John	Private	2nd Battalion, Parachute Regiment	562071	75305	Put in a cell until we told them what they wanted to know.
Shears	Charles Eli	Private	10th Battalion, Parachute Regiment	5623548		Interrogated by General of the SS Division in a German headquarters in Holland.
Shedden	William	Lance Corporal	7th Battalion, King's Own Scottish Borderers Regiment	3191038	90550	At Limberg 28/9/44. Promises of immediate transport two main prison camp where conditions were much better, as at Limberg Camp (St XII A) we were under terrible conditions.
Sheilds	John Williams	Private	16th Parachute Field Ambulance	14272469	91321	Yes.
Shepherd	Joseph	Private	11th Battalion, Parachute Regiment	14647522	75987	At Arnhem privately by SS Officer on what Airborne Divs we had in England abroad and on equipment we had in the airborne.
Silvester	Vernon John Bellis	Lieutenant	156th Battalion, Parachute Regiment	204917	91013	Routine interrogation at German brigade headquarters after capture.
Simons	Denis Harold	Staff Sergeant	Glider Pilot Regiment	119641		Luftwaffe Interrogation Centre, Oberursel. Oct 2nd 1944. Threats of solitary confinement – persuasion – promises of good treatment.
Simpson	David Anderson	Captain	Glider Pilot Regiment	193137	8494	Dulag Luft Oct '44 Oberursel – direct questioning.
Simpson	Albert	Staff Sergeant	Glider Pilot Regiment	856791		Dulag-Luft Nov + Dec '45. Solitary confinement very little rations. Threatened with being turned over to the Gestapo.
Small	Eric Lyng	Private	10th Battalion, Parachute Regiment	5682652	88909	Not officially interrogated – German interrogating officer attempted to trick me into giving information by stating that if I did I would go to an RAF camp.

Surname	First name	Rank	Regiment	Number	Number	Notes
Smith	Frederick Lawrence Spencer	Private	Royal Army Medical Corps	7349477		Usual routine questions on being captured.
Smith	James	Private	2nd Battalion, Parachute Regiment	14206353		By Luftwaffe Officers.
Smith	John Thomas	Private	156th Battalion, Parachute Regiment	14665924	90483	They told me what batt I was in.
Smith	Norman Peter	Private	7th Battalion, King's Own Scottish Borderers Regiment	3191832	90175	At Limburg on 28th Sept '44. Inter officer tried hard to receive information concerning unit and division, especially concerning where we took off from.
Smith	William	Private	4th Battalion, Dorset Regiment	3245456	17563	Arnhem 25th Sept 1944 by personal photographs and army pay books AB 64.
Smithson	Douglas	Sergeant	Glider Pilot Regiment	1886189		Normal interrogation.
Southwell	Frank	Trooper	1st Airborne Reconnaissance Squadron	10601898	88786	At 12 A camp shortly after capture, persuasion bribery.
Staff	Harry Victor William	Private	1st Battalion, Parachute Regiment	6015570		7 days solitary confinement at Oberursel.
Stanislaus	George	Private	3rd Battalion, Parachute Regiment	5672402	?	XII A Limburg. September. they knew all about us, but they were seeking confirmation. We was told to act dumb.
Stark	Ronnie Leslie	Major	1st Battalion, Parachute Regiment	167154	531	Interrogated at Oberusel (Air Force). Normal. Interrogated at Dietz (Army) – when giving name etc was reminded that other methods were used in England.
Stead	John Edward	Staff Sergeant	Glider Pilot Regiment	794717		At Luftwaffe Interrogation Centre. Used promise of food and baths also solitary confinement to try to extract information.

Name	Forename	Rank	Unit	Army number	POW number	Answer given on Questionnaire
Stephenson	James Airen	Sergeant	Glider Pilot Regiment	4616329		Luft interrogation name Oberurlzen solitary confinement.
Stephenson	Charles Richard	Lance Corporal	4th Parachute Brigade HQ	3711558		Frankfurt Doolag Luft (sic). Solitary confinement.
Stevens	Daniel Donne	Sapper	4th Parachute Squadron, Royal Engineers	1877687	90690	Limburg Sept. quick questioning in hopes of catching a slipped word or two.
Still	Blake Edwin Charles	Private	10th Battalion, Parachute Regiment	2323483		Nr Arnhem, Limburg. Only questioned were very hungry.
Stokes	Reginald	Private	2nd Battalion, South Staffordshire Regiment	5051452	89713	At 12 A Stalag Limburg. 4th October 1944. Method was questions devised to try and catch me, which of course failed. Was threatened by other methods, using force, etc.
Stones	Horace Ryan	Sergeant	Glider Pilot Regiment	4337089		Interrogation by Luftwaffe at Oberustle left in solitary confinement 2 days with very little or no food.
Storey	Sidney Joseph	Private	2nd Battalion, South Staffordshire Regiment	4922800	89283	Yes.
Stubbs	Herbert Henry	Lance Corporal	Provost Company, 1st Airborne Div	4803335	90844	Routine interrogation by Luftwaffe Officer.
Sullivan	Joseph Vincent	Private	133rd Parachute Field Ambulance	7265333	90387	Usual interrogation at Frankfurt on Main Sept 24th. In office with Luftwaffe Officer who threatened to shoot me if questions not answered.
Sully	Reginald Gordon	Lance Corporal	3rd Battalion, Parachute Regiment	7958094		Holland.
Sunderland	Abram	Private	4th Battalion, Dorset Regiment	3658220	26067	Holland. By Dutch SS Troops of the German Army. Methods: threats and hints of better treatment in exchange for information.

Surname	First Name	Rank	Unit	Number	Number	Notes
Swan	John	Private	10th Battalion, Parachute Regiment	2986583	140114	In hospital in Ensheda HOLLAND. Asked where I was captured when I landed. What Regt I was in. Where I stayed in England, was I married. Wanted information on V2s.
Swiney	George Henry	Private	181st Airlanding Field Ambulance	2366607		Lindberg November 1944. Questions of the nature of damage done by V1 and V2.
Tams	Leonard James	Private	2nd Battalion, South Staffordshire Regiment	4918801		Limburg. Threats of being shot.
Tasker	David Ritchie	Company Sergeant Major	2nd Battalion, Parachute Regiment	2882737		At Limberg on arrival. Were told would go to an RAF camp if we gave information. Said we would be shot if we refused information.
Taylor	Gordon Erich	Corporal	1st Parachute Squadron, Royal Engineers	5184742		At Wetzlow. Method used for information was to be put in dark cell for 7 days.
Taylor	John Alfred	Driver	Royal Army Service Corps	14403352	25803	Heelsum. Holland. 8.9.44 kicked in stomach by officer for not divulging name of O.C Division.
Taylor	Eric	Gunner	1st Airlanding Light Regiment Royal Artillery	974904	118496	No special interrogation. Stalag XI B 10/10/44 wanted particulars of Army life & Civvy life.
Taylor	Frederick	Gunner	1st Airlanding Anti-Tank Battery	1684407	92087	ARNHEIM. 26-9-44. ASKED UNIT and how we got Holland. What we carried in planes. also if we were Glider or Para.
Tebbutt	Richard Henry	Gunner	1st Airlanding Light Regiment	14329479	75820	Stamlager XII A. I was just asked my army number name and rank.
Telfer	James	Private	10th Battalion, Parachute Regiment	10583514		Limberg 9 Oct 44.
Tennet	Arthur	Lance Corporal	2nd Battalion, Parachute Regiment	4271165		Limburg as IIX A.
Terry	Fred Dolphin	Sergeant	1st Battalion, Border Regiment	3602936		Malag Bremen Nov 8 Dec 1944. Information required for notifying next of kin. Civilian masquerading as a Canadian Red Cross Representatives. Solitary confinement. (6 days)

Name	Forename	Rank	Unit	Army number	POW number	Answer given on Questionnaire
Thomas	Geoffrey Ramsden	Leading Aircraftman	Light Warning Set Unit No. 6080, RAF	1009701	92596	At Dulag (Oberursal nr Frankfurt on Main) solitary confinement (Brief duration) bogus Red Cross form.
Thomas	Frederick George	Private	Parachute Regiment	6089619		Frankfurt 19/9/1944 Solitary Confinement.
Thompson	Harold	Corporal	10th Battalion, Parachute Regiment	4372953	90421	At Limberg 27.9.44 (Method) Questionnaire by Luftwaffe.
Thompson	Harry	Sapper	9th Field Company, Royal Engineers Airborne	4858665		Frankfurt trick questions.
Thornley	Robert	Private	1st Battalion, Border Regiment	3598842	75560	Limburg 26/9/1944.
Thorpe	Russell Ambrose	Private	2nd Battalion, South Staffordshire Regiment	4914617		
Thrussell	Joseph	Private	7th Battalion, King's Own Scottish Borderers Regiment	3191825		Luftwaffe officer at Limburg.
Tillotson	John Willie	Private	133rd Parachute Field Ambulance	168025	89206	All A/B passing through Limberg were interrogated by Luftwaffe. Oct 2nd. Threatened but not carried out.
Timothy	John	Major	1st Battalion, Parachute Regiment	164812	530	Arnhem (Conversational) Oberersal (Luft Interrogation – normal).
Tims	Eric	Sergeant	3rd Battalion, Parachute Regiment	3526756		Dulag Luft Frankfurt 20.9.1944 verbal interrogation.
Tingey	Aubrey Henry	Private	2nd Battalion, South Staffordshire Regiment	14695003	75848	Limbura/Lahn Germany Oct 2nd 1944 by private interview.

Surname	Forename	Rank	Unit	Number	No.	Notes
Tobin	John O'Hara	Captain	Royal Army Medical Corps	263459	90863	At Oberusel on 25/9/44 at 2 am 24 hours solitary confinement on 1/2 litre watery soup two slices bread.
Tomblin	Bryan Alan	Sergeant	Glider Pilot Regiment	14259326	1005	Oberursal – direct questioning and solitary confinement.
Towns	Spencer Albert	Corporal	2nd Battalion, Parachute Regiment	4035901	89439	At Frankfort. Methods used – the promise of better camps and treatment etc.
Tracy	John	Private	7th Battalion, King's Own Scottish Borderers Regiment	14205520	90686	Limberg on 28th Sep 1944. They gave us cigarettes then told us that if we told them the truth we would be sent to a good camp and given good food.
Trim	Henry George	Lance Corporal	261st Field Park Company, Royal Engineers	2077679	90624	At Limburg, September '44. Friendly attitude and assurances that they really knew all they wanted. Pro forma for details of airborne landing.
Trotter	Andrew Carmochan?	Corporal	7th Battalion, King's Own Scottish Borderers Regiment	19414344	88788	1. Doitrisch (Holland) 2. Limburg (12A). Method of interrogation. Questions.
Ungi	Albert	Private	16th Parachute Field Ambulance	14560365	90154	Luftwaffe camp.
Unsworth	Joseph	Lance Corporal	1st Airborne Provost Company	19411962		Not especially interrogated. Interrogation carried out by German Luftwaffe.
Urquhart	James Alex	Staff Sergeant	Glider Pilot Regiment	5185152	?	Interrogated as per RAF aircrew at Interrogation Centre OBERUSAL. Germany.
Vale	Edwin John	Private	2nd Battalion, Parachute Regiment	13026704		Normal.
Vaugan	Thomas	Signalman	4th Parachute Brigade, Royal Signals	4034124	90845	Limburg. September 29th. Questions asked.
Vaughan	Thomas Charles	Private	2nd Battalion, South Staffordshire Regiment	4928042	93418	Frankfurt. Sept. Sweat Chambers.

Name	Forename	Rank	Unit	Army number	POW number	Answer given on Questionnaire
Vaughan	Peter	Trooper	1st Airborne Reconnaissance Squadron	13116352	75803	At Dulag Luft and AKdo 806/Stalag III D by Foreign Officer personnel. Nature of Interrogation was political, methods not coercive.
Veal	Robert William	Private	4th Battalion, Dorset Regiment	14441359		At Mühlburg by a German Officer on 10/10/44 who asked a variety of questions both military and personal.
Wagstaff	Jack	Private	2nd Battalion, South Staffordshire Regiment	4955931	89186	Limburg 26/9/1944.
Walker-Cook	Alfred	Staff Sergeant	Army Physical Training Corps	4689266		Neubrandenburg 22.9.44. German interpreter. Spoke to myself and 3 ORs of places in England. (socially).
Wallis	William	Sergeant	3rd Battalion, Parachute Regiment	5048129		At Limburg by Luftwaffe Officer.
Walsh	Richard	Private	2nd Battalion, Parachute Regiment	6409551		Frankford. (sic) Just by talking with no food.
Walton	Frank Thomas	Private	1st Battalion, Parachute Regiment	6015864		Arnhem Oct 1, 44 straight forward. Westlau October 3, 44 solitary confinement. Limburg Oct 12, 44 Straight forward.
Ward	William Edward	Private	10th Battalion, Parachute Regiment	6026817		Lindburg. Sept 23rd 1944. By questioning.
Warwick	Herbert	Private	156th Battalion, Parachute Regiment	3448671		Frankfurt threats. Shut up in a room for one week & one meal a day.
Watkinson	Charles Rollett	Staff Sergeant	Glider Pilot Regiment	809931		Close confinement.
Watson	Frank Campbell	Sergeant	Glider Pilot Regiment	2082989	15256	At Stalag XIII C generally on conditions in England.

Surname	First Name	Rank	Unit	Service No.	No.	Notes
Watson	Raymond	Private	3rd Battalion, Parachute Regiment	11425065		Arnhem threatening attitude.
Wayte	Frederick John	Lance Corporal	3rd Battalion, Parachute Regiment	5890044		Normal interrogation Dulag Luft.
Weallans	Arthur Edward	Sergeant	11th Battalion, Parachute Regiment	2660102		Interrogated by Luftwaffe NCO.
Weaver	Raymond Ernest	Driver	93 Company, RASC	14368841		At Limburg 12 A 3rd Oct. Each man filled in a form. British Sergeant assured us everything was in order.
Webb	Alan Kenneth	Private	1st Battalion, Border Regiment	14424829	91622	I was interrogated by German army and airforce officers. Method was questioning was not compelled to answer.
Webb	Arthur Stanley	Private	181st Airlanding Field Ambulance	7387237	77358	Stalag XII A Limburg. October 1944. Individual interviews with person dressed in civilian clothes who spoke good English.
Weiland	Douglas	Lance Corporal	156th Battalion, Parachute Regiment	6896313		Limberg Stalag 12 A. Luftwaffe officials. Cross questioning and promise of better treatment if information was volunteered.
Welham	Hubert Edward	Lance Corporal	1st Airborne Reconnaissance Squadron	6854308		Dulag-Luft. Frankfurt on Main. Dulag-Luft Wetzlar October 1944 Normal method.
Welsh	James	Driver	800 Company Air Despatch RASC	11251580	91794	Yes.
Whadcoat	Ernest Frederick	Private	10th Battalion, Parachute Regiment	6351604		Limburg Normal methods.
Whippy	John Walter	Sergeant	Glider Pilot Regiment	2044661		Oberusel 25-28 Sept 44. Solitary confinement for 5 days & then good treatment by G. Int Officer who made it appear that he knew everything about us and our organisation.

Name	Forename	Rank	Unit	Army number	POW number	Answer given on Questionnaire
White	Kenneth Grayston	Lieutenant	1st Airlanding Light Regiment	258890	2200	Not specially but I was informed in hospital at Apeldoorn that my next of kin could not be informed about me unless I gave fuller particulars (unit) than I was prepared to give.
White	George	Regimental Sergeant Major	10th Battalion, Parachute Regiment	4387779		At Limburg. About 1st Oct 44. Soft soap. Promise of a RAF Stalag. No work etc. By shouting and verbal threats (nothing further).
Widdowson	George	Major	10th Battalion, Parachute Regiment	49397	91001	Luftwaffe Interrogation Centre - Oberursal 5-9 Oct 45. Arnhem Plan + Airborne Troops. Diez 15-20 Oct 45 as above. Methods conciliatory and half threatening.
Willett	Lewis Alfred	Driver	250th Airborne Light Company, RASC	64737		Stalag XII A Lindberg. Enemy tried to gain information by promising better camp conditions and food for all airborne troops in receipt of a completed form from us.
Williams	Arthur	Private	2nd Battalion, South Staffordshire Regiment	14389591	92044	Lindberg. Trying to bribe us with English cigs. When that failed by threats.
Willoughby	Leslie	Private	3rd Battalion, Parachute Regiment	4466448		Ordinary questions.
Wilson	James McWhirter	Private	7th Battalion, King's Own Scottish Borderers Regiment	3131140		Holland.
Wilson	Joseph Leonard	Sergeant	Glider Pilot Regiment	1675969		Frankfurt 24/9/44 Solitary confinement.
Wilson	Rayment John	Sergeant	Glider Pilot Regiment	7366948		Oberursal Sept 44 Interview.
Wilson	Kenneth	Corporal	16th Parachute Field Ambulance	7263793		At an RAF camp near Frankfurt. Ordinary methods.

Surname	First names	Rank	Unit	Number		Notes
Wilson	Thomas Frederick	Corporal	1st Parachute Brigade, Royal Signals	2583477		At Limburg Germany Sep '44. General int as to unit, strength Company Comds and tactics.
Wilson	Thomas Alan	Private	1st Battalion, Parachute Regiment	7366147	89418	Limburg, by German Air-Force officer, also Mülberg.
Windsor	Ronald	Gunner	Forward Obs Unit, Royal Artillery	14261766		Just normal interrogation at Stalags 12A, 8C and Luft lag at Frankfurt.
Winslow	Jack Robert	Lance Corporal	156th Battalion, Parachute Regiment	6896410		Limberg XII A. Threatened to lose rations to go in the Bunker and not to be transferred to a proper Stalag.
Withnall	Patrick Brereton	Staff Sergeant	Glider Pilot Regiment	2332442		Dulag/Luft 1.10.44 Solitary confinement.
Wood	Jack	Private	2nd Battalion, South Staffordshire Regiment	4914111		Just a few questions on where we flew from and when. They were browned off of insults by the time it was my turn.
Wood	Harold George	Corporal	2nd Battalion, Parachute Regiment	6350557		Normal.
Woodard	Ronald Alan George	Private	156th Battalion, Parachute Regiment	5826728		Questions on conditions of living in England. At Limburg by civilian German.
Woodward	Robert Lisle	Private	156th Battalion, Parachute Regiment	3711157		Limberg. October 1944. Continuous questioning by a relay of Luftwaffe Officers. (Catch questions)
Woolford	Stanley Benjiman	Driver	Royal Artillery	11050415		Muhlberg general questions.
Worrall	James Ambrose	Private	2nd Battalion, Parachute Regiment	5835036	91659	At the Dulag-Luft camp at Wetzlar near Frankfurt. I was held for roughly 14 days in solitary confinement by Gestapo with one soup two slices of black bread & one cup of Ersatz coffee per day.
Wright	Leonard William	Lieutenant	3rd Battalion, Parachute Regiment	276874	90944	Oberursal Int Centre on 25/9/1944. Direct questioning & asking for confirmation of facts.
Wright	Stanley Winston	Sergeant Major	2nd Battalion, South Staffordshire Regiment	4913782		Sagan Nov 1944 Ordinary interrogation.
Young	Graham Ferguson	Leading Aircraftman	Light Warning Set Unit No. 6341	971682		Not specially interrogated 5 1/2 months after capture.

Chapter 4

Prison Camps

Dulags

Most men were at a Dulag for three to four weeks, before being transferred to a permanent camp. The precise dates for arriving at Dulags and permanent camps given in the questionnaires cannot be relied upon, for example, four men give dates for arrival at a Stalag before the start of Market Garden. However, it appears that Limburg started transferring men to Stalags as early as around 20 September, but as the numbers arriving increased men were held longer at the Dulag.

Conditions at Limburg were poor. The sudden influx of Arnhem prisoners took the camp far beyond its normal capacity:

> Sergeant Arthur Williams, Glider Pilot Regiment, 'Bad living conditions in Stalag 12A. Overcrowded tents and barrack huts. Bad and unsatisfactory food. Sanitation practically non-existent.'

> Private Leonard Cannon, 1st Battalion, Parachute Regiment, 'Living conditions bad. Very little food water shortage. No lights. Sanitation poor. Only one blanket issued.'

> Staff Sergeant Stanley Hann, Glider Pilot Regiment, 'Inability of German staff at Stalag XII to provide hot showers and delousing for POW who contacted lice owing to filthy living conditions over a period of eight weeks.'

Able-bodied officers sent to Hadamar via Limburg spent up to two weeks at Limburg before transfer, although some were moved more quickly. Presumably, this was caused by the Germans working through the backlog of arriving men:

> Captain John Killick, 89 Parachute Security Section, 'Stalag XII A Limburg 21st Sept–4 Oct: Oflag XII B Hadamar 4 Oct–16 Oct.'

> Captain Reverend Alastair Menzies, Royal Army Chaplains' Department, 'Stalag XII A Limburg 24 Sept–12 Oct?: XII B Dulag Hadamar 12 Oct–22 Oct?'

Captain William Mallett, Forward Observation Unit Royal Artillery, '2 Oct–5 Oct Limburg: 5 Oct–16 Oct Hadamar.'

The walking wounded officers sent to Fallingbostel were the exception. After a few days they were transferred to Oflag IX A/H or IX A/Z:

Lieutenant George Guyon, 1st Battalion, Parachute Regiment, 'Stalag XIC (sic) Fallingbostel 9.10.44–10.19.44: Oflag IX A/Z Rotenburg/Fulda 11.10.44.'

Lieutenant Alan Green, 1st Battalion. Border Regiment, 'Stalag XI B Fallingbostel 13 Oct–15 Oct: Oflag IX A/Z Rotenburg 15 Oct.'

Men did not stay long at Dulag Luft. They were in solitary confinement when not being interrogated and there was little food. Staff Sergeant George Cobbold, Glider Pilot Regiment, recorded spending three days in solitary. Staff Sergeant John Ellis, Glider Pilot Regiment, spent two days in solitary. But Staff Sergeant Healey spent almost two weeks at Oberursel:

Staff Sergeant Edwin Healey, Glider Pilot Regiment, 'Auber Ruzel (sic) – Sept 30th–Oct 13th 1944 solitary confinement.'

Food was scarce. During his twenty-four hours at Oberursel, Captain John Tobin, RAMC, received, 'Half a litre of watery soup and two slices of bread.'

Sergeant Horace Stones, Glider Pilot Regiment, 'Interrogation by Luftwaffe at Oberustle (sic) left in solitary confinement 2 days with very little or no food.'

Unlike at Limburg, NCOs and Other Ranks who were sent to Fallingbostel often stayed at the camp for the rest of the war. Conditions at the camp were not much better than Limburg, though there are no mentions of tents:

Sergeant Charles Lyons, Glider Pilot Regiment, 'for the first 2 months after capture 400 wounded men of 1st Airborne Div packed in a filthy room with inadequate food and medical treatment. One British M.O. but no medical supplies.'

Corporal Albert Austin, Light Warning Set No. 60680, RAF, was at Fallingbostel from 28 September until 4 December, before being transferred to Dulag Luft. He had been wounded and this accounted for some of the delay. But other men from the Light Warning unit were moved to Dulag in December, which suggests either a sudden understanding of their role or a delay in getting an appropriate technical interrogator. Sergeant Quigley, Light Warning Set No. 6341, RAF, recorded waiting a week at Dulag Luft for a German radar specialist to interview him. Leading Aircraftsman Graham Young, Light Warning Set No. 6341, RAF, had been seriously wounded and was held in several hospitals from 19 September until 9 March 1945. He was transferred to Dulag Luft in March 1945.

Selecting Men for Permanent Camps

Following interrogation and registration, men were moved to prison camps. It is clear that the Germans selected men for specific camps. As well as the separation of officers from Other Ranks, and of men deemed to be Air Force, there was a pattern in the camps where NCOs and wounded men were held. The selection was made centrally. The German prisoner numbers show that these were allocated at the main reception camps – Dulag XII A, Dulag XII B, Stalag XI B and Dulag Luft – before transfer to permanent camps. Wounded officers transferred to Oflag IX A/H and A/Z were allocated their numbers at these camps. Men who went to Dulag Luft from Limburg have POW numbers from Limburg sequences.

The High Command of the Army (OKH) and Luftwaffe (OKL) used information on camp capacity, facilities, and of the ability of camps to manage the different ranks of prisoner. Decisions taken by OKH and OKL were then modified depending on the Dulag that men passed through. Senior NCOs, men who were less malleable than younger men, from Limburg were sent to Stalag XVIII C. From Fallingbostel they went to Stalag II A. The Commandant of Stalag XVIII C at Markt Pongau, in what is now Austria, penalised men who refused to work. The Geneva Convention allowed NCOs the choice of not working. The *kommandos* managed by the Stalag included work on the railway and clearing debris, presumably from air raids, at Kundl, 80 miles west of the camp:

> Regimental Sergeant Major George White, 10th Battalion, Parachute Regiment, 'XVIII C under special guards and orders, when all we were was none working W.O.s [Warrant Officers] NCOs and men (as NCOs). They went to special pains to make our lot as uncomfortable and as unbearable as possible.'

There are no similar complaints from Stalag II A, however, this camp managed *kommandos* on farms. At this camp, several men mention volunteering to work because they thought there would be chances to escape:

> Lance Corporal Harold Black, 2nd Battalion, Parachute Regiment, '3 other men (Pte Carr Cpl Dell and L/Cpl Killen) and myself escaped from a komando (sic) on the farm for which we volunteered, with the purpose of escaping. This was at or rather twenty miles from Neubrandenburg.'

> Lance Sergeant George Kite, 2nd Battalion, South Staffordshire Regiment, 'My reason for volunteering for work was to escape but my release came before my plans were complete.'

Officers from Oflag IX A/Z complete their Liberation Questionnaires in Brussels. Photographed by Leighton 'Lee' Hill, NZ Expeditionary Force. (Author's Collection)

Right: Members of 1st Airborne Division being marched away from Oosterbeek into Arnhem. (Cumbria's Museum of Military Life Collection)

Below: Newly captured airborne men at a "Sammelstelle" a battlefield collecting point. (Bundesarchive)

Left: Quarter Master Sergeant David Morris 11 Parachute Regiment being questioned in the Arnhem area. The men immediate left and right of Morris are members of the Luftwaffe. (Regionaal Archief Nijmegen, Creative Commons)

Below: The main Luftwaffe interrogation centre at Oberursel, in the outskirts of Frankfurt. Primarily used to interrogate aircrew. (Univeristy of Lincoln, Bomber Command Archive)

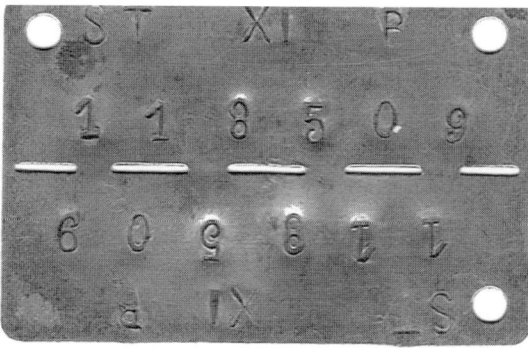

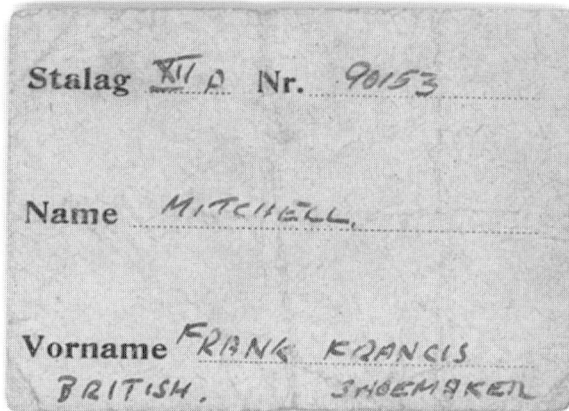

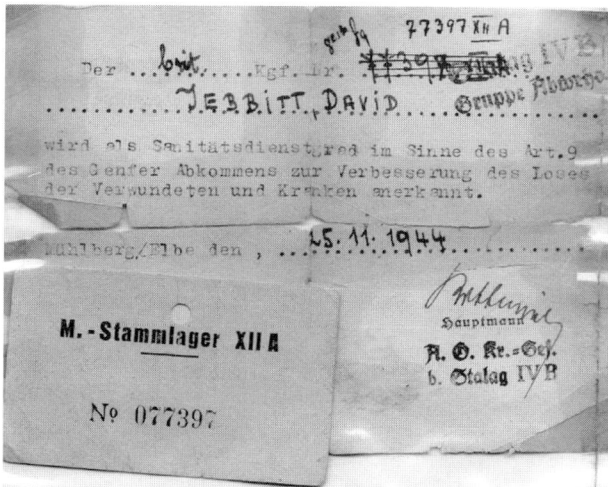

Different styles of German POW identity tags An oval ID tag issued at Stalag XI B Private Edgar Dellar 3rd Battalion The Parachute Regiment. Ian Dellar Collection. A rectangular metal identity tag issued at Stalag XIB to Private Arthur Locke 1st Battalion The Border Regiment. Derek Locke Collection. A card tag issued Sergeant Alan Mitchell, Glider Pilot Regiment at Stalag XII A - Richard Hollingworth Collection. Private David Jebbitt's recognition of his status under the Geneva Convention as a member of the Royal Army Medical Service from Stalag IV B, with a paper ID issued at Stalag XII A. (Stuart Jebbitt Collection)

APPENDIX II

Exhibit X

ARRIVAL REPORT FORM

Date:

Name:　　　　　　　Surname:　　　　　　Service Number:

Rank:

Trade:

R.A.F., R.C.A.F., R.A.A.F., R.N.Z.A.F., S.A.A.F., U.S.A.A.F., U.S.N.A.F., F.A.A.

Date of birth:

Where born

Profession:

Relion:

Married:

How many children:

Home address:

Next of kin:

What was your payment during the war:

When shot down:

Where shot down:

By:

Where taken prisoner:

By:

Squadron:　　　　　Group:　　　　　　Command:

Station:　　　　　　Station No:

Letter and number of aircraft:

Type of aircraft:

How is your health:　　　　　　　　Wounded:

Members of the crew:

Name:　Surname:　Number:　Wounded:　Killed:　P.O.W.:

....

....

....

Date.................................　　　　**Signature**................................

The fake Red Cross Form used at Dulag Luft. This version is taken from the 'The Dulag Luft Trial'. (Author Collection)

XMAS PARADE

Above: Roll call at Oflag IX, Christmas 1944, by Gordon Horner, from 'For you the War is over'. (Author Collection)

Right: Edward Beattie's drawing of his own interrogation at OB West from 'Diary of a Kriegie'. (Author Collection)

Oflag IX A/H Lower camp that had been a farm and then a holiday work camp for members of the Nazi Party. It was at the bottom of the hill on which Spangenberg Castle, Oflag IX A/H Upper Camp stood. By Borrett, from 'Backwater Borrett. (Author Collection)

Oflag IX A/Z, a requisitioned secondary school, by McIndoe. (Author Collection)

Block III at Eichstatt Oflag VII B. The camp consisted of huts in the grounds of a large house previously used by the German Army by Jimmy Graham from 'Joe in Germany'. (Author Collection)

Above left: German poster issued after the escape from Stalag Luft 3 warning prisoners of the risks escapers faced. (Author Collection)

Above right: The work of the Red Cross made a great difference to the life of POWs. (Red Cross)

Men from Oflag IX A/Z during their evacuation march east by the Germans in 1945. Photographed by Leighton 'Lee' Hill NZ Expeditionary Force. (Author's Collection)

Men from Oflag IX A/Z board USAAF Dakotas at Esperstedt airfield in April 1945 before flying to Belgium. Photographed by Leighton 'Lee' Hill NZ Expeditionary Force. (Author's Collection)

The Geneva Convention required prisoners to be managed by their equivalent troops, but since the Luftwaffe managed airborne troops it was understandable that, despite the OKW instruction, following their interrogation some airborne POWs were sent to Luftwaffe camps. This may have been caused by some men continuing to wear their regimental insignia during the battle and the similarity of the glider pilot wings and Royal Air Force insignia. The questionnaires show that the confusion was limited to the status of glider pilots, who were sent to both Army and Luftwaffe camps. Glider pilots who were interrogated at Dulag Luft all went to Luftwaffe camps. Only a small number went to Luftwaffe camps from Dulag XII A at Limburg. Since some men went to Dulag Luft via Limburg it is clear that the Germans identified some of their prisoners as Air Force, both on the battlefield and at Limburg.

Glider Pilot Regiment Camps	
Dulag Luft then Luftwaffe camp	70
Dulag XII A then Army camp	59
Unknown Dulag to Luftwaffe camp	23
Unknown Dulag to Army camp	27

Apart from glider pilots, no Army men were sent directly to Luftwaffe camps. Glider pilots who were sent to Army camps from the Dulag Luft were given Army POW numbers.

Non-Commisioned Officers and Other Ranks

The allocation of NCOs to camps was looser than for officers to Oflags. Stalag XVIII C held most warrant officers but it also held lance corporals, corporals and sergeants. It also had at least one private masquerading as a corporal.

> Private Eric Small, 10th Parachute Battalion, 'during my incarceration at Stalag 18 C and with approximately 200 other POW (NCO) was imprisoned separately in a special barracks for no other reason than that we would not work for them – at the time of capture I had stated my rank to be that of a full corporal in order to avoid necessity of assisting the enemies' war effort.'

The camps that took most Arnhem men were in the industrial areas of Silesia, centred on Stalag IV B at Mühlberg, and the mines and steelworks around Fallingbostel. Fallingbostel took walking wounded directly from Arnhem and able-bodied men on transfer from the main Dulag at Stalag XII A at Limburg.

Transfers from Dulags

The transfer from Dulag to permanent camp is described by very few questionnaires. For most it followed the same pattern as their move to Limburg, in locked in boxcars. The journey could take a considerable time. Private William Gibb, 181st Airlanding Field Ambulance, recorded his journey from Limburg to Mühlberg as taking ten days. Corporal Arthur Jones, 1st Battalion, Parachute Regiment, listed frostbite from ten days in a 'cattle wagon', as a medical condition he suffered while a POW. Today the 300-mile journey would take around five hours by train:

> Private Albert Dyer, 2nd Battalion, Parachute Regiment, 'Bad treatment when transported from one Stalag to another. i.e. Terrific overcrowding in cattle trucks. No sanitation allowed for. No food or water.'

> Private John Godden, 1st Battalion, Parachute Regiment, 'The way we were kept short of food & water during transportation from Limburg to Stalag IV B ie 2 issues of bread and water in 5 days travelling. Also during that period we were locked in cattle trucks with almost no ventilation, we were allowed no exercise during journey.'

> Private George Green, 2nd Battalion, South Staffordshire Regiment, 'I was moved from Stalag XII A Limburg to Stalag IV B Muhlberg on Elbe, arriving there on 15 Oct/44. We travelled in dirty cattle trucks, 50 men to a truck. Only twice during the whole journey were we allowed out of the truck for 5 minutes. Drinking water was only given to us once during the day, we had only 2/3 of a loaf each, and 1 1/2 small cheeses for the whole trip. Many men in the truck were ill, but no medical attention was given them on the journey.'

Officers might also have been transported by boxcar. Lieutenant Doig was moved from Dulag XII B to Oflag 79 in this way:

> Lieutenant Charles Doig, 7th Battalion, King's Own, 'Accommodating 22 officers in one third of a cattle truck for a journey of 5 days and nights.'

Walking wounded officers transferred from Fallingbostel to Oflag IX A/Z travelled by passenger train, but in no great comfort:

> Lieutenant George Guyon, 1st Battalion, Parachute Regiment, 'I was moved, together with approximately 30 other officers from Stalag XI C (sic) to Oflag IX A/Z, we were all wounded, some seriously. No attempt was made to provide adequate covering for those of us who had had our clothing cut away. Also we were forced to stand nearly the whole of one night in a draughty hallway of a station, which had a stone floor, and few benches.'

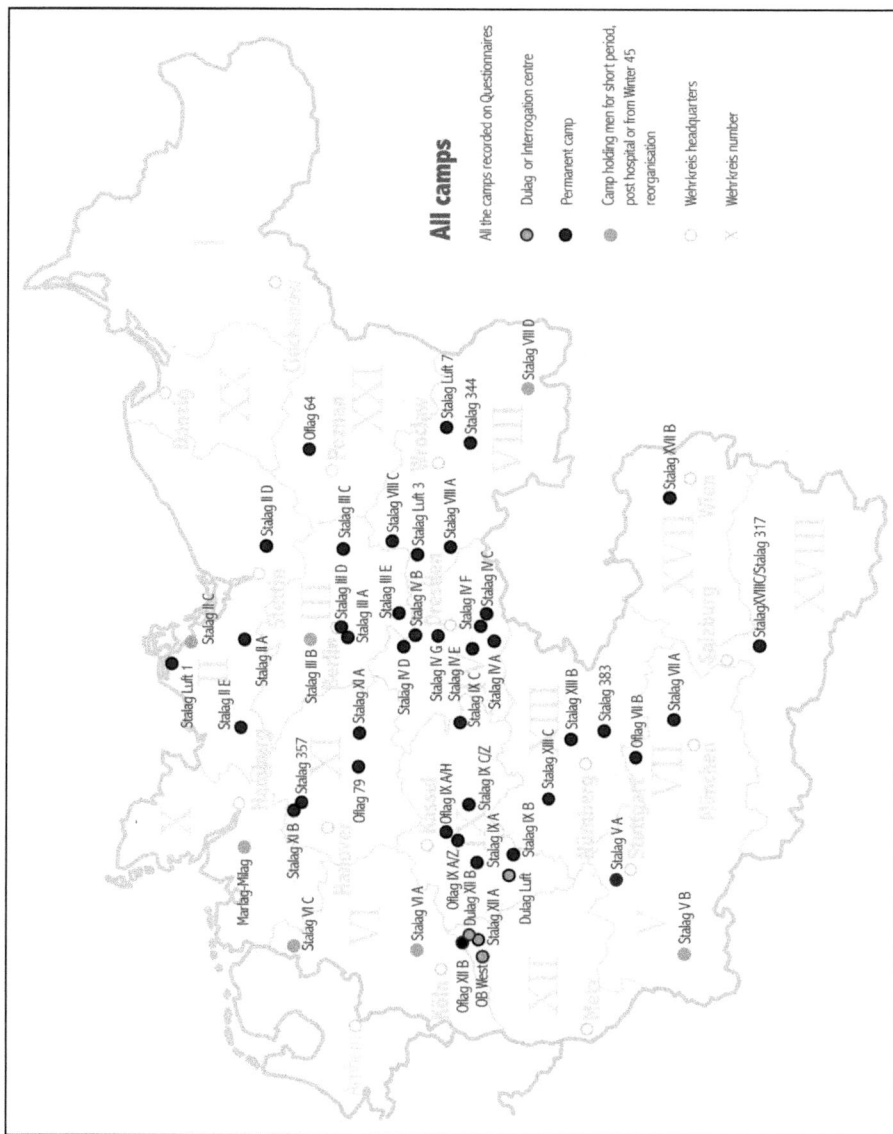

Map 3: Camps that held men captured at Arnhem.

All camps

All the camps recorded on Questionnaires

- Dulag or Interrogation centre
- Permanent camp
- Camp holding men for short period, post hospital or from Winter 45 reorganisation
- Wehrkreis headquarters
- X Wehrkreis number

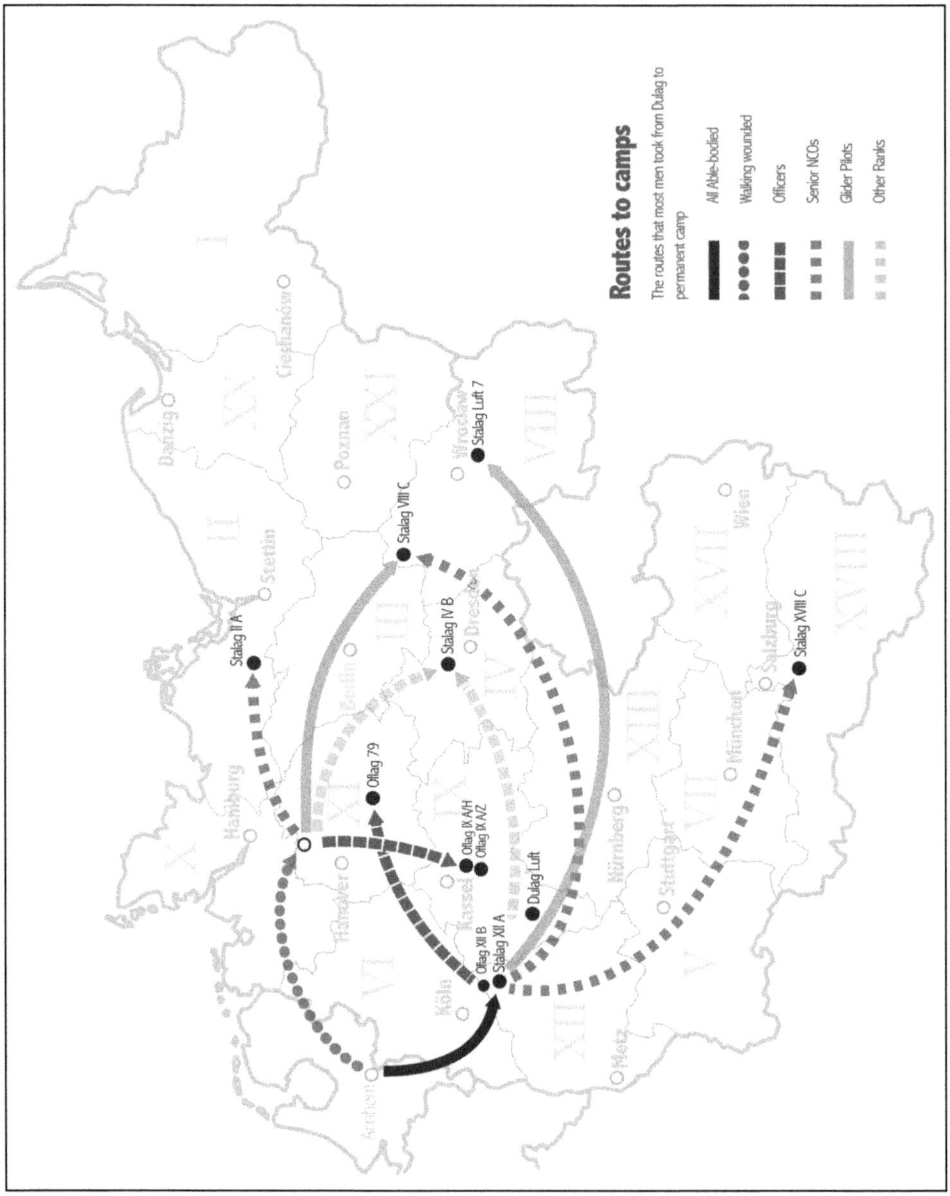

Map 4: Main routes to permanent camps.

Permanent Camps – Oflags

The questionnaires record officers at four permanent camps: Oflag 79 at Braunschweig, Oflag IX A/Z at Rotenburg an der Fulda, Oflag VII B at Eichstätt, and one officer at Oflag 64. No questionnaires exist for Oflag XII, where Lieutenant Colonel Tommy Haddon, 1st Battalion, Border Regiment, who had taken on the task of organising Dulag XII B, moved to in March 1945, or for Oflag IX A/H. Both camps were liberated before the repatriation scheme had begun.

Only one officer's questionnaire doesn't fit this pattern. Lieutenant Peter Mason, 7th Battalion, King's Own Scottish Borderers Regiment, was captured attempting to escape from hospital in Apeldoorn. He went first to Stalag XIII D, before being transferred to Oflag 64 at Szubin in Poland during October. Oflag 64 was a camp that held predominantly Americans. Mason was a CANLOAN: Canadian officers serving in the British Army.

Officers who were transferred to Oflag VII B were moved in January 1945. Lieutenant Colonel Haddon's own account describes the formal closure of the Dulag as being in March, but that the stream of British prisoners had been 'drying up' before then.

Oflag IX A/H and A/Z

The Oflag had three sites: IX A/H Upper Camp in Spangenberg Castle; IX A/H Lower Camp in a former hostel in the village of Elbersdorf on the north side of Spangenberg hill; and a Zweilager – subsidiary camp – IX A/Z, in a former school at Rotenburg, 20km to the south. No questionnaires exist for men held at Oflag IX A/H. Representatives of the Swiss Foreign Office visited the camp on 8 November 1944 and reported that twenty-eight new prisoners had arrived at the Upper Camp and 34 at Lower Camp from Arnhem[6]. They included three members of the Polish Parachute Brigade. Officers from Fallingbostel all have POW numbers in the 21XX series and by using the War Office list it is possible to identify eighty-three men who were sent to one of IX A's sites. Thirty of these went on to IX A/Z. There are questionnaires for twenty-one of these. The camp was marched east in late March and leaked escapees from the first day. The early escapees were repatriated before the Endor system got under way, which accounts for their questionnaires being missing.

There is only one reference to life in IX A/Z on the questionnaires. This refers to escape tunnels. It is puzzling because the last tunnel at Rotenburg was discovered in June 1944.[7] It started in a first-floor toilet and went down inside the wall:

> Captain John Burley Dickinson, 1st Airlanding Light Battery, 'Assisted to dig tunnels. However discovered before completion.'

---

6   WO 224/78.
7   Green, Peter, *The March East: the final days of Oflag IX A/H and A/Z* (History Press, 2012).

Other than transfers to hospitals, none of the POWs from IX A/Z were moved to other Oflags. Both camps were evacuated by the Germans in late March and marched eastwards away from the Americans. IX A/H was liberated on 4 April 1945. IX A/Z was liberated on 13 April 1945 and twenty-one questionnaires exist from this group.

Oflag 79 – Braunschweig

Oflag 79 was created in May 1944 when Oflag VIII F was transferred from Marisch-Trubau (now Moravská Třebová) in eastern Czechoslovakia. The camp history in the National Archives[8] describes it being housed in former 'Air Training Barracks' at Querum. Querum was on the north-eastern edge of Braunschweig.

The camp was bombed on 24 August by the USAAF. It had been mistaken for one of several aviation industry targets near Brunswick. Despite causing considerable damage to the buildings, no prisoners were killed.

There are seventy-seven questionnaires from men held at Oflag 79. As well as fifty-four officers, there were two NCOs and twenty-one Other Ranks as orderlies. The Fallingbostel[9] files record a transfer of forty-four NCOs and Other Ranks to Oflag 79 on 23 November 1944. Private Michael Baxendale 156th Battalion, Parachute Regiment, who was one of this group, gives Oflag 79 as his working camp and his work as 'batman'. The orderlies were all men who had been wounded and gone direct to Fallingbostel from Apeldoorn.

Nine officers record being wounded on capture, yet were transferred to Oflag 79. Seven travelled via Hadamar but they also include Major Robert Pott, 156th Battalion, Parachute Regiment, who spent almost three months in a hospital at Gronau before being sent directly to this Oflag in December 1944. His POW number, 2193, is one of the sequences allocated to officers who went to Oflag IX A. Also in this number was Captain Thomas Miller, 4th Parachute Brigade Royal Artillery, who went from a hospital at Seigburg to Hadamar and then to Oflag 79. His POW number is one of the usual Hadamar series, 608. One questionnaire records a man being transferred from Oflag 79. This was Major Thomas Courtney, 133 Parachute Field Ambulance, who was moved to work at Reserve Lazarett Leipzig-Wahren. He had moved again in March to Reserve Lazarett Halle.

Major Courtney is one of the few men to record anything about life at Oflag 79 in his questionnaire:

> 'Before leaving OFLAG 79 (Brunswick) German information shared by rumour, that the camp would probably be moved to the mountains in south Germany shortly. The date of this rumour would be about Jan 15 1945.'

---

8   WO 208/3292.
9   WO 361/1797/2.

The other references to the camp are an escape by Major Christopher Perrin-Brown in February 1945, and praise for the Senior British Officer's handling of the camp's liberation. This came on 12 April with the arrival of the US Ninth Army.

Oflag VII B – Eichstätt

Eichstätt is between Nuremburg and Munich, in Bavaria. Sixteen men record time at Oflag VII B. They are all men who left Hadamar in January 1945. It would be tempting to see this group as the permanent staff of Dulag XII B, however the absence of the Senior British Officer, Lieutenant Colonel Thomas Haddon, from the group argues against this.

The Germans evacuated the camp on 14 April 1945. Four American Mustangs that had been shooting up a nearby railway station attacked the column of prisoners thinking them German troops. The prisoners failed to realize the danger they were in until the very last minute and many were caught in the open. Ten were killed and more than forty wounded. The attack provided cover for an escape, though sadly the escaper was recaptured:

> Captain Richard Birchenough, 11th Battalion, Parachute Regiment, 'one escape made from line of march when officers were leaving OFLAG VII B for South on 14 April 45 – escape made alone under cover of machine-gunning of column by Allied planes. Captured 36 hours later.'

Permanent Camps – Stalags

Four camps dominated the list of those receiving NCOs and Other Ranks: Stalag II A, Stalag IV B, Stalag VIII C and some were retained at, or transferred to, Stalag XI B. Stalag IV B acted as a clearing-house for other Stalags in the large industrial area that ran from the mines of the eastern Harz into the Sudetenland. Finally, some NCOs and Other Ranks were transferred to Oflags as orderlies.

Glider pilot NCOs who had passed through Dulag Luft were sent to Stalag Luft 7.

NCOs and Other Ranks were moved between camps, but above all they suffered most from the winter evacuations. Those who went to Stalag XI B and Stalag IV B were particularly liable to be moved. The remaining camp files of Stalag XI B[10] show considerable movement into, and away from, the camp in the last six months of the war. Stalag IV B's role as a transit camp for Wehrkreis IV inflates the numbers of men who recorded it as a camp, before moving to other stalags in the Wehrkreis.

---

10 WO 361/1797/1 and WO 361/1797/2, National Archives, Kew.

Stalag II A – Neubrandenburg

Neubrandenburg between Berlin and the Baltic coast was a complex of camps holding French, Serb, Russian, Italian and American prisoners as well as British. In the last stages of the war it came a stopping point for men marched west away from the Russians. The camp managed agricultural working parties mainly, though one man records his work as 'Liepen joiner'. Others refer to Liepen as 'farm work'. Liepen is a small village 30 miles north of Neubrandenburg.

The Geneva Convention made working optional for NCOs. Some refused work because they felt it was assisting the enemy, while others could see advantages to being outside the camp:

> Lance Corporal Harald Back, 2nd Battalion, Parachute Regiment, '3 other men (Pte Carr Cpl Dell and L/Cpl Killen) and myself escaped from kommando on the farm for which we volunteered with the purpose of escaping.'

Lance Corporal Back's account is supported by that of the Man of Confidence of the *kommando*:

> Company Sergeant Major Frederick Meredith, 1st Battalion, Parachute Regiment, Escape, 'I was the confidence man to commando No. 221/17. Four men wished to escape before the entire commando was ready. I forced the door open and the four men went. The men's names are as follows: – Cpl Dell Cpl Carr Cpl Back Cpl Kill.'

Kommando 806, Stalag III D, Berlin

Stalag III D consisted of a group of small camps in the Berlin suburbs. They are described as *kommandos* by their inmates, but were not *arbeitkommandos* (working groups). They were used for a variety of intelligence and propaganda purposes, including attempts to create a British Free Corps, to fight alongside the Germans.[11] Trooper Peter Vaughan, 1st Airborne Recce Squadron, is the only man to record time in Kommando 806. He described the camp as the 'Berlin Interrogation Commando'. Trooper Vaughan was transferred to the *kommando* from Dulag Luft West. Edward Beattie, who was also held in Kommando 806,[12] describes the *kommando* as a very small camp:

> Kommando 806 is a very special group which lives in a separate compound. At the present moment it consists of eighteen Italian military priests, three Italian officers, a few Frenchmen, about a dozen

---

11 Weale, Adrian, *Renegades: Hitler's Englishmen*, Weidenfeld & Nicolson, London, 1994.
12 Beattie describes Vaughan as 'Sergeant Peter Vaughan of Colchester, Essex, England, a parachutist captured at Arnhem.' Beattie, Edward *op cit.*

Russians, officers or NCOs, who class as convinced Communists, two South African captains, myself, and an individual who shall be called Ponti, and who will one day rate an entry all to himself.

Nobody in Kommando 806 knows quite why he is here instead of being in a permanent camp, and nobody can ever get any satisfaction out of the Germans.

Why Trooper Vaughan was sent to the camp is unknown. He was a student before joining the army. Edward Beattie met Vaughan at Kommando 806, but he too throws no light on why Vaughan was there. On his questionnaire Vaughan gave his occupation as 'student': was he considered open to ideas or just very communicative? He certainly had no German sympathies and his questionnaire includes this statement:

> Have fairly extensive and detailed information relating to the endeavours and methods of a special department to the German foreign office and military to gain the collaboration of Allied P.O.W.s. For information on that subject I also beg to refer to other Officers and O.R.s of the American and British forces who – against their wishes – were kept in the Berlin interrogation commando.

Wehrkreis III did have another intelligence interest: it provided an unusual Reserve Army unit, Propaganda Ersatz und Ausbildung Abteilung (Propaganda Training Battalion).

Stalag IV B – Mühlberg

Stalag IV B acted as a Dulag for the camps and working parties in the industrial area that ran from the eastern Harz Mountains, around Dresden and Leipzig, and on into the Sudetenland. The questionnaires clearly show Stalag IV B a transit camp.[13] Men arrived at IV B and within a month transferred to one of its satellite camps: Stalags IVA, B, C, D, E, F or G. The International Red Cross, in their report on the camp in November 1944,[14] described it as a 'transit camp' and recorded that it held 11,532 men, of whom 7,262 were British. The questionnaires show 1,498 Arnhem men were held at any camp in Wehrkreis IV and 596 who remained at IV B.

As well as its administrative role for all Stalags in Wehrkreis IV, Mühlberg also managed *arbeitskommandos* directly. The questionnaires list sixty of these *kommandos*. Unlike the *kommandos* managed by Stalag XI B or Stalag IX C, where the *kommandos* had a simple number identifier, they used a three-figure code. For example, a general labouring *kommando* at Merseberg just outside Leipzig was 'Me 49 E': 'Me' for Merseberg, '49' as an accession number and 'E' for English, as the nationality of the labourers. 'Ei 116 E' was a British copper-mining *kommando*

---

13 Kilian, *Achim Mühlberg 1939–1948: Ein Gefangenenlager mitten in Deutschland*, Böhlau Verlag, 2011.
14 WO 224/12.

in the eastern Harz near Eisleben. The geographic spread of Mühlberg's own *kommandos* overlaps with those of its subordinate Stalags, suggesting that these were created ad hoc to manage the large number of *kommandos* in the district.

Stalag VIII C – Sagan

The camp was built close to Stalag Luft 3, the site of the 'Great Escape' of early 1944. It held predominatly British and Commonwealth troops. The Arnhem POWs were NCOs, mainly sergeants. In October 1944, 475 NCOs were transferred to Sagan from Fallingbostel,[15] the journey taking five days. Men were subject to further interrogations at Sagan, though the descriptions of these were that they were 'casual' or 'informal talks with civilians'.

Sagan managed working parties in the Sudetenland. Several questionnaires record men being punished for refusing to work. The issue of making NCOs work is also recorded at Stalag XVIII C, another camp that received large numbers of senior NCOs:

> Corporal Clifford Fairweather, 250th Airborne Light Company, RASC, 'Reprisals were taken by the Germans at Sagan in January 1945 against all NCOs refusing to work, in the form of taking all NCOs blankets away from them.'

> Lance Corporal Thomas Thomas, RAMC, 'At 8C the Commandant Hauptmann Hart took reprisals against prisoners captured at Arnhem and refused to issue Red Cross Supplies. Sick men were forced to parade in the snow. And conditions were generally terrible. No Bedding or under clothes.'

One man gave a different explanation of the punishments:

> Lance Sergeant Eric Chesterton, Royal Signals, 'Reprisals against PWs of Stalag VIII C. Explanation:- Suffering endured by German PWs held in Egypt.'

Stalag VIII C was evacuated in February 1945. One man records a special food issue before they left the camp, but then later of poor treatment during the march:

> Sergeant Major Stanley Wright, 2nd Battalion, South Staffordshire Regiment, 'The issue of Argentine Bulk Rations at Sagan before starting forced march. Treatment of Britishers on march as compared to other nationalities. No medical treatment on march.'

> Sergeant Donald McLeavy, Glider Pilot Regiment, 'On the march from Sagan to Falkenburg there was a serious lack of food. Medical attention. I myself having a festered foot. This situation was due partially to the German Commandant.'

---

15 WO 61/1797/2.

Stalag XI B – Fallingbostel

Fallingbostel's role as a Dulag for walking wounded from Arnhem was in addition to its standard function as a Stalag managing working parties. It was a large camp close to the Bergen-Belson concentration camp. There were other POW camps in the area, including Stalag 357, which took men from Fallingbostel.

The questionnaires show men being sent from Fallingbostel to working parties at nearby sugar beet factories during the beet processing season from October to December 1944. But it also sent men to the Herman Göring Steel Works at Hallendorf, the lead ore mines at Bad Grund and to groups carrying out repairs to railways damaged by bombing, including 'Arbeitskommando Katastrophen-Einsatz-Ülsen', a disaster response working detail at Ülsen. The work at Hallendorf extended beyond the steelworks. Questionnaires record forestry work, bomb damage, rebuilding an arms factory and demolishing bombed buildings.

Fallingbostel took some men who had been marched west in the winter of 1945, including WOII David Morris, 11th Battalion, Parachute Regiment, who had evaded capture until November, and then went to Stalag XII A, Dulag Luft, Stalag VIII C before arriving at Fallingbostel in March 1945.

Stalag XVIII – Markt Pongau

Stalag XVIII C, also known as Stalag 317, is now in Austria. Its Arnhem POWs were mainly senior NCOs. As with Stalag VIII C, there was friction over non-working NCOs:

> Regimental Sergeant Major George White, 10th Battalion, Parachute Regiment, 'confined in the Sonder [Special] Barracks at 317. XVIII C under special guards and orders when all we were was none working. W.O.s NCOs and men (as NCOs). They went to special pains to make our lot as uncomfortable and as unbearable as possible.'

> Company Sergeant Major George Lott, 10th Battalion, Parachute Regiment, 'I with others were without any consideration put into a compound at Markt Pongau with only hundred and 50 yards in which to walk and were not allowed outside of this compound. We were classified as 'work refusing NCOs' which we considered it a duty to be. Sanitary arrangements were bad. We were locked up like this for eight months.'

The questionnaires give the impression of a very unpleasant camp:

> Corporal Edward Oliver, 1st Parachute Squadron, Royal Engineers, 'We were once forced out to work by a German Sgt Major, at the pistol point.'

Kommandos – Working Parties

Arbeitskommandos (AK), were administered by Stalags. They could be a considerable distance away from their parent camp. Stalag XI B, Fallingbostel, supervised *kommandos* in lead mines at Bad Grund, 130km away in the north-western Harz mountains, and Stalag IX C at Bad Sulsa, near Weimar, managed *kommandos* at potash mines 100km to the west, despite having a sub camp Stalag IX C/Z at Muhlhausen that was nearer. Stalag IX C/Z managed *kommandos* on the south-western edge of the Harz Mountains.

Unlike Stalags, whose number related to their Wehrkreis, there was no standard numbering system for *kommandos*. In Wehrkreis IV, which had a large number of *kommandos*, a three-part system was used: location, number, language of POWs.

In other Wehrkreis, *kommandos* have only numbers, for example AK7002, managed by Stalag XI B, worked on canal repairs, while AK0395 worked on railway repairs in the Sudetenland and was managed by Stalag IV C. The questionnaires do not always record *kommandos* by their number or in the case of Wehrkreis IV their full title. Men in *kommandos* at Merseburg refer to their work – tunnelling, clearing debris, demolition, building air-raid shelters, canal-building, boot repairing – as well as three numbers, Me 40 E, Me 41 E and Me 49 E.

Men were transferred between *kommandos* to meet demands for labour. Lance Corporal George Miller, 1st Battalion, Border Regiment, went to Stalag IV B in October. A month later he was at a blanket factory at Kirschau, 60km east of Dresden. He then spent part of December doing agricultural work, before ending his captivity at a tin plate factory 10km north-west of Dresden. Private Daniel Tracey, 4th Battalion, Dorset Regiment, transferred from Stalag IV B to Stalag IV F before spending December to February on forestry work at Gunnersdorf, then February to early April at Neiderweisa cement work and then from April to May at railway repairs near Chemnitz.

Permanent Camps – Hospitals

Seriously wounded men were retained in hospitals in the Netherlands and Germany, and remained outside the system of Dulags until their condition allowed them to be moved. Seventy-four questionnaires show wounded men continuing to be held at hospitals in the Netherlands or Germany other than Fallingbostel. Many did not pass through Dulags; going from hospital direct to permanent camps in the winter of 1944–45.

The length of time men were held at hospitals depended on their medical condition. The largest single group of men that were transferred from one camp to another were the thirty-six who were moved from hospitals close to Arnhem to the Reserve Lazarett Freising, the camp hospital at Stalag VII A in Bavaria. Sergeant Kenneth White, Glider Pilot Regiment, went to the hospital at Freising in

September and was only transferred to the Stalag VII A in March 1945. Company Sergeant Major Thomas Courtie, 10th Battalion, Parachute Regiment, went to Freising in October. He was transferred to Stalag 383 in February 1945.

The hospital furthest from Arnhem was at Teupitz, just south-east of Berlin. This held seven men from November 1944 until Christmas Day:

> Sapper Conway Jones, 1st Parachute Squadron, Royal Engineers, '6 of my pals and myself were taken from Turpitz (sic) hospital with only a pair of pyjamas on Christmas Day travel by train to Frankfurt on Maine …'

As well as Sapper Jones', the questionnaires of Private Craig, 3rd Battalion, Parachute Regiment, and Lance Corporal Lloyd, 156th Battalion, Parachute Regiment, exist. Jones had shrapnel in his head: 'head wound shrapnel 4 months'. Like the others, he described his medical treatment as good. In conversations with his son, Craig described how he had been close to an exploding mortar bomb and needed an operation to remove shrapnel from his skull. For a time he had been blind.[16] Presumably all seven required surgery. Craig, Jones and Lloyd had been held at St Joseph's Hospital, Enschede before transfer to Teupitz.

The Teupitz men were all considered well enough to return to Dulag Luft in late December for interrogation. Craig described his interrogation as being 'Ordinary'. Lloyd did not refer to Dulag Luft or interrogation, but he has a month gap in the dates he gives as being at camps that matches Craig's time at Dulag Luft. Jones' interrogation experience was different:

> Sapper Conway Jones, 1st Parachute Squadron Royal Engineers, 'Ober Roosel (sic) Dulag Luft near Frankfurt on Maine. Confinement for one day still weak from wound. Just plain method and questions.'

All three men give hospitals and then Stalag IX C/Z at Mühlhausen from January 1945, suggesting that their transfer from Teupitz was premature. The transfer, though not in a boxcar, was not pleasant. Jones provides evidence of guards for men in transit coming from the destination camp, not their departure one:

> Sapper Conway Jones, 1st Parachute Squadron Royal Engineers, '… travel by train to Frankfurt on Maine. We were absolutely freezing with cold. No food and drink for 28 hrs. The guards were Luftwaffe Sgts very rough. They came from Ober Roosel (sic) Camp Frankfurt.'

The questionnaires often fail to distinguish between men being held at a Stalag or at a hospital associated with a Stalag, hence the number of men held in hospitals for long periods may be understated. Hospital medical teams made up of POWs were considered *arbeitskommandos* under the management of a Stalag and they may be listed by men as a Stalag and *kommando* rather than a hospital. For example, the

---

16 Pegasus, www.pegasusarchive.org/arnhem/frames.htm, accessed March 2021.

medical team at Obermaßfeld were Kommando 1249, managed by Stalag IX C at Sulza, 70 miles to the east. Only two men give 1249 as being a *kommando* at Obermaßfeld. Neither Sergeant Arthur Truman, Glider Pilot Regiment, nor Lance Sergeant Arthur Shepley, 156th Battalion Parachute Regiment, record being in a work camp, but both record being held at Obermaßfeld and Meiningen, and both give them their *kommando* numbers.

Officers from the RAMC held at Stalags can be assumed to be working as camp doctors. For example, Captain Stanley Lawrence, 16th Parachute Field Ambulance, RAMC, who gives his camp from January 1945 as Stalag XVII B at Krems in Austria, or Captain John Tobin, RAMC, at Stalag IV D.

Just over 10 per cent of the questionnaires include a hospital as a 'main camp'. These include men who also recorded being wounded on capture as well as a small number of others who describe their stay in hospital as being to a post-capture illness or injury.

Stalag VII A and Stalag XIII B, C and D took men from hospitals and it may be that their mentions on questionnaires are recording them as the Stalag that managed a *lazarett*, for example Reserve Lazarett Freising was managed by Stalag VII A at Moosburg. Nine officers record being at Stalag VII A in the last month of the war.

There are twenty-four questionnaires where men from the Royal Army Medical Corps did not record being wounded on capture but refer to hospitals, implying that the man spent time in captivity working in a hospital. Several men complained that their protected status as medical was not recognised by the Germans:

> Lance Corporal Eric Potts, 181st Airlanding Field Ambulance, 'Many men in the Medical Corps were unrecognised as medical men because their Red Cross cards were inadequately filled in or out of date. When these men were detailed to go on Kommando they had to go, although officially protected personnel.'

> Private William Evans, 181st Airlanding Field Ambulance, 'Not treated as protected personnel my identification card not being properly stamped by my unit.'

> Sergeant William Kerswell, RAMC, 'As a protected personnel, the only privilege granted was the double issue of writing materials to send home. No pay or walks out of stalag were granted.'

> Lance Corporal Stanley Kirk, 16th Parachute Field Ambulance, 'It was very difficult for R.A.M.C. personnel especially paratroops to get recognised as 'protected' personnel by the detaining power. When captured and I had with me A. B. 64 and A. P.W 3050 but I was never recognised as R.A.M.C.'

The question of medical personnel not being recognised was referred to in the 1949 revision of the Convention:

> Whereas Article 33 of the Geneva Convention of 27th July 1929, for the Relief of the Wounded and Sick in Armies in the Field, concerning

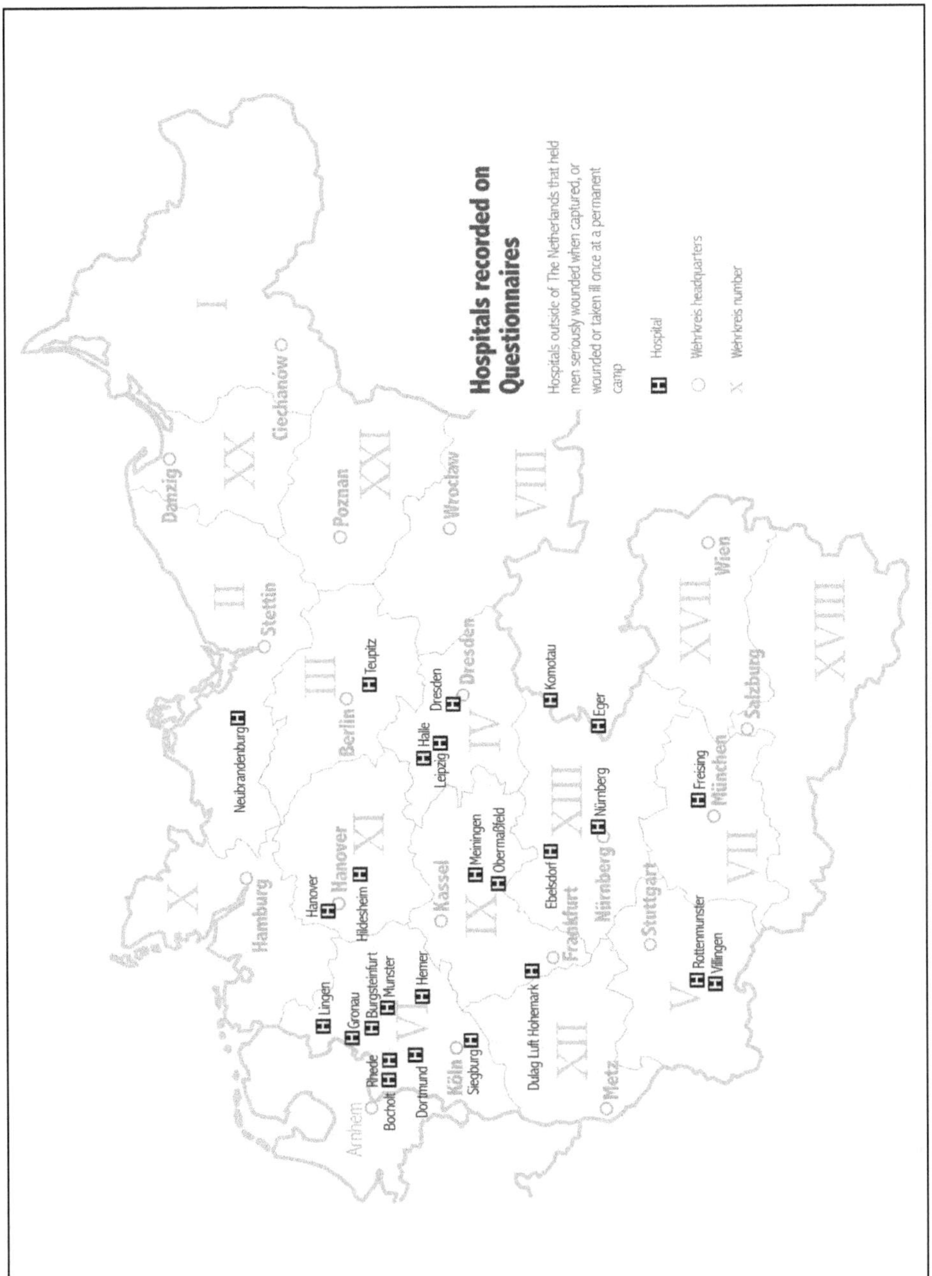

Map 5: Hospitals outside the Netherlands recorded on questionnaires.

the identity documents to be carried by medical personnel, was only partially observed during the course of the recent war, thus creating serious difficulties for many members of such personnel, the Conference recommends that States and National Red Cross Societies take all necessary steps in time of peace to have medical personnel duly provided with badges and identity cards prescribed in Article 40 of the new Convention.

The imprecise way men answered the 'main camps' question makes it difficult to distinguish between those who were patients and those who were working at hospitals. Three members of the medical team at Kriegslazarett 4/686 can be identified. This was the hospital manned by members of 181st Airlanding Field Ambulance that served German and Allied wounded alike until the end of the war. Initially at Apeldoorn, it was latterly moved to Heemstede. Private Arnold Jackson, 181st Airlanding Field Ambulance, gives the date for the move as 1 April 1945. Lance Corporal Budd, also 181st, had been working at the hospital in Apeldoorn. In the 'special notes' section he wrote:

> Lance Corporal Frederick Budd, 181st Airlanding Field Ambulance, '2 weeks before hospital liberated, Germans took 40 patients, 1 surgeon, padre and 1 orderly to Haarlam. Surgeon Major Rigby Jones.'

Permanent Camps-Stalag Lufts

Men record their interrogators offering to send them to 'better camps' if they answered all their questions. This was a reference to men held in Luftwaffe camps not working, whereas Other Ranks held in army camps would be required to work:

> Driver Lewis Willett, 250th Airborne Light Company, RASC, 'Enemy tried to gain information by promising better camp conditions and food for all airborne troops in receipt of a completed form from us.'

> Private John Hately, 156th Battalion, Parachute Regiment, '[interrogated] by Luftwaffe officer at Stalag XII A. I was informed that it was only a routine statement that was being taken in order to ascertain whether I belong to the A/B [airborne] Division so that I could be sent to a Stalag Luft.'

None referred to life at a Stalag Luft.

Chapter 5

Camp Life

Food and Health

The dominant factor in all the prisoners' lives, whether, officers, NCOs or Other Ranks, was food. Food was short throughout Germany and the prisoner of war system was no exception. Men had recorded being given little to eat at Dulags and this now continued:

> Private Harry Purdy, 3rd Battalion, Parachute Regiment, 'Lack of food in camp [i.e.] bread 1500 grm soup between seven men six days & no extra rations for working.'

> Lieutenant Edward Clapham MC, 1st Airlanding Anti-Tank battery Royal Artillery, 'Throughout the period of captivity, German rations were inadequate and subject to frequent "cuts".'

Once at a permanent camp, men could hope to receive a Red Cross parcel. The parcels contained tinned meat and fruits, dried milk, chocolate and cigarettes:

> Sergeant Stephen Garrard, Glider Pilot Regiment, 'German food rations inadequate: Red Cross food parcels our salvation.'

> Private Arthur Johnson, 2nd Battalion, South Staffordshire Regiment, 'I want to pay tribute to the Red Cross for the parcels I got, they were a godsend.'

Unfortunately for the men, delivery of Red Cross parcels was patchy and became even more so from the winter of 1944:

> Sergeant John Coates, 2nd Battalion, Parachute Regiment, 'Inadequate German ration last winter. No Red Cross parcels had arrived for months Jan. Feb. March.'

Private Boynes spoke for all prisoners of all nationalities:

> Private Albert Boynes, 10th Battalion, Parachute Regiment, 'The great work accomplished by the Red Cross. It is my firm conviction that without the aid rendered by that organisation our life in prison camps would have been even more difficult.'

After food or its absence, there were medical concerns. Many men had been wounded when captured: 567 men answered yes to the question, 'Were you wounded when captured?' Not surprisingly, men praised the treatment they received in Dutch hospitals:

> Sergeant Archibald Lyon, Glider Pilot Regiment, 'The nursing staff in Enschede Convent in Holland did everything to make us more comfortable than the Germans. They smuggled in food, fruit & general army communiques. The Dutch people did everything possible for me.'

However, when transferred to German hospitals for some men their treatment continued to be good. Freising was a hospital close to Stalag VII A at Moosburg, north-east of Munich, that took many seriously wounded men. Sapper Ellard seemed surprised he was treated well:

> Sapper Frank Paine, Royal Engineers, 'Extremely good treatment by German doctor and nuns in Freising Hospital.'

> Sapper Joseph Ellard, 4th Parachute Squadron, Royal Engineers, 'My treatment has fortunately been good.'

For men who were injured or ill after their arrival, ordinary camp hospitals could be very poor:

> Private Ernest Redman, 3rd Battalion, Parachute Regiment, 'Pte Morris Para Rgt died through neglect of injuries received whilst working in sugar beet factory at Dinklar near Hildesheim. Pte Morris was left in billets 2 or 3 days before being removed to hospital. In the opinion of myself and comrades he should have been taken to the hospital immediately after receiving injury.'

> Private Fred Pitt, 3rd Battalion, Parachute Regiment, 'I wish to bring to notice that I was discharged by hospital in Stalag VII A with my wound still open, by doctor KUNKER Jerry Dr and was working with it open.'

> Private Arnold Scott, 156th Battalion, Parachute Regiment, 'Wish to express the good work done night and day by POW Polish people in hospital Stalag II A when Germans were not looking after our wounded at all.'

Table 4: Medical

The answers to the Question 12 'Did you suffer any serious illnesses as a Prisoner of War? Nature of illness, cause, duration. (b) Did you receive adequate medical treatment?'

Name	Forename	Rank	Unit	Army number	POW number	Notes
Betts	George	Sergeant	Glider Pilot Regiment	14233066		Feverish camp conditions 1 week Dysentery Food 14 days
Bridgewater	Ernest Edward	Corporal	11th Battalion, Parachute Regiment	7262084		Skin disease bug bites Not adequate. Medical supplies had to be obtained from the French and we received very small quantities which were inadequate
Brook	William Henry	Driver	63rd Company, RASC	163198	75501	Dysentery insanitary state of camp (Limberg) 4 weeks
Caldwell	John Gibson McCoy	Private	2nd Battalion, South Staffs	274850		Dysentery Bad Food Yes at present [Treatment?] Definitely not
Carroll	William James	Private	11th Battalion, Parachute Regiment	2932551	117761	Tendons of left hand work in [illegible]
Chapman	Walter Frederick	Private	7th Battalion, King's Own Scottish Borderers	4751017		Chicken pox, scarlet fever and Tonsillitis for 5 weeks all caused by lack of food [Treatment?] Yes
Clifton	William	Corporal	9th Field Company, Royal Engineers	2077843	91313	Outbreak of boils 3 weeks [Treatment] No
Coidan	Denis Gabriel Andrew	Sapper	4th Parachute Squadron, Royal Engineers	1986027	117355	Septic head Lack of treatment to war wounds [Treatment?]When I was eventually able to see a British M.O.
Cole	Stanley Reginald	Lance Bombardier	Royal Artillery	14262654	93708	Dysentery bad food 8½ weeks [Treatment?] No

295

Name	Forename	Rank	Unit	Army number	POW number	Notes
Collins	Sydney George	Private	2nd Battalion, South Staffs	4699064	89288	Rheumatic fever 6 weeks [Treatment?] Yes
Courcha	William Alexander	Private	10th Battalion, Parachute Regiment	14665231	75407	Dysentery cause food, about 3 weeks The British Doctor did the best he could under the conditions, which were appalling
Courtney	Thomas Richard Brian	Major	133rd Parachute Field Ambulance, Royal Army Medical Corps	112406	91202	Crushed chest and fractured ribs. Buried in bomb explosion on 31 March. 3 weeks [Treatment?] Yes
Craig	John Alexander	Private	1st Battalion, Parachute Regiment	7046503	92185	Pleurisy and complications in the lungs. Exposure in the cold winter 11.1.45 – 1.5.45 [Treatment?] Yes adequate as afar as possible supplies were short
Crane	Ernest	Private	156th Battalion, Parachute Regiment	14420927	18658	Quinsy for 2 weeks [Treatment?] Yes
Cull	George William	Private	1st Parachute Regiment Brigade	14410678		Cut head in mine, underground [Treatment?] No. They made us work when we had dysentery & when we was so weak, couldn't stand up, only time they let us off work was if we had a very high temperature.
Cunliffe	Roger	Private	1st Battalion, Border Regiment	14402790		Stomach pains, lack and kind of food Had good treatment from Dutch
Daye	Russell Robert	Private	7th Battalion, King's Own Scottish Borderers	14620635	118419	Bad feet and weak r/leg wounds 3 months [Treatment?] No
Delea	Eric Michael Desmond	Private	156th Battalion, Parachute Regiment	3778794		Diphtheria 9 weeks Bronchitis 5 weeks [Treatment?] No
Down	Percy	Corporal	1st Battalion, Parachute Regiment	5671339	118257	Dysentery

Surname	Forename	Rank	Unit	Number	Number	Notes
Fishwick	William	Private	2nd Battalion, Parachute Regiment	3774446	91425	Jaundice catarrh (3 times)
Gordon	William James	Staff Sergeant	GHQ Liaison Regiment (Phantom)	5391601		Diphtheria lack off food? 26 days [Treatment?] Yes from French Medical Officer
Gore	Denis Edmund	Private	4th Battalion, Dorset Regiment	14723664	14948	Weakness & stomach trouble insufficient food 1/4/45 – 23/4/45 [Treatment?] No
Grant	Alexander	Private	7th Battalion, King's Own Scottish Borderers	14210847	91393	Running ears unknown 6 weeks treatment
Green	George	Private	2nd Battalion, South Staffs	7523335	90559	Chest trouble Cold weather chiefly. Nov 44 to March 44 (sic) [Treatment?] Treatment very poor
Greenall	John	Private	1st Battalion, Border Regiment	3606248	75398	Diphtheria – weakness – 6 weeks Palpitation – from Dip – 7 weeks [Treatment?] Yes
Gregg	Victor	Private	10th Battalion, Parachute Regiment	6913933	92043	Malaria 5 weeks [Treatment?] Yes
Gristwood	William John	Driver	1st Airlanding Anti-Tank Battery, Royal Artillery	1524980		Leg swelling lack of food still the same
Harbour	Frederick Spencer	Sergeant	10th Battalion, Parachute Regiment	6402134		Reoccurrence of frost-bite, received in 1940. The severe cold and lack of food and warmth. 8 months. [Treatment?] No
Harris	Douglas George	Private	3rd Battalion, Parachute Regiment	3967311		Pleurisy P/W treatment 5-2-45 till 18-5-1945 [Treatment?]
Harrison	Thomas	Private	3rd Battalion, Parachute Regiment	4273328	91739	Poisoned leg. Mine. 4 months' [Treatment?] Yes
Hartley	Benjamin	Driver	1st Airlanding Anti-Tank Battery, Royal Artillery	3712207		Blood – rheumatism Food and damp 15 weeks [Treatment?] No

Name	Forename	Rank	Unit	Army number	POW number	Notes
Hartley	Kenneth Wrightson	Lance Corporal	9th Field Company, Royal Engineers Airborne	2017149	75812	Medical supplies very few & poor
Harvey	Stanley Trevelyan	Private	11th Battalion, Parachute Regiment	865935	91530	Unknown – Glass in throat – While POW still bring up blood [Treatment?] Best English MO could provide
Holmes	Robert	Private	1st Battalion, Parachute Regiment	5891275	92008	Medical treatment adequate? [Treatment?] Yes at all camps except Limburg where we were not allowed to report sick
Howard	Leslie Frederick	Private	1st Battalion, Parachute Regiment	15327223		Rheumatism Boils [Treatment?] Yes
Hoyle	Kenneth H	Private	7th Battalion, King's Own Scottish Borderers	14424034		Dysentery 6 weeks Frostbite in feet [Treatment?] Yes when possible
Humpherson	Stanley Richmond	Private	7th Battalion, King's Own Scottish Borderers	3197733	90684	Discharge ears – Cold – 4 weeks Swollen legs – Knock – 3 weeks
Hunter	Robert	Private	156th Battalion, Parachute Regiment	3128295	89547	Pneumonia Chill 28-2-44 – 27-3-44 (sic) [Treatment?] Yes
Hutton	William Alfred	Private	2nd Battalion, South Staffs	4923158	25554	Bronchitis from working in cement water. Bad clothing 2 weeks [Treatment?] No. Paid doctor examination
Hyslop	Eric	Sergeant	7th Battalion, King's Own Scottish Borderers	3190541	75874	Battle exhaustion Dysentery Quinsy [illegible] abscess [Treatment?] Yes by British
Jackson	Empsall	Private	1st Parachute Regiment Brigade	2042543		Skin trouble [Treatment?] No. Lady doctor at Dresden wouldn't be troubled with English. Madame Funk.

Surname	First name(s)	Rank	Unit	Service No.	Camp No.	Notes
James	Alec Arnold	Sergeant	Glider Pilot Regiment	5891664	140210	Shrapnel wound in arm – all the time in captivity [Treatment?] Yes
James	Joseph James	Lance Corporal	2nd Battalion, South Staffs	4929053	75839	Diphtheria 60 days Scarlet Fever Diphtheria 40 days [Treatment?] Yes
Johnson	Horace	Private	2nd Battalion, South Staffs	4923187	9190	Enteritis food and conditions at XII A 7 weeks [Treatment ?] Yes by British and South African staff at IV B
Jones	Dewi Llewellyn	Sergeant	1st Airlanding Brigade, Royal Signals	2362597	91555	Dysentery living conditions 1 Jan 44 – 10 Jan 44 (sic) Diptheria living conditions 10 Jan 44 – release by Russians 17 February [Treatment ?] Best possible under the conditions under which we existed – treated by British MOs.
Jones	Conway Thomas	Sapper	1st Parachute Squadron, Royal Engineers	1909450		Head wound Shrapnel 4 months [Treatment ?] Good
Jones	Hugh	Private	10th Battalion, Parachute Regiment	4199324	140154	Wounded mortar bomb 5 months hospital [Treatment ?] Very good by English MO
Jorden	Leonard	Private	2nd Battalion, South Staffs	1655164	91558	Broken collar bone Action 30/9 – 19/12 44 [Treatment ?] Yes British MO
Keeler	Norman Arthur	Sergeant, Lance	4th Parachute Squadron, Royal Engineers	2031950	21705	Dysentery Bad Food on and off for 2 months [Treatment ?] No
Keenan	James Mullan	Private	156th Battalion, Parachute Regiment	3189614	118364	No [Treatment ?] No
Kerr	Harry Alexander	Trooper	1st Airborne Recce Squadron	7020098	118345	[Treatment ?] No. Supplies totally inadequate and no apparent efforts were made to remedy the situation.
King	Joseph Bertie	Corporal	16th Parachute Field Ambulance, Royal Army Medical Corps	7347201	118427	? Scarlet fever unknown [Treatment ?] Yes

Name	Forename	Rank	Unit	Army number	POW number	Notes
Lancaster	Joseph	Private	11th Battalion, Parachute Regiment	935934		Eye righteous – Lime and Cement – 3 months [Treatment ?] Yes
Lune	Albert	Private	181st Airlanding Field Ambulance, Royal Army Medical Corps	14672958	140058	Diphtheria bad living conditions seven weeks [Treatment?] Yes
Lupton	Thomas	Private	7th Battalion, King's Own Scottish Borderers	3195317	90508	Dermatitis and eczema 3 months [Treatment ?] The best at the MOs disposal
Marriott	Charles Edward	Private	1st Battalion, Border Regiment	4277974	117642	Operation on elbow taking shrapnel from elbow in Fallingbostel British Medical officer [Treatment ?] Yes RAMC
McAndrew	John Edward	Driver	250th Airborne Light Company, RASC	70518	117962	Gastric – Food – 6 months [Treatment ?] No
McKail	William	Private	7th Battalion, King's Own Scottish Borderers	14415428	91789	Fractured shoulder railway [Treatment ?] No
McLean	George Falconer	Lance Corporal	1st Battalion, Parachute Regiment	2937656	118411	Wound left arm SH [shrapnel] 5 Months [Treatment ?] No
Miller	Christopher Alfred	Staff Sergeant	Glider Pilot Regiment	937499	117770	Concussion and shock Glider crash 3 or 4 weeks from date of capture. [Treatment ?] None from German authorities
Moore	Alfred George Golden	Sergeant	1st Battalion, Parachute Regiment	6461833	140083	Seriously wounded 25-9-44 – 14-4-45 [Treatment ?] Yes
Perkins	Arthur Wallace	Gunner	1st Airlanding Light Regiment, Royal Artillery	14245682		Nutritional oedema – lack of food – three weeks Dysentery – ? – Fortnight [Treatment ?] No

Surname	First name(s)	Rank	Regiment		Details
Phillips	Ronald John	Private	2nd Battalion, Parachute Regiment	5510064	117829	Crushed hand – [illegible] – still [illegible] [Treatment ?] No [Notes] My period in Hildesheim Hospital 10-11-44 – 18-12-1944 was due to my crushing and breaking three fingers of my left hand. The treatment was very slipshod and my left hand is very weak
Potts	Edmund	Private	11th Battalion, Parachute Regiment	10582732	117943	Left wrist operated on still bad whilst working at Stalag [Treatment ?] Yes
Reed	Ronald	Private	1st Battalion, Border Regiment	4469834	118362	[Treatment ?] No Very bad
Roberts	Leslie	Driver	Royal Signals	14532593	90430	Dysentery travelling in the cattle trucks 2 weeks Boils Food and water still suffering from them Hearing impaired possibly caused by drilling in the morning [Treatment ?] No
Rouse	Edwin	Corporal	7th Battalion, King's Own Scottish Borderers	3191861	91783	Dysentery Filth 6 weeks [Treatment ?] No
Ryan	Edward Joseph	Private	10th Battalion, Parachute Regiment	6914029	118579	Wounds shrapnel 3 months [Treatment ?] No
Sander	Gustave	Private	11th Battalion, Parachute Regiment	13807937	91694	No treatment received after battle injury till 17/10/44 [Treatment ?] No
Scott	William Mawhinnie	Private	2nd Battalion, South Staffs	997574	75351	Dysentery Bad Food 3 weeks [Treatment ?] No
Sloan	Alexander	Private	7th Battalion, King's Own Scottish Borderers	3189499	92645	Back & stomach access caused by bullet & shrapnel [Treatment ?] Yes by British doctors
Sproson	Ernest Travis	Private	156th Battalion, Parachute Regiment	5109576		Frost bite no boots or socks [Treatment ?] No

Name	Forename	Rank	Unit	Army number	POW number	Notes
Staff	Harry Victor William	Private	1st Battalion, Parachute Regiment	6015570		Medical: Pneumonia Peritonsillar abscess General weakness for 2 months [Treatment ?] Excellent treatment by British medics at Stalag IV B.
Stanley	Dennis	Private	7th Battalion, King's Own Scottish Borderers	5255876		Oedema caused by malnutrition for 6 weeks. [Treatment ?] Yes
Stevens	Walter William	Private	2nd Battalion, Parachute Regiment	6203483	91187	Dysentery Bad Food 2/10/44 – 18/11/44 [Treatment ?] Yes
Sullivan	Edward	Private	11th Battalion, Parachute Regiment	4124947	91723	Poisoned hand wood splinter [Treatment ?] Yes
Sullivan	Joseph Vincent	Private	133rd Parachute Field Ambulance, Royal Army Medical Corps	7265333	90387	Dysentery caused by food [Treatment ?] Yes
Tedds	Frederick Arthur	Private	3rd Battalion, Parachute Regiment	5116659	91534	Jaundice Adequate medical treatment
Thorpe	Russell Ambrose	Private	2nd Battalion, South Staffs	4914617		Nervous breakdown – Action – Still prevails [Treatment ?] No
Tingey	Aubrey Henry	Private	2nd Battalion, South Staffs	14695003	75848	Dysentery poor food 2 weeks Injure left arm Sept 24 1944 still affected [Treatment ?] No
Towler	Walter	Private	3rd Battalion, Parachute Regiment	1452410	90034	[Treatment ?] Medical treatment very poor
Turnbull	Albert	Signalman	1st Airlanding Anti-Tank Battery Royal Artillery	14321818		Rheumatic fever – Damp and cold – 8 weeks [Treatment ?] Yes

Turner	Henry Charles	Private	10th Battalion, Parachute Regiment	14429950	75473	Pleurisy – didn't know cause good treatment – 3 months [Treatment ?] Yes
Turrell	Leslie	Private	11th Battalion, Parachute Regiment	3770461	117767	Synovitis knee parachute drop 4 months [Treatment ?] Yes as far as British MO [illegible] equipped could do
Vernon	Stanley	Lance Corporal	2nd Battalion, Parachute Regiment	1427411		Malaria 8 days [Treatment ?] Under the circumstances Yes
White	George	Regimental Sergeant Major	10th Battalion, Parachute Regiment	4387779		Gastric – Food – 3 months [Treatment ?] Whilst at XII A treatment V. Poor. Whilst at XVIII C treatment good
Whittaker	James	Lance Corporal	4th Battalion, Dorset Regiment	4271899	17582	Pains in back and kidneys – Caused by work to much straining and heavy – 1 week [Treatment ?] No
Williams	David Meredith	Private	10th Battalion, Parachute Regiment	14219148	52884	Sprained knee Fall 4 week no work still troubles [Treatment ?] Not from the Germans
Willoughby	Leslie	Private	3rd Battalion, Parachute Regiment	4466448		Appendicitis Lung trouble 12 weeks
Wren	Jack Francis	Private	2nd Battalion, Parachute Regiment	6853864	75337	Appendicitis & bleeding piles – Bad food – 6 weeks [Treatment ?] No
Wright	Stanley Winston	Sergeant Major	2nd Battalion, South Staffs	4913782		Malaria 14 days Dysentery Bad food 21 days [Treatment ?] No
Young	John	Private	7th Battalion, King's Own Scottish Borderers	3192130	75941	Pneumonia working outside in snow and not having enough nourishment 2 months [Treatment ?] 'Yes after I got to British hospital in Hohenstein'

Prison Work

NCOs and Other Ranks provided 95 per cent of all the questionnaires. For these men arrival at permanent camps meant they were liable to be transferred to *arbeitskommandos* (working parties), based outside the Stalag. The commandos provided labour for German factories, artificial oil plants, mines and railways, on farms or helping to maintain some semblance of order in cities being turned into rubble by Allied bombers. One commando managed from Stalag XI B was 50 miles away at Ülzen on the main railway line from Hamburg to Frankfurt and men record that they were repairing the tracks. Fallingbostel's records[17] show that 475 men, mainly Arnhem POWs, were sent to the *katastrophen kommando* (disaster work party) at Ülzen on 9 March 1945.

The Geneva Convention stipulated that prisoners should not do work that directly aided the military. Only one man reported that he had been made to carry out this kind of work:

> Sergeant Jack Hayes, 156th Battalion Parachute Regiment, 'Breaking Geneva Convention by making men dig anti-tank ditches and building road blocks.'

The *kommandos* were numbered. It is possible that men did not record the full title of their *kommando*, but on the basis of what is in the questionnaires, it appears that two numbering schemes were used for those recorded. Mostly *kommandos* were given simple three- or four-figure numbers. For example 1088 was a labouring group at Bralitz, north-east of Berlin, in Wehrkreis III; 137 was a mining group at Unterbreizbach in Thuringia, Wehrkreis IX; and 7002 was a labouring group at Üfingen in Wehrkreis XI. In Wehrkreis IV many, but not all, *kommandos* had a more complex system. A railway labouring group at Zwikau, south-west of Chemnitz, was numbered 'Z 131 E'. The prefix denoted the location and the suffix the nationality of the group, in this case English, ie British and Commonwealth. 'ME 41 E' cleared bomb debris and was located at Merseburg. But some *kommandos* in Wehrkreis IV were given as plain numbers in questionnaires; for example, 1193 laboured at a paper mill at Sebnitz, south-east of Dresden.

No men record belonging to formal *kommandos* attached to the Dulag at Limburg, but several refer to working while at Stalag XII A:

> Private Ted Few, 156th Battalion, Parachute Regiment, 'Made to bury decomposed corpses thrown up by bombs in graveyard. Limberg 1944.'

> Private John Tillotson, 133rd Parachute Field Ambulance, 'Protected personnel forced to work on bomb damage at revolver point.'

---

17 WO 361/1797/ 2.

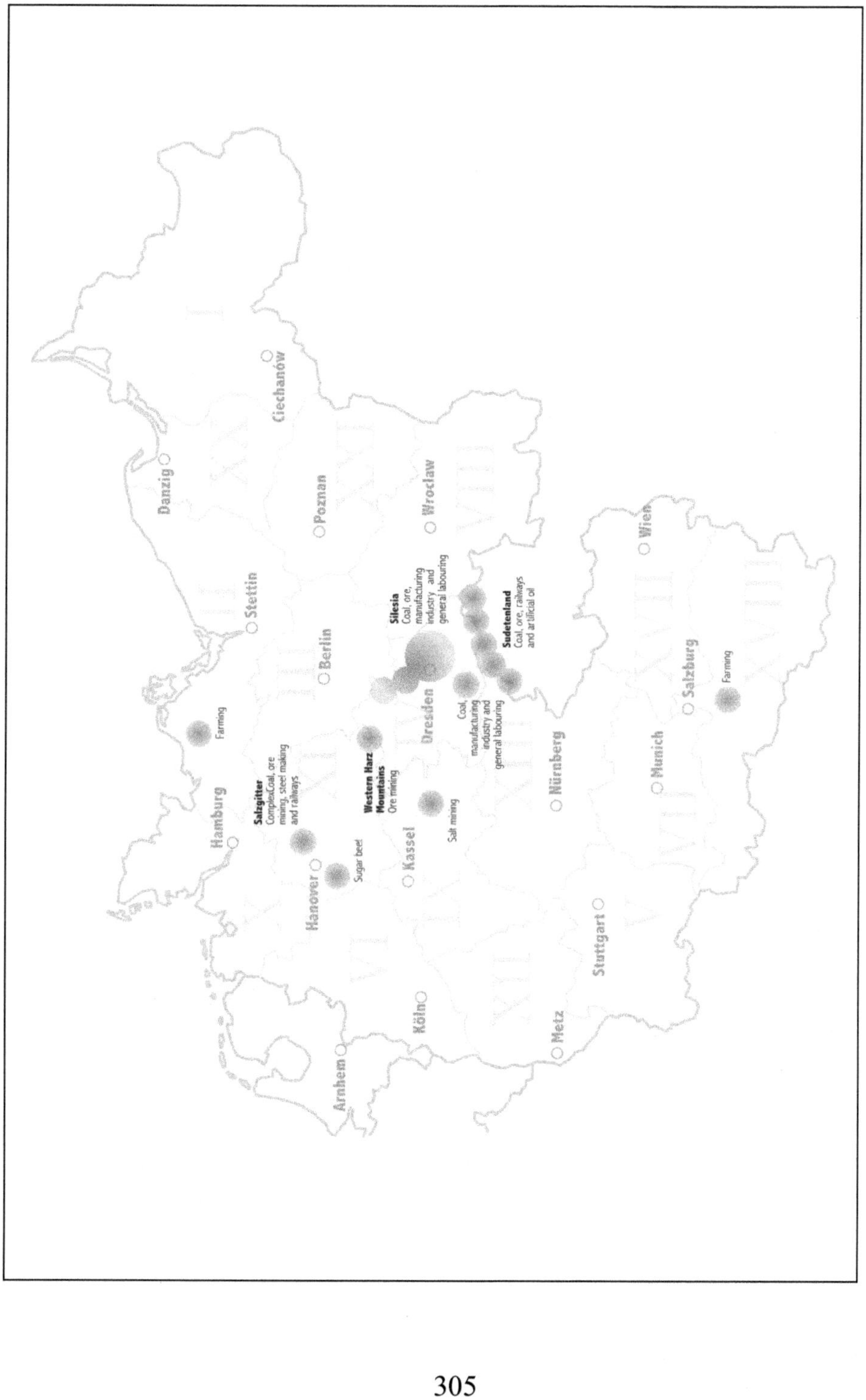

Map 6: Principal German industrial areas that used Arnhem POW labour.

Men would be transferred between camps and commandos as workloads changed. This was particularly the case in Wehrkreis IV, where Stalag IV B served as a transit camp for other Stalags. Time at a *kommando* could also be short, for example Private Benjamin Hawkins, 2nd Battalion, South Staffordshire Regiment, worked in a cement factory at Löbau for two weeks in January 1945.

All Stalags had *kommandos*, but Arnhem men worked at one of four main concentrations: Silesia and the Sudetenland; the Herman Göring Works near Fallingbostel; mines in the western Harz Mountains; and salt mines in western Thuringia. The questionnaires usually only give one- or two-word descriptions of the type of work done by the prisoners. These concentrate on how the men and others were treated, and sabotage:

> Private William Headland, 3rd Battalion, Parachute Regiment, 'We was working at a factory from 06:00 hrs to 17:00 hrs daily, to which was a 45 mins walk – with total rations of half litre soup and 350 grams German bread.'

> Private Roland Swinburn, 2nd Battalion, South Staffordshire Regiment, 'Yes We were under fed Rations being 900 grams of bread a day and 25 grams of marge a day and a bowl of soup a day. I lost a lot of weight. We had to work in coal, mine railways from 6 am to 6 pm.'

> Private Arthur Applin, 2nd Battalion, Parachute Regiment, 'we were employed on bomb damage in Leipsic [Leipzig] railway yards compelled to work under heavy air bombardment and that the German guards had orders to shoot any man attempting to take cover until the last possible moment. We were also compelled to work as many as 18 hours a day rising at 3:30 AM.'

Ill Treatment of Others

The men saw the way the Nazis treated political prisoners and Russians POWs:

> Private Fred Jackson, 10th Battalion, Parachute Regiment, 'I only wish to bring to notice the treatment of the men and women of Lager Eine und Zwanzig and the political lager where even in the bitterest weather the only thing that they were allowed to wear was boiler suits. I have seen SS men beat the women and club the men over their heads with rifle butts.'

> Private Malcolm Cuthbertson, 4th Battalion, Dorset Regiment, 'Long working hours, heavy work, with insufficient food. Witnessed brutal treatment of Russians and other nationalities who were not protected by Geneva convention. Also seen bodies of political prisoners who were shot by the enemy before the Russian advance.'

Signalman Charles Steven, 1st Parachute Brigade, Royal Signals, 'Foreign workers in Germany kept production going without pressure from SS, Gestapo, etc,'

Private Michael Hughes, 2nd Battalion, South Staffordshire Regiment, 'French POWs were working in collaboration with Germans in the Brux Benzine works such as brick-laying laying, welding, and draining engines.'

Private Hughes's comment about French POWs is odd. It is far more probable the French were forced labour and had been in captivity for five years. Germany depended on foreign labour. Some were prisoners, some came from concentration camps, others were recruited from occupied territories. Russian prisoners might be worked to death. Polish labourers were traditionally recruited for the harvest in eastern Germany but by 1944 foreigners could be found in all parts of the German economy. That did not make them collaborators, just victims of harsh economic fact.

The questionnaires provide no evidence that airborne prisoners were employed under 'special supervision', as the OKW orders required:

Private Herbert Ingham, 156th Battalion, Parachute Regiment, 'While on Work Party 7012 from XI B many men were struck by hand and bayonet, while being struck an armed guard was always near in case of our retaliating.'

Private Sydney Clements, 11th Battalion, Parachute Regiment, 'Hit by a Director of the sugar beet factory Dr Baul with a black jack for talking etc, work was 3 months outdoors.'

Sergeant George Nicklin, Glider Pilot Regiment, 'The employment of Alsatian dogs at Brick factory at Duderstadt to clear passage for German guards. Many prisoners, French, Russian and British badly bitten.'

The Geneva Convention gave NCOs the choice of working or not. The commandants of Stalag VIII C and Stalag XVIII C took exception to this and punished the non-working NCOS:

Corporal Clifford Fairweather, 250th Airborne Light Company, RASC, 'Reprisals were taken by the Germans at Sagan in January 1945 against all NCOs refusing to work, in the form of taking all NCOs' blankets away from them.' [Stalag VIII C]

Regimental Sergeant Major George White, 10th Battalion, Parachute Regiment, 'under special guards and orders when all we were was none working. W.O.s NCOs and men (as NCOs). They went to special pains to make our lot as un-comfortable and as unbearable as possible.' [Stalag XVIII C]

Table 5: Arbeitskommandos Named in Questionnaires

Place name spellings have been corrected. A spelling or identification that is uncertain it is shown (?). Numbers are those given on questionnaires.

Arbeitskommando	Number as given on questionnaires	Managing Stalag	Activity as described on questionnaire and comments	Location
	36 A	Stalag IV B	Mining	
	Camp 59 A	Stalag VII A		
Algermissen		Stalag XI B	Railway repairs	South-east of Hanover
Altenhain	57	Stalag IV G	Stone quarry	North-west of Frankfurt
Apeldoorn			Hospital maintained until the end of the war for British and German patients	
Aue	0 87	Stalag IV F	Timber yard	South-west of Chemnitz
Augsburg			Clearing bomb damage, railway repairs	
Aussig		Stalag IV G	Railway repairs	Now Ústí nad Labem, Czech Republic, south of Dresden
Bad Grund	7013	Stalag XI B	Lead mine	South-east of Hanover
Barum		Stalag XI B	Sugar factory. There was also part of Reichswerke Hermann Göring in Barum.	Suburb of Salzgitter
Basepohl		Stalag II A	Farm work	North-west of Neubrandenburg
Betty Schacht		Stalag IV C	Mine. *Schacht* = shaft, near Wurzmes	Now Vrskmaň Czech Republic, south-east of Chemnitz
Bischofferode	1015	Stalag IX C	Potash mine	West of Nordhausen
Bitterfeld	Be 6	Stalag IV D	Coal mine	North of Leipzig
Blechhammer	E3	Stalag VIII B	Artificial petroleum – Oberschllesische Hydrierwerke AG	Now Sławięcice, in Poland, west of Katowice
Bockwitz	L101	Stalag IV B	Garage work	South-east of Leipzig
Böhlen		Stalag IV G	Clearing bomb damage	South of Leipzig

Arbeitskommando	Number as given on questionnaires	Managing Stalag	Activity as described on questionnaire and comments	Location
Böhlen		Stalag IV G	Hydrogenation plant – artificial petroleum	South of Leipzig
Böhlen			Coal mining	South of Leipzig
Borna		Stalag IV G	Mining	District of Leipzig
Borstendorf			Saw mill, see also Floßmühle	South-east of Chemnitz
Bralitz	1088	Stalag III C	Railway, factory and street cleaning	North-east of Berlin
Breslau		Stalag VIII C	Quarry	
Brunswick/ Braunschweig		Stalag XI B	Railway	East of Hanover
Brüx	50	Stalag IV C	Coal mining and railway repairs	Now Most, Czech Republic, South-east of Chemnitz
Brüx	Lager 22	Stalag IV C	Coal mining	Now Most, Czech Republic, South-east of Chemnitz
Brüx	Lager 51	Stalag IV C	'Kolumbus Mine'	Now Most, Czech Republic, South-east of Chemnitz
Brüx		Stalag IV B	Demolition	Now Most, Czech Republic, South-east of Chemnitz
Brüx Benzine		Stalag IV C	Labouring and mining for hydrogenation plant (artificial petroleum plant) at Maltheuern	Now Most, Czech Republic, South-east of Chemnitz
BRABEG			Braunkohlen-Benzin AG, mining and synthetic fuel company that operated across Germany	
Celle		Stalag XI B	Salt mine	North-east of Hanover
Chouseche?		Stalag IV C	Digging	Tschausch, Czech Republic?
Clanylish?		Stalag IV B	Coal mine, Klein?	Unknown, Czech Republic?
Crossen		Stalag IV F	Paper	West of Chemnitz
Coswig	654	Stalag IV G	Automotive – Kirchbach'sche Werke	North-west of Dresden

Arbeitskommando	Number as given on questionnaires	Managing Stalag	Activity as described on questionnaire and comments	Location
Deutschlandsender Herzberg		Stalag IV B	High-powered radio transmitter	North-east Leipzig
Dinklar	7012	Stalag XI B	Sugar beet factory	South-east of Hanover
Ditmasdorf				West of Chemnitz
Döbeln			Labouring	West of Dresden
Döbeln			Stone work	West of Dresden
Döbeln			Building air-raid shelters	West of Dresden
Döbeln			Stone quarry	West of Dresden
Döbeln			Paper factory	West of Dresden
Dögnitz			Tile factory	East of Leipzig
Dögnitz			Bomb damage demolition	East of Leipzig
Dorndorf	143B	Stalag IX C	Potassium mine	West of Gotha
Dresden		Stalag IV B? or C?	Wood factory – artificial benzine?	Dresden
Dresden		Stalag IV A	Factory	Dresden
Dresden		Stalag IV A	Timber yard	Dresden
Dresden		Stalag IV B	Shoe repairs	Dresden
Dresden		Stalag IV A	Bomb debris clearing	Dresden
Dresden	1182	Stalag IV A	Odd jobs	Dresden
Dresden	1326	Stalag IV A	Bomb damage	Dresden
Dresden	1333	Stalag IV B	Tram repairs, water company pipe repairs, Clearing bomb damage	Dresden
Dresden	1335			Dresden
Dresden	Me 49 E	Stalag IV B	Clearing bomb damage and repairing sewers, tinplate factory	Dresden
Dresden Teplitz		Stalag IV B	Wood factory, see Teplitz	Dresden suburb
Düben		Stalag IV D	Sugar manufacture	North of Leipzig
Duderstadt			Brick works	West of Nordhausen
Eger		XIII B	Coal mine	Now Cheb, Czech Republic, east of Bayreuth
Eilenburg	D 608	Stalag IV D	Labouring	North-east Leipzig

Arbeitskommando	Number as given on questionnaires	Managing Stalag	Activity as described on questionnaire and comments	Location
Eisdorf		Stalag IV D	Sugar beet factory	West of Osterode
Eisdorf		Stalag IV D	Coal mine	West of Osterode
Eisleben	Ei 105 E	Stalag IV D	Copper mine	West of Halle
Eisleben	Ei 113 E	Stalag IV B	Copper mine	West of Halle
Elsterwerda		Stalag IV B	Stone making (sic)	East of Leipzig
Elsterhorst			Hospital	Now Nardt, north-east of Dresden
Eppendorf		Stalag IV F	Boot making	East of Chemnitz
Ereiwader?		Stalag VIII C	Clay pits	Saxony? or Poland?
Erfenschlag		Stalag IV B	Sectional housing woodwork, Timber yard	South-eastern suburb of Chemnitz
Erfenschlag	E 42	Stalag IV B	Cement works clearing bomb damage, repairing railway, filling bomb craters on farms	South-eastern suburb of Chemnitz
Etzdorf	Ei 116 E	Stalag IV B	Mining	South-west of Halle
Etzdorf		Stalag IV D	Coal and salt mine constructing tunnels	South-west of Halle
Falkenau		Stalag IV B and Stalag XIII B	Mine	Now Sokolov, Czech Republic, south of Leipzig
Falkenau	13 B	Stalag IV B and Stalag XIII B	Mine	Now Sokolov, Czech Republic, south of Leipzig
Fallingbostel		Stalag XI B	Camp repairs	Near Hanover
Flöha	N 90	Stalag IV F	Railway	East of Chemnitz
Floßmühle		Stalag IV F	Forestry, saw mill and paper mill	South-east of Chemnitz
Frankenberg		Stalag IV F	Forestry	North-east of Chemnitz
Frankleben		Stalag IV B	Canal building	West of Leipzig
Freiberg		Stalag IV B	Lead mine	South-west of Dresden
Freiberg	.	Stalag IV F	Leather, tannery	South-west of Dresden
Freiberg		Stalag IV D	Sugar factory, filling sacks	South-west of Dresden
Freiberg		Stalag IV F	Paper	South-west of Dresden

Arbeitskommando	Number as given on questionnaires	Managing Stalag	Activity as described on questionnaire and comments	Location
Freidwaldau		Stalag VIII C	Brick and tile works	Now Jeseník, Czech Republic, north-east of Brno
Glatz		Stalag VIII C	Stone quarry	Now Kłodzko in Poland, south of Wrocław
Gleina	G 123	Stalag IV F	Labouring 'pick and shovel'	South-west Leipzig
Grasseth		Stalag XIII B	Coal mine	Now Sokolov Czech Republic, south-west of Chemnitz
Grimma		Stalag IV G	Stone quarry	South-east of Leipzig
Grimma	39/386	Stalag IV G	Paper factory	South-east of Leipzig
Grossenhain		Stalag IV A	Stone breaking	North-west of Dresden
Groß Düngen	7011	Stalag XI B	Sugar beet factory	Near Hildesheim
Großröhrsdorf		Stalag IV B	Building work	North-east of Dresden
Großthiemig		Stalag IV D	Sand pit	North of Dresden
Großweitzschen	203	Stalag IV G	Building air raid shelters	North-west of Dresden
Grunau		Stalag IV B	Paper factory, also Döbeln	West of Dresden
Grünhainichen			Timber yard	South-east of Chemnitz
Gunnersdorf		Stalag IV F	Forestry	North-west of Vienna
Halbersdorf		Stalag IV F	Railway	North-west of Nurnberg
Halle		Stalag IV B	Building air raid shelters and burying dead from air raids	
Halle		Stalag IV B	Sewer repairs	
Halle		Stalag IV B	Brick factory	
Halle			Forestry	
Halle Trotha		Stalag IV D	Brickworks	A suburb of Halle
Halle Salle		Stalag IV D	Brickworks	A suburb of Halle
Hallendorf		Stalag XI B	General labouring	South-east of Hanover

Arbeitskommando	Number as given on questionnaires	Managing Stalag	Activity as described on questionnaire and comments	Location
Hallendorf	7001	Stalag XI B	Railway work, general labouring, and coal mine – part of Reichswerke Hermann Göring	South-east of Hanover
Hartha		Stalag IV G	Shoe factory	North of Chemnitz
Hartha	227	Stalag IV G	Loading and unloading railway wagons	North of Chemnitz
Hartmannsdorf		Stalag IV F	Timber yard	North-west of Chemnitz
Hemsburge?		Stalag IV D	Sand pits	
Herman Göring Works		Stalag XI B	Steelworks and associated iron ore and coal mines at Salzgitter, part of Reichswerke Hermann Göring	South-east of Hanover
Herzburg		Stalag IV B	Deutschlandsender Herzberg	North-east Leipzig
Herzburg		Stalag IV B	Demolition	North-east Leipzig
Herzburg	188	Stalag IV B	Railway, labouring and building	North-east Leipzig
Herzburg	Sch 188	Stalag IV B	Cooking	North-east Leipzig
Hettstedt	He 102 E	Stalag IV B	Copper smelter	North-west of Halle
Hildburghausen		Stalag IX C	Hospital	South of Gotha
Hildershiem		Stalag XI B	Sugar beet factory	South-east of Hanover
Hohenstein		Stalag IV E	Reserve Lazarett	West of Chemnitz
Jessen/Elster		Stalag IV B	Railway repairs, major railway junction	North-east of Leipzig
Jonsdorf		Stalag IV C	Coal mine	South-east of Dresden
Katastropheneinsatz Ülzen		Stalag XI B	'Disaster response' emergency repairs, Ülzen	North-east of Hanover
Kirchrode-Hannover	7010	Stalag XI B	Cement works and oil refinery	Suburb of Hannover
Kirschau	A1158	Stalag IV A	Blanket 'fabric' = fabrik, ie factory	Suburb of Lauchhammer, north of Dresden
Kleinleipisch		Stalag IV B	Open cast coal mine	Suburb of Lauchhammer, north of Dresden
Klitschmar	D 602	Stalag IV B?		North-west of Leipzig

313

Arbeitskommando	Number as given on questionnaires	Managing Stalag	Activity as described on questionnaire and comments	Location
Kolumbus	51	Stalag IV C	The name of a coal mine at Wurzmes and Brüx	Now Most, Czech Republic, South-east of Chemnitz
Komotau		Stalag IV C	Surface coal mine	Now Most, Czech Republic, South-east of Chemnitz
Komotau	395 A	Stalag IV C	Railway, also recorded as 0395 A	Now Most, Czech Republic, South-east of Chemnitz
Königswalde		Stalag IV C	Stone quarry	South of Chemnitz
Kriebethal	231	Stalag IV G	Paper factory	South-east of Leipzig
Krugersall	Ei 114E	Stalag IV B	The name of a copper mine	North-east of Halle
Kugel		Stalag II E	Forestry	South-west of Neubrandenburg
Kundl	25272	Stalag XVIII C	Pick and shovel, general labouring	North-east of Innsbruck
Lauchhammer			Briquet factory, coal?	North of Dresden
Lauchhammer	L 25	Stalag IV B	Steel works, Mitteldeutsche Stahlwerke GmbH, Riesa	North of Dresden
Liepen		Stalag II A	Farming	North-east of Neubrandenburg
Liepen		Stalag II A	Joinery	North-east of Neubrandenburg
Leipzig		Stalag IV G	Sawmill	
Lengenfeld	E43	Stalag IV F	Cleaning wool	South-west of Chemnitz
Liebau		Stalag IV A	Textile factory	Now Libina Czech Republic, north-east of Brno
Liebenwerda		Stalag IV D	Sand, Bad Liebenwerda	East of Leipzig
Lilianstien		Stalag IV A	Labouring	South East Dresden
Löbau		Stalag IV A	Cement works	East of Dresden
Löbau			Linen factory	East of Dresden
Löbau		Stalag IV A	Dye works	East of Dresden
Löbau		Stalag IV A	Textile factory	East of Dresden
Laucha	Re 21	Stalag IV D	Coal mine	South of Halle
Lohnde	7009	Stalag XI B	Railway repairs, see Algermissen	Suburb of Hanover

Arbeitskommando	Number as given on questionnaires	Managing Stalag	Activity as described on questionnaire and comments	Location
Lößnitz	L106	Stalag IV F		South-west of Chemnitz
Lubeck		Stalag II E	Forestry	On the Baltic coast
Lubtiz		Stalag IV G	Brickworks	Saxony?
Malchin		Stalag II A	Farm	South-east of Rostock
Malitzsch			Coke ovens	East of Dresden
Maltheuern		Stalag IV C		Now Záluží Czech Republic, south-east of Prague
Maltsch		Stalag VIII C	Sugar factory	Now Malczyce Poland, south of Poznań
Maschau		Stalag IV F	Coal mine	Now Mašťov, Czech Republic, south-west of Chemnitz
Meiningen	1288	Stalag IX C	Hospital	South-west of Gotha
Menzengraben	123B	Stalag IX C	Salt mine	West of Gotha
Merseburg		Stalag IV B	Air raid shelters, also tunnelling?	South of Halle
Merseburg		Stalag IV D	General labouring	South of Halle
Merseburg		Stalag IV B	Boot repairs	South of Halle
Merseburg		Stalag IV B	Brick laying	South of Halle
Merseburg	ME 41 E	Stalag IV B	Clearing bomb debris	South of Halle
Merseburg	Me 49 E	Stalag IV B	Labouring	South of Halle
Metzdorf		Stalag IV D	Coal mine	East of Chemnitz
Meuschau	Me 40 E	Stalag IV D	Construction of air raid shelters	South of Halle
Mitteldeutsche Stahlwerke	L 25	Stalag IV B	'Mitteldeutsche Stahlwerke', a company with several steelworks and lignite coal mines	
Mittenwald		Stalag VIII A	Construction of air raid shelters	South-west of Munich
Mittenwald		Stalag VII A	Labouring	South-west of Munich
Mittweida		Stalag IV F	Labouring	South-east of Leipzig

Arbeitskommando	Number as given on questionnaires	Managing Stalag	Activity as described on questionnaire and comments	Location
Mittweida	M 107	Stalag IV F	Labouring	South-east of Leipzig
Mochau		Stalag IV F?	Labouring	South-east of Leipzig
Moosburg		Stalag VII A	Stalag	North-east of Munich
Mückenberg		Stalag IV B	Lignite briquette	Now Lauchhammer, renamed 1950
Mückenberg		Stalag IV B	Coal mine	Now Lauchhammer, renamed 1950
Mühltroff	M 104	Stalag IV F	'Mixed work mostly timber', labouring	South-west of Leipzig
Mühlbach		Stalag IV F	Quarry	Now Pomezí nad Ohří, Czech Republic, south-east of Dresden
Mühlberg			Sugar factory	North-east of Leipzig
München			Road work	Munich
München Pasing	3785	Stalag VII A	Chaplain to all *kommandos* in Munich area	Pasing is a district of Munich
Mutschau	M 79	Stalag IV F	Open cast mine	South-west of Leipzig
Neundorf		Stalag IV A		South-east of Dresden
Niederwiesa		Stalag IV B	Cement works	Suburb of Chemnitz
Niederwiesa		Stalag IV F	Cement stone, presumably Neiderwiesa	Suburb of Chemnitz
Nieder-Georgenthal	51	Stalag IV C	Open cast coal mining	Now Most, Czech Republic, South-east of Chemnitz
Niedersedlitz	1124	Stalag IV A	Coal heaving and delivering	Suburb of Dresden
Niedersedlitz	1209	Stalag IV A	Timber work	Suburb of Dresden
Nonnewitz		Stalag IV B?	Open cast coal mining	South-west of Leipzig
Oberglogau	E600	Stalag VIIIB	Sugar beet factory	Now Głogówek, Poland, south-east of Wrocław
Obermaßfeld	1249	Stalag IX C	Hospital	South-west of Gotha

Arbeitskommando	Number as given on questionnaires	Managing Stalag	Activity as described on questionnaire and comments	Location
Oederan		Stalag IV F	Straw fabric? straw cooking?	North-east of Chemnitz
Ohlendorf		Stalag XI B	Iron ore mine, part of Salzgitter complex	South-east of Hanover
Ortrand		Stalag IV B	Saw mill	North of Dresden
Ortrand		Stalag IV D	Sand works	North of Dresden
Ortrand	L 48	Stalag IV B	Cement works	North of Dresden
Penig	P 5	Stalag IV F	Sand quarry	South-east of Leipzig
Penig	P 87	Stalag IV F	*Fahrbereitschaft* = garage, vehicle pool	South-east of Leipzig
Pirkau	U12		Railway sleepers	South-west of Leipzig
Pirna		Stalag IV A	Tree felling, for cellulose	Suburb of Dresden
Plauen	C114	Stalag IV F	Heavy labour on roads, air raid shelters	South-west of Chemnitz
Prossen		Stalag IV B	Labouring	South-east of Dresden
Radebeul		Stalag IV B	Tin plate factory	Suburb of Dresden
Rautenkranz		Stalag IV F	Tree felling	South-west of Chemnitz
Regis		Stalag VII A	Now Regis-Breitingen	South of Leipzig
Reideburg	Rei 104 E	Stalag IV D	Brick factory	A suburb of Halle
Reideburg	Rei 113E	Stalag IV D	Building air raid shelters, also forestry, grave digging and drains sewage	A suburb of Halle
Reinersdorf	453	Stalag IV A	Stone Quarry	North-west of Dresden
Reserve Lazarett			Military hospital	
Reserve Lazarett, Apeldoorn			'Airborne Hospital', continued in use under German control to the end of the war	Arnhem, Netherlands
Reserve Lazarett Meiningen	1288	Stalag IX C	A *kommando* providing labour to the hospital	South-west of Gotha
Reserve Lazarett Obermaßfeld	1249	Stalag IX C	A *kommando* providing labour to the hospital	South-west of Gotha
Roachercroats?		Stalag IV B	Timber yard, also spelt Rohchencroats on same questionnaire	Saxony?

Arbeitskommando	Number as given on questionnaires	Managing Stalag	Activity as described on questionnaire and comments	Location
Robert Schacht		Stalag IV C	Company involved in constructing synthetic fuel plant or Robert 'Schacht' (shaft) a mine, near Brüx	Now Most, Czech Republic, South-east of Chemnitz
Rochsburg		Stalag IV F	Paper mill	North-west of Chemnitz
Röhrsdorf	R 123	Stalag IV F	Timber yard and wood factory	North-west of Chemnitz
Roitsch		Stalag IV F	Labouring	North-east of Leipzig
Salzgitter	7005	Stalag XI B	Mine	South-east of Hanover
Schlachthof		Stalag IV A	*Schlachthof* = abattoir	Dresden
Sebnitz	1193	Stalag IV B	Paper mill	East of Dresden
Seestadtl		Stalag IV F	Mine. The village, north-east of Wurzmes, has been destroyed by mining	Was Ervínice, Czech Republic, south-east of Chemnitz
Stalag 357		Stalag 357	Joiner	South of Fallingbostel
Stecher's		Stalag IV E	The name of a leather company, Freiberg	South-west of Dresden
Straffe Lager		Stalag IV A	Punishment camp	
Stützengrün		Stalag IV B?	Lumber	South-west of Chemnitz
Stützengrün		Stalag IV F	Gas from wood	South-west of Chemnitz
Techwitz		Stalag IV B?		South-west of Leipzig
Teplitz		Stalag IV C	Benzine production	Now Teplice, Czech Republic, south of Dresden
Teplitz		Stalag IV B	Wood factory	Now Teplice, Czech Republic, south of Dresden
Teutschenthal	Ei 114 E	Stalag IV D	Salt mine	West of Halle
Teutschenthal	Ei 30	Stalag IV B	Salt Mine	West of Halle
Tolkewiz		Stalag IV A	Strassenbahn – Tram repairs	Suburb of Dresden

Arbeitskommando	Number as given on questionnaires	Managing Stalag	Activity as described on questionnaire and comments	Location
Togehentall?			Coal mine? Misspelling of Teutschenthal?	Saxony? Sudetenland?
Torgau		Stalag IV D	Air raid shelter tunnelling	North-east of Leipzig
Trebsen	39/386	Stalag IV G	Labouring paper factory	South-east of Leipzig
Trebsen Mulde		Stalag IV G	Paper factory, by the River Mulde	South-east of Leipzig
Tröglitz		Stalag IV F	Petrol factory – artificial fuel plant	South-west of Leipzig
Tröglitz	T 35	Stalag IV F		South-west of Leipzig
Trotha	Na 33 E		Brick laying and quarrying	Suburb of Halle
Tschausch	3 or III	Stalag IV C	Open cast mining	Now Souš, Czech Republic, south of Dresden
Tyssa		Stalag IV A		Now Tisá, Czech Republic, south-east of Dresden
Üfingen		Stalag XI B		South-east of Hanover
Üfingen	7002	Stalag XI B	Labouring at Salzgitter	South-east of Hanover
Üfingen	7002	Stalag XI B	Canal work	South-east of Hanover
Ülzen		Stalag XI B	Railway line repair	North-west of Hanover
Uelzen		Stalag XI B	Synonym for Ülzen, Railway line repair	North-west of Hanover
Unterbreizbach	137	Stalag IX C	Potassium salt mine	South-east of Gotha
Unterröblingen		Stalag IV B	Railway labouring	West of Halle
Unterschwöditz		Stalag IV F	Railway	South-west of Leipzig
Unterschwöditz	U 12	Stalag IV B	Open cast coal mine	South-west of Leipzig
Varchentin		Stalag II A	Farm work	East of Neubrandenburg
Velsen		Stalag XI B	Clearing bomb damage and laying railway line	East of Münster
Wallwitz	58	Stalag IV D	Railway work	East of Magdeburg

Arbeitskommando	Number as given on questionnaires	Managing Stalag	Activity as described on questionnaire and comments	Location
Weißenborn		Stalag IV F		North-east of Chemnitz
Weißenfels		Stalag IV F	Boot and shoe	South-west of Leipzig
Wilischthal		Stalag IV B	Paper works	South-east of Chemnitz
Wittenberg		Stalag IV B	Saw mill	North of Leipzig
Wörgl		Stalag XVIII C	Railway, close to Kundl	North-east of Innsbruck
Wurzen		Stalag IV G	Paper mill	South-east of Leipzig
Wurzmes		Stalag IV C	Brick yard	Now Vrskmaň, Czech Republic, south-east of Chemnitz
Wurzmes		Stalag IV C	Demolition	Now Vrskmaň, Czech Republic, south-east of Chemnitz
Wurzmes		Stalag IV C	Repairing bomb damage	Now Vrskmaň, Czech Republic, south-east of Chemnitz
Wurzmes		Stalag IV C	Brickworks	Now Vrskmaň, Czech Republic, south-east of Chemnitz
Wurzmes	50	Stalag IV C	Coal mining	Now Vrskmaň, Czech Republic, south-east of Chemnitz
Zahna	W 610	Stalag IV F	Brick works	North-east of Leipzig
Zeitz		Stalag IV F	Coal mining, also bomb hole filling	South-west of Leipzig
Zeitz			Braunkohlen-Benzin AG (BRABEG), coal gasification plant	South-west of Leipzig
Zeitz			Hydrogenation plant	South-west of Leipzig
Zeitz		Stalag IV B	Labourer	South-west of Leipzig

Arbeitskommando	Number as given on questionnaires	Managing Stalag	Activity as described on questionnaire and comments	Location
Zeitz	T 35	Stalag IV F	Labouring	South-west of Leipzig
Zeitz	U 12	Stalag IV F	Surface coal mine laying railway lines	South-west of Leipzig
Ziegenhain				West of Dresden
Zingfield?	8002	Stalag VII A	Medical orderly	Bavaria?
Ziplast? Komotau		Stalag IV C	Labouring, 'Ziplast' a company? Or job?	Now Most, Czech Republic, South-east of Chemnitz
Zschornewitz		Stalag IV B		North of Leipzig
Zugspitze	Z 55	Stalag IV B	Leather work	East of Chemnitz
Zwickau		Stalag IV F	Demolition	South of Leipzig
Zwickau	C58	Stalag IV B	Wood work	South of Leipzig
Zwickau	Z 131	Stalag IV F	Wood gasification	South of Leipzig
Zwikau	Z 131 E	Stalag IV F	Railway labouring	South of Leipzig
Zwikau		Stalag IV F	Paper factory	South of Leipzig

Table 6: Men and their *Kommandos*

The *kommando*'s name, activity and or number is as given on the questionnaires.

Family Name	Forename	Rank	Unit	Army number	POW number	All kommandos
Ackerman	Donald Henry Edwin	Gunner	1st Airborne Div, Light Regiment, Royal Artillery	14334539	88742	Rei 113 building air raid shelters
Acton	John	Private	1st Battalion, Border Regiment	3605400		Miner, Road repairs
Adams	Arthur Richard	Lance Corporal	7th Battalion, King's Own Scottish Borderers	14211553	18661	Munich Railways
Adams	Donald	Staff Sergeant	Glider Pilot Regiment	136331		
Addis	John	Private	1st Battalion, Border Regiment	4697979	92114	Brüx coal mine
Agar	Godfrey Stewart	Staff Sergeant	Glider Pilot Regiment	2151406	118668	
Aggleton	Michael John	Private	2nd Battalion, South Staffordshire Regiment	4929070	91754	Halle Trotha, Rei 104E Brick factory Reideburg
Airey	John	Private	11th Battalion, Parachute Regiment	3596766	91574	Grasseth Coal mine Sudetenland
Aitcheson	Frederick George	Private	2nd Battalion, Parachute Regiment	2931605	140150	Augsburg railway
Aitken	George Cecil	Private	1st Battalion, Parachute Regiment	4208372		Üfingen, Bomb damage clearing factory
Aitken	John	Private	7th Battalion, King's Own Scottish Borderers	14415429		Me 41 E bomb debris
Aitken	Peter	Staff Sergeant	Glider Pilot Regiment	28799361		
Alcock	Norman	Driver	250th Airborne Light Company, Royal Army Service Corps	136798	88757	Sudetenland rail labouring
Aldcroft	Albert	Lance Corporal	Royal Engineers	2020229		Merseburg debris clearing

Surname	Forename(s)	Rank	Regiment			Work location
Allchurch	Charles Cedric	Driver	1st Airlanding Anti-Tank Battery, Royal Artillery	14565660	92011	Dresden bomb damage
Allchurch	William Henry	Private	133rd Parachute Field Ambulance	7360747		Obermaßfeld, Hillburghausen
Allen	Arthur	Signalman	1st Parachute Brigade, Royal Signals	2594068	89409	Ei 114E Krugersall mine
Allen	Ernest William	Lance Corporal	10th Battalion, Parachute Regiment	117618		Wurzmes demolition, Brüx railway
Allen	Geoffrey Richard Ernest	Sergeant	Glider Pilot Regiment	2579984		
Allen	John Charles	Private	The Parachute Regiment	5349777	117477	AK 7011 Groß Düngen sugar beet factory
Allen	Robert Arthur	Corporal	3rd Battalion, Parachute Regiment	2080592	89462	
Allen	Ronald Harry	Gunner	Royal Artillery	14325639	229759	Dresden labouring
Allen	Wilfred	Private	2nd Battalion, South Staffordshire Regiment	1815415		Teutschenthal salt mines
Alletson	Edward Charles Walter	Private	21st Independent Parachute Company	5832371	118900	
Allingham	Edward	Private	2nd Battalion, South Staffordshire Regiment	1815416	91758	
Allison	Thomas	Private	7th Battalion, King's Own Scottish Borderers	14414347		
Allwood	Henry	Gunner	Royal Artillery	15267128	15245	Factory
Allwright	Charles Norman	Sergeant	7th Battalion, King's Own Scottish Borderers	4751022		
Amos	Henry	Private	2nd Battalion, South Staffordshire Regiment	51254455	75909	Unterschwödiz
Anderson	Alexander	Sergeant	Royal Army Service Corps	292574	118863	
Anderson	Alexander Kennedy	Sergeant	1st Battalion, Parachute Regiment	5679174		
Anderson	Arthur	Private	2nd Battalion, Parachute Regiment	5783569		Eilenburg building
Anderson	Ivor Douglas	Private	7th Battalion, King's Own Scottish Borderers	3189214		Rei 113 Building air raid shelters Halle
Anderson	William	Private	7th Battalion, King's Own Scottish Borderers	3190405		

Family Name	Forename	Rank	Unit	Army number	POW number	All kommandos
Anderson	William Henry	Private	Royal Army Service Corps	14244352		
Andrews	John	Gunner	1st Airlanding Light Regiment, Royal Artillery	14326582	92218	Me 49E Merseburg labouring
Angell	Donald Francis	Private	1st Battalion, Border Regiment	14237266	91882	Dresden clearing bomb damage
Ansell	Lawrence Frank	Sergeant	2nd Battalion, Parachute Regiment	2042803	89854	
Anson	John Edward	Lance Corporal	1st Parachute Brigade, Royal Signals	2576520		
Anson	Joseph William	Private	10th Battalion, Parachute Regiment	14332028	92125	Halle brickyard, Halle salt factory, Halle gravedigging
Appleby	John	Private	1st Battalion, Border Regiment	14579657	75433	Stone pits
Applin	Arthur George	Private	2nd Battalion, Parachute Regiment	14421867	88787	AK 231 repairing railways
Archer	Cyril	Gunner	1st Airlanding Light Regiment, Royal Artillery	14507454	75998	Troglitz clearing bomb damage from petrol factory
Arnold	Jack Thomas	Gunner	1st Airlanding Light Regiment, Royal Artillery	985649	118061	Bad Grund mining 7013
Ash	Alfred George	Lance Corporal	3rd Battalion, Parachute Regiment	14200328	90030	Plauen labouring
Ash	Arthur Charles	Driver	Royal Electrical and Mechanical Engineers	14412395		Dresden clearing bomb debris
Ashcroft	Stanley	Private	156th Battalion, Parachute Regiment	321781	90117	Eilenburg labouring
Ashfield	Cyril Douglas	Private	2nd Battalion, Parachute Regiment	5837161		Brüx railway repairs
Ashington	George	Private	2nd Battalion, South Staffordshire Regiment	5109173	117515	Uelzen railways
Ashley	Neville Leonard	Sergeant	2nd Battalion, Parachute Regiment	4124109		
Ashton	Frederick	Gunner	2nd Airlanding Anti-Tank Battery, Royal Artillery	3530609	92233	Merseburg
Ashton	Frederick John	Private	1st Battalion, Border Regiment	3771829	117682	Bad Grund lead mining

Ashton	Gerard	Private	1st Battalion, Border Regiment	3603315		Halle Trotha brickworks, Halle Saale brickworks
Ashworth	Harvey	Sapper	1st Parachute Squadron, Royal Engineers	1881677		Wurzmes mining, Brüx Benzine works
Askew	Thomas Richard	Private	1st Parachute Brigade	14229144	89259	
Aston	George Frederick	Private	11th Battalion, Parachute Regiment	4927881		50 mining
Atherton	George Frederick	Private	1st Battalion, Border Regiment	14583624	91476	Railway
Atkinson	Frederick	Corporal	The Parachute Regiment	3447850	118756	
Austen	James	Private	The Parachute Regiment	6399160		Dresden bomb debris
Austin	Albert Henry	Corporal	Light Warning Unit No. 6080, RAF	919538		
Austin	Norris	Corporal	1st Battalion, Border Regiment	4455267		Dresden stone quarry street work
Auty	Sam	Sergeant	Glider Pilot Regiment	4617488		
Avann	Thomas Alfred Spencer	Private	3rd Battalion, Parachute Regiment	7617647	89724	Hallendorf 7001 bomb damage
Avis	Jack Robb	Sergeant	2nd Battalion, Parachute Regiment	5672958		
Ayres	David Ivor	Lance Corporal	250th Airborne Light Company, Royal Army Service Corps	123373		
Baal	Lloyd Wilson	Private	10th Battalion, Parachute Regiment	93872	89594	Brux surface coal mining and railway track laying
Back	Harold Ernest	Lance Corporal	2nd Battalion, Parachute Regiment	6473851		Neubrandenburg Farm
Bacon	Arthur Henry	Private	2nd Battalion, Parachute Regiment	6142669		
Bacon	Sydney Thomas	Corporal	156th Battalion, Parachute Regiment	6012161		
Badger	Peter George	Private	2nd Battalion, Parachute Regiment	469960	117561	

Family Name	Forename	Rank	Unit	Army number	POW number	All kommandos
Baggott	Ronald	Private	2nd Battalion, South Staffordshire Regiment	14654405	91176	
Bailey	Albert Herbert Charles	Driver	253rd Airborne Light Company, Royal Army Service Corps	170899		Dresden General work
Bailey	Walter Clement	Trooper	1st Airborne Reconnaissance Squadron	10603469		Reinersdorf quarry
Baldwin	John	Lieutenant	Glider Pilot Regiment	269414		
Baldwin	Ronald George	Private	11th Battalion, Parachute Regiment	4980004	92118	Brüx Czech mining
Ball	Donald	Private	The Parachute Regiment	3973863	118487	Uelzen Railway
Ball	Eric	Lance Corporal	10th Battalion, Parachute Regiment	865470	118290	Bad Grund lead mine 7013
Ball	George	Signalman	1st Airlanding Light Regiment, Royal Signals	2122492	118122	Bad Grund lead mine 7013
Ball	Richard Patrick	Gunner	1st Airlanding Light Regiment, Royal Artillery	1084454	117397	Bad Grund, Harz 7013 Mountains lead mine
Ballingall	Peter	Private	16th Parachute Field Ambulance	97004292	118595	
Barclay	Robert	Lance Corporal	1st Battalion, Parachute Regiment	3131984	140156	
Barham	Leonard Charles	Sergeant	1st Battalion, Parachute Regiment	6026001		
Barling	Anthony Seymour	Captain	133rd Parachute Field Ambulance	306036	40	
Barlow	Leslie George	Private	3rd Battalion, Parachute Regiment	7908100	91599	
Barnard	Harry	Private	3rd Battalion, Parachute Regiment	5511669		G114 labour
Barnbrook	James Stanley	Sergeant	2nd Battalion, Parachute Regiment	6016887		
Barnes	George	Private	2nd Battalion, Parachute Regiment	6145484	88941	Halle Demolition
Barningham	Sydney	Private	7th Battalion, King's Own Scottish Borderers	14414368		Z131 railway
Barr	John Dobbin	Private	7th Battalion, King's Own Scottish Borderers	14211045	75959	Unterschwöditz mining

326

Surname	First name	Rank	Regiment	Number	Number	Work
Barraclough	Charles	Private	2nd Battalion, Parachute Regiment	883950		Rei 113 Halle varied work
Barrett	Dennis George	Sergeant	1st Battalion, Parachute Regiment	5338896		
Barrett	Robert Ernest	Gunner	1st Airlanding Light Regiment, Royal Artillery	869862	92115	
Barritt	Harry Charlie	Lance Corporal	10th Battalion, Parachute Regiment	6412557		Brüx railway
Barron	Stanley	Lance Corporal	250th Airborne Light Company, Royal Army Service Corps	175762		Herxberg Building work
Barry	Philip Hanbury	Lieutenant	2nd Battalion, Parachute Regiment	240444	2182	
Barstow	Robert	Sergeant	3rd Battalion, Parachute Regiment	3392250		
Bashford	Stanley Thomas Howard	Sergeant	11th Battalion, Parachute Regiment	4857599	89784	Leipen Farm
Bass	Bertram	Gunner	1st Airlanding Anti-Tank Battery, Royal Artillery	998089		
Bastow	James Arthur	Signalman	1st Parachute Brigade, Royal Signals	6216630	117880	7012 Dinklar Sugar factory
Bates	John Bernard	Staff Sergeant	Glider Pilot Regiment	912044		
Bateson	Robert James	Private	1st Battalion, Border Regiment	3776362	975499	KDO 395A Komatau
Batten	John Samuel	Sergeant	Parachute Regiment	5435891	117981	
Battley	John Harold	Private	16th Parachute Field Ambulance	7387449	89574	Jessen/Elster Saxony railway repairs
Baudrey	Henry William	Private	156th Battalion, Parachute Regiment	841838	75328	T35 Troglitz Petro Factory
Baxendale	Michael Kenneth	Private	156th Battalion, Parachute Regiment	6849050	117855	Oflag 79 orderly
Baxter	Robert Valentine	Private	Parachute Regiment	2760375		Brüx Labouring
Bayford	George William	Regimental Sergeant Major	Glider Pilot Regiment	6843827		

Family Name	Forename	Rank	Unit	Army number	POW number	All kommandos
Bayley	Len Edward	Private	10th Battalion, Parachute Regiment	14646018		K. DO.7002 Brunswick canal work
Baylis	George Sidney	Staff Sergeant	Glider Pilot Regiment	6206242		
Baylis	Richard William Charles	Private	2nd Battalion, South Staffordshire Regiment	978278	140084	
Beach	James William Alfred	Private	3rd Battalion, Parachute Regiment	14203487		Zwikua railway
Beasley	Walter Leslies	Private	156th Battalion, Parachute Regiment	6981219	75509	Weißenfels boot and shoe
Beattie	James	Private	7th Battalion, King's Own Scottish Borderers	3197491	88795	ME 40 E Merseburgh building air raid shelters
Beckett	Owen Charles	Lance Corporal	10th Battalion, Parachute Regiment	7346270		
Beckett	Sydney Reginald Barker	Private	4th Battalion, Dorset Regiment	1506674	21874	Leipzig Labouring
Bedder	Walter Thomas	Private	7th Battalion, King's Own Scottish Borderers	1539436	90497	Komotau KDO 375A
Beddoe	William Glyndwr	Lieutenant	7th Battalion, King's Own Scottish Borderers	285618	524	
Bedford	Douglas Leslie	Private	1st Battalion, Parachute Regiment	14658474		Z 131 Zwikau railway labouring
Bedford	Francis Henry	Private	2nd Battalion, Parachute Regiment	7013778		Wittenburg Saw Mill, Wittenburg Brick Factory
Bedford	Stanley William	Private	2nd Battalion, South Staffordshire Regiment	4925203		Merseburg Tunnelling
Beeston	John Richard	Private	2nd Battalion, Parachute Regiment	11050096		Zwickau railway
Beet	Charles	Lance Corporal	2nd Battalion, South Staffordshire Regiment	5125139	99999	U 12 Pirkau railway labour
Beet	Walter Reginald	Private	10th Battalion, Parachute Regiment	6400246	75454	Komotau blacksmith

Surname	First Name	Rank	Regiment/Unit	Number	Number	Work
Beezum	Gordon	Sergeant	Glider Pilot Regiment	7904031		
Bell	Albert Percy	Private	16th Parachute Field Ambulance	69089	89949	
Bell	John Mitchell Kenyon	Lieutenant	156th Battalion, Parachute Regiment	217392		
Bell	Keith Foster	Lieutenant	11th Battalion, Parachute Regiment	172259	2179	
Bell	Robert	Aircraftman	Light Warning Unit No. 6080, RAF	1373392		
Bell	Robert	Private	7th Battalion, King's Own Scottish Borderers	3191588		Eger coal mine
Bellamy	John Desmond	Sergeant/W	16th Parachute Field Ambulance	7381695	89795	
Bellas	George Geoffrey	Private	7th Battalion, King's Own Scottish Borderers	3325532		A1158 Kirschau blanket factory, Zwickau
Bellew	Cyril	Craftsman	Royal Electrical and Mechanical Engineers	4081359	75843	Mühltroff – Ger labouring
Benham	Arthur James	Private	2nd Battalion, Parachute Regiment	58357880		Hallendorf camp worker
Bennett	Arthur	Private	2nd Battalion, South Staffordshire Regiment	4928716		Borne, coal mining
Bennett	Edward Harry	Private	156th Battalion, Parachute Regiment	14416157	90647	ME 41 E Merseburg labourer
Bennett	Harold George	Private	133rd Parachute Field Ambulance	7378123		
Bennett	Thomas	Private	3rd Battalion, Parachute Regiment	4129244	89557	Halle 110 general labouring, Merseburg Me 40 E building air raid shelters
Bennett	William James (?)	Private	Parachute Regiment	3459818		Kirschau (Sud) blanket factory, Dresden Jam factory, Dresden Bomb debris
Bent	William	Private	1st Battalion, Border Regiment	3596732	75926	U 12 Untterswodtiz
Berg	Alfred Ernest	Lance Corporal	250th Airborne Light Company, Royal Army Service Corps	6219285	91140	Legenfeld Voigtland Cotton Mill and Railway
Berg	Edward Horace	Private	2nd Battalion, South Staffordshire Regiment	6400036		Zeitz railway
Bernstein	Cyril	Lance Corporal	11th Battalion, Parachute Regiment	954033	92135	

Family Name	Forename	Rank	Unit	Army number	POW number	All kommandos
Berry	Cecil John	Lance Corporal	2nd Battalion, South Staffordshire Regiment	4921888		Brüx
Berry	George Albert	Lance Bombardier	1st Airlanding Anti-Tank Battery, Royal Artillery	3524816	92014	
Berry	Joseph Edward	Private	11th Battalion, Parachute Regiment	1428100	294932	
Berry	O'Neill Ferguson	Lance Corporal	7th Battalion, King's Own Scottish Borderers	3188546		AK 7005 salzgitter tunnelling
Best	Lawrence	Driver	250th Airborne Light Company, Royal Army Service Corps	10694171	76000	
Bett	John Myles	Sergeant, Lance	7th Battalion, King's Own Scottish Borderers	3196624	140133rd	
Betts	George	Sergeant	Glider Pilot Regiment	14233066		
Betts	Henry	Private	156th Battalion, Parachute Regiment	4345218		
Beveridge	Thomas McLeod	Lance Corporal	9th Field Company, Royal Engineers Airborne	2113967	75856	Bockwitz labourer
Beveridge	William	Private	1st Battalion, Parachute Regiment	2885410	140117	
Bevington	Bernard Leslie	Private	2nd Battalion, South Staffordshire Regiment	14397682		Maltsch sugar factory
Bicker	George Stanley	Corporal	Royal Signals	2324374		
Biddulph	James	Private	2nd Battalion, South Staffordshire Regiment	5051428		Maltch sugar beet
Bilsland	John	Private	3rd Battalion, Parachute Regiment	3196036		
Binge	Dudley Albert George	Sergeant	2nd Battalion, Parachute Regiment	1612710		
Binns	Arthur	Staff Sergeant	Glider Pilot Regiment	3390495		
Birchenough	Richard Alfred Godsal	Captain	11th Battalion, Parachute Regiment	112810	18650	

Surname	Forename	Rank	Regiment	Service No.	POW No.	Work
Bird	Charles Randle	Lance Corporal	5th Battalion, Dorset Regiment	4923658	93369	Messelung road labouring
Bird	Frederick Rudd	Gunner	1st Airlanding Light Regiment, Royal Artillery	14290006	118217	Bad Grund lead mining 7013
Bird	Roy Alexander	Corporal	16th Parachute Field Ambulance	85750	89654	
Birtwistle	Sam	Gunner	1st Airlanding Light Regiment, Royal Artillery	14254706	75966	REI 21 Lochoa coal mine
Bishop	Frank	Private	2nd Battalion, South Staffordshire Regiment	5681913	117804	Hildershiem Suagr factory
Bishop	Walter William	Lance Corporal	156th Battalion, Parachute Regiment	6086564		Dresden Labouring
Black	Bernard	Staff Sergeant	Glider Pilot Regiment	884545	7596	
Black	James Charles	Sapper	1st Parachute Squadron, Royal Engineers	1986005		Merseburg tunnelling
Black	John	Private	156th Battalion, Parachute Regiment	2939792		Dresden machinist
Blackie	James	Corporal	7th Battalion, King's Own Scottish Borderers	3185739		
Blackmore	John David	Private	10th Battalion, Parachute Regiment	4447335		M 104 tunnelling
Blackmore	Sydney George	Private	1st Battalion, Parachute Regiment	6853726	117793	Dinkler Sugar factory
Blacow	Ronald	Sergeant	156th Battalion, Parachute Regiment	3710567		
Blades	Ernest	Private	1st Battalion, Border Regiment	3602778	91628	Kirschau blanket factory, Frieberg Tannery
Bland	Percy	Private	156th Battalion, Parachute Regiment	4208563		Bad Grund lead mining 7013
Blanks	Joseph	Private	156th Battalion, Parachute Regiment	6146068	75506	Komatau railway
Blinko	George Henry	Private	21st Independent Parachute Company	5391704		Coal heaving
Blockwell	Albert Leslie	Lance Corporal	7th Battalion, King's Own Scottish Borderers	7622135	26090	Zietz labouring
Blouet	Donald	Private	133rd Parachute Field Ambulance	7349318	90112	
Bloys	William	Private	2nd Battalion, Parachute Regiment	6029487		Slate Mine
Blundell	Kenneth	Staff Sergeant	Glider Pilot Regiment	4460360		
Boddington	Wilfred	Private	156th Battalion, Parachute Regiment	103738		

331

Family Name	Forename	Rank	Unit	Army number	POW number	All kommandos
Boe	John Allan	Private	3rd Battalion, Parachute Regiment	5442182	117309	
Bollington	Robert	Gunner	1st Airlanding Light Regiment, Royal Artillery	14326060	118631	
Bolton	Joseph	Private	2nd Battalion, Parachute Regiment	1086471	117914	AK 7011 Groß Düngen sugar beet factory
Bonser	Frank	Private	11th Battalion, Parachute Regiment	4800484	117591	Groß Düngon
Boorman	Percy	Lance Corporal	4th Parachute Brigade	6286352	117660	Groß Düngon
Booth	Eric Charles	Driver	1st Parachute Squadron, Royal Engineers	1951655		Halle in a crematorium
Booth	Harry	Private	3rd Battalion, Parachute Regiment	892682		
Bourne	Derrick Arthur	Private	2nd Battalion, South Staffordshire Regiment	4925767		Me 49 E Merseburg
Bourne	Ernest Frederick	Lance Corporal	2nd Battalion, South Staffordshire Regiment	4918790	91638	Brüx coal miner
Boushear	James	Private	156th Battalion, Parachute Regiment	14255636		Zwikau Z 131 railway
Boustead	Albert Edward	Lieutenant	2nd Battalion, South Staffordshire Regiment	434	91844	
Bowden	Samuel Kenneth	Sergeant	Glider Pilot Regiment	71237		
Bower	Stanley	Sapper	4th Parachute Squadron, Royal Engineers	1951358	90698	133rd5 Dresden
Bowers	Raymond Francis	Captain Reverend	10th Battalion, Parachute Regiment	291627	140115	
Bowes	James Michael	Private	156th Battalion, Parachute Regiment	3653641	75343	Elsterwerder cement works, Maschau coal mine
Bowie	Alexander John	Private	3rd Battalion, Parachute Regiment	3318961		Rei 113 Halle air raid shelter labouring
Bowles	Charles Edward	Private	2nd Battalion, Oxfordshire and Buckinghamshire Light Infantry Regiment	5383183	118070	

Surname	First name	Rank	Unit	Number	Number	Work/location
Bowles	Dennis Arthur	Gunner	1st Airlanding Light Regiment, Royal Artillery	14257583		Zwickau Z131
Boyd	Douglas	Private	7th Battalion, King's Own Scottish Borderers	3197623		Neitz labouring
Boydell	Edward	Private	2nd Battalion, Parachute Regiment	2757701		Sebnitz paper factory
Boyle	Peter Bernard	Staff Sergeant	Glider Pilot Regiment	4983193		
Boyle	Ronald James	Private	2nd Battalion, Parachute Regiment	3598564	117376	AK 7012 Dinklar
Boynes	Albert Percival Michael	Private	10th Battalion, Parachute Regiment	5619030	26082	
Brackenboro	John Leonard	Private	Parachute Regiment	4123948		Torchentel salt mine, Etzdorf coal mine
Bradbeer	Albert Leslie	Sergeant	Glider Pilot Regiment	14230534	76284	
Bradbury	John Alfred	Sergeant	Glider Pilot Regiment	14547304		
Bradbury	William Henry George	Sapper	1st Parachute Squadron, Royal Engineers	14203066		REI 113 Halle labourer
Bradley	Edward	Sergeant	2nd Battalion, South Staffordshire Regiment	4913836	89848	
Bradley	Leslie	Sergeant	1st Battalion, Parachute Regiment	3654679	140113	
Bradley	Thomas Phazie	Lance Corporal	9th Field Company, Royal Engineers Airborne	2012016		Dresden fitter
Braithwaite	Gilbert Edmund	Private	2nd Battalion, South Staffordshire Regiment	6016356		Wurzmes surface coal mine, Tschausch
Braithwaite	Robert Raymond	Private	The Parachute Regiment	2084621		Sudetenland mining
Bramwell	Paul Eric	Gunner	1st Airlanding Light Regiment, Royal Artillery	935154	92068	
Breen	Thomas Francis	Lance Corporal	1st Airborne Provost Company	1917769		Menzengraben salt mine
Bremner	Francis Reginald John	Private	156th Battalion, Parachute Regiment	5348811		labouring
Brett	Frank Arthur	Gunner	1st Airlanding Anti-Tank Battery, Royal Artillery	1103757	75561	Großthiemig, sand quarry

Family Name	Forename	Rank	Unit	Army number	POW number	All kommandos
Brett	Thomas	Lance Corporal	1st Battalion, Border Regiment	3596764	91625	Dresden labourer
Brewin	Thomas Frderick	Private	2nd Battalion, South Staffordshire Regiment	14662825	91503	Brüx miner
Bricker	Denis Herbert	Driver	250th Airborne Light Company, Royal Army Service Corps	175632	118617	
Bridge	Joseph Edward	Private	2nd Battalion, South Staffordshire Regiment	4923097	89444	Zschornewitz
Bridgewater	Ernest Edward	Corporal	11th Battalion, Parachute Regiment	7262084		
Briggs	Kenneth William	Lance Corporal	1st Battalion, Border Regiment	4346036	75674	Dresden Tramways
Bright	Stanley	Private	2nd Battalion, South Staffordshire Regiment	5734258		
Bristow	Frank James	Private	156th Battalion, Parachute Regiment	6291433		
Britland	Sydney	Leading Aircraftman	Light Warning Unit No. 6080, RAF	1750457	1055	
Britnev	Vladimir Alexandroitcn	Lieutenant	1st Battalion, Parachute Regiment	162044	534	
Britton	Daniel James	Private	1st Battalion, Parachute Regiment	5672278	140088	
Broadfoot	Robert	Private	156th Battalion, Parachute Regiment	3189292		Eisleben Copper Mine, Hetzsted oxide
Broadhurst	William	Private	11th Battalion, Parachute Regiment	889617	9166	AK 50 Wurzmes coal mining, Elsterhorst hospital, Hoenstien Res Laz
Broadley	David Smith	Staff Sergeant	Glider Pilot Regiment	1468299		
Brock	Edwin Ward	Regimental Sergeant Major	16th Parachute Field Ambulance	7522897		
Brodie	James	Gunner	1st Airlanding Light Regiment, Royal Artillery	14957653		Wurzmes mining, Tschausch

Surname	Forename	Rank	Regiment	Number	Number 2	Work
Brodrick	Thomas Robert	Corporal	Army Catering Corps	7369184	140055	
Bromfield	Arthur	Sergeant	2nd Battalion, Parachute Regiment	6014527	88939	Kundl General labouring
Bromilow	Willis Vincent	Private	1st Battalion, Border Regiment	14653229	117623	Groß Düngon sugar factory
Brook	William Henry	Driver	63 Company, Royal Army Service Corps	163198	75501	Floßmühle paper mill
Brooker	Ronald James	Trooper	1st Airborne Reconnaissance Squadron	6354463	91435	Tröglitz general labourer
Brookes	Dennis Lionel	Corporal	11th Battalion, Parachute Regiment	4123596		
Brookfield	John	Staff Sergeant	Glider Pilot Regiment	85942	76289	
Brooks	Arthur	Private	2nd Battalion, South Staffordshire Regiment	5125767	92898	
Brooks	Clarence	Sergeant	Glider Pilot Regiment	7590893		
Brooks	David Arthur	Sergeant	2nd Battalion, Parachute Regiment	6349289		
Brooks	Edward Charles	Corporal	156th Battalion, Parachute Regiment	5437863		
Brooks	Jack	Private	1st Battalion, Border Regiment	14650833	117535	Groß Düngon sugar beet
Brooks	Jack Douglas	Driver	250th Airborne Light Company, Royal Army Service Corps	242720	91417	Dresden factory
Brooks	Stanley Donald	Private	2nd Battalion, Parachute Regiment	6104511	117266	
Broome	Alfred James	Private	10th Battalion, Parachute Regiment	6022185		Merseburg boot repairer
Brophy	Thomas	Private	156th Battalion, Parachute Regiment	65890		58 Wallwitz railway work
Brotherton	Arthur	Private	156th Battalion, Parachute Regiment	5054413		Merseburg brick layer
Brotherton	Donald	Private	3rd Battalion, Parachute Regiment	6018336	117523	7011 Groß Düngon
Brotherton	Walter	Craftsman	Royal Electrical and Mechanical Engineers	4273439	91760	1209 Niedersedlitz timber
Brown	Andrew Peddie Dunlop	Private	3rd Battalion, Parachute Regiment	3191772	65303	Komotau ARP repairs

Family Name	Forename	Rank	Unit	Army number	POW number	All kommandos
Brown	Arthur	Private	2nd Battalion, Parachute Regiment	7357412		
Brown	Charles Francis Leighton	Private	4th Battalion, Dorset Regiment	5956239		Brux miner
Brown	Cyril	Private	2nd Battalion, Parachute Regiment	920584		Hallendorf
Brown	Duncan	Corporal	3rd Battalion, Parachute Regiment	2931228	89926	
Brown	Edward Hubart	Gunner	1st Airlanding Light Regiment, Royal Artillery	1096863	118214	
Brown	George Andrew	Corporal	3rd Battalion, Parachute Regiment	3129190	75318	
Brown	George Reginald	Sergeant, Lance	2nd Battalion, South Staffordshire Regiment	4917565	89468	
Brown	Harold Stanley	Driver	253rd Airborne Light Company, Royal Army Service Corps	2897665		
Brown	Harry	Private	156th Battalion, Parachute Regiment	91516		Zwickau railway
Brown	Henry	Gunner	1st Airlanding Light Regiment, Royal Artillery	937082	75977	Mückanburg surface coal mine
Brown	James	Private	4th Parachute Brigade	2987572	90626	Herzberg building
Brown	John	Sapper	Royal Engineers	1895443	118186	7013 Bad Grund metal mine
Brown	John Redshaw	Private	11th Battalion, Parachute Regiment	4452924	91729	Merseberg labouring
Brown	Joseph Potter	Lance Corporal	1st Battalion, Border Regiment	4542186	77754	Stützengrün wood yard
Brown	Leonard	Private	7th Battalion, King's Own Scottish Borderers	14211781	89851	AK 7001 Hallendorf railway bomb damage
Brown	Norman	Private	2nd Battalion, South Staffordshire Regiment	4918535		Halle [C???] Employment
Brown	Norman	Private	7th Battalion, King's Own Scottish Borderers	3190181		Halle construction air raid shelters

Brown	Peter	Private	3rd Battalion, Parachute Regiment	3058097		Merseburg labouring in air raid shelters
Brown	Robert Miller	Private	16th Parachute Field Ambulance	14633706	90560	
Brown	Thomas Watson	Private	The Parachute Regiment	3858124	91582	Coal mining, Labouring
Brown	William Harold	Private	10th Battalion, Parachute Regiment	4535118	75502	Mückenberg rail laying
Browne	Daniel James	Private	1st Battalion, Border Regiment	14550679	14186	O 87 Hoffmannstof, Ayr wood yard
Browne	Edward William	Staff Sergeant	Glider Pilot Regiment	5730039		
Browne	Patrick	Private	7th Battalion, King's Own Scottish Borderers	1711838		Z 131 Zwickau railways
Brownsell	Anthony	Corporal	156th Battalion, Parachute Regiment	5670619		
Bruce	Arnold	Private	2nd Battalion, South Staffordshire Regiment	4919516	92113	Maulburge sugar beet factory, Merseburg bomb damage roads
Bruce	Jack	Sergeant	Glider Pilot Regiment	6211584		
Brunt	Derek	Private	1st Battalion, Parachute Regiment	4748060	92120	Dresden bomb damage
Bryan	Stephen Arthur	Lance Corporal	2nd Battalion, South Staffordshire Regiment	4919029	117965	kommando 7002 canal work
Bryans	William Howard	Private	2nd Battalion, Parachute Regiment	3325884	75427	Ziplast Komotau
Bryant	Reginald Ernest	Private	156th Battalion, Parachute Regiment	14428514		Frankenberg Lumberjack, Niedecwiera cement stone
Bryce	Charles	Staff Sergeant	Glider Pilot Regiment	3254730		
Bryson	Lionel Henry	Regimental Sergeant Major	Royal Army Medical Corps	7259229		
Buchanan	Peter Rhodes	Sergeant	2nd Battalion, Parachute Regiment	2931641		
Buck	Charles Reginald Harold	Craftsman	Advanced Workshop Detachment, Royal Electrical and Mechanical Engineers	7387240	89268	Eisdorf sugar beet factory, Unteroblingen coal mine

Family Name	Forename	Rank	Unit	Army number	POW number	All kommandos
Buck	Lawrence Fredrick	Corporal	1st Parachute Squadron, Royal Engineers	1883034		
Buckley	Charles	Private	1st Battalion, Border Regiment	3597954	91982	Dresden labouring
Budd	Frederick John	Lance Corporal	181st Airlanding Field Ambulance	7364587		
Budibent	Clement Bryan	Private	156th Battalion, Parachute Regiment	7674669	18655	
Buglass	James	Private	3rd Battalion, Parachute Regiment	4975389		Lager 51 Brux mining
Bull	Henry James	Private	156th Battalion, Parachute Regiment	6092624		Dresden tramways
Bull	Thomas James	Private	2nd Battalion, South Staffordshire Regiment	14200023	89515	Etzdorf
Bullas	Jack	Private	156th Battalion, Parachute Regiment	3387227		
Bunkall	Cecil Norman	Sergeant	Glider Pilot Regiment	911333		
Burdon	Jack Forster	Private	1st Battalion, Border Regiment	3191498	75438	Komatau railway
Burgess	Leonard	Private	3rd Battalion, Parachute Regiment	14693144	91690	36A
Burgoyne	William Ralph	Sergeant	Glider Pilot Regiment	4749099		
Burns	Peter	Private	3rd Battalion, Parachute Regiment	14569564	117458	Dinklar 7012
Burns	Robert Speed	Private	4th Parachute Brigade HQ	3452456	117659	Groß Düngen kommandos 7011
Burrell	Reginald George	Gunner	1st Airlanding Anti-Tank Battery, Royal Artillery	1109220		Brüx coal mine
Burridge	Bernard William	Sergeant	1st Battalion, Parachute Regiment	2620969	89213	
Burridge	Thomas William	Private	7th Battalion, King's Own Scottish Borderers	1076009	89213	Z 131 Zwicaku railway
Burton	Albert	Sapper	4th Parachute Squadron, Royal Engineers	1882104	140144	
Burton	George	Corporal	3rd Battalion, Parachute Regiment	4921199		

Surname	First name(s)	Rank	Regiment	Number	Number	Location / work
Burton	Thomas	Private	7th Battalion, King's Own Scottish Borderers	3450209	90249	
Butler	Dennis John	Private	1st Battalion, Parachute Regiment	14409701		Gunnersdorf timber cutting, Oederan general labourer
Butter	Arthur Anthony	Private	The Parachute Regiment	7960360	294117	Tschausch
Butterly	John James	Lance Corporal	1st Parachute Brigade, Royal Signals	796225	880906	Togehentall wagon tippler
Buttriss	George	Gunner	Forward Observation Unit, Royal Artillery	946892	90711	
Buxey	William Thomas	Sergeant	Glider Pilot Regiment	1876657		
Byrne	John	Private	1st Battalion, Parachute Regiment	4206915		Lager 22 Brüx mining
Byrne	Michael	Private	1st Battalion, Border Regiment	3782510	118304	Ülzen railway repairs
Byrne	Philip Stafford	Private	1st Battalion, Parachute Regiment	4206124	89957	Z 131 Zwickau, AK P5 Penig
Caddick	Ernest	Lance Corporal	156th Battalion, Parachute Regiment	3770832		G 123 Gleina
Cain	John	Private	1st Battalion, Parachute Regiment	3189138	75363	Sudetenland
Cairns	William	Corporal	7th Battalion, King's Own Scottish Borderers	3190460		
Calder	Ronald	Staff Sergeant	Glider Pilot Regiment	3859441		
Caldwell	John Gibson McCoy	Private	2nd Battalion, South Staffordshire Regiment	274850		Brüx Mines and factory
Callaghan	William	Private	1st Battalion, Border Regiment	37086684	75699	
Cameron	Alan James	Trooper	4th Parachute Brigade HQ	3536624	117367	Groß Düngon
Cameron	Andrew	Sapper	9th Field Company, Royal Engineers Airborne	2073139		
Cameron	Hugh McKenzie	Gunner	1st Airlanding Light Regiment, Royal Artillery	890053	75919	Unterschwöditz coal mine
Camp	Thomas Everard	Private	1st Battalion, Border Regiment	2619360	118320	Ülzen bomb clearance and railway

Family Name	Forename	Rank	Unit	Army number	POW number	All kommandos
Campbell	Henry	Sergeant	2nd Battalion, Parachute Regiment	3055067		
Campbell	John Joseph	Private	7th Battalion, King's Own Scottish Borderers	4539373	90498	Komotau labourer
Campbell	Robert Stewart	Lance Bombardier	1st Airlanding Light Regiment, Royal Artillery	1578886		
Campbell	Sidney Alex Albers	Gunner	1st Airlanding Light Regiment, Royal Artillery	6099334		Brüx surface coal mine
Campbell	Alec	Staff Sergeant	Glider Pilot Regiment	2694009		
Cannon	Leonard Alexander	Private	1st Battalion, Parachute Regiment	3964252		Fallingbostel labourer
Cansfield	Peter Evens	Signalman	1st Parachute Brigade, Royal Signals	4927573	91328	Zwieku 'Adolf Hitler Ring' labourer German railways pmt way
Canty	Roy	Private	3rd Battalion, Parachute Regiment	6015492		Me 40 air raid shelter work E
Capewell	Edward	Private	2nd Battalion, South Staffordshire Regiment	14642798	92703	Dresden clearing bomb debris
Cardwell	Edward Alfred	Sapper	4th Parachute Squadron, Royal Engineers	1952670	117909	Groß Düngon
Carlier	Leonard Thomas	Private	2nd Battalion, Parachute Regiment	5835317	89827	AK 7001 navying
Carmichael	John	Private	1st Battalion, Parachute Regiment	2879115	91559	
Carpenter	Richard	Private	11th Battalion, Parachute Regiment	5954520		Merseburg labourer
Carr	Jack	Sergeant	2nd Battalion, Parachute Regiment	2182264		
Carr	Joseph Stuart	Private	2nd Battalion, Parachute Regiment	6147869		Varchentin
Carr	Stephen Francis	Sapper	1st Parachute Squadron, Royal Engineers	2135069	117444	AK 7012 Dinklar
Carr	William	Signalman	4th Parachute Brigade, Royal Signals	4279044	91677	Dresden clearance of bomb debris
Carroll	Albert	Lance Corporal	2nd Battalion, South Staffordshire Regiment	14668753	89367	Wurzmes surface work coal, Brüx laying tram track

Surname	Forename	Rank	Regiment	Number	POW No.	Work location
Carroll	William James	Private	11th Battalion, Parachute Regiment	2932551	117761	AK 7001 Hallendorf railway
Carruthers	William George	Private	7th Battalion, King's Own Scottish Borderers	3194917	91509	Kirschau Kershaw (?) labour, Dresden labour
Carter	Frederick George Henry	Private	16th Parachute Field Ambulance	14264103	90150	
Carter	George Richard	Private	7th Battalion, King's Own Scottish Borderers	3326436		Mining Stalag IV C
Carter	James Henry	Driver	1st Airlanding Anti-Tank Battery, Royal Artillery	1142052		Konigswaide Stone Quarry
Carter	Stephen Wiliam	Private	181st Airlanding Field Ambulance	7392998		
Cartledge	Albert	Private	2nd Battalion, Parachute Regiment	14550580		Halle shelters
Cartmell	James	Private	156th Battalion, Parachute Regiment	3447716	118308	Bad Grund lead mine
Cartwright	Hugh Harry Langdon	Lieutenant	2nd Battalion, South Staffordshire Regiment	269402	2171	
Case	Alfred Ernest	Private	156th Battalion, Parachute Regiment	5380977	91759	Freidwaldau brick and tile
Cassells	William	Gunner	1st Airlanding Light Regiment, Royal Artillery	14283055	92092	Brux mine
Cattell	Frederick	Private	2nd Battalion, South Staffordshire Regiment	1557871	91751	Freiberg leather works
Cave	William Herbert	Driver	250th Airborne Light Company, Royal Army Service Corps	176447	118898	
Cawley	John	Driver	253rd Airborne Light Company, Royal Army Service Corps	10680840	90968	58 Wallwitz railway
Cawood	Donald Samuel	Private	1st Battalion, Border Regiment	14202522	91629	Kirschau [Kershaw] Blanket factory, Freiberg Leather factory,
Cawrey	Victor Frank	Private	21st Independent Parachute Company	4975875	118305	7012 Dinklar sugar beet
Chamberlain	Stanley Arthur	Private	3rd Battalion, Parachute Regiment	557436	89733	
Chambers	Talbot Alexander	Sergeant	89 Parachute Security Section	118933	93637	

Family Name	Forename	Rank	Unit	Army number	POW number	All kommandos
Chandler	Brian Gerald	Private	2nd Battalion, South Staffordshire Regiment	7607105		Grossenhain stone breaking
Chandler	William Francis	Trooper	1st Airborne Reconnaissance Squadron	6091692	118711	
Channon	William	Company Quartermaster Sergeant Major	4th Parachute Brigade HQ	5567123	88745	Kundl Austria clearing debris
Chant	James Stephen	Private	2nd Battalion, South Staffordshire Regiment	5498826	89337	Merseburg air raid shelters
Chaplin	Donald Arthur	Sergeant	11th Battalion, Parachute Regiment	3970424		
Chapman	Albert Henry	Gunner	1st Airlanding Light Regiment, Royal Artillery	1470053		Ortrand Concrete Works
Chapman	Harold	Trooper	GHQ Liaison Regiment (Phantom)	14521821		Zwickau Z 131, Ditmasdorf B 5
Chapman	Harry Arthur Frederick	Staff Sergeant	Glider Pilot Regiment	4267802		
Chapman	Ronald Anthony Francis	Private	3rd Battalion, Parachute Regiment	4914786		Kommando 23 Jessen
Chapman	Walter Frederick	Private	7th Battalion, King's Own Scottish Borderers	4751017		
Charles	Ernest	Private	1st Battalion, Parachute Regiment	5679630		Rei 113 Halle labouring
Chesterton	Eric	Sergeant, Lance	Royal Signals	2330939		
Chilcott	Frederick Henry	Bombardier	1st Airlanding Anti-Tank Battery, Royal Artillery	780594		
Chilton	Edward	Private	1st Battalion, Border Regiment	3191430	75497	Komatau railway
Chilton	Herbert James	Staff Sergeant	1st Airlanding Brigade	2012822	118889	

Surname	First names	Rank	Regiment/Unit	Number	Number	Work
Chilvers	George Williams	Lance Corporal	7th Battalion, King's Own Scottish Borderers	6922969		Sudetenland coal mining
Chivers	Laurence Herbert James	Sergeant	156th Battalion, Parachute Regiment	5673491		
Chivers	William Ernest	Private	2nd Battalion, South Staffordshire Regiment	4917934		Velsen clearing bomb damage laying railway line
Christie	George	Private	7th Battalion, King's Own Scottish Borderers	3190220	90556	Merseburg bomb damage
Christopher	James	Private	156th Battalion, Parachute Regiment	14425251	75700	Grosstheimig cement factory
Clamp	George Edward	Corporal	2nd Battalion, Parachute Regiment	4859690		Varchentin Farm work
Clancey	Philip Stafford	Private	10th Battalion, Parachute Regiment	6091449		
Clapham MC	Edward Eric	Lieutenant	1st Airlanding Anti-Tank Battery, Royal Artillery	258481	2175	
Clark	Andrew Basil	Company Quartermaster Sergeant Major	11th Battalion, Parachute Regiment	6397607		
Clark	Clifford Samuel	Leading Aircraftman	Light Warning Unit No. 6341, RAF	1675207		
Clark	Henry Pullman	Sergeant	1st Airlanding Light Regiment, Royal Artillery	997188	88740	
Clark	James	Private	7th Battalion, King's Own Scottish Borderers	3245281	90528	
Clark	John William	Private	3rd Battalion, Parachute Regiment	14219515	89172	Merseburg building air raid shelters
Clarke	Alfred Charles James	Private	3rd Battalion, Parachute Regiment	122644		
Clarke	Christopher	Private	3rd Battalion, Parachute Regiment	2049999	91517	Friburgh [sic] Freiberg tanner
Clarke	Donald	Sergeant	11th Battalion, Parachute Regiment	4450139	88788	
Clarke	Edward	Private	10th Battalion, Parachute Regiment	3191917	118830	

Family Name	Forename	Rank	Unit	Army number	POW number	All kommandos
Clarke	George	Driver	250th Airborne Light Company, Royal Army Service Corps	290806		13 B Coal Mine
Clarke	Peter	Staff Sergeant	Glider Pilot Regiment	7356321	118129	Braunsweig railway
Clarke	Reginald Eric	Sergeant	Glider Pilot Regiment	7949735		
Clarkson	Gordon	Private	2nd Battalion, Parachute Regiment	14682836		Wurzmes mining, Tschausch railway
Clegg	Thomas	Private	Royal Army Medical Corps	73918145		Leipzig labouring
Clements	Robert Stanley	Private	156th Battalion, Parachute Regiment	6293276	117709	AK 7011 Groß Düngen near Hildesheim sugar beet factory labourer
Clements	Sydney Peter	Private	11th Battalion, Parachute Regiment	14411807	117346	AK 7011 Groß Düngen Sugar Beet factory
Clifton	William	Corporal	9th Field Company, Royal Engineers Airborne	2077843	91313	
Clowes	Albert	Private	1st Battalion, Border Regiment	3780000	26085	Bailand Leipzig labourer
Coates	John Robert	Sergeant	2nd Battalion, Parachute Regiment	3771565		Kundl railway at Worgl
Cobbold	George Arthur	Staff Sergeant	Glider Pilot Regiment	2575349		
Cockroft	Frederick	Driver	1st Airborne Division Signals	14503023		Brüx coal miner
Cocks	Cecil	Private	1st Battalion, Border Regiment	14642494	91707	Brux coal mine
Coggins	Percy	Private	1st Battalion, Parachute Regiment	5047437	89331	
Coid	William	Private	7th Battalion, King's Own Scottish Borderers	3190234	75372	Mückenberg Bubiag lignite mining and laying railway lines
Coidan	Denis Gabriel Andrew	Sapper	4th Parachute Squadron, Royal Engineers	1986027	117355	7001 Hallendorf general labour
Colaluca	Angelo	Private	3rd Battalion, Parachute Regiment	4809747	117819	7013 Bad Gründ

Surname	First name	Rank	Regiment	Number	Number	Location
Cole	John Henry	Private	156th Battalion, Parachute Regiment	6896445		Halle (Rei 21?) coal mine
Cole	Stanley Reginald	Lance Bombardier	Royal Artillery	14262654	93708	
Coleman	Richard	Private	10th Battalion, Parachute Regiment	3658412	90520	Elsterwerda? labouring
Colkin	Billy	Private	7th Battalion, King's Own Scottish Borderers	11000947	91778	Sudetenland coal mining
Collier	Dennis	Private	156th Battalion, Parachute Regiment	5734402		Komatau railway
Collins	Herbert	Lance Corporal	7th Battalion, King's Own Scottish Borderers	3325401	99999	Dresden clearing bomb damage
Collins	Sydney George	Private	2nd Battalion, South Staffordshire Regiment	4699064	89288	Brüx Benzin
Colls	Douglas	Sergeant, Lance	1st Airlanding Anti-Tank Battery, Royal Artillery	1514892		
Colmer	Donald Bernard	Private	3rd Battalion, Parachute Regiment	2067681		
Coltart	David	Private	7th Battalion, King's Own Scottish Borderers	3191054		Germany coal mine
Combey	Simpson Alfred	Lance Corporal	4th Parachute Squadron, Royal Engineers	125981	117794	Hallendorf rebuilding arms factory
Common	Albert	Private	1st Battalion, Border Regiment	3191433	91457	D 395 A railway repair shops Komotau
Condon	George Walter	Private	11th Battalion, Parachute Regiment	7263856		
Connelly	Edward	Private	7th Battalion, King's Own Scottish Borderers	3325781		Brux mines
Connely	James Joseph	Gunner	1st Airlanding Anti-Tank Battery, Royal Artillery	3055590	91734	Halle brick factory
Connold	Norman Thomas	Private	3rd Battalion, Parachute Regiment	14427804		Wurtzmez open mine, Tschausch-Brux open mine, Coluitbus-Brux filling bomb craters
Connolly	John	Private	4th Battalion, Dorset Regiment	14710015	17562	Ortand Saw mill
Connor	Frank	Private	7th Battalion, King's Own Scottish Borderers	144336225	25479	Chemitz Soap Factory

Family Name	Forename	Rank	Unit	Army number	POW number	All kommandos
Conway	James Joseph	Staff Sergeant	Glider Pilot Regiment	7043131	117320	Hildesheim sugar factory, Uelzen railway station
Coogan	Allan McKenzie Smith	Gunner	1st Airlanding Light Regiment, Royal Artillery	1084529		Gleina Zeitz Petroleum Factory,
Cook	George	Private	3rd Battalion, Parachute Regiment	6214569	89173	Merseburg Air raid shelter labouring
Cook	James	Sapper	9th Field Company, Royal Engineers Airborne	2069925	91491	Brux mining
Cook	Noel	Sapper	4th Parachute Squadron, Royal Engineers	1903563	26021	Gunnerdorf forestry, Eppendorf boot making
Cook	William Mark	Lance Corporal	11th Battalion, Parachute Regiment	903583	92143	Maltheuern [Maltern] miner
Cooke	Archie William George	Lance Corporal	1st Parachute Squadron, Royal Engineers	1881045		Jessen railway work
Cooke	Charles Edward	Private	2nd Battalion, South Staffordshire Regiment	4917571		
Cooke	Clifford Kenneth	Private	11th Battalion, Parachute Regiment	10666764	89804	Uelzen railway
Cooke	Eric Finney	Private	2nd Battalion, Parachute Regiment	4197475	117278	
Cooke	Peter Sidney Victor	Corporal	3rd Battalion, Parachute Regiment	2080407	294120	
Coombe	Herbert Dorrien	Sergeant	3rd Battalion, Parachute Regiment	5435865	140301	
Cooper	Benjamin John Richard	Sergeant, Lance	2nd Battalion, South Staffordshire Regiment	4077803		

Cooper	Cyril	Driver	Airborne Light Company, Royal Army Service Corps	114167	140093	Mooseburg
Cooper	Dennis Patrick	Private	1st Battalion, Border Regiment	1437623	75685	U 12 mine Unterswaditx
Cooper	Gordon Michael	Private	4th Battalion, Dorset Regiment	14556629		Fackneau coal mining
Cooper	Herbert George	Private	2nd Battalion, South Staffordshire Regiment	5057632	91673	
Cooper	James	Trooper	1st Airborne Reconnaissance Squadron	1467133rd5	117414	Bad Grund mining 7013
Cooper	John Robert	Corporal	11th Battalion, Parachute Regiment	863102	140123	
Cooper	Robert Dudley	Private	10th Battalion, Parachute Regiment	1461847		AK 1326 Dresden demolition of bomb damage, Tyssa 'Open camp'
Cooper	Ronald Victor	Lance Corporal	1st Parachute Brigade, Royal Signals	5348617		Zwickau railway maintenance
Cooper	Stanley	Private	181st Airlanding Field Ambulance	7368352		POW hospital
Cooper	Thomas John	Private	10th Battalion, Parachute Regiment	897853	75654	
Copley	Stanley George	Signalman	1st Parachute Brigade, Royal Signals	2587283	117839	Kd 7012 Dinklar
Coppack	Philip Maurice	Staff Sergeant	Glider Pilot Regiment	937504		
Corfield	Ronald	Sergeant	Glider Pilot Regiment	14344873		
Cormack	George Burnet	Private	181st Airlanding Field Ambulance	7347023	140059	
Cornish	Denis	Sergeant	Glider Pilot Regiment	903724		
Corns	Charles Eric	Lance Corporal	2nd Battalion, South Staffordshire Regiment	4918495	91746	Kirschau, Zwickau paper factory February March April
Cortmann	Alexander	Private	3rd Battalion, Parachute Regiment	2890203	92100	Zwickau railway maintenance
Corton	Bernard	Private	1st Battalion, Border Regiment	14591265	91520	AK Z55 leather work Zugspitze
Cottam	John Philip	Private	4th Battalion, Dorset Regiment	14664309	25027	Zwikau railway labouring

Family Name	Forename	Rank	Unit	Army number	POW number	All kommandos
Cotten	George Henry Charles	Sapper	1st Parachute Squadron, Royal Engineers	14892438		Erfenschlag, Chemnirz sectional housing woodwork
Cottrell	William John	Bombardier	1st Airlanding Anti-Tank Battery, Royal Artillery	1514708		
Couch	Stanley Hugh	Private	2nd Battalion, South Staffordshire Regiment	5440744		
Coupe	Harold	Sapper	1st Parachute Squadron, Royal Engineers	1922268	89229	Halle Rei 113 labourer
Courcha	William Alexander	Private	10th Battalion, Parachute Regiment	14665231	75407	T 35 Zeitz filling in bomb holes
Course	Charles Joseph	Private	10th Battalion, Parachute Regiment	4986412		Halle
Courtie	Thomas	Company Sergeant Major	10th Battalion, Parachute Regiment	3768595	140153	
Courtney	Richard William	Gunner	2nd Airlanding Anti-Tank Battery, Royal Artillery	14268331	90921	Herzberg building
Courtney	Thomas Richard Brian	Major	133rd Parachute Field Ambulance	112406	91202	Kdo D 602 Klitzschmar
Cousins	Eric Robert	Sergeant	7th Battalion, King's Own Scottish Borderers	4751138	89427	
Cowie	David	Sergeant	2nd Battalion, Parachute Regiment	7886460		
Cox	Basil	Private	10th Battalion, Parachute Regiment	5671559	91757	
Cox	Denis Herbert	Sergeant, Acting	2nd Battalion, South Staffordshire Regiment	5051692	89424	Baspohl farm
Cox	Ronald Charles Percival	Private	2nd Battalion, Parachute Regiment	5832882		Kdo 133rd3 Dresden tramways fitter
Cox	Wilfred Douglas	Private	156th Battalion, Parachute Regiment	49191598	89935	7001 Hallendorf

Surname	Forename	Rank	Regiment	Number	Number	Work/Location
Coxon	Frank	Private	1st Battalion, Parachute Regiment	825718		Merseberg air raid shelters, Frankleben canal building
Craig	Daniel	Lance Bombardier	Forward Observation Unit, Royal Artillery	855981	75340	
Craig	Daniel	Private	7th Battalion, King's Own Scottish Borderers	14211595	90557	Merseburg demolition
Craig	James	Sergeant	2nd Battalion, Parachute Regiment	3246833	89139	
Craig	John Alexander	Private	1st Battalion, Parachute Regiment	7046503	92185	Brüx coal mine
Craig	Thomas John Lawson	Private	7th Battalion, King's Own Scottish Borderers	3194287	117380	7012 Dinklar
Craig	William	Private	3rd Battalion, Parachute Regiment	14246464		
Craik	James	Private	7th Battalion, King's Own Scottish Borderers	3190194		Halle Trotha Brick work
Cram	James Wilson	Sergeant	7th Battalion, King's Own Scottish Borderers	3193062	89988	
Crandles	Austin	Private	2nd Battalion, South Staffordshire Regiment	14340452	89261	Kdo 50 Brüx Benzine factory demolition
Crane	Douglas Broadway	Private	1st Battalion, Parachute Regiment	14577150	75160	Unterschwöditz surface mine (coal)
Crane	Ernest	Private	156th Battalion, Parachute Regiment	14420927	18658	Munich garage work
Crane	William	Private	2nd Battalion, Parachute Regiment	4398812	117851	
Crawford	Bert Victor	Private	2nd Battalion, Parachute Regiment	5731255		Halle outdoor labourer
Crawley	Leslie Stanley	Private	2nd Battalion, Parachute Regiment	1677621	75439	Nr Dresden labourer, Lilianstien labourer
Creasy	Reginald George	Corporal	3rd Battalion, Parachute Regiment	5623140	90102	
Cressey	Charles	Lance Corporal	1st Airborne Provost Company	2053082	14909	
Critchley	Arthur	Private	3rd Battalion, Parachute Regiment	7888645		Sebnitz paper mill
Crittenden	Robert Claude	Lieutenant	1st Battalion, Border Regiment	264942	2176	

Family Name	Forename	Rank	Unit	Army number	POW number	All kommandos
Crockett	Dennis George	Private	7th Battalion, King's Own Scottish Borderers	11001185	916141	Brüx coal mine
Crockford		Sergeant	Glider Pilot Regiment	2063433		
Cronshaw	Albert	Private	1st Battalion, Border Regiment	6471864		Gliena labouring
Crook	John Williams	Lance Bombardier	1st Airlanding Light Regiment, Royal Artillery	14256319		Z131 Zwickau plate layer
Cross	Bernard	Private	1st Battalion, Border Regiment	1146496	18654	Munchen road work
Crossland	Stanley	Lance Corporal	1st Battalion, Border Regiment	4691419	117619	
Crowe	Ronald Harry	Sergeant	1st Parachute Brigade, Royal Signals	2323334	18679	
Crudginton		Private	1st Battalion, Parachute Regiment	5439376		Johnsdorf mine work
Cuckle	Lionel	Private	11th Battalion, Parachute Regiment	4896515	75995	
Cull	George William	Private	1st Parachute Brigade	14410678		Falkenau coal mine
Cull	Peter Patrick	Private	1st Battalion, Border Regiment	3608321	14935	Tschausch heavy labouring on drainage system for coal washing plant
Culliton	Patrick	Private	3rd Battalion, Parachute Regiment	13098369		Merseburg air raid shelter construction
Cully	Christopher	Private	7th Battalion, King's Own Scottish Borderers	3196678	75541	Komotau locomotive repair
Culpan	Eric Hopkinson	Sergeant	Glider Pilot Regiment	2081536		
Cund	Edwin	Sergeant	2nd Battalion, South Staffordshire Regiment	4914618		Liepen farm work
Cunliffe	Roger	Private	1st Battalion, Border Regiment	14402790		Oederan Chemnitz 'Straw Factory'
Cunningham	Alexander	Corporal	10th Battalion, Parachute Regiment	4481938	90824	
Cunningham	Thomas	Lance Corporal	156th Battalion, Parachute Regiment	345429	90500	Chemnitz Wood Factory and bomb damage

Curtin	William Victor	Lance Corporal	11th Battalion, Parachute Regiment	62945308	95390	U 12 Zeitz surface coal mining
Curtis	Arthur	Private	11th Battalion, Parachute Regiment	6399339		El 116 E coal mine
Curtis	George	Private	1st Battalion, Border Regiment	3597790	118189	
Curtis	Leonard Arthur Cecil	Private	3rd Battalion, Parachute Regiment	2047378	117875	Hildesheim sugar beet factory
Cuthbertson	Malcolm	Private	4th Battalion, Dorset Regiment	3770561	91903	Kirschau textiles, Löbau cement works, Löbau textile factory
Cuthell	Stanley	Private	181st Airlanding Field Ambulance	7388028		Jessen railways
Cuttill	George Frederick	Corporal	10th Battalion, Parachute Regiment	6025196		
Dagwell	David Nicol	Private	156th Battalion, Parachute Regiment	5349578		Komotau 395A railway
Dale	John Arthur	Lance Corporal	2nd Battalion, South Staffordshire Regiment	4914922	89487	Commontour (sic) Komotau demolition, Brux railway
Dale	Ronald Richard	Staff Sergeant	Glider Pilot Regiment	5112070	900	
Daley	Joseph	Private	1st Battalion, Border Regiment	3599017	24651	Trebsen paper mill
Dalton	Christopher	Private	1st Battalion, Parachute Regiment	4348459		
Dance	Kenneth George	Private	2nd Battalion, South Staffordshire Regiment	4927983	25553	Halle brickyard
Dane	Ernest Victor	Sapper	9th Field Company, Royal Engineers Airborne	2135629	117886	7011 Groß Düngen
Daniels	Stanley	Private	2nd Battalion, South Staffordshire Regiment	14682944	89138	Komotau Surface coal mine, Brux railway repairs
Darkins	Arthur Robert	Private	156th Battalion, Parachute Regiment	6474749		
Davey	Edward Thomas	Private	181st Airlanding Field Ambulance	7358134	90173	Jessen/Elster railway repairs

Family Name	Forename	Rank	Unit	Army number	POW number	All kommandos
Davey	Roy	Corporal	2nd Battalion, South Staffordshire Regiment	5348839	89921	
Davidson	Charles	Private	10th Battalion, Parachute Regiment	4536073	75493	Dresden tramways
Davidson	Robert Mason	Private	156th Battalion, Parachute Regiment	61519	117713	Ohlendorf iron ore mining
Davies	Desmond Godfrey	Private	2nd Battalion, Parachute Regiment Royal Army Medical Corps	14389667	89420	
Davies	Eric	Private	1st Battalion, Parachute Regiment	4195158	117835	
Davies	Henry	Private	4th Battalion, Dorset Regiment	14723652		Kleinleipisch line laying surface coal mine
Davies	Robert William	Private	1st Battalion, Border Regiment	1454411	75695	Chemnitz
Davies	Sydney	Private	2nd Battalion, Parachute Regiment	14309397		Maltch sugar beet
Davies	William Peter	Private	3rd Battalion, Parachute Regiment	41796618		Stalag XII A Cookhouse
Davis	Alexander	Private	1st Battalion, Parachute Regiment	818745		Dresden labouring
Davis	George Ernest	Staff Sergeant	Glider Pilot Regiment	2045543		
Davis	James Robert	Private	7th Battalion, King's Own Scottish Borderers	11251840	75352	Gleina 'Pick and Shovel'
Davis	John Harold	Private	3rd Battalion, Parachute Regiment	5625908		Stutzengruh gas from wood
Davis	Samuel Wilfred	Private	181st Airlanding Field Ambulance	7362406	93720	
Dawson	Herbert	Private	2nd Battalion, South Staffordshire Regiment	1714784	89717	357 Fallingbostel labourer
Dawson	John Harold	Private	2nd Battalion, Parachute Regiment	11407811	75336	Mückenburg labouring coal mine
Dawson	Leonard William	Sergeant/W	156th Battalion, Parachute Regiment	800747		
Dawson	Robert Ridley	Corporal	Royal Army Medical Corps	7266914		

Surname	Forename	Rank	Regiment	Number	Number	Detail
Dawson	William Felix	Private	2nd Battalion, South Staffordshire Regiment	5053162	91698	Miner Sudetenland
Day	Frank Graham	Driver	261st Field Park Company, Royal Engineers	2013286		Z 131 Zwickau
Daye	Russell Robert	Private	7th Battalion, King's Own Scottish Borderers	14620635	118419	Kdo 7005 salzgitter railway line laying, Kdo 7001 hallendorf Lumberjack
Deacon	James	Corporal	7th Battalion, King's Own Scottish Borderers	3190690		
Deakin	Albert	Private	2nd Battalion, South Staffordshire Regiment	2621911	91483	Zwickau railway
Dean	William Arthur	Private	156th Battalion, Parachute Regiment	4974106		
Deasy	William Roy	Staff Sergeant	Glider Pilot Regiment	985314	118164	
Debnam	Thomas James	Private	3rd Battalion, Parachute Regiment	5435791	117979	
Deeley	George Alfred	Sergeant	Glider Pilot Regiment	5127622		
Delea	Eric Michael Desmond	Private	156th Battalion, Parachute Regiment	3778794		Roich labouring Wurzen
Dell	Edward	Corporal	2nd Battalion, Parachute Regiment	6203748		Farm labour
Denholm	James	Private	11th Battalion, Parachute Regiment	3314746	119639	
Dennis	Bernard George	Gunner	1st Airlanding Light Regiment, Royal Artillery	1076427	77371	Flossmüle B/Borsendorf saw mill
Dennis	Frank	Sergeant	Glider Pilot Regiment	5887705		
Dennis	Ronald Francis	Private	4th Battalion, Dorset Regiment	14710022	26048	Frakenberg forestry, Chemnitz railway
Dennison	Wilfred	Private	7th Battalion, King's Own Scottish Borderers	4539145	90639	Merseburg debris clearing
Denny	Thomas Bernard Philip	Private	2nd Battalion, South Staffordshire Regiment	14554721		Brüx coal mining
Derbyshire	Stanley	Private	3rd Battalion, Parachute Regiment	14375898	52885	Salt mine Menzengraben
Devey	John Raymond	Staff Sergeant	Glider Pilot Regiment	3601654	903	
Devine	John	Signalman	1st Parachute Brigade, Royal Signals	2574778	88905	

Family Name	Forename	Rank	Unit	Army number	POW number	All kommandos
Devlin	James	Private	7th Battalion, King's Own Scottish Borderers	14410841		Teutschental Salt mine
Di Paola	Joseph	Private	7th Battalion, King's Own Scottish Borderers	3323806		Zwicka railway
Dicken	Henry	Private	10th Battalion, Parachute Regiment	14410900	90516	
Dickens	John Raymond	Captain	2nd Battalion, South Staffordshire Regiment	180222	2201	
Dickin	James Leon	Private	2nd Battalion, South Staffordshire Regiment	4927982		
Dickinson	John Burley	Captain	1st Airlanding Light Regiment, Royal Artillery	138257	2199	
Dickson	Richard	Private	3rd Battalion, Parachute Regiment	4546716	92122	36A mining
Didsbury	Noran	Sergeant	Glider Pilot Regiment	14576025		
Dinwiddie	Gordon Maidland	Major	7th Battalion, King's Own Scottish Borderers	90195	2195	
Dixon	Eric Joseph	Private	2nd Battalion, South Staffordshire Regiment	4201186	75872	
Dixon	Frank Edwin	Lance Corporal	16th Parachute Field Ambulance	7381047		
Dixon	George	Corporal	1st Airborne Reconnaissance Squadron	14272599		
Dixon	John	Private	7th Battalion, King's Own Scottish Borderers	14203067	90692	Me 41 E debris clearing
Dixon	John Francis	Private	1st Battalion, Border Regiment	3602801		
Dixon	Joseph Albert	Private	3rd Battalion, Parachute Regiment	3915723		Wurzmes Labouring surface coal mine, Schaustlager Brüx tramways, Kolumbus lager open cast mine
Dixon	Thomas	Private	133rd Parachute Field Ambulance	7361998	89925	
Dixon	Robert Richard	Gunner	1st Airlanding Light Regiment, Royal Artillery	14600654		Ortrand cement works
Dodd	William Ronald	Private	3rd Battalion, Parachute Regiment	6404195		Merseberg Tunnelling air raid shelters

Surname	First name(s)	Rank	Unit	Number	POW No.	Work detail
Doig	Charles	Lieutenant	7th Battalion, King's Own Scottish Borderers	268306		
Doig	John	Private	156th Battalion, Parachute Regiment	14407490		Wittenberg saw mill
Dolaghan	Thomas Noel William Dowie	Private	4th Parachute Brigade	6977906	89826	kdo 7002 Üfingen labouring excavation
Donald	Colin	Private	Parachute Regiment	1467192	117417	
Donaldson	Edward	Private	7th Battalion, King's Own Scottish Borderers	14656612	89231	Building air raid shelters Merseburg
Donnelly	Moses	Private	1st Battalion, Parachute Regiment	4538622	91461	Hartha? Saxony Shoe Factory
Donnelly	Thomas Baker	Private	1st Battalion, Parachute Regiment	2981809		Rhorsdorf Tankholz [?]
Donovan		Private	2nd Battalion, Parachute Regiment	5953014	89358	Wurzmes Surface mine, Tchause railway
Donowho	William	Private	7th Battalion, King's Own Scottish Borderers	3190801		7001 Railway
Doughty	Leslie	Sergeant	1st Airlanding Anti-Tank Battery, Royal Artillery	842123	90131	
Douglas	Joseph	Lance Corporal	1st Parachute Squadron, Royal Engineers	1886957		
Douglas	William	Private	156th Battalion, Parachute Regiment	3189703	91481	Kirschau blanket fabric, Stechers Leather fabric
Douthwaite	Fred	Private	1st Battalion, Parachute Regiment	14587525	117657	Bad Gründ 7013
Dove	William Kenneth	Private	156th Battalion, Parachute Regiment	6981695		Zahna brick making, Mutschau coal mine
Dover	Victor	Major	2nd Battalion, Parachute Regiment	113514	521	
Down	Percy	Corporal	1st Battalion, Parachute Regiment	567133rd9	118257	Brunswick railway camp
Downton	William Henry	Private	2nd Battalion, South Staffordshire Regiment	14316550	92022	Dresden clearing bomb damage
Drayton	Frank	Private	2nd Battalion, Parachute Regiment	408160	89525	Neubrandenburg farm work
Dredge	Norman Victor	Private	2nd Battalion, South Staffordshire Regiment	14700066	92215	
Drew	Douglas John Archer	Private	3rd Battalion, Parachute Regiment	6468336		Teutschental salt mine, Eisdorf coal mine

Family Name	Forename	Rank	Unit	Army number	POW number	All kommandos
Drewitt	Arthur William	Private	11th Battalion, Parachute Regiment	518429	117485	7012 Dinklar sugar beet factory
Driscoll	Edward Dennis	Corporal	7th Battalion, King's Own Scottish Borderers	2751006	90567	
Drury	Robert	Private	10th Battalion, Parachute Regiment	5726456		Rei 113 Halle grave digging
Dryden	John James	Private	11th Battalion, Parachute Regiment	4451109		Halle sewage repair
Duck	John	Signalman	4 Para Brigade, Royal Signals	2573508	90737	Reinersdorf Stone quarrying
Duddy	George Victor	Private	181st Airlanding Field Ambulance	7402718	89573	
Dudley	Frank Thomas	Craftsman	Royal Electrical and Mechanical Engineers	5574814	91497	Kirschau blanket factory, Dresden clearing bomb debris, Dresden Tin Factory
Duffell	Edward George	Private	2nd Battalion, Parachute Regiment	5835781	89688	Railway Hallendorf 7001
Duffy	John	Sergeant	1st Parachute Brigade	7662893	90033	
Dukes	Benjamin William	Private	181st Airlanding Field Ambulance	7380299		Railway platelaying Jessen
Dunbar	William Shearer	Sergeant	Glider Pilot Regiment	2572042		
Dunford	Reginald Charles	Private	10th Battalion, Parachute Regiment	555639	77099	Dresden Tramways/salvage
Dunlop	John Paterson	Lance Bombardier	1st Airlanding Light Regiment, Royal Artillery	1084223	117403	7011 Groß Düngen
Dunn	Kenneth Harold	Private	2nd Battalion, Parachute Regiment	1828301		
Durant	George Edwin	Gunner	1st Airlanding Light Regiment, Royal Artillery	14284494	91884	Seestat (Wurzmes) coal mine, Bettyschacht, Tchaus & Brüx coal mine

Durkin	James	Private	1st Battalion, Border Regiment	4614317	26024	Muckenberg rail laying
Durnin	Charles	Private	1st Battalion, Border Regiment	4347257	91969	Dresden labouring
Dyall	William	Sergeant	Glider Pilot Regiment	853162		Stalag IV D work 'none done'
Dyer	Albert Jack	Private	2nd Battalion, Parachute Regiment	206567		Wurzmes surface coal mine, Tschausch 'Navvy'
Dyer	Thomas	Private	2nd Battalion, Parachute Regiment	4543023	89946	Zwickau railway
Eagleton	John	Private	1st Battalion, Border Regiment	14671556	91521	Freiberg Leather
Easton	William	Private	3rd Battalion, Parachute Regiment	5781435		Wurzmes repairing bomb damage, Brüx tramway
Eatwell	Horace Arthur	Regimental Sergeant Major	1st Battalion, Parachute Regiment	2613152	89402	Bruxe
Eccles	Cyril	Private	156th Battalion, Parachute Regiment	7617196		Wilischthal labourer in paper works
Edwards	Charles Percy	Lance Corporal	7th Battalion, King's Own Scottish Borderers	4921302	90763	Merseberg clearing debris
Edwards	James	Lance Corporal	2nd Battalion, South Staffordshire Regiment	4927985	76661	Wurzmes Miner, Chouse Stasenbarr
Edwards	John Iver	Gunner	1st Airlanding Light Regiment, Royal Artillery	14679928	118175	Kommando 7013 Bad Grund Harz lead mining
Edwards	John William Edward	Private	2nd Battalion, Parachute Regiment	5511508	117955	AK 7011 Groß Düngen sugar factory
Edwards	Thomas	Corporal	2nd Battalion, Parachute Regiment	4699004		
Edwards	William	Private	[Unit not given]	2100175		
Elder	Paul	Lance Corporal	4th Parachute Brigade, Royal Signals	2981146	118597	
Eley	John	Private	1st Airlanding Light Regiment, Royal Artillery	14316068	75818	Zieginine
Ellard	Joseph James	Sapper	4th Parachute Squadron, Royal Engineers	4448884	140111	
Elletson	John Edward	Lance Corporal	1st Parachute Brigade, Royal Signals	259133rd4	91296	
Elliott	Albert James	Private	3rd Battalion, Parachute Regiment	6207794		Falkenali coal mine

357

Family Name	Forename	Rank	Unit	Army number	POW number	All kommandos
Elliott	Arthur Lewis Shaw	Bandsman	1st Battalion, Border Regiment	3759659	118321	
Elliott	Charles Bridgeman	Private	156th Battalion, Parachute Regiment	4279607		IV B Blankets, IV F Leather
Elliott	Frederick Robert George	Corporal	10th Battalion, Parachute Regiment	5773317		
Elliott	John	Private	4th Parachute Brigade HQ	839439	90625	Herbbuge cook
Elliott	Robert	Private	1st Battalion, Border Regiment	3608489		
Elliott	Sidney Charlie Edwin	Private	2nd Battalion, Parachute Regiment	6153666	140131	
Ellis	Desmond	Private	2nd Battalion, South Staffordshire Regiment	6409401		Zwickau railway filling
Ellis	John Aloysius	Staff Sergeant	Glider Pilot Regiment	1901936		
Ellis	Leslie Henry	WO II	1st Parachute Squadron, Royal Engineers	1869692		Kundl near Wörgi Railway
Ellis	William George	Gunner	2nd Airlanding Anti-Tank Battery, Royal Artillery	1094054		Mickenburg surface coal mine
Ellison	Anthony	Private	1st Battalion, Border Regiment	4277251	91930	Dresden clearing bomb damage
Ellwood	Michael	Private	2nd Battalion, Parachute Regiment	14272883		Brüx coal mine
Elsey	George Douglas Jack	Craftsman	Royal Electrical and Mechanical Engineers	1574063	21901	Erfenschlag cement works clearing bomb damage, repairing railway, filling bomb craters on farms
Emmerton	Thomas Horace	Lance Corporal	2nd Battalion, Parachute Regiment	5831766		Torchental, Metzdorf
Entwistle	John	Private	1st Battalion, Border Regiment	14674222	91780	Brüx mines
Erangey	Patrick Joseph	Gunner	2nd Airlanding Anti-Tank Battery, Royal Artillery	1147917		Dresden-Niedersedlitz glazier

Surname	Forename	Rank	Unit	Number	Camp No.	Work detail
Evans	Ernest Philip	Signalman	4th Parachute Brigade, Royal Signals	14580106	117881	Gross Düngen sugar beet 7011
Evans	Frank	Private	1st Battalion, Border Regiment	3864100	91881	Kolumbus mining – Brux
Evans	Kenneth Charles	Lieutenant	4th Parachute Squadron, Royal Engineers	267949	2178	
Evans	Robert George	Private	1st Battalion, Parachute Regiment	6108197		
Evans	Thomas	Private	3rd Battalion, Parachute Regiment	4031655		
Evans	Trevor Parry	Sergeant, Lance	2nd Battalion, Parachute Regiment	3966276	89810	
Evans	Walter John	Private	156th Battalion, Parachute Regiment	5679918		Zarhest brick factory, Zlits railway lines
Evans	Wilfred Richard	Driver	1st Airlanding Light Regiment, Royal Artillery	14320758	75312	Chemnitz soap factory
Evans	William Henry	Corporal	1st Battalion, Border Regiment	3602813	140142	
Evans	William James	Private	181st Airlanding Field Ambulance	7361934		Jessen railway
Everest	Sydney John	Private	3rd Battalion, Parachute Regiment	6214961	90470	Stalag 357 joiner
Eves	Edward	Private	1st Parachute Brigade	3977266	75448	Lilienstein labouring
Ewing	Archibald	Private	2nd Battalion, Parachute Regiment	2937469		
Exley	Brian Harding	Gunner	1st Airlanding Light Regiment, Royal Artillery	14296963	75830	Erfenschlag timber yard, Grünhainichen Timber yard
Fail	Adam	Gunner	1st Airlanding Anti-Tank Battery, Royal Artillery	1491362	75543	
Fairbrass	Jack	Private	2nd Battalion, South Staffordshire Regiment	989345	17526	Stützengrün Production of gas from wood
Fairmington	Matthew	Lance Corporal	10th Battalion, Parachute Regiment	10602075		
Fairweather	Clifford	Corporal	250th Airborne Light Company, Royal Army Service Corps	229170	118846	
Faithorn	Peter	Private	21st Independent Parachute Company	5772762		Borna coal mining

Family Name	Forename	Rank	Unit	Army number	POW number	All kommandos
Farley	Peter	Private	1st Battalion, Border Regiment	3190506		Mückenberg
Farmer	Samuel	Private	10th Battalion, Parachute Regiment	6854355	92168	
Farr	Victor	Private	The Parachute Regiment	14650326		133rd3 Dresden Painter
Farrell	Alexander	Private	7th Battalion, King's Own Scottish Borderers	2884841	91898	Dresden labouring
Farrington	Bernard Haig	Private	2nd Battalion, South Staffordshire Regiment	4918377	118721	
Farrow	Kenneth Ronald	Private	21st Independent Parachute Company	4928276	117550	7012 Dinklar sugar back filling
Faulkner	Maurice Arthur	Private	2nd Battalion, South Staffordshire Regiment	4917591	91647	Kirschau blanket factory, Löbau cement factory, Löbau linen factory
Fellows	James	Private	1st Battalion, Border Regiment	14584168		Falknau coal mining
Fenton	John	Lance Corporal	2nd Battalion, South Staffordshire Regiment	491469	89849	'ARBKDO 7001' railway
Fenwick	George Rae	Corporal	250th Airborne Light Company, Royal Army Service Corps	108381	91188	
Fergus	Gerard John	Trooper	1st Airborne Reconnaissance Squadron	14282358	52935	123B Menzengraben, Dorndorf
Ferguson	David Drummond	Private	7th Battalion, King's Own Scottish Borderers	14210564	25480	
Ferguson	John	Sergeant, Lance	7th Battalion, King's Own Scottish Borderers	3190459		
Ferguson	Samuel	Sergeant	156th Battalion, Parachute Regiment	2754337		
Ferrari	Henry Felix	Signalman	Royal Signals	6352602		Dresden general labouring
Few	Ted	Private	156th Battalion, Parachute Regiment	5257174		Mittweida labourer
Fickling	Kenneth Bruce	Private	1st Battalion, Parachute Regiment	14568820		Gera labouring
Field	Albert Henry	Private	2nd Battalion, South Staffordshire Regiment	11006127	140211	Mittenwald shelters

Surname	First name	Rank	Regiment	Number	Number	Work
Finglass	Gordon	Private	21st Independent Parachute Company	6346424	117784	
Finlinson	Edwin	Private	10th Battalion, Parachute Regiment	1593916	294918	Döbeln stone work
Fisher	Donald Edwin	Private	10th Battalion, Parachute Regiment	5890901	91687	
Fisher	Patrick	Private	2nd Battalion, Parachute Regiment	5630343	294160	Tschausch III labourer
Fisher	Sidney Eugene	Private	2nd Battalion, Parachute Regiment	5771570		13 B Falkenau coal mine
Fishwick	William	Private	2nd Battalion, Parachute Regiment	3774446	91425	
Fitchett	Reginald Frank	Lance Corporal	3rd Battalion, Parachute Regiment	5337096	117876	Kmd 7011
Fitzgerald	Michael	Driver	1st Airlanding Anti-Tank battery	6854732		Arnhem loading looted goods, Ereiwader clay pits, Hannover filling bomb craters railways
Fitzgibbons	Maurice	Corporal	156th Battalion, Parachute Regiment	4617001		
Fitzpatrick	John Francis	Private	2nd Battalion, Parachute Regiment	4198450		Z 131 Zwickau railway
Flanaghan	Andrew	Private	11th Battalion, Parachute Regiment	1609685	91482	Wurzmes coal mining, Tschausch laying tramlines
Fleming	James	Private	2nd Battalion, Parachute Regiment	2985559		Sebnitz 1193
Fleming	Joseph	Private	7th Battalion, King's Own Scottish Borderers	14211103	75937	
Fleming	William James	Sergeant	2nd Battalion, Parachute Regiment	2989834		
Fletcher	Dugald	Private	156th Battalion, Parachute Regiment	2766219		Wallwitz
Fletcher	Ernest Leslie	Bombardier	2nd Airlanding Anti-Tank Battery, Royal Artillery	1525244	89756	
Flint	Thomas Joseph	Private	2nd Battalion, South Staffordshire Regiment	14682857	92093	? Mining
Flynn	Christopher Alexander	Private	1st Battalion, Border Regiment	3602818	53397	Menzengraben salt mine
Flynn	James	Private	1st Battalion, Border Regiment	3595760	140070	8002 Zingfield medical orderly

Family Name	Forename	Rank	Unit	Army number	POW number	All kommandos
Fogarty	Christopher Winthrop	Lieutenant	1st Airlanding Light Regiment, Royal Artillery	237353	93296	
Ford	Harry Gardner	Private	2nd Battalion, Parachute Regiment	14650990	91571	Brux mining
Ford	Jesse	Lance Corporal	Provost Company, 1st Airborne Division	7691865		Etzdorf Et 116 E
Ford	William	Lance Corporal	7th Battalion, King's Own Scottish Borderers	3188138	90720	Wallwitz railroad surface work
Forman	John Henry	Private	2nd Battalion, South Staffordshire Regiment	4920555	91701	Mining
Forman	Michael Bertram	Major	7th Battalion, King's Own Scottish Borderers	91061	90861	
Forsyth	Thomas Thomson	Private	7th Battalion, King's Own Scottish Borderers	14210830	90168	Hallendorf General Labouring
Fort	Eric Joseph	Corporal	2nd Battalion, South Staffordshire Regiment	4923320	89551	
Forwood	Charles	Corporal	7th Battalion, King's Own Scottish Borderers	3136134	88797	
Foster	Andrew	Private	156th Battalion, Parachute Regiment	3190000		
Foster	David William	Leading Aircraftman	Light Warning Unit No. 6080	1652764		
Foster	Edward James	Private	2nd Battalion, Parachute Regiment	6028848		Dresden tramways, waterworks
Foster	Eric	Staff Sergeant	Glider Pilot Regiment	6401145		
Foster	Harry	Private	1st Battalion, Border Regiment	14584171	75688	Stützengrün
Foster	James Henry	Private	7th Battalion, King's Own Scottish Borderers	144339540	91774	Kirschau blanket factory, Radebeul tin factory
Foster	Kenneth	Private	156th Battalion, Parachute Regiment	320416	140138	Driver for Int Red Cross
Foster	Williams	Gunner	1st Airlanding Light Regiment, Royal Artillery	14337091	975967	Stutzongrunn forestry
Foulke	Harold Bernard	Private	181st Airlanding Field Ambulance	7382422	140061	Augsburg removing bomb damage

362

Surname	First name(s)	Rank	Regiment	Service No.	POW No.	Work
Fowler	Colin	Private	1st Battalion, Border Regiment	4546551	91931	
Fowler	James Edward	Lance Corporal	3rd Battalion, Parachute Regiment	4076697	117176	
Fowler	Sydney John	Lance Corporal	3rd Battalion, Parachute Regiment	870732	89224	Merseburg – Camp Leader, Duben – Carter for sugar tablet factory
Fox	George	Private	Royal Engineers	14435314		Zeitz
Fox	John	Private	2nd Battalion, South Staffordshire Regiment	14437468	76799	Halle brick factory
Fox	Wilfred George	Private	2nd Battalion, South Staffordshire Regiment	4697023	92167	Neiderwiesa cement works
Foxon	James Arthur	Signalman	Royal Signals	2378460	91899	NA 33 Halle-Trotha bricks quarrying, REI 104 E Halle Brick loading
Franzel	Frank Charles	Private	11th Battalion, Parachute Regiment	3661561		Niedersedlitz General labourer,
Frary	Dennis	Private	133rd Parachute Field Ambulance	14351195		
Fraser	Homer Newell	Staff Sergeant	Glider Pilot Regiment	2135945	140099	
Freemantle	Albert Brendon	Private	156th Battalion, Parachute Regiment	888204		Zahna brick factory, Mutchau surface coal mine
Frewin	Eric Sidney	Private	1st Battalion, Border Regiment	1150793	25560	Kleinleipisch L 34E railway
Funnell	Harry Ronald	Private	10th Battalion, Parachute Regiment	6411360		Me 41 E Debris clearing
Furber	Tom	Private	2nd Battalion, South Staffordshire Regiment	14682861		Komotau surface coal mine, Brüx railway repairs
Furniss	Thomas	Driver	250th Airborne Light Company, Royal Army Service Corps	10694184	117594	Bad Grund lead mine
Gaitero	Allan	Corporal	3rd Battalion, Parachute Regiment	6466565	89523	
Garbutt	William Martyn	Sergeant	Glider Pilot Regiment	816515	76327	
Gardner	Cyril	Private	7th Battalion, King's Own Scottish Borderers	14204693	90577	Merseburg labouring
Gardner	Eric Sidney	Private	Royal Army Medical Corps	7382362	9171	

Family Name	Forename	Rank	Unit	Army number	POW number	All kommandos
Garnham	Ronald Arthur Douglas	Sergeant	Glider Pilot Regiment	3966566		
Garnsworthy	Leslie George	Sergeant	1st Airlanding Anti-Tank Battery, Royal Artillery	5671600		
Garrard	Stephen Walter	Sergeant	Glider Pilot Regiment	10677268		
Garvey	Thomas	Private	1st Battalion, Border Regiment	3596852	91984	Dresden shoe factory
Gascoyne	John William	Private	10th Battalion, Parachute Regiment	5734588	294913	Döbeln labourer
Gaunt	James	Sergeant, Lance	2nd Battalion, South Staffordshire Regiment	49133rd13	90025	
Gavin	Patrick Charles	Regimental Quartermaster Sergeant	133rd Parachute Field Ambulance	7263776		
Gaz	Jozef	Private	1st Polish Parachute Brigade	3143169		Halle labouring
Geoghan	Thomas	Private	2nd Battalion, South Staffordshire Regiment	1561803	91634	Brüx
Gethin	James Thomas	Private	1st Battalion, Parachute Regiment	4757644		
Gibb	Archibald Allan	Private	2nd Battalion, South Staffordshire Regiment	2880575	89435	Coal mine – surface, Coal mine surface
Gibb	William	Private	181st Airlanding Field Ambulance	7396628	90571	
Gibbins	Leonard Albert	Corporal	3rd Battalion, Parachute Regiment	2181072		
Gibbons	Ernest James Scott	Sergeant	9th Field Company, Royal Engineers Airborne	1867057	117182	Jessen railway
Gibbs	Frederick Michael	Captain	156th Battalion, Parachute Regiment	114084	91015	
Gibbs	Ronald Williams	Gunner	1st Airlanding Light Regiment, Royal Artillery	932645	118095	Bad Grund lead mine 7013

Surname	First name(s)	Rank	Regiment			Work
Gibney	James	Sergeant Major	Royal Signals	2582457	91575	Brüx Coal miner
Gibson	John	Signalman	4th Parachute Brigade, Royal Signals	2933959	117437	AK 7011 Groß Düngen sugar beet factory
Gibson	Robert	Private	156th Battalion, Parachute Regiment	14509289	90773	Hertzberg demolition
Gick	Bernard Joseph	Lieutenant	1st Battalion, Parachute Regiment	186283	91009	
Gilbert	William Ernest	Private	3rd Battalion, Parachute Regiment Royal Army Medical Corps	7372770	93701	
Gilchrist	David Alexander	Major/T	11th Battalion, Parachute Regiment	95588	545	
Gilchrist	James Gibson	Private	156th Battalion, Parachute Regiment	14415465	975697	Rocsburg Paper factory
Gilchrist	William	Lance Corporal	7th Battalion, King's Own Scottish Borderers	14410114	140136	
Giles	Dennis	Private	16th Parachute Field Ambulance	14548345	118432	Uelzen railway
Giles	Jess	Private	2nd Battalion, South Staffordshire Regiment	1686196		Oderan straw fabric
Gill	Stanley Albert	Private	2nd Battalion, South Staffordshire Regiment	4209968		
Gillard	Owen William	Private	156th Battalion, Parachute Regiment	295319		Herzberg labouring
Gillespie	George Whyte	Private	10th Battalion, Parachute Regiment	1478056	90535	Dresden tramways
Gillespie	Stanley	Lieutenant	3rd Battalion, Parachute Regiment	273249	556	
Gillies	Peter	Private	7th Battalion, King's Own Scottish Borderers	3196959	89449	Brüx surface [coal mine]
Gillies	William	Private	1st Battalion, Border Regiment	1799012	92007	Dresden bomb damage
Gillow	Charles	Staff Sergeant	Glider Pilot Regiment	894370		
Girgan	James	Private	7th Battalion, King's Own Scottish Borderers	3191075	294539	Railway
Girvin	Robert	Staff Sergeant	Glider Pilot Regiment	7022767		
Gleave	William	Private	2nd Battalion, Parachute Regiment	3855379	118637	Lubeck wood felling
Gledhill	Tom	Private	1st Battalion, Parachute Regiment	14333598	117528	Algermissen

Family Name	Forename	Rank	Unit	Army number	POW number	All kommandos
Glenn	James Joseph	Driver	250th Airborne Light Company, Royal Army Service Corps	6984399	91784	Halle brick factory
Glenn	John	Private	1st Battalion, Border Regiment	14401972	118102	
Glennon	Thomas	Private	7th Battalion, King's Own Scottish Borderers	3191300		
Glover	George H	Private	10th Battalion, Parachute Regiment	3913168	89593	Brüx labouring
Glover	James	Staff Sergeant	Glider Pilot Regiment	6970561		
Godbold	John William	Private	1st Battalion, Parachute Regiment	6215765	92131	Camp 51 coal mine
Goddard	Lawrence George	Lance Corporal	250th Airborne Light Company, Royal Army Service Corps	200409	89943	Hallendorf kommando 7001 labourer
Godden	John Herbert	Private	1st Battalion, Parachute Regiment	912836		
Godden	Sidney James	Private	1st Battalion, Parachute Regiment	6352588		
Gofton	Andrew Kay	Private	16th Parachute Field Ambulance	7390953	93686	
Goldstein	Sidney	Private	7th Battalion, King's Own Scottish Borderers	1527851		
Goode	Eric Henry	Sapper	1st Parachute Squadron, Royal Engineers	2073137	118286	Kommando 7013 lead
Goodger	Osmond Geoffrey	Private	2nd Battalion, South Staffordshire Regiment	14295823	91674	Dresden road work
Goodrich	Horace William	Corporal	1st Parachute Brigade	81635		
Goodwin	Roger	Private	3rd Battalion, Parachute Regiment	14434753	90028	Plauen air raid shelters
Gordon	William Dalziel	Staff Sergeant	Glider Pilot Regiment	934643	118350	
Gordon	William James	Staff Sergeant	GHQ Liaison Regiment (Phantom)	5391601		
Gore	Denis Edmund	Private	4th Battalion, Dorset Regiment	14723664	14948	Mückenberg open cast coal mine
Gorman	Alfred	Private	1st Battalion, Border Regiment	3186358	117406	Dinklar kommando 7012

Surname	First name(s)	Rank	Unit			
Gough	Charles Frederick Howard	Major	1st Airborne Reconnaissance Squadron	31420	595	
Gough	Samuel	Private	Forward Observation Unit, Royal Artillery	981355	89226	Merseburg air raid shelter digging,
Gould	Jack	Private	156th Battalion, Parachute Regiment	14204155		Reinersdorf stone quarry
Goulding	Denis	Sergeant	1st Battalion, Border Regiment	3599543	18678	
Gower	Geoffrey Ernest	Private	1st Battalion, Parachute Regiment	14418468	91373	Boklen coal mining
Grainger	Frederick	Private	7th Battalion, King's Own Scottish Borderers	14416704	90637	
Grant	Alexander	Private	7th Battalion, King's Own Scottish Borderers	14210847	91393	
Grant	Anthony	Private	1st Battalion, Parachute Regiment	2939381		Eilenburg labouring
Grant	Gerard	Private	1st Battalion, Border Regiment	3607117	91473	Dresden demolition
Grant	Patrick	Private	156th Battalion, Parachute Regiment	2820322		Kleinleipisch laying railway lines
Grant	Richard Sydney	Staff Sergeant	Glider Pilot Regiment	6474934		
Grant	Robert Henry	Private	156th Battalion, Parachute Regiment	14418394		Plauen labouring
Gray	Frederick	Private	156th Battalion, Parachute Regiment	6980488		Dresden tramways
Gray	James	Private	1st Battalion, Parachute Regiment	14417442		Zwikau railway
Gray	John Robert	Private	2nd Battalion, Parachute Regiment	5835364		Kommando EI 114E Teutschenthal, Kommando EI 116 E Etzdorf
Gray	Joseph Patrick	Private	11th Battalion, Parachute Regiment	697843	91588	Limburg bomb damage, Seestadl road repairs, Brüz mining
Gray	Percy Norman	Private	1st Battalion, Border Regiment	3603654	92033	Zietz labouring
Gray	Robert	Driver	2nd Airlanding Anti-Tank Battery, Royal Artillery	1441987		Zwikau railway
Green	Alan Thomas	Lieutenant	1st Battalion, Border Regiment	247201	2177	

Family Name	Forename	Rank	Unit	Army number	POW number	All kommandos
Green	George	Private	2nd Battalion, South Staffordshire Regiment	7523335	90559	
Green	George Stanley	Lance Corporal	1st Battalion, Parachute Regiment	2929195		Halle REI 113 navvy
Green	James Webster	Private	4th Parachute Brigade HQ	14403355	118728	
Green	John	Driver	250th Airborne Light Company, Royal Army Service Corps	10698160	117845	Kommando 7013
Green	Paul James	Private	11th Battalion, Parachute Regiment	2930629	91996	
Green	Stanley Clifford	Aircraftman	Light Warning Unit No. 6080	1877382		
Green	Walter	Corporal	181st Airlanding Field Ambulance	7399587	77329	Teplitz IV C medical orderly
Green	William Henry	Gunner	1st Airlanding Light Regiment, Royal Artillery	14326093	75829	Falkenau Coal Mine
Greenall	John	Private	1st Battalion, Border Regiment	3606248	75398	Zwikau railway
Greenbaum	Frank Ashley	Sergeant	Glider Pilot Regiment	14417002		
Greenhill	Douglas Crump	Private	16th Parachute Field Ambulance	7368666	284148	
Greensill	Joseph	Signalman	1st Parachute Brigade, Royal Signals	5572988	90035	Zwikau railway
Greenslade	George Charles	Staff Sergeant	Glider Pilot Regiment	6086559	75462	
Gregg	Victor	Private	10th Battalion, Parachute Regiment	6913933	92043	Kommando 1124 Niedersedlitz general labour
Gregory	Nicholas	Driver	1st Airlanding Anti-Tank Battery, Royal Artillery	1526957	91295	
Grewcock	Walter Kenneth	Corporal	1st Parachute Brigade, Royal Signals	2591584	89179	

Surname	Forename	Rank	Unit	Number		Work
Grieveson	John	Signalman	Royal Signals	862338		395B carpentry
Griffin	Joseph	Private	10th Battalion, Parachute Regiment	5619645	90078	Hallendorf
Griffith	Thomas David	Corporal	1st Battalion, Parachute Regiment	1695912		
Griffith	William Gordon	Sergeant	Glider Pilot Regiment	4192348		
Griffiths	Alan	Private	4th Battalion, Dorset Regiment	14723668	26032	Zwickau railway labourer
Griffiths	George William	Sergeant	1st Battalion, Parachute Regiment	4194806		Varchentin Farm and forestry
Griffiths	John Douglas	Sergeant	Glider Pilot Regiment	2570423		
Griffiths	William Henry	Private	7th Battalion, King's Own Scottish Borderers	14648339	90580	Merseberg debris clearing
Grindrod	John	Private	1st Battalion, Border Regiment	1739180		Wood work
Gristwood	William John	Driver	1st Airlanding Anti-Tank Battery, Royal Artillery	1524980		
Grounsell	William Charles Francis	Private	156th Battalion, Parachute Regiment	5672628		Merseberg debris clearing
Grove	Philip Nigel	Captain/T	1st Battalion, Parachute Regiment	85684	597	
Grundy	Benjamin	Private	2nd Battalion, Parachute Regiment	4748425		Halle cook
Guidi	David	Private	7th Battalion, King's Own Scottish Borderers	14435105		Walwitz railway
Guyatt	Eric George	Lance Bombardier	1st Airlanding Light Regiment, Royal Artillery	935260	92081	Brüx mining
Guyon	George Edmund	Lieutenant	1st Battalion, Parachute Regiment	184696	2183	
Gwilliam	William Henry	Private	4th Battalion, Dorset Regiment	14207817		Großthiemig sand quarry
Hackett	Andrew Dennistoun	Lance Corporal	Provost Company, 1st Airborne Division	3320391	117430	
Hackett	Henry	Gunner	Forward Observation Unit, Royal Artillery	876593		

Family Name	Forename	Rank	Unit	Army number	POW number	All kommandos
Hadfield	Frank Charles	Gunner	1st Airlanding Light Regiment, Royal Artillery	14399107	117708	Hildesheim sugar beet factory
Hadfield	George Frederick	Sergeant	Glider Pilot Regiment	3531592	140112	
Hailes	George Greener	Private	11th Battalion, Parachute Regiment	4470510	117933	
Hale	George John	Private	1st Battalion, Parachute Regiment	5989841	92054	Dresden stone quarry
Hale	Roland John	Private	2nd Battalion, Parachute Regiment	5512642		Merseburg digging air raid shelters
Hales	Albert Charles	Lance Corporal	4th Battalion, Dorset Regiment	6014349	91914	
Hales	Clifford	Signalman	1st Parachute Brigade, Royal Signals	3782726	91929	Dresden sewer & refuse
Haley	John Michael William	Private	156th Battalion, Parachute Regiment	14391649		AK Me 41E clearing bomb damage
Halford	Fred Victor	Gunner	2nd Airlanding Anti-Tank Battery, Royal Artillery	4917794		Zwickau railway
Hall	Bertie Kenneth	Private	2nd Battalion, South Staffordshire Regiment	4032739	89187	Sudetenland open coal mine
Hall	David	Private	2nd Battalion, South Staffordshire Regiment	5124942	90257	AK 7005 labouring
Hall	Edward	Driver	250th Airborne Light Company, Royal Army Service Corps	213094	117844	
Hall	Harry George	Private	2nd Battalion, South Staffordshire Regiment	4928572	93202	Frywaldo brick works
Hall	Joseph Kenneth	Private	2nd Battalion, Parachute Regiment	975632		Kornotau coal mine, Baüx tram way
Hall	Joseph Stanley	Private	16th Parachute Field Ambulance	7366937		
Hall	Kevin Kenneth	Private	156th Battalion, Parachute Regiment	4344015		Dresden tarma workshop, Pirna wood clearing, Neundorf no work
Haller	Bernard John Frederick	Staff Sergeant	Glider Pilot Regiment	14291815		

Surname	First name	Rank	Regiment	Number	Number	Work
Hallett	Hugh Anthony	Private	2nd Battalion, Parachute Regiment	6465318	89693	Hallendorf kommando 7001 building
Halley-Frame	Thomas Sidney	Lance Corporal	3rd Battalion, Parachute Regiment	6013288	91532	
Halliday	Leslie Albert	Private	3rd Battalion, Parachute Regiment	5952211	118495	
Halliwell	Stanley	Sergeant, Lance	1st Parachute Squadron, Royal Engineers	2000549	89623	
Halmshaw	Raymond	Gunner	1st Airlanding Light Regiment, Royal Artillery	1155912	75562	Efenchlag timber yard
Halstead	Richard Angus	Lieutenant	1st Battalion, Parachute Regiment	203705	2198	
Hamer	Mal Dwyn	Lance Corporal	1st Parachute Brigade	6921343	75451	Komotau engineer
Hamilton	John	Gunner	1st Airlanding Light Regiment, Royal Artillery	14709137	75912	Clanylish coal mine
Hamilton	Reginald Thomas	Private	7th Battalion, King's Own Scottish Borderers	14437879		Merseburg tunnelling
Hamlett	Ernest	Private	1st Battalion, Border Regiment	4462122	118075	Bad Grund 7013
Hampton	Leslie Robert	Gunner	1st Airlanding Light Regiment, Royal Artillery	14249030	75969	Rochsburg (Sachs) Paper Mill
Hancock	Kenneth	Private	2nd Battalion, South Staffordshire Regiment	14642711		Maltch (sic) Coke Oven
Handforth	John Collin	Private	7th Battalion, King's Own Scottish Borderers	3325396	90714	M10 labouring Mittriedir
Hann	Alfred John	Signalman	Royal Signals	2384029	91967	Dresden clearing bomb damage
Hann	Stanley	Staff Sergeant	Glider Pilot Regiment	44692164	76307	
Hannah	Andrew	Private	1st Battalion, Border Regiment	3192167	140096	
Hannah	James Alexander	Private	1st Battalion, Border Regiment	3192337	117450	Groß Düngon sugar
Harbour	Frederick Spencer	Sergeant	10th Battalion, Parachute Regiment	6402134		
Hardie	John	Driver	112 Field Regiment, Royal Artillery	873582		Menzengraben salt mine

Family Name	Forename	Rank	Unit	Army number	POW number	All kommandos
Harding	Henry	Private	10th Battalion, Parachute Regiment	14623902	88779	Wurzmes Betty Schacht mine, Tschausch nr Brüx railway repairs
Harding	Kenneth Arthur Gordon	Private	2nd Battalion, Parachute Regiment	6148830		
Hardwick	John Geoffrey	Sergeant	Glider Pilot Regiment	3054186		
Hardy	Harry	Private	156th Battalion, Parachute Regiment	4343700	117894	
Hare	Ronald	Gunner	1st Airlanding Anti-Tank Battery, Royal Artillery	4698349	92013	Dresden clearing bomb damage
Hares	Myrddin Edward	Trooper	1st Airborne Reconnaissance Squadron	6852442	75683	U 12 Ziet
Hargrave	Francis Richard	Private	2nd Battalion, South Staffordshire Regiment	7013354	89576	Halle tunnelling
Hargreaves	Alan Wilson	Sergeant	Glider Pilot Regiment	1922641		
Harley	William Douglas	Lance Corporal	2nd Battalion, South Staffordshire Regiment	14202780	118289	Kmdo 7013 Bad Grund
Harlow	Albert Wiliam(?) Harrison	Major Reverend	Royal Army Chaplains' Department	131946	640	
Harper	Charles	Private	7th Battalion, King's Own Scottish Borderers	3190813	75984	Erfanslag joiner
Harper	Gordon Thomas	Private	2nd Battalion, South Staffordshire Regiment	14692209	17566	Gunnersdorf Forestry, Chemnitz Cement Works
Harper	John Everard	Lance Corporal	2nd Battalion, Parachute Regiment	497226	88485	Halle building air raid shelters, Merzurg building air raid shelters
Harris	Douglas George	Private	3rd Battalion, Parachute Regiment	3967311		Wurmes coal mine labourer

Harris	George William	Staff Sergeant	Army Physical Training Corps	3767430	89164	
Harris	James Phillip	Private	1st Battalion, Parachute Regiment	854121	117846	Hildesheim sugar factory
Harris	John Edward	Private	2nd Battalion, South Staffordshire Regiment	1786237	89999	L106 Lossnitz labourer
Harris	Kenneth Wesley	Private	10th Battalion, Parachute Regiment	14425014	80092	Hersburg AK 188 labouring
Harris	Norman	Lance Corporal	1st Parachute Brigade	83502		
Harris	Percy Victor	Private	4th Battalion, Dorset Regiment	5735127		Gleina G123 nr Zeitz pick and shovel
Harris	Ronald Maxwell	Sergeant	Parachute Regiment	911930	89342	
Harrison	Alan Aubrey	Private	3rd Battalion, Parachute Regiment	4624721	89838	Fallingbostel odd jobs
Harrison	Eric George	Private	1st Battalion, Border Regiment	14579662	175991	
Harrison	Ivan	Lance Corporal	1st Battalion, Border Regiment	3603444	91800	Brüx coal mine
Harrison	James William	Private	4th Parachute Brigade	4697029		Mittweida labouring
Harrison	Robert	Private	7th Battalion, King's Own Scottish Borderers	14210604	90725	
Harrison	Thomas	Private	3rd Battalion, Parachute Regiment	4273328	91739	Brüx mine
Harrop	James Edward	Private	4th Battalion, Dorset Regiment	1723369	25988	Zwikau railway
Hart	George Briggs	Private	7th Battalion, King's Own Scottish Borderers	1115868	75425	Railway
Hartley	Alfred Harold	Private	156th Battalion, Parachute Regiment	14413724	14069	Dresden tram maintenance in tram sheds, Pirna tree felling
Hartley	Benjamin	Driver	1st Airlanding Anti-Tank Battery, Royal Artillery	3712207		Brüx
Hartley	Kenneth Wrightson	Lance Corporal	9th Field Company, Royal Engineers Airborne	2017149	75812	Unterschwöditz coal outcrop railway
Hartley	William	Driver	1st Airlanding Anti-Tank Battery, Royal Artillery	1514908	919294	

Family Name	Forename	Rank	Unit	Army number	POW number	All kommandos
Hartman	John Victor	Corporal	2nd Battalion, Parachute Regiment	14231235		
Harvey	Arthur Edwin	Private	2nd Battalion, South Staffordshire Regiment	4918973	91640	lager 51, Nieder-Georgenthal Brüx
Harvey	Clifford	Private	181st Airlanding Field Ambulance	7263046	93691	
Harvey	Richard	Sapper	9th Field Company, Royal Engineers Airborne	2152263		Wallwitz railway
Harvey	Robert	Private	2nd Battalion, South Staffordshire Regiment	5192902	117318	
Harvey	Stanley Trevelyan	Private	11th Battalion, Parachute Regiment	865935	91530	Stalag XII A working on bombed houses
Harwood	Alfred George	Private	2nd Battalion, South Staffordshire Regiment	5391715		Working groups at Stalag 357
Haslam	Reginald Alfred	Bombardier	1st Airlanding Anti-Tank Battery, Royal Artillery	1115969		
Hastings	Benjamin	Driver	253rd Airborne Light Company, Royal Army Service Corps	993266	140078	
Hastings	Thomas Ernest	Corporal	Royal Army Medical Corps Para	7381574	118445	
Hatcher	Arthur	Corporal	16th Parachute Field Ambulance	7264821		
Hately	John Frederick	Private	156th Battalion, Parachute Regiment	6896966	221694	W 610 Zahna brick works – Stalag IV D, M79 Stalag IV F Mutschau surface coal mine
Haunch	George William Edgar	Lance Corporal	7th Battalion, King's Own Scottish Borderers	3325597	90713	Mittweida labourer
Hawkins	Benjamin Edward	Private	2nd Battalion, South Staffordshire Regiment	4922840	91639	Kirschau blanket factory yard gang, Löbau Cement factory yard gang, Löbau dye factory yard gang
Hawley	Ernest William	Lance Bombardier	1st Airlanding Anti-Tank Battery, Royal Artillery	1545256	92036	

Surname	First name(s)	Rank	Unit	Number	Number	Work/Location
Hayes	Frederick George	Sergeant	156th Battalion, Parachute Regiment	5249918		
Hayes	George	Driver	250th Airborne Light Company, Royal Army Service Corps	183151	75950	Leipzig saw mill, Leipzig post office
Hayes	Joseph	Private	11th Battalion, Parachute Regiment	2984852	92028	
Hayes	William Jack	Sergeant	156th Battalion, Parachute Regiment	5108162	52932	
Hayman	Ronald Walter	Private	3rd Battalion, Parachute Regiment	602704	117823	Sugar Beet factory Dinklar AK 7012
Haynes	John Henry	Private	11th Battalion, Parachute Regiment	7888568	75980	Zwikau demolition, Mühlbach quarry
Haysom	James	Signalman	1st Parachute Brigade, Royal Signals	2573777		
Hayward	Charles Henry	Private	7th Battalion, King's Own Scottish Borderers	14649274		Merseburg air raid shelters
Hayward	John Spencer Victor	Private	250th Airborne Light Company, Royal Army Service Corps	107853	140066	
Hayward	William Charles	Gunner	2nd Airlanding Anti-Tank Battery, Royal Artillery	781029	117653	
Headland	William George	Private	3rd Battalion, Parachute Regiment	1435227		Wurzmes coalmine, Brux benzine factory
Healey	Edwin	Staff Sergeant	Glider Pilot Regiment	3775315		
Heaney	Kevin Joseph	Private	Royal Army Ordnance Corps	14335886		Merseburg labourer
Heath	Joseph Henry	Private	10th Battalion, Parachute Regiment	945801		Dresden tramway repairs
Heaton	Joseph	Private	2nd Battalion, Parachute Regiment	7899398		Hallendorf labouring
Hedgecock	Leonard	Staff Sergeant	Glider Pilot Regiment	2584748		
Hedley	John	Private	11th Battalion, Parachute Regiment	4279331	75974	Erfenschlag E 42
Hellier	Wally James	Private	2nd Battalion, Parachute Regiment	6148710		Herzberg building
Henderson	Duncan	Private	156th Battalion, Parachute Regiment	853860		RE 113 Halle sewage drains

Family Name	Forename	Rank	Unit	Army number	POW number	All kommandos
Hendry	John	Gunner	1st Airlanding Light Regiment, Royal Artillery	877914	118044	Radgrund Mines
Hendy	Arthur Sydney	Lance Corporal	1st Parachute Squadron, Royal Engineers	1874248		Seestadtl mining, Brüx railway building
Henley	Reginald French	Private	10th Battalion, Parachute Regiment	5568074	89389	Halle Rei 113 forestry
Hepworth	Jack	Private	156th Battalion, Parachute Regiment	7263996	90926	
Herbert	Allan George	Private	2nd Battalion, South Staffordshire Regiment	4915809	118538	Forestry
Herbert	Henry Charles	Private	11th Battalion, Parachute Regiment	14405294		Dresden tramways
Hewerdine	Walter	Driver	1st Airlanding Anti-Tank Battery, Royal Artillery	1527073		Brux surface coal mine
Hewish	Robert Harvey	Lance Corporal	4th Parachute Brigade, Royal Signals	6469323		Me 40E
Heyes	Stanley	Signalman	1st Parachute Brigade, Royal Signals	4132010	118696	Velzen railway repairs
Hickman	Thomas Victor	Lance Corporal	1st Airlanding Anti-Tank Battery, Royal Artillery	893124	75855	Unterschwöditz
Hicks	Albert Edward	Driver	63 Company, Royal Army Service Corps	14318934	91432	Trebsen paper factory
Higginbotham	James	Staff Sergeant	Glider Pilot Regiment	905927		
Higginbottom	Ernest	Lance Corporal	2nd Battalion, Parachute Regiment	1798347		Wurzmes demolition, Tschausch surface mine
Higgins	Geoffrey	Sergeant	Glider Pilot Regiment	7911243		
Higginson	Walter	Private	11th Battalion, Parachute Regiment	3452978	117687	AK 7011 Groß Düngen
Hill	Cecil	Corporal	2nd Battalion, Parachute Regiment	6401664		Brux general labour
Hill	David McNair	Private	7th Battalion, King's Own Scottish Borderers	14210611	75837	Trebsen Muldie paper
Hill	Francis Edwin	Private	3rd Battalion, Parachute Regiment	5389890	75327	Komotau railway

Surname	First name	Rank	Unit	Number	Number	Location
Hill	Henry Samuel	Driver	253rd Airborne Light Company, Royal Army Service Corps	5949386		
Hill	Leslie Thomas	Private	2nd Battalion, Parachute Regiment	5391983	117847	7001 Groß Dungeon
Hill	Norris Williams	Private	1st Parachute Brigade	11007637		Halle camp carpenter
Hill	William	Lance Corporal	1st Airlanding Brigade	14283573	91724	Dresden labourer
Hill	William	Lance Corporal	16th Parachute Field Ambulance	7264147		
Hill	William	Private	Royal Army Medical Corps	7376940	75664	
Hillman	Albert Edward	Private	2nd Battalion, Parachute Regiment	14207392	117308	
Hills	James Alfred	Private	7th Battalion, King's Own Scottish Borderers	2883680		Dresden factory
Hilton	Harry	Lance Corporal	4th Battalion, Dorset Regiment	5962248	26050	Falkaneu coal mine
Hilton	Wallace George	Private	7th Battalion, King's Own Scottish Borderers	1542155	90499	188 Herzburg
Hindmarsh	Henry	Private	2nd Battalion, Parachute Regiment	4461927		Deutschlandsender Herzberg labouring
Hinsley	William Alfred	Private	4th Battalion, Dorset Regiment	1584800	14223	Großthiemig labouring
Hippisley	William James	Company Quartermaster Sergeant Major	156th Battalion, Parachute Regiment	5671303		
Hoare	Leonard Leslie	Private	2nd Battalion, Parachute Regiment	6351050	90672	Frieberg factory
Hobson	Frank	Private	7th Battalion, King's Own Scottish Borderers	14415862	75921	Großthiemig sand quarry
Hockley	Ernest Harold	Sergeant	Glider Pilot Regiment	2323238		
Hoddinott	Brinkley	Private	11th Battalion, Parachute Regiment	14284895	117763	
Hodge	Donald Hugh	Private	1st Battalion, Border Regiment	3866321	15231	Döbeln labouring
Hodges	Joseph	Private	Royal Army Ordnance Corps	10573941		Dresden Bomb damage repair
Hodgkins	Basil Royston	Lieutenant	4th Battalion, Dorset Regiment	315216	583	
Hodgson	Frank Douglas	Corporal	1st Airborne Provost Company	4537324	15450	Frieberg lead mines

Family Name	Forename	Rank	Unit	Army number	POW number	All kommandos
Hodgson	Geoffrey	Private	156th Battalion, Parachute Regiment	14291625		Floßmühle wood clearing
Hogan	Michael Patrick William	Private	10th Battalion, Parachute Regiment	14429149	75748	
Hogger	Albert Cornelius	Lance Corporal	4th Battalion, Dorset Regiment	5888643	17538	
Hogwood	Ralph Herbert	Sergeant	7th Battalion, King's Own Scottish Borderers	5052938	88746	
Holcombe	John	Private	3rd Battalion, Parachute Regiment	2089989	91616	Dresden clearing bomb damage
Holden	James	Private	Parachute Regiment	3458392	92147	Merseburg canal building
Holding	Thomas Wilfred	Private	1st Battalion, Border Regiment	3782686		Coal mining
Holdsworth	Kenneth	Lance Corporal	181st Airlanding Field Ambulance	7399450		
Hole	Edward Stanley	Private	3rd Battalion, Parachute Regiment	5672174		Rei 113 Halle laying sewer pipes
Holgate	Norman	Private	4th Battalion, Dorset Regiment	1767939		
Holland	Donald Kitson	Sergeant	2nd Battalion, South Staffordshire Regiment	4921819		
Holland	James	Driver	Royal Artillery	14321655	75880	Unterswodurzje coal mine
Hollands	Frank Richard	Private	156th Battalion, Parachute Regiment	6104597		Röhrsdorf timber yard
Hollinshead	Douglas	Private	11th Battalion, Parachute Regiment	844968	118171	Bad Grund electrician
Hollis	William	Private	1st Battalion, Parachute Regiment	14367454	118051	Bad Grund lead mine 7013
Holmes	Robert	Private	1st Battalion, Parachute Regiment	5891275	92008	Brux coal mine
Holmes	William John	Private	11th Battalion, Parachute Regiment	2821375	140126	
Holt	Arthur	Private	7th Battalion, King's Own Scottish Borderers	3716068	90489	Dresden general fitter
Holt	Ronald Charles Neville	Private	2nd Battalion, Parachute Regiment	2766005	93727	Brunswik railway

378

Surname	First names	Rank	Unit	Number	Camp no.	Notes
Hooker	Gerald Sidney Herbert	Sergeant	Glider Pilot Regiment	2600495	117490	
Hooper	James Michael	Staff Sergeant	Glider Pilot Regiment	2584037		
Hooper	Tom	Private	1st Battalion, Border Regiment	3599167	92110	Dresden labour
Hooson	Gwilyn	Private	7th Battalion, King's Own Scottish Borderers	14374202	89535	Falkenau mines
Hope	James	Private	2nd Battalion, South Staffordshire Regiment	14340464	91504	Sudatenland miner
Hope	John William	Driver	250th Airborne Light Company, Royal Army Service Corps	241767	90820	ME 41E Merseberg bomb craters debris
Hope	Thomas Rogers	Lance Corporal	1st Airborne Provost Company	6206756		
Hope-Jones	Ronald Christopher	Lieutenant	1st Battalion, Border Regiment	187403	602	
Hopkins	Kenneth Arthur	Private	181st Airlanding Field Ambulance	14672266		Jessen on Elster
Hornbuckle		Private	4th Battalion, Dorset Regiment	4922862	26054	Enfenslaigh cement works
Horne	George Minta	Signalman	1st Parachute Brigade, Royal Signals	2598143	91952	Dresden bomb debris, Zwickau railway bomb damage
Horne	Robert William Peter	Private	156th Battalion, Parachute Regiment	6087103	90562	
Horsburgh	Robert	Corporal	7th Battalion, King's Own Scottish Borderers	3192345	9133rd4	
Horsfield	James	Private	10th Battalion, Parachute Regiment	14632609	17	Dobeln stone quarry
Horsley	James	Private	11th Battalion, Parachute Regiment	6010893		7013 Bad Grund lead mining
Horton	Charles Henry	Private	16th Parachute Field Ambulance	7357394	93681	
Horton	John	Sergeant	Glider Pilot Regiment	14413159	21	
Hosker	Thomas Herbert	Private	7th Battalion, King's Own Scottish Borderers	14573434		Dresden bomb damage
Hotine	Robert Edward	Driver	4th Parachute Brigade, Royal Signals	2600066	90802	Dresden AK 133rd3 garage labourer

Family Name	Forename	Rank	Unit	Army number	POW number	All kommandos
Houghton	Norman Edwin	Private	11th Battalion, Parachute Regiment	996560		Dresden clearing bomb debris
Hounslow	Edward Charles	Private	3rd Battalion, Parachute Regiment	5502730	89562	Re1 113 Halle air raid shelter building, Me 40E Merseburg air raid shelter building
Hounslow	Harold	Private	2nd Battalion, Oxfordshire and Buckinghamshire Light Infantry Regiment	5385947		
Howard	Ernest	Corporal	156th Battalion, Parachute Regiment	5884952	90688	Basepohl farm
Howard	Harold	Lance Corporal	4th Parachute Squadron, Royal Engineers	1904106	117582	AK 7011 Groß Düngen
Howard	John James	Lance Corporal	1st Battalion, Parachute Regiment	3598966	89855	NCOs camp Fallingbostel general
Howard	Leslie Frederick	Private	1st Battalion, Parachute Regiment	15327223		
Howard	Stanley Victor	Private	2nd Battalion, Parachute Regiment	6029634		
Howard	Thomas Henry	Private	10th Battalion, Parachute Regiment	14417045		Halle forestry
Howe	Henry	Private	181st Airlanding Field Ambulance	14679982		Jessen bomb damage on railway
Howell	Derek Martin	Gunner	1st Airlanding Anti-Tank Battery, Royal Artillery	5835348	118694	Ulzen railway repair
Howells	John	Lance Corporal	1st Airborne Provost Company	4078592	118226	Bad Grund 7013
Howes	Raymond Cuthbert	Lance Corporal	2nd Battalion, South Staffordshire Regiment	4919552	118205	7011 Bad Grund lead mines, 7009 Lohnde railway
Howson	Victor	Private	11th Battalion, Parachute Regiment	14499916	75690	Elsterwerda railway, Mochau labouring
Hoyer Millar MC	Francis Kinglake	Captain	2nd Battalion, Parachute Regiment	85213	90872	
Hoyland	Frank Charles	Private	4th Parachute Brigade HQ	14292326		Dresden tram

Surname	First name	Rank	Regiment	Number	Number	Work
Hoyle	Kenneth H	Private	7th Battalion, King's Own Scottish Borderers	14424034		
Hoyne	William	Sergeant	1st Battalion, Border Regiment	3596668	140120	
Hudson	Arthur George	Private	2nd Battalion, Parachute Regiment	1507796	75409	Komotau railway
Hudson	Francis	Lance Corporal	2nd Battalion, South Staffordshire Regiment	5046543	91637	Brux Coal mining
Hudson	Frederick Philip	Sergeant	Glider Pilot Regiment	14218054		
Hudson	George Ernest	Sapper	9th Field Company, Royal Engineers	2124141	75840	Zeitz U12 surface coal mine
Huggett	William Arthur	Lance Corporal	1st Parachute Brigade, Royal Signals	5572488	89408	Salt mine near Halle
Hughes	Anthony Cecil	Private	3rd Battalion, Parachute Regiment	5125630	77095	Brux coal mining
Hughes	Edward	Lance Corporal	1st Battalion, Border Regiment	3596264	75689	Nr Leipzig railway
Hughes	Ernest	Corporal	11th Battalion, Parachute Regiment	3718667	140294	
Hughes	Ernest Edward	Sapper	1st Parachute Squadron, Royal Engineers	14644896	140116	
Hughes	Gwyn	Gunner	2nd Airlanding Anti-Tank Battery, Royal Artillery	14519116		Plauen
Hughes	Michael Frederick	Private	2nd Battalion, South Staffordshire Regiment	5891442		Benzine Brux Robert Stacht, Chouseche Digging
Hughes	Peter	Private	7th Battalion, King's Own Scottish Borderers	14212001		Dresden waterworks and trams
Hughes	Richard Francis	Private	Parachute Regiment	4127229	75676	Ortrand sand works
Hughes	Thomas	Private	2nd Battalion, Parachute Regiment	3969834	91184	Falkeneu underground coal mine
Hughes	Thomas	Private	11th Battalion, Parachute Regiment	4127126	117585	Hildesheim sugar beet
Hughes	William Horace	Private	2nd Battalion, South Staffordshire Regiment	14316562	92212	RE 133rd Halle brickworks
Hull	Charles Cecil	Private	181st Airlanding Field Ambulance	7387687		Worked in hospitals at all above
Hume	William	Private	7th Battalion, King's Own Scottish Borderers	3190812	90486	Komotau locomotive AK 0395 A

Family Name	Forename	Rank	Unit	Army number	POW number	All kommandos
Humpherson	Stanley Richmond	Private	7th Battalion, King's Own Scottish Borderers	3197733	90684	Kd Arb 1124 Dresden soap factory
Humphreys	William	Private	2nd Battalion, Parachute Regiment	5835367	117578	
Hunt	Harry James	Private	2nd Battalion, Parachute Regiment	6848386		Komotau working in railway workshops repairing boiler pipes for locomotives
Hunt	William	Private	1st Battalion, Border Regiment	4626714	91979	Dresden bomb debris
Hunter	Edward Donaldson	Private	7th Battalion, King's Own Scottish Borderers	14204706	117703	Hallendorf labouring
Hunter	Robert	Private	156th Battalion, Parachute Regiment	3128295	89547	Jessen railway repairs
Hunton	Alfred Frederick	Gunner	2nd Airlanding Anti-Tank Battery, Royal Artillery	1094022	90896	AK 58 Wallwitzl
Hurst	Norman Frank	Private	1st Battalion, Parachute Regiment	4123041	91749	Sudetenland coal mine
Husband	Desmond John	Private	156th Battalion, Parachute Regiment	14519026		Me 41 E clearing bomb damage
Hutchinson	Ronald	Private	2nd Battalion, Parachute Regiment	4455745	89908	Hallendorf, Barum – also Herman Göring Works
Hutton	James Brownlie	Private	156th Battalion, Parachute Regiment	14350633	90762	Dresden repair work on tramcars and labouring with elect and water supply
Hutton	James Gordon	Private	Royal Army Medical Corps	7365933	90826	
Hutton	Matthew	Private	2nd Battalion, Parachute Regiment	4467557	75411	Trebsen (Wurzen) bricklayer paper mill
Hutton	William Alfred	Private	2nd Battalion, South Staffordshire Regiment	4923158	25554	Freyberg (sic) timber Freiberg paper?
Hyams	Meyer John	Private	10th Battalion, Parachute Regiment	6410376	117971	

Surname	First name	Rank	Regiment	No. 1	No. 2	Work/Camp
Hyde	Thomas	Private	7th Battalion, King's Own Scottish Borderers	975812	90578	Grunau/Dobeln paper factory
Hyland	Thomas	Sapper	Royal Engineers	2004091		
Hymes	Douglas	Private	1st Battalion, Parachute Regiment	7402136		
Hyslop	Eric	Sergeant	7th Battalion, King's Own Scottish Borderers	3190541	75874	
Infield	Gerald Maurice	Lieutenant	3rd Battalion, Parachute Regiment	174451	522	
Ingham	Herbert	Private	156th Battalion, Parachute Regiment	14382007	117977	AK 7012 Dinklar
Ingham	Hubert Leslie	Private	1st Battalion, Border Regiment	3718775	975357	AK 395A Komotau wagon repairs
Ingham	Ralph Taylor	Private	11th Battalion, Parachute Regiment	147330064		Üfingen Brunswick tunnelling
Ingle	John Ernest	Driver	Royal Army Service Corps	14506862		Railway Stalag IV C
Ingram	Stanley	Lance Bombardier	1st Airlanding Light Regiment, Royal Artillery	14306817	75871	Etzdorf Ei 116E railway work
Install	Alfred Charles	Sergeant	Glider Pilot Regiment	5734412		
Ireland	Albert	Private	181st Airlanding Field Ambulance	7372142	140054	
Isherwood	Reginald	Sergeant	1st Battalion, Parachute Regiment	893585		Hanover repairing bombed railway at Hanover – Linden
Ives	Andrews Robert	Private	11th Battalion, Parachute Regiment	5576559	117581	Dinklar
Ivey	Alan Wilfred	Staff Sergeant	Glider Pilot Regiment	1480721		
Izzard	Cyril James	Private	2nd Battalion, Parachute Regiment	6029653	91397	
Jackson	Albert	Private	156th Battalion, Parachute Regiment	4278961		Flossmuhle Saxony Tree felling
Jackson	Arnold Phillip	Private	181st Airlanding Field Ambulance	14275901		
Jackson	Arthur	Private	Royal Army Service Corps	10694198		Lubtich Brickworks. Blacksmith
Jackson	Arthur Henry	Private	133rd Parachute Field Ambulance	7357319	90690	
Jackson	Charles James	Sergeant	Glider Pilot Regiment	2583498	76300	

Family Name	Forename	Rank	Unit	Army number	POW number	All kommandos
Jackson	Empsall	Private	1st Parachute Brigade	2042543		Dresden bomb damage and navvying
Jackson	Fred Duncan	Private	10th Battalion, Parachute Regiment	81614	117524	Hallendorf iron plate AK 7001
Jackson	John Henry	Corporal	7th Battalion, King's Own Scottish Borderers	4750981		
Jackson	Peter Joseph	Private	181st Airlanding Field Ambulance	7260275		Worked English POW hospital at Stalag IVB
Jackson	Sydney	Lance Corporal	2nd Battalion, South Staffordshire Regiment	4124815		Halle building air raid shelters, Merseburg building air raid shelters
Jackson	William Marshall	Private	7th Battalion, King's Own Scottish Borderers	3194093	117852	7012 Dinklar sugar beet factory
James	Alec Arnold	Sergeant	Glider Pilot Regiment	5891664	140210	
James	Arthur Bert	Private	21st Independent Parachute Company	7022654	75364	
James	David William Mervyn	Staff Sergeant	Glider Pilot Regiment	944489		
James	Edward Henry	Private	21st Independent Parachute Company	1602953	75365	
James	George	Private	2nd Battalion, Parachute Regiment	6153238	89279	Sudetenland – Brüx
James	Joseph James	Lance Corporal	2nd Battalion, South Staffordshire Regiment	4929053	75839	
James	Robert John	Private	2nd Battalion, South Staffordshire Regiment	6095111		Fallingbostel camp repairs
James	Stanley Ernest George	Private	11th Battalion, Parachute Regiment	14051444	52921	Menzengraben 123B
Jamieson	Peter Dunlop	Sergeant	156th Battalion, Parachute Regiment	2884343		
Janovsky	Roland	Private	2nd Battalion, Parachute Regiment	6848274		Rei 113 bomb damage labouring

Surname	First name(s)	Rank	Unit	Service number	POW number	Work
Jarvis	Ronald Eric	Sergeant	11th Battalion, Parachute Regiment	6292520	92145	
Jeavons	Sidney Thomas	Private	2nd Battalion, South Staffordshire Regiment	4923382		Brüx coal mining
Jebbitt	David Owen	Private	181st Airlanding Field Ambulance	7265533		
Jeffery	Norman Dennis	Private	4th Battalion, Dorset Regiment	14592676	17581	Chemnitz coal shovelling
Jeffries	John Patrick	Signalman	Royal Signals	2379610	117314	Groß Düngon
Jenkins	Griffith	Private	1st Battalion, Parachute Regiment	929213	91462	Zwickau railway
Jenkins	Kenneth George	Gunner	1st Airlanding Anti-Tank Battery, Royal Artillery	14384421	75957	
Jenkins	Ronald William	Lance Corporal	156th Battalion, Parachute Regiment	7437345		Me 41E Merseburg
Jenkinson	Horace	Private	2nd Battalion, Oxfordshire and Buckinghamshire Light Infantry Regiment	5891203	920009	Doesden general labour
Jenkinson	Wilfred	Driver	223 Company, Royal Army Service Corps	3860067		Ordrun
Jervis	Harold	Private	2nd Battalion, South Staffordshire Regiment	5067977		Wurzmes AK 50 demolition, Tschause 3 labouring
Jessup	Geoffrey Frederick George	Private	156th Battalion, Parachute Regiment	6460489	118209	Bad Grund lead mine
Jeuchner	Albert George	Private	2nd Battalion, Parachute Regiment	6352988	91162	Döbeln paper factory
John	John Edward	Private	Royal Army Medical Corps	7357904	88911	Jesson railway
Johnson	Arthur	Private	2nd Battalion, South Staffordshire Regiment	1568699	92045	Me 49 E clearing bomb damage repairing sewers
Johnson	Douglas Frederick William	Private	2nd Battalion, South Staffordshire Regiment	867876		Wurzmes coal mining, Wurzmes demolition, Brüx benzine factory, railway
Johnson	Horace	Private	2nd Battalion, South Staffordshire Regiment	4923187	9190	Reinersdorf stone quarry

Family Name	Forename	Rank	Unit	Army number	POW number	All kommandos
Johnson	Peter	Private	1st Battalion, Parachute Regiment	5388969	89242	Merseburg air raid shelters
Johnston	Harold	Private	4th Battalion, Dorset Regiment	3709037	17569	Etzdorf labouring railway, Unteroblingen, labouring railway
Johnstone	Robert	Private	Parachute Regiment	4279221	117304	Hallendorf railway repairs. Unloading steel
Johnstone	William Tait	Signalman	1st Parachute Brigade, Royal Signals	2378622		Kleinleipisch, surface coal mine
Jolly	Arthur Charles Edward	Private	156th Battalion, Parachute Regiment	320647		Z 131 Railway Zwickau, P 5 Penig sand quarry
Jolly	Frank Ronald	Signalman	1st Airlanding Light Regiment, Royal Artillery	14280533	92067	Brüx miner
Jonas	John James	Corporal	2nd Battalion, Parachute Regiment	1876407	93725	
Jones	Alfred Redgewell	Corporal	2nd Battalion, South Staffordshire Regiment	4922888	89509	
Jones	Anthony	Private	2nd Battalion, Parachute Regiment	1595342	117692	Hildemsheim sugar factory
Jones	Arthur	Corporal	1st Battalion, Parachute Regiment	3957377		
Jones	Conway Thomas	Sapper	1st Parachute Squadron, Royal Engineers	1909450		
Jones	Cyril	Gunner	2nd Airlanding Anti-Tank Battery, Royal Artillery	14319790	91777	Merseburg sewer repair
Jones	Dewi Llewellyn	Sergeant	1st Airlanding Brigade, Royal Signals	2362597	91555	
Jones	Donald	Sergeant	Glider Pilot Regiment	14395807		
Jones	Edgar	Driver	1st Airlanding Anti-Tank Battery, Royal Artillery	11053201	118272	Bad Grund miner
Jones	Ernest George	Lance Corporal	21st Independent Parachute Company	7360854	117260	Hallendorf ak 7001

Surname	First name(s)	Rank	Unit	Number	Camp no.	Work
Jones	George	Sapper	1st Parachute Squadron, Royal Engineers	2193549	91490	Kirschau labourer, Weissonborne labourer
Jones	Harry Thomas	Private	1st Battalion, Parachute Regiment	5192697		Johnsdorf mine work
Jones	Howard Franklyn	Lance Corporal	16th Parachute Field Ambulance	7518016	89789	
Jones	Hugh	Private	10th Battalion, Parachute Regiment	4199324	140154	
Jones	John	Private	1st Battalion, Parachute Regiment	14418927		Waldheim paper factory
Jones	John Alfred	Gunner	2nd Airlanding Anti-Tank Battery, Royal Artillery	14281117	91703	Brüx coal mining
Jones	John Campbell	Signalman	4th Parachute Brigade, Royal Signals	324396	77367	Floha N90 Railway
Jones	John Richard	Private	156th Battalion, Parachute Regiment	14316790	75691	Halbersdorf railway (coaling)
Jones	Peter	Private	2nd Battalion, Parachute Regiment	3388690	52922	
Jones	Robert	Sapper	Royal Engineers	5733483	88932	Merseburg building air raid shelters
Jones	Robert Hobdell	Sergeant	2nd Battalion, Parachute Regiment	4975220	88902	
Jones	Robert John	Corporal	2nd Battalion, South Staffordshire Regiment	5886650		
Jones	Stephen Samuel	Private	156th Battalion, Parachute Regiment	5575919	21903	Eger coal mine
Jones	Thomas Edward	Driver	250th Airborne Light Company, Royal Army Service Corps	277972	91094	Dresden
Jones	Thomas Leslie	Private	3rd Battalion, Parachute Regiment	3911512		Erfenshlag Timber Yard
Jones	Wilfred Richard George	Private	181st Airlanding Field Ambulance	7364540	90558	
Jones	William Arthur	Driver	Royal Army Service Corps	14435505	91795	Sudetenland miner
Jordan	William Edwin	Private	4th Battalion, Dorset Regiment	14227233	17594	
Jorden	Leonard	Private	2nd Battalion, South Staffordshire Regiment	1655164	91558	Borna colliers
Jorimann	Reginald Percy	Private	2nd Battalion, South Staffordshire Regiment	5504266		Teutschenthal salt mine

Family Name	Forename	Rank	Unit	Army number	POW number	All kommandos
Josephs	Daniel	Private	156th Battalion, Parachute Regiment	6849171		
Jukes	George William	Signalman	1st Parachute Brigade, Royal Signals	2069539		
Kane	John Patrick	Private	2nd Battalion, Parachute Regiment	4690202		Dresden timber work
Kane	Lawrence Patrick	Lieutenant	7th Battalion, King's Own Scottish Borderers	482	569	
Kay	George Edward	Private	3rd Battalion, Parachute Regiment	4974938	88758	
Kay	John	Private	Parachute Regiment	915487	89731	Fallingbostel brick layer
Kaye	Stanley Lawrence	Captain	16th Parachute Field Ambulance	246299	618	
Kean	Alexander Brown	Lance Corporal	1st Parachute Brigade, Royal Signals	2699469		Zwickau railway
Kearns	James Thomas	Private	1st Battalion, Parachute Regiment	4808363	89495	AK Re 113 Halle forestry
Keddie	John	Private	10th Battalion, Parachute Regiment	2758803		Sudetenland labourer
Keeler	Norman Arthur	Sergeant, Lance	4th Parachute Squadron, Royal Engineers	2031950	21705	
Keenan	James Mullan	Private	156th Battalion, Parachute Regiment	3189614	118364	
Keens	Norman	Private	2nd Battalion, Parachute Regiment	14310355		Wurzmes surface coal mine, Brüx tramway
Kellett	Edgar	Trooper	1st Airborne Reconnaissance Squadron	14253215	75684	Unterschwöditz surface coal mine
Kelly	Charles	Gunner	1st Airlanding Anti-Tank Battery, Royal Artillery	14504062	75468	Komotau engine sheds
Kelly	Dennis	Private	2nd Battalion, Parachute Regiment	4616630		133rd3 kommando Dresden garage

Surname	Forename	Rank	Regiment	Service no.	POW no.	Notes
Kelly	James	Lance Corporal	10th Battalion, Parachute Regiment	2930968	90505	Komotau labourer
Kelly	Patrick Joseph	Sergeant	1st Battalion, Parachute Regiment	7012461		
Kemley	Peter William	Private	2nd Battalion, Parachute Regiment	14584652	118154	
Kennedy	George	Lance Corporal	7th Battalion, King's Own Scottish Borderers	2930509		Brüx coal
Kennedy	Simon James	Private	11th Battalion, Parachute Regiment	5885331	92158	
Kennedy	Wilfred	Private	156th Battalion, Parachute Regiment	2877369	90579	Merseberg clearing debris
Kenworthy	Joseph	Private	1st Battalion, Border Regiment	4467370	118066	Bad Grund mines
Kerr	Charles Cole	Private	7th Battalion, King's Own Scottish Borderers	3188450		
Kerr	Harry Alexander	Trooper	1st Airborne Reconnaissance Squadron	7020098	118345	
Kerr	James Edward	Sergeant, Lance	1st Battalion, Border Regiment	3602996	118836	
Kerswell	William John	Sergeant	Royal Army Medical Corps	7523088	77338	
Keys	Harry	Private	2nd Battalion, South Staffordshire Regiment	4208715		7001 kommando railway work
Kidd	James	Private	7th Battalion, King's Own Scottish Borderers	3194226	89317	Merseburg labouring air raid shelters
Kidds	Charles Frederick	Private	2nd Battalion, Parachute Regiment	7021470	294155	Brüx
Kidley	Jack	Private	2nd Battalion, South Staffordshire Regiment	14441082		Dresden bomb damage
Kilbryde	George Howard	Sergeant	Glider Pilot Regiment	4922900		
Kill	William	Sergeant, Lance	1st Airlanding Anti-Tank Battery, Royal Artillery	1107611	89415	
Killick	John Edward	Captain	89 Parachute Security Section	137467	628	
Kilner	Melville Gordon	Corporal	1st Battalion, Parachute Regiment	3910374		

Family Name	Forename	Rank	Unit	Army number	POW number	All kommandos
King	Charles	Private	156th Battalion, Parachute Regiment	5338048	75537	Merseburg Brickwork
King	Charles Davis	Lance Corporal	1st Airborne Reconnaissance Squadron	5347510	118626	
King	David John	Private	1st Battalion, Parachute Regiment	6148512	92159	
King	Frank Douglas	Captain	11th Battalion, Parachute Regiment	138204	585	
King	George Richard	Private	Parachute Regiment	5510137		Floßmühle paper mill tree felling
King	Joseph Bertie	Corporal	16th Parachute Field Ambulance	7347201	118427	
King	Leonard William	Signalman	4th Parachute Brigade, Royal Signals	2588983		Döbeln labouring
Kirk	Duncan	Private	7th Battalion, King's Own Scottish Borderers	14211437	91487	Z 131 Zwickau railway
Kirk	George Milton	Sapper	1st Parachute Squadron, Royal Engineers	1948638		Wallwitz stone breaking on railway
Kirk	Stanley Harry	Lance Corporal	16th Parachute Field Ambulance	7349841		Erfenschlag wood factory
Kirlew	Alfred Harry	Private	156th Battalion, Parachute Regiment	405893		Dresden stone quarry
Kirlow	Alfred	Private	2nd Battalion, Parachute Regiment	14437450		Halle REI 113
Kitchener	Robert Anthony	Private	2nd Battalion, Parachute Regiment	6145647		
Kite	George Anthony	Sergeant, Lance	2nd Battalion, South Staffordshire Regiment	5498368		Basepohl
Klamph	Samuel	Private	156th Battalion, Parachute Regiment	5953101		Merseburg carpentering
Knapp	Frederick Frank	Private	11th Battalion, Parachute Regiment	14670639		Chemnitz labour in factory
Knight	James	Private	2nd Battalion, Parachute Regiment	5735190	117865	7011 Groß Düngen
Knight	James Downie	Private	7th Battalion, King's Own Scottish Borderers	14211438	75939	Lauchhammer brickette fabrication

Knight	Joseph William	Sapper	9th Field Company, Royal Engineers Airborne	2058280	91610	Brüx Fitter in mine
Knight	Lawrence Alfred	Sergeant, Lance	2nd Battalion, Parachute Regiment	7016898		
Knight	Leonard Davies	Signalman	1st Parachute Brigade, Royal Signals	14200119	89308	Halle Rei113 labouring on air raid shelters
Knox	William Hutchinson	Sergeant	Glider Pilot Regiment	11000594	1070	
Lacey	Sidney Herbert	Sergeant, Lance	2nd Battalion, South Staffordshire Regiment	4917620	89474	
Laidlaw	Robert James	Private	7th Battalion, King's Own Scottish Borderers	3194137	140238	
Laing	Herbert Alexander	Private	21st Independent Parachute Company	879322	118030	Ülzen
Laing	Robert	Private	1st Battalion, Parachute Regiment	888389		
Laing	Robert Hutt	Lance Bombardier	2nd Airlanding Anti-Tank Battery, Royal Artillery	14554942	91695	Kirschau blanket factory, Dresden farm work, Dresden Tin factory
Lakin	Bernard Lamplugh	Private	Royal Army Medical Corps	7522252	88910	
Lamb	Lionel Edward	Private	10th Battalion, Parachute Regiment	1806297	117689	Dinklar sugar beet
Lancaster	Alexander Albert	Corporal	9th Field Company, Royal Engineers Airborne	1899732		
Lancaster	Clarke Albert	Corporal	Parachute Regiment	4389325	117978	
Lancaster	Joseph	Private	11th Battalion, Parachute Regiment	935934		Rei 113
Lane	Henry Sidney	Private	181st Airlanding Field Ambulance	7384160		Jessen railway
Lane	Philip George Oliver	Corporal	1st Parachute Squadron, Royal Engineers	2009968		
Lang	Robert	Private	1st Battalion, Border Regiment	3606642	117504	Ülzen railway repairs
Langford	Alfred Joseph	Private	2nd Battalion, South Staffordshire Regiment	4919269		

Family Name	Forename	Rank	Unit	Army number	POW number	All kommandos
Langford	John Adair	Captain	Forward Observation Unit, Royal Artillery	158269	90871	
Langford	Samuel	Private	2nd Battalion, Parachute Regiment	5952886	91076	Hemsburge sand pit
Lasenby	James Joseph	Lieutenant	1st Battalion, Parachute Regiment	297337	91000	
Lashmar	Reginald Douglas	Private	156th Battalion, Parachute Regiment	6846980		AK 181 blanket factory, AK Z 131 railway
Latto	James	Lance Corporal	1st Battalion, Parachute Regiment	6353770	118810	Celle saltmining
Laughland	Thomas Anderson	Sergeant	2nd Battalion, Parachute Regiment	2989237		
Launder	Philip Ernest Stephen	Private	2nd Battalion, South Staffordshire Regiment	14673092	77081	Dresden – various
Law	Sidney Albert	Private	2nd Battalion, South Staffordshire Regiment	1790572		Plate laying railway
Lawrence	Henry Philip	Private	2nd Battalion, South Staffordshire Regiment	4922180		Plauen labourer
Lawson	Albert	Private	2nd Battalion, South Staffordshire Regiment	1789246	91169	Dresden bomb damage
Lawson	George Steele	Signalman	Royal Signals	2382692		Niedersedlitz stone quarry
Lawson	Wilfred McLellen	Private	156th Battalion, Parachute Regiment	7948335	118001	Ülzen railway bomb damage
Lawton	John William	Lance Corporal	1st Airborne Provost Company	7691899		
Layland	Frederick	Gunner	2nd Airlanding Anti-Tank Battery, Royal Artillery	1092475	92062	Me 49 E clearing bomb debris and repairing sewers
Layton	Ernest	Private	Parachute Regiment	14224910		
Ledger	James	Staff Sergeant	Glider Pilot Regiment	5111304	140080	
Lee	Idwal	Driver	1st Airlanding Anti-Tank Battery, Royal Artillery	5188617	75540	
Lee	John Henry Dixon	Captain	1st Airlanding Light Regiment, Royal Artillery	94122	587	

Leece	Albert Edward	Gunner	Royal Artillery	14667137	91887	Brüx coal mines
Leech	James	Private	156th Battalion, Parachute Regiment	4343831		Limburg labouring
Leeder	Roberto Cedric	Sergeant	Glider Pilot Regiment	6293746		
Lees	Fred	Sergeant	Glider Pilot Regiment	109626		
Lees	Herbert	Corporal	10th Battalion, Parachute Regiment	7014234		
Lees	Norman Alfred	Lance Corporal	156th Battalion, Parachute Regiment	14377390	90542	Zahna brick making, Mutchau coal mines
Lees	Robert Brownlee	Corporal	156th Battalion, Parachute Regiment	3190642		
Leggett	Clarence Leslie	Corporal	11th Battalion, Parachute Regiment	4691420	75986	Leipzig Balen 2 coal miner
Leith	James Park	Lance Corporal	7th Battalion, King's Own Scottish Borderers	14211442	118744	
Lemon	Arthur	Private	7th Battalion, King's Own Scottish Borderers	14633797	88770	Demolition Mines
Lennie	George Dougan	Private	3rd Battalion, Parachute Regiment	3187549		
Leslie	James	Private	10th Battalion, Parachute Regiment	14432451	92072	Germany coal mine
Leslie	John	Lance Corporal	10th Battalion, Parachute Regiment	2930008	75795	
Leslie	Thomas Mackie	Sergeant	2nd Battalion, Parachute Regiment	7343202		
Letchford	Arthur Nugent	Private	2nd Battalion, Parachute Regiment	6854730		Zwickau railway
Lever	Benjamin	Lance Corporal	1st Battalion, Border Regiment	3776422	26083	Bailand labourer
Levien	Robert Hugh	Lieutenant	2nd Battalion, Parachute Regiment	73127	554	
Lewington	John William	Private	10th Battalion, Parachute Regiment	14641541		
Lewington	William Bert	Lance Corporal	4th Battalion, Dorset Regiment	5953107	17534	Dresden bomb damage
Lewis	Harry	Private	None	2939511		Hallendorf railway and bomb damage

Family Name	Forename	Rank	Unit	Army number	POW number	All kommandos
Lewis	Harry Leslie	Private	4th Battalion, Dorset Regiment	14702331	20533	Eisleben copper mine
Lewis	John	Corporal	1st Battalion, Parachute Regiment	4032087	92129	AK 133rd3 Bomb work, Schlachthof, Strafp
Lewis	Stanley Edward	Lance Corporal	Parachute Regiment	2929796	118522	
Lewis	Vivian	Corporal	1st Battalion, Parachute Regiment	890079		
Lewis	William	Private	1st Battalion, Border Regiment	14431937	92111	Wurzmes coal mine, Brüx tramway repairs
Linden	Jack Alfred	Corporal	89 Parachute Security Section	918417		
Linden	Thomas	Private	7th Battalion, King's Own Scottish Borderers	3197468	90495	Dresden joinery work
Lindley	Francis William	Major	10th Battalion, Parachute Regiment	226192	2194	
Lindsay	Allan Barr	Staff Sergeant	Glider Pilot Regiment	918329	76335	
Lines	Stanley	Lance Corporal	2nd Battalion, South Staffordshire Regiment	5440800	75356	Borna railway repairs
Lintern	Ronald Jack	Corporal	156th Battalion, Parachute Regiment	3959419		
Lister	Benjamin	Corporal	250th Airborne Light Company, Royal Army Service Corps	178990	17547	
Little	David Richardson	Private	3rd Battalion, Parachute Regiment	3190427		
Little	Wilfred	Private	1st Battalion, Border Regiment	4621936	91710	Kirschau, Crossen paper, Zwickau railway
Littlewood	Harold	Lance Corporal	156th Battalion, Parachute Regiment	4127282		Merseburg demolition
Livesey	Stanley	Lance Corporal	7th Battalion, King's Own Scottish Borderers	14427536		Eilenburg construction air raid shelter

Surname	First name(s)	Rank	Regiment	Number	Number	Location
Livesey	Trevor John	Captain	1st Parachute Squadron, Royal Engineers	222702	611	
Lloyd	Arthur	Lance Corporal	156th Battalion, Parachute Regiment	5888980		
Lloyd	Clifford Walter	Private	4th Battalion, Dorset Regiment	5726668	20035	Gunnersdorf forestry, Chemnitz railway
Lloyd	Philip Isaac	Signalman	Royal Signals	558280	90805	Dresden tram and water main repairs
Lloyd	Samuel	Gunner	1st Airlanding Anti-Tank Battery, Royal Artillery	14268055		Brüx coal mine
Lochery	John Aiken	Private	7th Battalion, King's Own Scottish Borderers	14327588	91779	Wurzmes Miner, Brux Snouse
Lock	Bert Edward	Private	11th Battalion, Parachute Regiment	2081300	117961	Hildeshiem sugar beet factory
Lockwood	Joseph William	Gunner	1st Airlanding Light Regiment Royal Artillery	14329838		Liebenwerda Sand and ?, Ziegtz coal mine
Logan	Thomas Dvison	Private	2nd Battalion, Parachute Regiment	1433668	118681	
Long	Albert Edward	Private	4th Battalion, Dorset Regiment	5950672		Falkenau coal mines
Long	Reginald Arthur	Staff Sergeant	Glider Pilot Regiment	10538193		
Long	Thomas Edwin	Private	2nd Battalion, Parachute Regiment	14918167	117576	7011 Groß Düngen
Longson	James	Private	1st Battalion, Border Regiment	3782025	75994	Komatau railway workshops
Losty	Patrick Alfred	Sergeant	Glider Pilot Regiment	1436976		
Lothian	James Charles Ogilvie	Lance Corporal	7th Battalion, King's Own Scottish Borderers	14212249	75383	Harzberg building and demolition
Lott	George Henry	Company Sergeant Major	10th Battalion, Parachute Regiment	6395878		
Lovatt	George	Private	7th Battalion, King's Own Scottish Borderers	14201968	90691	Dresden bomb damage
Lovett	James	Staff Sergeant	Glider Pilot Regiment	128577		
Lowe	Alfred	Private	2nd Battalion, South Staffordshire Regiment	14700220		Clay pits

Family Name	Forename	Rank	Unit	Army number	POW number	All kommandos
Lowe	David Borwell	Staff Sergeant	Glider Pilot Regiment	2084363	76332	
Lowe	Eric Leslie	Gunner	1st Airlanding Light Regiment, Royal Artillery	14552349	91444	
Lowrie	James	Lance Corporal	1st Parachute Brigade, Royal Signals	2351489		Zwickau railway
Lumb	Donald	Corporal	3rd Battalion, Parachute Regiment	3780397		
Lumb	Vernon	Sergeant	3rd Battalion, Parachute Regiment	137755		
Lumsden	Albert Edward	Private	2nd Battalion, Parachute Regiment	941821		Herzberg
Lund	James	Private	2nd Battalion, Parachute Regiment	843710		
Lund	Robert	Staff Sergeant	Glider Pilot Regiment	2005243		
Lune	Albert	Private	181st Airlanding Field Ambulance	14672958	140058	
Lupton	Thomas	Private	7th Battalion, King's Own Scottish Borderers	3195317	90508	
Lynch	Peter Patrick	Sergeant	7th Battalion, King's Own Scottish Borderers	3192399	89987	
Lyndon	Edwin Charles	Sapper	9th Field Company, Royal Engineers Airborne	2115530		Zwickau railway
Lynes	Frank Herbert	Lance Corporal	7th Battalion, King's Own Scottish Borderers	2563317		
Lyon	Archibald Davidson	Sergeant	Glider Pilot Regiment	14216954	15246	
Lyons	Charles Howard Cecil	Sergeant	Glider Pilot Regiment	427924	118524	
Lyons	Leslie William Herbert	Sergeant	Parachute Regiment	5573769		
Lyons	Robert	Private	7th Battalion, King's Own Scottish Borderers	4698363	90786	Merseburg demolition
Macdonald	John Forbes	Sergeant	Glider Pilot Regiment	2881342		
Macdonnell	Charles James	Lieutenant	2nd Battalion, South Staffordshire Regiment	294983	2173	

Surname	First name(s)	Rank	Regiment/Unit	Number	Number 2	Note
Mackay	Ernest Henry	Private	2nd Battalion, Parachute Regiment	6922282	91676	Dresden bomb clearance
Mackenzie	John Alexander	Private	3rd Battalion, Parachute Regiment	2820366	89961	Jessen/Elster railway
Madden	Harald	Private	Parachute Regiment	14658029		Brüx miner
Magee	Alfred	Private	156th Battalion, Parachute Regiment	1439453		Mittweida
Maguire	Joseph	Private	1st Battalion, Border Regiment	14583475	24938	AK 131 Zwickau Reichsbahn Labourer Electrician
Maidens	William Edward	Private	16th Parachute Field Ambulance	7403380		Jessen railway
Mallett	William John	Captain	Forward Observation Unit, Royal Artillery	249340	568	
Malley	James	Private	7th Battalion, King's Own Scottish Borderers	14211489		Halle air raid shelter construction
Mallison	Geoffrey Norman	Staff Sergeant	Glider Pilot Regiment	4348337		
Maloney	Robert	Signalman	1st Parachute Brigade, Royal Signals	2328785		Hallendorf labourer
Manders	Jesse Ewart	Leading Aircraftman	Light Warning Unit No. 6080, RAF	1206626	1255	
Manley	George	Private	7th Battalion, King's Own Scottish Borderers	10602371	91781	Sudetenland
Manley	John	Private	3rd Battalion, Parachute Regiment	5833839		
Mann	Sydney George	Corporal	1st Battalion, Border Regiment	4276920	18675	
Manning	Alfred Ernest	Gunner	2nd Airlanding Anti-Tank Battery, Royal Artillery	1155826		Dresden clearing bomb debris
Manuel	Henry Thomas	Private	11th Battalion, Parachute Regiment	320899	140073	
Mapplebeck	Thomas	Private	3rd Battalion, Parachute Regiment	2067264	118599	
Mardell	George Henry	Sergeant	2nd Battalion, South Staffordshire Regiment	6201240	89425	
Markham	Leonard	Private	Parachute Regiment	5962142	89799	Fallingbostel odd jobs

Family Name	Forename	Rank	Unit	Army number	POW number	All kommandos
Marks	Geoffrey George	Private	1st Battalion, Parachute Regiment	6853688		Brüx labourer
Marr	William	Sapper	1st Parachute Squadron, Royal Engineers	2110349	89232	
Marriott	Charles Edward	Private	1st Battalion, Border Regiment	4277974	117642	
Marriott	Charles Edward	Private	11th Battalion, Parachute Regiment	4399906		Plauen laying pipe lines
Marriott	James Harold	Private	156th Battalion, Parachute Regiment	4987520		Mittweida corporation
Marsden	James	Gunner	2nd Airlanding Anti-Tank Battery, Royal Artillery	1152480		Chemnitz saw mill
Marshall	James	Private	7th Battalion, King's Own Scottish Borderers	14608077	90576	Me 41 E Merseburg bomb debris
Marshall	Reginald	Private	7th Battalion, King's Own Scottish Borderers	3326129	91782	Germany coal mining
Martin	Frederick George	Company Sergeant Major	1st Battalion, Parachute Regiment	6285361	89411	Varchentin farm work AK 221/17
Martin	Joseph	Private	1st Battalion, Parachute Regiment	2615745	118725	
Martin	Reginald	Driver	Advanced Workshop Detachment, Royal Electrical and Mechanical Engineers	115945	91173	Dresden AK 1124 flour mill
Martin	Reginald Alfred	Lance Corporal	253rd Airborne Light Company, Royal Army Service Corps	171029		Straw factory
Maskell	William	Private	7th Battalion, King's Own Scottish Borderers	14403967	118174	Bad Grund mine
Mason	Arthur	Private	7th Battalion, King's Own Scottish Borderers	1525984	88754	Merseburg air raid shelter work
Mason	Edward	Private	1st Battalion, Border Regiment	3660775	91524	Dresden road repairs
Mason	Harry Pearson	Corporal	1st Battalion, Parachute Regiment	3601962		
Mason	Herbert Advad	Staff Sergeant	181st Airlanding Field Ambulance	7249904	77340	

Surname	Forename	Rank	Regiment	176	15258	Location
Mason	Peter Brown	Lieutenant	7th Battalion, King's Own Scottish Borderers	176	15258	
Mason	William Frederick	Private	2nd Battalion, Parachute Regiment	11002192	75309	Komotau railway
Maston	Edward Peel	Private	156th Battalion, Parachute Regiment	14414353		Stalag XII A demolition, Teplitz coal mine
Mather	Denis	Private	3rd Battalion, Parachute Regiment	14221140	91745	Maltheuern
Matthew	Douglas	Private	Parachute Regiment	2884596	294131	Brüx railway
Matthews	Frederick George	Private	1st Battalion, Border Regiment	3392036	117499	Ülzen
Matthews	Ronald George	Private	7th Battalion, King's Own Scottish Borderers	4750960		Dresden clearing bomb debris
Matthews	William Lawrence	Corporal	1st Battalion, Parachute Regiment	2618797		Varchentin farming
Maughan	Albert Sidney	Sergeant	Glider Pilot Regiment	4270235		
Mawditt	Norman Denis	Lance Corporal	181st Airlanding Field Ambulance	7519050		Reserve Lazarett Appeldoorn
Mawhinney	Herbert	Sergeant	156th Battalion, Parachute Regiment	5109805		
Maxwell	John	Private	3rd Battalion, Parachute Regiment	2928375	75316	
Maxwell	Thomas Williams	Private	2nd Battalion, South Staffordshire Regiment	987046	118027	Bad Grund AK 7013 mine
May	Dennis Roy	Private	2nd Battalion, Parachute Regiment	14331381		
May	Kenneth	Sergeant, Lance	156th Battalion, Parachute Regiment	1430419	90746	
May	William Albert Henry	Staff Sergeant	Glider Pilot Regiment	854844		
McAlindon	Joseph	Private	10th Battalion, Parachute Regiment	7346837	89950	Jessen bomb damage on railway
McAndrew	John Edward	Driver	250th Airborne Light Company, Royal Army Service Corps	70518	117962	Kommando 7013 Bad Grund

Family Name	Forename	Rank	Unit	Army number	POW number	All kommandos
McCall	Jack Miller	Corporal	7th Battalion, King's Own Scottish Borderers	14211456		
McCallum	John	Private	133rd Parachute Field Ambulance	7348139	90691	
McCalmont	Edwin John Terance	Corporal	11th Battalion, Parachute Regiment	1136790		
McCandlish	Andrew Holen	Sergeant	Glider Pilot Regiment	3320419	88476	
McCarner	William Hector	Sergeant	1st Airlanding Anti-Tank Battery, Royal Artillery	3711379	91316	
McCarron	Joseph Gerald	Private	1st Battalion, Parachute Regiment	6985449		Limburg?, Brix coal mine
McClure	Robert Hammond	Corporal	7th Battalion, King's Own Scottish Borderers	14211457	118754	
McClure	William	Private	2nd Battalion, Parachute Regiment	7022065		Herzberg Elster
McCluskie	John	Sergeant	1st Battalion, Border Regiment	3596965	117454	
McCooke	John Brewster	Captain	2nd Battalion, South Staffordshire Regiment	140490	91006	
McCool	John Gerald	Gunner	2nd Airlanding Anti-Tank Battery, Royal Artillery	5392324	117398	Bad Grund lead mining
McCormack	James Laurence	Private	2nd Battalion, Parachute Regiment	6983201		
McCourt	James Frederick	Captain	7th Battalion, King's Own Scottish Borderers	465	465	
McCreedy	Richard James	Lance Bombardier	1st Airlanding Anti-Tank Battery, Royal Artillery	3711048		P87 Fahrbereitschaft
McDonald	Allan Gosland	Private	7th Battalion, King's Own Scottish Borderers	3326607		Teutschental salt mine, Etzdorf coal mine
McDonald	James Pennie	Private	Parachute Regiment	879673	75692	

McDonald	John	Sapper	1st Parachute Squadron, Royal Engineers	2931360		Erfenschlag labouring
McDonald	Robert Hector	Private	1st Battalion, Border Regiment	3772203	914753	Brüx miner
McDonald	Thomas	Private	7th Battalion, King's Own Scottish Borderers	3189884		
McDonnell	Patrick	Private	2nd Battalion, Parachute Regiment	7047377		Teutschenthal salt mine, Etzdorf coal mine
McDowell	James	Private	7th Battalion, King's Own Scottish Borderers	3193938	91896	Zwickau railway
McEvoy	Anthony	Private	21st Independent Parachute Company	14002666	75314	Mückenberg rail line laying surface mine
McFarlane	Roland	Corporal	Royal Army Medical Corps	7377807	77327	
McGaugie	Robert	Private	7th Battalion, King's Own Scottish Borderers	33233736	90068	Zwickau railway
McGaw	John Sibbald	Lance Corporal	1st Airborne Provost Company	7691875		Basepohl farm
McGivern	George Simon Patrick	Lance Corporal	1st Parachute Squadron, Royal Engineers	2000959	117217	
McGowan	Walter	Private	181st Airlanding Field Ambulance	7407324	90158	Jessen railway maintenance
McGrath	Terence Ronald Forbes	Sergeant	4th Parachute Squadron, Royal Engineers	1875005	21753	
McGurk	John	Private	7th Battalion, King's Own Scottish Borderers	3194113	99999	Herzberg building and demolition
McHale	John	Private	2nd Battalion, Parachute Regiment	14563648	75428	Großröhrsdorf building, Lilianstein labouring
McHardy	Charles	Private	7th Battalion, King's Own Scottish Borderers	14214324	90579	Me 41 E Merseburg debris
McHugh	James	Private	1st Battalion, Border Regiment	3599165	91948	Dresden labourer
McInally	John Andrew	Private	7th Battalion, King's Own Scottish Borderers	3190240	118035	
McIntosh	Donald Dinnie	Private	1st Battalion, Parachute Regiment	2880411		Heiotberg demolition
McIntosh	William Downie	Private	3rd Battalion, Parachute Regiment	5191914		Brüx surface coal mine
McIntyre	Hugh	Corporal	7th Battalion, King's Own Scottish Borderers	3187559		Inschin farm

Family Name	Forename	Rank	Unit	Army number	POW number	All kommandos
McIvor	Hugh	Sergeant	2nd Airlanding Anti-Tank Battery, Royal Artillery	3179804		
McKail	William	Private	7th Battalion, King's Own Scottish Borderers	14415428	91789	Zwickau railway
McKay	James Maxwell	Staff Sergeant	Glider Pilot Regiment	2823181		
McKee	William	Private	Parachute Regiment	1445760		
McKendrick	John Lindsay	Private	7th Battalion, King's Own Scottish Borderers	14211200	18657	
McKenna	William Tarrant	Sapper	4th Parachute Squadron, Royal Engineers	3055480	140103	
McKnight	John	Lance Corporal	7th Battalion, King's Own Scottish Borderers	3715834	26062	Böhlen Leipzig labouring
McKnight	John	Private	133rd Parachute Field Ambulance	7360808		
McLachlan	Frederick	Gunner	Royal Artillery	14587240	19535	
McLaren	Ernest	Lance Corporal	7th Battalion, King's Own Scottish Borderers	14211475		Wurzmes, Tschausch building railway for new factory
McLay	James	Corporal	7th Battalion, King's Own Scottish Borderers	14211476	90563	
McLean	Charles Harris	Corporal	Royal Army Medical Corps	7517370	118377	
McLean	Duncan	Captain	2nd Battalion, Parachute Regiment	94824	616	
McLean	George Falconer	Lance Corporal	1st Battalion, Parachute Regiment	2937656	118411	
McLeavy	Donald	Sergeant	Glider Pilot Regiment	0	117758	
McLellan	John	Private	7th Battalion, King's Own Scottish Borderers	3190228	15460	Königswalde quarrying, Brüx clearing bomb debris
McLoughlin	David	Private	2nd Battalion, Parachute Regiment	7047407		Hallendorf mining
McLoughlin	Patrick Bernard	Private	10th Battalion, Parachute Regiment	6412159	75600	Zeitz filling bomb holes

McLure	James	Private	156th Battalion, Parachute Regiment	2454564		Breslau quarry
McNeilage	Robert	Private	7th Battalion, King's Own Scottish Borderers	14327083	90490	AK 133rd3 Dresden tramways electric motor repairs
McNeill	George Cuthill	Corporal	1st Battalion, Parachute Regiment	3130965		Neubrandenburg agricultural
McQuilian	Alexander	Private	11th Battalion, Parachute Regiment	7901172	91663	Sudetenland coal mine
McTavish	Alexander	Gunner	1st Airlanding Light Regiment, Royal Artillery	1156883	75563	Erfenschlag timber yards
McVicar	Archibald Lamont	Private	10th Battalion, Parachute Regiment	2933355		Komatau labourer
McWilliam	Thomas Andrew	Corporal	156th Battalion, Parachute Regiment	3771531		
McWilliams	Robert	Private	Royal Army Medical Corps	7378039	118405	
Mead	Kenneth Andrew	Sergeant	Glicer Pilot Regiment	1878306		
Meakin	Reginald	Lieutenant	Glider Pilot Regiment	314146		
Meakings	Frank Howard	Lance Corporal	16th Parachute Field Ambulance	861740	90088	7001 Hallendorf various labour
Meen	Bernard George Henry	Lance Corporal	3rd Battalion, Parachute Regiment	6025548		Wurzmes, repairing bomb damage, Brüx building tramway
Meiklejohn	John	Private	7th Battalion, King's Own Scottish Borderers	3185236	80652	Me 41 E clearing bomb debris
Meiklejon	Robert Smith	Private	11th Battalion, Parachute Regiment	2990761	75434	
Mellor	William Frederick	Private	Royal Army Medical Corps, attached 2nd Battalion, Parachute Regiment	14381095	294176	
Mellors	Wilfred	Lance Corporal	2nd Battalion, South Staffordshire Regiment	5052769	89599	
Melrose	William George	Staff Sergeant	Glider Pilot Regiment	1464667		
Melvin	Ronald Cameron	Corporal	2nd Battalion, South Staffordshire Regiment	4923341	90415	

Family Name	Forename	Rank	Unit	Army number	POW number	All kommandos
Menzies	Harry	Corporal	2nd Battalion, Parachute Regiment	3247104		
Mercer	Kenneth Walter	Private	4th Battalion, Dorset Regiment	14656451	14227	Stalag IV F Wood worker
Meredith	Clifford Desmond	Private	2nd Battalion, South Staffordshire Regiment	5260457		Wurzmes, Brüx
Merignac	Louis	Private	7th Battalion, King's Own Scottish Borderers	3184987		
Merrick	Albert John	Driver	1st Parachute Brigade, Royal Signals	7896485	91619	Sudetenland coal mine
Metcalfe	Edwin	Private	1st Battalion, Border Regiment	3602861	118844	Ülzen railway
Middleton	Alan James	Driver	250th Airborne Light Company, Royal Army Service Corps	10680515		Dresden bomb debris
Middleton	Horace	Private	156th Battalion, Parachute Regiment	5048758	117507	
Midgley	Jack	Private	2nd Battalion, Parachute Regiment	1597944		
Miles	Ashley Bertram	Private	1st Parachute Brigade HQ	888755	75517	Stützengrün
Miles	Ronald Frederick	Trooper	1st Airborne Reconnaissance Squadron	6853948	118494	
Millard	Jack	Private	3rd Battalion, Parachute Regiment	3388645	294177	
Miller	Brian	Staff Sergeant	16th Parachute Field Ambulance	7349554	89671	
Miller	Christopher Alfred	Staff Sergeant	Glider Pilot Regiment	937499	117770	
Miller	George	Lance Corporal	1st Battalion, Border Regiment	2980246	918718	Kersche blanket factory, Dresden agricultural work, Radebeul tin factory

Surname	First name(s)	Rank	Regiment	Service No.	Camp No.	Work
Miller	Percy Frank	Private	1st Battalion, Parachute Regiment	14503578	75406	
Miller	Philip Anthony Alfred	Sapper	1st Parachute Squadron, Royal Engineers	1947386		Halle Rei 113 grave digging, bomb damage, labouring
Miller	Thomas Visgen	Captain	4th Parachute Brigade Royal Artillery	89054	608	
Miller	Walter	Private	2nd Battalion, Parachute Regiment	4926652	75339	Etzdorf mining
Milligan	William John	Private	7th Battalion, King's Own Scottish Borderers	3197078	117381	7011 Groß Dügen sugar factory
Millington	Arthur	Private	1st Battalion, Border Regiment	3856104	91880	Sudetenland mines
Mills	James	Driver	16th Parachute Field Ambulance	3973384	118439	
Mills	Kenneth Henry George	Staff Sergeant	Glider Pilot Regiment	551404		
Milne	Alexander Noble	Gunner	1st Airlanding Light Regiment, Royal Artillery	919655	75976	Muckinberg laying railway lines
Milne	George	Private	7th Battalion, King's Own Scottish Borderers	2878859	117412	
Milner	Charles	Private	7th Battalion, King's Own Scottish Borderers	14327609		Gognitz
Milner	Denis Herbert	Private	16th Parachute Field Ambulance	7397106	90554	
Milner	Eric	Driver	1st Airlanding Anti-Tank Battery, Royal Artillery	1144982	75098	Bockwitz repairing lorries
Milner	Ernest Leonard	Private	156th Battalion, Parachute Regiment	5334959	140129	
Minto	James Henry	Private	7th Battalion, King's Own Scottish Borderers	14204716	91485	Brüx Zentrum Mine
Mirylees	Geoffrey Keith	Private	1st Battalion, Parachute Regiment	6898405	75819	
Mitchell	Alan	Sergeant	Glider Pilot Regiment	10538003	858	
Mitchell	Charles Maurice	Private	7th Battalion, King's Own Scottish Borderers	14636263	25194	Grasseth coal mining
Mitchell	Edward	Sergeant	Glider Pilot Regiment	10555051	76321	

Family Name	Forename	Rank	Unit	Army number	POW number	All kommandos
Mitchell	Geoffrey Ernest	Private	2nd Battalion, Parachute Regiment	5782772	89423	
Mitchell	Harry	Private	21st Independent Parachute Company	6986281	117626	Dinklar sugar factory
Mitchell	James	Private	7th Battalion, King's Own Scottish Borderers	3186927		Kolumbus mines
Mitchell	William	Driver	250th Airborne Light Company, Royal Army Service Corps	80574	91351	Plauen C114 air raid shelters
Mitchelmore	Albert Henry	Private	3rd Battalion, Parachute Regiment	6460413	75317	Pirkau surface coal mine
Mobsby	William	Private	3rd Battalion, Parachute Regiment	6410136	92032	Brüx mining
Mock	George	Gunner	1st Airlanding Anti-Tank Battery, Royal Artillery	14708487	92012	Wallwits
Moffat	Alexander	Lance Corporal	1st Parachute Squadron, Royal Engineers	2067621	117420	AK 7012 Sugar beet dinkla
Moffat	Walter	Private	Parachute Regiment	14255679	75417	
Monsell	John Humphrey Arnold	Lieutenant	2nd Battalion, Parachute Regiment	112889	562	
Montgomery	Samuel	Private	2nd Battalion, South Staffordshire Regiment	7013157	90005	Mülhtroff building railway sidings
Montgomery	Terence	Private	1st Battalion, Parachute Regiment	7013242	92037	
Moody	Albert Doanld Urquhart	Signalman	Royal Signals	6349280	140217	
Moon	Raymond Jack	Private	250th Airborne Light Company, Royal Army Service Corps	14566626	91459	Zwickau railway
Moore	Albert James	Lance Corporal	3rd Battalion, Parachute Regiment	5832722		
Moore	Alfred George Golden	Sergeant	1st Battalion, Parachute Regiment	6461833	140083	

Surname	First names	Rank	Regiment	Number	Number	Location
Moore	Arthur Reginald	Private	Parachute Regiment	14218858	75324	Komatau labouring
Moore	Eric Charles Arthur	Sergeant	2nd Airlanding Anti-Tank Battery, Royal Artillery	868114	91788	
Moore	William	Private	7th Battalion, King's Own Scottish Borderers	14201431	90694	Kirschau cloth factory, Liebau cloth factory
Morait	Peter John	Private	156th Battalion, Parachute Regiment	59816		Dresden maintenance in garage
Moran	Joseph	Signalman	1st Parachute Brigade, Royal Signals	2320146	91620	Brux valley Sudetenland miner
Mordle	Alfred Augustus	Corporal	7th Battalion, King's Own Scottish Borderers	14204397	118624	
Morgan	Edward	Gunner	1st Airlanding Light Regiment, Royal Artillery	1116829	92937	Erfenschlag Germany wood factory
Morgan	Michael Joseph	Gunner	1st Airlanding Anti-Tank Battery, Royal Artillery	868311	91479	
Morgan	Stephen	Private	2nd Battalion, Parachute Regiment	14436780		Herzberg railways
Morris	David	WO II	11th Battalion, Parachute Regiment	5946742		
Morris	Edmund Barker	Lance Corporal	1st Airborne Reconnaissance Squadron	14279106		
Morris	Gordon Hollister	Private	11th Battalion, Parachute Regiment	14339316	118673	
Morris	John Alyn	Private	3rd Battalion, Parachute Regiment	4198194	92170	Maltern Brux mining
Morrison	George	Private	10th Battalion, Parachute Regiment	2981937	92038	
Morrison	John Alexander	Captain	Glider Pilot Regiment	88880	5979	
Morrison	Roderick Dickson	Driver	1st Airlanding Light Regiment, Royal Artillery	882484		Plauen C115 labour roads etc
Morton	Albert Alfred	Private	2nd Battalion, Parachute Regiment	6853588	117956	Groß Düngon sugar factory

Family Name	Forename	Rank	Unit	Army number	POW number	All kommandos
Moscou	David Beaconsfield	Lance Corporal	7th Battalion, King's Own Scottish Borderers	14610927		
Moses	Ernest	Sergeant	10th Battalion, Parachute Regiment	4124796	117856	
Mossie	Robert	Private	2nd Battalion, South Staffordshire Regiment	3191185	92058	Dresden labourer in bombed areas
Mountford	William Frederick	Lance Corporal	2nd Battalion, South Staffordshire Regiment	5439497	91644	
Mowat	Billy Bruce	Leading Aircraftman	Light Warning Unit No. 6341, RAF	168468		
Mowat	John Robert	Staff Sergeant	Glider Pilot Regiment	2818874		
Muirhead	Archibald	Sergeant	7th Battalion, King's Own Scottish Borderers	3187718	89533	
Mulcahy	Thomas	Private	1st Battalion, Parachute Regiment	3393711		Sudetenland coal mining
Mullender	James William	Private	11th Battalion, Parachute Regiment	4399431	52908	Menzengraben
Mullineux	William	Private	3rd Battalion, Parachute Regiment	3866182		Kolumbus Lager 51 Brüx coal mining
Mullins	Thomas Harald	Private	Parachute Regiment	1691988		AK 231 Kriebethal, Rautenkranz lumberjack
Mumford	Ernest Frank	Private	16th Parachute Field Ambulance	7266759	118628	Medical orderly XI B
Munro	Alexander	Private	11th Battalion, Parachute Regiment	7370319	117167	
Munro	James L	Private	10th Battalion, Parachute Regiment	3318030		Zwickau railway works
Murphy	Alfred Victor	Private	2nd Battalion, Parachute Regiment	14218919	25964	Zwickau railway
Murphy	Andrew	Private	7th Battalion, King's Own Scottish Borderers	14327614	93376	Dresden labourer
Murray	Alistair George	Private	2nd Battalion, Parachute Regiment	2926439		
Murray	James	Private	Parachute Regiment?	14530543		

Surname	Forename	Rank	Unit	Number	Number 2	Camp/Work
Murray MC	Douglas Campbell	Major/T	1st Parachute Squadron, Royal Engineers	106883	607	
Mustard	Alfred	Private	156th Battalion, Parachute Regiment	3770819		Merseburg clearing debris
Musto	Ronald Herbert	Private	11th Battalion, Parachute Regiment	924313		
Mynett	Leonard	Private	11th Battalion, Parachute Regiment	6985800	91412	
Nadin	George Edmund	Private	1st Battalion, Border Regiment	3866328		Merseburg sewage
Naish	Bernard Cyril	Private	4th Battalion, Dorset Regiment	14376654	17588	Chemnitz wood and bomb damage,
Nash	William	Private	250th Airborne Light Company, Royal Army Service Corps	2597427		Kirschau blanket factory, Löpbau textiles
Naylor		Private	10th Battalion, Parachute Regiment	6349458	89595	Grimma stone quarry
Needham	George Henry	Sapper	1st Parachute Squadron, Royal Engineers	2133rd390		
Neil	George Currie	Corporal	1st Battalion, Parachute Regiment	7394382		
Neild	Harry	Private	156th Battalion, Parachute Regiment	4539879		Dresden Rex tramways
Nelson	Albert	Gunner	1st Airlanding Light Regiment, Royal Artillery	14264847	75838	Erfenschlag timber yards
Neve	George Thomas	Private	181st Airlanding Field Ambulance	7370817		
Nevins	Daniel	Private	10th Battalion, Parachute Regiment	4275543		
Newell	Cecil	Private	2nd Battalion, Parachute Regiment	1559998		Wurzmes surface mine labouring, Tschausch labouring in a factory
Newell	Douglas George Valentine	Lance Corporal	11th Battalion, Parachute Regiment	165223	89349	Halle air riad shelter
Newham	Leslie	Driver	1st Airlanding Light Regiment, Royal Artillery	14609703		Liebenwerda sand, Unterswodtz mine

Family Name	Forename	Rank	Unit	Army number	POW number	All kommandos
Newhouse	Frank	Private	10th Battalion, Parachute Regiment	14557569	14188	Dresden
Newman	Arthur Royston 'Roy'	Private	16th Parachute Field Ambulance	198333	22044	
Newman	James	Private	181st Airlanding Field Ambulance	7397436		Jessen railways
Newman	Robert Eugène	Private	Royal Army Medical Corps	7533134		
Newman	Walter Roy	Lance Corporal	10th Battalion, Parachute Regiment	6407101	118206	Ülzen railway line repair
Newport	Edward Selwyn	Lieutenant	1st Battalion, Border Regiment	96393	630	
Newton	Arthur	Staff Sergeant	Glider Pilot Regiment	913044		
Newton	George Robert	Private	Royal Army Medical Corps	7262642	140300	
Newton	Herbert Leonard	Trooper	1st Airborne Reconnaissance Squadron	6028646	118477	Ülzen railway work
Newton	Kenneth Ernest	Private	181st Airlanding Field Ambulance	14672306		
Newton	Peter	Private	156th Battalion, Parachute Regiment	3194733		G 123 Gleina
Newton	William Ewart	Private	2nd Battalion, South Staffordshire Regiment	1714799	89400	Etzdorf, Teutschenthal coal and salt mine
Nichollas	Lewis	Private	2nd Battalion, Parachute Regiment	4390380	117336	Groß Düngon sugar factory
Nichols	Henry William	Private	2nd Battalion, Parachute Regiment	2083033		Dresden tramways and waterworks
Nicholson	John	Private	Parachute Regiment	10601868	75341	Zwickau railway
Nicholson	William John Ainsley	Driver	63 Company, Royal Army Service Corps	10662795		Zwickau railways
Nicklin	George Lewis	Sergeant	Glider Pilot Regiment	7955175	117174	
Nicklin	William Harry	Lance Corporal	Royal Army Service Corps	290769	90584	Merseburg clearing bomb debris
Niel	Marshall	Private	3rd Battalion, Parachute Regiment	4461059	118193	

Surname	First names	Rank	Regiment	Number	Number	Work
Nightingale	Cyril	Private	3rd Battalion, Parachute Regiment	4694319	91511	Eilenburg labouring
Nimmo	Tristram	Private	1st Battalion, Parachute Regiment	2938274		
Nixon	Charles	Private	1st Battalion, Border Regiment	3600613	91944	
Noble	Barry Denis	Private	156th Battalion, Parachute Regiment	14641561		Meresburg bomb debris
Noble	Charles Bruce	Captain	133rd Parachute Field Ambulance	279738		Arbeitskommando 7001 medical officer
Noble	Jeffrey Fraser	Lieutenant	156th Battalion, Parachute Regiment	276375	91017	
Nolan	Harold	Lance Corporal	1st Battalion, Border Regiment	767839	118802	Ülzen railway
Nolan	William Gregory	Lance Corporal	2nd Battalion, South Staffordshire Regiment	4919088		Wurzmes demolition, Tschausch rail repair
Norris	Donald Eric	Staff Sergeant	Glider Pilot Regiment	1470905	118693	
North	Albert Joseph William	Sergeant	Glider Pilot Regiment	14269986	118614	
Noton	Montagu John	Private	156th Battalion, Parachute Regiment	899551		Floßmühle timber yard stacker
Nullis	John Robert	Lance Corporal	2nd Battalion, South Staffordshire Regiment	5729659		Ülzen railway
Nurse	George	Private	156th Battalion, Parachute Regiment	3977282		Dresden loading waggons
Nyman	Hugo Oscar	Private	4th Battalion, Dorset Regiment	14512195	14176	Hartha shoe factory
O'Brian	Robert Gerard	Private	1st Battalion, Parachute Regiment	2049245		
O'Brien	Cyril	Private	1st Parachute Brigade	14411394		Chemnitz labourer
O'Brien	Michael	Driver	16th Parachute Field Ambulance	1466843	90151	
O'Brien	William Arthur	Private	11th Battalion, Parachute Regiment	5989720	72149	Mulberg sugar factory, Merseburg clearing debris, Wittenberg Host
O'Dell	Charles John	Private	11th Battalion, Parachute Regiment	866848	118054	AK 7005 Salzgitter
O'Donnell	Edward	Private	The Parachute Regiment	3065854		Komotau labouring January February March April May

411

Family Name	Forename	Rank	Unit	Army number	POW number	All kommandos
O'Hanlon	Henry	Private	1st Battalion, Border Regiment	3783776		
O'Leary	Peter	Sergeant	1st Battalion, Parachute Regiment	4206855	140128	
O'Malley	Hamilton Joseph Keyes	Captain	Glider Pilot Regiment	44556		
O'Neill	Peter	Private	1st Battalion, Border Regiment	3772654		Dresden bomb damage
O'Neill	William	Private	7th Battalion, King's Own Scottish Borderers	3195748	14202	Dresden clearing bomb debris
O'Quinn	Bernard Patrick	Lance Corporal	1st Airborne Provost Company	7687579		
Oakes	William Arthur	Sergeant	Glider Pilot Regiment	14573970		
Oakley	Albert William Frank	Private	10th Battalion, Parachute Regiment	14204428	92042	Niedersedlitz general labourer
Oakley	Harry	Corporal	2nd Battalion, South Staffordshire Regiment	5124863		
Oates	Jack	Private	Parachute Regiment	2089524		Wurzmes pick and shovel, Brüx pits (coal)
Ogden	Ernest Alvin	Trooper	1st Airborne Reconnaissance Squadron	3599015	117719	
Oldbury	James Thomas	Sapper	1st Parachute Squadron, Royal Engineers	1871921		
Oldfield	William Thomas	Gunner	Royal Artillery	1457697	91538	? Location miner
Oliver	Edward James	Corporal	1st Parachute Squadron, Royal Engineers	2093811		Kundl
Oliver	James	Private	2nd Battalion, Parachute Regiment	3189025	140079	
Oliver	Leslie	Private	1st Battalion, Border Regiment	3537403	91793	Dresden bomb demolition
Oram	Arthur William	Sergeant	Glider Pilot Regiment	14416890		

Surname	First name	Rank	Regiment	Service number	POW number	Work
Orchard	Edward John	Private	7th Battalion, King's Own Scottish Borderers	14209984	117553	
Orrell	Herbert	Private	2nd Battalion, Parachute Regiment	14643075	91319	Leipzig hospital orderly
Osborn	Frank	Private	2nd Battalion, South Staffordshire Regiment	14316895	75927	Nonnewitz coal mine
Osborne	Raymond Frederick	Staff Sergeant	Glider Pilot Regiment	922174		
Owen	Albert	Private	10th Battalion, Parachute Regiment	14367248		Dreden welding odd jobs
Owen	Frederick Richard	Private	2nd Battalion, South Staffordshire Regiment	993170	89600	Bockwitz Garage work
Owen	Geoffrey Grenvelle Jonfi	Lance Corporal	181st Airlanding Field Ambulance	7399699		Apeldoorn Hospital
Owen	Russell	Signalman	1st Parachute Brigade, Royal Signals	7013739	117877	7012 Dinklar Sugar Beet factory
Owens	Cecil	Private	7th Battalion, King's Own Scottish Borderers	14201305	90045	Grunau near Dobeln paper factory
Oxford	Cecil James	Sergeant	Glider Pilot Regiment	4859963		
Paddon	Walter Charles Frank	Lance Corporal	2nd Battalion, Parachute Regiment	6153239		
Padfield	Harold	Sergeant, Lance	1st Parachute Squadron, Royal Engineers	1873564		Kundl
Paffett	James Henry	Sergeant	9th Field Company, Royal Engineers Airborne	1870477	117208	
Paine	Frank Thomas	Sapper	Royal Engineers	2090115	140152	
Painter	Frederick Thomas	Private	2nd Battalion, Parachute Regiment	7893694		Dresden Goods yard, railway
Painting	Harold	Lance Corporal	2nd Battalion, South Staffordshire Regiment	5111673	91422	Trebsen paper factory
Palframan	Arthur Kenneth	Gunner	1st Airlanding Light Regiment, Royal Artillery	14312127	91541	Kirschau blanket factory, Freiburg leather factory
Palmer	Albert Edgar	Sergeant	Glider Pilot Regiment	4803786		

413

Family Name	Forename	Rank	Unit	Army number	POW number	All kommandos
Palmer	Charles Thomas Albert	Lance Corporal	7th Battalion, King's Own Scottish Borderers	4750869	91083	Dresden clearing bomb damage
Palmer	David Edward	Lance Corporal	11th Battalion, Parachute Regiment	6343456	89812	
Palmer	Harry	Private	3rd Battalion, Parachute Regiment	5382027		Merseberg fuel work
Palmer	Raymond	Private	4th Battalion, Dorset Regiment	4399530	75898	
Panter	Stanley Charles	Captain	2nd Battalion, Parachute Regiment	165617	91002	
Parfitt	Cecil	Gunner	2nd Airlanding Anti-Tank Battery, Royal Artillery	5392331	91790	4 D 4 B
Pargeter	Albert Raymond	Private	2nd Battalion, South Staffordshire Regiment	4917639	91734	
Park	William	Gunner	Forward Observation Unit, Royal Artillery	1152141		Dresden stone quarry
Parker	Donald Sydney	Sergeant	Glider Pilot Regiment	5886465		
Parker	Frederick John	Lance Corporal	4th Parachute Brigade, Royal Electrical and Mechanical Engineers	7623305	117862	
Parker	George	Private	1st Battalion, Border Regiment	14560262		Brux coal mine
Parker	Thomas	Private	156th Battalion, Parachute Regiment	14632653	90745	Dresden tramways
Parker MM	Harry Frank	Corporal	3rd Battalion, Parachute Regiment	4620407		Basepol farm work
Parkes	William Henry	Sergeant	2nd Battalion, South Staffordshire Regiment	4917868		
Parkin	Godfrey	Sapper	9th Field Unit, Royal Engineers	2135831	117638	AK 7011 Groß Düngen sugar beet factory
Parkin	Harold Cosford	Private	2nd Battalion, Parachute Regiment	910905		Packing Stalag IV F
Parkin	William	Corporal	7th Battalion, King's Own Scottish Borderers	47509191	90784	

Surname	First name	Rank	Regiment	Number	Number	Camp/Work
Parrack	Peter Adolphus	Private	156th Battalion, Parachute Regiment	5113809		
Parrish	George Frederick	Private	3rd Battalion, Parachute Regiment	14661418	117895	
Parry	George	Private	2nd Battalion, South Staffordshire Regiment	4919190		Komotau railway workshops
Parry	William Reginald	Private	16th Parachute Field Ambulance	97005169		
Parsons	Maurice Charles	Sergeant	1st Battalion, Parachute Regiment	6018096	89455	
Partridge	Felix Frederick	Sapper	Royal Engineers	1915238		Halle Wood yard
Paterson	George	Private	11th Battalion, Parachute Regiment	2820870	117263	Dinklar sugar beet
Paterson	Robert	Sergeant	156th Battalion, Parachute Regiment	3244907	89820	
Paterson	Robert	Sapper	4th Parachute Squadron, Royal Engineers	14644253	118403	Ülzen bomb damage (railway)
Paterson	William	Signalman	1st Parachute Brigade, Royal Signals	2348020	91340	AK M 104 Mühltroff mixed mostly timber
Patterson	Donald	Lance Corporal	7th Battalion, King's Own Scottish Borderers	3193858	91477	Kirschau blanket factory, Freiberg leather factory
Patterson	Kenneth	Driver	Royal Artillery	14321751	91372	Teplitz Coal mine and railway
Pattle	Reginald Stanley	Driver	133rd Parachute Field Ambulance	5124019	90849	
Pauling	Leonard James	Gunner	1st Airlanding Light Regiment, Royal Artillery	14376919		kommando 112 Dresden clearing bomb debris
Paull	George Arthur	Lieutenant	2nd Airlanding Anti-Tank Battery, Royal Artillery	268829	90870	
Pavey	Charles	Gunner	2nd Airlanding Anti-Tank Battery, Royal Artillery	6400146	91702	Brüx coal mining
Payne	Albert Stanley	Private	2nd Battalion, Parachute Regiment	5835225		Brüx coal mine
Peacock	Claude Victor	Lance Corporal	11th Battalion, Parachute Regiment	6142921	117771	Dinklar sugar factory

Family Name	Forename	Rank	Unit	Army number	POW number	All kommandos
Peacock	Frank William	Sapper	4th Parachute Squadron, Royal Engineers	2070914	117908	Groß Düngon
Peacock	Frederick William	Private	1st Battalion, Border Regiment	4808802	25559	Unterschwöditz coal mine
Pearce	Leslie James	Lance Corporal	3rd Battalion, Parachute Regiment	4917641	117826	
Pearce	Reginald	Private	156th Battalion, Parachute Regiment	5826606	117615	Groß Düngon sugar beet factory
Pearce	William Charles	Private	11th Battalion, Parachute Regiment	4750999	117233	
Pearson	Ambrose	Private	1st Battalion, Parachute Regiment	4695232	90779	Dresden factory
Pearson	Herbert James	Private	4th Battalion, Dorset Regiment	14723722	17597	
Pearson	Michael David	Private	Parachute Regiment	4699298	75445	Halle labouring in oil pump factory
Pearson	George William	Private	1st Battalion, Border Regiment	3602871	75470	Komatau locomotive repair sheds
Peck	Jack	Lance Corporal	1st Parachute Brigade, Royal Signals	4803722	91314	
Peers	James	Corporal	Provost Company, 1st Airborne Division	1735900	89866	
Peet	Charles William	Private	3rd Battalion, Parachute Regiment	14242974	117281	
Penfold	Kenneth	Private	2nd Battalion, Parachute Regiment	4865420		Chemnitz saw mill
Penman	James	Private	Army Catering Corps, 1st Airborne Division	29990978		
Penney	Ronald Edward	Private	11th Battalion, Parachute Regiment	860215	14218	Dresden flour mill
Pennington	Alfred	Private	1st Battalion, Border Regiment	3390631	118309	
Pentney	Trevor George Harcourt	Lance Corporal	Provost Company, 1st Airborne Division	14688685		Dresden bomb damage

Surname	First names	Rank	Regiment	Service No.	POW No.	Work
Pepper	Maurice Raymond	Sergeant	Glider Pilot Regiment	7595239		
Percy	Victor Douglas	Staff Sergeant	Glider Pilot Regiment	5951478	118488	
Perkins	Arthur Wallace	Gunner	1st Airlanding Light Regiment, Royal Artillery	14245682		
Perkins	George	Private	7th Battalion, King's Own Scottish Borderers	14422898	117785	Sugar factory
Perks	Victor	Private	133rd Parachute Field Ambulance	14630044	90042	Jesen railway
Perrin-Brown	Christopher	Major	1st Battalion, Parachute Regiment	121945	572	
Perry	Charles Edward	Private	3rd Battalion, Parachute Regiment	14207893	75531	Bockwitz reps to army trucks
Perry	George Herbert	Corporal	3rd Battalion, Parachute Regiment	4622196		
Perry	Norman	Private	2nd Battalion, South Staffordshire Regiment	4916676		Rei 113 Halle manual labour
Perry	Stanley	Lance Corporal	2nd Battalion, Parachute Regiment	6353005	89792	Hallendorf AK 7001 labouring
Perse	Peter John	Captain	11th Battalion, Parachute Regiment	148840	2200	
Peters	Thomas Charles	Private	2nd Battalion, Parachute Regiment	14343574	117799	Groß Düngon
Petrie	Lewis	Sergeant	7th Battalion, King's Own Scottish Borderers	3185683		
Pettitt	Thomas Joseph	Private	2nd Battalion, Parachute Regiment	14397946		Trebsen 39/386 paper works
Phillips	Alfred Henry	Private	156th Battalion, Parachute Regiment	14578642	118212	
Phillips	Bernard	Corporal	1st Airborne Provost Company	7373821	89395	
Phillips	Edward Leigh	Captain Reverend	3rd Battalion, Parachute Regiment	163854	558	
Phillips	Patrick Mannix	Private	2nd Battalion, Parachute Regiment	6462931	117509	Groß Düngon
Phillips	Ronald John	Private	2nd Battalion, Parachute Regiment	5510064	117829	Dinklar 7012, AK 7005 Salzgitter joiner

Family Name	Forename	Rank	Unit	Army number	POW number	All kommandos
Phillips	Thomas John	Private	181st Airlanding Field Ambulance	7374379		
Phipps	Dennis Edward	Private	Parachute Regiment	14539342		Dresden clearing bomb damage
Pick	Robert Baxter Paterson	Private	1st Battalion, Parachute Regiment	7367569	91495	
Pierce	Gordon Basil	Corporal	7th Battalion, King's Own Scottish Borderers	4750968	89154	Kundl (No 25272) general work
Pilbeam	Henry Frank James	Craftsman	Royal Electrical and Mechanical Engineers	7590939	91494	Kirschau woollen factory, Frieberg leather work
Pilbeam	Reginald	Private	133rd Parachute Field Ambulance	7361895	118451	
Pinguet	Robert Sidney Paul	Sergeant	89 Parachute Security Section	10350914		
Pitcher	Richard Eric	Private	10th Battalion, Parachute Regiment	7369253		
Pitman	Kenneth Frederick	Driver	1st Airlanding Anti-Tank Battery, Royal Artillery	1462957		
Pitt	Fred	Private	3rd Battalion, Parachute Regiment	3455442	140134	Railway work
Pitt	Harry	Private	7th Battalion, King's Own Scottish Borderers	3197317		Merseburg clearing debris
Plenderleith	John	Private	3rd Battalion, Parachute Regiment	3449604		Ortrand saw mills
Plunton	Charles Frederick	Sapper	1st Parachute Squadron, Royal Engineers	1912650	118771	
Pocklington	George Edward	Lance Corporal	3rd Battalion, Parachute Regiment	4754286		
Ponting	Joseph Bernard	Private	3rd Battalion, Parachute Regiment	5193231	91656	Dresden clearing bomb damage
Poole	Granville	Gunner	2nd Airlanding Anti-Tank Battery, Royal Artillery	14583325	91888	Brüx miner

Pooley	Kenneth Walter	Private	Royal Army Ordnance Corps	14235531	117502	7013 mining
Pope	Robert Edward	Private	2nd Battalion, Parachute Regiment	5388849	75412	Unterschwödiz railway
Poplett	William Alfred	Private	3rd Battalion, Parachute Regiment	5113895	91512	Wurzmes, Teplitz Benzine
Postans	Charles	Sapper	9th Field Company, Royal Engineers Airborne	1867233	117153	
Pott	Robert Lailett John	Major	156th Battalion, Parachute Regiment	95241	2193	
Potter	Joseph William Dominic	Signalman	1st Airborne Division Signals	2590125	118138	Bad Grund
Potts	Dennis	Private	1st Parachute Brigade	6354479	75519	Limburg bomb damage labour, Stützengrün wood yard
Potts	Edmund	Private	11th Battalion, Parachute Regiment	10582732	117943	AK 7001 Hallendorf labour
Potts	Eric	Lance Corporal	181st Airlanding Field Ambulance	7399495		Jessen railway
Potts	John Reginald	Private	1st Parachute Brigade	5962036	89583	Halle air raid shelters
Poulton	William Lawrence	Private	2nd Battalion, South Staffordshire Regiment	4929079	91738	Kirschau blankets
Powell	Charles	Lance Corporal	2nd Battalion, Parachute Regiment	4035583	117800	Groß Düngen
Powell	Francis	Sergeant	Glider Pilot Regiment	190364		
Poynton	Joseph	Private	1st Airlanding Anti-Tank Battery, Royal Artillery	3386146	92076	Dresden road work
Prentice	Eric	Sergeant	1st Airlanding Light Regiment Royal Artillery	838595	118523	Freiberg lead mine
Presley	Leslie	Private	1st Battalion, Parachute Regiment	5672364	92261	Halle
Pressly	Ian Leith	Private	10th Battalion, Parachute Regiment	14420876	93261	Wallawitz Reichbahn [railways]
Preston	Lawrence	Private	1st Battalion, Border Regiment	3600079	75484	Germany carpenter
Preston	Tom	Corporal	7th Battalion, King's Own Scottish Borderers	3715814	88747	

Family Name	Forename	Rank	Unit	Army number	POW number	All kommandos
Price	Douglas	Private	3rd Battalion, Parachute Regiment	14286857	75429	Komatau labourer
Price	Raymond	Trooper	1st Airborne Reconnaissance Squadron	4919635	118715	
Price	Raymond William	Private	3rd Battalion, Parachute Regiment	5252678	91598	Kolumbus Brux coal mine
Price	Sidney Robert	Sergeant	Glider Pilot Regiment	2388139		
Prigmore	Frederick	Private	10th Battalion, Parachute Regiment	5512177		Torgua area air raid shelter tunnelling
Prince	Charles Henry	Private	181st Airlanding Field Ambulance	14672756		Jessen railway
Prior	Mark James	Sergeant/W	3rd Battalion, Parachute Regiment	6094195		Liepen farming
Pritchard	Thomas	Private	1st Battalion, Parachute Regiment	4802222	92155	
Prosho	Thomas George	Private	1st Parachute Brigade	6148592		
Prosser	John Edward	Private	4th Parachute Brigade	6202091	117339	AK 7011 Groß Düngen
Proudfoot	William	Staff Sergeant	Glider Pilot Regiment	922985	76320	
Proudlock	James	Private	156th Battalion, Parachute Regiment	101687		
Proven	Robert	Private	7th Battalion, King's Own Scottish Borderers	3192121	140107	
Pruden	Ernest Edward	Quartermaster Sergeant	16th Parachute Field Ambulance	7348767		
Pryce	John Ivor	Lieutenant	3rd Battalion, Parachute Regiment	177861	550	
Pugh	George Everton	Quartermaster Sergeant	Army Physical Training Corps	3710537	140127	
Pullen	Arthur Harvey	Private	2nd Battalion, Parachute Regiment	5445475		kdo 123 B Menzengraben salt mine
Pullinger	Albert	Private	2nd Battalion, Parachute Regiment	5836763		

Surname	First name(s)	Rank	Regiment/Unit	Service No.	POW No.	Notes
Pummell	Joseph Walter	Lance Corporal	1st Airborne Provost Company	6025654		
Purdie	John	Corporal	7th Battalion, King's Own Scottish Borderers	3193054		
Purdy	Harry	Private	3rd Battalion, Parachute Regiment	6203365	89831	kommando at Stalag 357 electrical maintenance then all kinds of labour
Purnell	Desmond James George	Gunner	1st Airlanding Anti-Tank Battery, Royal Artillery	4194052	117351	7012 Dinklar sugar beet
Purnell	William Tom	Private	7th Battalion, King's Own Scottish Borderers	3190949	90350	Salzgitter miner
Purvis	James Anderson	Private	2nd Battalion, South Staffordshire Regiment	557747		Zwickau labour
Pusser	David Stanley James	Sergeant	Royal Army Medical Corps	7370765		
Pye	George	Staff Sergeant	181st Airlanding Field Ambulance	7261693		
Quigley	Edmund	Sergeant	Light Warning Unit No. 6341, RAF	1149134	943	
Quinn	Albert Edward	Private	1st Battalion, Border Regiment	4546937	75350	Bockwitz labouring, Lauchhammer steel works
Quinn	Hugh	Lance Corporal	4th Parachute Squadron, Royal Engineers	1875356	117372	7001 Hallendorf clearing bombed buildings
Rafferty	Henry	Lance Corporal	1st Battalion, Border Regiment	3597639	118090	
Rafferty	William	Private	1st Battalion, Border Regiment	14642750		Oederan straw fabric
Rainbow	Edmund Hubert	Private	181st Airlanding Field Ambulance	7401241		Wallwitz railway repairs
Rainford	Arthur	Gunner	1st Airlanding Light Regiment, Royal Artillery	14302795		Erfenschlag nr Chemnitz timber yard, Grünhainichen
Ralph	Edward Ernest Sidney	Staff Sergeant	Glider Pilot Regiment	1434775	117299	
Ramsbottom	Harold Bocek?	Private	2nd Battalion, South Staffordshire Regiment	4207102	75682	Dresden shoe factory

Family Name	Forename	Rank	Unit	Army number	POW number	All kommandos
Ramsbottom	Walter James	Staff Sergeant	Glider Pilot Regiment	920299		Working party at Arnhem
Ramsey	Sydney	Private	2nd Battalion, Parachute Regiment	3249012		Forest working parties sent Chemnitz Freybourg forest
Randle	Oliver	Sapper	4th Parachute Squadron, Royal Engineers	2009716	117588	7011 Groß Düngen
Rands	Leslie Briton	Driver	Royal Army Service Corps	14425027		Railway
Rankin	William John Begg	Private	7th Battalion, King's Own Scottish Borderers	3190180	117583	7011 Groß Düngen
Ransom	James Leslie	Lance Corporal	250th Airborne Light Company, Royal Army Service Corps	10694205	91189	Kommando 133rd3
Ratchford	William	Private	11th Battalion, Parachute Regiment	14400554		Zwickau track laying Reichbahn
Rathband	Herbert Henry	Sergeant/W	Glider Pilot Regiment	1544344	103967	
Raven	William James	Private	3rd Battalion, Parachute Regiment	5679281	117827	AK 7012 sugar factory
Rawding	Harold	Private	2nd Battalion, South Staffordshire Regiment	4910663	17593	Kriebethal paper mill, Rohchencroats lumber yard
Rea	Henry William	Signalman	1st Airborne Division Signals	10547340	91900	Brux coal mine
Read	Lewis Allen	Sergeant	10th Battalion, Parachute Regiment	6402998		
Read	Victor Henry William	Signalman	1st Parachute Brigade, Royal Signals	2586247	89797	Hallendorf general labour steel works
Reading	Charles	Private	Parachute Regiment	262549		Zwickau railway
Reading	Kenneth	Private	21st Independent Parachute Company	143133rd29	91380	Brüx
Reast	Stanley Albert Barradell	Lance Corporal	1st Airborne Provost Company	986562	14904	
Reay	Harrison James	Private	11th Battalion, Parachute Regiment	3716400	75990	Kriebethal paper factory

Surname	First name	Rank	Unit	Service no.	POW no.	Notes
Reay	John James	Private	16th Parachute Field Ambulance	4451377	88937	Hildesheim sugar beet factory
Redman	Ernest	Private	3rd Battalion, Parachute Regiment	3862185	117983	
Reed	Ronald	Private	1st Battalion, Border Regiment	4469834	118362	
Reed	Samuel	Private	4th Parachute Brigade HQ	64180	118177	7013 Bad Gründ lead mining
Reeves	Reginald Henry	Sapper	9th Field Company, Royal Engineers Airborne	1883104	75854	
Reeves	Richard George	Private	3rd Battalion, Parachute Regiment	3968883	92171	Brux
Reid	George	Sapper	4th Parachute Squadron, Royal Engineers	2067721		M/S 51 steel erection
Reid	James Bruce	Private	7th Battalion, King's Own Scottish Borderers	14416765		Wurzen bomb damage, Dögnitz [bomb damage?]
Reid	William	Private	156th Battalion, Parachute Regiment	3131283		AK 133rd3 Dresden, tram depot repairs and water company pipe damage
Reilly	John	Craftsman	Royal Electrical and Mechanical Engineers	889575		Brux
Rendle	William	Private	181st Airlanding Field Ambulance	7399502		
Rennie	David Brown	Private	10th Battalion, Parachute Regiment	14423029		AK 188 Hertzburgh
Renton	John	Private	1st Battalion, Border Regiment	3192256	75503	AK 395A Komatau wagon repairs
Reynolds	Cyril Wilfred	Private	1st Battalion, Border Regiment	14645531		Dresden bomb damage
Reynolds	Jack	Lieutenant	2nd Battalion, South Staffordshire Regiment	190738	538	
Rhydderch	Verdun	Private	250th Airborne Light Company, Royal Army Service Corps	190586		
Rice	Ronald Edward	Corporal	2nd Battalion, South Staffordshire Regiment	5627473	89382	
Richards	John Thomas	Sergeant	1st Battalion, Parachute Regiment	4195046		Nr Hanover no number repairing railway tracks
Richardson	Ernest James	Private	Parachute Regiment	4979999		
Richey	James	Captain	1st Battalion, Parachute Regiment	151648	547	

Family Name	Forename	Rank	Unit	Army number	POW number	All kommandos
Riding	Cedric Kenneth	Private	1st Battalion, Border Regiment	3606398	118052	
Rigby-Jones MC	Guy	Major/T	181st Airlanding Field Ambulance	216228		
Riley	Bernard	Private	1st Battalion, Border Regiment	4546122	118191	AK 7013 Bad Gründ
Riley	Hugh	Private	1st Battalion, Border Regiment	3866213	75496	
Ring	Ronald	Private	156th Battalion, Parachute Regiment	4345252		
Roan	Cyril Charles	Lance Corporal	2nd Battalion, Parachute Regiment	5891392		Weißenfels boot and shoe
Robbie	William George	Private	10th Battalion, Parachute Regiment	2879256		Zeitz labour benzine factory
Robbins	James	Lance Corporal	181st Airlanding Field Ambulance	7366512	76659	Jessen
Roberts	Andrew	Lieutenant	2nd Battalion, Parachute Regiment	251878		
Roberts	Christopher William	Private	156th Battalion, Parachute Regiment	5253355		Wallwitz railway
Roberts	David Norman	Private	1st Battalion, Parachute Regiment	1678453		
Roberts	Geoffrey William	Private	7th Battalion, King's Own Scottish Borderers	14434693	92103	Brüx coal mining
Roberts	Harry Royston	Lieutenant	1st Airborne Divisional Workshop, Royal Electrical and Mechanical Engineers	281104	2188	
Roberts	John	Lance Corporal	2nd Battalion, South Staffordshire Regiment	4913467		Halle brick factory
Roberts	Leslie	Driver	Royal Signals	14532593	90430	AK 7005 Salzgitter mine
Roberts	Robert William	Lance Bombardier	Forward Observation Unit, Royal Artillery	924830	92050	AK Dresden 1326 clearing bomb damage, AK Dresden 1182 odd jobs

Surname	First name(s)	Rank	Unit	Number	POW No.	Work/Location
Roberts	Wilfred Clifford	Corporal	3rd Battalion, Parachute Regiment	7343865	118551	Regis Saxony
Robertson	Arthur	Gunner	2nd Airlanding Anti-Tank Battery, Royal Artillery	5392231		Dresden (sic) Teplitz? wood factory
Robertson	Matthew	Corporal	7th Battalion, King's Own Scottish Borderers	3192156		
Robertson	Robert Dickson	Corporal	7th Battalion, King's Own Scottish Borderers	3195880	118369	
Robertson	Stanley	Private	1st Parachute Brigade HQ	3603869	75447	Halle labouring
Robertson	Thomas Hood	Lance Corporal	156th Battalion, Parachute Regiment	91664		
Robinson	Cyril Bernard	Sergeant Major	1st Battalion, Parachute Regiment Brigade	4698977		Z 131 railway track laying
Robinson	Cyril Frederick	Sergeant	Glider Pilot Regiment	5830482		
Robinson	Michael William Patrick	Sapper	9th Field Company, Royal Engineers Airborne	1944654	76252	Brüx coal mining
Robson	Joseph	Lance Corporal	11th Battalion, Parachute Regiment	14644631	92139	Dresden bomb damage
Robson	Ronald	Driver	253rd Airborne Light Company, Royal Army Service Corps	174394		Wallwitz railway labourer
Rock	Ernest	Private	2nd Battalion, Parachute Regiment	3607396		Hallendorf AK 7001
Roddick	Roy Alistair	Corporal	10th Battalion, Parachute Regiment	6403044		
Rodgers	Harry	Lance Corporal	1st Parachute Brigade HQ	886051	89080	AK 7001 railway
Roger	James Charles	Private	10th Battalion, Parachute Regiment	4619865	117190	Ülzen bombed damage railway
Rogers	Arthur	Private	2nd Battalion, South Staffordshire Regiment	1811751	91421	Egar coal mine 13 B
Roissetter	Fredrick	Private	2nd Battalion, Parachute Regiment	875919	117234	
Rollins	Robert	Private	156th Battalion, Parachute Regiment	4748127		Komotau railway yard
Rook	Walter Ernest	Private	2nd Battalion, Parachute Regiment	5956703		Herzberg builder's labourer
Rose	John William	Private	181st Airlanding Field Ambulance	7404654	90026	Jessen/Elstar railway repairs

Family Name	Forename	Rank	Unit	Army number	POW number	All kommandos
Rose	Stanley Edward	Private	11th Battalion, Parachute Regiment	6854552	117584	kmd 7012 Hildesheim
Ross	John	Private	156th Battalion, Parachute Regiment	2823352	75658	Zeitz Labour
Ross	Ronald	Sergeant	7th Battalion, King's Own Scottish Borderers	3184652	88798	
Roughton	John Kenneth	Corporal	10th Battalion, Parachute Regiment	7886696		L101 Bockwitz auto repair shop, L25 Mitteldeutsche Stahlwerke
Rouse	Edwin	Corporal	7th Battalion, King's Own Scottish Borderers	3191861	91783	
Rouse	Ronald	Sergeant	11th Battalion, Parachute Regiment	4981946		
Routledge	James	Sergeant	3rd Battalion, Parachute Regiment	4275722		
Rowan	Gerald	Private	181st Airlanding Field Ambulance	144401865		
Rowbottom	Frank	Lance Corporal	2nd Battalion, South Staffordshire Regiment	5050824	52836	
Rowley	Ernest	Private	10th Battalion, Parachute Regiment	5347202		
Rowthorn	Aubrey Owen	Corporal	3rd Battalion, Parachute Regiment	5890319		
Royall	Arthur Robert	Lieutenant	1st Battalion, Border Regiment	269802	632	
Royle	James Harold Ernest	Private	2nd Battalion, Parachute Regiment	3454348	140132	
Rubin	Leonard Sidney	Private	181st Airlanding Field Ambulance	7403928		
Rumney	Albert Edward	Gunner	1st Airlanding Light Regiment, Royal Artillery	1103814	118160	Bad Grund miner
Rumsey	Reginald	Private	10th Battalion, Parachute Regiment	6407115	117600	Germany sugar beet factory
Rushforth	George	Lance Corporal	250th Airborne Light Company, Royal Army Service Corps	99987		
Russell	Andrew McCallum	Private	7th Battalion, King's Own Scottish Borderers	14607803	15459	Jessen railway work
Russell	Arthur Eli	Private	10th Battalion, Parachute Regiment	2048220	75423	Unterschwöditz

Russell	Ralph Frederick	Private	2nd Battalion, Parachute Regiment	5731487	89294	Halle REi 113 labourer out door
Russon	John Edward	Private	2nd Battalion, Parachute Regiment	4928328	140076	Mittenwald general clearing
Rutter	Jeffrey Raymond	Private	10th Battalion, Parachute Regiment	5836591		Merseburg clearing bomb damage
Ryan	Edward	Private	10th Battalion, Parachute Regiment	3961505		Menzel. Elsterwera
Ryan	Edward Joseph	Private	10th Battalion, Parachute Regiment	6914029	118579	
Ryan	Ronald William	Sergeant	Glider Pilot Regiment	2589852		
Saabye	Jack	Sapper	Royal Engineers	1864157	118238	
Sadler	Charles	Sergeant	156th Battalion, Parachute Regiment	4387908		
Salt	Bernard Frederick	Private	2nd Battalion, Parachute Regiment	14660885	117150	
Saltman	Jack	Private	7th Battalion, King's Own Scottish Borderers	14213424	89885	357 joiner
Salton	James	Private	10th Battalion, Parachute Regiment	3056379	75694	Elsterwerda stone making (sic)
Sander	Gustave	Private	11th Battalion, Parachute Regiment	13807937	91694	Dresden sawmill
Sanders	Samuel John Frederick	Staff Sergeant	181st Airlanding Field Ambulance	7348718	77583	
Sanderson	Ellison	Sergeant	Glider Pilot Regiment	937039		
Sankey	Walter	Private	2nd Battalion, South Staffordshire Regiment	14480882	91180	Wallwitz
Sargant	Raymond	Sergeant	Glider Pilot Regiment	4617321		
Sargent	Reginald Arthur	Driver	181st Airlanding Field Ambulance	199690		Dresden road work
Saunders	Charles Stanley	Private	3rd Battalion, Parachute Regiment	5381500	1249	AK 123B Menzengraben
Saunders	John Richard	Private	2nd Battalion, South Staffordshire Regiment	14397706	92173	Brüx mining

Family Name	Forename	Rank	Unit	Army number	POW number	All kommandos
Saunders	Leslie Percy	Sergeant	Glider Pilot Regiment	4804127		
Saunders	William	Private	2nd Battalion, Parachute Regiment	7018194		Salzgitter labouring stone tunnel
Savage	Henry Owen	Corporal	1st Battalion, Parachute Regiment	2057101		
Sawyer	James George	Lance Corporal	250th Airborne Light Company, Royal Army Service Corps	289543	91153	Dresden factory work
Sawyer	John	Private	2nd Battalion, South Staffordshire Regiment	5047154	89803	Hallendorf labourer 7001
Sawyers	Edward	Private	3rd Battalion, Parachute Regiment	4456749		Wurzmes surface mine, Aussig railways
Sayles	Bennett	Staff Sergeant	Glider Pilot Regiment	850767		
Scholfield	John	Private	181st Airlanding Field Ambulance	7407356		
Scott	Andrew	Sergeant	7th Battalion, King's Own Scottish Borderers	3191998		
Scott	Arnold	Private	156th Battalion, Parachute Regiment	4746709		
Scott	Joseph James	Private	1st Battalion, Border Regiment	3603978	118152	Bad Gründ 7013
Scott	Joseph Rowland	Gunner	1st Airlanding Light Regiment, Royal Artillery	14322051		Zeitz Halle surface coal quarry
Scott	William Mawhinnie	Private	2nd Battalion, South Staffordshire Regiment	997574	75351	Lengenfeld E43 wool cleaning
Scrivener	Edmund Filford	Lieutenant	1st Battalion, Border Regiment	292013	601	
Scutt	Henry John	Private	10th Battalion, Parachute Regiment	6395492		Merseberg tunnelling
Seabridge	Thomas Cyril	Private	2nd Battalion, South Staffordshire Regiment	5050452	117514	Ülzen railway repair
Seale	Joseph Alexander	Private	1st Battalion, Border Regiment	14645417	118574	
Seaman	Frederick George	Sergeant	Glider Pilot Regiment	876231		

Surname	First name(s)	Rank	Regiment			Work/Location
Searle	Ivan John	Private	2nd Battalion, Parachute Regiment	562071	75305	Komatau railway work
Sefton	Stanley	Private	11th Battalion, Parachute Regiment	4042163	90948	D608 Eilenburg
Seymour	George Harry	Private	11th Battalion, Parachute Regiment	6464228	118672	
Seymour	Tom Henry	Lance Corporal	1st Battalion, Border Regiment	14574818	75687	Falkenau mining
Sharkey	James	Private	2nd Battalion, Parachute Regiment	14540464	294149	
Sharlott	Ronald Cyril Walter	Private	21st Independent Parachute Company	14663891	117627	Hildesheim sugar beet
Shaw	Albert	Private	7th Battalion, King's Own Scottish Borderers	10602461		123B Menzengraben salt mine
Shaw	Neil Buchanan	Corporal	7th Battalion, King's Own Scottish Borderers	14435379	89618	
Shaw	Robert	Private	2nd Battalion, Parachute Regiment	13041806		
Shearer	George	Lance Corporal	7th Battalion, King's Own Scottish Borderers	4268582	91488	Kirschau blanket factory, Dresden agriculture Radebeul tin plate factory
Shears	Charles Eli	Private	10th Battalion, Parachute Regiment	5623548		Dresden clearing up bomb damage under the SS
Shedden	William	Lance Corporal	7th Battalion, King's Own Scottish Borderers	3191038	90550	
Sheilds	John Williams	Private	16th Parachute Field Ambulance	14272469	91321	
Shelbourne	James Ernest	Private	1st Battalion, Parachute Regiment	6914183		Ei 114 salt mine, Be 6 Bitterfeld coal mine
Sheldon	Walter	Private	1st Battalion, Border Regiment	14201232	91951	Dresden labouring
Shell	Lionel	Sergeant	Glider Pilot Regiment	319389		
Shelton	Albert Stanley	Lance Corporal	1st Battalion, Parachute Regiment Brigade	6107546		Chemnitz soap factory
Shephard	Wallis James	Private	1st Battalion, Border Regiment	3604890	91785	Brickyard
Shepherd	Frank	Staff Sergeant	Glider Pilot Regiment	932328		
Shepherd	Joseph	Private	11th Battalion, Parachute Regiment	14647522	75987	Dresden wood factory

429

Family Name	Forename	Rank	Unit	Army number	POW number	All kommandos
Shepherd	Robert	Driver	250th Airborne Light Company, Royal Army Service Corps	240955	89511	Halle building air raid shelters
Shepley	Arthur	Sergeant, Lance	156th Battalion, Parachute Regiment	4344978	52919	
Sherret	Richard	Private	7th Battalion, King's Own Scottish Borderers	3196547	9133rd3	
Sherwood	Reginald Douglas	Gunner	1st Airlanding Light Regiment, Royal Artillery	904283	117636	Groß Düngon 7011
Short	Edward Richard	Private	11th Battalion, Parachute Regiment	5954640	117579	Dinkler sugar beet factory
Silvester	Vernon John Bellis	Lieutenant	156th Battalion, Parachute Regiment	204917	91013	
Simonds	William Robert	Private	156th Battalion, Parachute Regiment	5884494	75416	Komatu railway
Simons	Denis Harold	Staff Sergeant	Glider Pilot Regiment	119641		
Simpson	Albert	Staff Sergeant	Glider Pilot Regiment	856791		
Simpson	David Anderson	Captain	Glider Pilot Regiment	193137	8494	
Simpson	David Richard	Trooper	1st Airborne Reconnaissance Squadron	4807155	91436	Zwickau lager staff
Skelly	Matthew	Private	Royal Army Medical Corps	59586	118404	
Skidmore	Leonard	Private	2nd Battalion, South Staffordshire Regiment	14286891	92165	Dresden bomb damage
Slatter	Reginald	Private	2nd Battalion, South Staffordshire Regiment	5509858	91700	Zwikau railway
Sloan	Alexander	Private	7th Battalion, King's Own Scottish Borderers	3189499	92645	
Small	Eric Lyng	Private	10th Battalion, Parachute Regiment	5682652	88909	
Small	William Desmond	Private	1st Battalion, Parachute Regiment	2616873		Torgau salt mine, Torgau coal mine

Smallwood	Leonard	Bombardier	1st Airlanding Anti-Tank Battery, Royal Artillery	2077387	91537	
Smart	Daniel Penman	Lance Corporal	4th Battalion, Dorset Regiment	4923884		
Smith	Arthur John Alan	Staff Sergeant	Glider Pilot Regiment	14206556		
Smith	Claude Albert	Sergeant	Glider Pilot Regiment	6400991		
Smith	Frederick Lawrence Spencer	Private	Royal Army Medical Corps	7349477		
Smith	Gerald	Private	2nd Battalion, Parachute Regiment	895906	90561	
Smith	Hugh	Private	3rd Battalion, Parachute Regiment	972248	117441	Kommando 7012 Dinkler sugar beet
Smith	James	Private	2nd Battalion, Parachute Regiment	14206353		Eilenburg labouring
Smith	John Lawrence	Private	156th Battalion, Parachute Regiment	3781730	75511	
Smith	John Thomas	Private	156th Battalion, Parachute Regiment	14665924	90483	Brabag-Zeitz filling in yankee bomb holes
Smith	Leslie	Private	10th Battalion, Parachute Regiment	6103769	117868	
Smith	Norman	Private	2nd Battalion, Parachute Regiment	7367390	89422	Jessen railway
Smith	Norman Peter	Private	7th Battalion, King's Own Scottish Borderers	3191832	90175	Me 41 E bomb debris
Smith	Reginald Albert	Driver	250th Airborne Light Company, Royal Army Service Corps	6405247	90822	Mersburg sand pit
Smith	Richard Arthur	Private	11th Battalion, Parachute Regiment	14406654	118292	Bad Grund lead mine 7013
Smith	Ronald Arthur	Private	4th Parachute Brigade	5891105		Dresden road works
Smith	Stanley	Private	11th Battalion, Parachute Regiment	6286753	140256	
Smith	Stephen Knowles	Sergeant	1st Parachute Squadron, Royal Engineers	869950		
Smith	Thomas	Private	3rd Battalion, Parachute Regiment	3244188	75318	Wallwitz railway

Family Name	Forename	Rank	Unit	Army number	POW number	All kommandos
Smith	William	Private	4th Battalion, Dorset Regiment	3245456	17563	
Smith	William Henry	Private	2nd Battalion, South Staffordshire Regiment	14700136		Halle Trotha Na 33 E brick works
Smithson	Douglas	Sergeant	Glider Pilot Regiment	1886189		
Smyth	John Michael	Private	10th Battalion, Parachute Regiment	3961524	75686	Elsterwerder stone making, Mouchow coal mine
Snape	William	Private	11th Battalion, Parachute Regiment	4200916	140074	
Snell	William	Private	3rd Battalion, Parachute Regiment	14395715		Brüx surface mine
Snelson	John Alfred	Private	4th Battalion, Dorset Regiment	3654902	19485	Kleinleipisch railways in coalfield
Snoding	Victor Henry	Private	16th Parachute Field Ambulance	14679808		Jessen railway
Southwell	Frank	Trooper	1st Airborne Reconnaissance Squadron	10601898	88786	Halle air raid shelter construction, Merseburg air raid shelter construction
Speedie	William	Gunner	1st Airlanding Light Regiment, Royal Artillery	14297015	77092	Ei 113E Eisleben copper mining, He 102 E Hettstedt factory smelting copper
Spencer	John Robert	Private	156th Battalion, Parachute Regiment	3448672		Mückenberg coal mine
Spicer	Joseph Henry	Private	3rd Battalion, Parachute Regiment	3773429		Ortrand saw mills
Sproson	Ernest Travis	Private	156th Battalion, Parachute Regiment	5109576		Zwickau railway
Staddon	Roy Glinn	Lieutenant	1st Airlanding Light Regiment, Royal Artillery	258888	2203	
Staff	Harry Victor William	Private	1st Battalion, Parachute Regiment	6015570		
Stanislaus	George	Private	3rd Battalion, Parachute Regiment	5672402		Merseburg air raid shelters
Stanley	Dennis	Private	7th Battalion, King's Own Scottish Borderers	5255876		Gunnersdorf forestry, Oderan straw cooking

Surname	First name	Rank	Unit	Number	Number	Work/Camp
Stark	Ronnie Leslie	Major	1st Battalion, Parachute Regiment	167154	531	
Start	Arthur Edward	Driver	Royal Army Service Corps	106686628	25680	Stützengrün
Stead	John Edward	Staff Sergeant	Glider Pilot Regiment	794717		
Steel	Henry	Private	7th Battalion, King's Own Scottish Borderers	3190845	75879	Kalkenau coal mines
Steel	James	Lieutenant	Royal Engineers	256839	11453	
Steer	George William	Captain	7th Battalion, King's Own Scottish Borderers	121441	580	
Steirn	Aubrey Edward	Private	4th Battalion, Dorset Regiment	5734516	117345	
Stephens	Douglas	Driver	Royal Army Service Corps	10689300	91454	
Stephens	John Howard	Lieutenant	Glider Pilot Regiment	166162	5868	
Stephenson	Charles Richard	Lance Corporal	4th Parachute Brigade HQ	3711558		Floßmühle
Stephenson	Fredrick John	Private	2nd Battalion, Parachute Regiment	4461913		Merseburg mining and air raid shelters
Stephenson	James Airen	Sergeant	Glider Pilot Regiment	4616329		
Stevens	Charles Edward	Signalman	1st Parachute Brigade, Royal Signals	2587250	9133rd5	Kriebethal packing labourer, Rautenkranz tree felling
Stevens	Daniel Donne	Sapper	4th Parachute Squadron, Royal Engineers	1877687	90690	Tolkewitz Dresden Omnibus, Schlachthof –slaughterhouse, Straffe Lager digging air raid shelters
Stevens	Reginald Charles	Sergeant	3rd Battalion, Parachute Regiment	3908419		
Stevens	Reginald John	Private	HQ 1st Airlanding Brigade	5441106	91453	Zwikau railway
Stevens	Thomas Birdsall	Sergeant	Glider Pilot Regiment	3713627		

Family Name	Forename	Rank	Unit	Army number	POW number	All kommandos
Stevens	Walter Wiliam	Private	2nd Battalion, Parachute Regiment	6203483	91187	Zeitz bomb holes
Stewart	Edward	Private	4th Parachute Brigade HQ	2882576	90551	Herzberg demolition
Stewart	Lachlan McIntyre	Private	2nd Airlanding Anti-Tank Battery, Royal Artillery	1440083	91696	Kirschau Blanket factory, Dresden bomb damage
Stidson	Bert James George	Lance Corporal	3rd Battalion, Parachute Regiment	859567	91531	
Still	Blake Edwin Charles	Private	10th Battalion, Parachute Regiment	2323483		Dresden tramways and salvage
Stillwell	John James	Private	10th Battalion, Parachute Regiment	6412179		Halle air raid shelters
Stimpson	John William	Private	1st Battalion, Border Regiment	4756947	91797	4/C Railway
Stockbridge	Stanley Gordon	Lance Corporal	1st Battalion, Parachute Regiment	5050289	90411	Salzgitter tunnelling
Stokes	Jack	Private	2nd Battalion, Parachute Regiment	5726302	140087	
Stokes	Reginald	Private	2nd Battalion, South Staffordshire Regiment	5051452	89713	Working party Stalag 357 labouring
Stone	Charles	Private	3rd Battalion, Parachute Regiment	5125422	118806	
Stone	Frank John	Corporal	250th Airborne Light Company, Royal Army Service Corps	176054	117625	
Stones	Horace Ryan	Sergeant	Glider Pilot Regiment	4337089		
Storey	Sidney Joseph	Private	2nd Battalion, South Staffordshire Regiment	4922800	89283	Wurzmes mines and demolition, Brüx mines and demolition
Stott	William Patrick	Lieutenant	1st Battalion, Border Regiment	228611	619	
Streeter	Fred Henry	Private	1st Battalion, Border Regiment	14319170	91725	Wurzmes coal mining, Tschausch general labouring, Kolumbus coal mining

Surname	First names	Rank	Regiment	Number	Number	Notes
Stripp	Ronald Sidney	Private	1st Battalion, Border Regiment	6412612	75518	Glina? general labouring
Strong	Gordon Thomas Piney	Sergeant	1st Battalion, Parachute Regiment	7901320	89413	Varchentin
Stubbs	Herbert Henry	Lance Corporal	Provost Company, 1st Airborne Division	4803335	90844	
Such	Albert George	Gunner	1st Airlanding Light Regiment, Royal Artillery	14318215	52917	
Suffolk	Douglas Evan Gabe	Driver	250th Airborne Light Company, Royal Army Service Corps	243335		
Sullivan	David	Private	133rd Parachute Field Ambulance	14584840	90705	
Sullivan	Edward	Private	11th Battalion, Parachute Regiment	4124947	91723	Merseburg labouring
Sullivan	Henry	Private	2nd Battalion, Parachute Regiment	5445367		Dresden tramways
Sullivan	John Anthony	Sergeant	Glider Pilot Regiment	6915850	118814	
Sullivan	Joseph Vincent	Private	133rd Parachute Field Ambulance	7265333	90387	
Sully	Reginald Gordon	Lance Corporal	3rd Battalion, Parachute Regiment	7958094		Zwickay Railway
Sumner	James	Private	1st Battalion, Parachute Regiment	4206313	75167	Komotau fitter
Sunderland	Abram	Private	4th Battalion, Dorset Regiment	3658220	26067	
Sutherberry	Stanley	Trooper	1st Airborne Reconnaissance Squadron	37775079	118190	Bad Grund mining 7013
Sutton	Peter Francis	Private	1st Battalion, Parachute Regiment	1509534	52880	Menzengraben 123 salt mine
Swan	John	Private	10th Battalion, Parachute Regiment	2986583	140114	
Sweeney	Frederick Thomas	Lance Corporal	2nd Battalion, Parachute Regiment	4128770	89687	Hallendorf labourer
Sweeney	James	Private	2nd Battalion, Parachute Regiment	14314297	119302	
Sweeney	Joseph	Private	3rd Battalion, Parachute Regiment	7015510		
Swinburn	Roland Alfred	Private	2nd Battalion, South Staffordshire Regiment	4914462	89281	Chech (sic) railways
Swiney	George Henry	Private	181st Airlanding Field Ambulance	2366607		

Family Name	Forename	Rank	Unit	Army number	POW number	All kommandos
Swire	Leonard Robert	Private	1st Battalion, Border Regiment	14677968	75557	Gliena pick and shovel
Sykes	Jack	Corporal	10th Battalion, Parachute Regiment	4613278	88923	
Symes	Donald Douglas	Private	4th Parachute Brigade HQ	3969910		Coal heaving
Tait	Thomas Henry	Private	2nd Battalion, Parachute Regiment	1700964		Herzberg carpenter
Tall	Anthony Harold	Private	Parachute Regiment	5509604	91419	Wurzmes surface coal mine, Tschausch railway line repair
Tallant	George William	Private	133rd Parachute Field Ambulance	14580854		
Tams	Leonard James	Private	2nd Battalion, South Staffordshire Regiment	4918801		Merseburg ARP shelters
Tandy	Bernard Raymond	Private	4th Battalion, Dorset Regiment	4922073	117679	AK 7001 Hallendorf
Tarbitten	John Walter	Staff Sergeant	Glider Pilot Regiment	7363554		
Tasker	David Ritchie	Company Sergeant Major	2nd Battalion, Parachute Regiment	2882737		
Tate	Alfred	Private	2nd Battalion, Parachute Regiment	4747547	117923	Salzgitter Labourer, Barum labourer
Tate	George Cooper	Private	1st Battalion, Border Regiment	3602897	24253	Mückenberg surface coal mine
Taylor	Amos	Private	Parachute Regiment	4127008	91561	AK 49 A Merseburg
Taylor	Clifford James	Lance Corporal	2nd Battalion, South Staffordshire Regiment	4919628	89432	Sudetenland 50, Sudetenland
Taylor	Eric	Gunner	1st Airlanding Light Regiment, Royal Artillery	974904	118496	
Taylor	Frederick	Gunner	1st Airlanding Anti-Tank Battery, Royal Artillery	1684407	92087	Dresden bomb debris

Surname	Given names	Rank	Unit	No. 1	No. 2	Work/Location
Taylor	Gordon Erich	Corporal	1st Parachute Squadron, Royal Engineers	5184742		Merseburg bomb damage
Taylor	Harry	Private	1st Battalion, Border Regiment	1560536	117656	
Taylor	James William	Lieutenant	7th Battalion, King's Own Scottish Borderers	489	2197	
Taylor	John Alfred	Driver	Royal Army Service Corps	14403352	25803	087 Aue timber yard
Taylor	Kenneth	Gunner	2nd Airlanding Anti-Tank Battery, Royal Artillery	14545649		Sudetenland miner
Taylor	Kenneth Joseph	Private	21st Independent Parachute Company	6148344	93412	Trebsen (Sachs) Labouring paper factory
Taylor	Perry	Private	11th Battalion, Parachute Regiment	6095347	91577	Dresden bomb damage
Taylor	William Mons	Private	156th Battalion, Parachute Regiment	14625060	90423	Brick laying 357
Tebbutt	Richard Henry	Gunner	1st Airlanding Light Regiment, Royal Artillery	14329479	75820	Zeitz Surface coal mine
Tedds	Frederick Arthur	Private	3rd Battalion, Parachute Regiment	5116659	91534	Wurzmes (S'land) coal mines and brick works, Tschausch Brüx railway
Teece	Percy James	Lance Corporal	1st Airborne Provost Company	7398111	118232	Bad Grund lead mine 7013
Telfer	James	Private	10th Battalion, Parachute Regiment	10583514		Dresden labour
Temple	Stanley James	Sapper	1st Parachute Squadron, Royal Engineers	1876271	117889	Nr Hildestum, Hannover sugar beet factory
Tennet	Arthur	Lance Corporal	2nd Battalion, Parachute Regiment	4271165		Herzberg labourer
Terry	Fred Dolphin	Sergeant	1st Battalion, Border Regiment	3602936		
Tew	Leonard Ira	Lance Corporal	2nd Battalion, South Staffordshire Regiment	1603718	89146	Brüx surface mining
Thackeray	Charles Louis	Staff Sergeant	Glider Pilot Regiment	87484		
Thatcher	Laurence Albion	Private	2nd Battalion, Parachute Regiment	14270226		
Thelwell	Arthur	Lance Corporal	Provost Company, 1st Airborne Division	3976695		Brüx mines demolition, Brüx railway laying
Thickens	Trevor	Gunner	1st Airlanding Brigade, Royal Signals	14319564		Zeitz labouring

Family Name	Forename	Rank	Unit	Army number	POW number	All kommandos
Thomas	Frederick George	Private	Parachute Regiment	6089619		Brüx miner
Thomas	Frederick H G	Private	10th Battalion, Parachute Regiment	4749339	75495	Jesson rail road
Thomas	Geoffrey Ramsden	Leading Aircraftman	Light Warning Unit No. 6080, RAF	1009701	92596	
Thomas	Jack	Private	1st Battalion, Parachute Regiment	2616730	117732	AK 7013 Bad Grund lead
Thomas	John Arthur	Lance Corporal	1st Airborne Reconnaissance Squadron	7664756		
Thomas	Thomas David	Lance Corporal	Royal Army Medical Corps	7402758		
Thomas	William	Lance Corporal	16th Parachute Field Ambulance	90752	89991	
Thompson	Albert	Sergeant	3rd Battalion, Parachute Regiment	4802925	89546	
Thompson	Harold	Corporal	10th Battalion, Parachute Regiment	4372953	90421	
Thompson	Harry	Private	4th Battalion, Dorset Regiment	5953745	17537	
Thompson	Harry	Sapper	9th Field Company, Royal Engineers Airborne	4858665		Glaze stone quarry, Bruux labouring
Thompson	Horace	Private	3rd Battalion, Parachute Regiment	1513648		Dresden 'Pat: Medicine'
Thompson	John	Corporal	156th Battalion, Parachute Regiment	5725314	117361	
Thompson	William Robert	Driver	250th Airborne Light Company, Royal Army Service Corps	75968	91124	AK Sch188 Herzburg cooking
Thomson	John	Staff Sergeant	Glider Pilot Regiment	3194205		
Thomson	John	Private	Royal Army Medical Corps	3052830	118773	
Thornley	Robert	Private	1st Battalion, Border Regiment	3598842	75560	Urterswoduzje coal mine
Thornton	Cyril Williams	Private	1st Battalion, Parachute Regiment	6408334	75789	Unterswodish coal mine
Thornton	Frederick George	Driver	1st Parachute Brigade, Royal Signals	2572006	92249	

438

Surname	First name	Rank	Regiment	Number	Number	Location
Thorpe	Russell Ambrose	Private	2nd Battalion, South Staffordshire Regiment	4914617		Jesson railway
Thrussell	Joseph	Private	7th Battalion, King's Own Scottish Borderers	3191825		Wurzmes mining, Tschauch Brüx Corporation
Tidball	Ronald	Private	Royal Army Medical Corps, attached 1st Battalion, Parachute Regiment	14590201	294182	
Tidswell	Peter James	Private	2nd Battalion, South Staffordshire Regiment	4928642	91743	Kirschau blanket factory, Zwickau Paper Factory
Tidy	Harold	Private	3rd Battalion, Parachute Regiment	3858993		
Tillotson	John Willie	Private	133rd Parachute Field Ambulance	168025	89206	
Timothy	John	Major	1st Battalion, Parachute Regiment	164812	530	
Tims	Eric	Sergeant	3rd Battalion, Parachute Regiment	3526756		
Tindale	William	Private	7th Battalion, King's Own Scottish Borderers	3194092	89484	Merseburg air raid shelters
Tingey	Aubrey Henry	Private	2nd Battalion, South Staffordshire Regiment	14695003	75848	39/386 Paper factory Grmma
Tipler	Jack	Sapper	9th Field Company, Royal Engineers Airborne	1875910		Stützengrün gaz halts platz
Tobin	John O'Hara	Captain	Royal Army Medical Corps	263459	90863	Bralitz AK 1088 (Stalag III C)
Tobin	Montague	Staff Sergeant	Glider Pilot Regiment	7596863	76330	
Tolcher	Cecil	Private	3rd Battalion, Parachute Regiment	5109776	117899	7011 Groß Düngen
Tomblin	Bryan Alan	Sergeant	Glider Pilot Regiment	14259326	1005	
Tomlinson	John William	Sergeant	2nd Battalion, Parachute Regiment	3457129		
Tonks	Jack	Sergeant	Glider Pilot Regiment	1533350		
Topp	Edward	Private	Royal Army Medical Corps, attached 11th Battalion, Parachute Regiment	7366381		
Towler	Walter	Private	3rd Battalion, Parachute Regiment	1452410	90034	Hallendord
Towns	Spencer Albert	Corporal	2nd Battalion, Parachute Regiment	4035901	89439	

439

Family Name	Forename	Rank	Unit	Army number	POW number	All kommandos
Townsend	Arthur Sidney	Private	2nd Battalion, South Staffordshire Regiment	4928172		Ei 114 E salt mine
Townsend	Reginald George	Driver	1st Airlanding Anti-Tank Battery, Royal Artillery	14260506	91712	Brüx coal mines
Townsley	Arthur	Private	156th Battalion, Parachute Regiment	14632673	90526	Wittenburg brick works, Mutchaw coal mines
Tracey	Daniel Edward	Private	4th Battalion, Dorset Regiment	3663292	19473	Gunnersdorf Forestry, Neiderweisa cement factory, Chemnitz railway
Tracy	John	Private	7th Battalion, King's Own Scottish Borderers	14205520	90686	Dognitz labourer tile factory
Travers	Thomas	Lance Corporal	2nd Battalion, Parachute Regiment	14290146	91395	G123 Labourer
Travis	Geoffrey Edwards	Private	1st Battalion, Border Regiment	3783718	92124	Brüx mine
Travis-Davison	Kenneth	Sergeant	Glider Pilot Regiment	1779501		
Trayfoot	Albert John	Private	2nd Battalion, South Staffordshire Regiment	6098705		Wurzmes mining, Tschaus railway
Treherne	Leslie Edward Sidley	Lieutenant	10th Battalion, Parachute Regiment	224515	91219	
Trevis	John Thomas	Private	4th Battalion, Dorset Regiment	5050843	17552	Gunnersdorf, Neiderwiesa
Trim	Henry George	Lance Corporal	261st Field Park Company, Royal Engineers	2077679	90624	Z 131 Zwickau Saxony Reichbahn
Trotter	Andrew Carmochan?	Corporal	7th Battalion, King's Own Scottish Borderers	19414344	88788	
Troughear	John Joseph	Private	1st Battalion, Border Regiment	14206269	75419	Techwitz Navvy work
Troy	Sidney Richard	Gunner	2nd Airlanding Anti-Tank Battery, Royal Artillery	1524961	117721	AK 7012 Dinklar sugar beet labourer
Trueman	Arthur	Sergeant	Glider Pilot Regiment	101997	52909	1249 Obermaßfeld

Surname	Forename	Rank	Unit	Number	Number	Camp work
Truscott	James Sidney	Private	2nd Battalion, Parachute Regiment	5732326		Sudetenland mine
Tucker	Percy Henry	Corporal	1st Battalion, Parachute Regiment	5436835	118466	
Tucker	Sidney Francis	Lance Corporal	2nd Battalion, South Staffordshire Regiment	5672376		Rei 113 air raid shelters, Me 40 E air raid shelters
Tuckwood	Robert George	Private	1st Battalion, Parachute Regiment	2082225		Dresden Timber Yard
Tunningley	Adino	Sapper	9th Field Company, Royal Engineers Airborne	2126746	91350	Z 131 Zwickau railway
Turnbull	Albert	Signalman	1st Airlanding Anti-Tank Battery, Royal Artillery	14321818		Wurzmes surface mining, Brüx constructing shelters
Turner	Arthur	Sergeant	1st Battalion, Parachute Regiment	2612567		Varchentin farming
Turner	Henry Charles	Private	10th Battalion, Parachute Regiment	14429950	75473	Komotau Factory
Turner	John Henry	Private	10th Battalion, Parachute Regiment	4126773	90517	AK 453 Reinersdorf
Turner	Ronald	Sapper	9th Field Company, Royal Engineers Airborne	2006480		T35 Zeitz labouring
Turner	Stanley Reginald	Craftsman	Royal Electrical and Mechanical Engineers	5124014	75833	Mulhtroff Timber yard
Turner	William	Driver	250th Airborne Light Company, Royal Army Service Corps	11057252	91122	Herzberg labour
Turnidge	Benjamin Basil	Private	1st Battalion, Parachute Regiment	6012580		Dresden timber yard
Turrell	Leslie	Private	11th Battalion, Parachute Regiment	3770461	117767	Hallendorf
Twort	James Alfred	Lance Corporal	3rd Battalion, Parachute Regiment	2037852		
Tyson	Geoffrey	Gunner	1st Airlanding Light Regiment, Royal Artillery	4390649		REI 113 air raid shelters
Underwood	Frederick Ernest	Signalman	1st Airlanding Brigade, Royal Signals	10579286	118893	
Ungi	Albert	Private	16th Parachute Field Ambulance	14560365	90154	Tschausch III digging

Family Name	Forename	Rank	Unit	Army number	POW number	All kommandos
Unsworth	Joseph	Lance Corporal	1st Airborne Provost Company	19411962		
Urquhart	David	Sergeant, Lance	1st Parachute Squadron, Royal Engineers	2136258	89621	Liepen joiner
Urquhart	James Alex	Staff Sergeant	Glider Pilot Regiment	5185152		
Vale	Edwin John	Private	2nd Battalion, Parachute Regiment	13026704		Halle air raid shelters
Vardy	Harold	Private	2nd Battalion, Parachute Regiment	4747822	89909	Hallendorf 7001 iron ingots, Barum bomb damage
Varney	Charles Norman	Bombardier	Royal Artillery	14311471	117328	Hanover kommando but not working
Vaugan	Thomas	Signalman	4th Parachute Brigade, Royal Signals	4034124	90845	Königswalde, Brüx benzine factory
Vaughan	Peter	Trooper	1st Airborne Reconnaissance Squadron	13116352	75803	Kdo 806
Vaughan	Thomas Charles	Private	2nd Battalion, South Staffordshire Regiment	4928042	93418	Friewaldau brickworks
Veal	Robert William	Private	4th Battalion, Dorset Regiment	14441359		Floßmühle forestry
Vernon	Stanley	Lance Corporal	2nd Battalion, Parachute Regiment	1427411		Rei 113 Halle
Verrall	Cyril Albert Douglas	Private	1st Battalion, Border Regiment	7023138	75483	Großröhrsdorf, Prossen
Vick	Arthur James	Sergeant, Lance	7th Battalion, King's Own Scottish Borderers	4750885	89592	
Vincent	Stanley Maurice	Private	2nd Battalion, Parachute Regiment	549942		Erfenschlag timber yard
Vine	James	Private	1st Battalion, Border Regiment	3771185		Headstead
Vooght	Leslie John	Lance Corporal	2nd Battalion, Parachute Regiment	6402898		

CAMP LIFE

Surname	First names	Rank	Unit	Number	Number	Work
Vowles	Frederick Harry	Private	10th Battalion, Parachute Regiment	53337249	75677	Ortrand saw mill
Wade	Richard Samuel	Staff Sergeant	Glider Pilot Regiment	6969360	117350	
Wadling	Ronald Francis	Private	2nd Battalion, South Staffordshire Regiment	5631222	118222	7012 Dinklar
Wagstaff	Jack	Private	2nd Battalion, South Staffordshire Regiment	4955931	89186	Merseburg air raid shelters
Wainright	Lawrence	Lance Corporal	2nd Battalion, Parachute Regiment	5783535		D 608 Eilenburg labouring
Wake	Lewis James	Lance Corporal	4th Battalion, Dorset Regiment	5725542	99899	Water works
Walker-Cook	Alfred	Staff Sergeant	Army Physical Training Corps	4689266		
Wallace	Samuel	Private	1st Battalion, Border Regiment	14671726	24363	Halle brick factory
Wallis	Stanley Percival	Private	1st Battalion, Parachute Regiment	14565828		Z 131 Zwikau railway [?????]
Wallis	William	Sergeant	3rd Battalion, Parachute Regiment	5048129		
Walpole	Robert Holland	Lieutenant	1st Parachute Squadron, Royal Engineers	299883	570	
Walsh	Richard	Private	2nd Battalion, Parachute Regiment	6409551		Chemnitz labour
Walsh	William Marston	Driver	1st Parachute Brigade	3975544		Röhrsdorf wood factory
Walters	Ernest Frederick	Lieutenant	2nd Battalion, South Staffordshire Regiment	247035	625	
Walton	Frank Thomas	Private	1st Battalion, Parachute Regiment	6015864		Königswalde, Brüx builders labourers
Ward	Cyril Thomas James	Driver	253rd Airborne Light Company, Royal Army Service Corps	191887	91660	Coal mining
Ward	Douglas Edward Newman	Staff Sergeant	Glider Pilot Regiment	1878308		

443

Family Name	Forename	Rank	Unit	Army number	POW number	All kommandos
Ward	Frederick Ernest	Private	4th Battalion, Dorset Regiment	5959729	17577	
Ward	Jack	Corporal	10th Battalion, Parachute Regiment	4122698		
Ward	Kenneth Alan	Private	2nd Battalion, Parachute Regiment	14401199	90990	Komotau railway repairs
Ward	Raymond John	Staff Sergeant	Glider Pilot Regiment	961033	117493	
Ward	William Edward	Private	10th Battalion, Parachute Regiment	6026817		Merseburg air raid shelters
Wardle	George Henry	Private	181st Airlanding Field Ambulance	7399634	77376	
Wardle	Harry	Private	2nd Battalion, South Staffordshire Regiment	14386178	92096	Dresden bomb damage glazing
Wareham	James Anthony	Signalman	1st Parachute Brigade, Royal Signals	14650390	90046	Z 131 Zwickau railway
Warren	Ernest Edward	Corporal	1st Parachute Brigade	2736584		Kundl pick and shovel
Warren	Hector George	Corporal	2nd Battalion, Parachute Regiment	5836132	117205	
Warren	Horace	Driver	1st Airlanding Light Regiment, Royal Artillery	797724	118215	Bad Grund 7013 silver and lead mine
Warren	James William Sidney	Private	156th Battalion, Parachute Regiment	5826438		Merseburg demolition
Warrender	Alfred George	Private	2nd Airlanding Anti-Tank Battery, Royal Artillery	1469862		Floßmühle saw mill
Warrener	Reginald	Private	1st Battalion, Border Regiment	4279142		
Warwick	Herbert	Private	156th Battalion, Parachute Regiment	3448671		Freiberg sugar filling, Ei 105 E Eisleben copper mine, Hettstedt He 102 E lead works
Washer	Kenneth Edwin	Trooper	1st Airborne Reconnaissance Squadron	14370214	75816	Grasseth mining

Surname	First name	Rank	Regiment/Unit			Camp/Location
Wassell	Douglas	Driver	800 Company Air Despatch, Royal Army Service Corps	407727	117432	Bad Grund 7013
Waters	John	Gunner	1st Airlanding Light Regiment, Royal Artillery	14311629	75333	
Watkins	Herbert	Staff Sergeant	Glider Pilot Regiment	3660659		
Watkinson	Charles Rollett	Staff Sergeant	Glider Pilot Regiment	809931		
Watson	Charles Garth	Sergeant	Glider Pilot Regiment	1591231		
Watson	Frank Campbell	Sergeant	Glider Pilot Regiment	2082989	15256	
Watson	Horace Richard	Private	Army Catering Corps	1712902	91708	Brüx
Watson	John	Private	7th Battalion, King's Own Scottish Borderers	14327664		Falkenau coal mine
Watson	John Leslie	Private	2nd Battalion, South Staffordshire Regiment	14573619	90414	
Watson	Raymond	Private	3rd Battalion, Parachute Regiment	11425065		Salzgitter 7005
Watson	Thomas	Private	1st Battalion, Border Regiment	3533468	75696	Stützengrün labourer wood
Watson	William Alexander	Corporal	1st Airborne Reconnaissance Squadron	10603591	89835	
Watt	William	Private	1st Battalion, Parachute Regiment	923891	118445	Ülzen railway bomb damage
Watton	Norman Ralph	Private	2nd Battalion, South Staffordshire Regiment	14265948	91508	Brüx miner
Watts	James Percival	Private	2nd Battalion, Parachute Regiment	2061552		Kolumbus ak 51
Wayte	Frederick John	Lance Corporal	3rd Battalion, Parachute Regiment	5890044		
Weallans	Arthur Edward	Sergeant	11th Battalion, Parachute Regiment	2660102		Kugel forestry
Weatherburn	Eric	Private	4th Battalion, Dorset Regiment	3780290	14985	Mückenberg coal
Weaver	Raymond Ernest	Driver	93 Company Royal Army Service Corps	14368841		Brüx coalmine
Webb	Alan Kenneth	Private	1st Battalion, Border Regiment	14424829	91622	Dresden Bomb damage (civil)

Family Name	Forename	Rank	Unit	Army number	POW number	All kommandos
Webb	Arthur Stanley	Private	181st Airlanding Field Ambulance	7387237	77358	
Webb	Charles	Private	11th Battalion, Parachute Regiment	11001276	117762	Hildesheim sugar beet
Webb	Maurice William	Private	2nd Battalion, Parachute Regiment	5392996		Erfenschlag wood hauling
Webb	Norman Harold	Lance Corporal	2nd Battalion, Parachute Regiment	5391635		Maltsch sugar beet
Webber	Daniel Robert Wynham	Major	11th Battalion, Parachute Regiment	63580	552	
Wedgbury	Albert Edward	Private	2nd Battalion, South Staffordshire Regiment	4039812	75936	Jesson railway
Weiland	Douglas	Lance Corporal	156th Battalion, Parachute Regiment	6896313		W 610 Zahna brick factory, M 79 Mutschau surface coal mine
Welch	William Gordon	Captain	1st Battalion, Border Regiment	132473	2186	
Welham	Hubert Edward	Lance Corporal	1st Airborne Reconnaissance Squadron	6854308		Döbeln digging air raid shelters
Wellington	William	Private	7th Battalion, King's Own Scottish Borderers	4622033	91769	Germany labourer
Wells	Joseph	Private	4th Battalion, Dorset Regiment	14631903	14221	Liebenwalder railway work
Welsh	James	Driver	800 Company Air Despatch, Royal Army Service Corps	11251580	91794	Brüx coal mining
Wesson	Harry	Private	2nd Battalion, South Staffordshire Regiment	14660102	91753	Kirschau blanket, Freiburg
West	George	Corporal	11th Battalion, Parachute Regiment	4460064		
West	Percy	Private	156th Battalion, Parachute Regiment	558672		Zwickau Z 131 railway
West	William Samuel	Private	1st Battalion, Parachute Regiment	10582814	118148	Velsen labouring

Surname	First name(s)	Rank	Regiment			Work location
Wetherall	John Aubrey Bruce	Sergeant	Glider Pilot Regiment	14414511	1087	
Wetherall		Private	2nd Battalion, South Staffordshire Regiment	14334858	90347	Salzgitter
Whadcoat	Ernest Frederick	Private	10th Battalion, Parachute Regiment	6351604		C. Germany salt imine, C. Germany coal mine
Whaites	Albert George	Signalman	Royal Signals	14264165	91554	Brüx coal mine
Whalley	Walter	Lance Corporal	Advanced Workshop Detachment, Royal Electrical and Mechanical Engineers	5950306	75041	Hartmannsdorf Timber yard (Gas Halte), Stützengrum Timber yard (Gas Halte)
Wharam	Denis	Driver	250th Airborne Light Company, Royal Army Service Corps	268832	75385	
Whatmore	Reginald	Private	2nd Battalion, Parachute Regiment	5110657		Seestatl surface mine reparing houses, Brüx Benzine factory
Wheeler	Henry	Private	3rd Battalion, Parachute Regiment	6089379	91565	Warwitch railway
Wheeler	Leonard Ernest	Sergeant	2nd Battalion, South Staffordshire Regiment	7014846	117552	
Wheeler	William	Lance Corporal	1st Battalion, Border Regiment	4693666	91950	Plauen shoe repairing
Whelan	John James	Private	156th Battalion, Parachute Regiment	14436631		Niedersedlitz Dresden coal heaving and deliveries
Wheldon	Roland Alfred	Staff Sergeant	Glider Pilot Regiment	3715219		
Whippy	John Walter	Sergeant	Glider Pilot Regiment	2044661		
White	Bernard	Private	1st Battalion, Border Regiment	4547299	117501	Salzgitter iron ore factory
White	George	Regimental Sergeant Major	10th Battalion, Parachute Regiment	4387779		
White	Kenneth Grayston	Lieutenant	1st Airlanding Light Regiment, Royal Artillery	258890	2200	
White	Kenneth James	Sergeant	Glider Pilot Regiment	1891554	140212	
White	Leslie Philip	Lance Corporal	Royal Army Service Corps	276402	90997	Komotau railway

447

Family Name	Forename	Rank	Unit	Army number	POW number	All kommandos
White	Wilfred	Private	1st Battalion, Border Regiment	4467262	92004	Merseburg sewerage
Whitlock	Sydney Edward	Private	11th Battalion, Parachute Regiment	231982	91309	Dresden trams
Whittaker	James	Lance Corporal	4th Battalion, Dorset Regiment	4271899	17582	Stutzengrien Saxony lumber
Whittaker	Solomon	Private	2nd Battalion, South Staffordshire Regiment	4914442	92098	Dresden Bomb Debris
Whittaker	Stanley James	Private	4th Parachute Brigade	14618322		Komotau bricklayer's mate
Whittaker	Thomas	Private	10th Battalion, Parachute Regiment	3655345		
Whittam	Albert	Gunner	1st Airlanding Light Regiment, Royal Artillery	1791277	118695	Ülzen railway repair
Whyatt	Norman	Lance Corporal	1st Battalion, Parachute Regiment	5504900	92150	
Widdowson	George	Major	10th Battalion, Parachute Regiment	49397	91001	
Widdowson	Herbert	Lance Corporal	2nd Battalion, South Staffordshire Regiment	5050919		
Wiedericks	Benjamin James	Private	156th Battalion, Parachute Regiment	2766217		Wallwitz
Wild	John Richard Wilcock	Sergeant	Glider Pilot Regiment	14428935	76319	
Wilde	Cyril	Private	3rd Battalion, Parachute Regiment	14207950	75585	Jessen railway
Wilde	Jack	Private	2nd Battalion, South Staffordshire Regiment	14682977	89140	Hallendorf
Wilder	Leslie Maurice	Lance Corporal	1st Parachute Brigade, Royal Signals	2583200		AK 231 Kriebethal paper manufacturing
Wilding	Albert Geoffrey	Signalman	Royal Signals	5125376	91668	Brüx coal mining
Wildman	John Alfred	Private	1st Battalion, Parachute Regiment	14227447	140242	
Wilkinson	Richard	Sergeant, Lance	3rd Battalion, Parachute Regiment	408654		Basepohl farm

Surname	First name	Rank	Regiment	Service No.	Camp No.	Work
Willcock	Douglas Brian	Lieutenant	156th Battalion, Parachute Regiment	176224	76777	
Willcocks	Arthur Hambly	Captain	2nd Battalion, South Staffordshire Regiment	187080	544	
Willett	Lewis Alfred	Driver	250th Airborne Light Company, Royal Army Service Corps	64737		Herzberg labourer
Williams	Arthur	Private	2nd Battalion, South Staffordshire Regiment	14389591	92044	Sudetenland coal mining
Williams	Arthur Morley	Sergeant	Glider Pilot Regiment	4208939		
Williams	David Meredith	Private	10th Battalion, Parachute Regiment	14219148	52884	AK 123 B Menzengraben
Williams	Dennis Harold	Private	7th Battalion, King's Own Scottish Borderers	14313606	140068	
Williams	Jeffrey Arthur James	Trooper	1st Airborne Reconnaissance Squadron	14208949	117735	Dinkler sugar beet
Williams	Kenneth	Private	2nd Battalion, South Staffordshire Regiment	5829632	89601	Coal mine
Williams	Mervyn Lionel	Private	156th Battalion, Parachute Regiment	14664091		Z 131 Zwickau railway gritting
Williamson	John	Private	1st Battalion, Parachute Regiment	14251983	140072	
Williamson	Robert Hugh	Private	1st Battalion, Border Regiment	3596704	75948	
Willis	Jack	Private	3rd Battalion, Parachute Regiment	843584		Sudetenland coal mine
Willoughby	Bryan	Private	1st Battalion, Parachute Regiment	5679967	140110	
Willoughby	Leslie	Private	3rd Battalion, Parachute Regiment	4466448		
Willoughby	Norman	Private	1st Parachute Brigade HQ	4699350	75162	
Wilmot	Harold Francis Thomas	Staff Sergeant	Glider Pilot Regiment	7016404		
Wilson	Alexander Outridge	Private	10th Battalion, Parachute Regiment	5873605		Wrzmes Repairing bomb damage, Brux General labouring Herman Goering Benzine Fabrik
Wilson	Baldwin	Captain	1st Battalion, Border Regiment	182276	2192	
Wilson	Clement John	Sapper	9th Independent Company, Royal Engineers	1896106	81179	F 67 Flossmüle forestry Friburg

Family Name	Forename	Rank	Unit	Army number	POW number	All kommandos
Wilson	Ernest	Private	2nd Battalion, South Staffordshire Regiment	4919216		Merseburg tunnelling for air raid shelters
Wilson	James Archibald	Sergeant	Glider Pilot Regiment	3247627		
Wilson	James McWhirter	Private	7th Battalion, King's Own Scottish Borderers	3131140		
Wilson	John	Private	21st Independent Parachute Company	14551208	91672	Wurzmes (Komotau) mining, Brux general labouring
Wilson	Joseph Leonard	Sergeant	Glider Pilot Regiment	1675969		
Wilson	Kenneth	Corporal	16th Parachute Field Ambulance	7263793		
Wilson	Rayment John	Sergeant	Glider Pilot Regiment	7366948		
Wilson	Thomas Alan	Private	1st Battalion, Parachute Regiment	7366147	89418	Jessen railway
Wilson	Thomas Frederick	Corporal	1st Parachute Brigade, Royal Signals	2583477		
Wilson	William Herbert	Sapper	9th Field Company, Royal Engineers Airborne	6461773	118897	
Wiltshire	Reginald William	Lance Corporal	4th Parachute Brigade HQ	7349096		
Windsor	Ronald	Gunner	Forward Observation Unit, Royal Artillery	14261766		Königswalde stone quarry, Brüx factory
Wink	John	Private	7th Battalion, King's Own Scottish Borderers	14554656		Großthiemig
Winslow	Jack Robert	Lance Corporal	156th Battalion, Parachute Regiment	6896410		Kundl General
Winter	Victor Norman	Private	181st Airlanding Field Ambulance	7370800	140060	
Winterbottom	Leslie	Private	3rd Battalion, Parachute Regiment	14218354		

Surname	First name(s)	Rank	Unit	Number 1	Number 2	Work
Wise	Ernest Leslie	Private	3rd Battalion, Parachute Regiment	870497		Sestadl coal mine, Brüx tramway building
Wise	Thomas James	Private	2nd Battalion, South Staffordshire Regiment	4928047	91742	Coal mining
Witham	Cornelius Robert	Private	11th Battalion, Parachute Regiment	14411380	118537	Velsen railway
Withey	Leslie George	Lance Corporal	250th Airborne Light Company, Royal Army Service Corps	277631	14201	Dresden bomb debris
Withnall	Patrick Brereton	Staff Sergeant	Glider Pilot Regiment	2332442		
Withnall	William Charles	Lieutenant	2nd Battalion, South Staffordshire Regiment	5050853	548	
Witty	Thomas Alfred	Private	7th Battalion, King's Own Scottish Borderers	4540232	75958	Plauen air raid shelters
Wood	Albert Edward	Private	156th Battalion, Parachute Regiment	5672565		REI 113 Halle road making
Wood	Alfred Robert	Private	3rd Battalion, Parachute Regiment	1498245	118699	
Wood	David	Private	2nd Battalion, South Staffordshire Regiment	4928653	93263	54 Bruxe coal mining
Wood	Ernest	Private	1st Battalion, Border Regiment	3603488	26084	Böhlen, nr Leipzig clearing bomb damage
Wood	Ernest John	Private	1st Battalion, Border Regiment	14671738		
Wood	Harold George	Corporal	2nd Battalion, Parachute Regiment	6350557		Digging XIB
Wood	Jack	Private	2nd Battalion, South Staffordshire Regiment	4914111		
Wood	Joseph	Private	1st Battalion, Parachute Regiment	1440598	117745	Dinklar sugar beet
Woodard	Ronald Alan George	Private	156th Battalion, Parachute Regiment	5826728		Komotau engine repairs
Woodhouse	Francis	Lance Bombardier	1st Airlanding Light Regiment, Royal Artillery	14249662	52921	Menzengraben salt mine
Woodland	Alfred Arthur	Private	4th Battalion, Dorset Regiment	6150553	26069	Dresden fitter's mate and labourer

Family Name	Forename	Rank	Unit	Army number	POW number	All kommandos
Woodmansey	Frederick	Sergeant	10th Battalion, Parachute Regiment	4537265		
Woods	Kenneth	Driver	253rd Airborne Light Company, Royal Army Service Corps	10683067		Dresden bombed damage
Woods	Leslie Harold	Corporal	2nd Battalion, Parachute Regiment	5949111		
Woodward	Robert Lisle	Private	156th Battalion, Parachute Regiment	3711157		G 123 Glina, labouring bomb clearance
Woolford	Stanley Benjiman	Driver	Royal Artillery	11050415		
Woolrich	Herbert	Driver	4th Parachute Brigade, Royal Signals	10698347	90741	Dresden garage labourer
Worrall	James Ambrose	Private	2nd Battalion, Parachute Regiment	5835036	91659	Brüx Sudetenland coal mining
Worsfold	Gerald Percy	Private	7th Battalion, King's Own Scottish Borderers	14440258	91478	Limburg debris clearing, Conningswaldi stone quarry, Brüx Benzine Fabrik
Wren	Jack Francis	Private	2nd Battalion, Parachute Regiment	6853864	75337	Kleinleipisch railway line laying at coal mine
Wright	David	Captain	1st Parachute Brigade HQ	218952	571	
Wright	Gerald Arthur	Private	3rd Battalion, Parachute Regiment	6346044	91484	AK 51 Brüx coal mine
Wright	James Holt	Sapper	1st Parachute Squadron, Royal Engineers	2182781	91493	
Wright	Leonard William	Lieutenant	3rd Battalion, Parachute Regiment	276874	90944	
Wright	Leslie Edward	Private	Royal Army Ordnance Corps	14655624	118678	
Wright	Stanley Winston	Sergeant Major	2nd Battalion, South Staffordshire Regiment	4913782		
Wrighton	Raymond Bernard	Private	1st Battalion, Border Regiment	14595060		Gliena labouring

Wyard	Raymond Russell	Private	156th Battalion, Parachute Regiment	7344919		Dresden shoe repairs
Wyke	Peter	Private	10th Battalion, Parachute Regiment	14219746	75336	Zwickau AK Z 131 railway
Yarman	Andrew	Private	1st Battalion, Border Regiment	3597286	75659	Leipzig?
Yates	Dewar Galloway	Private	7th Battalion, King's Own Scottish Borderers	14211034	118414	
Young	Graham Ferguson	Leading Aircraftman	Light Warning Unit No. 6341, RAF	971682		
Young	James Walker	Lance Corporal	Royal Army Service Corps	220847	14097	
Young	John	Private	7th Battalion, King's Own Scottish Borderers	3192130	75941	Stützengrün timber yard
Young	John James	Private	1st Battalion, Border Regiment	4547346	91971	Dresden bomb debris clearance
Young	William Gibb	Private	7th Battalion, King's Own Scottish Borderers	3190173	117451	
Younger	John Charles	Private	2nd Battalion, South Staffordshire Regiment	4913643	89465	Stedstdal, Tschausch
Youngman	Ronald	Lance Corporal	2nd Battalion, Parachute Regiment	6354216	75338	Lauchhammer general labouring at surface coal mine

Sabotage

Sabotage obviously carried risks, it is rarely recorded:

> Sapper George Cotton, 1st Parachute Squadron, Royal Engineers, 'When ordered to save our factory by German civilian, we refused. In some cases we put wood on the fire, the German civilian threatened us with a revolver, but he didn't use it.'

> Private Stanley Brooks, 2nd Battalion, Parachute Regiment, 'Punished with 3 days in strafflager[18] for burning wood destined for railway wagons October.'

For others the sabotage appears to be very matter of fact:

> Private Arthur Curtis, 11th Battalion, Parachute Regiment, 'cut electricity supply in mine at 5 places mine stopped for 2 days.'

> Sapper Joseph Knight, 9th Field Company, Royal Engineers Airborne, 'Coal dust in winch bearings on several occasions and losing tools, at Himmel Furst Mine, Tohnsdorf Brüx area.'

> Private Leonard Curtis, 3rd Battalion, Parachute Regiment, 'Refused to assist Germans to stop fire at sugar beet factory at Hildesheim Nov 1944.'

The men were often working alongside other Arnhem POWs. For example, seventeen men refer to being part of a *kommando*, repairing rail lines, that performed an impressive piece of sabotage. They derailed a train:

> Private Robert Hunter, 156th Battalion, Parachute Regiment, 'Our working party derailed a passenger train by replacing old rail across the track when it was due, And the train ran onto it and off the rail. No one was injured or killed but the train was derailed.'

> Private Walter McGowan, 181st Airlanding Field Ambulance, 'Derailed passenger and goods train on line from Elster to Wittenberg blocking line for 4 days (Time 20.45 hrs) commando from Jesson.'

---

18 *Straff lager* = punishment camp or compound.

Table 7: Sabotage

Answers to Question 5 Sabotage

Did you do any sabotage or destruction of enemy factory plant, war material, communications, etc, when employed on working parties or during escape? (Give details, places and dates.)

Name	Forename	Rank	Unit	Army number	POW number	Notes
Aitken	George Cecil	Private	1st Battalion, Parachute Regiment	4208372		Whilst engaged on repairs of underground electric cable tunnel disconnecting wires and causing tunnel to collapse by undermining shoring up beams
Allen	John Charles	Private	Parachute Regiment	5349777	117477	Minor efforts at sugar factory. Broke machines and held up work several times whilst working there.
Avann	Thomas Alfred Spencer	Private	3rd Battalion, Parachute Regiment	7617647	89724	Inefficient work
Bailey	Walter Clement	Trooper	1st Airborne Reconnaissance Squadron	10603469		Constantly loading large stones barrows causing machines to break down for considerable periods against threats to stop food.
Ball	Richard Patrick	Gunner	1st Airlanding Light Battery Royal Artillery	1084454	117397	Smashed mining machinery. Stall dynamite, fuses, detonators while work party in Bad Grund. Between the months of Nov 1944 until April 1945.

Name	Forename	Rank	Unit	Army number	POW number	Notes
Betts	George	Sergeant	Glider Pilot Regiment	14233066		At Limburg, unloading concrete blocks for building from trucks, breaking alternate ones in Oct 44
Black	James Charles	Sapper	1st Parachute Squadron Royal Engineers	1986005		Cut underground telephone cable at Merseburg on 18th of April 1944 App. In the air raid shelters repeatedly during raids in Merseburg to cause confusion.
Booth	Eric Charles	Driver	1st Parachute Squadron Royal Engineers	1951655		When marching along road I sabotaged a German anti-tank weapon, causing injury myself, (Broke electrical switches + equipment, when on working parties)
Breen	Thomas Francis	Lance Corporal	1st Airborne Provost Company	1917769		I manage electrical machines of the machinery out of action that was used for the movement of salt in the mine.
Brett	Frank Arthur	Gunner	1st Airlanding Anti-Tank Battery Royal Artillery	1103757	75561	Sabotage "General sabotage where possible"
Bridge	Joseph Edward	Private	2nd Battalion, South Staffordshire Regiment	4923097	89444	Scrapping of enemy work and general go slow policy at all times
Broadhurst	William	Private	11th Battalion, Parachute Regiment	889617	9166	Bent rails in coal mine causing several trucks to capsize. Buried tools. Dec '44 - Jan '45. Changed destination labels on priority railway trucks. Komotau. Dec '44.

Surname	Forename	Rank	Unit	Number	Number 2	Description
Brooks	Arthur	Private	2nd Battalion, South Staffordshire Regiment	5125767	92898	Broke up bedsteads - bed boards & usted lights
Bryans	William Howard	Private	2nd Battalion, Parachute Regiment	3325884	75427	Sabotage "Slow on the job"
Burns	Peter	Private	3rd Battalion, Parachute Regiment	14569564	117458	I threw sand in a high dynamo at Dinklar Sugar factory with hopes it would blow up.
Byrne	Michael	Private	1st Battalion, Border Regiment	3782510	118304	Yes it has already been reported
Carroll	William James	Private	11th Battalion, Parachute Regiment	2932551	117761	Whilst working clearing up bombed factory damaged [illegible] of machines
Cawrey	Victor Frank	Private	21st Independent Parachute Company	4975875	118305	Cut conveyor belts in sugar factory to hamper production Dinklar Nov 12th approx
Chapman	Ronald Anthony Francis	Private	3rd Battalion, Parachute Regiment	4914786		Derailed troop train bound for Wittenberg on April 5th 2100 hrs. at Elster. By placing rail across the track.
Chivers	William Ernest	Private	2nd Battalion, South Staffordshire Regiment	4917934		Whilst working with the railway gang. Destroying acetylene apparatus, cutting wires & burying nuts and bolts.
Christie	George	Private	7th Battalion, King's Own Scottish Borderers Regiment	3190220	90556	Stealing food from goods trains after the RAF raid 6.12.44 till April 1945 st Merseburg goods station while on working party.party."
Clements	Robert Stanley	Private	156th Battalion, Parachute Regiment	6293276	117709	Minor acts

Name	Forename	Rank	Unit	Army number	POW number	Notes
Connely	James Joseph	Gunner	1st Airlanding Anti-Tank Battery Royal Artillery	3055590	91734	Occasionally damaged presses at factory by placing bolts among cla. (Damage only temporary)
Cooke	Archie William George	Lance Corporal	1st Parachute Squadron Royal Engineers	1881045		Derailed train while working on line repairing at Elster. Friday 13th April at about 23:30 hrs. Left rail across track.
Cotten	George Henry Charles	Sapper	1st Parachute Squadron Royal Engineers	14892438		When ordered to save our factory by German civilian, we refused. In some cases we put wood on the fire, the German civilian threatened us with a revolver, but he didn't use it.
Cox	Ronald Charles Percival	Private	2nd Battalion, Parachute Regiment	5832882		Smashing tools whilst in the workshops of the tramways
Cox	Denis Herbert	Sergeant, Acting	2nd Battalion, South Staffordshire Regiment	5051692	89424	Food sabotage. Potatoes, cabbages, threshing machines etc
Craig	Daniel	Private	7th Battalion, King's Own Scottish Borderers Regiment	14211595	90557	Stole food while on work party, at food depot in Merseburg on 4.3.45
Curtis	Arthur	Private	11th Battalion, Parachute Regiment	6399339		Stop the mine working for two days by cutting the main electricall cable in five place
Curtis	Leonard Arthur Cecil	Private	3rd Battalion, Parachute Regiment	2047378	117875	Refused to assist Germans to stop fire at sugar beet factory at Hildesheim Nov 1944
Cuthbertson	Malcolm	Private	4th Battalion, Dorset Regiment	3770561	91903	Only general slackness during working hours. Throwing tools etc away, while working camps.

Surname	First name(s)	Rank	Regiment	Service No.	Camp No.	Details
Davey	Edward Thomas	Private	181st Airlanding Field Ambulance	7358134	90173	Accidentally left a length of rail partly over open track at night at Elster. Causing derailment of train and blocking of both tracks Friday 13 April 45
Davis	James Robert	Private	7th Battalion, King's Own Scottish Borderers Regiment	11251840	75352	Broke tools, worked no more than was necessary
Daye	Russell Robert	Private	7th Battalion, King's Own Scottish Borderers Regiment	14620635	118419	I was working at Brunswick Steel Werke at Watenstedt [part of name Salzgitter] Germany. We were clearing up bomb damage made by RAF. All the machinery was still in workable conditions. I did my best to make them unworkable.
Derbyshire	Stanley	Private	3rd Battalion, Parachute Regiment	14375898	52885	Bars of metal were hidden in salt wagons which would damage the mill when salt was tipped. Wintersbach Salt Works Menzengraben Germany. Oct 44 to March 45.
Donnelly	Moses	Private	1st Battalion, Parachute Regiment	4538622	91461	In the factory where I worked refusing to work and wasting material. Paul Otto Shoe Factory March to April 1945
Dove	William Kenneth	Private	156th Battalion, Parachute Regiment	6981695		Destruction of tools in factory Zahna, Wittenberg, Germmay 25/10/44 - 30/1/45
Dredge	Norman Victor	Private	2nd Battalion, South Staffordshire Regiment	14700066	92215	The destruction of Telegraph cops at CV issues of all description warehouses Holland (forced work) dates places unknowing.

Name	Forename	Rank	Unit	Army number	POW number	Notes
Drury	Robert	Private	10th Battalion, Parachute Regiment	5726456		Sabotage field telephone wires on road while being evacuated. Broke up Building Materials and wasted all cement possible.
Dukes	Benjamin William	Private	181st Airlanding Field Ambulance	7380299		Derailing of (troop & ammo) train during night 16-4-45 while working on line at Elster
Dunford	Reginald Charles	Private	10th Battalion, Parachute Regiment	555639	77099	Severed to communication wires. (Dresden) deliberately. On various occasions destroyed electrical equipment.
Dyer	Albert Jack	Private	2nd Battalion, Parachute Regiment	206567		Set coal heap on fire. Selstadl December 1944
Eagleton	John	Private	1st Battalion, Border	14671556	91521	General everyday sabotage
Eatwell	Horace Arthur	Regimental Sergeant Major	1st Battalion, Parachute Regiment	2613152	89402	Electrical power house Waldenburg 1 Dyno damaged short of explosives only there a fortnight 31st of Jan—approx 14 Feb 45
Elliott	Albert James	Private	3rd Battalion, Parachute Regiment	6207794		Went slow
Elsey	George Douglas Jack	Craftsman	Royal Electrical and Mechanical Engineers	1574063	21901	While making cement slabs mixing wrong materials and breaking finished article in transport. Not assisting to put out fires when factory was bombed.
Fellows	James	Private	1st Battalion, Border Regiment	14584168		Destroying supports and causing cave-ins down the mine - derailing wagons dates unknown.

Surname	First name	Rank	Regiment	Number	Number	Notes
Few	Ted	Private	156th Battalion, Parachute Regiment	5257174		Breaking of tools etc, mild sabotage
Fitzgerald	Michael	Driver	1st Airlanding Anti-Tank battery	6854732		Arnhem loading inner tubes for cars looted from Holland cutting them with knives.
Furniss	Thomas	Driver	250th Airborne Light Company, Royal Army Service Corps	10694184	117594	Pushed wagon down shaft in the mine on 6.2.45 stopped production for 1 hour
Giles	Jess	Private	2nd Battalion, South Staffordshire Regiment	1686196		General
Girvin	Robert	Staff Sergeant	Glider Pilot Regiment	7022767		Stole ammo and buried it on march from Bankau to Luckenwalde in January '45
Godbold	John William	Private	1st Battalion, Parachute Regiment	6215765	92131	Fusing lights and damaging mine trucks and equipment
Guidi	David	Private	7th Battalion, King's Own Scottish Borderers Regiment	14435105		At Walwitz on the railroad by loosening rail joints and breaking equipment
Hamilton	Reginald Thomas	Private	7th Battalion, King's Own Scottish Borderers Regiment	14437879		Refused to work
Hartley	Benjamin	Driver	1st Airlanding Anti-Tank Battery Royal Artillery	3712207		Turned on valve of main water pipe causing shortages of water stopping use of cranes at least 12 hrs. Burying bolts used for laying track. Not easy to replace.
Hately	John Frederick	Private	156th Battalion, Parachute Regiment	6896966	221694	At W610 overloading conveyor belt causing to break Fused conveyor band

Name	Forename	Rank	Unit	Army number	POW number	Notes
Heath	Joseph Henry	Private	10th Battalion, Parachute Regiment	945801		Making belts break
Hill	Francis Edwin	Private	3rd Battalion, Parachute Regiment	5389890	75327	Picked up various tools (spanner etc) and lost them
Hindmarsh	Henry	Private	2nd Battalion, Parachute Regiment	4461927		Minor sabotage at Deutchland sender Herzberg [transmitter], ie sand and gravel in axle boxes of wireless coaches etc
Hobson	Frank	Private	7th Battalion, King's Own Scottish Borderers Regiment	14415862	75921	General sabotage
Hollinshead	Douglas	Private	11th Battalion, Parachute Regiment	844968	118171	Fuzzed transformer station Burnt out electrical motor" [comment in different handwriting "Nov '44"]
Hopkins	Kenneth Arthur	Private	181st Airlanding Field Ambulance	14672266		One Railway train derailed at Elster April 13th 1945 while on a working party at night repairing bomb damage.
Hunt	Harry James	Private	2nd Battalion, Parachute Regiment	6848386		Cut pipes for engines too short in length; passed though faulty pipes while testing. Always worked slow. Mislaid tools.
Hunter	Robert	Private	156th Battalion, Parachute Regiment	3128295	89547	Our working party derailed a passenger train by replacing old rail across the track when it was due, And the train ran onto it and off the rail. No one was injured or killed but the train was derailed.

Surname	First Name	Rank	Regiment	Number 1	Number 2	Description
Ingham	Herbert	Private	156th Battalion, Parachute Regiment	14382007	117977	While on Work Party 7012 from XI B many men were struck by hand and bayonet while being struck an armed guard was always near in case of our retaliating
Jackson	Fred Duncan	Private	10th Battalion, Parachute Regiment	81614	117524	While working on loading railway wagons in Herman Göring Werks Braunsweig. While working on No 9 party for Einezats clone.
Jeffries	John Patrick	Signalman	Royal Signals	2379610	117314	Used Electric home-made cookers when Germans informed us it was sabotage punishable as such.
John	John Edward	Private	Royal Army Medical Corps	7357904	88911	Derailed a passenger whilst repairing a line at Elster on Friday April 13th 1945 at about 23.30 hrs at night
Johnson	Arthur	Private	2nd Battalion, South Staffordshire Regiment	1568699	92045	Smashed new sewer pipes, shovels, picks and looted food.
Johnson	Horace	Private	2nd Battalion, South Staffordshire Regiment	4923187	9190	By continually clogging machinery"
Johnston	Harold	Private	4th Battalion, Dorset Regiment	3709037	17569	All our working party at Etzdorf from 11-11-44 till 28-3-45 damaged and destroyed tools issued to us for working purposes
Kay	John	Private	Parachute Regiment	915487	89731	Little when chances were there
Kelly	Dennis	Private	2nd Battalion, Parachute Regiment	4616630		On buses puncturing gas bags
Knight	Joseph William	Sapper	9th Field Company (Airborne), Royal Engineers	2058280	91610	Coal dust in winch bearings on several occasions and losing tools, at Himmel Furst Mine, Tohnsdorf Brüx area

Name	Forename	Rank	Unit	Army number	POW number	Notes
Lashmar	Reginald Douglas	Private	156th Battalion, Parachute Regiment	6846980		General small scale
Layland	Frederick	Gunner	2nd Airlanding Anti-Tank Battery Royal Artillery	1092475	92062	Broke new sewer pipes and, shovels, picks and looted food at night, getting out through the barbed wire at the commando.
Lees	Norman Alfred	Lance Corporal	156th Battalion, Parachute Regiment	14377390	90542	Destruction of tools. Zahna Wittenberg Germany 25.10.44 - 20.1.45
Lock	Bert Edward	Private	11th Battalion, Parachute Regiment	2081300	117961	Superficial damage only to unloading machinery. Dinkler Sugar Fabric
Longson	James	Private	1st Battalion, Border Regiment	3782025	75994	Sabotage "Destruction of working materials"
Lowrie	James	Lance Corporal	1st Parachute Brigade Royal Signals	2351489		Always buried tools such as shovels, pics, etc, when chance occurred. When employed on bomb damage took everything that had escaped the bombing
Lumsden	Albert Edward	Private	2nd Battalion, Parachute Regiment	941821		Throwing tools in canal
Lyons	Robert	Private	7th Battalion, King's Own Scottish Borderers Regiment	4698363	90786	Stole food from railroad goods yard, and in the town of Merseburg whilst on working party after RAF raid 6-12-44 until May 1945.
Mackenzie	John Alexander	Private	3rd Battalion, Parachute Regiment	2820366	89961	Derailed troop train at Elster/Elbe on or about 15/4/1945

Surname	First name	Rank	Unit	Service No.		Notes
Maguire	Joseph	Private	1st Battalion, Border Regiment	14583475	24938	Minor sabotage eg damaging electrical and signalling equipment at various stations in Saxony
Maidens	William Edward	Private	16th Para Field Ambulance	7403380		Jesson Commando: Derailed train with cut up track between 15th & 20th April 44
Matthews	Ronald George	Private	7th Battalion, King's Own Scottish Borderers Regiment	4750960		Broke shovels and picks etc Dresden
McClure	William	Private	2nd Battalion, Parachute Regiment	7022065		Small only
McCreedy	Richard James	Lance Bombardier	1st Airlanding Anti-Tank Battery Royal Artillery	3711048		Slight but effectual damage of goods arriving for unloading by members of our commando
McGowan	Walter	Private	181st Airlanding Field Ambulance	7407324	90158	Derailed passenger and goods train on line from Elster to Wittenberg blocking line for 4 days (Time 20.45 hrs) commando from Jesson. (Refused to work after Allied strafing).
McKenna	William Tarrant	Sapper	4th Para Squadron Royal Engineers	3055480	140103	When unloading [illegible] sets broke nearly them all
McLure	James	Private	156th Battalion, Parachute Regiment	2454564		With Czechoslavakian partisans
McVicar	Archibald Lamont	Private	10th Battalion, Parachute Regiment	2933355		Lost tools whilst working. Put outside in the snow to work for punishment
Miller	Philip Anthony Alfred	Sapper	1st Parachute Squadron Royal Engineers	1947386		Sabotaged field telephone lines on raod whilst being evacuated. Broke building material and wasted cement.

Name	Forename	Rank	Unit	Army number	POW number	Notes
Mitchell	Edward	Sergeant	Glider Pilot Regiment	10555051	76321	At Muhlburg Railway station whilst unloading cement blocks with about 6 other POWs made certain that we drop them heavily call breaking 5/6 the top one of each pile being left whole.
Montgomery	Terence	Private	1st Battalion, Parachute Regiment	7013242	92037	Change of identity Nov 1944
Moore	Arthur Reginald	Private	Parachute Regiment	14218858	75324	Removal of cotton waste from oiling boxes on trucks and engines causing them to get overheated, Dates not known
Morait	Peter John	Private	156th Battalion, Parachute Regiment	59816		Caused successful sabotage to a battery maintenance plant causing disruption for some weeks in Dresden. Jan 15 1944.
Mullineux	William	Private	3rd Battalion, Parachute Regiment	3866182		Sabotaged anything I thought I could get away with down the coal mine over a period Nov 44 May 44. Hercules Coal Mine Brüx
Neild	Harry	Private	156th Battalion, Parachute Regiment	4539879		While working laithe and milling machines (NATURE) deliberate mistakes in manufacturing [illegible] and screw cutting and breakages to machines delayed production.
Newell	Cecil	Private	2nd Battalion, Parachute Regiment	1559998		Breaking of tools on jobs which was called sabotage by German masters
Nolan	Harold	Lance Corporal	1st Battalion, Border Regiment	767839	118802	Filled axle boxes on railway trucks with sand having [let] the grease out

Parkes	William Henry	Sergeant	2nd Battalion, South Staffordshire Regiment	4917868		Food sabotage when dealing with food for the towns such as potatoes and cabbages. Breaking farm implements
Parkin	Harold Cosford	Private	2nd Battalion, Parachute Regiment	910905		Damaging goods which were loaded daily wagons [… illegible]
Pearson	Michael David	Private	Parachute Regiment	4699298	75445	When working in oil pump factory (IVEISE u MONSKIE) in Halle damaged pumps and tools and any useful material by rough handling.
Perks	Victor	Private	133rd Para Field Ambulance	14630044	90042	Working at night on railway at Elster April 1945 we left railway line on the track and derailed a train it took 2 days to clear the line again
Pettitt	Thomas Joseph	Private	2nd Battalion, Parachute Regiment	14397946		This only was done on a small scale by myself and companions by deliberately doing slow work on a call loading therefore slowing down the machines that were driven by steam, Stealing potatoes etc from clamps that were intended to feed this factories workers.
Phillips	Ronald John	Private	2nd Battalion, Parachute Regiment	5510064	117829	Bar going slow and wasting materials
Potts	Eric	Lance Corporal	181st Airlanding Field Ambulance	7399495		Working party on railway derailed train at Elster outside Wittenberg whilst reparing a line; rendering both lines useless.

Name	Forename	Rank	Unit	Army number	POW number	Notes
Prince	Charles Henry	Private	181st Airlanding Field Ambulance	14672756		One passenger train derailed engine destroyed Elster Friday 13 April 1945
Rafferty	William	Private	1st Battalion, Border Regiment	14642750		General
Ramsbottom	Walter James	Staff Sergeant	Glider Pilot Regiment	920299		Was in charge of working party at Arnhem 26/9/1944-9/10/1944, the whole party destroyed thousands of telegraph pole accessories while loading them onto railway wagons"
Ransom	James Leslie	Lance Corporal	250th Airborne Light Company, Royal Army Service Corps	10694205	91189	Breaking of tools and machinery whilts in Tram repair shops in Dresden from November 1944 to April 1945.
Rathband	Herbert Henry	Sergeant/W	Glider Pilot Regiment	1544344	103967	Placed sand in axle boxes of goods wagons loaded with white metal at an Arnheim factory where we were made to work before being taken to POW camps
Reed	Samuel	Private	4th Parachute Brigade HQ	64180	118177	Boring machines, drills, electrical appliances dropped down shaft and disuued workings, duiurng work in lead mine 7013 Bad Grund
Reid	William	Private	156th Battalion, Parachute Regiment	3131283		When working on bomb damage areas we all burst the pipes which were not already damaged. Water & Sewage

Surname	First name	Rank	Unit			Remarks
Riley	Bernard	Private	1st Battalion, Border Regiment	4546122	118191	Used to go down the mine with the afternoon shift and return up with the morning shift which had finished. Derailed trucks. Worked slow. Acted dumb.
Riley	Hugh	Private	1st Battalion, Border Regiment	3866213	75496	Whenever possible
Robbins	James	Lance Corporal	181st Airlanding Field Ambulance	7366512	76659	Derailing of train at Elster approx April 16th 45
Rose	John William	Private	181st Airlanding Field Ambulance	7404654	90026	Derailed train full of troops & officers at Jessen whilst on kommando. Left line on good track whilst repairing damaged ones 16.4.45
Russell	Arthur Eli	Private	10th Battalion, Parachute Regiment	2048220	75423	When employed on working party damage to [illegible] Breaking of shovel picks, loosening of railway nuts. At Rubeaks surface coal mine
Russell	Andrew McCallum	Private	7th Battalion, King's Own Scottish Borderers Regiment	14607803	15459	Derailed train at Elster 13/4/45 whilst repairing bomb damage
Shears	Charles Eli	Private	10th Battalion, Parachute Regiment	5623548		Destroyed a printing press in Dresden and cut off a electric supply in Dresden from the Gestapo.
Smith	Reginald Albert	Driver	250th Airborne Light Company, Royal Army Service Corps	6405247	90822	Passive resistance. Very slow work
Smith	John Thomas	Private	156th Battalion, Parachute Regiment	14665924	90483	We sabotaged all the time thay just could not make us work. When filling in bomb holes which were half full of water, we used to make them look solid. A truck went over oned day and found out that it was not solid

Name	Forename	Rank	Unit	Army number	POW number	Notes
Smith	Norman	Private	2nd Battalion, Parachute Regiment	7367390	89422	Derailing a train during work on line at Elster approx April 16th '45
Smyth	John Michael	Private	10th Battalion, Parachute Regiment	3961524	75686	The last job we were on, Sabotage was done by the cutting of cables
Snoding	Victor Henry	Private	16th Para Field Ambulance	14679808		HMSO has XII A. In a hospital working till 29/10/1944? Sabotage "Derailing a train at Elster on Elbe April 16th 1945"
Sproson	Ernest Travis	Private	156th Battalion, Parachute Regiment	5109576		Stealing food. Zwickau railway goods yard
Stead	John Edward	Staff Sergeant	Glider Pilot Regiment	794717		Placed sugar in petrol tank of enemy vehicle 2 hours after capture.
Still	Blake Edwin Charles	Private	10th Battalion, Parachute Regiment	2323483		Deliberately damaged electrical equipment while working at tram depot"
Tams	Leonard James	Private	2nd Battalion, South Staffordshire Regiment	4918801		Broke tools and machines
Taylor	Kenneth Joseph	Private	21st Independent Parachute Company	6148344	93412	Whilst on Working Party at Paper Factory, in Terbsen, Saxony about 8 Jan 1945 by feeding logs with large nails into hacking machine destroyed some [illegible] blades of said machine and put it out of operation for a day.

Surname	Forename	Rank	Regiment	Number	Number	Description
Taylor	Perry	Private	11th Battalion, Parachute Regiment	6095347	91577	Destroying cement with water breaking tools etc at Dresden Xmas time
Teece	Percy James	Lance Corporal	1st Airborne Provost Company	7398111	118232	Caused a crushing machine to be out of commission for 3 weeks
Thelwell	Arthur	Lance Corporal	1st Airborne Provost Company	3976695		While working as Railway Platelayers, such things as not butting joints up. Not making the bedding firm, causing delay in shipment from from Feb 18th-May. Hydra Works Brüx Sudetenland
Thorpe	Russell Ambrose	Private	2nd Battalion, South Staffordshire Regiment	4914617		One train (passenger) derailed at Elster whilst on working party
Tracey	Daniel Edward	Private	4th Battalion, Dorset Regiment	3663292	19473	Fusing & breaking mixing machines in cement factory
Turner	Stanley Reginald	Craftsman	Royal Electrical and Mechanical Engineers	5124014	75833	Only little things of no importance
Turner	John Henry	Private	10th Battalion, Parachute Regiment	4126773	90517	During my period as quarry worker. Breaking tools, + belts driving stone breaking machinery + failing to work as hard + efficient as expected by Quarry Foreman
Turrell	Leslie	Private	11th Battalion, Parachute Regiment	3770461	117767	Burning railway sleepers. Breaking water spirit levels. Shovelling earth on steel nuts and bolts to prevent them being used
Wallace	Samuel	Private	1st Battalion, Border Regiment	14671726	24363	By destroying the bricks while wet. And therefore they had to be put through the machine again, slowly up production

Name	Forename	Rank	Unit	Army number	POW number	Notes
Walsh	William Marston	Driver	1st Parachute Brigade	3975544		Me and my friend burned 3 dynamos and damaged the cutting machine and 1 driveing belt also general sabotage at Rorhsdorf. Commando no R 123
Ward	Douglas Edward Newman	Staff Sergeant	Glider Pilot Regiment	1878308		Destruction of barbed wire round defence posts Muhlberg. Dates not Royal Electrical and Mechanical Engineersmberd.
Wareham	James Anthony	Signalman	1st Parachute Brigade Royal Signals	14650390	90046	Burying vital tools Keys on railway premises and minor stuff
Warwick	Herbert	Private	156th Battalion, Parachute Regiment	3448671		In copper mine upsetting wagons breaking tools etc
Wassell	Douglas	Driver	800th Company Air Despatch Royal Army Service Corps	407727	117432	I have thrown any amount of lamps down the mine shaft at Bad Grund. Oberharz.
Wayte	Frederick John	Lance Corporal	3rd Battalion, Parachute Regiment	5890044		General sabotage
Weiland	Douglas	Lance Corporal	156th Battalion, Parachute Regiment	6896313		At brick factory Zahna. Continuous fusing of electrical equipment. Damage to conveyor belts and minor nuisances
Wesson	Harry	Private	2nd Battalion, South Staffordshire Regiment	14660102	91753	Broken into potato store. Received 5 days straff. Food 400 grams of bread and water a day. Place Brant.

White	Bernard	Private	1st Battalion, Border Regiment	4547299	117501	Four electric motors broken by allowing as small bogey to run into place of storage at a reasonably fast speed. Place Nassau Bereitung, Galbecht, Nr Brunswick. Jan 1945
Whittaker	Stanley James	Private	4th Parachute Brigade	14618322		The job I was doing I knew could not be completed before the end of the War
Wilde	Cyril	Private	3rd Battalion, Parachute Regiment	14207950	75585	Derailed train while repairing track during black out Friday 13th 23.30 hrs
Williams	David Meredith	Private	10th Battalion, Parachute Regiment	14219148	52884	Only in small ways. Such as breaking and losing tools and equipment. By accident once cut main power cable for mine
Wilson	Thomas Alan	Private	1st Battalion, Parachute Regiment	7366147	89418	Derailed troop train at Elster 14-4-45 (approx)
Wink	John	Private	7th Battalion, King's Own Scottish Borderers Regiment	14554656		Kept pushing wagons over embankment when at work
Wood	Jack	Private	2nd Battalion, South Staffordshire Regiment	4914111		I smashed an overhead crane controls at the Herman Goering Works at Hallendorf in February and buried all tools where ever possible
Woodward	Robert Lisle	Private	156th Battalion, Parachute Regiment	3711157		Emptied 137 Oxygen bottles, cut 3 mains power cables and broke 5 underground Benzine Pipes - from January 45 to March 45.

Name	Forename	Rank	Unit	Army number	POW number	Notes
Worrall	James Ambrose	Private	2nd Battalion, Parachute Regiment	5835036	91659	When working in the coal-mines of Quido + Herkvees at Malthern, Brüx Sudetenland I cut telephone & electrical supply wires in the mine. I also had a good term of "One for Churchill" mainly dodging work. This form of dodging was a camp plan
Wright	Stanley Winston	SergeantMajor	2nd Battalion, South Staffordshire Regiment	4913782		Cutting barbed wire at Sagan Dec 1944. Jan 45 looted bread store for Civilians at Hanover on March 25th
Youngman	Ronald	Lance Corporal	2nd Battalion, Parachute Regiment	6354216	75338	General sabotage whenever possible

Collaboration and War Crimes

The questions about collaboration and war crimes produced few answers. There were only seventeen examples of collaboration and ten of war crimes.

Eight of the answers to the collaboration question concentrate on Red Cross parcels at Limburg. The answers were more about unequal treatment than collaboration with the enemy. The combination of men who had no experience of camp life in a camp that held men only temporarily was a fertile ground for rumours of wrongdoing and when food was short Red Cross parcels were very desirable. Lance Corporal Whyatt was so angry about the situation at Limburg that he answered twice: once to the question and then this from the final catch-all question on any other matters:

> Lance Corporal Norman Whyatt, 1st Battalion, Parachute Regiment, 'I would like to report that the distribution of Red Cross parcels at Stalag 12A, in October 1944 was very unsatisfactorily carried out and the British Man of Confidence (Sgt Amery 6th Airborne Div) was greatly criticised by all British POWs for the manner in which he conducted himself.'

> Captain James McCourt, 7th Battalion, King's Own Scottish Borderers, 'Cannot name them but the MEN OF CONFIDENCE at Limburg obviously were fraternising with the enemy & trading Red Cross Parcels.'

One man gave a clear example of collaboration. However, his evidence is then slightly undermined by another complaint that the senior British prisoners – the Men of Confidence – were collaborating:

> Driver Reginald Pattle, 133rd Parachute Field Ambulance, Royal Army Medical Corps, 'At Limburg 12A 28/9/44 to 13/10/44 there was a Sikh who wore a revolver and a Nazi armband. And the camp leaders, an Airborne Sgt and a Marine Commando RSM, were of doubtful sentiments.'

The ten records of war crimes describe five men being shot without warning or at least insufficient warning by guards. Private Shears is the only man to record this incident at Limburg. He did it in the space for any other comments:

> Private Charles Eli Shears, 10th Battalion, Parachute Regiment, 'Have seen my own comrades shot by the SS in prison camp in Limburg in Germany. For asking for more bread. We were starving for the want of food.'

Three of the reports appear to be describing the same incident:

> Gunner John Hendry, 1st Airlanding Light Regiment Royal Artillery, 'A Glider Pilot was shot by an unknown German sentry at Stalag XI B early in October 1944 and died. This sentry had shouted orders to us which we did not understand so he opened fire and shot the Glider Pilot. I gave evidence at an enquiry at the Stalag shortly afterwards for Red Cross and German Intelligence officer.'

Major Murray, Royal Engineers, offered information about an incident where men in a lorry carrying POWs were shot by a guard when one, Major Hibbert, escaped.

Table 8: Collaboration

Answers to Question 6: Collaboration with enemy

Do you know of any British or American personnel who collaborated with the enemy or in any way helped the enemy against other Allied Prisoners of War? (Give details, names of person(s) concerned, camp(s), dates and nature of collaboration or help given to the enemy).

Name	Forename	Rank	Unit	Army number	POW number	Answers
Britnev	Vladimir Alexandroitcn	Lieutenant	1st Battalion, Parachute Regiment	162044	534	[Report on collaboration] Brought back to England six weeks ago now by other members of the organisation in Oflag 79. No need to report.
Brooker	Ronald James	Trooper	1st Airborne Recce Squadron	6354463	91435	Henry Du Bier South African. Drove lorry for enemy and went everywhere without sentry. Working camp T 35 Tröglitz near Zeitz.
Courtney	Thomas Richard Brian	Major	133rd Parachute Field Ambulance, Royal Army Medical Corps	112406	91202	I was warned against a VAN ZUCKE (? spelling and rank) who was posing as a Med. Officer who was in reality collaborating with the enemy.
Dodd	William Ronald	Private	3rd Battalion, Parachute Regiment	6404195		When our Con man [man of confidence] and 6 others escaped Pte Coxon (Green Howards) gave information to the Feldwebel. Sentries told us 'Nix Good command.' Shifted to another W Party. Information given about Dec 20th 44.
Forwood	Charles	Corporal	7th Battalion, King's Own Scottish Borderers	3136134	88797	Sgt (name unknown) 6th Airborne Div gave false information to prisoners so that they would work for the Germans. (He was acting Dolmich [?] at 12 A).
Gillow	Charles	Staff Sergeant	Glider Pilot Regiment	894370		On the departure from Stalag III A collaboration by the French was proved – (documentary) – I myself can quote no actual instance but feel assured that such a state existed & that documentary proof will be obtainable when the whole camp is evacuated.

Surname	First name(s)	Rank	Unit	Number	Number	Notes
Harvey	Stanley Trevelyan	Private	11th Battalion, Parachute Regiment	865935	91530	British POWs sold us Red Cross food for rings and watches, this was reported at my last camp Limberg 12A.
Hughes	Michael Frederick	Private	2nd Battalion, South Staffordshire Regiment	5891442		French POWs were working in collaboration with Germans in the Brux Benzine works such as bricks laying, welding, and draining engines, on the nearing of Allied troops they put on their uniforms, they also refused to transport to Br & US POWs who had to walk i.e. Brux to Kalsbad (sic).
McCourt	James Frederick	Captain	7th Battalion, King's Own Scottish Borderers	465	465	Cannot name them but the MEN OF CONFIDENCE at Limburg obviously were fraternising with the enemy & trading Red Cross Parcels – Ref Col Food – US Army.
Tillotson	John Willie	Private	133rd Parachute Field Ambulance, Royal Army Medical Corps	168025	89206	Limberg camp very badly organised. R. M. Commando (RSM) & 6 A/B Div Sgt in charge. Protected personnel forced to work on bomb damaged (sic) at revolver point. Reported but to no effect.
Tobin	John O'Hara	Captain	Royal Army Medical Corps	263459	90863	Security Officer at Oflag 79 gave me two names to carry to Senior British Medical Officer at Stalag III C as suspected enemy agents. Names are 1) Pollock 2) Van Sickle.
Pattle	Reginald Stanley	Driver	133rd Parachute Field Ambulance, Royal Army Medical Corps	5124019	90849	At Limburg 12A 28/9/44 to 13/10/44 there was a Sikh who wore a revolver and a Nazi armband. And the camp leaders, an Airborne Sgt and a Marine Commando RSM were of doubtful sentiments. [Notes alongside from War Officer MI5.]
Smith	John Lawrence	Private	156th Battalion, Parachute Regiment	3781730	75511	Sgt Amos. At Stalag XII A Limberg, Sept 30 1944, also RSM name unknown but in charge of camp. Giving Red Cross food parcels to Germans food belonging to other POWS [Has MI5 in blue pencil and text outlined.]
Vaughan	Peter	Trooper	1st Airborne Recce Squadron	13116352	75803	Have fairly extensive and detailed information relating to the endeavour and methods of a special department of the German Foreign office and military to gain the collaboration of Allied POWs. For information on that subject I also beg to refer to other officers and ORs of the American and British Forces who – against their wish – were kept in the Berlin Interrogation Commando.

Name	Forename	Rank	Unit	Army number	POW number	Answers
White	Bernard	Private	1st Battalion, Border Regiment	4547299	117501	A Corporal name unknown, probably known by RSM Lord 1st Airborne Div. Paroled 3 days per week, believed engaged to German.
Whyatt	Norman	Lance Corporal	1st Battalion, Parachute Regiment	5504900	92150	I think that Sgt Amery British M of C [Man of Confidence] at Stalag 12A Limburg collaborated with the enemy. My friend L/C Young, A. shares my opinion. Date 1-10-44 – 20-10-44 I would like to report that the distribution of Red Cross parcels at Stalag 12A, in October 1944 was very unsatisfactorily carried out and the British Man of Confidence (Sgt Amery 6th Airborne Div) was greatly criticised by all British POWs for the manner in which he conducted himself.
Jones	Stephen Samuel	Private	156th Battalion, Parachute Regiment	5575919	21903	Americans treated us very bad in front of Germans.
Pettitt	Thomas Joseph	Private	2nd Battalion, Parachute Regiment	14397946		Only hearsay only. Of British W.O + hut leaders in Stalag IV B by fawning and giving as much help as possible to the Germans. Names not known but they were hut to leaders of 24B and 26 B.
Pick	Robert Baxter Paterson	Private	1st Battalion, Parachute Regiment	7367569	91495	Stalag XII A. Two Britain's and two Americans acting as men of confidence October 44. Refused to do distribute food parcels. No attempts was made by those in any way to help their fellow prisoners. A lot of food parcels were in the camp they were only distributed on the [illegible]. Particulars were WO I No 4 Royal Marine Commando & Sgt [illegible] 6th Airborne Div. [Blue pencilled outline and MI 5 on questionnaire.]

Table 9: War Crimes

Question 7: War Crimes

If you have any information or evidence of bad treatment by the enemy to yourself or to others, or knowledge of any enemy violation of Geneva Convention you should ask for a copy of 'Form Q' on which to make your statement. (Note: Form Q is a separate form inviting information on 'War Crimes' and describes the kinds of offences coming under this title.)

Name	Forename	Rank	Unit	Army number	POW number	Notes
Ashington	George	Private	2nd Battalion, South Staffordshire Regiment	5109173	117515	One glider pilot shot dead in Stalag XI B by God without warning. RSM Lord of Parachute Regt has full particulars of guard.
Aston	George Frederick	Private	11th Battalion, Parachute Regiment	4927881		At IV C Stalag I saw a Russian shot at Aussig station by a German sentry 573 Regt Wehrmacht.
Brown	John	Sapper	Royal Engineers	1895443	118186	Insufficient warning of POW standing orders when captured. Caused unnecessary death of one Sgt (G.P.).
Courtney	Thomas Richard Brian	Major	133rd Parachute Field Ambulance, Royal Army Medical Corps	112406	91202	I was informed about April 13 that there is a British Major (Secret Service) at Torgau who is awaiting execution about the second week in May.
Hendry	John	Gunner	1st Airlanding Light Regiment Royal Artillery	877914	118044	A Glider Pilot was shot by an unknown German sentry at Stalag XI B early in October 1944 and died. This sentry had shouted orders to us which we did not understand so he opened fire and shot the Glider Pilot. I gave evidence at an enquiry at the Stalag shortly afterwards for Red Cross and German Intelligence officer.
Keeler	Norman Arthur	Sergeant, Lance	4th Parachute Squadron Royal Engineers	2031950	21705	Distributing Red Cross parcels contents to German civilians and refusing POWs.
Livesey	Trevor John	Captain	1st Parachute Squadron Royal Engineers	222702	611	Information on war crimes has been written in the form of a statement and is held by Major Cassels (S. A. Army) at Oflag 79.

479

Name	Forename	Rank	Unit	Army number	POW number	Notes
Matthews	Ronald George	Private	7th Battalion King's Own Scottish Borderers	4750960		A comrade being shot for looting without being given a trial. [On Questionnaire in red is a note 'A French Canadian Bouvi'].
Monsell	John Humphrey Arnold	Lieutenant	2nd Battalion, Parachute Regiment	112889	562	No that has already been dealt with.
Murray MC	Douglas Campbell	Major/T	1st Parachute Squadron, Royal Engineers	106883	607	I have evidence to the Major A Hibbert escape.
Whittam	Albert	Gunner	1st Airlanding Light Regiment, Royal Artillery	1791277	118695	Whilst at a working camp at Uelzen Pte Chisholm died through lack of medical treatment. German MO refused to treat him. Pte Chisholm was suffering from an abscess in his throat which burst and choked him, he died 21st March 1945 (approx).

Table 10: Assistance

People, other than Allied servicemen, who helped the POWS

Name	Forename	Rank	Unit	Army number	POW number	Notes
Birchenough	Richard Alfred Godsal	Captain	11th Battalion, Parachute Regiment	112810	18650	When recaptured on 15th April 45 and marching back I was given moral encouragement by German officer cadet who could speak fair English and was helping [eligible] captured by the Allied troops. He gave me information about Allied troops and their position. I made a note of his name and address. Harald von Wallenburg-Pachalý, Castle Furstlich-Drehna, Kreis Kialau, Post Crinitz Silesia.
Conway	James Joseph	Staff Sergeant	Glider Pilot Regiment	7043131	117320	2 Polish girls helped in last escape …

Dalton	Christopher	Private	1st Battalion, Parachute Regiment	4348459		... we were very well treated by civilian jailers for 10 days at Brunfels/Lahn the name of the people is Shleifer [Schlierfer]. Our jailer was a [pai ... or Ma ...] called Shleifer, both the man and his son & daughter were very kind, they did not like the Nazi, the mother commiting suicide when Hitler declared war. Others in the village who were very kind, bringing food to us, was the English wife of the Doctor and the inspector of Police.
Edwards	John William Edward	Private	2nd Battalion, Parachute Regiment	5511508	117955	... when we escaped after 1 week we were without food for 4 days until we met a Frenchman who kept us in food & gave us clothing for 1 week his name & address – R. Gazeilz, Champagne Fabrik, Bordeaux, Gironde, France. he came through with us to the US troops & we left him with them.
Gough	Charles Frederick Howard	Major	1st Airborne Recce Squadron	31420	595	I should like to mention the Yugo Slavs and a Czech girl at Ertzgarten. I did not have time to get their names as each time we had to leave in a hurry. Also French Commando (sic) at Geisenheim. Man of Confidence was Henri Saunier of Blamont – Meurthe et Moselle. In each case they took considerable risks to feed and hide me.
Harvey	Robert	Private	2nd Battalion, South Staffordshire Regiment	5192902	117318	I was help to escape with my companion Cpl Carter by Mrs [Els?] Schafer Dresden, she was pick up by the Gestapo for helping us to escape.
James	Bert		21st Independent Parachute Company	7022654	075364	When the Russians did not seem to feed us very well, I was taken in by a German family, I was fed and treated excellently. The family was Herr Martin Richter, 18 Guttenbergstrafe, Risa/Elbe, Deutchland.
Johnson	Arthur	Private	2nd Battalion, South Staffordshire Regiment	1568699	92045	I want to pay tribute to the Red Cross for the parcels I got they were a godsend.
Jones	Samuel		156th Battalion, Parachute Regiment	5575919	21903	Was helped by Check (sic) partisans along with four other British. Check was a hero – Františeit Kutil Javor CII PP Janovice N/Uhlavou.

Name	Forename	Rank	Unit	Army number	POW number	Notes
Layland	Frederick	Gunner	2nd Airlanding Anti-Tank Battery, Royal Artillery	1092475	92062	I wish to thank the Red Cross Society for the parcels I received. Could not have lived on German rations …
Lyon	Archibald Davidson	Sergeant	Glider Pilot Regiment	14216954	15246	The nursing staff in Enschede Convent in Holland did everything to make us more comfortable than the Germans. They smuggled in food, fruit & general army communiques. The Dutch people did everything possible for me.
Miller	Philip Anthony Alfred	Sapper	1st Parachute Squadron, Royal Engineers	1947386		Appreciation and thanks to International Red Cross.
Newton	Kenneth Ernest	Private	181st Airlanding Field Ambulance, Royal Army Medical Corps	14672306		I would also like to thank the Red Cross for the many ways in which they make POW life more bearable.
Nicholas	Lewis	Private	2nd Battalion, Parachute Regiment	4390380	117336	… after our escape for one week we were without food or water. We met a French soldier, who fed us and supplied us with clothes. His address is R. Cayeily, Champagne Fabrique, Bordeaux, Gironde, France.
Pettitt	Thomas Joseph	Private	2nd Battalion, Parachute Regiment	14397946		… the Chec people in general did great work for the POWs marching through their towns and villages.
Pott	Robert Lailett John	Major	156th Battalion, Parachute Regiment	95241	2193	The following people helped me. At Arnhem on 20.9.44. I was picked up by a stretcher party of 6 Dutchman including one named Rob Ruef. Was fed and looked after for some hours at monastery of Millhill Brethren (NW of Arnheim on Ede Road). Leg put in splint by Dr? (monastery would know name) received further treatment for one night at big hospital in Arnheim one of the surgeons name was Van Haaften. At Gronau Hauptlazeret

Surname	Forename	Rank	Unit	Number	Number	Remarks
Quigley	Edmund	Sergeant	Light Warning Unit No. 6341, RAF	1149134	943	received good treatment and nursing from Oberazt, Oberstßazt, Red +, Fransiscan nuns, + German orderly called Fräulein from near Basle. Major Elfering of the SS who was also undergoing treatment in the hospital did a lot for me including the loan of his wireless by which I was able to listen to BBC.
						The help given to me by Yugoslavian girl workers helping me to evade work by giving numerous excuses to the German overseer during my absence.
Scott	Arnold	Private	156th Battalion, Parachute Regiment	4746709	?	Wish to express the good work done night and day by POW Polish people in hospital Stalag II A when Germans were not looking after our wounded at all.
Seymour	Tom Henry	Lance Corporal	1st Battalion, Border Regiment	14574818	75687	… helped by 3 civilians given compass and directions for contacting Yanks.
Stark	Ronnie Leslie	Major	1st Battalion, Parachute Regiment	167154	531	I received help in escaping by Anton Weltmerer of ENSELHAUSEN HALLERTAY – BAYERNNE. Bavaria. This German was most helpful and gave me shelter and food in spite of SS troops being in the vicinity of his house. He was well aware of the risk he was taking and showed calmness and courage throughout. A French soldier who works for this German also gave valuable assistance his name is Pierre VALARIER, 65 Rue la Crevalerts Paris 13.
Thornton	Frederick George	Driver	1st Parachute Brigade, Royal Signals	2572006	92249	During imprisonment in civilian prison I was treated with every respect and given the best food possible in Germany. The civilian jailer Mr Shleifer and family had all suffered imprisonment etc through the Nazi government. The address of the above jail Braunfels on Lahn near Frankfurt.
Wood	Jack	Private	2nd Battalion, South Staffordshire Regiment	4914111		I would like to thank the Red Cross for all they have done for us.

Assistance

Several men recorded their thanks to the Red Cross:

> Gunner Frederick Layland, 2nd Airlanding Anti-Tank Battery, 'I wish to thank the Red Cross Society for the parcels I received, Could not have lived on German rations ...'

Others took the opportunity to record the names of those, other than Allied servicemen, who had helped them while in captivity. These were often, but not always, Allies. Two men record being helped by what appears to be the same man, though difficulties of spelling non-English names gave their helper two surnames: 'Cayeily' and 'Gazeilz'.

The help provided by the local inhabitants to men held in the East was also recorded:

> Lance Corporal Tom Seymour, 1st Battalion, Border Regiment, 'The good work done by Sgt G Rafferty in the miners work camp. Also the Chec [sic]people in general did great work for the POWs marching through their towns and villages.'

> Private Arnold Scott, 156th Battalion, Parachute Regiment, 'Wish to express the good work done night and day by POW Polish people in hospital Stalag II A when Germans were not looking after our wounded at all.'

Chapter 6

Escapes, Winter, Freedom

Escaping and Evasion

The British Army encouraged escaping. Men were lectured on evasion techniques as well as how to behave if captured. And although most escapers were not free for long, escapers helped tie down German internal security forces and generally made a nuisance of themselves. It also raised prisoners' morale. The questionnaires include descriptions of escapes in similar terms and others identify their escape companions as airborne, showing that Arnhem men were not separated at camps. Nevertheless, of 2,357 questionnaires, only 13 per cent (315) record at least one escape attempt.

Although it was policy to encourage escape attempts, two factors combined to make escape less likely from autumn 1944 onwards. The war was obviously coming to an end, even with the setback at Arnhem and later in the Ardennes. Why take any risk? And the risk factor was reinforced by German threats to treat POWs as saboteurs and shoot them. This caution was formal British policy and instructions to discourage escaping were sent to camps:

> Staff Sergeant John Devey, Glider Pilot Regiment, 'Escapes discouraged according to official sources via Camp Leader.'

What is striking is that some men were serial escapers. Private Kevin Hall, 156th Battalion, Parachute Regiment, made four attempts between February and April 1945. Regimental Sergeant Major Horace Eatwell, 1st Battalion, Parachute Regiment, made three in 1945. Some men provided detailed accounts of their escapes with extra sheets added to their questionnaires, while others were more succinct. Private James Kearns, 1st Battalion, Parachute Regiment, answered the escape question, 'Only for a few days.'

Perhaps the most incredible escape carried out at any time was that of Major Pott in October 1944 from a hospital at Gronau just over the Dutch border in Germany. At the time he was on crutches:

> Major Robert Pott, 156th Battalion, Parachute Regiment, 'On the morning I was due to leave GRONAU hospital at approx 0200 hrs I got out of window about 10' from the ground went on crutches to Dutch frontier, crossed a stream near ENTSCHEDE (approx 5 kms) attempted to obtain help from Dutch, but they reported to

Dutch police who reported to German police who collected me and returned me to GRONAU (approx 1300 hrs). Gunner Clark helped me to dress. He was unable to come with me as he had one leg off. My left thigh and stomach was in plaster and my left knee would only bend a few degrees at the time of the escape.'

Major Pott's questionnaire also included this unusual comment about hospital life: 'Major Elfering of the SS who was also undergoing treatment in the hospital did a lot for me including the loan of his wireless by which I was able to listen to BBC.'

Of the 393 escapes recorded in the questionnaires, forty took place around the battlefield; twenty-two in transit to a Dulag; 162 during transfer to or at a permanent camp or *kommando*; and 150 during an evacuation march. Nineteen escapes give no location.

Battlefield Escapes

Since the man subsequently became a POW, most of the early escapes recorded in the questionnaires will be ones where the escapee was recaptured:

> Sergeant James Barnbrick, 2nd Battalion, Parachute Regiment, 'Attempted immediately on captured. (Arnhem) Holland. Used the Germans own slit trench at the HQ but men were counted.'

> Bombardier William Cottrell, 1st Airlanding Anti-Tank Battery, Royal Artillery, 'At Arnhem. Captured first on Sept 20th held for around an hour in cellar escaped through grating into street. Re-captured next day.'

Corporal Edwards' escape attempt deserved to succeed because of its sheer cheek. Sadly it did not:

> Corporal Thomas Edwards, 1st Battalion, Parachute Regiment, 'At Arnhem with unknown Airborne officer 1 day after capture. Joined up with German SS unit on the march.'

However, a few men with questionnaires evaded capture at Arnhem and remained at large for some time. In some cases they remained with their liberators until the war ended. Staff Sergeant Bernard Haller, Glider Pilot Regiment, was liberated by the Canadian Army, having been with the Dutch underground since he escaped from Apeldoorn hospital in October 1944.

In the East, men who escaped were helped by the Czech underground. In some cases they too spent time with their liberators before being repatriated:

> Regimental Sergeant Major Horace Eatwell, 1st Battalion, Parachute Regiment, 'Imprisoned by the Gestapo at Praha & Kladno for 26 days from 15 April 45 until released by Czech Patriots on 6 May. Fought in the defence of Praha for 3 days.'

Escapers in the West also stayed with their liberators, in Craftsman Bellew's case for three weeks:

> Craftsman Cyril Bellew, REME, 'Escaped from column with companion Alex Ramsey on April 14 1945 and joined 'E' Coy 2 Batt 359th (USA) Infantry Reg, 90th Division and served with them as a rifleman till the end of the War.'

In Transit

Men continued to try to escape from trains to the Dulags and then again on trains across Germany to their permanent camps. Without maps, food or money and in British uniforms they were not likely to get very far:

> Private William O'Neill, 7th Battalion, King's Own Scottish Borderers, 'Being told that proper time to escape was soon after capture, some of us tried to get away during train journey to 1st camp (XII A). We were allowed out of wagon (train) for urinal purposes and attempted to hide until train moved on. Discovered by guards. Names of companions not known.'

> Sergeant Edward Mitchell, Glider Pilot Regiment, 'Attempted to break out of railway wagon on way to Mulburg [sic] nailed ventilator was wrenched open but discovered by guard who struck a Polish corporal with a bayonet and nailed the board back up again.'

The Policy Changes

On arrival at their permanent camps, men found that official policy had changed. Now the orders were not to escape. It was felt that the end of the war was close and escaping was not a justified risk. There was also the awful outcome of the escape from Stalag Luft 3, in March 1944, where fifty recaptured escapers were shot.

Following the escape the Germans had produced a poster addressed to all POWs and headlined 'The escape from prison camps is no longer a sport!' The identification of gangsters and terrorists as a threat to Germany was the basis for ensuring men captured at Arnhem were members of the Allied armed forces and the reason men were threatened with the Gestapo if their captors weren't satisfied with their identification.

Some men record that the stay-put order had come from General Fortune, who had commanded 51st Highland Division captured at Saint Valery-en-Caux in 1940 and was seen by many as the senior British POW:

> Lieutenant Roy Standdon, 1st Airlanding Light Regiment, Royal Artillery. 'On orders from General Fortune no escapes attempted during my period of actual imprisonment.'

> Lance Corporal Howard Jones, 16th Parachute Field Ambulance, 'Instructed by British Office in touch with Conf. Man <u>not</u> to escape owing to the shooting of captured escapers & the end of the War approaching.'

Nevertheless, some men attempted escapes from their camps or *kommandos*. Gunner Ackerman escaped from Stalag IV D:

> Gunner Donald Ackerman, Royal Artillery, 'Myself and six pals, we were absent for three days making our way to Kassel. We were picked up by the Jerry Air Force, we were threatened but later returned to our Stalag. We moved at night only.'

Helped by a German family, two men did manage to successfully evade capture until liberation by American troops:

> Sergeant Reginald Isherwood, 1st Battalion, Parachute Regiment, 'Myself and Sgt Richards got French uniform when sentry reached end of his beat nipped through our hole in the wire. Weren't noticed in streets because there are many French POW in Hanover where the camp was. I spoke French and contacted French POW. He told us the news and advised us not to make for the front as they would be here soon. He was working on a bombed house. Took us there told the family and they hid and fed us from then 1/4/45 till the Americans arrived on the 10/4/45. The family were Germans.'

Evacuation Marches

Walking away from their camps offered men the best escape opportunities, especially during April, when the sounds of the front line were evident to the men. This was despite repeated German warnings that escapers would be shot and the orders from senior officers:

> Sergeant Eric Culpan, Glider Pilot Regiment, 'On our march from Bankau the Germans threatened to shoot the 5 men nearest to any who escaped. We were told the orders not to escape had come from higher up.'

The original questionnaires had no question about the camp evacuation marches that started in the snow as the Russians threatened to liberate POW camps in Eastern Prussia and Poland from early 1945 onwards, and which, for some, continued until the end of the war. Four of the Arnhem questionnaires have an extra question added by duplicator: 'Have you taken part in any marches in or into GERMANY? If so please write names of any personnel who you saw fallout, giving if possible, place, name, and date.' Unfortunately the four with the extra question are from men held in western or central Germany and none answered it. However, 172 men did refer to marches while a POW using other questions. Although referred to as 'marches', men who took part in them emphasized that they were not marches in the military sense. They were trudges, treks or, in the better weather of April and May, ambles. Oflag IX A/Z deliberately put the oldest men at the front of the column to ensure it did not travel quickly.

Stalag Luft 3, Stalag Luft 7 and Stalag VIII all were evacuated in the winter. Men from these camps would be expected to refer to being evacuated but of the six questionnaires from Stalag Luft 3 only one refers to the march west, in the additional information section:

> Staff Sergeant John Devey, Glider Pilot Regiment, 'Deplorable treatment by Germans from 19 Jan ''45 to 8 Feb '45 during march from Bankau …'

References to marches in the questionnaires also come in the lists of camps, for example Company Sergeant Major Thomas Courtie, who gave this as his last entry, 'Line of March 16th April 45 – 1st May 45.'

But the most detail of marches comes in the final additional information question on the questionnaire:

> Staff Sergeant Bennett Sayles, Glider Pilot Regiment, 'Forced to march in severe snowstorm with barometer [sic] reading -30° several men were struck by guards on arrival at Luckenwalde we were all severe malnutrition cases …'

> Bombardier Charles Varney, Royal Artillery, 'March from 7 February 1944 [sic] – 14 March [sic] approx 450 miles. Food 500 gr Bread per day & this ration not issued on at least 12 occasions. No hot drinks or soups for practically whole journey. No medical attention (dysentery & septic dermatitis). Thrashing by German posterns when unable to keep pace with main column. Four men of my group of 30 died from dysentery accentuated by lack of medical attention during & immediately following this march.'

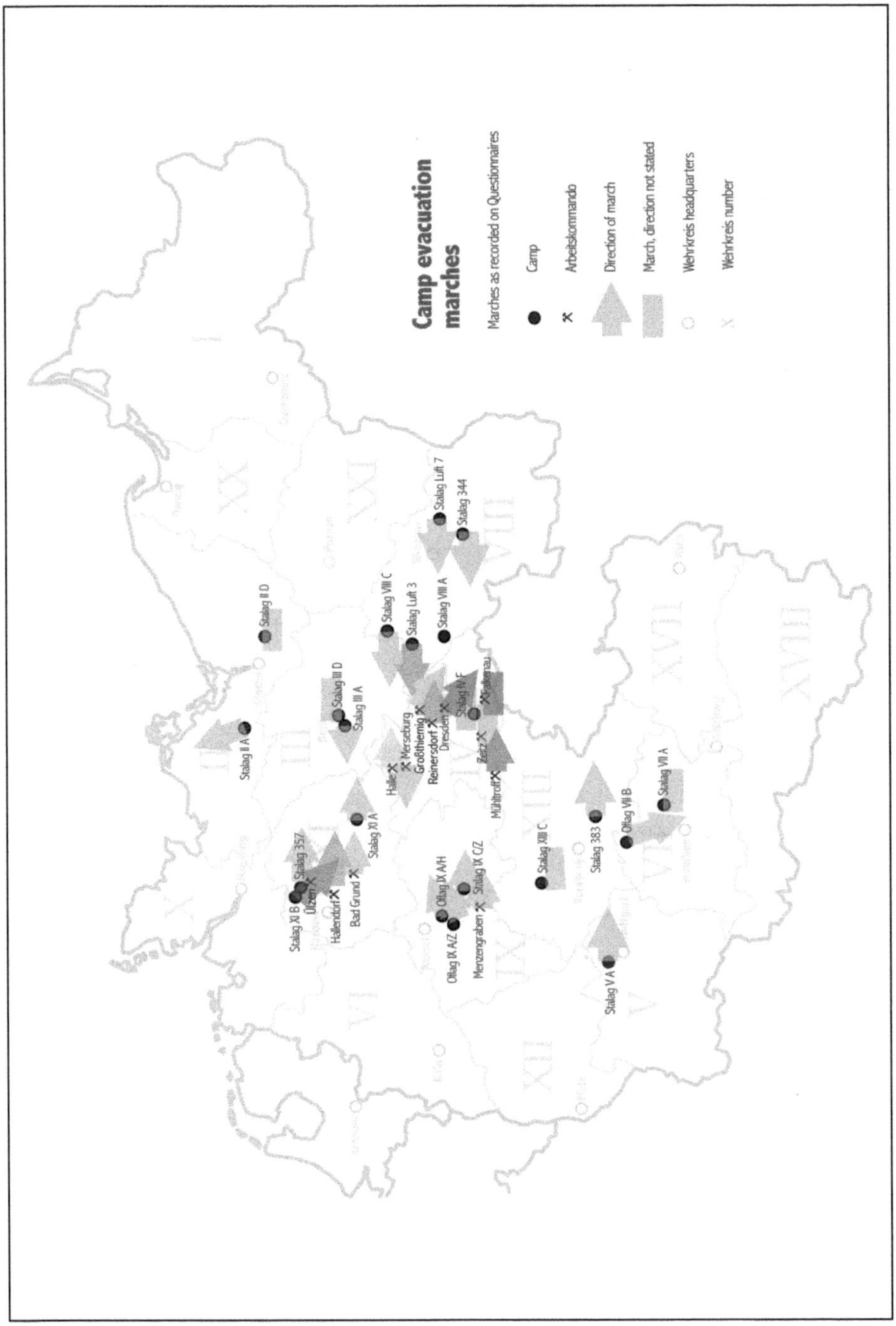

Camp evacuation marches

Marches as recorded on Questionnaires

● Camp

✗ Arbeitskommando

▲ Direction of march

▬ March, direction not stated

○ Wehrkreis headquarters

✗ Wehrkreis number

Map 7: Camp evacuation marches recorded in the questionnaires.

Table 11: References to Evacuation Marches

Most references are given under the final question, 'Have you any other matter of any kind you wish to bring to notice?' Where they come from other questions they are shown by a title in square brackets.

Name	Forename	Rank	Unit	Army number	POW number	References to evacuation marches given as direct quotations from Liberation Questionnaires.
Aitken	Peter	Staff Sergeant	Glider Pilot Regiment	28799361		The exceptionally good behaviour of the CoE Padre to Luft 7, Captain Colins, during the march from Bankau to the West. [Captain Reverend J B Collins RACD, Stalag XVIIA Army Number 3014 army number 111558].
Beveridge	Thomas McLeod	Lance Corporal	9th Field Company, Royal Engineers Airborne	2113967	75856	[Escapes] Escaped at Worldorf near Doblin 27 April 45 during march at 03.30 hrs met American Army same day.
Bevington	Bernard Leslie	Private	2nd Battalion, South Staffordshire Regiment	14397682		[Escapes] On the march recaptured + joined another column. General bad treatment of prisoners no medical attention on march sick forced forward.
Booth	Eric Charles	Driver	1st Parachute Squadron, Royal Engineers	1951655		[Escapes] Yes partial escape, owing to being evacuated hid up in wood, object to wait for American army.
Brotherton	Donald	Private	3rd Battalion, Parachute Regiment	6018336	117523	[Escapes] 12.4.45 From column marching from XI A near Belzig with four others.
Buxey	William Thomas	Sergeant	Glider Pilot Regiment	1876657		Magnificent work done by medical officer of Luft 7 whilst marching from Luft to III A needs recommendation.

491

Name	Forename	Rank	Unit	Army number	POW number	References to evacuation marches given as direct quotations from Liberation Questionnaires.
Chambers	Talbot Alexander	Sergeant	89th Parachute Field Security Section	118933	93637	[Escapes] Yes. Alone. Feb 10, from wood 2nd night of Stalag's march W from Sagan. Method – evasion of guards by crawling 1/2 a mile from lightly guarded Indian enclosure. Recaptured Feb 17 SORAU (Silesia) by SS troops retreating W while crossing road to improve hideout. Not physically fit.
Clapham MC	Edward Eric	Lieutenant	1st Airlanding Anti-tank Battery, Royal Artillery	258481	2175	The whole of Oflag IX A/Z were marched for 14 days before the American advance, causing unnecessary suffering to many of the older and less fit officers of the camp.
Clarke	Peter	Staff Sergeant	Glider Pilot Regiment	7356321	118129	I have in my possession a fairly full diary of the period 8 Feb – 13th April 1945. The period during which I was marching.
Courtie	Thomas	Company Sergeant Major	10th Battalion, Parachute Regiment	3768595	140153	[List of camps] Line of march 16th April 44 – 1st May 45.
Crowe	Ronald Harry	Sergeant	1st Parachute Brigade, Royal Signals	2323334	18679	[List of camps] on march until released 1–May 45.
Cull	George William	Private	1st Parachute Brigade	14410678		[Escapes] We escaped while Jerry had us on the march. We escaped to the hills on 27th April & slept the night & returned to the village in the morning & found he had shot one chap who tried to get away, so went on for about 3 miles and met the Yanks, Tpr John Folwer 2nd NY.
Culpan	Eric Hopkinson	Sergeant	Glider Pilot Regiment	2081536		On our march from Bankau the Germans threatened to shoot the 5 men nearest to any who escaped. We were told the orders not to escape had come from higher up.
Deasy	William Roy	Staff Sergeant	Glider Pilot Regiment	985314	118164	[Medical] Dysentery and malnutrition during march west.

Surname	First name(s)	Rank	Regiment	Service No.	POW No.	Account
Derbyshire	Stanley	Private	3rd Battalion, Parachute Regiment	14375898	52885	[Escapes] My camp had marched away from the front for a month. Whilst sleeping in a barn we were told to prepare to move at 3 am. Gunfire in near distance denoted closeness of Allied troops so Pte P. Sutton & I hid in the straw. Pte Sutton was discovered before he had time to hide & had to join the column which marched away.
Devey	John Raymond	Staff Sergeant	Glider Pilot Regiment	3601654	903	Deplorable treatment by Germans from 19 Jan '45 to 8 Feb '45 during march from Bankau to Luckenwalde. Night marches (a) one of 41 KMS in intense cold. (b) one of 21 KMS in blizzard. Food :- 31/2 loaves of bread (1500 grm loaves) a few ozs of margarine 1/2 cup of soup every other day during 3 weeks. Train journey of 4 days after capture without food or water.
Down	Percy	Corporal	1st Battalion, Parachute Regiment	5671339	118257	Marched from Sagan to Brunswick not physically fit – and lack of food.
Elliott	Sidney Charlie Edwin	Private	2nd Battalion, Parachute Regiment	6153666	140131	[List of camps] Transit March 1945 – 27.4.1945.
Green	Alan Thomas	Lieutenant	1st Battalion, Border Regiment	247201	2177	The march which all ranks had to undertake when in an unfit condition. Rations supplied by the Germans were negligible, we lived mainly on the Red Cross stores held in the camp prior to our move. Billets were poor.
Greenbaum	Frank Ashley	Sergeant	Glider Pilot Regiment	14417002		The actions carried out by Captain Howatson RAMC (99321) and Captain Collins R A Ch D (111558) on the forced walk from Bankau to Goldberg in my opinion deserves the highest praise.
Griffith	William Gordon	Sergeant	Glider Pilot Regiment	4192348		Received very poor treatment during evacuation from Silesia, starvation rations and long forced marches under severe weather conditions. I wish to commend Padre Collins CoE for exceptional work during the march. It was far above anything expected of a fellow prisoner.

493

Name	Forename	Rank	Unit	Army number	POW number	References to evacuation marches given as direct quotations from Liberation Questionnaires.
Hadfield	George Frederick	Sergeant	Glider Pilot Regiment	3531592	140112	I desire to bring to the notice of the authorities, the exceedingly good work done by C.S.M. McKenzie, R.A.S.C. in the capacity of 'man of confidence', during our stay in Stalag 383 and afterwards on the line of march
Harley	William Douglas	Lance Corporal	2nd Battalion, South Staffordshire Regiment	14202780	118289	Escaped on the morning of the 11th April outside of Derenberg with L/C Wyatt, when we had done three days marching. We were physically fit. We met the Americans approx 4 pm same day.
Heath	Joseph Henry	Private	10th Battalion, Parachute Regiment	945801		[Escapes] Yes 7/8/45 while marching from Dresden with Tpr Williams also with me met up with Russians.
Heaton	Joseph	Private	2nd Battalion, Parachute Regiment	7899398		[Escapes] Escaped at night whilst being marched away from advancing troops.
Howard	John James	Lance Corporal	1st Battalion, Parachute Regiment	3598966	89855	[Escapes] Latter end of captivity from column when being marched towards (Sweden?) stayed at a State Farm for food during march. Walked off with three companions into woods. Contacted Seventh Armoured Div. near Bergen. Names of mates. L/Cpl Hall, Pte Purdy Pte Stokes.
Isherwood	Reginald	Sergeant	1st Battalion, Parachute Regiment	893585		[Escapes] Yes. 1) when being marched from Sagen about 5/2/45 spent the first night in a brick factory near Maskau.
Jones	Peter	Private	2nd Battalion, Parachute Regiment	3388690	52922	On march after Meiningen.
Kerswell	William John	Sergeant	Royal Army Medical Corps	7523088	77338	[Escapes] On the night of 27/28 March 1945 7377807 Cpl McFarlane RAMC, Pte Starksmeth, and self, by pretence of sickness managed to fall out of column marching away from XIII C.
Lang	Robert	Private	1st Battalion, Border Regiment	3606642	117504	[Escapes] Yes on the march from Uelzen (Friday 13 April) Breaking away from the column at night time.

Surname	Forename	Rank	Regiment	Number	POW No.	Notes
Lawson	Wilfred McLellen	Private	156th Battalion, Parachute Regiment	7948335	118001	[Escapes] Yes escaped on march from Uelzen with Pte Roger 8 kilos from town.
Lewis	John	Corporal	1st Battalion, Parachute Regiment	4032087	92129	[Escapes] On April 14th we were march out of Dresden for good to Czecho Slavakia. We marched 50 km that day and on the same night we escaped, going all night and all the next day.
Lyons	Charles Howard Cecil	Sergeant	Glider Pilot Regiment	427924	118524	[List of camps] 27 March '45 – Released whilst on march.
Matthews	William Lawrence	Corporal	1st Battalion, Parachute Regiment	2618797		On 28 April 1945 we commence in march from Varchentin in the custody of our guards on reaching Stavenhagen we were turned off the roads by German military authorities here our guards left us.
McLeavy	Donald	Sergeant	Glider Pilot Regiment	5350002	117758	On the march from Sagan to Falkenburg there was a serious lack of food. Medical attention. I myself having a festered foot. This situation was due partially to the German Commandant.
Metcalfe	Edwin	Private	1st Battalion, Border Regiment	3602861	118844	[Escapes] Yes. When the troops came near to our camp, the Germans marched us away there were 500 men. Four of us escaped into the woods and waited until our troops came.
Miller	Christopher Alfred	Staff Sergeant	Glider Pilot Regiment	937499	117770	Ill treatment of POWs whilst marching for period of three months. Including lack of food and medical attention.
Mullender	James William	Private	11th Battalion, Parachute Regiment	4399431	52908	[List of camps] Marching from 1 April to 2 May.
Nicklin	George Lewis	Sergeant	Glider Pilot Regiment	7955175	117174	[Escapes] Yes. 3 kilos past Spremsberg left column alone on 12.2.1945 and attempted to lie up waiting for Russian forces. Recaptured 22.2.1945 by Gestapo. 2nd attempt (successful) 8 kilos past Hanover on 8.4.1945 joined American forces 10.4.1945.

Name	Forename	Rank	Unit	Army number	POW number	References to evacuation marches given as direct quotations from Liberation Questionnaires.
Paterson	William	Signalman	1st Parachute Brigade, Royal Signals	2348020	91340	[Escapes] 15 April 45 Sachgrün – from column of March.
Potter	Joseph William Dominic	Signalman	1st Airborne Division, Signals	2590125	118138	[Escapes] At Derenburg we got information that the USA troops were four kilometres away, we were on the march. We made a mass break and hid. G Ball and E Ball were my companions. We were liberated the same day.
Powell	Charles	Lance Corporal	2nd Battalion, Parachute Regiment	4035583	117800	[Escapes] I escaped on the Thursday evening of the third week of April whilst marching about 1 1/2 mile beyond Gorzke heading for Belzig.
Prosho	Thomas George	Private	1st Parachute Brigade	6148592		[Escapes] Escaped 15th of April from marching column while halted during the day with three other POW.
Ransom	James Leslie	Lance Corporal	250th Airborne Light Company, Royal Army Service Corps	10694205	91189	[Escapes] Escape from Kommando whilst on evacuation march from Dresden.
Sayles	Bennett	Staff Sergeant	Glider Pilot Regiment	850767		Very bad treatment received from guards of Stalag Luft 7 whilst on March from Bankau to Luckenwalde Forced to march in severe snowstorm with barometer reading -30° several men were struck by guards on arrival at Luckenwaldewe were all severe malnutrition cases all this was reported to the protecting power.
Shepley	Arthur	Sergeant, Lance	156th Battalion, Parachute Regiment	4344978	52919	[Escapes] Whilst on the march through Germany 13/4/44 released by Americans on 16/4/44.
Smith	John Thomas	Private	156th Battalion, Parachute Regiment	14665924	90483	I escaped three days before the Yanks took Zeitz. The Germans marched us away. I slipped away at night and met the Americans on my way back.

Surname	First names	Rank	Regiment			Notes
Smith	Norman Peter	Private	7th Battalion, King's Own Scottish Borderers Regiment	3191832	90175	Left Merseburg on 13th April '44 and marched for six days without any proper food. Only a few potatoes each day. Conditions at Dahlen Stalag very bad. The Germans had no rations to give us.
Stead	John Edward	Staff Sergeant	Glider Pilot Regiment	794717		[Escapes] Attempted escape at Carlsru during march from Bauhau to Luckenwalde.
Stokes	Reginald	Private	2nd Battalion, South Staffordshire Regiment	5051452	89713	[Escapes] Escaped from line of march from Stammlager 357 to Eastern Germany, slipped into woods with three pals at Bergen.
Stones	Horace Ryan	Sergeant	Glider Pilot Regiment	4337089		The treatment of NCOs from Stalag Luft 7 on their march from Bankau East of Breslau to 70 km S. of Sagan food was bad if any. Men were suffering with poor treatment and intense cold and lack of food.
Such	Albert George	Gunner	1st Airlanding Light Regiment, Royal Artillery	14318215	52917	On 13 April escaped from the march and made for the village of Weisendorf and was picked up by the American troops on 16 April 45.
Teece	Percy James	Lance Corporal	1st Airborne Provost Company	7398111	118232	Broke away from column of March on 11 April 1945 at Derenburg and relieved by America 331st Infantry Regt 2 hours later. I was physically fit.
Trueman	Arthur	Sergeant	Glider Pilot Regiment	101997	52909	[Escapes] Made escape whilst on the march through Germany on 13.4.45 with 3130647 Cpl Waight 2nd Bn RSF and 4344978 Sgt Shipley 156 Bn Parachute. Were relieved by the Americans at Steitz (Zietz?) 16.4.44. Was semi-fit condition – Companions alive and well.
Tucker	Percy Henry	Corporal	1st Battalion, Parachute Regiment	5436835	118466	[Escapes] 2 Escapes. 1st attempt from Sagan evacuation, 9 Feb 44. Kept to woods aid of escape compass with S/Sgt Wade G/Pilot. 2nd attempt whilst on march from Leipzig with four Frenchmen. Contacted US troops at Wurzen. Weak condition.

Name	Forename	Rank	Unit	Army number	POW number	References to evacuation marches given as direct quotations from Liberation Questionnaires.
Turnridge	Benjamin Basil	Private	1st Battalion, Parachute Regiment	6012580		[Escapes] 8.4.45 Dipoldiswold during evacuation march of working camp.
Varney	Charles Norman	Bombardier	Royal Artillery	14311471	117328	March from 7 February 1944 (sic) – 14 March (sic) approx 450 miles. Food 500 gr Bread per day & this ration not issued on at least 12 occasions. No hot drinks or soups for practically whole journey. No medical attention (dysentery & septic dermatitis). Thrashing by German posterns when unable to keep pace with main column. Four men of my group of 30 died from dysentery accentuated by lack of medical attention during & immediately following this march.
Wright	Stanley Winston	Sergeant Major	2nd Battalion, South Staffordshire Regiment	4913782		[Escapes] Feb On the march free for 5 days recaptured by Volkstrohme – Fit April 8th at Hannover, successful picked up by Americans April 10th. The issue of Argentine Bulk Rations at Sagan before starting forced march. … Treatment of Britishers on march as compared to other nationalities. No medical treatment on march.
Wright	Leslie Edward	Private	Royal Army Ordnance Corps	14655624	118678	[List of camps] Marching from 6th Feb 1945 to 3rd May 1945.

Escapes During Marches

There were two classic techniques to escape from evacuation columns: hide in the camp when it was evacuated or hide during a rest, under a culvert or in bushes or in a pile of hay:

> Corporal George Bicker, Royal Signals, 'hid in cellar under cookhouse and awaited Russians ...'

> Captain Philip Barry, 2nd Battalion, Parachute Regiment, 'At Rockensus 30 March 45 at 1100 hrs tunnelled into haystack with Capt Lauder. Found by locals at 1330 hrs. I was fit.'

Attacking the guard was not recommended, but two incidents are recorded. Perhaps Sapper Daniels' 'hit' is better understood as 'pushed'; even so it was still potentially dangerous:

> Sapper Daniel Stevens, 4th Parachute Squadron, Royal Engineers, 'About 3 km from our jail over night. I hit the guard into a ditch & the boys disarmed him.'

> Lance Corporal Tom Seymour, 1st Battalion, Border Regiment, '... placed in barns in Klatovy Checoslovakia from here we overpowered the guards on the night of the 6th of May ...'

Eight men describe the same large-scale escape from a column of prisoners from Stalag XI B at Derenburg, about 100 miles south-east of Fallingbostel on their way to the Harz mountains. For a short period the Germans saw the Harz as a potential safe redoubt. It was also the destination for Oflag IX A/Z:

> Lance Corporal William Harley, 2nd Battalion, South Staffordshire Regiment, 'At Derenburg 11/4/45 Whilst on march. Civilians were in a panic. This enabled me (and many others) to slip away through side streets to the outskirts of the village where we hid out until the arrival of the American armoured column the same day. I was with L/Cpl E. Ball and Sigmn J. W. D. Potter.'

As well as the men Lance Corporal Harley mentions, Lance Corporals Teece, Howells, Signalman Ball, Privates Riley and Cartmell also describe the Derenburg escape.

Table 12: Escapes Attempted

The answers to the question 'Did you make any attempted or partly successful escapes'? (Give details of each attempt escape, stating where, when, method employed, names of your companions, where and when recaptured and by whom. Were you physically fit? What happened to your companions?' Most men Most men, if they answered, started started their answer with 'Yes'. This has been omitted, although Private Joseph Wood's single word 'Yes' has been included.

Where the escape took place
Arnhem = A
In transit = T
Camp = C
On march = M
No location given = nk

Name	Forename	Rank	Unit	Army number	POW number	Escape location	Answers given as direct quotations from Liberation Questionnaires
Ackerman	Donald Henry Edwin	Gunner	Royal Artillery	14334539	88742	C	Myself and six pals, we were absent for three days making our way to Kassel. We were picked up by the Jerry Air Force, we were threatened but later returned to our Stalag. We moved at night only.
Agar	Godfrey Stewart	Staff Sergeant	Glider Pilot Regiment	2151406	118668	C	Partial attempt frustrated by capture of French comrades the day before I was due to leave. I was on fit. Stalag IV B Mulhberg.
Austin	Norris	Corporal	1st Battalion, Border Regiment	4455267		C	Pte Hart S/A Army, Pte Ponting, Pte Houghton and myself escaped while in Czec but after 10 days & nights we gave up to police because of hunger and our physical state (26-4-45 to 6-5-45).

Surname	First name	Rank	Regiment			Account
Back	Harold Ernest	Lance Corporal	2nd Battalion, Parachute Regiment	6473851		C	3 other men (Pte Carr Cpl Dell and L/Cpl Killen) and myself escaped from kommando on the farm for which we volunteered with the purpose of escaping. This was at or rather twenty miles from Neubrandenburg on Jan 13th 1945. A method was to break the lock from the inside of the lager door which is not too difficult. And we made our way due west with the aid of a Parachutist's escape compass. We kept going for six days and reach south-west of Hamburg some miles from the river Elbe. We were recaptured, outskirts in a village in this area the name of which has escaped my memory. [Our] captors were the Volkstürm troops, who it seemed to us, had been warned of our approach. We were quite fit when we escaped, but on being recaptured we were suffering from slight exposure and although I didn't realise it at the time I had a bad touch of frostbite in my toes. Myself and my companions were taken back to Stalag II A at Luckenwalde.
Ball	Eric	Lance Corporal	10th Battalion, Parachute Regiment	865470	118290	M	At Darenburg by lengthening the column of marching labour (about 1000) until the guards lost control. The end of column (about 200) turning right instead of left. Then we went into hiding until the American column arrived a few hours later. Companions Sig Potter Sig Ball.
Ball	George	Signalman	1st Airlanding Light Regiment, Royal Signals	2122492	118122	M	At Darenburg 11/4/45. Whilst on march. Civilians were in a panic. This enabled me (and many others) to slip away through side streets to the outskirts of the village where we hid out until the arrival of the American armoured column the same day. I was with L/Cpl E. Ball and Sigmn J. W. D. Potter.

501

Name	Forename	Rank	Unit	Army number	POW number	Escape location	Answers given as direct quotations from Liberation Questionnaires
Ball	Richard Patrick	Gunner	1st Airlanding Light Regiment, Royal Artillery	1084454	117397	M	Along with Private J Cartmell Left a column of prisoners on the march 11 April. Relieved by American 331 Inf Div 11 April 1945.
Barham	Leonard Charles	Sergeant	1st Battalion, Parachute Regiment	6026001		C	Escaped with Pte Laing of 1st Btn Para Regt on 19th Feb 1945 by changing identities with two Ptes on Working Camp detail in Jan 1945 from a coal-mine camp at Borna, nr Leipzig. Recaptured a couple of days later on the Dresden main road; place name I've forgotten. My companion was with me all through until liberation.
Barnbrook	James Stanley	Sergeant	2nd Battalion, Parachute Regiment	6016887		A	Attempted immediately on captured. (Arnhem) Holland. Used the Germans own slit trench at the HQ but men were counted. Old wound gave considerable trouble.
Barnes	George	Private	2nd Battalion, Parachute Regiment	6145484	88941	M	Escaped 10/4/45. After bombing of camp with Ray Paine, South African captured 5 miles from camp by civil police after evacuation of Camp. Paine did not come have not seen since.
Barraclough	Charles	Private	2nd Battalion, Parachute Regiment	883950		C	Escaped from Halle on 13 April. Walked out of the camp during confusion of evacuation, the wire had previously been blown by American bombing. Companion Harold Coupe met up with Americans forces 16/4/45 quite fit.
Barry	Philip Hanbury	Lieutenant	2nd Battalion, Parachute Regiment	240444	2182	M	1. Line of March between Rotenberg and Rockensus, 29th March 45 at approximate at approx 2300 hrs. Hid in hedge. No companions, Recaptured by sentry with dog at end of column. 2. At Rockensus 30 March 45 at 1100 hrs tunnelled into haystack with Capt Lauder. Found by locals at 1330 hrs. I was fit. Companion okay with us.

Surname	Given names	Rank	Regiment	Service No.	No.	Cat.	Details
Batten	John Samuel	Sergeant	The Parachute Regiment	5435891	117981	M	Escaped on march 30kms east of Leipzig, was recaptured too weak at Brandis.
Bedford	Stanley William	Private	2nd Battalion, South Staffordshire Regiment	4925203		M	Escaped whilst being marched. 17th of April 1945 by hiding in woods after making dash for it. Pte Smith Pte Wagstaff Pte Johnson finally met the Americans Wurzon 24 April 1945.
Bellew	Cyril	Craftsman	Royal Electrical and Mechanical Engineers	4081359	75843	M	Escaped from column with companion Alex Ramsey on April 14 1945 and joined 'E' Coy 2 Batt 359th (USA) Infantry Reg, 90th Division and served with them as a rifleman till the end of the War.
Berry	Joseph Edward	Private	11th Battalion, Parachute Regiment	1428100	294932	A	Two days after capture jumped train with Victor Moore. Contacted Dutch underground. Recaptured 20th in November. Moore believed escaped. Underground tried to get us over Rhine but run into German outpost. Was unfit at time. Attempted escape two days later in another train 4 got away but guard was suspicious attempt failed for remaining number.
Beveridge	Thomas McLeod	Lance Corporal	9th Field Company, Royal Engineers Airborne	2113967	75856	M	Escaped at Worldorf near Doblin 27 April 45 during march at 03.30 hrs met American Army same day. Companions Pte Perry, Gunner Milner, Pte Brown, Pte Darling. I was physically fit. Companions got through as well.
Bicker	George Stanley	Corporal	Royal Signals	2324374		C M	(1) Stalag 8G 1st Jan 45, Cut compound wires crossed to compounds to outer wire cut outside wire and when awaiting favourable moment for final breakthrough 5 men from my compound made a quick escape through hole 1 cut of wire captured just outside wire had to return own compound. (2) tried again Feb 10th 45 when Jerry threatening to march all fit men away, hid in cellar under cookhouse and awaited Russians liberated on the 17th very hungry, into Russian hospital with bronchitis.

503

Name	Forename	Rank	Unit	Army number	POW number	Escape location	Answers given as direct quotations from Liberation Questionnaires
Birchenough	Richard Alfred Godsal	Captain	11th Battalion, Parachute Regiment	112810	18650	M	One escape made from line of march when officers were leaving OFLAG VII B for South on 14 April 45 – escape made alone under cover of machine-gunning of column by Allied planes. Captured 36 hours later by German youths armed with .22 rifles 28 km from ANSBACH at GRAPSTEINBORG. Condition fairly good though all equipment mislaid during air attack and lost.
Bishop	Walter William	Lance Corporal	156th Battalion, Parachute Regiment	6086564		A	I escaped in Holland, recaptured after two days by German SS troops we were fighting in that sector.
Black	John	Private	156th Battalion, Parachute Regiment	2939792		C	Escaped Hellensdorf, 18/4/45 with Pte Hutton, LCpl Bradley and Pte Smith. Captured 22/4/1945 15km from Altenberg, fit, Companions returned with me.
Black	James Charles	Sapper	1st Parachute Squadron, Royal Engineers	1986005		M C	Escaped near Leipzig while being evacuated from Merseburg 22 April app. Recaptured at Wurzen 27 April. Escaped from Oschatze 30 April reached American Lines across the Elbe at Grimma 1 May on my own.
Bloys	William	Private	2nd Battalion, Parachute Regiment	6029487		C	I made my escape in Halle my companion was Delaney. I never see him after we were brought back to our camp.
Booth	Eric Charles	Driver	1st Parachute Squadron, Royal Engineers	1951655		M	Yes partial escape, owing to being evacuated hid up in wood, object to wait for American army. Separated from my companion R Drury 5726456 P. Miller 1947386. Was caught by two SS officers.
Bradbury	William Henry George	Sapper	1st Parachute Squadron, Royal Engineers	14203066		M	Prison camp Halle REI 113. Escaped from enemy and contacted American jeep patrol 5 days later. Lived most of the time on Red Cross supplies which we had manage to saved. Physically (sic). One comrade Spr Coupe.

Bradley	Thomas Phazie	Lance Corporal	9th Field Company, Royal Engineers Airborne	2012016		C	On the 18.4.45 from the farm at Hebendorf We escaped through the farm window when the guard went to sleep. My companions were Jim Smith, John Black, Pte Hatton, we were all recaptured on 22.4.45 by artillery troops 10 or 15 kilos from Altenburg. We were physically fit.
Breen	Thomas Francis	Lance Corporal	1st Airborne Provost Company	1917769		M	Escaped on Friday 20th of April '45 accompanied by Paul Emile Turgeon (Canadian Army) about 2 miles from Floss, Bavaria, and succeeded in reaching 90 Division American Army on Sunday 22nd April '45. Turgeon now in Allied hands.
Bromfield	Arthur	Sergeant	2nd Battalion, Parachute Regiment	6014527	88939	C	Escaped from working Kommando (Kundl). 17 men attempted escape out of 29. Went with Cpl Warren. 2736584. 1st The Parachute. Bde. 17/4/45 Cut wire at night, travelled for 3 days and, dressed as French workers, Recaptured by German soldiers at ZILLERBRUCH. 20/4/45. (Fit) both recaptured.
Brooker	Ronald James	Trooper	1st Airborne Reconnaissance Squadron	6354463	91435	T C M	On transit from hospital, was recaptured same day by SS troops. Was still suffering from wounds. Escaped from work camp 3 days before the Americans arrived. Escaped on transit (at liberty 13th-16th April accompanied by Sigman Eddyshaw, Pte Sykes, Pte Withey).
Brooks	Stanley Donald	Private	2nd Battalion, Parachute Regiment	6104511	117266	C	From Stalag XI B 10th April 45 walked out of main gate and to make out we were French labourers. Pte CURTIS & Pte BURNHAM (both USA) recaptured by SS troops in Railway Depot, SS School Fallingbostel. 10 April. [Were you physically fit?] No they are safe and have gone back to the USA.
Brown	Leonard	Private	7th Battalion, King's Own Scottish Borderers	14211781	89851	nk	When the US 2nd Div moved up. Wolfunbottle area. Not physically fit.

Name	Forename	Rank	Unit	Army number	POW number	Escape location	Answers given as direct quotations from Liberation Questionnaires
Brown	Norman	Private	2nd Battalion, South Staffordshire Regiment	4918535		C	I & others on the night escaped, The dates are being 12.4.45 during an air raid warning to the fields outside of Halle with A Russell, B [illegible]. P Dettmar. Three days after the Americans came and Russell and myself fought with them for three days.
Buck	Lawrence Fredrick	Corporal	1st Parachute Squadron, Royal Engineers	1883034		C	Markt Pongau 6/5/45. By taking bath party from one lager to another. Bdr Hood 1456647 Bdr Savory. L/ Cpr Hirst 2126716. Met scouts of 101st American Airborne Div. at SAALFELDON Wed 9/5/45. Fit. Americans sent us to Munich POW centre.
Buglass	James	Private	3rd Battalion, Parachute Regiment	4975389		C	With Brian Hill 2nd Para Btt but recaptured by Civil Volkstraum. Physically fit.
Butler	Dennis John	Private	1st Battalion, Parachute Regiment	14409701		C	[Escape details illegible but from *kommando* near Chemnitz dressed as French worker.]
Byrne	Mchael	Private	1st Battalion, Border Regiment	3782510	118304	M	On the night of April 13th my two companions and I were on the march towards the river Elbe when we stopped for the night we managed to slip round the side of a farm and took to the woods. We moved from 1 wood to another for two days and nights and then took to the main highway. On reaching a small village 14 KILOS from UELZEN we were hidden in a house by a Frenchman until our own troops enter the village. My companions names were Pte Matthews and Pte Lang. We were not fit.
Caldwell	John Gibson McCoy	Private	2nd Battalion, South Staffordshire Regiment	274850		nk	Once successful as a civilian. Relieved at Louwy By Red Army and then carried on to Pilson to the US Army.

Surname	First name	Rank	Unit	Service No.	No.	Cat	Details
Campbell	Henry	Sergeant	2nd Battalion, Parachute Regiment	3055067		C	Attempted to escape on Friday, 2nd May 1945 with two other companions from Stalag 317 18C. Method employed masqueraded as camp staff. Lost my two companions on Tuesday 6th May 1945. Met an American troops on Wednesday, 7 May 1945. Physically fit.
Campbell	Sidney Alex Albers	Gunner	1st Airlanding Light Regiment, Royal Artillery	6099334		C	Twice. Brüx Sudatenland 23rd March 45 walked off working group in morning mist. Pte G James Caught 24 March in woods by Gerry civvie with pistol, 2nd time caught 4 hrs after. Alone.
Carlier	Leonard Thomas	Private	2nd Battalion, Parachute Regiment	5835317	89827	C	Successful. Escaped on 8.4.45 with five others Also attempt on 7.4.45 from camp but guard trebled.
Carr	Joseph Stuart	Private	2nd Battalion, Parachute Regiment	6147869		C	From commando work. Jan 15th 1945 Varchentin accompanied by corporal Dell, LCpl Back both of same unit and LCpl Killen Airborne Military Police. Recaptured at Witenburg by Wehrmacht. Yes. Returned to Luckenwade with my companions.
Carr	William	Signalman	4th Parachute Brigade, Royal Signals	4279044	91677	C	Escaped during March from working commando with Pvt D. James 1st The Parachute Bn. Recaptured by police after three days in woods. Escape from camp in Tysa 30 April and made way to Russian lines near Chemnitz, where learnt by wireless that war was over. Companions - Pvt L Norton 2nd Battalion, Parachute Regiment Bn, Pvt R O'Dwyer 10th Battalion, Parachute Regiment Bn. Joined by 3 Americans while passing their camp.
Cartmell	James	Private	156th Battalion, Parachute Regiment	3447716	118308	M	Escaped on the morning of the 11 April outside of Derenberg with Pte Ball, met our forces one hour later, in Derenberg.

Name	Forename	Rank	Unit	Army number	POW number	Escape location	Answers given as direct quotations from Liberation Questionnaires
Cawrey	Victor Frank	Private	21st Independent Parachute Company	4975875	118305	M	Given orders to evacuate Stalag when American forces were imminent. Started marching and ducked column in company of Pte Humphreys 2nd Batt Pte Finglass 21st Ind Para. Captured at Zerbst by SS 22 April. All three. Yes was fit.
Chambers	Talbot Alexander	Sergeant	89th Parachute Field Security Section	118933	93637	M	Alone. Feb 10, from wood 2nd night of Stalag's march W from Sagan. Method – evasion of guards by crawling 1/2 a mile from lightly guarded Indian enclosure. Recaptured Feb 17 SORAU (Silesia) by SS troops retreating W while crossing road to improve hideout. Not physically ft.
Channon	William	Company Quartermaster Sergeant Major	4th Parachute Brigade HQ	5567123	88745	C	Escaped successfully on 16/4/44 [sic] from KUNDL AUSTRIA with 5184774 Sgt G Wright 43 Reccy Rgt. Travelled by night, walked all the way, through SCHRANZ INNESBRUCK ZIRL TELPS NAZARIETH LERMOS REUTTE, were able to link up with 7th US Army and gave valuable information to US Army Intelligence Off.
Chapman	Harry Arthur Frederick	Staff Sergeant	Glider Pilot Regiment	4267802		T	On the train from Limberg to Muhlberg detected by sentry.
Chesterton	Eric	Sergeant, Lance	Royal Signals	2330939		C	(1) Stalag VIII C – Jan 1 1945 – Escape through compound and perimeter wires under cover of snow blizzard – 2324374 Cpl Bicker G.S.M. – returned Camp owing lack of food insufficient clothing under inclement weather conditions with view to further escape. (2) Stalag VIII C – 10 Feb 45 – seclusion in cellar when Camp evacuated 2324374 Cpl Bicker G.S.M. – awaited arrival of Russian forces – liberated 17 Feb 45.

Chivers	William Ernest	Private	2nd Battalion, South Staffordshire Regiment	4917934		C	Recaptured after 3 days. On entering Stalag 12 [?], escaped notice of guards who were deciding upon huts etc, prisoner, w/o companions dashed off. Kept away from main roads, etc, & lived on swedes etc. Escaped 22/9/44. Recaptured name of village unknown 25/9/44. Fairly fit.
Clark	Henry Pullman	Sergeant	1st Airlanding Light Regiment, Royal Artillery	997188	88740	C	May 3rd 45 on hearing the American army was expected in Pongau, along with Cpl Lindon and Corp [?] Hughes The Parachute Regt [?]. Went Salzburg route Heard Americans were in Pongau May 6. [?] Berchesgarden.
Clark	James	Private	7th Battalion, King's Own Scottish Borderers	3245281	90528	M	I escaped on the 7.2.45, while being withdrawn from one camp to another, at night. J McLure of the 156th Battalion, Parachute Regiment Reg was with me. We were fit. We were never recaptured.
Clarke	Peter	Staff Sergeant	Glider Pilot Regiment	7356321	118129	A	Escaped With two other Glider Pilots from Kaiser Wilhelm Barracks at Appeldorn At 21:30 hours Sat 1st of October and we were all recaptured at 19:00 hours Sunday, second October 1944. The escape was affected by crawling under two belts of wire. Companions Sgt Blunthorne Sgt Eason. Recaptured in woods 12 miles north-west of Apeldoorn by local Wehrmacht was physically fit and [?].
Coates	John Robert	Sergeant	2nd Battalion, Parachute Regiment	3771565		C	Attempted escape from Stalag XVIII C in early March. Broke out of compound and mixed with a working party which was going out in the night. Companion Sgt Mulhall 1 Grenadier Guards. Caught at last gate. Not very fit. No parcels for months. Bare German Russians.
Conway	James Joseph	Staff Sergeant	Glider Pilot Regiment	7043131	117320	nk	Escaped three times – caught twice – two Polish girls helped in last one.

509

Name	Forename	Rank	Unit	Army number	POW number	Escape location	Answers given as direct quotations from Liberation Questionnaires
Cook	George	Private	3rd Battalion, Parachute Regiment	6214569	89173	M	Escaped from WALLMAIN whilst on the march to 12 G [sic] from Merseburg. 6979407 N Robinson, and L Hemings. Both safe in Allied hands.
Cooke	Clifford Kenneth	Private	11th Battalion, Parachute Regiment	10666764	89804	C	13/4/45 Escaped 12 kms north-west of Uelzen. Evaded German troops for five day regained our lines 18/4/45. L/C Newman, WR L/C Nullis, J R, Pte Stanton, M.
Cottrell	William John	Bombardier	1st Airlanding Anti-Tank Battery, Royal Artillery	1514708		A	At Arnhem. Captured first on Sept 20th held for around an hour in cellar escaped through grating into street. Re-captured next day. Being knocked out by mortar bomb blast near main bridge. SS medical personnel treated me.
Coupe	Harold	Sapper	1st Parachute Squadron, Royal Engineers	1922268	89229	C	Escaped from Halle camp Rei 113 on the 12.5.45 Contacted a jeep patrol 5 days later. Reideburg. Bradbury, G. Physically fit.
Critchley	Arthur	Private	3rd Battalion, Parachute Regiment	7888645		M	Escaped from camp on the move, made our way across country towards Freiberg was picked up by German soldiers nine miles from Freiberg. Pte Gaven (English) 2 Americans for 4 days.
Cull	George William	Private	1st Parachute Brigade	14410678		M	We escaped while Jerry had us on the march. We escaped to the hills on 27th April & slept the night & returned to the village in the morning & found he had shot one chap who tried to get away, so went on for about 3 miles and met the Yanks, Tpr John Folwer 2nd NY.
Culliton	Patrick	Private	3rd Battalion, Parachute Regiment	13098369		nk	3 Times. First time by myself. Second time 2 of us. Third time 12 of us. Details too long. No room to write.

Cunliffe	Roger	Private	1st Battalion, Border Regiment	14402790		C	Escape 26/4/1945 from Oederan with King, Jenkinson, Recapt Mitvida German airforce troops. Not physically fit. Remained with companions.
Cunningham	Thomas	Lance Corporal	156th Battalion, Parachute Regiment	345429	90500	M	1st Attempt escape from evacuation to Floha April 22nd (44). 2nd Attempt escaped from Floha to Chemnitz May 6th Information from forced labourers (Smith other names unknown).
Curtis	Arthur	Private	11th Battalion, Parachute Regiment	6399339		M	I escaped on 8 March 1945 recaptured 15th March.
Curtis	Leonard Arthur Cecil	Private	3rd Battalion, Parachute Regiment	2047378	117875	M	Escaped on march into woods on hearing Allied gunfire. Recaptured next day. Partially fit. Escaped about middle of March.
Cuthbertson	Malcolm	Private	4th Battalion, Dorsetshire Regiment	3770561	91903	M	8.5.45. We were being moved under guard away from Russian battle area. Made our way to nearest USA unit following a Russian air attack on a column. Remainder of party also dispersed 17 men in our party. One man of our party killed three wounded by air attack.
Dalton	Christopher	Private	1st Battalion, Parachute Regiment	4348459		T	I escaped with Pte Thornton 1st The Parachute Brigade when leaving Limburg on the 13th November by jumping off a train. We had to climb through the window of a cattle truck. Captured the same day by a Gamekeeper, we were very well treated by civilian jailers for 10 days at Brunfels/Lahn. The name of the people is Schliefer. Our jailer was a painter or [illegible] called SHLEIFER, both the man and his son & daughter were very kind, they did not like the Nazi, the mother commiting suicide when Hitler declared war. Others in the village who were very kind, bringing food to us, was the English wife of the Doctor and the inspector of Police.

511

Name	Forename	Rank	Unit	Army number	POW number	Escape location	Answers given as direct quotations from Liberation Questionnaires
Davidson	Charles	Private	10th Battalion, Parachute Regiment	4536073	75493	M	Escaped from column on 4th May near Lauenstein reached Russian lines 10 May 1945 Name of friends Gillesbie, Oswald, Moody, Geddis, Nesbi. Yes. Liberated.
Davies	Sydney	Private	2nd Battalion, Parachute Regiment	14309397		T	Arnheim captured in the morning 21st escaped for 4 hrs. Hanover (M Fitzgerald) Repat) escaped 2 o clock through the wire jumped on the Hanover-Hamburg express. Got off at Neimburg. Had eats in farm. Picked up 6 o clock and taken to French Larger.
Dell	Edward	Corporal	2nd Battalion, Parachute Regiment	6203748		C	Escaped from commando 14.1.44 [sic]. Recaptured by civi Gestapo on 21.1.44. Physically fit. Companions L/Cpl Beck. Cpl Carr. L/Cpl Killen.
Denholm	James	Private	11th Battalion, Parachute Regiment	3314746	119639	A	I escaped from hospital with my pal Pte Norman's same regiment on first Oct 44 by hiding in an air raid shelter till dusk, and then climbing the wall surrounding camp we got away, the following day we were picked up by the underground [illegible] then taken to a house where medical treatment was given to us. For weeks, we were kept there, until the doctor said we were fit to move, after we left there we went to Apeldoorn and stayed two days from there to Barnaveldt [Barneveld] by bicycle. We had a dinner there and seven o'clock that night the underground came, and took us to a farmhouse about five kilos away. We stayed there for about two weeks when notice came that we should get ready to move prior to attempt to cross the Rhine. On Saturday morning 18th Nov. we found ourselves in a forest with a lot of people of different nationalities, and were told that we would all be moving at half past five that night to cross the Rhine. We started off that night [illegible], but finally about twelve o'clock, we ran into a German patrol and got captured.

Surname	First name	Rank	Unit	Service No.			Narrative
Derbyshire	Stanley	Private	3rd Battalion, Parachute Regiment	14375898	52885	M	One successful. My camp had marched away from the front for a month. Whilst sleeping in a barn we were told to prepare to move at 3 am. Gunfire in near distance denoted closeness of Allied troops so Pte P. Sutton & I hid in the straw. Pte Sutton was discovered before he had time to hide & had to join the column which marched away. On 1st May 45 was relieved by American troops.
Devine	John	Signalman	1st Parachute Brigade, Royal Signals	2574778	88905	A	Was placed in barn of a farm about 20 kilometres German side of Arnheim. Escaped through roof caught following morning by SS. Companions were seriously wounded RE officers who couldn't move.
Dixon	Robert Richard	Gunner	1st Airlanding Light Regiment, Royal Artillery	14600654		M	When marching from Sagan VIII C Albert Chapman and myself (same regt.) got out of column at Ortrande. Played crank. 13-2-45. free for two days. Both fit. Both sent to working commando. Recaptured by 2 Volksturm (Home Guards).
Dolaghan	Thomas Noel William Dowie	Private	4th Parachute Brigade	6977906	89826	M	SUCCESSFUL ESCAPE on 11th April 45 to American Lines 2nd Armd Div when they were 10 kms from MATHIERZOL German guards panicked when they heard guns getting closer. Escaped during excitement about 200 companions escaped about the same time from MATHIERZOL.
Donowho	William	Private	7th Battalion, King's Own Scottish Borderers	3190801		M	I escaped before evacuation of the camp 8.4.45 with J Coplande Pte by lifting the floor of our hut and lying under it until the Jerrys had gone. Then we got civil clothing and walked about the area until the Americans came in and then we gave ourselves up to the Americans.
Drayton	Frank	Private	2nd Battalion, Parachute Regiment	408160	89525	M	Yes April 29 1945. Line of march Basepohl. Americans. Scheirin 2-5-45. Yes. Don't know.

Name	Forename	Rank	Unit	Army number	POW number	Escape location	Answers given as direct quotations from Liberation Questionnaires
Drury	Robert	Private	10th Battalion, Parachute Regiment	5726456		C	Partial escape on Friday 13 April 45 at 4a.m. owing to evacuation. Hid in a wood locally (Halle). Object to hide up till liberated. Companion R Drury (5726456), E. Booth (1951655). Recaptured locally by Volksturm. E. Booth separated at sunrise and was captured by Luftwaffe (same Day).
Dunford	Reginald Charles	Private	10th Battalion, Parachute Regiment	555639	77099	A C	1st Escape Arnhem 30/9/44. Hid in Barn at dusk in hosp stalag at Apeldoorn 26 K N Arnhem, crawled through wire evading sentries successfully received food, support from the Dutchman. Companion Pte – 11th Batt (Name forgotten) recaptured Oosterbeek (Holl) 4/10/44 German bicycle patrol. 2nd Escape. Dresden 8/1/45 alone recaptured Aussig(nk) civil police 11/1/45. 3rd Escape 16/2/45 34 hrs free. 4th Escape 18/3/45 72 hrs free. 5th Escape 28/4/45 6 dys free. 6th Escape 5/5/45 Free till hostilities ceased.
Dunn	Kenneth Harold	Private	2nd Battalion, Parachute Regiment	1828301		A	Attempted to escape on second day of capture en route from assembly camp to railway station but was recaptured and returned to camp.
Dyall	William	Sergeant	Glider Pilot Regiment	853162		nk	One successful escape.
Eatwell	Horace Arthur	Regimental Sergeant Major	1st Battalion, Parachute Regiment	2613152	89402	M C	1st Breslau, line of March 18th Jan 44 with Pte Wright R.T. Regt, 29th Jan 44. Luftwaffe officer recaptured both at Waldenburg Fit. 2nd Czechoslovakia one day loose. 3rd attempt Lager from 22 Bruxe helped by Czechs into the Protectorate. 10 days freedom from 4th April-15th April 45.

Surname	First Name	Rank	Unit	No. 1	No. 2	Code	Notes
Edwards	John William Edward	Private	2nd Battalion, Parachute Regiment	5511508	117955	C	Escaped in company with Ptes Morton & Nicholas (of my unit) 12/4/1845 from Altingrabou reached the American bridgehead over the River Elbe on the 29/4/1945.
Edwards	Thomas	Corporal	2nd Battalion, Parachute Regiment	4699004		A	At Arnhem with unknown Airborne officer 1 day after capture. Joined up with German SS unit on the march. Where we were given away by Dutch civilians. Companion believed to be now an POW.
Elliott	Charles Bridgeman	Private	156th Battalion, Parachute Regiment	4279607		nk	[Answered no to escape question, then added this under 'any other information'] Escaped 6/5/44 [sic] and was successful in reaching Russian lines between Dresden and Chemnitz.
Ellis	Leslie Henry	WO II	1st Parachute Squadron, Royal Engineers	1869692		C	I escaped from working camp at Kundl on 18 April 1945 with QMS. Milson E. A. A.P.T.C. We were being transported to new location by train at night. We jumped off train while on the move just outside Kundl station. We were recaptured at Rattenberg. I escaped again from XVIII C on 3/5/45 with Sgt T Bushell & Sapper Euerton and Gunner Woods.
Ellwood	Michael	Private	2nd Battalion, Parachute Regiment	14272883		A	After 5 days medical treatment I tried to reach the Rhine, but was caught within 36 hrs by the SS. I had just received my sight after 6 days blindness.
Evans	Trevor Parry	Lance Sergeant,	2nd Battalion, Parachute Regiment	3966276	89810	A	Yes after capture at Arnheim.
Evans	Wilfred Richard	Driver	1st Airlanding Light Regiment, Royal Artillery	14320758	75312	C	From Lager at Chemnitz March 13th 45 Broke out of window and scaled the wooden wall around the lager, captured 30 kilos from Chemnitz. Pte Harry Hill 1st The Parachute Brig. Partly fit been repatriated about the same time as myself.

515

Name	Forename	Rank	Unit	Army number	POW number	Escape location	Answers given as direct quotations from Liberation Questionnaires
Eves	Edward	Private	1st Parachute Brigade	3977266	75448	C	From working camp at Lilianstein by cutting barbed wire on April 8th 45 recaptured again April 9th by Flak regiment. We were physically fit (IJ Turney, W Richmond G Anderson J Mucklin).
Fellows	James	Private	1st Battalion, Border Regiment	14584168		M	Made successful escape from prison column 25/5/1945, 10 miles from Müchdorf.
Fergus	Gerard John	Trooper	1st Airborne Reconnaissance Squadron	14282358	52935	A	Jeep was captured on 19.9.44. I managed to escape into the woods but had a bad leg and could not walk far. I got trench feet from exposure. Some civilians picked me up and handed me over to the Germans.
Fitzgerald	Michael	Driver	1st Airlanding Anti-Tank battery	6854732		nk	Captured Apeldoorn Holland 25 Sept '45 Handover (Davis) re-pat). Escaped at 2 o'clock breaking wire jumped on the Hanover Hamburg express. Eats in farm taken to French lager.
Fleming	William James	Sergeant	2nd Battalion, Parachute Regiment	2989834		C	At Kundl Austria. Whilst in transit back to Stalag walked away from sentry. Was free from 18/5/1945 and 21/5/1945 then picked up by civilians at Kufstein Austria.
Fowler	Sydney John	Lance Corporal	3rd Battalion, Parachute Regiment	870732	89224	C	I escaped from Merseburg Dec 14th. With Pe. Deviin AIF & Sprs Paine, Woods & Hetbury. 1st Bde Para Reg. We separated after escaping Devlin & I keeping together. We were helped by two Poles. Who then gave us over to police in Leipzig. whilst on way to Czechoslovakia. We were sent to a new camp after our punishment where they escaped further twice whilst I was in hospital. Devlin was killed later at another camp.

Surname	First name	Rank	Unit	Service no.	POW no.	Cat.	Notes
Fox	George	Private	Royal Engineers	14435314		C	Escaped on 21.3.45. From working camp Zeitz with Walter Stevens POW no 91187. Was captured again on 23.3.45 at Leipzig. Left companion when relieved.
Fox	Wilfred George	Private	2nd Battalion, South Staffordshire Regiment	4697023	92167	C	With two other men 6/5/45. Made own lines 7/5/45, Chemnitz. Fairly fit.
Foxon	James Arthur	Signalman	Royal Signals	2378460	91899	C	One week after arrival at Halle-Trotha Pte Carroll & Pte Smith D, Pte Lilley J and I escaped, but were seen crossing wire. Guard turned out, police all informed. We separated but were all recaptured after four or five hours at liberty.
Franzel	Frank Charles	Private	11th Battalion, Parachute Regiment	3661561		M	One attempt whilst being evacuated from Dresden in April. Caught four hours later in woods around Moldau. By four Volkssturm. One companion Ron Penny.
Funnell	Harry Ronald	Private	10th Battalion, Parachute Regiment	6411360		C	I escaped successfully on Thursday 12 April last, hiding with one other man in a cellar until Sunday Apl 15th when American spearhead entered Merseburg. I was physically fit, and my comrades name is L/Cpl Rotherham 156 Bn, Para, who came from England with me.
Furniss	Thomas	Driver	250th Airborne Light Company, Royal Army Service Corps	10694184	117594	M	On the 10th April 45 while we was marching in a *column we heard tanks very near so we disorganised the column and took cover in the civilian houses for two hours then we were relieved by the Americans. *About 600 men.
Giles	Dennis	Private	16th Parachute Field Ambulance, RAMC	14548345	118432	C	At Uelzen by jumping of Goods Train on 15 Feb 1945 approx was recaptured two days later by German troops. I was physically fit.

Name	Forename	Rank	Unit	Army number	POW number	Escape location	Answers given as direct quotations from Liberation Questionnaires
Gillow	Charles	Staff Sergeant	Glider Pilot Regiment	894370		M	In April '45 – When ordered by the Germans to entrain for evacuation from Stalag III A – I donned French clothes & lived with French Kommandos in Luckenwald – the evacuation subsequently proved impossible so I returned to camp – subsequently moving off with the advancing Russian forces.
Gledhill	Tom	Private	1st Battalion, Parachute Regiment	14333598	117528	C	We escaped four of us from our working place. Pte Eastham, L/Corp Howes, Pte Dixon. We was caught by a famer. And all of us put in a Strafe Commando.
Goode	Eric Henry	Sapper	1st Parachute Squadron, Royal Engineers	2073137	118286	C	Once, at Bad Grund while unloading sleepers, hid in wood, was recaptured after 4 hours, practically fit. Companion Pte Banks recaptured.
Goodwin	Roger	Private	3rd Battalion, Parachute Regiment	14434753	90028	C	From Plauen on Dec 28. I escaped whilst at work. I was recaptured near Nuremberg.
Gough	Charles Frederick Howard	Major	1st Airborne Reconnaissance Squadron	31420	595	C M	Oct 44. Attempts to get through floor of hut at HADAMAR. Discovered through an [illegible] which was due to lack of experience in 'stooging' whilst at work. Apr 17th 1944 [sic]. Made successful break from column of P's OW on march from EICHSTATT to MOUSSEBERG. Locality ERTSGARDEN 6 kms S of INGOLSTADT. No companion. Heat in civilian air raid shelter first night and received valuable assistance from JUGO SLAV P's OW working in village. Had to escape following afternoon as the village was being searched. Spent four days on the banks of small tributary R. DANUBE 2 kms

Surname	Forename	Rank	Unit	Number	Ref	Code	Account
Green	George Stanley	Lance Corporal	1st Battalion, Parachute Regiment	2929195		nk	N ERTZGARDEN & joined up with two escaped Americans Sgt FEATHERSTONE AMERICAN AIR CORPS & a 2nd Lt whose surname I cannot remember. We then posed as French workers stayed one night in barn at ERTSGARDEN & 1 nights in a cowshed walked about quite openly in daytime and talk to an SS FELDWEBEL telling him we came from BORDEAUX. On 23 April stopped by SS CHECK PATROL and taken to GEISENHEIM where we escaped & were hidden and fed by FRENCH P.O.W COMMANDO in the town. On 28 Apr made contact with Americans 86 Div Blackhawks & handed over two German officers and 3 ORs to them whom we had captured that morning. Escaped when American 1st Army was 30 kilos away. Hid out in fields for 5 days until sighting American armour.
Green	John	Driver	250th Airborne Light Company, Royal Army Service Corps	10698160	117845	M	Escaped from column while we was marching, we heard that our tanks was nead [sic], so we disorganised and took cover in civilian house for two hours, then we was relieved by the Americans.
Gregg	Victor	Private	10th Battalion, Parachute Regiment	6913933	92043	nk	April 45 failure after 5 days owing to lack of food. May 45 Yes Escaped to Russian Lines at Freiburg Abroad one week.
Grove	Philip Nigel	Captain/T	1st Battalion, Parachute Regiment	85684	597	A	From hospital at Arnhem 19 Sept 1944. Noticing that no sentry was guarding me whilst awaiting medical attention outside hospital, I managed to walk into hospital grounds. Recaptured in hospital grounds by a sentry I did not see when rounding a clump of bushes.

Name	Forename	Rank	Unit	Army number	POW number	Escape location	Answers given as direct quotations from Liberation Questionnaires
Grundy	Benjamin	Private	2nd Battalion, Parachute Regiment	4748425		C	1st From Halle on March 29th after bombing of billets 3 Americans and I walked 30 kilometres hid in a wood and were discovered by Hitler Youth on April 1st then brought Volkssturm soldiers at the village of Nunets. Taken back to lager in Halle. 2nd escaped from lager hid in country for 2 days when picked up by Americans.
Guyatt	Eric George	Lance Bombardier	1st Airlanding Light Regiment, Royal Artillery	935260	92081	C	Columbus Lager Brüx on the way to work report there then tried to escape captured by Volkssturm (alone).
Hall	Kevin Kenneth	Private	156th Battalion, Parachute Regiment	4344015		C C M	4 attempts 1st from Dresden 13.2.45. Walking. Pte Hartley recapt. Prina. 2nd Dresden 17.3.45 alone, 21.3.45 German Unter-offizier not fit. 3rd Dresden 4-4-45 with Pte Sweet 6-4-45 control officer taken to Koma at Neundorf. 4th Neundorf 1.5.45 alone made contact with Russians at Teplitz on 4.5.45.
Haller	Bernard John Frederick	Staff Sergeant	Glider Pilot Regiment	14291815		A	Escaped from Apeldoorn Hospital (Kaiser Wilhelm Kaserne) Holland Oct 6th 44 In company with Pte J Hardy RAMC att 1st Batt 1st The Parachute Brig. Not recaptured Pte Hardy returned to UK February 1945. After escape remained in enemy occupied Holland until liberated by Canadian 1st Army May 8, 1945.
Hamilton	Reginald Thomas	Private	7th Battalion, King's Own Scottish Borderers	14437879		C	Merseburg. R. T. Hamilton and L/C Cook DLI caught by civilians February 26th it was an individual attempt.

Surname	First name	Rank	Regiment				Notes
Harley	William Douglas	Lance Corporal	2nd Battalion, South Staffordshire Regiment	14202780	118289	M	Escaped on the morning of the 11th April outside of Derenberg with L/C Wyatt, when we had done three days marching. We were physically fit. We met the Americans approx 4 pm same day.
Harper	Charles	Private	7th Battalion, King's Own Scottish Borderers	3190813	75984	nk	Once – can't remember any details.
Harper	John Everard	Lance Corporal	2nd Battalion, Parachute Regiment	497226	88485	C	At Merzburg I tried to escape but was picked up by civilian police one day after. I had with me last of a food parcel, my physical fitness was not too bad. I was not punished.
Hartley	Alfred Harold	Private	156th Battalion, Parachute Regiment	14413724	14069	C	12-2-45 – 14-2-45 with Pte K Hall (Para) sent to working party. To follow the Elbe to Prague + then to Russian lines. Captured 20 km Pirna. Without food, compass, didn't speak German, no greatcoat.
Harvey	Stanley Trevelyan	Private	11th Battalion, Parachute Regiment	865935	91530	C	From working party alone for three or four hours, from Limberg. Going for a pick, recaptured at station by two Germans. Not fit.
Haslam	Reginald Alfred	Bombardier	1st Airlanding Anti-Tank Battery, Royal Artillery	1115969		C C	Attempted escape Nov 2nd 44 with T/Sgt Robert A Leaf US Army. Recaptured by Mil personal (7th-11-144). Escaped from XII A camp Muhlberg from working party marched on foot. T/Sgt Leaf was transported to USA NCOs camp after completion of solitary confinement.
Hawkins	Benjamin Edward	Private	2nd Battalion, South Staffordshire Regiment	4922840	91639	M	Broke away from column 6th May 45 Made way to Dresden, with two other men, no knowledge of others. One man George Elliot badly wounded in arm – in hospital at Bodenbach under Russian care.

Name	Forename	Rank	Unit	Army number	POW number	Escape location	Answers given as direct quotations from Liberation Questionnaires
Hayes	Frederick George	Sergeant	156th Battalion, Parachute Regiment	5249918		A	On the 20-9-44 when captured managed to arrange to accompany a wounded officer placed him in a German ambulance, while the sentries were thus occupied, escaped into the woods, stumbled on German patrol 24-9-44 was shot at, slightly wounded, recaptured, near Arnhem.
Hayes	William Jack	Sergeant	156th Battalion, Parachute Regiment	5108162	52932	M M	Attempted to escape on 15-4-45 but was too unfit through lack of food to travel fast enough eventually caught by six German Volksturm who threatened to shoot me and my companion (S/Sgt Vickers). Escaped off a column at Jena Thuringen and succeeded after two days to contact American tanks.
Headland	William George	Private	3rd Battalion, Parachute Regiment	1435227		C	From Brux factory with a Pte Hughes we met up with the Russians, and from there the Yanks at Karlsbad, Hughes is also repatriated We were very unfit owing to food shortage.
Heath	Joseph Henry	Private	10th Battalion, Parachute Regiment	945801		M	7/8/45 while marching from Dresden with Tpr Williams also with me met up with Russians.
Heaton	Joseph	Private	2nd Battalion, Parachute Regiment	7899398		C M	Attempt made on 7th of April 1945 but failed, due to the fact that one fellow was caught, the guards were then trebled and dogs were put into the camp. 8/4/44 [sic] Escaped at night whilst being marched away from advancing troops. 5 of us got away. Reached American 2 Armoured Brigade at Solder on Wednesday 11/4/45.

Surname	Forename	Rank	Unit	Number	Number	Code	Narrative
Henderson	Duncan	Private	156th Battalion, Parachute Regiment	853860		C C	From Halle Rei-113. Lager bombed so took the opportunity. Volksturm searching haystacks found us near Delistch escaped again by travelling with a railway kommando to Halle crossed railway bridges at night recaptured near Eisleben my companion was Nicholas WEBER American. Escaped later concealed by Poles until arrival of Americans app. date March-April.
Heyes	Stanley	Signalman	1st Parachute Brigade, Royal Signals	4132010	118696	C	We escaped from Working camp on 10/4/45. We escaped while on cookhouse fatigues, and made our way to the Allied lines. It took us three days to get to front. We were picked up by German front line infantry and taken to Munster Larger [sic] where we were liberated by 11th Armoured Div (18/4/1944). Companions were Gnr HOWELL Gnr WHITTAM.
Hill	Cecil	Corporal	2nd Battalion, Parachute Regiment	6401664		C	Wurzmes Dec 3rd by cutting the wire (with assistance of con. man). Pte Buglass 3rd Parare-caught by civil police at Seestadtl Dec 4th. Fairly fit. I don't know.
Hill	Norris Williams	Private	1st Parachute Brigade	11007637		nk	Escaped successful on 13/4/45 companions name John Potts got to American lines on 15/4/45.
Hill	William	Lance Corporal	16th Parachute Field Ambulance, RAMC	7264147		T	By myself going through Cologne 19 Sept 1944 recaptured 21st (trying to get back to Arnhem) Herman Goering Panzer Grenadiers.
Hinsley	William Alfred	Private	4th Battalion, Dorsetshire Regiment	1584800	14223	M	Escaped with seven comrades from evacuation column at Riesa, recaptured by military four days later at Dobeln, were all fit and were sent to a military camp, from where we were evacuated to Sudatanland.
Hodge	Donald Hugh	Private	1st Battalion, Border Regiment	3866321	15231	M	I escaped at night time whilst marching near MIESON ON ELBE and picked up next day by German home guard, I was weak from hunger and hadn't had food for days.

Name	Forename	Rank	Unit	Army number	POW number	Escape location	Answers given as direct quotations from Liberation Questionnaires
Hole	Edward Stanley	Private	3rd Battalion, Parachute Regiment	5672174		M	Escaped 13/4/1945. We were told to pack our kit 3 O'Clock on 13-4-45. Contacted to the Americans on 16-4-45 given food and accommodation by Capt Blumhart 802d F.A Bn U.S. Army. Pte Charles and Pte Lancaster escaped with me.
Hollinshead	Douglas	Private	11th Battalion, Parachute Regiment	844968	118171	M	Escaped from column 10-4-45. Hid in houses for 24 hrs until US Army came.
Holt	Ronald Charles Neville	Private	2nd Battalion, Parachute Regiment	2766005	93727	C	Brunswick, April, through the wire. WO/1 Tracey (RAF) recaptured by German Paras, also previously by German Guards but released after bribery and threats; left by German Paras in Ampleben. Took command of village after troops left & US troops took in.
Horne	George Minta	Signalman	1st Parachute Brigade, Royal Signals	2598143	91952	C	Dresden Feb 18: From working party companion Cpl Lewis; recaptured 23 kilometres from Gorlitz: Russian front 26 Feb 1944: interrogated at IV A I was fit. Cpl Lewis sent to another camp.
Houghton	Norman Edwin	Private	11th Battalion, Parachute Regiment	996560		C	Escaped from Tyssa on 27/4/1945 with Pte Ponting, Corps Hart and Austin. Was recaptured by SS unit at Mulda on 1/5/1945. I was physically fit. Remained with companions until liberation.
Howard	John James	Lance Corporal	1st Battalion, Parachute Regiment	3598966	89855	M	Latter end of captivity from column when being marched towards (Swedemnk) stayed at a State Farm for food during march. Walked off with three companions into woods. Contacted Seventh Armoured Div. near Bergen. Names of mates. L/Cpl Hall, Pte Purdy Pte Stokes.

Howell	Derek Martin	Gunner	1st Airlanding Anti-Tank Battery, Royal Artillery	5835348	118694	C	We escaped from working camp on 10-4-45. Escaped while on Cookhouse fatigues. Made our way to our own lines. with Signalman Heyes and Gunner Whittham recaptured by the German front line infantry on 13-4-45 and sent to Munster lager where we were liberated by the 11th Armoured on the 18-4-45.
Howells	John	Lance Corporal	1st Airborne Provost Company	4078592	118226	M	Broke away from column on march on April 11th 1945 at Derenberg & relieved by the American 331st Infantry Regt. after 2 hours. I was physically fit.
Howes	Raymond Cuthbert	Lance Corporal	2nd Battalion, South Staffordshire Regiment	4919552	118205	C	One attempt. From Bad Grund, working. 3-11-44 caught 5-11-44 Einbeck by Volksstorm. Unfit. Companions Pt Dixon, Pte Gledhill, Pte Eastham. All caught together.
Hughes	Anthony Cecil	Private	3rd Battalion, Parachute Regiment	5125630	77095	A	Just after captured recaptured Arnheim Dutch Nazis.
Hughes	Ernest Edward	Sapper	1st Parachute Squadron, Royal Engineers	14644896	140116	A C	Arnhem 21st Sept 1944 24 Sept 1944 SS Troops. Augsburg 13th April 15 April 45. Airforce Augsburg 15th. Not physically fit.
Hughes	Richard Francis	Private	The Parachute Regiment	4127229	75676	C	Escaped. Deserted sentries made for the Russian lines successful Hersfeld April 12 1945. I was fit. My companions made a successful escape.
Humphreys	William	Private	2nd Battalion, Parachute Regiment	5835367	117578	C	Altengrowbow. 13-3-45. Hid under a bridge Tom Curry, L Finglass captured in wood 18.3.45 by patrol. Yes. Companions alright.
Hunt	William	Private	1st Battalion, Border Regiment	4626714	91979	C	Escaped April 21st 45 from Tysa with Walter Sheldon + Harry Jenkinson. Lost companions at Beroun.

Name	Forename	Rank	Unit	Army number	POW number	Escape location	Answers given as direct quotations from Liberation Questionnaires
Husband	Desmond John	Private	156th Battalion, Parachute Regiment	14519026		M	Escaped from temporary camp near Dahlen, Travelled through woods, and with refugee convoy (Civil) at some points. Contacted USA troops at Wurzen, Pte Warner and L/Cpl Littlewood escaped with me.
Hutton	James Brownlie	Private	156th Battalion, Parachute Regiment	14350633	90762	C	Once 18-4-45 from a farm at Halendorf escaped through the farm window when the guard went to [illegible]. My companions were Tom Bradley, Jim Smith and John Black. We were all recaptured on 22-4-45 by artillery trucks 10 or 15 kilos from Altenburg. We were physically fit.
Hymes	Douglas	Private	1st Battalion, Parachute Regiment	7402136		T	In boxcar travelling between Limburgh + Mulburgh had floor removed. Unsuccessful as other occupants threatened calling for guards. Companions names forgot. Phys Fit No.
Jackson	Fred Duncan	Private	10th Battalion, Parachute Regiment	81614	117524	C	Once while at work the RAF made a raid and instead of going to the shelter I made off along the railway but I had a bit of bad luck and I walked into the werks police who detained me.
Janovsky	Roland	Private	2nd Battalion, Parachute Regiment	6848274		M	13-4-45 evacuated from Halle by Germans. Escaped from main party same evening. Hiding the village of Quis 11 kilos from Halle. East. Relieved by American Recce. Group 18-4-44 (Kitchener, R Knight) released with me. All were physically fit.
Jeffries	John Patrick	Signalman	Royal Signals	2379610	117314	M	Whilst we were being moved from the front at XI A, nr Magdeburg, on 4 April Pte Powell of the Second Btn and myself escaped off the march and were captured 5 days later by the Luftwaffe who treated us pretty decently.

Surname	First name	Rank	Regiment	Number	Number	Code	Notes
Jenkinson	Horace	Private	The Oxfordshire and Buckinghamshire Light Infantry	5891203	920009	M	From Dresden to Prage [sic]. Pte Sheldon Pte Hunt.
Johnson	Arthur	Private	2nd Battalion, South Staffordshire Regiment	1568699	92045	C	Tried to escape while the big R.A.F. Raid was on Leuna Works at night, but caught next morning in a barn. Confined to cells for seven days on half rations.
Johnson	Peter	Private	1st Battalion, Parachute Regiment	5388969	89242	M	Escaped whilst being marched from Merseburg 17/4/45. Dived into woods on roadside, hiding until column of prisoners had marched past. Contacted Americans 24.4.45 at Wurzren. Accompanied by Ptes Wagstaff, Smith, Bedford.
Jonas	John James	Corporal	2nd Battalion, Parachute Regiment	1876407	93725	C	January 2nd attempted escape, but only managed to get out of compound. Recaptured by Postern on sentry go. Bayoneted on recapture. Perfectly fit. Companions recaptured same time. Escaped Feb 16th 1944 [sic].
Jones	George	Sapper	1st Parachute Squadron, Royal Engineers	2193549	91490	A	Escape attempt 25.10.45 [sic] from SS Captors. Captured same night by SS. Physically fit.
Jones	John Campbell	Signalman	4th Parachute Brigade, Royal Signals	324396	77367	C	Successful. Disguised as French soldiers from Niederwiesa Lager through German lines to Mitwieda where we met American Recce. C. Snow (RA) J. Senior (RCS) 6/5/45 arriving 7/5/45 all safe.
Jones	Stephen	Samuel	156th Battalion, Parachute Regiment	5575919	21903		Was helped by Check (sic) partisans along with four other British. Check was a hero – Františeit Kutil Javor CII PP Janovice N/Úhlavou.
Jones	Thomas Leslie	Private	3rd Battalion, Parachute Regiment	3911512		M	Escaped whilst being evacuated from Erfenshlag with Ptes Vincent and O'Brian Recaptured 24 hours later by German Volksturm at Augsburg. (Yes) Captured with me.

527

Name	Forename	Rank	Unit	Army number	POW number	Escape location	Answers given as direct quotations from Liberation Questionnaires
Kane	John Patrick	Private	2nd Battalion, Parachute Regiment	4690202		M	On April 17th the Allied armies were advancing fast and the Germans decided to move us to Teplitz but I escaped with 2819656 Pte ORTON, J only got as far as FRIEBERG. Russians arrived.
Kearns	James Thomas	Private	1st Battalion, Parachute Regiment	4808363	89495	nk	Only for a few days.
Keeler	Norman Arthur	Sergeant, Lance	4th Parachute Squadron, Royal Engineers	2031950	21705	C	Hanover. 8/4/45. Hid in roof. S/Sgt Lawson, Sgt Wight, Sgt Jackman, S/Sgt Elliot. S/Sgt Hannon Hanover. German Home Guard 8/4/45. Weak from lack of food. Companions recaptured.
Killick	John Edward	Captain	89th Parachute Field Security Section	137467	628	A	I made one attempt to escape whilst being moved by M.T. from Arnhem to Zutphen. When the M.T unloaded at Zutphen I concealed myself alone under a tarpaulin and succeeded in being carried on in the truck, in the hope of being able to jump off under cover of dark. Unfortunately, when we had nearly reached Hengelo, the truck driver came to the back of the truck for petrol and discovered me. No court of enquiries or official proceedings followed, and I was returned to Zutphen and received no punishment.
King	Leonard William	Signalman	4th Parachute Brigade, Royal Signals	2588983		A	I escaped from hospital Utrecht Holland by way of tunnel underneath the hospital with three Americans one Dutch and one Scotsman. It was organised by the Dutch underground movement. I stay for three weeks with Mlle Stay, 93 Ledeschekade, Utrecht, in company with the Scotsman. I was treated very well indeed.

Surname	First names	Rank	Unit	Number	Initials	Narrative
Kirk	Stanley Harry	Lance Corporal	16th Parachute Field Ambulance, RAMC	7349841	T C	A futile attempt at Limburg on or about 15/11/44 jumping on the train whilst walking on railway station. I was alone and was observed immediately by railway guard. I was fit but rather weak. Broke away from working camp on 15/4/45 and made towards gunfire. Contacted American troops about 15 kilometres away.
Kirlew	Alfred Harry	Private	156th Battalion, Parachute Regiment	405893	C M	I escaped from Erfenschlag Germany on 14-3-45. Recaptured 16-3-45 buy Home Guard. Pte Penfold, Para Reg and Pte Bruley, Seaforth Highlanders were with me. I did eight days imprisonment and escaped again I was with Pte Hill Para Reg. On the first escape from Hartendorf and was away 14 days round Chemnitz Germany. I was recaptured by the German soldiers. I escaped while on the march from there, And joined the Americans at Rochlize Germany on the 5-5-45. I was with Pte Morgan and Pte Hill Para Reg. On the first escape I was beaten with a stick around the head and shoulders. First escape was through window Second we hid in the straw whilst on the March, And which broke the wire of the lager.
Kitchener	Robert Anthony	Private	2nd Battalion, Parachute Regiment	6145647	M	13-4-45 evacuated from Halle, managed to get away from main party of about 1000 same night, was picked up by American Recce 17-4-45 with L. Knight and R. Janovsky.
Knapp	Frederick Frank	Private	11th Battalion, Parachute Regiment	14670639	C	Attempted escape at Marrienburg 14 April. Bluffed our way out to pass the Guard. E Faulkner. Recaptured in about 5 miles away 15 April by a German Sgt. Yes. Same as myself.

Name	Forename	Rank	Unit	Army number	POW number	Escape location	Answers given as direct quotations from Liberation Questionnaires
Knight	Leonard Davies	Signalman	1st Parachute Brigade, Royal Signals	14200119	89308	M	13-4-1945 Evacuated from Halle by German troops, escaped from party same evening at Queis, hid in barn until relieved by American troops on 18/4/1945 (Kitchiner Janovsky) relieved with me. All were physically fit.
Lancaster	Joseph	Private	11th Battalion, Parachute Regiment	935934		M	Escaped on 13-4-44. Contacted Americans on 16-4-44 at 03-00 hrs. 13-4-45 we were told we were to evacuate. So Pte Hole, Pte Charles, myself escaped and hid in a quarry until the others had gone, then return to lager and hid there till USA over ran us.
Lane	Philip George Oliver	Corporal	1st Parachute Squadron, Royal Engineers	2009968		M	On 3rd/5/45 while in column from one larger to another 1 left with Sgt Sanford S/152/753 and made our way to Hallein where we met the Americans.
Lang	Robert	Private	1st Battalion, Border Regiment	3606642	117504	M	On the march from Uelzen (Friday 13 April) Breaking away from the column at night time hid in some woods for two nights with Pte Mathews and Pte Bryne. Then made for the village about 4 kilos from Uelzen. Stayed in farm with Russian and French workers. German troops took up position around the village. They did not bother us. Their morale was very low and everyone carried a white piece of cloth. The Recce Corps of the 11th Armd Div then entered the village on 18th April.
Lawson	George Steele	Signalman	Royal Signals	2382692		M M	On 17/4/45 with 5 companions – Bensley, McWilliams, Black, Painter & Ralphs got to 600 metres of American front at Frankenburg. Then with companion Carmichael two days before war finished to Czechoslovakia.

Surname	First name	Rank	Unit	Number	Number	Code	Details
Lawson	Wilfred McLellen	Private	156th Battalion, Parachute Regiment	7948335	118001	M	Yes escaped on march from Uelzen with Pte Roger 8 kilos from town.
Layland	Frederick	Gunner	2nd Airlanding Anti-Tank Battery, Royal Artillery	1092475	92062	C	Attempted to escape when the RAF were bombing Leuna works at night was caught two days later in a railway truck. Given seven days straffe, but only did five.
Lees	Norman Alfred	Lance Corporal	156th Battalion, Parachute Regiment	14377390	90542	A	Failed owing to strained muscles left leg Holland.
Lewis	John	Corporal	1st Battalion, Parachute Regiment	4032087		C C M	(1) I got as far as Bouxion from Dresden 20-2-1945. (2) I got to Gorlitz on the 22-3-1945. I had to give up no food. (3) I got away again on the 14.4.1945 and I got in to the US Army on the 18-4-1945 with two men. On April 14th we were march out of Dresden for good to Czecho Slavakia. We marched 50 km that day and on the same night we escaped, going all night and all the next day going by compass moon. Reached Deffaldisch. Next day we again [illegible] making of Freidburg when we were surrounded by police, put into jail. Sapper Stevens + two companions and now is with me.
Linden	Jack Alfred	Corporal	89th Parachute Field Security Section	918417		C	Left Markt Pongau with Sgt Clark, Light Airborne Artillery approx 3-5-45 to contact our troops in Salzburg area. Turned back by SS patrols approximately 30 kms W of Bischoshten where met Sgt Hughes 3rd The Parachute BTN. Returned to Bischoshten On way to Bischoshten where waited for Americans who didn't arrive [illegible] returned to camp with American 10-5-45. Physically unfit.

Name	Forename	Rank	Unit	Army number	POW number	Escape location	Answers given as direct quotations from Liberation Questionnaires
Lowe	Alfred	Private	2nd Battalion, South Staffordshire Regiment	14700220		C	Recaptured [sic] by Yanks April 10th 45 at Hanover.
Mallison	Geoffrey Norman	Staff Sergeant	Glider Pilot Regiment	4348337		A	One-successful. Apeldoorn Hospital. Alone whilst fetching beds from German barracks to prisoners' barracks. Remained in German barracks in attic. At night Germans asleep came down, outside and away over camp fence. Wound not healed. [Plus long escape note with details of time with the resistance, that ends PS] I was never recaptured, being liberated by the Canadians at SLIEDRECHT].
Matthews	Frederick George	Private	1st Battalion, Border Regiment	3392036	117499	M	On the march from Uelzen on Friday Apr 13th 45. Breaking away from column at night time hid in woods for two nights with Ptes. LANG & BRYNE saying that made for village about 4 killo from Uelzen.
Matthews	William Lawrence	Corporal	1st Battalion, Parachute Regiment		2618797	M	On 28 April 1945 we commence in march from Varchentin in the custody of our guards on reaching Stavenhagen we were turned off the roads by German military authorities here our guards left us and so we decided to make our way to the nearest Allied lines by various routes avoiding main roads this we did and eventually reached Schwerin on 2 May.
May	William Albert Henry	Staff Sergeant	Glider Pilot Regiment	854844		T	Escape Yes. Train journey from Limburg to Muhlberg. Discovered after forcing rail truck windows. S/Sergt Jenko Chapman, Sert Loback, Cpl Pileach. Last mentioned beaten by Feldwebel all interned in IV B.

Surname	First name(s)	Rank	Unit	Number	Number	Code	Notes
McCreedy	Richard James	Lance Bombardier	1st Airlanding Anti-Tank Battery, Royal Artillery	3711048		C	Alone February 45 from Plauen. Myself from working party on station stowed away on Holzburner but was suspected immediately because of unknown stop in Plauen and that I had not allowed for.
McLure	James	Private	156th Battalion, Parachute Regiment	2454564		M	Escaped from the enemy on Feb 18th and remained at large until contacted by the Russian forces, with Pte Clark KOSB.
Menzies	Harry	Corporal	2nd Battalion, Parachute Regiment	3247104		C	2-1-45 8C seven men cut wires recaptured outside Jones and Priestly.
Metcalfe	Edwin	Private	1st Battalion, Border Regiment	3602861	118844	M	When the troops came near to our camp, the Germans marched us away there were 500 men. Four of us escaped into the woods and waited until our troops came.
Miller	Christopher Alfred	Staff Sergeant	Glider Pilot Regiment	937499	117770	nk	Personal attempt only.
Miller	Philip Anthony Alfred	Sapper	1st Parachute Squadron, Royal Engineers	1947386		M	Partial escape on Friday 13 April 45 at 4a.m. owing to evacuation. Hid in a wood locally (Halle). Object to hide up till liberated. Companion R Drury (5726456), E. Booth (1951655). Recaptured locally by Volksturm. E. Booth separated at sunrise and was captured by Luftwaffe (same Day).
Milne	George	Private	7th Battalion, King's Own Scottish Borderers	2878859	117412	M	Pte Herd Pte Perkins and myself escaped from our camp after we had orders to evacuate. We reached Russian lines 2 days later. We were physically fit.
Milner	Eric	Driver	1st Airlanding Anti-Tank Battery, Royal Artillery	1144982	75098	M	Escaped April 27th 45 companion was C Perry. We were physically fit.
Mitchell	Edward	Sergeant	Glider Pilot Regiment	10555051	76321	T	Attempted to break out of railway wagon on way to Mulburg nailed ventilator was wrenched open but discovered by guard who struck a Polish corporal with a bayonet and nailed the board back up again.

Name	Forename	Rank	Unit	Army number	POW number	Escape location	Answers given as direct quotations from Liberation Questionnaires
Morait	Peter John	Private	156th Battalion, Parachute Regiment	59816		A M	Escaped on first day of capture alone retaken next morning. Escaped second time from the column on the march. Retaken 23 hours later by Volksturm near Dresden.
Morris	David	WO II	11th Battalion, Parachute Regiment	5946742		T	24 hrs after I was taken prisoner on 24 Sept I escaped by jumping from a train accompanied by CQMS Cox of my own unit, and we made our way to a Dutch farm owned by pro-British people, was looked after by Underground Movement. I was, from September 25, 1944 until November 17, 1944 at large in Apeldoorn and Barnes out being cared for by the Dutch underground movement. On November 17 a party about 92 strong led by Major Maguire tried to cross lock over the river (Rhinenk) Near Oosterbeek but on the way were ambushed by Germans and most of the party taken prisoner a number of casualties were suffered. [Plus four-page letter describing his escape.]
Morton	Albert Alfred	Private	2nd Battalion, Parachute Regiment	6853588	117956	C	Escaped from Altongrabow 12/4/45 in company with Pte Edwards & Pte Nicholes same unit reached American bridgehead over Elbe 29/4/45.
Naylor	Alf	Private	10th Battalion, Parachute Regiment	6349458	89595	C	The first time unsuccessful, the second time OK. the first time was when the Russians advanced to the river Oder and were threatening the town of Glogen some 27 kilos away. The jerries came in one night about two in the morning and said we were to be ready to march at seven the next morning. [Plus two-page description of escapes, which includes concern for German guard being held by Americans.]

Surname	Forename(s)	Rank	Unit	Number		Category	Account
Neil	George Currie	Corporal	1st Battalion, Parachute Regiment	7394382		M	On line of march from Arnheim (sic). I escaped off a column while I was with a company of soldiers. It was on 19 April. I reached the American lines on the 4th April.
Newell	Douglas George Valentine	Lance Corporal	11th Battalion, Parachute Regiment	165223	89349	C	Escaped 13-4-45 from Halle with 6412179 Pte Stillwell J. Made our way successfully to the American Lines on 15th-4-45 at Reiderburg.
Newman	Robert Eugène	Private	Royal Army Medical Corps	7533134		A T	Tried to escape three times. Twice in Arnhem on my own and once with two companions on leaving Limberg. First two escapes recaptured by SS men, third time by one Canadian [sic]. Two mates. Henry the Pale [sic] & Harry, a Londoner.
Nichollas	Lewis	Private	2nd Battalion, Parachute Regiment	4390380	117336	C	Escape from XI A Altengrabow, with Ptes Moston, H & Edwards, W, on the 12/4/45 of the same unit. Reached American bridgehead of Elbe 29/4/45.
Noble	Charles Bruce	Captain	133rd Parachute Field Ambulance	279738		A	Sept 23 44. Evaded recapture until Jan 2nd 45. Do not known fate of the 8 people with whom captured in Jan. In particular Sgt Benwell, AAC (reported sent back to Gestapo in Holland from Stalag XI B).
Nullis	John Robert	Lance Corporal	2nd Battalion, South Staffordshire Regiment	5729659		nk	Escape 13/4/45.
O'Brian	Robert Gerard	Private	1st Battalion, Parachute Regiment	2049245		A T	Whilst I was making my way I was challenged by a German sentry. I evaded him but was stopped by others. I attempted to escape on the way to Muhlberg but was stopped by some of my own companions.

535

Name	Forename	Rank	Unit	Army number	POW number	Escape location	Answers given as direct quotations from Liberation Questionnaires
O'Brien	Cyril	Private	1st Parachute Brigade	14411394		C	Twice, unsuccessfully on 11/2/1945, broke the side of the lager & got out. Recaptured after 24 hrs near Czech border, companions name Pte Thompson 156 Batt. Second time 29/4/1945 broke down door panel, recaptured 24 hrs after by Volkstürm, companions names Pte Jones, 3rd Para Batt & Pte Vincent 2nd Para Battn, 1st Para Battn companions captured with me.
O'Brien	William Arthur	Private	11th Battalion, Parachute Regiment	5989720	72149	M	I escaped 3 weeks before liberation. The Germans were marching us and I hid in the woods until the Americans came. No companions.
O'Dell	Charles John	Private	11th Battalion, Parachute Regiment	866848	118054	A	From Holland but was retaken again before I was registered was retaken in Holland. No I was not physically fit I had a small hole in leg, was retaken by SS Troops.
O'Hanlon	Henry	Private	1st Battalion, Border Regiment	3783776		T	Jumped from train going from Holland to Germany 24-9/-944, with John Corless. Recaptured 20th Nov 44 also John Corless by the Germans. Place Rhine Arnhem.
O'Neill	William	Private	7th Battalion, King's Own Scottish Borderers	3195748	14202	T	Being told that proper time to escape was soon after capture, some of us tried to get away during train journey to 1st camp (XII A). We were allowed out of wagon (train) for urinal purposes and attempted to hide until train moved on. Discovered by guards. Names of companions not known.
Oakley	Albert William Frank	Private	10th Battalion, Parachute Regiment	14204428	92042	nk	Once.

Oliver	Edward James	Corporal	1st Parachute Squadron Royal Engineers	2093811	M	No real escape attempted prior to 3 May 1944. We walked out of camp on 3 May 44. Guards was very slack and we lived in the civilians until we got picked up by U.S. Army. 6 escaped. 3 of us are well. I do not know what happened to our three companions as we split up at NERFEN.
Padfield	Harold	Sergeant, Lance	1st Parachute Squadron Royal Engineers	1873564	C	No attempts made before 3rd May. Camp was very slack at the time. Guards weren't so strict and we just walked out with the bath party. We met American Peace delegation at Zett am See 7.5.45. C/S Lidel.
Palmer	David Edward	Lance Corporal	11th Battalion, Parachute Regiment	6343456	M	By following a column of men out and reaching Stendall with them then hiding in the woods and an old barn until the Americans were nearby and getting through to them. Successful.
Palmer	Harry	Private	3rd Battalion, Parachute Regiment	5382027	nk	On 23.8.45 [sic] till the 29.8.45 [sic] recaptured at Wurzen 29.8.45.
Paterson	William	Signalman	1st Parachute Brigade, Royal Signals	2348020	M	Sachgrün – from column of March – 15 April 45 hiding in the woods. Lt. W .O. Terry 383579 (US Army HQ 607 TD Bn), W.O J Benson (RAF), Pvte. T Prosho (1st The Parachute Bde). Physical condition of all good – attempt successful.
Penfold	Kenneth	Private	2nd Battalion, Parachute Regiment	4865420	C	First attempt from Chemnitz to Gluaco re-captured by civil police, good treatment by Police. Broke out of camp. 2nd time as 1st on 17 got 4 kilos. 3rd time I escape with Sgt Lanver 7 S. African airforces, we hid in a cellar in Hartmansdorf until the Yanks came in tanks.

Name	Forename	Rank	Unit	Army number	POW number	Escape location	Answers given as direct quotations from Liberation Questionnaires
Perrin-Brown	Christopher	Major	1st Battalion, Parachute Regiment	121945	572	C	I escaped from Oflag 79 on Feb 25th for details see back page. On Feb 25th 1945 at 1000hrs I dress myself in blue trousers (dyed pyjamas) and coat. I had a German F.S. And a sack on my back. In the sack I had a suit or brown dungarees and a BD jacket. I walked up to the first gate of the camp having organised for Killick 1st Airborne to harass the sentry with questions. The sentry looked at me – I said Ave – and he opened the gate. The guardroom behind which was a temporary urinal I walked behind the guardroom to the urinal thence behind the guardroom to the second gate … [details on extra page; got to Bielefeld where recaptured and then returned to Oflag 79 in March.]
Perry	Charles Edward	Private	3rd Battalion, Parachute Regiment	14207893	75531	M	Escaped April 27th 45. While being marched away from the Front by guards. Escaped at night from farm barns where were to sleep for the night. Reached American patrol the following day. Companion Drv E. Milner.
Perry	Norman	Private	2nd Battalion, South Staffordshire Regiment	4916676		M	I escaped from Working Camp Rei 113 (Halle) on April 12th with John Telther of 3rd Btn Para as the camp was being evacuated. We eventually came into contact with American armour on April 15th.
Perry	Stanley	Lance Corporal	2nd Battalion, Parachute Regiment	6353005	89792	C M	Attempted on 7/4/45 managed to get through barbed wire except last fence. One man caught as guards were trebled. Escape on night 8/4/45 with 4 other The Parachute troops whilst being marched away from advancing armies. Reached USA 2nd Armd Div at Salder on Wednesday 11.4.45. Names of other comrades Ptes Heaton, Carlier, Smith, Kennedy.

Peters	Thomas Charles	Private	2nd Battalion, Parachute Regiment	14343574	117799	M	Escaped April 12th (45) from marching column near 'BELZIG' at night, WO Goodall RAF, Ptes Brotherton, Davies, 1 American. Captured nr Magdenburg by German SS Officer. Apr. 23/4/45.
Petrie	Lewis	Sergeant	7th Battalion, King's Own Scottish Borderers	3185683		C	Captured near Kuftstein by a civvy again I escape from Mark Pongau and was hidden by French patriots and then released when American 7th army patrol took WORGL AUSTRIA. About three weeks in all.
Pettitt	Thomas Joseph	Private	2nd Battalion, Parachute Regiment	14397946		T M	Whilst being taken to Germany. Escape failed as the first man got stuck in the aperture we made. We were not physically fit one man was taken away & nothing happened to anyone else. I've not seen this man. Escape on the March on 23rd April 45. By going through the roof of a barn and marching to American lines in plain view of the enemy.
Phillips	Ronald John	Private	2nd Battalion, Parachute Regiment	5510064	117829	C	Once. Attempted alone. I left the hospital in Hildesheim about 1730 hrs 18-12-44 and was retaken about 1730 hrs 19-12-44 by two German soldiers. I was quite fit.
Pilbeam	Henry Frank James	Craftsman	REME	7590939	91494	C	Once at Freiberg, about March 25th Walked away from factory with Cfm George Ducker. Recaptured next day about 30 miles away, by the Civilian Police. Moderately fit, 5 days hard labour.
Ponting	Joseph Bernard	Private	3rd Battalion, Parachute Regiment	5193231	91656	C	From Tyssa in Czecho on the 27.4.45 with three others Pte Houghton, Pte Austin, Pte Hart S.A. Army. Recaptured by SS at Muldo 1.5.45. Evaded guards. Fit. Remain together until released.

Name	Forename	Rank	Unit	Army number	POW number	Escape location	Answers given as direct quotations from Liberation Questionnaires
Pott	Robert Lailett John	Major	156th Battalion, Parachute Regiment	95241	2193	A	On the morning I was due to leave GRONAU hospital at approx 0200 hrs I got out of window about 10' from the ground went on crutches to Dutch frontier, crossed a stream near ENTSCHEDE (approx 5 kms) attempted to obtain help from Dutch, but they reported to Dutch police who reported me to German police who collected me and returned me to GRONAU (approx 1300 hrs). Gunner Clark helped me to dress. He was unable to come with me as he had one leg off. My left thigh and stomach was in plaster and my left knee would only bend a few degrees at the time of the escape.
Potter	Joseph William Dominic	Signalman	1st Airborne Division Signals	2590125	118138	M	At Derenburg we got information that the USA troops were four kilometres away, we were on the march. We made a mass break and hid. G Ball and E Ball were my companions. We were liberated the same day.
Potts	John Reginald	Private	1st Parachute Brigade	5962036	89583	nk	Escaped successfully on 13 April 1945 together with Norris Hill. Reached American lines on 15th of April 1945.
Powell	Charles	Lance Corporal	2nd Battalion, Parachute Regiment	4035583	117800	M	I escaped on the Thursday evening of the third week of April whilst marching about 1 1/2 mile beyond Gorzke heading for Belzig and was recaptured on a Pick-a-back Bomb airfield SW of Altengrabow. Was picked up by Luftwaffe personnel. My companion was J Jeffries POW No/117615 and he was in my company throughout my POW service.
Powell	Francis	Sergeant	Glider Pilot Regiment	190364		A	On first day of capture escaped swam the Rhine and made about 30 kilos in two days. Had the bad luck to be found in a deserted barn by a section of Huns out looking for loot.

Surname	First name	Rank	Unit	Number	Number	Medal	Account
Poynton	Joseph	Private	1st Airlanding Anti-Tank Battery, Royal Artillery	3386146	92076	C	I was help to escape with my companion Cpl Carter by Mrs [illegible] Schafer Dresden, she was pick up by the Gestapo for helping us to escape.
Presley	Leslie	Private	1st Battalion, Parachute Regiment	5672364	92261	C C	9/1/45 made escape recaptured 11/1/45 from Halle to River Sale. Took all my clothing after recapture beat with a rifle and sticks, not fit, escape on my own, then escaped again from Halle hospital to the US Armys [sic] took 14 days through enemy lines approx 1/4/45.
Prosho	Thomas George	Private	1st Parachute Brigade	6148592		M	Escaped 15th of April from marching column while halted during the day with three other POW Pt W Patterson, WO J Benson, Lt Terry (USA) the officer is still with own unit.
Purdy	Harry	Private	3rd Battalion, Parachute Regiment	6203365	89831	M	From line of march from camp and at halt slipped into woods with three other comrades and were relieved by the 7th Armour division at a spot approximately 15 kilo from Bergan was fairly fit.
Ralph	Edward Ernest Sidney	Staff Sergeant	Glider Pilot Regiment	1434775	117299	M M M M C	1. Escapes one escaped from Sprenburgschule[nk] on March from Sagan South Sgt Hodgson (REME). 2. Escaped from Aurneberg [nk] after recapture the Sgt H with Hodgson. 3. Escaped Riseau with same person. 4. Escaped at Ouchty with same person (continued on after shots) 5. Escaped from Muhlberg with Sgt Grifiths (GPR) and Sgt Garnhem (GPR) in this escape I was successful in reaching the 69th division of the American army. In each attempt we escaped at night crawling through the wire. Recaptured in first case by SS In the second third and fourth by the Wehrmacht. I was fairly fit but week.

Name	Forename	Rank	Unit	Army number	POW number	Escape location	Answers given as direct quotations from Liberation Questionnaires
Ramsey	Sydney	Private	2nd Battalion, Parachute Regiment	3249012			Attempted to escape but owing to a leg injury could not carry on.
Ransom	James Leslie	Lance Corporal	250th Airborne Light Company, Royal Army Service Corps	10694205	91189	C M	From Dresden recaptured in 48 hrs. in Dresden area by Volksturm under cover of darkness. Escape from Kommando whilst on evacuation march from Dresden.
Redman	Ernest	Private	3rd Battalion, Parachute Regiment	3862185	117983	M	Escaped April 12, 45 when Stalag XI A moved camp. When darkness fell ran into woods outside of road with Pte L Thomas, RWF 4th Btn. Invaded capture until relieved by Russian army 4th May, 45. Was fit at the time of escape.
Reid	William	Private	156th Battalion, Parachute Regiment	3131283		C	From Hillensdorf in April. Released by Russians on May 8th. Cpl Hutchison REME.
Reilly	John	Craftsman	REME	889575		C	Escape Yes successful from Brüx 29 April 1945. Companion Pte Worsfield (14440258) K.O.S.B. Got through to the Russians in Czecoslovakia who sent us to the American on 12-5-45.
Riley	Bernard	Private	1st Battalion, Border Regiment	4546122	118191	M	Escaped from marching column 11/4/45. After 3 or 4 days freedom. Met up with advanced American forces at Derenburgh.
Roan	Cyril Charles	Lance Corporal	2nd Battalion, Parachute Regiment	5891392		T	Escaped from train transporting POW s to Germany from Apeldoorn (Holland). I jumped from a freight coach and was free 10 days when I was discovered by a Luftwaffe patrol three miles from Arnhem on the 5.10.44. I was physically fit and alone.

Surname	Forename	Rank	Regiment	Service No.	POW No.	Code	Notes
Roberts	Christopher William	Private	156th Battalion, Parachute Regiment	5253355		M	Made for direction of gunfire on 15-4-45 and contacted American tanks 2200 hrs 15-4-45.
Robertson	Arthur	Gunner	2nd Airlanding Anti-tank Battery, Royal Artillery	5392231		C	On 17 APRIL 1945, myself and four comrades, escaped from near Teplitze and proceeded to American lines, but we were detained at Freyburg on 21 April by Germans, and was released by the Russians on V day.
Robertson	Robert Dickson	Corporal	7th Battalion, King's Own Scottish Borderers	3195880	118369	M	I left the column near Spremberg 11.2.45 retaken by Volkstraum at a village near Probus. 2nd attempt. Left the column outside Hanover 8.4.45 and met American forces 10.4.45. Companions Sgt Nicklin Glider Pilot Reg, Sgt Potter 2nd Batt Essex.
Roger	James Charles	Private	10th Battalion, Parachute Regiment	4619865	117190	M	Escaped from commando while on march with Pte Lawson about 8 kilos from Uelzen.
Ross	John	Private	156th Battalion, Parachute Regiment	2823352	75658	C	Escaped on 24 Sept [sic] picked up by Americans 26 Sept [sic] [Ross was in a kommando at Zeitz January-April 1945].
Roughton	John Kenneth	Corporal	10th Battalion, Parachute Regiment	7886696		A	Arnheim 22.9.44 Removal of the postern (forcibly). Nil. 25.9.94 Arnhem by SS troops. Yes. I do not know.
Sander	Gustave	Private	11th Battalion, Parachute Regiment	13807937	91694	T C M M M	After leaving Limburg in Nov 1944 for Mühlberg with 6090123 Pte LAIRD Jwe decided to escape from the truck, but were frustrated by the others in the truck. On 10 April 45 I again tried with Pte Laird from the working party Dresden, but got caught in Freital same day by Civil Police and taken to their station. During search Pte Laird was struck with a rubber truncheon money taken the latter was given to both by Major Pierpoint US army for escape purpose, also our watches. Next we were handed over to the military and sentenced to 5 days by Capt Mülee 6 Coy 396

Name	Forename	Rank	Unit	Army number	POW number	Escape location	Answers given as direct quotations from Liberation Questionnaires
							Landschutzen Bn. On 15th April we were evacuated from arrest to Zimmerwald Sudetenland and on 16th escaped en route again with Pt Laird reached Klingenberg and got caught again. On first May 45 I tried again with Pte Laird and Bdr Muir from Zinmwald, we had to pass through the wire heavily guarded by guards and dogs and marched all night in snow till reaching Dippoldiswalde, on our travels we passed through woods used by the German army for dumps etc. Roads were blown and also bridges. On 3 May we reached Klingenberg and after having been without food we were recaptured and placed in a cellar of a hotel. Escaped by unscrewing the door leaving Bdr Muir behind being too exhausted to carry on. On 5 May we reached Hainchen crossing through the German armour formations which were fighting on the outskirts and met the Russian forces towards noon. With then went to Oelerau, on 6 May we carried on towards Chemnitz and linked up with the American army and were taken to ex POW collecting centre.
Sargant	Raymond	Sergeant	Glider Pilot Regiment	4617321		C	Luckenwalde, made by walking out as French worker successful. S/Sgt Browne. Yes.
Scott	Arnold	Private	156th Battalion, Parachute Regiment	4746709		C	Successful escape from Stalag with Polish boy – joined Russian army at Pritawalk with them until meeting Americans. Companion wished to come to England but sent to Polish in Brussels.
Seymour	Tom Henry	Lance Corporal	1st Battalion, Border Regiment	14574818	75687	M	We placed in barns in Klatovy Checoslovakia from here we overpowered the guards on the night of the 6th of May it. We then heard the town SUSICE a few miles were appeal for our help to round up the

						Details
						Germans in the town. This we did to the best our ability. There were a few SS whom we dare not tackle as they were very heavily armed and they're only 10 of us British Canadians. The only names I know are Ptes Gudgon The Border RGt, Pte Doyle, Cpl Bartlett, rest 6th Airborne Div and myself L/Cpl Seymour. When we had cleared the town they asked for three volunteers to go out and meet the American troops and reminded to stay in town in case anything happened. Myself Cpl Bartlett and another Englishman went out contacted the Americans about 4 miles. The first person Matt was an American captain of whom I have a photograph. From then on I could not describe.
Shears	Charles Eli	Private	10th Battalion, Parachute Regiment	5623548	M	On the 6th of March under guard away from Russian advance, near Dresden. We were strafed by SU planes during one of these raids. Ten of us escaped. After two days reaches SU troops.
Shelbourne	James Ernest	Private	1st Battalion, Parachute Regiment	6914183	C	1. Teutscenthal; Nov 16 '44; Breaking out of camp at night with Pte Small Pte Whitehead 1st The Parachute Bn recaptured 50 kg distant on November 19 by German air raid warden. All received 10 day solitary. 2. Town Jail; Wansleben Nov 24 44; Breaking out of jail at night with Pte R. de Berry Canadian Black Watch recaptured November 29 in railway truck by 3 SS men at Halle (three weeks bread and water in Torgau). 3. Coal mine, Bittefeild 13-4-45. Escaped into woods during intended evacuation. Alone. Met American front-line troops in Hohweissif 21-4-45. [Plus letter with escape details.]

Name	Forename	Rank	Unit	Army number	POW number	Escape location	Answers given as direct quotations from Liberation Questionnaires
Sheldon	Walter	Private	1st Battalion, Border Regiment	14201232	91951	M	From Dresden to Prague Pte Hunt Pte Jenkinson.
Shepherd	Joseph	Private	11th Battalion, Parachute Regiment	14647522	75987	M	Were evacuated from Dresden escaped with Pte Carslike Picked up by Hitler Youth 5 days later. We were straffed by fighters.
Shepley	Arthur	Sergeant, Lance	156th Battalion, Parachute Regiment	4344978	52919	M	Whilst on the march through Germany 13/4/44 released by Americans on 16/4/44 at Staitz. Companions Sgt Trueman Glider Pilot Rgt 101997 Cpl Waight RSF 3130617.
Simpson	Albert	Staff Sergeant	Glider Pilot Regiment	856791		A T	Escaped from hospital at Apeldoorn with Sgt Dowling GPR recaptured by Germans after 48 hrs near Amersfort. Escaped from train with Lt G P Rgt name unknown. Lost contact in dark after escape 1.10.44. Contacted Dutch underground movement after 11 days. Recaptured near Renkum Nov 19th in an attempt to cross Rhine with organised party.
Smith	John Thomas	Private	156th Battalion, Parachute Regiment	14665924	90483	M	I escaped three days before the Yanks took Zeitz. The Germans marched us away. I slipped away at night and met the Americans on my way back.
Smith	Thomas	Private	3rd Battalion, Parachute Regiment	3244188	75318	C	I went out on a working party to Wallwitz was there for a week, and the Americans broke through, they were only a few miles from us, and we went to meet them and contacted some tankmen, all companions safe.
Speedie	William	Gunner	1st Airlanding Light Regiment, Royal Artillery	14297015		C	One attempt from mine Isleben (sic) recaptured 2 days later. No special method employed. Recaptured trying to get food. By civilians. Physically fit.

Staff	Harry Victor William	Private	1st Battalion, Parachute Regiment	6015570		T	Pte Carmichael, Pte O'Brien & 14 others in a carriage but were frustrated owing to cowardice of 1 Canadian NCO and 3 British
Stanley	Dennis	Private	7th Battalion, King's Own Scottish Borderers	5255876		C	Oderan 30/4/45. Through bars in window. Tpr Cronje, W. 6 SAACR, Pte Painter, W. The Parachutechute. Hetsdorf 1/5/1945 by Volksturm. Semi-starving, companions recaptured with me.
Stark	Ronnie Leslie	Major	1st Battalion, Parachute Regiment	167154	531	M	Escaped from marching column at ROTTENEGG with Maj Timothy MC. We had been resting for the day in barns, and at about 19:00 hours we worked our way through what cover there was available to a nearby wood. Major Timothy and I hid in this wood until about 2200 hrs and then we ran away across country in the direction of our own lines. On previous occasions the Germans had searched the area of rest with Volkssturm so we made as much ground as possible for first night. For three days we lay up in a wood about 10 miles south of the Danube hoping our own troops would soon breakthrough. Our provisions were nearly finished so we decided to move nearer the Danube. On our way we contacted a French worker who gave us food and later took us to a German house where he was employed. This German gave a shelter for the night and allowed us to use his shooting lodge in a wood just outside the village. We were fed by this man for three days, when we joined up with a French working commando and live with them for three days. German and Hungarian troops used the farm we were at, the whole time we kept a careful check on all troop movements so as we could give up-to-date information to our own troops. When the American spearhead arrived Maj Timothy and I reported to the commander and gave him all the information we had gained during our stay in the area. We were asked to stay by the Americans to report to the regimental commander on his arrival but regimental headquarters did not arrive in the town so we made our way back to NURNBERG and later were evacuated back in the normal channels.

Name	Forename	Rank	Unit	Army number	POW number	Escape location	Answers given as direct quotations from Liberation Questionnaires
Stead	John Edward	Staff Sergeant	Glider Pilot Regiment	794717		M	Attempted escape at Carlsrui during march from Bauhau to Luckenwalde. Twisted ankle in large pot-hole & was caught by German Guard who returned me to column.
Steel	James	Lieutenant	Royal Engineers	256839	11453	M	Escaped on line of march at Rottenegg on the 19th April 1944.
Stevens	Daniel Donne	Sapper	4th Parachute Squadron, Royal Engineers	1877687	90690	C M	1945 Feb19 1. One partly recaptured leaving lager Feb 20 2. One unsuccessful escaped for 7 days & got 120 km from Dresden, recaptured by police. DAVID HOUSE. JOHN PATERSON. April 14th 3. One successful broke through German & American lines on April 18th. DAVID HOUSE. John Paterson. John Lewis & T. Coles. On April 14th we were marched out of Dresden proceeding to Czecho-Slovakia. We marched for about 50 kms & broke away from the column at night. 5 men (David House, T Coles, John Paterson J Lewis & myself) we proceeded over country working by compass and moon – reached Dippalsdorf. Next day we again proceeded making for Frieburg when we were surrounded by police & civilians, put into jail and were marched out in the morning by a guard. About 3 km from our jail over night. I hit the guard into a ditch & the boys disarmed him. We broke away and found that David House was not amongst us. We stayed for an hour & things got too dangerous so we proceeded further towards the gunfire, which seemed about 20 km away. As we were marching along on the night of April 17th we spotted the German lines and crawled through them. We were within 20 yards of the

Surname	First names	Rank	Regiment				Notes
							American lines when the Americans opened fire on us & we lost T. Coles. Next morning we broke through the American lines and asked them if they had found any dead or injured parachutists but the answer was in the negative. April 18th, 1945.
Stevens	Walter William	Private	2nd Battalion, Parachute Regiment	6203483	91187	C	I escaped from working party 18/3/44 [sic] captured 23/3/45 by Farm workers at Leipzig sent to prison 21/3/45 to 23/4/45. I had travelled 60 kilos had to come into the open for food.
Still	Blake Edwin Charles	Private	10th Battalion, Parachute Regiment	2323483		C C CM	Four attempted escapes. 16/2/45 from lager Dresden with No 555639 Pte Dunford. Sawed window bars. All escapes made in uniform. Second escape from same lager 18/3/45. Third time from Hollstein 28/4/45. Fourth escape from Stn approx 20 kilo E of Segnitz.
Stillwell	John James	Private	10th Battalion, Parachute Regiment	6412179		C	Escaped 13-4-45 from Halle with L/Cp Newell no 165223. Made our way through to the American Lines on 15th-4-45 at Reiderburg.
Stokes	Reginald	Private	2nd Battalion, South Staffordshire Regiment	5051452	89713	M	From line of march from Stammlager 357 to Eastern Germany, slipped into woods with three pals at Bergen. Were relieved by 7th Armoured Div at a spot approx near Dorfmark. Was fairly fit. Fed off farms and state farms.
Stripp	Ronald Sidney	Private	1st Battalion, Border Regiment	6412612	75518	A M	Whilst being escorted back to German lines could not make own lines, recaptured still wounded. Whilst being evacuated from Glina April 13th recaptured [sic] by American troops April 16th.
Such	Albert George	Gunner	1st Airlanding Light Regiment, Royal Artillery	14318215	52917	M	On 13 April escaped from the march and made for the village of Weisendorf and was picked up by the American troops on 16 April 45.

Name	Forename	Rank	Unit	Army number	POW number	Escape location	Answers given as direct quotations from Liberation Questionnaires
Taylor	John Alfred	Driver	Royal Army Service Corps	14403352	25803	T	Attempted escape at Amersfoort 9.9.44 while being marched to Barracks, hid in cellar till 11.9.44 given away by Dutch civilian who had previously offered help. No companions.
Teece	Percy James	Lance Corporal	1st Airborne Provost Company	7398111	118232	M	Broke away from column of march on 11 April 1945 at Derenburg and relived by America 331st Infantry Regt 2 hours later. I was physically fit.
Thornton	Frederick George	Driver	1st Parachute Brigade, Royal Signals	2572006	92249	A T	Evaded capture Arnhem Holland for 15 days lived in an evacuated part of the City. No contact was made with civilians. Escaped from train en route to Mulberg from Limberg. Broke through truck window 13/11/1944 recaptured 13/11/1944.
Timothy	John	Major	1st Battalion, Parachute Regiment	164812	530	M	Escaped while camp was being more from EICHSTATT to MOOSBURG. Left column at ROTTENEGG with Major Stack MC. We had been marching by night … [continued as long note, see Major Stark MC.]
Tingey	Aubrey Henry	Private	2nd Battalion, South Staffordshire Regiment	14695003	75848	C	Escaped from Falkenhein Germany. Apr 24th 1945. Escaped through roof of barn then hiked to Wurzen. Rogers. Whitton. Reynolds. Smith. Greenhaugh. All reached Wurzen. Apr 24 1945. US Army. Not fit.
Travers	Thomas	Lance Corporal	2nd Battalion, Parachute Regiment	14290146	91395	M	During evacuation. Met Americans.
Trueman	Arthur	Sergeant	Glider Pilot Regiment	101997	52909	M	Made escape whilst on the march through Germany on 13.4.45 with 3130647 Cpl Waight 2nd Bn RSF and 4344978 Sgt Shipley 156th Battalion, Parachute Regiment. Were relieved by the Americans at Steitz (Zietznk) 16.4.44. Was semi-fit condition – Companions alive and well.

Surname	First name(s)	Rank	Regiment	Number	Number 2	Cat	Notes
Tucker	Percy Henry	Corporal	1st Battalion, Parachute Regiment	5436835	118466	M	1st attempt from Sagan evacuation, 9 Feb 44. Kept to woods aid of escape compass with S/Sgt Wade G/Pilot. 2nd attempt whilst on march from Leipzig with four Frenchmen. Contacted US troops at Wurzen. Weak condition.
Tuckwood	Robert George	Private	1st Battalion, Parachute Regiment	2082225		M	8.4.45 DIPPOLDSWALDE during evacuation of Camp. Benjamin Turnidge, Frederick Melas. Relieved by Russian forcers 9.5.45 at FREIBERG. Weak through hunger. Remained together.
Turnidge	Benjamin Basil	Private	1st Battalion, Parachute Regiment	6012580		M	8.4.45 Dipoldiswold during evacuation march of working camp. Robert Tuckwwod Frederick Males Relieved by Russian forces on 7.5.1945 at Freiberg. Weak through hunger. Remained together.
Tyson	Geoffrey	Gunner	1st Airlanding Light Regiment, Royal Artillery	4390649		M	From Halle broke away from line of march hid in barn for 6 days in village of Kockwitz. Companions marched on in direction of Leipzig. Tyson Vale Vernon Fitzpatrick Speller Markey.
Vaugan	Thomas	Signalman	4th Parachute Brigade, Royal Signals	4034124	90845	C	Made escape end of Feb in Protectorate Czechoslovakia. Recaptured end of April by SS troops. I was fit. No companion.
Vernon	Stanley	Lance Corporal	2nd Battalion, Parachute Regiment	1427411		M	From Halle. Broke away from the line of march. Hid in Barn in village of Kockwitz for 6 days. Companions marched on. Other small parties escaped I believe. Pte Vale, Gnr Tyson, Pte Fitzpatrick, Trp Spellers, Pte Markey.
Vick	Arthur James	Sergeant, Lance	7th Battalion, King's Own Scottish Borderers	4750885	89592	A	On line of march from Arnhiem.

Name	Forename	Rank	Unit	Army number	POW number	Escape location	Answers given as direct quotations from Liberation Questionnaires
Vincent	Stanley Maurice	Private	2nd Battalion, Parachute Regiment	549942		M	Escaped while being evacuated from Erfenschlag with Pte Jones and O'Brian. Recaptured 24 hrs later by German Volksturm at Augsburg. (Yes) Recaptured with me.
Wade	Richard Samuel	Staff Sergeant	Glider Pilot Regiment	6969360	117350	A C	1. General hospital in Arnhem. Captured after 10 mins down Side road. 2. On 2nd day of March from Sagan. Free 4 days, 6 kilos from Russians. Recaptured – travelled with German company (556) for 7 weeks–treated well–then sent to Muhlberg. (Cpl Tucker 1st The Parachute as companion).
Wallace	Samuel	Private	1st Battalion, Border Regiment	14671726	24363	M	We made a bid for freedom on the 9th May, while on the march from Halle. We were picked up in Leipzig by civilians and taken to a French commando. Where we got relieved by the American company airborne [illegible] 70th [illegible].
Walsh	Richard	Private	2nd Battalion, Parachute Regiment	6409551		C	I made one escape on May 5th 45 with L. A. C. Johnson and was recaptured 15 hrs later at Chemnitz. Johnson was caught up to do for me. I was weak from loss of food.
Walsh	William Marston	Driver	1st Parachute Brigade	3975544		M	The Germans tried to evacuate our commando which had the strength of 30 men on marching into Chemnitz me and my friend that's Pte Roy Fox evaded the column and made our way to the lines we left the column on the 12th and got through on the 14th.
Walton	Frank Thomas	Private	1st Battalion, Parachute Regiment	6015864		C	Brüx, April 22, as Frenchmen, John Ross. Relieved by Russians, No, Arrived in England.

Surname	First name	Rank	Unit	Service no.		Code	Remarks
Ward	William Edward	Private	10th Battalion, Parachute Regiment	6026817		C	In Eilenburg on 18.4.45. By dressing as a civilian. Surrendered to enemy on 21.4.45 through lack of food with Pte McCormick of Durham Light Infantry.
Warren	Ernest Edward	Corporal	1st Parachute Brigade	2736584		A C	Arnhem. 21/9/44. Faked seriously wounded in leg escaped in dark recaptured night 22/23/9/44 Slight leg wound no companions. Kundl 17/4/45 17 escaped cut wire travelled on foot 3 days as French workers. Recaptured Zillerbrook (German soldier) 20/4/1945. Com Sgt Bromfield 6016537.
Watt	William	Private	1st Battalion, Parachute Regiment	923891	118445	C	At Uelzen on 13.4.45/Travelling overnight and hiding by day/Harry Lingard/Recaptured by Cameronians [sic] at Uelzen on 18.4.45
Weallans	Arthur Edward	Sergeant	11th Battalion, Parachute Regiment	2660102		M	Escaped from Stalag II A 3 March 1945 by joining marching columns of British POWs coming from Poland.
Welham	Hubert Edward	Lance Corporal	1st Airborne Reconnaissance Squadron	6854308		M M	Fraunstein Saxony 29 April 1945. No companions. Recaptured Eppendorf Saxony 3 May 1945 by German cavalry unit. Physically fit.
Whadcoat	Ernest Frederick	Private	10th Battalion, Parachute Regiment	6351604		nk	Recaptured after 3 days. Name of companion Pte D Dupont.
Whittaker	Stanley James	Private	4th Parachute Brigade	14618322		M	The whole camp made a break for the American lines on the 8.5.45. The enemy was disorganised and some were going [to] the Americans to give themselves up. I travelled with one such Driver. I do not know what happened to my camp companions.
Whittam	Albert	Gunner	1st Airlanding Light Regiment, Royal Artillery	1791277	118695	C	Escaped from working camp at Uelzen on 10.4.1945 with Sig Heyes and Gnr Howell. Recaptured 13.4.45 by German front line infantry. Liberated from Munster lager by 11th Armoured Div 18.4.45.

Name	Forename	Rank	Unit	Army number	POW number	Escape location	Answers given as direct quotations from Liberation Questionnaires
Wiedericks	Benjamin James	Private	156th Battalion, Parachute Regiment	2766217		M	Heard gun fire on 15/4/45 and made for the direction of the guns. Reached the American lines about ten that night.
Wilder	Leslie Maurice	Lance Corporal	1st Parachute Brigade, Royal Signals	2583200		M	May 30th 1945 [sic] whilst marching from Meissen to Czechoslovkia. No companions, hid under bridge after halt and then walked N.W. Recaptured April 3 near Döbeln by German patrol, held in Frieburg until released by Russian forces. I was fit.
Willett	Lewis Alfred	Driver	250th Airborne Light Company, Royal Army Service Corps	64737		C	Escaped from prison camp near Torgau 22/4/45 through barbed wire enclosure. Made way to Werzen where 69 American Div liberated me 25/4/45. I was physically fit.
Williams	David Meredith	Private	10th Battalion, Parachute Regiment	14219148	52884	M	Fredichroda Thuringia whilst marching away from Americans 4/4/45. Ran away from column (Oliver, John Stephen – Jim Brown, George Waterhouse – Skinner) freed by French troops. Recaptured by SS on 7/4/45 2 with me – 3 missing.
Wiltshire	Reginald William	Lance Corporal	4th Parachute Brigade HQ	7349096		T	In transit from Holland to Germany. Climbed to roof of train & made way to rear with two crew of Flying Fort. Blankets wrapped around feet as boots confiscated. One jumped I escaped but train passed Germany flak train whose gun crew saw us in truck & informed guards. Names of companions unknown & nothing heard of men who jumped last seen rolling down railway bank.
Withey	Leslie George	Lance Corporal	250th Airborne Light Company, Royal Army Service Corps	277631	14201	M	Yes about March 45 with Gunner Manning (The Parachute Artillery) arrested by Chechnk civilian landwatch not very fit. Area north west Czecho border.

Surname	Forename	Rank	Unit	Number		Code	Details
Wood	Harold George	Corporal	2nd Battalion, Parachute Regiment	6350557		M	Whilst evacuating camp at Sagan 10 Feb 44 Recaptured by civil police. No.
Wood	Jack	Private	2nd Battalion, South Staffordshire Regiment	4914111		M	One attempt, we were on the march and at midnight an unknown friend and myself rolled into a ditch. Lights from flares discovered us and we were rifle butted back into the column.
Wood	Joseph	Private	1st Battalion, Parachute Regiment	1440598		M	Yes.
Worsfold	Gerald Percy	Private	7th Battalion, King's Own Scottish Borderers	14440258	91478	C	Successful from Brüx 29 April 1945. Companion Pt J. Reilly (889575) REME. My companion and myself got safely through to American lines at Pilsen on 12 May 1945.
Wright	Stanley Winston	Sergeant Major	2nd Battalion, South Staffordshire Regiment	4913782		C M C	Jan 3rd 1945 Sagan failure – Sgt Flowers P.T.C. 21 days strafe. I was fit – avoided detection. Feb On the march free for 5 days recaptured by Volkstrohme – Fit. April 8th at Hanover, successful picked up by Americans April 10th.
Wyard	Raymond Russell	Private	156th Battalion, Parachute Regiment	7344919		M	April 16 from SCHEEBURG with Charles Deadman – J Bosik walk by main road to Dresden then on the way to Chemnitz when we was recaptured on April 22 by SS. Suffered with bad knees fell down on a cliff. Companions caught also.

Freedom

Men captured earlier in the war would have welcomed liberation as an opportunity to return home. For some, and perhaps especially recent captives like the men from Arnhem, liberation was an opportunity to re-join the war. As well as Craftsman Berry, REME, and Regimental Sergeant Major Eatwell mentioned earlier, Lance Corporal Seymour and his comrades' exploits after they escaped were impressive:

> Lance Corporal Thomas Seymour, 1 Border, 'We then heard the town SUSICE a few miles were appeal for our help to round up the Germans in the town. This we did to the best our ability. There were a few SS whom we dare not tackle as they were very heavily armed and they're only 10 of us British Canadians … When we had cleared the town they asked for three volunteers to go out and meet the American troops and remainder to stay in town in case anything happened.'

The questionnaires did not include a question about how men had performed in combat. Sergeant Garbutt, Glider Pilot Regiment, used the 'Any other information' question to record the performance of his comrades during Market Garden:

> Sergeant William Garbutt, Glider Pilot Regiment, 'Magnificent work of Major Croot (Glider Pilot Regt) during fighting and splendid work of Sgt A Allenbury (Glider Pilot) in attending to our & enemy wounded under heavy bombardment from enemy.'

Praise for the Red Cross and their food parcels occurs throughout the questionnaires, but some men mention the exemplary performance of other prisoners:

> Private William Davies, 3rd Battalion, Parachute Regiment, 'The camp leader RSM Lord did really good work for all prisoners and defied the German commandant on very many occasions also Red Cross parcels provided help kept us alive as German rations were very low.'

Sadly, we don't have the questionnaire of Regimental Sergeant Major Lord. It seems unlikely that he would have failed to complete one if asked, so presumably the liberation of men remaining at Fallingbostel was too early for Operation Endor:

> Sergeant George Hadfield, Glider Pilot Regiment, 'I desire to bring to the notice of the authorities, the exceedingly good work done by C.S.M. McKenzie, R.A.S.C. in the capacity of 'man of confidence', during our stay in Stalag 383 and afterwards on the line of march.'

> Corporal Bernard Phillips, 1st Airborne Provost Company, 'I would like to recommend the good work done to the whole camp by the man of confidence. Mr J Barker ['YMCA' added in another hand].'

Appendix 1

General Questionnaires for British/ American Ex-Prisoners of War

PART I.

GENERAL QUESTIONNAIRE FOR BRITISH/AMERICAN EX-PRISONERS OF WAR

1. No.................. RANK............................. SURNAME ....

CHRISTIAN NAMES..

DECORATIONS...

2. SHIP (R.N., U.S.N. or MERCHANT NAVY)..

UNIT (Army)..

SQUADRON (RAF or AAF)..

3. DIVISION (Army), COMMAND (RAF or AAF)..

4. DATE OF BIRTH...

5. DATE OF ENLISTMENT...

6. CIVILIAN TRADE OR PROFESSION ....

(OR EXAMINATIONS PASSED WHILE P/W)

....

7. PRIVATE ADDRESS...

8. PLACE AND DATE OF ORIGINAL CAPTURE ....

9. WERE YOU WOUNDED WHEN CAPTURED? ....

10. MAIN CAMPS OR HOSPITALS IN WHICH IMPRISONED

Camp No.	Location	From	Till

11. WERE YOU IN A WORK CAMP?

Location	From	Till	Nature of work

12. DID YOU SUFFER ANY SERIOUS ILLNESSES WHILE A P/W?

Nature of illness	Cause	Duration

(b) DID YOU RECEIVE ADEQUATE MEDICAL TREATMENT?

....

TOP SECRET

GENERAL QUESTIONNAIRE. PART II. TOP SECRET   M.I.9/Gen

MIS X

1. No.......................... RANK........................ SURNAME...

           CHRISTIAN NAMES..

2. LECTURES before Capture :
     (a) Were you lectured in your unit on how to behave in the event of capture?
        (state where, when and by whom).

....

....

     (b) Were you lectured on escape and evasion? (state where, when and by whom).

....

....

3. INTERROGATION after capture :
    Were you specially interrogated by the enemy? (state where, when and methods used by enemy).

....

....

....

4. ESCAPES attempted :
    Did you make any attempted or partly successful escapes? (give details of each attempt separately, stating
      where, when, method employed, names of your companions, where and when recaptured and by whom.
      Were you physically fit? What happened to your companions?

....

....

....

....

5. SABOTAGE :
    Did you do any sabotage or destruction of enemy factory plant, war material, communications, etc, when
      employed on working parties or during escape? (Give details, places and dates.)

....

....

....

6. COLLABORATION with enemy:
    Do you know of any British or American personnel who collaborated with the enemy or in any way helped
      the enemy against other allied prisoners of war? (give details, names of person (s) concerned, camp (s),
      dates and nature of collaboration or help given to the enemy).

....

....

....

7. WAR CRIMES:
    If you have any information or evidence of bad treatment by the enemy to yourself or to others, or
      knowledge of any enemy violation of Geneva Convention you should ask for a copy of "Form Q" on
      which to make your statement.
     (NOTE: Form Q is a separate form inviting information on *War Crimes* and describes the kinds of offences
      coming under this title.)

GENERAL QUESTIONNAIRE. PART II. TOP SECRET
(continued)

8. Have you any other matter of any kind you wish to bring to notice?

....

....

....

....

....

....

SECURITY UNDERTAKING

I fully realise that all information relating to the matters covered by the questions in Part II. are of a highly secret and official nature.
I have had explained to me and fully understand that under Defence Regulations or U.S.A.R. 380-5 I am forbidden to publish or communicate any information concerning these matters.

Date... *Signature*..

Appendix 2

German POW Number Sequences for Arnhem POWs

Camp	Type of prisoner	German POW number series	Notes
Dulag XII A Limburg	NCOs and other ranks – able bodied	14XXX, 15XXX, 17XXX, 19XXX, 24XXX, 075XXX, 88XXX, 89XXX, 90XXX, 91XXX, 92XXX, 93XXX, 221XXX, 916XXX, 920XXX, 975XXX	The series 15XXX was duplicated and used by Stalag XII A and Stalag XIII D.
Dulag XII A Limburg	19 officers	908XX	
Dulag XII B Hadamar	Officers – able-bodied	5XX, 6XX, 90XXX, 93XXX	
Dulag-Luft	RAF and Glider Pilot Officers – treated as Royal Air Force	58XX	
Dulag-Luft	RAF and Glider Pilot NCOs – treated as Royal Air Force	8XX, 9XX, 10XX	
Oflag IX A	Officers – walking wounded and officers from Obermaßfeld and Meiningen	21XX	The 21XX series was mainly used for wounded who were sent to Fallingbostel and after a brief time were moved to Oflag IX A, but Major Pott received a duplicate number in this series. In a further complication the sequence had also been used for men captured in Normandy in 1944.

GERMAN POW NUMBER SEQUENCES FOR ARNHEM POWS

Camp	Type of prisoner	German POW number series	Notes
Stalag IX C/Z Severely wounded men from hospitals at Obermaßfeld and Meiningen	NCOs and Other Ranks – severely wounded	5XXXX	
Stalag XI B Fallingbostel	NCOs and Other Ranks – walking wounded	117XXX, 118XXX, 119XXX	Fallingbostel were still using the 119XXX series in October for prisoners captured after 'Market Garden'.
Stalag XIII D	All ranks – wounded	15XXX	The series 15XXX was duplicated and used by Stalag XII A and Stalag XIII D.
Stalag VII A Severely wounded men from several hospitals across Germany	All ranks – severely wounded	18XXX, 140XXX	

Glossary

AK: abbreviation for *arbeitskommando.*

Arbeitskommando or kommando: a working party.

Camp numbers: The camp's number, XII, came from the military district in which it was located and the suffix 'A' distinguished it from other camps in the district. H was an abbreviation for Hauptlager 'Main camp': Z was an abbreviation for Zweilager 'Second or junior camp'. Later in the war, new camps and some existing camps were given Arabic numbers. When Oflag VIII F was transferred westwards in 1943 it was renamed Oflag 79.

Dulag: German abbreviation for Durchgangslager, reception camp.

Dulag Luft: German abbreviation for Durchgangslager der Luftwaffe, reception camp for aircrew.

Dulag Oberbefehlshaber West: the Supreme Commander West's Interrogation Centre, at Diez.

Ersatzheer: Reserve Army, including territorial troops, provided the guards to OKW camps.

Feldwebel: Sergeant.

Frontstalag: a temporary reception camp close to the battlefield.

Heer: German Army.

Kommando: a specialist group or task force; abbreviation for *arbeitskommando* (work commando).

Kriegsgefangen: Prisoner of war.

Kriegsgefangenennummer: Prisoner of war's German identity number.

Kriegsmarine: Germany Navy.

Kriegy: Prisoners' own nickname for themselves.

Landesschützen: Territorial army units, part of the Reserve Army (Ersatzheer); provided the guards at OKW camps.

Lazarett: Hospital.

Luftwaffe: German air force.

GLOSSARY

Man of Confidence: The 'Man of Confidence' was the prisoners' representative and used as the leader of the prisoners by the Germans in camps for NCOs and Other Ranks. The equivalent in Oflags was the 'Senior British Officer'.

Milag: Abbreviation of Marinelager, the camp for naval personal, part of Marlag und Milag Nord maintained by Oberkommando der Kriegsmarine, which held Navy and Merchant Navy prisoners. Merchant Navy men were held in the Marlag – Marineinterniertenlager.

Oberbefehlshaber: Supreme Commander.

Oberkommando der Wehrmacht – OKW: Supreme Command of the German Armed Forces.

Oberkommando der Heer – OKH: Supreme Command of the German Army.

Oberkommando der Luftwaffe – OKL: Supreme Command of the German Air Forces.

Oflag: the German abbreviation for Offizierslager, a camp for officers.

Protecting Power: the country safeguarding the interests of prisoners of war. From 1942 until the end of the war the Protecting Power for British and Empire men was Switzerland.

Reichssicherheitshauptamt – RHSA: Head office of the Nazi German security services.

Reserve Lazarett: Military hospital, Prison camp hospital.

Revier: a medical facility providing simple treatment.

Senior British Officer: the prisoners' representative used as the leader of the prisoners by the Germans in camps for officers. The equivalent in Stalags was the 'Man of confidence'.

Sammelstelle: temporary holding camp for newly captured men close to the battlefield.

Sicherheitsdienst: German security services outside the Nazi party.

Stalag: the German abbreviation for Mannschafts-Stammlager, a permanent camp for NCOs and Other Ranks, with many men located in working parties (arbeitskommandos) outside the camp.

Stalag Luft: Camps maintained by the Oberkommando der Luftwaffe, with Luftwaffe guards that held captured aircrew.

Strafe Lager: Punishment camp.

Wehrkreis: German military district.

Wehrmacht: German armed forces.

Zweiglager: subsidiary camp.

/Z: see Zweiglager.

References

The National Archives, Kew

Liberation Questionnaires
These are at the War Office: Directorate of Military Intelligence: Liberated Prisoner of War Interrogation Questionnaires WO 344. They are arranged alphabetically and by Army Number.

Camps
Dulag Luft Camp History AIR 40/2466
Dulag Luft Oberursel Camp History WO 344/101/2
Dulag Luft Wetzlar WO 32/18503
Dulag Luft War Crimes WO 208/4642
Dulag Luft Interrogation Reports AIR 40/238
Dulag Luft Oberursel War Crimes WO 208/4642
Oflag 79 Camp History WO 208/3292
Oflag 79 Protecting Power Reports WO 361/1844
Oflag IX A/H Camp History WO 208/3293
Oflag IX A/H Protecting Power Reports WO 224/78
Oflag IX A/Z Camp History WO 208/3294
Oflag IX A/Z Protecting Power Reports WO 224/79
Oflag XII B Camp History WO 208/3295
Dulag XII B Hadamar Protecting Power Reports WO 261/1845
Stalag XI B Protecting Power Reports WO 224/35
Stalag XIB Fallingbostel; miscellaneous collection of nominal rolls WO 361/17971
Stalag IV B Mühlberg Protecting Power Reports WO 224/12
Hospitals in Wehrkreis IV Protecting Power Reports WO 224/208
Stalag VIII B Protecting Power Reports WO 224/27
Obermaßfeld Miscellaneous correspondence WO 216/827
Obermaßfeld Protecting Power Report FO 916/1154

Online Sources
Stalag IV G Protecting Power Reports, on Pegasus www.pegasusarchive.org/pow/cSt_4G_report1.htm

Bibliography

Bankhead, Harry, *A Salute to the Steadfast*, Ramsay Press, 1999.

Beattie, Edward W., *Diary of a Kriegie*, Thomas Y Crowell, 1946.

Blockwell, Albert, *Diary of a Red Devil*, Helion, 2005.

Borgsen, Werner and Volland, Klaus, *Stalag XB Sandbostel*, Edition Temmen, 2010.

Borrie, John, *Despite Captivity*, William Kimber, 1975.

Breloer (ed.), *Mein Tagebuch: Geschichten vom Überleben 1939–1947*, Verlagsgesellschaft Schulferns, 1984.

Carruthers, Bob (ed.), *Handbook of German Military Forces*, Pen and Sword, 2013.

Charles Rollings, *Prisoners of War – Voices of captivity during the Second World War*, Ebury Press, 2007.

Cherry, Niall, *Red Berets and Red Crosses*, R. N. Sigmond, reprinted 2000.

Clutton-Brook, Oliver, *Footprints on the Sands of Time*, Grub Street, 2013.

Cooper, Alan, *Air Battle for Arnhem*, Pen and Sword, 2012.

Cuddon, Eric (ed.), *Trial of Erich Killinger, Heinz Junge, Otto Boehriner, Heinrich Eberhardt, Gustav Bauer-Schlichtegroll (The Dulag Luft Trial)*, William Hodge and Company, 1952.

Dancocks, Daniel G., *In Enemy Hands: Canadian Prisoners of War 1939–45*, Hurtig, 1983.

Dover, Victor, *The Silken Canopy*, Cassell, 1979.

Dugdale, J. and Emery, A. (ed.), *Art in the bag*, Privately printed for the Oflag 79 Art Club.

Eastwood, S., Gray, C., and Green, A. T., W*hen Dragons Flew: an illustrated history of the 1st Battalion, Border Regiment 1939–45*, Silverlink Publishing, 1994.

Edgar, Donald, *The Stalag Men*, John Clare, 1982.

Fairley, John, *Remember Arnhem*, Pegasus Journal, 1978.

Foot and Langley, *MI9: Escape and Evasion 1939–1945*, Bodley Head, 1979.

Frost, John, *A Drop too Many*, Stackpole Books, 1982.

Geck, Stefan, *Dulag Luft/Auswertestelle West: Vernehmungslager der Luftwaffe für westalliierte Kriegsgefangene im Zweiten Weltkrieg*, Peter Lang, 2008.

Gerritsen-Teunissen, M., *Dagboek in krijgsgevangenschap*, Self-published.

Graham, Jimmy and Thomas, Jack, *Joe in Germany*, Surrey Fine Art Press, 1946.

Gray, Jenny, *Major Cotterell at Arnhem*, Spellmount, 2012.

Green, Peter, *A Fragment of a Life*, Self-published, 2008.

Gregg, Victor and Stroud, *Rick, Rifleman: a front-line life from Alamein and Dresden to the fall of the Berlin Wall*, Bloomsbury, 2011.

Hacket, John, *I Was a Stranger*, Chatto & Windus, 1977.

Hall, Colin, *Dropped in it*, Self-published, 2010.

Heaps, Leo, *The Grey Goose of Arnhem*, Weidenfeld and Nicholson Ltd., 1976.

Hey, J. A., *Roll of Honour: Battle of Arnhem September 1944*, 5th edition, The Society of Friends of the Airborne Museum Oosterbeek, 2011.

Hicks, Norman, *Captured at Arnhem*, Pen and Sword, 2013.

Horner, Gordon, *For You the War is Over*, Falcon Press, 1948.

Hunt, Leslie, *Prisoners' Progress: an illustrated diary of the March into captivity of the last of the British Army in France June 1940*, Hutchinson, 1941.

Ishee, A. W., *Stalag IV-B*, AuthorHouse, 2004.

Junier, A. and Smulders, B., *By Land, Sea and Air*, R. N. Sigmond Publishing, 2003.

Kahn, David, *Hitler's Spies: German military intelligence in World War II*, Da Capo Press, 2000.

Kelly, Frank, *Private Kelly*, Evans Brothers, 1954.

Kessel, Lipmann, *Surgeon at Arms*, Pen and Sword, 1976.

Kindersley, Philip, *For You the War is Over*, Midas, 1983.

Kochavi, Arieh, *Confronting Captivity*, University of North Carolina Press, 2005.

Laekas, Michael John, *A Soldier's Journey (1940–1945)*, Kindle.

Lindsay, Arthur, *The Diary: escape from the Black March*, iUniverse Inc., 2010.

Longden, Sean, *Hitler's British Slaves*, Constable, 2005.

Longson, Jim & Taylor, Christine, *An Arnhem Odyssey*, Leo Cooper, 1991.

Mattiello & Vogt, *Deutsche Kriegesgefangen – und Internierten einrichtungen 1939–1945*, Handbuch und Katalog Lagergeschite und Lagerzensurstempel, Wolfgang Vogt, 1987.

Mattiello, G. and Vogt, W., *Deutsche Kriegsgefangen-und Internierten einrichtungen 1939–1945*, Wolfgang Vogt, 1987.

Mawson, Stuart, *Arnhem Doctor*, Spellmount, 2007.

Mawson, Stuart, *Doctor after Arnhem*, Spellmount, 2006.

Moore, Bob and Fedorwich, Kent (ed.), *Prisoners of War and their Captors in World War II*, Berg, 1996.

Morrison, Alexander, *Silent Invader*, Airlife, 1999.

Nichol, J. and Rennel, T., *The Last Escape*, Penguin, 2002.

O'Reilly, John, *156 Parachute Battalion: From Delhi to Arnhem*, Thoroton, 2009.

Oliver Clutton-Brock & Raymond Crompton, *The Long Road*, Grub Street, 2013.

Otway, T. B. H., *Airborne Forces*, Imperial War Museum (reprint), 1990.

Overy, R. J., *War and Economy in the Third Reich*, OUP, 1994.

Peatling, Robert, *Without Tradition: 2 Para – 1941–1945*, Leo Cooper Ltd, 2004.

Peters, Mike and Buist, Luke, *Glider Pilots at Arnhem*, Pen and Sword, 2010.

Pijpers, G. & Truesdale, D., *Arnhem their Final Battle: the 11th Parachute Battalion*, Sigmond, 2012.

Powell, Geoffrey, *Men at Arnhem*, Pen and Sword, 2003.

BIBLIOGRAPHY

Prouse, Robert, *Ticket to Hell via Dieppe*, Van Nostrznd Reinhold, 1982.

Reynolds, Michael, *Sons of the Reich: 11 SS Panzer Corps*, Spellmount, 2002.

Ritchie, Sebastian, *Arnhem Myth and Reality*, Hale, 2011.

Roberts, Harry, *Capture at Arnhem*, Windrush Press, 1999.

Roger Payne, *Paras: Voices of the British Airborne Forces in the Second World War*, Amberley, 2014.

Rossiter, Mike, *We Fought at Arnhem*, Corgi, 2012.

Schmidt, Haks Walburgh, *No Return Flight: 134 Platoon at Arnhem 1944*, Aspekt, 2009.

Sigmond, Robert, *Off at Last*, R. N. Sigmond Publishing, 1997.

Sims, James, *Arnhem Spearhead: a private soldier's story*, Imperial War Museum, 1978.

Spinelli, Angelo and Carlson, Lewis, *Life Behind Barbed Wire*, Fordham University Press, 2004.

Stainforth, Peter, *Wings of the Wind*, The Falcon Press, 1952.

Stranges, Anthony, (ed.) Lesch, *Germany's Synthetic fuel industry, 1927–1945. The German Chemical Industry in the Twentieth Century*, Springer, 2000.Tooze, Adam, *The Wages of Destruction*, Penguin, 2006.

van Roekel, C., *Who Was Who During the Battle of Arnhem*, The Society of Friends of the Airborne Museum, 1996.

Vercoe, Tony, *Survival at Stalag IVB*, McFarland & Company Ltd, 2006.

Vourkoutiotis, Vasilis, *The Prisoners of War and German High Command*, Palgrave, 2003.

War Office, *Prisoners of War British Army 1939–1945*, HMSO/Imperial War Museum, 1990.

Warrack, Graeme, *Travel by Dark: after Arnhem*, Harvill, 1963.

Weale, Adrian, *Renegades: Hitler's Englishmen*, Weidenfeld & Nicholson, 1994.

Weinmann, Martin et. al., *Das nationalsozialistische Lagersystem*, Zweitausendeins, 1990.

Wylie, Neville, *Barbed Wire Diplomacy*, OUP, 2010.

Index

Only the text sections have been indexed. The tables are available to search online at https://tinyurl.com/yzfayeac.

INDEX

INDEX

People

INDEX

Military Units